CAMBRIDGE STUDIES IN AMERICAN LITERATURE AND CULTURE

Ideology and Classic American Literature

Cambridge Studies in American Literature and Culture

Editor:
Albert Gelpi, Stanford University

Advisory Board

Nina Baym, *University of Illinois, Champaign–Urbana*
Sacvan Bercovitch, *Harvard University*
Richard Bridgman, *University of California, Berkeley*
David Levin, *University of Virginia*
Joel Porte, *Harvard University*
Mike Weaver, *Oxford University*

Other books in the series

Ideology and
Classic American
Literature

Edited by

SACVAN BERCOVITCH
Harvard University

and

MYRA JEHLEN
Rutgers University

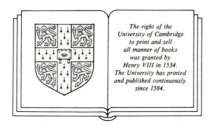

The right of the
University of Cambridge
to print and sell
all manner of books
was granted by
Henry VIII in 1534.
The University has printed
and published continuously
since 1584.

CAMBRIDGE UNIVERSITY PRESS

Cambridge
London   New York   New Rochelle
Melbourne   Sydney

Published by the Press Syndicate of the University of Cambridge
The Pitt Building, Trumpington Street, Cambridge CB2 1RP
32 East 57th Street, New York, NY 10022, USA
10 Stamford Road, Oakleigh, Melbourne 3166, Australia

First published 1986
First paperback edition 1987

Printed in the United States of America

Library of Congress Cataloging in Publication Data
Main entry under title:
Ideology and classic American literature.

(Cambridge studies in American literature and culture)
Bibliography: p.
Includes index.

1. American literature – 19th century – History and
criticism – Addresses, essays, lectures. 2. Politics
in literature – Addresses, essays, lectures.
I. Bercovitch, Sacvan. II. Jehlen, Myra. III. Series.
PS217.P64I36 1986   810'.9'358   85-21247

British Library Cataloguing in Publication Data
Bercovitch, Sacvan

Ideology and classic American literature – (Cambridge studies in
American literature and culture)
1. American literature – 19th century – History
and criticism
I. Title II. Jehlen, Myra
810.9'003   PS201
ISBN 0 521 25221 0 hard covers
ISBN 0 521 27309 9 paperback

For Eytan and Jessica

Contents

Acknowledgments

The following chapters have appeared in other books or journals. Grateful acknowledgment is made to the publishers for permission to reprint them here.

Chapter 4, "Myth and the Production of History," by Richard Slotkin, is adapted from his introduction to *The Fatal Environment: The Myth of the Frontier in the Age of Industrialization* (New York: Atheneum, 1985).

Chapter 6, "The Novel and the Middle Class in America," by Myra Jehlen, first appeared in *Salmagundi* 36 (1977).

Chapter 7, "Figurations for a New American Literary History," by Houston A. Baker, Jr., appeared as a chapter in his *Blues, Ideology, and Afro-American Literature: A Vernacular Theory* (Chicago: University of Chicago Press, 1984).

Chapter 9, "Reification and American Literature," © 1981 by Carolyn Porter, is reprinted with some changes from *Seeing and Being: The Plight of the Participant Observer in Emerson, James, Adams, and Faulkner* (Middletown, Conn.: Wesleyan University Press).

Chapter 12, "Sentimental Power: *Uncle Tom's Cabin* and the Politics of Literary History," by Jane Tompkins, is adapted from a chapter in her *Sensational Designs: The Cultural Work of American Fiction, 1790–1860* (New York: Oxford University Press, 1985) and originally appeared in *Glyph* 9 (1981), published by Johns Hopkins University Press.

Chapter 13, "*Walden* and the 'Curse of Trade,' " by Michael T. Gilmore, appeared in a slightly different version in his *American Romanticism and the Marketplace* (Chicago: University of Chicago Press, 1985).

Chapter 16, "That Hive of Subtlety," by James H. Kavanagh, is a revised version of an essay by the same title that appeared in *The Bucknell Review* 29, no. 1 (1984).

List of Contributors

JONATHAN ARAC teaches at the University of Illinois at Chicago. He has edited and contributed to several volumes on literary theory, and is the author of *Commissioned Spirits: The Shaping of Social Motion in Dickens, Carlyle, Melville, and Hawthorne* (1979) and *Contemporary Criticism and the Figuration of History* (1986).

HOUSTON A. BAKER, JR. teaches at the University of Pennsylvania. He has published several books of poetry, and is the author of *The Journey Back: Issues in Black Literature and Criticism* (1980), and *Blues, Ideology, and Afro-American Literature: A Vernacular Theory* (1984), and other scholarly works.

SACVAN BERCOVITCH teaches at Harvard University. He has edited several books in early American literature, and is the author of *The Puritan Origins of the American Self* (1975) and *The American Jeremiad* (1979).

ROBERT H. BYER teaches at the University of Southern California. He is the author of *The Man in the Crowd: Edgar Allan Poe in His Culture* (1986).

EMORY ELLIOTT teaches at Princeton University. He has edited various works in American literature and culture, and is the author of *Power and the Pulpit in Puritan New England* (1975) and *Revolutionary Writers: Literature and Authority in the New Republic* (1982).

MICHAEL T. GILMORE teaches at Brandeis University. He has edited several books on colonial and nineteenth-century literature, and is the author of *The Middle Way: Puritanism and Ideology in American Romantic Fiction* (1977) and *American Romanticism and the Marketplace* (1985).

GERALD GRAFF teaches at Northwestern University. He has published widely on literary theory, and is the author of *Poetic Statement and Critical Dogma* (1970) and *Literature Against Itself: Literary Ideas in Modern Society* (1979).

MYRA JEHLEN teaches at Rutgers University. She has written on feminist theory, and is the author of *Class and Character in Faulkner's South* (1976) and *American Incarnation* (1986).

JAMES H. KAVANAGH teaches at Carnegie-Mellon University. He has published various essays on literary theory and comparative literature, and is the author of *Emily Brontë* (1985).

LEO MARX teaches at the Massachusetts Institute of Technology. He has published widely on American literature and culture, and is the author of *The Machine in the Garden: Technology and the Pastoral Ideal in America* (1964).

DONALD E. PEASE teaches at Dartmouth College. He has edited and contributed to various publications, and is the author of *American Visionary Contracts* (1986), a study of nineteenth-century American literature.

CAROLYN PORTER teaches at the University of California at Berkeley. She is the author of a forthcoming study of Melville and of *Seeing and Being: The Plight of the Participant Observer in Emerson, James, Adams, and Faulkner* (1981).

PAUL ROYSTER is Production Manager of The Library of America. He is the author of "Political Economy in American Literature: The Rhetoric of Emerson and Melville" (Ph.D. dissertation, Columbia University, 1984).

RICHARD SLOTKIN teaches at Wesleyan University. He has published a novel, edited a collection of early American writings, and is the author of *Regeneration Through Violence: The Mythology of the American Frontier, 1600–1860* (1973) and *The Fatal Environment: The Myth of the Frontier in the Age of Industrialization* (1985).

HENRY NASH SMITH is Professor Emeritus of English at the University of California at Berkeley. He is the author of *Virgin Land: The American West as Symbol and Myth* (1950), *Mark Twain: The Development of a Writer* (1962), and *Democracy and the Novel* (1978), and other works. His reassessment of *Virgin Land* in this volume was solicited by the editors.

JANE TOMPKINS teaches at Duke University. She has written on literary theory and women's literature, and is the author of *Sensational Designs: The Cultural Work of American Fiction, 1790–1860* (1985).

ALAN TRACHTENBERG teaches at Yale University. He has edited and contributed to various books and journals, and is the author of *Brooklyn Bridge: Fact and Symbol* (1965), *America and Lewis Hines* (1977), and *The Incorporation of America: Culture and Society in the Gilded Age* (1982).

1

Introduction:
Beyond Transcendence

MYRA JEHLEN

Two contemporary developments may be said to have inspired this collection. The first is an increasing recognition that the political categories of race, gender, and class enter into the formal making of American literature such that they underlie not only its themes, not only its characters and events, but its very language. The ideological dimension of literary works has emerged, therefore, as integral to their entire composition. This redefinition of literature obviously has formal implications for criticism as well, and recent ideological readings, such as those gathered here, project besides new interpretations, new methods. The construction of these methods has benefited from the second development referred to, the education of American critics in European theories of culture including a complex tradition of ideological theory. Moreover, in recent times, this tradition has been evolving a definition of ideology that seems especially congenial to literary analysis. Thus, these collected essays bespeak a fortunate junction between a newly felt need and the discovery of a new tool for analysis.

In a sense, of course, the study of American literature has always had an ideological component. Van Wyck Brooks's contention that native writing constituted a distinct tradition meriting its own criticism contrasted a democratic and progressive America with an aristocratic, conservative England and enlisted the critic on the democratic side.[1] Proudly Anglophile, the Southern conservative manifesto *I'll Take My Stand* projected the same dichotomy when it boasted that the South had preserved an elite culture by remaining within the English tradition.[2] And in the thirties, Granville Hicks's *The Great Tradition*[3] continued to identify American literature as such with democracy by applauding a mainstream tradition that rejected the highbrow values and styles of English authors in favor of the plain but vigorous language of the

1

common man. In more nuanced terms, Malcolm Cowley and Edmund Wilson agreed that the American writer was ideally a democrat.

The background for the criticism in this volume is not the twenties and thirties, however, but the forties and fifties. This is a crucial distinction because the forties and fifties – characterized first by war-inspired nationalism, later by the jingoism of the McCarthy period – essentially reversed the dominant ideological and cultural thinking of the twenties and thirties. In the methods and attitudes of literary criticism, the change occurred gradually, and might have appeared at first only to represent a broader consensus. F. O. Matthiessen, whose *American Renaissance*[4] ushered in the forties and a new classical canon, shared the politically left attitudes of many of his predecessors. But unlike them he did not deal directly with political issues. Instead he recast these issues as artistic problems within a separate literary frame of reference. Writers as well as critics, Cowley and Wilson had also distinguished between literature and history. To Matthiessen, however, different meant apart: The language of literature was not only distinct, it was also self-sufficiently self-contained. If he located individual works and traditions in their historical context, he then read them as transcendent visions. While on one hand continuing the cultural history of Brooks by proposing a model of American literary identity, therefore, he was responding on the other hand to an opposite thirties tendency codified in the New Criticism.

Theoretically the New Critics were militantly anti-ideological. They maintained that the meaning of art had nothing to do with its social interpretation but lay within the individual work that constituted a world of its own. In the political world outside the text, however, the New Critics typically took right-wing stands and, reflecting the alignment described earlier, endorsed English styles and cultural traditions. Although *American Renaissance* stands opposed to them on both counts, it adopts their method in its close focus on a few works that represent the classic American tradition primarily by virtue of their literary sophistication. In a corollary sense, if Matthiessen's canon-building did not necessarily contradict the concept of a democratic culture, it rendered such a culture paradoxically hierarchical. Ten years later Henry Nash Smith's magisterial *Virgin Land*[5] made this paradox explicit when it defined a complementary category of popular writing characterized pejoratively by a lack of artistic consciousness. By the beginning of the fifties, ideological analysis and literary criticism appeared inherently contradictory to most critics of American literature who had adapted two crucial aspects of their earlier formalist opposition: a structural distinction between "serious" and "popular" writings, and the technique of textual close reading (for the explication of serious writing) as the appropriate approach to a work of art that is a discrete entity whose primary meanings lie within.

In *Virgin Land,* which discusses both elite and popular writings, Smith developed the notion of a cultural common language composed of myths and symbols. Because these myths and symbols were themselves already linguistic – not history but legends of history – the critical enterprise could take place entirely in the realm of language. In this realm, aesthetic evaluation appeared to be independent of social and political factors. The historical life of the myths and symbols might well be proffered as a gloss on their life in literature, but this was not essential to a coherent account of the literature and certainly not to a judgment of its artistic merit. *Virgin Land* is excellent history as well as excellent criticism, but it need not have been the former in order to be the latter.

For the Americanists of what came to be known as "the myth and symbol school," this separation was what identified them as literary critics: They began their work by stipulating the formal difference between literary and historical texts.[6] It must be stressed that this new formalism produced an extraordinary body of critical works. *American Renaissance* virtually ushered in a critical renaissance. Such studies as R. W. B. Lewis's *The American Adam*[7] attested at once to the rich interest of the literature and the sophistication of the criticism. Indeed, in token of its new seriousness, American literature now became a common doctoral subject. Through this period, students of American literature remained historically conscious, perhaps more so than those who studied English and European writing. But the common critical wisdom was that in literature, ideology was a trace of incomplete combustion in the transformation of the material of history into the spirit of literature. To call a writer "ideological" was to mean that he or she was less accomplished; an "ideological" work was by that definition less literary.

Treated as "background" or "context" rather than as an integral part of the literary language, history devolves into either disparate facts or all-encompassing trends that tend to confirm the established readings. The sidelining of history in the criticism of the forties and fifties, or its removal to the periphery of analysis, combined with the period's general ideological conformity, produced an account of American literature that was probing and acute about its artistic qualities but hardly even aware of its ideology or of its representation of social issues. In studies of individual works, the critics discovered authorial ambiguity and ambivalence, but seldom saw in them reflections of larger contradictions.

Then in the sixties and seventies such contradictions became paramount concerns. Racial, class, and political conflicts revealed a heterogeneity that pluralism did not always reconcile. The notion of an
all-encompassing American identity, in literature as in society, now
appeared not only incomplete but, in its denial of nonhegemonic difference, actually repressive. In the way that universal "man" subsumes
subuniversal "woman," the universal "American" was now seen to
subsume "others" to whom it denied universality. The criticism of this
period tended to discover literature's formative principles in tension and
contradiction.[8] Richard Slotkin's iconoclastic *Regeneration Through Violence*[9] exposed the fabled settling of the West as the founding paradigm
of national imperialism. In *The Lay of the Land*,[10] Annette Kolodny
examined the widespread representation of the continent as a woman
awaiting masculine possession, in terms of oppressive gender stereotypes. (Earlier, Leslie Fiedler did not think to question the female status
of the wilderness but on the contrary was troubled by the inadequate
manhood of "her" conquerors.) John Cawelti explored the popular
Westerns and discovered that their brashness masked uncertainty and
unresolved conflicts.[11] The cultural historian Nathan Huggins, focusing
on literature, added his *Harlem Renaissance*[12] to the list that had begun
with *American Renaissance*.

Thus the recognition of conflict in America had doubled the terms of
critical inquiry. In these books there are two central agents, two sets of
interactive perspectives and terms: The erstwhile objects – women,
blacks, even the continent itself and its first owners – have become at
least potential subjects in their own right. From this doubled perspective, critics who earlier had observed ambivalence, as between a
writer's celebration of individual autonomy and his concern for the
community, now saw the reflection of real conflicts in the surrounding
society. Literary ambiguities that had seemed to connote only a complex authorial sensibility appeared in the new context more urgently
engaged in a dialectical search for resolution. On the other hand, terms
like "America" and "American," when they were revealed to be not
only encompassing but also exclusive, represented even the "universal"
as limited. In a word, the "ideal" of the earlier critical era now emerged
as "ideology."

At first, however, few critics who dealt with ideology would
have identified it as their focus, and even fewer would have described
their analyses as ideological. The emergence of ideological literary criticism as an approach in its own right represents a special coincidence
between a sense that "social context" was both illuminating and prob-

lematical in the study of literature and the development of an analytical method that rendered ideology as an interpretive, indeed a linguistic, construction in many ways analogous to literature itself.

To suggest an analogy between literature and ideology, however, contradicts both their most common definitions. Literature, we have been taught, is a vehicle for abiding truths, and ideology, a system of interested deceit. In this regard, it should be noted that the concept of ideology has been especially suspect in this country, where the very consciousness of history has been repudiated for making unacceptable inroads on self-determination. Any conception of ideology implies that class and convention are intimate components of individual behavior, so that ideological analysis is inevitably a study of the limits of self-definition. Even in contextual criticism we are more comfortable with transhistorical concepts like "democracy" and "individualism," which tend to affirm the transcendence of ideas and of the mind.

Ironically, the original definition of ideology implied just that.[13] In the program of the French Revolution's Institut de France, ideology was the generic study of ideas that existed as universals in the realm of reason (rather than of history). Indeed, the savants of the Institut, established in 1795, represented Enlightenment idealism so well that they ran afoul of Napoleon's more immanent need to fortify his regime by restoring a degree of censorship and an established religion. To these reactionary moves, the ideologues, for whom the Revolution meant above all the right to think and speak freely, formed a liberal opposition that championed the embattled ideals of Enlightenment liberalism. Because these ideals were associated with a class, the bourgeoisie, their championship now came to represent a class attitude. Approximately fifty years after the coining of the term "ideology," Marx completed the reversal of its meaning when he denounced, as ideology, the self-serving "world view" of the middle class (which he believed the bourgeoisie had foisted on the proletariat). Ideology now meant "false consciousness," a system of beliefs about the world and one's relation to it that represented the interests of the dominant social class. The explication and exposition of this system were therefore crucial parts of political agitation: To change the world, the insurgents needed to prove that its present order was neither naturally good nor necessary.

The development of the theory of ideology has been mainly the work of Marxists concerned with finding ways to expose its misrepresentations and false ideals, to strip away the lie and expose the liar. But this is an ambiguous mission for a literary critic, who thereby becomes, at least positionally, a sort of adversary of the work she or he analyzes.[14] In practice, of course, ideological criticism has seldom been this simplistic and has sought to illuminate rather than merely to expose, to decode rather than debunk. Still, the possibility of reducing literary fictions into historical lies is there in the basic conflict between the notion of "false consciousness" and the root word "art," which, as Stephen Daedalus pointed out, extends into "artifice." In short, there is some basic opposition in intellectual impulse between those who erect imaginary worlds and those who seek to excavate the foundations of this one. As reading invites and may require a suspension of disbelief, criticism implies an appreciation of the writer's power to persuade the reader to that suspension. So long, then, as ideology essentially meant false consciousness, its relationship to reading and criticism – that is, to an engagement with the text that would value precisely its invention – remained problematical; though Marx himself and most Marxist critics understood very well the special value of literary creation.

In part this difficulty in dealing with literature, and with aesthetic issues generally, arose from the fact that Marx modeled his scientific analysis of society on the mechanistic and deterministic science of the nineteenth century. In that image, Marxism intended to discover an objective history ruled by the laws of causality. Ideology needed to be understood for its objective impact in permitting and even fueling the work of these laws, but as a subjectivity it was only an obstacle to be removed: an opiate. This definition of science, however, no longer prevails. In fact, the current definition essentially denies the possibility of objective knowledge. Thus, when recently the English Marxist Terence Eagleton sought to develop a "science of the text,"[15] he did not need to specify that his model was the science of relativity and quantum mechanics, which is neither absolute nor deterministic, on behalf either of the world or of the observer. In the abstract terms in which contemporary scientific ideas enter the general discussion, the change from nineteenth- to twentieth-century scientific models has invited an abrogation of the division between the evaluative, interpretive act and the facts it produces. Much as the dream life of the unconscious has come to be seen as a crucial aspect of consciousness, subjectivity now constitutes an inextricable part of our understanding of reality.

In the evolution of scientific Marxism and its concept of ideology, the Marxists of the Frankfurt Institute of Social Research (founded in 1923) might be described as a sort of interregnum, for they did not directly address the question of scientific models but rather moved to recast Marxism from a science into a social philosophy. In doing so, Max Horkheimer and his colleagues were perhaps reacting to post–World War I disillusionment with scientific authority as well as all totalizing absolutes. At any rate, putting aside the scientific Marxism inherited

from the nineteenth century, they disengaged a cultural and philosophical Marxism with its own problems and possibly its own laws. The
results of this emancipation were dramatic, though perhaps not fully
evident until after World War II. In relation to a concept of ideology,
the sense that Marxists were making social and cultural rather than
scientific analyses broadened the examination of false consciousness into
one of consciousness per se. "Today," Theodor Adorno would write,
"ideology means society as appearance."[16] In this formulation, ideology
was a terminus of investigation rather than a pass-through to the reality
it masked. The logic of this was much greater interest in literary and
cultural forms, and in language as such.

Of course, the predecessors of the Frankfurt Marxists would not have
denied the significance of language and form. The issue is not whether
language matters, but how: how literary style and form participate in
meaning. And although there is by no means a clear division between
nineteenth- and twentieth-century Marxist views of this question, the
wide-ranging debate in the thirties over the ethical and political value of
modernism can be seen as expressing a disagreement over the nature of
language and its relation to the material world. The most revealing
antagonists in this debate are perhaps Georg Lukács and Walter Benjamin.[17] Lukács's hostility to modernism (and in relation to Benjamin, to
the experimental theater of Bertolt Brecht, which Benjamin greatly
admired) and his endorsement of realism implement a Hegelian understanding of the way the mind engages history by seeking a reconciliation between the material and the ideal. As amended by Marx to make
the material primary, this concept becomes still more committed to an
external reality that it is the mission of art to illuminate, and not to
supplant with its own imaginary world. But reality was at once more
elusive and more malleable for Benjamin, who considered Brecht's use
of the latest techniques in style and form "progressive" precisely in its
experimentation, because that way the theater participated, in the same
way as industrial innovation, in the radical reconstruction of history.
Implicit in this view is the notion that language is not merely the
vehicle, or even only the agent, but part of the material of historical
process, more than an account of things, an aspect of the thing itself.[18]
In the same vein, Fredric Jameson has shown that Adorno sought
through a "negative dialectic" to transform the dialectical method into a
way of deconstructing the manifest (positive) content of established
ideas in order to reveal the conditions in which they arose, and in which
they might have taken other forms.[19]

Thus the greater power these critics ascribe to language imparts more
fluidity to the realm of the concrete as well. It is important to recognize

that neither Benjamin nor Adorno stresses the subjective *over* the objective. Their alternative to an unmasking approach is not to remain within the realm of perception. By questioning realism as a literary mode and empirical content as the primary site of artistic meaning, and instead focusing on form via experimentation, both intended to move toward a more direct apprehension of the concrete. The paradox that is today virtually common sense – that the power to name is the power to know, but that conversely knowledge is limited by language – is already implied by the Frankfurt revision of the nature of art, and it represented then as it does now the enhanced reality of both form and its object. For although in the terms of this paradox the concrete is forever inaccessible, it achieves a greater autonomy in the measure of the power that language has to re-create it interpretively. More powerful and more autonomous, the concept of language developed by such ideological critics as Benjamin and Adorno is thus also more modest in defining its relation to the "real" world.[20] On the other hand, in this revision, ideology becomes a newly important, indeed a crucial, category of knowledge, mediating terms – "subjectivity" and "external reality" – that are otherwise irreconcilable. This amounts really to a reversal of the earlier conception: Instead of obscuring reality, ideology now is just what in fact reveals it.

This reversal, whose process is exemplified here in the disagreement between Lukács and Benjamin over Brecht, is by now so widespread that it characterizes as well some more recent revisions of Marx that might be seen as moving in a direction opposite to that of the Frankfurt School, toward a more scientific Marxism. Although Louis Althusser, for instance, stresses the materialist economist Marx over the social historian, he also finds real substance in ideology where Marx saw "an imaginary assemblage . . . a pure dream, empty and vain, constituted by the 'day's residues' from the only full and positive reality, that of the concrete history of concrete material individuals materially producing their existence."[21] For Althusser, this empty and vain negativity has become positive. Ideology is real, albeit "a non-historical reality," by which he means that it is "omnipresent, trans-historical," not composed of any particular content but rather the constant structure of social knowledge. In the same way Freud meant that the unconscious is eternal, Althusser proposes that "ideology is eternal," that is, always there as the "'representation' of the imaginary relationship of individuals to their real conditions of existence." Reflecting a radical transformation in conceptions of reality itself and in the role of language in relation to reality, the crux of the difference between Althusser and Marx lies in the fact that for Althusser the imaginary, like a dream for

Freud, is its own reality, indeed, one that is not so much dependent "on the real conditions of existence" as more potently another account of them.

Along this line, the French critic Pierre Macherey (*A Theory of Literary Production*) carried the recognition of the substantive reality of ideological structures one step farther by his suggestion that the literary representation of ideology, in giving it the specific shape of this story or that drama, in turn enables the work to project, by juxtaposition, its own alternative structures. That is, the effort to embody an ideology in literature can expose some of its problematical or controversial aspects – for at some points, the work, becoming incompatible with the ideology it represents, falls silent. Having refused to take ideology's dictation, the work is left at those points without any language at all, and in its silences and ruptures, reveals the limits of the ideology. The literary form outlines ideological form within the work; and although the line is broken and in places disappears altogether, what is important in this context is that it is wholly formal, a silenced and unconscious context paradoxically embodied in form. Ironically, if the objection to an older mode of ideological criticism was that it tended to reduce meaning to message, this kind is so conscious of the unceasingly creative meaningfulness of form that it is loath even to specify meaning, and wants only to point in its direction and to indicate its condition and categories.

To be sure, Macherey continues to define ideology as an interested account intended to rationalize or bolster or win political power, and therefore as suppressive. It "exists because there are certain things which must not be spoken of,"[22] namely the things that literature says by not-saying them. But in this rendition, the presence of ideology in literature calls for an even closer and more formal reading. As with the definition of ideology described above, so too the analytical process has been almost reversed: We are not to ask whether literature accords with history but are to read in order to discover history. Literature so considered is not about sensuous experience but about understanding and perception; and perception is about structures, limits, and forms.

Indeed, this ideological formalism may be in danger of generating its own reductionism. Far from there being any need to argue the unity of form and content, it now seems rather that critics are in danger of ignoring the more explicit content of a work as superficial or even as misleading. The marriage of form and content has made them one, and that one is form.[23] In the structured literary universe, ideology is basically represented by available forms and their possible permutations, by styles and modes, in other words the "mechanisms of aesthetic production," that generate the range of possible ideological meanings. What all this seems to indicate is that writing is a process of forms interacting and intersecting with forms; and that critical reading, however ideological, is essentially a formal exegesis of which the elucidation of the content of literature is a by-product. The work that presents its conception of the world as natural through the apparent spontaneity of character and story conceals that way "its real ideological determinants," which it is the critic's task to reveal. The ideal and apparently absolute imaginary world orbits an ideological star in a contingent universe.

So the word by which Destutt de Tracy and his eighteenth-century confreres meant to indicate the study of the mind's eternal universe has come down to us as in itself a historical system structuring the way the mind interacts with nature and society to make and continuously remake a relativistic history. From its Enlightenment origin in a vision of infinitely free ideas, "ideology" has become a term that mediates the finite entities of text and context, and also of individual author and cultural history; that is, a term that demarcates the limits of individualism and the imagination.

At the same time, however, the ideological dimension of a work is also the site or the means for at least a degree of imaginative freedom. Indeed, in Macherey's nice concept of literary silences that speak or hint of alternatives otherwise unimaginable, the literary encounter with ideology seems to produce a version of transcendence. Jameson stresses that Marxism offers not only a negative or demystifying but a positive, Utopian hermeneutic: Even as an ideological analysis uncovers the political argument couched in apparently natural forms, it also aspires to transcend that opposition between ideology and ideal, and to project a Utopian "collective logic beyond good and evil."[24] Insofar as the literary object of analysis is material, this kind of transcendence is perhaps rather an ultimate penetration to structural first principles. The alternative visions that succeed such a harrowing of the ideological underworld appear as shadows cast forward by history from the edge of this world. Thus they are not freely imagined in the old sense, nor do they construct new worlds. They only reveal that this one is finite and incomplete. Precisely by taking us to the limits of ideology, literature may offer a way to look a little beyond. The ideological analysis of literature would then be particularly perceptive even of literary "transcendence."

The Marxist tradition has been the primary context for the development of the concept of ideology, but both as word and as meaning it has a prior and concurrent independent history. Indeed, probably the best-known analysis of capitalist ideology was done by the sociologist Max Weber, who was not a Marxist, and his analysis implies a concept of ideology at least as powerful as the one projected by Marx. For whereas Marx had denounced ideology as mainly an apologia for the existing social system, Weber described it, in *The Protestant Ethic and the Spirit of Capitalism*,[25] as the positive force that had enabled and inspired the emergence of a new system. In this guise, ideology early acquired a substance of its own, and became not only rationale but reason.

On one level, Marx's and Weber's definitions might be seen as two sides of a coin: rather than opposite definitions, only opposite perspectives. The Marxists, having adopted the perspective of the working class, would then be describing the way ideology deluded workers into quiescence, whereas Weber, looking at things from the standpoint of the middle class, sought to explain how it had acquired and maintained its hegemony. But in fact the two accounts are not entirely complementary, Weber's positive version of ideology going beyond Marx's negative, to add to instrumentality the capacity both for self-generation and for giving rise to history. Elsewhere, Weber explicitly criticized Marxists for what he described as their one-sided materialist conception of causality, which reduced ideology to a creature of economic interests.

He himself placed ideology at the origin of things. If men make history, ideologies make men. His examination of the history of capitalism starts not with the material formation of classes but with the making of individuals by "the influence of those psychological sanctions which, originating in religious belief and the practice of religion, gave a direction to practical conduct and held the individual to it" (p. 97). Although he did not claim that ascetic Protestantism had actually created economic capitalism, he did ascribe to it the power not only to abet but to enact material transformations. Thus for him, ideas, such as the one that hard work and simple living are pleasing to God, have the power to initiate economic activity and even to deter expected behavior. Weber stressed the irrationality of mortal beings accumulating wealth they would never consume, that indeed they intended never to consume, as the measure of the extraordinary power of the "spirit of capitalism" precisely to rationalize.

Weber's Protestant ideology was an autonomous system that "stood at the cradle of the modern economic man" (p. 174). In a formulation that epitomizes his difference with Marx, he found that Protestant asceticism had "created the force which was alone decisive" for the success of "the idea that faithful labour, even at low wages, on the part of those whom life offers no other opportunities, is highly pleasing to God," an idea that flowed from "the conception of this labour as a calling, as the best, often in the last analysis the only means of attaining certainty of grace" (p. 178). This translation of what Marx dubbed the "opiate" of religion that ensured the passivity of the oppressed proletariat, into the proletariat's positive inspiration to work hard and cheap, dramatizes the way, once thought is taken to be not only reproductive but productive, false consciousness itself may acquire a positive meaning.

The Weberian definition of ideology as a historical and cultural agent in its own right proved a congenial basis for the construction of subsequent definitions that also stressed the positive power of ideas. In his *Ideology and Utopia*,[26] Karl Mannheim took Weber's concept to its logical conclusion by totalizing it so that it absorbed the entire universe of historical experience. All that we know, we know through the prism of ideology, he argued, "the thought of all parties in all epochs is of an ideological character" (p. 77). We had better, then, abandon "the vain hope of discovering truth in a form which is independent of an historically and socially determined set of meanings." The analysis of ideology is not an unmasking but a historical explanation of claims and attitudes that only present themselves as transcendent. Where for Weber ideology was a particular perspective among others, for Mannheim it became all-pervasive: "All historical knowledge is relational knowledge, and can only be formulated with reference to the position of the observer" (p. 79). Thus encompassing all social thinking and understanding, the study of ideology is really a "sociology of knowledge"; the analyst's goal is "to understand the narrowness of each individual point of view and the interplay between these distinctive attitudes in the total social process" (p. 81).

Mannheim's concept of ideology permits a material analysis that still realizes the substantiality of ideas and mental forms. But this reconciliation of thought and experience has its cost, or at least it runs a risk that Clifford Geertz dubbed "Mannheim's Paradox."[27] The paradox is simply that if all knowledge is ideological, no analysis can rise above the level of its own ideology: It cannot then be fully analytical. For all his insistence that, despite the relative nature of all evaluation, one must still make moral and political judgments, Mannheim lacked firm ground on which to base such judgments.[28] If all knowledge is relative, how can we even know that we know, let alone commit ourselves to it, as Mannheim continued to urge?

Geertz's conception of ideology might be considered in our context a third stage of non-Marxist descent. He proposed to resolve Mannheim's paradox, which had emerged from the totalization of Weber's ideology, by what amounts to a further totalitization. Mannheim had

16 Theodor Adorno, *Prisms,* translated from the German by Samuel and Sherry Weber, (Cambridge, Mass.: MIT Press, 1982; originally published 1967), p. 31.

17 Walter Benjamin (1892–1940) was a member of the group of critics known as the "Frankfurt School" (although in the thirties he lived mainly in Paris) and wrote literary and cultural criticism. He was closely associated with Bertolt Brecht. Attempting to flee Nazi-occupied France, he was caught at the border and committed suicide. Georg Lukács (1885–1971) was a Marxist literary critic and an important contributor to the development of what is sometimes referred to as "Western Marxism" in order to suggest its Western European orientation with its weight of Enlightenment and Romantic traditions and values. Some accounts divide Lukács's career between early and late in a way that refers to this heritage, characterizing the early period as first Kantian and then Hegelian in contrast to the Marxism and Leninism of his later thought.

18 Hannah Arendt's introduction to Benjamin's *Illuminations* (see Selected Bibliography) is particularly useful.

19 Fredric Jameson, *Marxism and Form: Twentieth-Century Dialectical Theories of Literature* (Princeton, N.J.: Princeton University Press, 1971), chapter 1, pp. 38–59.

20 In the historical context, this represents a criticism of Romantic definitions of language that render it as all-powerful in the image of an all-knowable world.

21 Louis Althusser, "Ideology and Ideological State Apparatuses," in *Lenin and Philosophy and Other Essays,* translated from the French by Ben Brewster (London: New Left Books, 1971), pp. 127–86.

22 This is Terence Eagleton's paraphrase of Macherey, *Criticism and Ideology,* p. 90. *Pour une théorie de la production litteraire* was originally published in a series edited by Louis Althusser (Paris: François Maspero, 1966; English translation by Geoffrey Wall, London: Routledge & Kegan Paul, 1978).

23 For Eagleton, "to explain the literary work in terms of the ideological structure of which it is a part, yet which it transforms in its art . . . means grasping the literary work as a *formal* structure." (*Marxism and Literary Criticism* [Berkeley: University of California Press, 1976], p. 19.)

24 Fredric Jameson, *The Political Unconscious: Narrative as a Socially Symbolic Act* (Ithaca, N.Y.: Cornell University Press, 1981), p. 286.

25 Max Weber, *The Protestant Ethic and the Spirit of Capitalism,* translated by Talcott Parsons with a foreword by R. H. Tawney (New York: Scribner, 1958; originally published 1904–05.)

26 Karl Mannheim, *Ideology and Utopia: An Introduction to the Sociology of Knowledge,* Translated from the German by Louis Wirth and Edward Shils, (New York, Harcourt Brace, n.d.; originally published 1936).

27 Clifford Geertz, "Ideology as a Cultural System," in *The Interpretation of Cultures* (New York: Basic Books, 1973), pp. 193–233.

28 As protection against this predicament, Marx and his followers had their

vision of the Utopian future as a solid external standpoint, and Weber had other modes of thought and value from which to evaluate the ideological.

29   Indeed, the method Geertz developed for anthropological investigation mimics textual exegesis. "Thick description" might be described as an *explication du texte sociale* whose synchronic complexity stands in for Mannheim's dialectical process.

30   Daniel Bell, "The End of Ideology in the West, An Epilogue," in *The End of Ideology: On the Exhaustion of Ideas in the Fifties* (New York: Free Press, 1960), pp. 393–407.

I

Reassessments

2

Symbol and Idea in *Virgin Land*

HENRY NASH SMITH

Myth and ideology have often been linked in political discussion, sometimes as antonyms, sometimes as synonyms. It is therefore surprising, as one critic has pointed out, that the word "ideology" does not appear in my book *Virgin Land: The American West as Symbol and Myth* (1950).[1] The apparent neglect of this topic raises a question bearing on the central concerns of the book. It is true that "ideology" is used loosely nowadays to designate the assumptions underlying a given writer's view of almost any topic, but the term still has polemic overtones recalling the fact that it became current in this country as a result of the growing interest in Marxist theory following the Russian revolution. If *Virgin Land* systematically avoids dealing with conflicts that are ideological in the political sense, it lies open to the charge occasionally brought against it of being an example of "consensus history."[2] The present chapter addresses this question.

In an article entitled " 'Myth' and 'Ideology' in Modern Usage," Ben Halpern presents a brief history of the terms, from which I draw a few salient facts.[3] The word "ideology" was first used by Destutt de Tracy in his *Éléments d'idéologie* (1803–17), where it meant "the system of purely objective true ideas built up from the clear and distinct elements of perception." Thereafter it figured prominently in French and German political controversy. Marx used "ideology" to designate "the whole system of religion, morality and law, whereby a ruling class 'justifies' and upholds the social system dictated by its interest."[4] Specifically, he intended to contrast the received ideas constituting the false consciousness of the bourgeoisie with the truth revealed in the doctrines of dialectical materialism and of the primacy of the class struggle as a motivating force in history. Controversy continues into the present between those who affirm and those who deny that these doctrines embody "scientific"

21

truth. Louis Feuer's hostile *Ideology and the Ideologists* (1975), for example, maintains that in our day it is the orthodox Marxists who are the ideologues.[5] Fortunately, there is no need for me to venture into the enchanted forest of this debate, because both "myth" and "ideology" are now widely used without reference to theoretical subtleties. Thus W. J. T. Mitchell, editor of *Critical Inquiry,* in a recent article discussing that respected journal, while recognizing that "the notion of an 'ideological pluralism' seems self-contradictory, for the ideologue must deny the possibility of pure pluralism," nevertheless insists that his editorial policy is precisely that, transcending ideology.[6]

Against this background, let me turn to a consideration of ideology in relation to *Virgin Land.* In the preface to the book, I proposed to use the terms "symbol" and "myth" to designate "larger or smaller units of the same kind of thing, namely an intellectual construction that fuses concept and emotion into an image."[7] I might have avoided some misunderstandings of what I was about if I had introduced the term "ideology" at this point by adding that the intellectual constructions under consideration could not be sharply categorized but should be thought of as occupying positions along a spectrum extending from myth at one end, characterized by the dominance of image and emotion, to ideology at the other end, characterized by emphasis on concepts, on abstract ideas.[8] The unfortunate additional statement that I did not "mean to raise the question whether such products of the imagination accurately reflect empirical fact" was a clumsy effort to distinguish both these kinds of intellectual construction from the intellectual constructions of historians who accept the constraint of refutability by reference to recorded data about past events. From this point of view the distinction between myth and ideology is less important than that between both myth and ideology on one hand and what I call "empirical fact" on the other. I was undertaking not to add to the vast methodologically controlled record of past events and behavior produced by professional historians, but rather to chart what I called (in an unpublished prospectus written in 1939) "the superstructure of the Westward Movement."

Yet the Marxist term "superstructure" oversimplifies the argument of *Virgin Land* because it classifies the symbols and myths described in the book as mere rationalizations, hermetically enclosed within a false consciousness. My thesis is more complex. I present the collective representations I discuss as having quite various relations to the reality of American history as this is defined by scholars, and I do not accord to that reality a "scientific" accuracy. The book does indeed assume that both myth and ideology in American culture belong wholly or partly to what Fredric Jameson has recently labeled the "political unconscious."[9]

But within the category of collective representations I maintain a rough distinction between myth and symbol as structures of concrete images and a set of abstract ideas that has remained relatively constant in its outlines from the seventeenth century to the present. Thus I point out that the conception of "free land" beyond the frontier as a "safety valve" for tensions and conflicts within the settled parts of the United States was "an imaginative construction which masked poverty and industrial strife with the pleasing suggestion that a beneficent nature stronger than any human agency, the ancient resource of Americans, the power that had made the country rich and great, would solve the new problems of industrialism."[10]

The ideas involved here belong to what Sacvan Bercovitch calls "the American consensus" that "has often served, rhetorically, as a defence against the facts of pluralism and conflict."[11] This structure of beliefs has given special emphasis from the beginning to the West and the Westward Movement, placing the British occupation of North America within a world-historical frame. It appeared as a constituent of high culture in seventeenth-century New England Puritan discourse and gradually became diffused throughout popular culture. Connecting the Puritan idea of an errand into the wilderness that Perry Miller analyzed with the "Hebrew exodus" in a typology of America's mission, Bercovitch has more recently asserted its importance in the political theory of the Revolution.[12] David Levin recognizes a similar set of ideas in the work of the nineteenth-century Romantic historians,[13] and Albert Weinberg produced a classic monograph on the subject as early as 1935 in *Manifest Destiny: A Study of Nationalist Expansionism in American History*. Bercovitch has identified this " 'consensus view' of American history" as "the context of the American literary renaissance," calling it "neither a myth nor a statistic, but an ideology" and "an ideology that links the myth-maker and the census-taker."[14]

This cluster of concepts, which I would call an American ideology, is constantly present in *Virgin Land,* but, so to speak, offstage, only occasionally given explicit recognition. The structure of the book is basically a conflict between an assumed historical reality and the ideology, myths, and symbols generated in American culture by contemplation of the moving frontier of settlement and the territory beyond. Because this ideology is usually taken for granted in *Virgin Land,* I shall present a few quotations from various other sources that exhibit it more fully.

I begin with David Levin's sketch of the cosmic frame within which the mission of America was conceived by the historians he discusses: "History was the unfolding of a vast Providential plan, and the laws of the moral world were the links between the ages, forming 'the guiding principle of civilization, which marshals incongruous incidents into their just places and arranges checkered groups in clear and harmonious order.' " Furthermore,

> Human progress had proceeded westward, from the Middle East to North America. And all along the way, whether they knew it or not, the people of the vanguard had carried with them a new principle: Christianity in the "German woods," nationality in the Iberian peninsula, the Reformation in the Netherlands and England, Democracy (or Liberty) in the American colonies.[15]

Richard Hofstadter summarizes the thesis of George Bancroft's ten-volume *History of the United States* (1834–76): "The unifying principle [of American history] was progress ordained and planned by God – the advance of liberty, justice, and humanity, all of which were particularly exemplified in American history, where providential guidance had brought together a singularly fit people and fit institutions."[16] The operative word here is "progress." Its most obvious referent was the development of American political institutions and economic growth, which were set in motion immediately with the planting of the original colonies along the Atlantic seaboard. But it had a more striking, because more visible and dramatic, horizontal dimension in the Westward Movement, the advance of "civilization" across the continent. In Tocqueville's *Democracy in America* (1835; first American edition 1838) he says that the eyes of the American people are fixed upon the majestic spectacle of "its own march" into the wilderness, "drying swamps, turning the course of rivers, peopling solitudes, and subduing Nature."

> This magnificent image of themselves [declares Tocqueville] does not meet the gaze of the Americans at intervals only: it may be said to haunt every one of them in his least as well as in his most important actions, and to be always flitting before his mind. Nothing conceivable is so petty, so insipid, so crowded with paltry interests, in one word so anti-poetic, as the life of a man in the United States. But among the thoughts which it suggests there is always one which is full of poetry, and that is the hidden nerve which gives vigor to the frame.[17]

Tocqueville's description applies to what might be called the domestic aspect of the American ideology. The outward-looking aspect would become more prominent in the following decade, which saw the invention of the slogan "Manifest Destiny," the war against Mexico, and the American acquisition of the vast area stretching from the Great

Plains to the Pacific Coast. A Currier and Ives print of 1868 entitled "Across the Continent: 'Westward the Course of Empire Takes Its Way'," from a lithograph by Fanny Palmer, shows an apparently limitless flat empty space with a railroad stretching into a haze of distance. A range of mountains borders the plain on one side, with a river at its base on which a lone Indian is paddling a canoe. On the bank are two Indians on horseback with lance and bow, but they are simply picturesque, not menacing. In the middle distance covered wagons follow a primitive road paralleling the tracks. The foreground is occupied by a steam locomotive headed west with a train of cars, standing beside a cluster of log cabins from which additional covered wagons are setting out. Men are wielding shovels and axes to fell a small grove near the cabins, the largest of which is prominently labeled "Public School." Children are entering the school, while townspeople beside the train greet newcomers.[18]

In this allegorical picture the white settlers are not engaged in hostilities with the natives, but as the frontier of settlement moved out upon the Great Plains after the Civil War, formidable campaigns were mounted against the Plains Indians.[19] The names of Geronimo and Sitting Bull, along with that of Custer, became household words. The melodrama of dime-novel Indian fighting was transferred to the stage in the 1870s in a play called *Buffalo Bill, King of Bordermen,* which starred William F. Cody himself, and in the following decade Cody took his own Wild West Show on the road, with immense success in the East and in Europe. This prime example of popular art was of course a dramatization of the ideology of Manifest Destiny. At the Trans-Mississippi Exposition at Omaha, Nebraska, in 1898 a Cody Day was proclaimed with the hero as guest of honor. Senator John M. Thurston delivered an address in which he proclaimed:

> You have been a great national and international educator of men. . . . We remember that when this whole western land was a wilderness, when these representatives of the aborigines were attempting to hold their own against the onward tide of civilization, the settler and the hardy pioneer, the women and the children, felt safe whenever Cody rode along the frontier; he was their protector and defender.[20]

Cody was fully equal to the role assigned him by Senator Thurston. In his reply he said that "we who are old men, we who are called old-timers, cannot forget the trials and tribulations which we had to encounter while paving the path for civilization and national prosperity." The American ideology either ignored the existence of the native inhabitants of the continent or cast them as subhuman foes. As Thurston's allusion indicates, one of the acts in Cody's show presented a band of Indian horsemen attacking a stagecoach or covered wagons bearing white settlers. Richard Slotkin has shown that such a ritual combat had been a feature of the Western story from its origins in seventeenth-century narratives of Indian captivities and wars.[21] The point demands emphasis because with the passage of time the exciting physical combat acquired a more and more elaborate rationale, usually covert, for which the word "civilization" was the code designation. Something of this sort must be what Thurston had in mind when he called Buffalo Bill "a great national and international educator of men."[22]

For a final example of the pervasive presence of the American ideology made into a myth, I turn to a speech delivered in September 1980 by the candidate who would be elected president in November. In the so-called television debate with John Anderson, Ronald Reagan declared:

> I have always believed that this land was placed here between the two great oceans by some divine plan. It was placed here to be found by a special kind of people – people who had a special love for freedom and who had the courage to uproot themselves and leave hearth and homeland and come to what in the beginning was the most undeveloped wilderness possible. We spoke a multitude of tongues – landed on this eastern shore and then went out over the mountains and the prairies and the deserts and the far Western mountains of the Pacific building cities and towns and farms and schools and churches.
>
> If wind, water or fire destroyed them, we built them again. And in so doing at the same time we built a new breed of human called an American – a proud, an independent and a most compassionate individual for the most part. Two hundred years ago Tom Paine, when the thirteen tiny colonies were trying to become a nation, said we have it in our power to begin the world over again.[23]

The providential mission, the rebirth of a new and guiltless type of man, the American, in the New World after the ritual death of tearing up roots – these are easily recognizable, even without the reference to Tom Paine. And if it seems odd that the candidate favored by fundamentalist Protestant sects should invoke the name of a notorious infidel, Reagan reestablishes his connection with religious tradition by declaring in conclusion, "together we can begin the world over again. We can meet our destiny and that destiny can build a land here that will be for all mankind a shining city on a hill. I think we ought to get at it."

The materials dealt with in *Virgin Land* are all in one way or another connected with this central ideology or myth of America – for the most part as embodiments of it, but in a few instances as competing myths, the principal examples being the notion of a Great American Desert east of the Rockies and the pre–Civil War Southern vision of a slave empire on the shores of the Caribbean. The content of the book was dictated by what I found when I embarked on a naïvely inductive examination of nineteenth-century American attitudes toward the West. Believing that I was operating without hypotheses, I set about reading all published descriptions of or comments on the Great Plains and the Rocky Mountains – all the narratives of travel and residence in these areas, articles in magazines, poems and stories and novels that I could lay my hands on. Of course, this proved to be an impossibly ambitious project, especially as my roughly chronological approach revealed an increasing proliferation of such materials with every passing decade. Furthermore, as I reread *Virgin Land* now I realize that my own attitudes were influenced by the basic myth or ideology of America to a greater extent than I had realized. This conditioning was the perhaps inevitable result of the intellectual climate of the academic community within which I had received my formal training in American history. As late as the 1930s, the study and teaching of the subject were still largely controlled by the ideas of Frederick Jackson Turner, who, although retired from teaching, had been active as a scholar up to his death in 1932.[24] The very choice of the subject of *Virgin Land* may well have been suggested by the pervasive interest in the frontier generated by his work.

At any rate, when I imagined I was operating without hypotheses, I was sometimes unwittingly using those of Turner. I recognized that the immense poetic resonance of Turner's work owed much to the mass of discussion of the West lying behind it. I noted that he was a Middle Westerner speaking "from the distilled experience of his people," and added:

> If the myth of the garden embodied certain erroneous judgments made by these people concerning the economic forces that had come to dominate American life, it was still true to their experience in the large, because it expressed beliefs and aspirations as well as statistics. This is not the only kind of historical truth, but it is a kind historians need never find contemptible.[25]

In calling some elements of the myth of the garden simply erroneous, I felt myself to be standing apart from them as a neutral observer. But I was not entirely detached from the "beliefs and aspirations" expressed

by Turner. The oversimplified term "statistics" and the hint of elevation in the archaic phrase "need never" reveal an emotional contagion, a
note of rhetoric replacing thought.

An even more important failure on my part to comprehend fully the
assumptions underlying Turner's view of American history concerned
the celebrated declaration that "the existence of an area of free land, its
continuous recession, and the advance of American settlement westward explain American development."[26] The term "free land" is integral to Turner's definition of the frontier as the dividing line between
civilization and savagery. I recognized that "civilization" brought with
it the theory of a fixed typology of social stages through which every
society must pass as it develops from a state of nature upward toward
the level of complexity and refinement represented by the nations of
Europe and the eastern United States. But I did not realize to what
extent the notion of civilization embodied a doctrine of inevitable progress so deeply buried it was almost inaccessible to critical examination.
Thus I took over from Turner the attitude that Ursula Brumm has
found to be characteristic of American culture, a refusal to acknowledge
the guilt intrinsic to the national errand into the wilderness.[27] Like my
teachers and academic colleagues, I had in this fashion lost the capacity
for facing up to the tragic dimensions of the Westward Movement.

I had acquired an even more important contagion from Turner's
conception of the wilderness beyond the frontier as free land: the tendency to assume that this area was in effect devoid of human inhabitants. As Richard Hofstadter observes, in Turner's *Rise of the New West*
(and in his work generally), "the Indian has almost entirely disappeared
as an actor or a victim from American history."[28] *Virgin Land* suffers to
some extent from Turner's tunnel vision. It would be a much better
book if it showed even a partial awareness of the materials that would
be brought together in subsequent years by Roy Harvey Pearce in *The
Savages of America: A Study of the Indian and the Idea of Civilization*,[29] and
especially by Richard Drinnon's impressive *Facing West*, which surveys
American policy toward nonwhite races from the Pequots in the seventeenth century to the Vietnamese in the twentieth.[30]

From these observations about pervasive ideological distortion in *Virgin Land,* I turn to more particular comments on the three main sections
into which the book is divided. I regret that in the first (and shortest) of
these, entitled "Passage to India," I did not follow the consequences of
the idea of Manifest Destiny beyond a discussion of Whitman's mystical
vision of a brotherhood of nations and races brought about by the
American advance across the Pacific. It is a defect in my study that I did
not at least glance at the grimly ironic later history of the cult of

Manifest Destiny, which Drinnon and others have shown to have had great influence in the twentieth century.

The next section of *Virgin Land*, "The Sons of Leatherstocking," introduces the vast subject of fictional treatments of the Wild West. This aspect of American experience has, of course, been seized upon by the popular cultures of nations literally throughout the world, and has accordingly attracted much scholarly attention in recent decades.[31] Two books have a particular relevance to my own work – so much relevance, in fact, that condensations of them might conceivably be added as first and last chapters to *Virgin Land*. Richard Slotkin's *Regeneration Through Violence* is an embarrassment to me because it reveals how massive a body of writing about the West lies behind the documents considered in my own study. And John G. Cawelti's *Adventure, Mystery, and Romance*[32] surveys and analyzes the fortunes of the Western story in the twentieth century, with ample attention to the movies as well as to literary versions. Both Slotkin and Cawelti have observations about the American cult of violence – legitimized violence, to use Cawelti's phrase recalling our desperate need to believe in our own innocence[33] – that strike me as profound. Both these scholars raise in an acute form a question that has been endlessly debated: What is the significance of the fact that the western two-gun man has been during much of the twentieth century, and remains in some degree today, a national folk hero? Does the evolution of this mythical figure (from dime novels to the movies and then to television series) merely reflect cultural changes rooted in economic and social processes, or do the imaginative products of popular culture play a part in shaping the attitudes of the populace at large?

The last paragraph of Slotkin's book states the problem eloquently without offering an answer. In memory, transformed by imagination, the American frontiersmen have an air of "simplicity and purity that makes them seen finely heroic expressions of an admirable quality of the human spirit." But the actual effect of "our passage through the land" has been to exalt "the warfare between man and nature, between race and race," as "a kind of heroic ideal": The Westward Movement has built railways and cities and factories but has left "the land and its people, its 'dark' people especially, economically exploited and wasted."[34]

Book Three of *Virgin Land*, "The Garden of the World," is the longest of the three sections, and the one containing the most frequent references to the impact of myths and symbols on the processes of history, particularly on political history. It is in this section, therefore, that the question of the possible effect of a nonmaterial force on actual events arises in its most tangible form. Let me consider a few representative passages. In summarizing the attack on slavery made by Charles J. Faulkner in the Virginia legislature in 1832, I assert that his recital of the clichés of agrarian theory and the ideal of a freehold yeoman society was "true enough . . . to constitute an accurate prediction of the intellectual history of the free-soil West for the next half-century."[35] This rather obscure statement does not exactly claim that Faulkner's speech determined the course of history, but a later passage is less ambiguous:

> The agrarian ideal had supplanted mercantilist theory in the latter part of the eighteenth century because at that time it had corresponded more closely to the actual state of affairs in the North American interior and had provided a much more reliable basis for charting the course of Western history in the immediate future. One index to its adequacy was the vigor and persuasive power of the symbol of the yeoman that had been developed from its premises.[36]

The references to "persuasive power" and to "charting the course of Western history" (whatever "charting" may be taken to mean) suggest that the agrarian ideology exerted an influence on the minds of numerous individuals, especially perhaps of voters and even of legislators. I feel now that I should have been more explicit, but this passage stands in the context of a good deal of evidence concerning the climate of opinion in the United States during the decades preceding the Civil War. Leo Marx is correct in finding in *Virgin Land* the contention that "Americans, so far as they shared an idea of what they were doing as a people, actually saw themselves creating a society in the image of a garden" and indeed that "down to the twentieth century the imagination of Americans was dominated by the idea of transforming the heartland into . . . a new 'Garden of the World'."[37]

My most direct assertion of the influence of the agrarian myth or ideology on actual events concerns the election of 1860. I quote briefly from *Virgin Land:* "The platform of 1860, demanding free homesteads for actual settlers, showed that the Republicans meant to capture the myth of the garden and the symbol of the hardy yeoman, and thus to command the imaginations of the Northwestern farmers." Or, more elaborately:

> The seizure of this symbol [of the yeoman] by Republican orators in the campaign of 1860 enlisted in their cause the undefined but powerful force which the imagination of the masses of voters always exerts in political crises. Advocates of the Homestead Bill sincerely believed that the yeoman depicted in

the myth of the garden was an accurate representation of the common man of the Northwest and this belief was evidentally shared by thousands of voters.[38]

There are enough monographs about the campaign of 1860 to provide at least some support for these statements. I do, however, run the danger of oversimplifying the election by implying that the homestead proposal was the dominant if not the only contested issue.

As a final example of my assertion of the influence of symbolic structures on group behavior, let me mention the chapter entitled "The Myth of the Garden and Reform of the Land System." I observe that

> The ghosts of outmoded idealisms . . . are not easily laid. As they lose their pertinence to a changed social setting, they often become bad influences by lending themselves to the uses of men who wish merely to confuse issues. The myth of the garden suffered this fate. By the 1870s it could already be invoked to prevent reform of the land system.[39]

In this instance debates in Congress, unpublished correspondence concerning the creation of the United States Geological Survey, reports of various federally supported scientific surveys, and promotional pamphlets furnish a good deal of documentation concerning the motives of the more prominent antagonists in the controversy over John Wesley Powell's proposals for adapting the homestead system to the conditions of soil and climate beyond the one-hundredth meridian. My analysis is reasonably circumstantial and I am able to maintain with some confidence that "the unimpaired survival of the dream of a yeoman society, with its idealism only slightly tarnished as yet by the sordid collapse of the homestead system, threw over the facts an imaginative veil which furnished the pretext for a sincere, if shallow, opposition to so drastic a reforming program as Powell's."[40] In the end, the myth of the garden prevailed. Both the testimony concerning rainfall on the Great Plains delivered at hearings before the Public Land Commission in 1879 and debates on the floor of Congress seem to me to demonstrate conclusively the power of an ideology, deriving in unbroken continuity from the Puritan notion of a divine errand into the wilderness, to serve the selfish interests of skillful manipulators. The manipulators would have been powerless if the ideology, with its imaginative aura of myth, had not survived to some degree as a collective representation in the minds of a considerable fraction of the general public.

I conclude with a quotation from a review by George M. Fredrickson that I find highly congenial:

The questions Frederick Jackson Turner raised about the lasting impact of the westward movement on European-American culture and society deserve reconsideration from a new perspective that would be less given to emphasis on triumphs of the frontiersmen. To what extent is the careless and wasteful exploitation of natural resources in the U.S. an inheritance from the frontier scramble for seemingly endless wealth? Does the resurgent American ethic of "looking out for number one" in any way represent a carry-over of frontier individualism? Are we bellicose and moralistic in international relations partly because of habits of mind acquired during the conquest of North America? Do liberal fears of "a cowboy in the White House" represent more than a loose metaphor? . . .

If we look upon the frontier as a place where the spirit of capitalistic accumulation could flower without restraint, we can perhaps begin to recapture its significance for American history in general.[41]

Notes

1   "Smith might have gone further in relating the myth to actuality by showing it function, for example, as an ideology (a term strikingly absent from the book, though the concept of it is hinted)" (Alan Trachtenberg, "Myth, History, and Literature in *Virgin Land,*" in *Prospects* 3 [1977]: 127).

2   For example, in an anonymous article in *Time* magazine (February 2, 1970, pp. 14–15) entitled "Revisionism: A New, Angry Look at the American Past." Among the "revisionist" historians named are Staughton Lynd, Leon Litwak, Eugene Genovese, Gabriel Kolko, Bernard Bernstein, Barrington Moore, Jr., and William Appleman Williams. Some revisionists are said to be influenced by Marxism. The "consensus historians" named in the article, besides myself, are Richard Hofstadter, Daniel Boorstin, and George Kennan. John Higham had broached this topic a decade earlier in "The Cult of the 'American Consensus': Homogenizing Our History" (*Commentary* 27 [February 1959]: 93–100), citing Daniel Boorstin as his principal example.

3   Ben Halpern, " 'Myth' and 'Ideology' in Modern Usage," *History and Theory* 1 (1961): 129–49.

4   Paraphrased by Halpern (*History and Theory* 1 [1961]: 148, n. 27) from Marx's *The Eighteenth Brumaire of Louis Napoleon.*

5   Louis Feuer, *Ideology and the Ideologists* (New York, 1975), esp. pp. 96–97.

6   W. J. T. Mitchell, "*Critical Inquiry* and the Ideology of Pluralism," *Critical Inquiry* 8 (Summer 1982): 612–13.

7   Henry Nash Smith, *Virgin Land: The American West as Symbol and Myth* (Cambridge, Mass., 1950), p. vii.

8   This model corresponds to Halpern's statement that "the basic distinction
    is that between rationality ('ideology') and irrationality ('myth') as two
    limits in a continuum which may be designated by the name of 'historically
    significant value' " (*History and Theory* 1 [1961]: 144). James O. Robertson,
    citing G. S. Kirk, *Myth: Its Meaning and Functions in Ancient and Other
    Cultures* (1970), proposes a definition of myth that seems to embrace the
    entire spectrum I have described, extending from myth to ideology:
    "Myths are by their nature vague. . . . They are the available images
    which pervade the culture of every nation, every group, every family, and
    every individual." (Robertson, *American Myth, American Reality* [New
    York, 1980], p. 347). And Robertson's description of myth seems reason-
    ably close to Roland Barthes's conception in *Mythologies,* trans. Annette
    Lavers (New York, 1972; first published 1954–56).

9   Fredric Jameson, *The Political Unconscious: Narrative as a Socially Symbolic
    Act* (Ithaca, N.Y., 1981), esp. p. 87. Feuer quotes Friedrich Engels to the
    effect that "Ideology is a process accomplished by the so-called thinker
    consciously, it is true, but with a false consciousness. The real motive force
    impelling him remains unknown to him; otherwise it simply would not be
    an ideological process. Hence he invents false or seeming motives" (*Ideol-
    ogy and the Ideologists,* p. 180).

10 Smith, *Virgin Land,* pp. 205–6.

11 Sacvan Bercovitch, "The Ideological Context of the American Renais-
    sance," in Winfred Fluck, Jürgen Peper, and Willi Paul Adams, eds., *Forms
    and Functions of History in American Literature: Essays in Honor of Ursula
    Brumm* (Berlin, 1981), p. 1.

12 Sacvan Bercovitch, "The Typology of America's Mission," *American Quar-
    terly* 30 (Summer 1978): 135–55, esp. 151.

13 David Levin, *History as Romantic Art: Bancroft, Prescott, Motley, Parkman*
    (Stanford, 1959), esp. pp. 27–28, 32, 36.

14 Bercovitch, "Ideological Context," pp. 1–2.

15 Levin, *History as Romantic Art,* pp. 26–27.

16 Richard Hofstadter, *The Progressive Historians: Turner, Beard, Parrington*
    (New York, 1963), p. 16.

17 Alexis de Tocqueville, *Democracy in America,* trans. Henry Reeve, ed.
    Henry S. Commager, Galaxy edition (New York, 1947), p. 292. Berco-
    vitch ("Ideological Context," p. 19) quotes an observation of Emerson that
    expresses almost exactly the same idea: "They [who] complain about the
    flatness of American life have no perception of its destiny. They are not
    Americans" (*Works,* ed. E. W. Emerson, 12 vols. [1903–4], 11:544).

18 Reproduced at p. 90 of Susan D. Walker, *The Railroad in the American
    Landscape: 1850–1950* (catalogue of an exhibit in the Wellesley College
    Museum, Wellesley, Mass., 1981).

19 Samuel Eliot Morison and Henry S. Commager, *The Growth of the Ameri-
    can Republic,* 5th ed., 2 vols. (New York, 1962), 2:135–40.

20 Richard J. Walsh, in collaboration with Milton J. Salisbury, *The Making of
    Buffalo Bill: A Study in Heroics* (Indianapolis, 1928), p. 319. The stability of

the myth of the Westward Movement is demonstrated by the fidelity of Senator Thurston's monstrous fiction to the beliefs represented in the sculptured "Rescue Group" by Horatio Greenough that had been installed in the national Capitol in 1853. It depicts a Daniel Boone larger than life-size wrestling with an Indian warrior armed with a tomahawk who is attempting to murder a white mother with her babe in her arms. Photographs of this sculpture appear in Roy H. Pearce, *The Savages of America: A Study of the Indian and the Idea of Civilization*, rev. ed. (Baltimore, 1965), facing p. 3, and in Robert H. Berkhofer, Jr., *The White Man's Indian. Images of the American Indian from Columbus to the Present* (New York, 1978), plate 7 following p. 138. See also Robert W. Rydell, "The Trans-Mississippi and International Exposition: 'To Work Out the Problem of Universal Civilization,' " *American Quarterly* 33 (Winter 1981): 587–607.

21 Richard Slotkin, *Regeneration Through Violence: The Mythology of the American Frontier, 1600–1850* (Middletown, Conn.: 1973), esp. p. 68: "The Indian wars proved to be the most acceptable metaphor for the American experience."

22 The scenario derived from the myth of Manifest Destiny could be revised to keep pace with history. When the Wild West Show played in Madison Square Garden in 1901, it included "a reproduction of the storming of Tientsin in the recent Boxer Rebellion." The Indians were "reluctantly made up as Chinamen" in order to defend the Chinese city. Mark Twain was reported to have "left the house looking 'sour as a pickle' " to show his "dislike for the Chinese policy of the government" (Walsh and Salisbury, *The Making of Buffalo Bill*, p. 326).

23 Text in the *New York Times*, September 22, 1980, p. B7. The speech was, of course, probably composed by a ghost or a committee employed by the Republican National Committee, but as a collective utterance of expert students of public opinion it gains in force. I cannot forbear quoting Ernest Tuveson's remark in his *Redeemer Nation: The Idea of America's Millennial Role* (Chicago, 1968, p. 205) that "the belief in national apotheosis had become fixed in the national mind, having entered the sacrosanct area of creedal conviction; . . . and the halo of manifest destiny around the head of Columbia is not wholly gone even yet."

24 Full details in Roy A. Billington, *Frederick Jackson Turner: Historian, Scholar, Teacher* (New York, 1973), esp. chap. 16, "The Twilight Years," and chap. 19, "The Significance of Frederick Jackson Turner in American History."

25 Smith, *Virgin Land*, p. 251.

26 Frederick Jackson Turner, *Early Writings*, ed. Fulmer Mood (Madison, Wis., 1938), p. 186.

27 Brumm notes that Turner views the Westward Movement as unalloyed progress: "Damit sind die tragischen und auch die schuldhaften Aspekte des Wildnisuntergangs beseiteingeschoben" (Ursula Brumm, *Geschichte und Wildnis in der amerikanischen literatur* [Berlin, 1980], p. 23).

28 Hofstadter, *Progressive Historians,* p. 105.
29 It should be noted that Pearce's commitment to the historical method ("the history of ideas") developed by Arthur O. Lovejoy led him to pay less attention than might be desired to social and economic factors.
30 Richard Drinnon, *Facing West: The Metaphysics of Indian-hating and Empire-building* (Minneapolis, 1980). Drinnon acknowledges a special debt to Michael P. Rogin, *Fathers and Children: Andrew Jackson and the Subjugation of the American Indian* (New York, 1975), restricted to a much shorter chronological period but with ample documentation concerning land-hunger of white settlers as a factor in "Indian removal"; and to Robert F. Berkhofer, Jr., *The White Man's Indian: Images of the American Indian from Columbus to the Present* (New York, 1978), which takes advantage of much recent investigation of the history of American ethnography. The even more recent study by Lee C. Mitchell, *Witnesses to a Vanishing America: The Nineteenth-Century Response* (Princeton, N.J., 1981), traces in yet greater detail the development of scientific study of native American cultures, and extends Pearce's discussion of the treatment of the Indian in Cooper, Melville, and Mark Twain.
31 Ray A. Billington, *Land of Savagery, Land of Promise: The European Imagery of the American Frontier in the Nineteenth Century* (New York, 1981); William T. Pilkington, ed., *Critical Essays on the Western American Novel* (Boston, 1981).
32 John G. Cawelti, *Adventure, Mystery, and Romance: Formula Stories as Art and Popular Culture* (Chicago, 1976).
33 Cawelti, *Adventure, Mystery, and Romance,* p. 249. Elsewhere, Cawelti speaks of "a climate of justifiable violence" in "the classic Western," which he identifies with the novels of Zane Grey and the films starring William S. Hart (p. 235).
34 Slotkin, *Regeneration Through Violence,* p. 565.
35 Smith, *Virgin Land,* p. 134.
36 Ibid., p. 156.
37 Leo Marx, *The Machine in the Garden: Technology and the Pastoral Ideal in America* (New York, 1964), pp. 141, 143.
38 Smith, *Virgin Land,* pp. 168, 172.
39 Ibid., p. 195.
40 Ibid., p. 200.
41 George M. Fredrickson, " 'Settlers' and 'Savages' on Two Frontiers," *New York Review of Books* (March 18, 1972), p. 53.

3

Pastoralism in America

LEO MARX

> The social function of science vis-à-vis ideologies is first to understand
> them – what they are, how they work, what gives rise to them – and
> second to criticize them, to force them to come to terms with (but not
> necessarily to surrender to) reality.
>
> Clifford Geertz,
> "Ideology as a
> Cultural System"

The question in distant view here is whether pastoralism might
yet provide the basis for an effective ideology in the United States. (By
"effective" I mean an ideology capable of winning the adherence of at
least one significant social group.) Less distant, or more nearly answerable, are these related questions: How shall we understand the appeal of
pastoralism to a growing minority of Americans in recent years? How
shall we compare pastoralism, as a nascent left-wing ideology, with the
ideologies arising from the traditional European (Marxist) left tradition?
To what extent is the attraction exerted by pastoralism on the American
left another expression of "American exceptionalism"? What is the relationship between this political pastoralism and the mentality figured
forth by our "classic" American literature? What light does a close
reading of that body of writing throw on the adequacy – the strength
and weakness – of the pastoral view of reality? Or, put differently, what
connections are there between the conceptual and aesthetic shortcomings of pastoralism? What indeed *is* pastoralism?

In some part these questions arise from an awareness of the shortcomings of my earlier treatment of the subject in *The Machine in the
Garden* (1964).[1] There I concentrated on the ambivalent responses of
certain Americans, especially writers, artists, and intellectuals, to the

36

onset of industrialism.[2] I tried to demonstrate how this articulate minority consistently inverted the standard, one might almost say "official," interpretation of the "representative event" of that Great Transformation. By a representative event I mean a distinctive episode of an era that serves to epitomize and to legitimate a widely shared, potentially comprehensive view of what is happening.[3]

The representative event alluded to in my title was the sudden, dramatic appearance of the new machine technology in the native landscape. Between 1820 and 1860 such events became a part of the everyday experience of many people, and variants of the complex machine-in-the-landscape image became an omnipresent feature of American popular culture. This was a time when the widespread awareness of the accelerating pace of change far exceeded most people's capacity to describe, much less explain, those changes. Most of the words and catchphrases we have come to rely on to designate the transition to modernity—industrialization, industrial revolution, the rise of industrial capitalism, urbanization, rationalization, mechanization, bureaucratization, modernization, and so on—either had not yet been coined or had not yet won currency. To read widely in the public discourse of the period is to become conscious of a large conceptual void and a yearning to fill it. Hence the strong appeal of a representative event whose very sensory attributes seemed to embody the essential character of that change. No image caught the mood better than the familiar Currier and Ives prints of locomotives hurtling across the western prairie: They showed a machine (composed of iron, fire, smoke, steam) bringing man-made power to bear on the native terrain (composed of irregular, unmodified, wild but potentially life-enhancing forms)—on nature itself.

As described by spokesmen for the more influential élites, this event represented an exhilarating, extravagantly optimistic conception of history as a record of steady, cumulative, and (for the truest of true believers) preordained expansion of human knowledge and power. The implication was that such new knowledge and power would be used to enhance the well-being of Americans and, eventually, of people everywhere. In the dominant culture,[4] in other words, the transition to industrialism was enthusiastically endorsed as the stage of history when the direction of change finally, unmistakably acquired the character of continuous, predictable *progress*. As described by the dissident intellectual minority, however, the same event evoked feelings of dislocation, anxiety, alienation, and foreboding.

In characterizing this dissident mentality I emphasized its striking affinities with the mentality embodied in a time-honored literary mode – the pastoral. The point was not to supplant but to enlarge the conventional view that equated the literary recoil from industrialization with the relatively local viewpoint of the "romantic movement." But in retrospect my explanation for the close affinity between the American responses and pastoralism seems parochial and finally misleading. If American artists and intellectuals were attracted to the pastoral mode, I argued, it was because of the compelling similarity between the unusually promising geopolitical situation in which they had found themselves – the actual and potential conditions of life they enjoyed – and the ideal vision embodied in the classic, Virgilian pastoral.

In the New World, in other words, it actually seemed possible, as never before, for migrating Europeans to establish a society that might realize the ancient pastoral dream of harmony: a *via media* between decadence and wildness, too much and too little civilization. For the revolutionary generation of Americans, notably Thomas Jefferson, this Rousseauistic possibility was represented by the captivating topographical image, or mental map, of the new nation as an ideal society of the "middle landscape" midway between *l'ancien régime* and the wild frontier. Hence the citizens of such a nation might reasonably aspire to the hitherto unattainable balance of the classic mean: the best of art combined with the best of nature. The chronological center of *The Machine in the Garden* was the mid-nineteenth century, but the book ended in the present tense with a suggestion that today, in the era of high technology, pastoralism almost certainly had become anachronistic, even less feasible as the basis for a political ideology than it had been in Jefferson's time, and therefore it soon might be expected to lose its hold on the minds of disaffected Americans.

That tacit prediction hardly could have been more quickly contraverted by events. On December 2, 1964, a few weeks after the publication of *The Machine in the Garden,* the Berkeley student rebellion began. The manifest continuity between the extremist rhetoric of the rebellious students' leader, Mario Savio ("You've got to put your bodies upon the [machine] and make it stop") and that of Henry Thoreau ("Let your life be a counter friction to stop the machine") turned out to be the mere surface expression of a much deeper ideological continuity between our nineteenth-century pastoralism and the radical movement (or counterculture) of the 1960s.[5] I will come back to the point. For the moment it is necessary only to suggest that insofar as the inchoate radicalism of the Vietnam era was an expression of a shared world view – and perhaps an incipient ideology – that set of beliefs may be thought of as a further updated version of the romantic pastoralism with which many of our greatest nineteenth-century writers, artists, and intellectuals had reacted to the onset of industrialism.

Since the great upheaval of the Vietnam era, furthermore, aspects of the same collective mentality have informed most of the dissident tendencies and movements adhered to by discontented members of the white middle class in the United States. I am thinking of environmentalism, the antinuclear movements (against both nuclear power and nuclear weaponry), the voluntary simplicity movement, the "small is beautiful" and "stable state" economic doctrines, as well as the quest for "soft energy paths" and for alternative (or appropriate) technologies. Much the same viewpoint has found expression in the widespread inclination of privileged but morally troubled Americans to "recover the natural," and to repudiate the Calvinist work ethic in favor of a "new" set of rules – an ethic of "self-fulfillment."[6]

Taken together, these movements and tendencies would seem to herald a change in the prevailing national ethos. Like the political and cultural radicalism of the 1960s, these recent movements represent a marked departure from the characteristic dissident movements of the industrializing era. They differ from the trade union, populist, progressive, or New Deal movements of the previous century and a half in that they do not arise from, or centrally involve, antagonistic economic interests; they have little or nothing to do with the conflict between labor and capital. Most of the people they attract identify their interests neither with the owners and managers of the great corporations, the small minority comprising the richest and most powerful Americans, nor with the unskilled or semiskilled workers who depend for their livelihood on selling their labor by the month, week, or day. As Alain Touraine observes of these "new" social movements that have arisen since World War II, the chief conflict they represent "is not so much that which sets the worker against the head of the organization as that which opposes a population to the apparatus by which it is dominated."[7]

The emergence of these new movements and tendencies seems to coincide with the loss of credibility suffered by the idea of material progress, fulcrum of what has been the dominant national belief system, in the aftermath of Hiroshima, Vietnam, Watergate, and the serial economic and political crises that continue to threaten the stability of the democratic capitalist system. At the same time, I believe, this change represents a shift of allegiance toward the antitechnocratic, pastoral mentality prefigured by many of the writers whose work we have canonized as "classic" American literature.

All of these new developments suggest the need for a serious reconsideration of pastoralism. We need to look at this collective mentality in both its synchronic form, as an ancient and recurrent response to the more or less steadily increasing power and complexity of organized society, and its diachronic form, as it has been adapted to the distinctive character of advanced industrial society in the United States. In what follows I shall argue that pastoralism, so far from being an anachronism in the era of high technology, may be particularly well suited to the ideological needs of a large, educated, relatively affluent, mobile, yet morally and spiritually troubled segment of the white middle class. First, however, I will explain my use of the concepts of "world view" and "ideology."

The Concepts of "World View" and "Ideology"

These terms, along with "myth," "ethos," or "utopia," refer to forms in which self-conscious groups of people have lent expression to collective mentalities.[8] In the increasingly skeptical, secular cultures of the modern era, it should be said, prevailing ideas about the character and direction of social change – of history – may play a part similar to that played by "myth" in traditional, preindustrial cultures. An obvious example, already mentioned, is the idea of history as a record of continuous progress that was energetically promoted by spokesmen for many of the leading American elites in the nineteenth century. (The most conspicuous exceptions were the slave-owning planters of the South and the dissident intelligentsia of the North.) They did so, for one thing, because it served their immediate interests. A wholehearted commitment to "progress," after all, was tantamount to an unqualified endorsement of what then were called "internal improvements," or what a developmental economist nowadays would call "building the industrial infrastructure." As deployed by skillful rhetoreticians such as Edward Everett and Daniel Webster, "progress" became a code word for the entire program of industrial development.

But we cannot begin to account for the powerful grip that the progressive viewpoint has had on the minds of Americans if we think of it only as an expression of narrow class interests. Quite apart from its manifest usefulness to enterprising capitalists, the idea of history as a record of progress was attractive to many other Americans for many other reasons. To begin with, it was – is – intrinsically appealing. Its implicit confidence in human rationality is flattering enough but its cosmic hopefulness, when joined, as it had been by the *philosophes* of the Enlightenment, with the idea of liberation from the oppressive rule of monarchs, aristocrats, and priests – which is to say, with a vision of a more just and egalitarian society – lends the idea of progress the enormously gratifying quality of unconstrained moral generosity. To believe that things are, or soon will be, getting better for most people was particularly desirable in a culture freeing itself from the strong hold of Calvinism and its tortuous, finally hypocritical way of justifying self-centered behavior. The belief in progress not only helped to assuage the guilt arising from self-concern, it gave self-advancement a warrant of innocence. In nineteenth-century America, indeed, the progressive world view provided a kind of conceptual umbrella for a large cluster of prevalent attitudes: the imperatives of the quasi-religious work ethic; the idea that equality of opportunity, or upward social mobility, was available to any industrious (white male) adult; and the distinctive millennial fantasies nurtured by evangelical Protestantism – the nation's largest and most dynamic religious dispensation. In the populistic religion of the period a version of fundamentalist Christianity was neatly blended with an opportunistic and worldly progressivism.

In the United States, then, the belief in progress became a central feature of the dominant world view. To paraphrase an anthropologist's definition of "world view," the vision of history as a record of continuous progress has been taken by many Americans as a picture of the way things in sheer actuality are, and of their shared assumptions about the relations among nature, self, and society or, in other words, "their most comprehensive ideas of order."[9] But this world view also has been the basis of any number of divergent ideologies. The distinction is a matter of both scope and function. A world view is the more comprehensive, indeed expressly or tacitly cosmological, mentality. An ideology, on the other hand, is by comparison narrow and programmatic. It is a much more explicit belief system, and its adherents often recognize such an authoritative promulgation of those beliefs as the doctrines of Adam Smith or Karl Marx. When a particular social group, or coalition of social groups, uses a shared world view as the basis for a program of action, they in effect shape it into an ideology. In our time, for example, many liberals, who are committed to some variant of market capitalism, adhere to essentially the same progressive world view as their political antagonists, the socialists or communists who are committed to some form of collectivism. If the function of a world view is to provide a credible picture of reality, the function of an ideology is to guide its adherents in changing that reality, or at least the (social) segment of reality thought to be changeable. In sum, then, a world view is descriptive and metaphysical, an ideology, prescriptive and political.

What Is Pastoralism?

In its root meaning "pastoralism" refers to the ways of herds-men, and today anthropologists and historians invoke that literal sense of the word to describe the way of life of peoples who usually do not practice agriculture, who tend to be nomadic, and whose basic economic activity is animal husbandry. But that straightforward descriptive usage is rarely invoked by anyone except the scholarly experts who study premodern cultures. The meaning of pastoralism that prevails in ordinary discourse nowadays, and that I have in view here, is fundamentally different. It derives from the concept, initially formulated during the Renaissance, of the pastoral, or shepherd poem, as a distinct literary kind. Thus pastoral-*ism* in this sense refers, at a second remove, to the worthy life represented by such fictive shepherds and, by extension, to the viewpoint of anyone (whether an actual, historical person or a fictitious character) with a similar, as it were, shepherdlike view of life. In origin and meaning this outlook was closely bound up with the widespread tendency of early cultures to idealize the herdsman and his ways.

During the last twenty years students of pastoralism have begun to assimilate the impressive store of new and precise information acquired during the previous century of investigation into the cultural life of the earliest literate peoples. The decipherment of cuneiform writing; the progress in the translation of Babylonian and Assyrian languages, now presumed to have been dialects of Akkadian, as well as other ancient Near Eastern languages; the seminal modern archaeological finds, notably the discovery of Sumer – all of these scholarly achievements are being brought to bear on the subject of pastoralism and its literary embodiment, the pastoral mode.

In a cogent summary of the new scholarship and its implications, David Halperin observes that we now can legitimately push back the origin of pastoralism as far as the earliest known uses of writing in Mesopotamia near the end of the fourth millennium (roughly 3100 B.C.).[10] This chronological expansion of our knowledge is bound to alter the way we think about pastoralism and the literary mode it nurtured. So far from having been the late and peripheral development depicted in most scholarly writing on the subject, the pastoral must now be granted its true status as one of the oldest and most characteristic forms of human expression. The obvious starting point for a theory of pastoralism consonant with the new evidence is in fact its deep-rooted, elemental, immemorial character. That evidence lends strong support to the commonsense assumption that *pastoral-ism,* a widely shared viewpoint that cast favor on the herdsman and his ways, existed apart from, and before, the development of those expressive and thematic conventions that were to constitute the distinctive literary kind retrospectively named "the pastoral." The point requires emphasis because it in effect reverses the conception of pastoral origins implicit in most modern literary–critical writing on the subject. In other words, the existence of pastoral conventions almost certainly was a consequence of the enormous appeal exerted by the herdsman and his way of life, not the other way around.

From the time of its earliest known manifestation the meaning of pastoralism turned upon the figure of the shepherd as an efficacious mediator between the realm of organized society and the realm of nature. The herdsman of the ancient Near East characteristically is a "liminal figure" who moves back and forth across the borderland between civilization and nature.[11] Seen against the background of the wilderness, he appears to be a representative of a complex, hierarchical, urban society. His job is to protect his flock from such menaces of nature as storms, drought, and predatory animals. Seen from the opposite vantage, however, against the background of the settled community with its ordered, sophisticated ways and its power, he appears to epitomize the virtues of a simple unworldly life disengaged from civilization and lived, as we now might say, "close to nature." On this view he becomes something of an ascetic; he is independent, self-sufficient, and, like Henry Thoreau or the rugged western hero of American mythology, a man singularly endowed with the qualities needed to endure long periods of solitude, discomfort, and deprivation. In his character and behavior this liminal figure combines traits that result from his having lived as both a part of, and apart from, nature; from his having lived as both a part of, and apart from, society.

Most features of pastoralism that now appear to have been relatively constant over time were present, if only in embryonic form, in the mediating functions attributed to the idealized herdsmen by cultures of the ancient Near East. To mediate in this context means, quite literally, to resolve the root tension between civilization and nature by living in the borderland between them. The mediation is two-directional. In the earliest documents there are instances of a shepherd helping to effect the passage of people moving either to or from the organized community. In the old Babylonian version of the Epic of Gilgamesh, for example, the shepherd's hut becomes "a cultural half-way house," scene of the conversion of the epic hero's friend, Enkidu.

When he arrives at the hut, Enkidu is a truly *wild* man, but by the time he leaves he has been partly domesticated or, as we say, civilized.[12] By implication the liminal function of the shepherd thus may help to acculturate uncouth, primitive persons, or to help – what? "pastoralize" or "naturalize"? (we seem to lack a satisfactory name for this role) – excessively worldly persons.

The ancient shepherd's liminal position accounts for his superior grasp of metaphysical reality. To move away from the organized community and its mundane concerns is to gain – or regain – access to the mysterious energy and potency presumed to reside in the part of the world that is Not-Man. Of course nature, in the sense of the biophysical environment, figures in these early texts as the habitat of the gods as well as malevolent creatures and forces. As did the Graeco-Roman religion, the cultures of the ancient Near East characteristically recognized withdrawal into an unmodified terrain as a way of achieving holiness and oracular wisdom.

But no good purpose would be served by trying to distill the new knowledge into a formal definition. As Nietzsche once remarked, only that which has no history can be defined. To be sure, pastoralism, like any idea or mentality, has a history, but it is a history that makes sense only if we take account of the distinctive meaning it acquires in each specific social context in which it is reactivated. To revise the Nietzschean dictum, then: Only the relatively unchanging core of a collective mentality – its synchronic form – can be satisfactorily defined. When – if – we know enough to frame such a definition, it surely will presuppose, as a primary fact of the human situation, our inescapable confinement to a symbolic border country such as that initially associated with the herdsmen of the ancient Near East. The ethos that would accompany such a world view, the "moral and aesthetic style" its adherents would exhibit, also would be likely to vary from one time and place to another.[13] But the underlying attitude surely would imply acceptance of the need, in virtually all aspects of experience, to mediate – to strive for acceptable if transitory resolutions – between the constraints of society and the constraints of nature. From the beginning pastoralism was grounded in the presumed opposition between the realm of the collective, the organized, and the worldly on the one hand, and the personal, the spontaneous, and the inward on the other. As the temporary, two-directional, back-and-forthness of the idealized herdsman's life suggests, pastoralism comports with a dialectical mode of perception. If this world view can be said to have a constant feature, it may well be a recognition of the ineradicable, ultimately irresolvable nature of the conflict at its heart.

Pastoralism and the Demise of the Old Pastoral

To leap from the pastoralism of antiquity to that of the early modern era is not quite as presumptuous as it may seem. So far as we know, in fact, the appeal of pastoralism in the sense used here—a secular or at least non-theological mentality that lends expression to people's shared understanding of their relationship to their surroundings, their beliefs and ideals—had gradually ebbed, or had been lost to view, after the fall of Rome. (So far as pastoral impulses manifested themselves during the Christian era, they were primarily assimilated to an explicitly theological system of ideas.)[14] In any case, the modern history of the subject begins in sixteenth-century Europe. Stimulated by the recovery of classical literature, and the secular spirit of such seminal works of the pastoral imagination as Virgil's *Eclogues,* scholars formulated the concept of the shepherd poem, or pastoral, as a discrete literary kind. For the next two centuries—roughly from 1550 to 1750—the expression of secular pastoralism was largely confined to formal works of literature and art "about" shepherds and their ways. Critics were justifiably impressed and puzzled by this resurgence of an ancient, seemingly anachronistic form, and in an effort to explain its meaning and function they produced a large body of theoretical writing.[15] In retrospect, and simplifying greatly, we may assign most of the critical theories and the aesthetic practice of pastoral during the early modern period to one of two categories representing opposed conceptions of the form and the motives behind it.

Adherents of the more popular conception simply equated the pastoral, its meaning and function, with its conventions. For reasons these theorists seldom bothered to explore, shepherds and their lives are a pleasing subject, and works that "imitate" them are pastorals. For this school the inviolable principle of pastoral identity was the tacit motto, "no shepherd, no pastoral." Adherents of the other school asserted, or more often intimated, that all of the business about shepherds was the mere outward expression of some deeper propensity of mind and spirit. Thus, Shakespeare in the scene where Polonius comes rushing on stage, excited and breathless, to tell Hamlet what he already knows—that the players have arrived: "The best actors in the world, either for tragedy, comedy, history, pastoral, pastoral-comical, historical-pastoral, tragical-historical, tragical-comical-historical-pastoral, scene individable or poem unlimited" (II, ii, 385–90).

For all of the lord chamberlain's fatuity, his splendidly concise critical theory is pregnant with insight into the messiness of literature, the instability and mutability of literary kinds, and, most significant here, the essential character of pastoral.[16] He spontaneously accords the pastoral the status of a mode comparable, in its importance and seriousness – in its universality – to the historic (epic), comic, and tragic modes. The crux, for our purposes, is precisely the Polonian assumption that pastoral is not a genre but a mode – the broadest, most inclusive category of composition: It derives its identity not from any formal convention but from a particular perspective on human experience, one that focuses upon certain conditions, aspects, or qualities of life (to the relative neglect, necessarily, of others). That there is such a thing as a pastoral perspective, or pastoral-*ism,* and that it exists independent of any particular genre or form of expression, is confirmed by our ready use of the concept adjectively to describe a kind of (pastoral) poem, drama, novel, painting, opera, ballet, garden, landscape, character, film, or for that matter, just about any made thing. The point, in short, is that the essence of the mode does not reside in any particular form or convention or body of conventions. By the middle of the eighteenth century the old pastoral, weighted down by the precious, tedious, artificial, anachronistic shepherd convention, quietly sank out of sight. At the risk of seeming to slight some great achievements of the human imagination, one might sum up what had happened to European pastoralism between 1550 and 1750 as the final severing of the ties that had for so long bound the mentality to the specific conditions of life surrounding its origin in the ancient Near East.

This view of pastoralism and its history was initiated by the seminal work of William Empson in the 1930s.[17] Now it may be said that the demise of the old pastoral in effect had liberated the mentality it had been designed to express. That this death and resurrection coincided with what Karl Polanyi so aptly called the Great Transformation is a fact whose implications we have scarcely begun to explore.[18]

American Exceptionalism

The idea of "American exceptionalism" derives from the marked difference between the critical reaction to the Great Transformation in western Europe and in the United States. By 1848 it had become apparent that in Europe the strongest opposition to industrial capitalism would come from the revolutionary socialist movement. In the United States, however, such a movement then had not and, indeed, never has developed comparable strength. Awareness of this difference led to the repeated posing of the historic question recently posed

once again by C. Vann Woodward. "Why," he asks, "of all the advanced capitalist countries of the world," is the United States "the only
one where socialism never gained a mass following, where Marxism
never caught on, and where the working class has never produced a
mass-based party of its own?"[19]

At first, admittedly, this looks like just the right question to ask if
one is interested in accounting for the seeming ineffectuality of the
radical left in the United States. A review of the explanations given by
historians and other scholars, however, proves not to be as helpful as
one might wish. Their explanatory theories may be placed along a
continuum between those that emphasize relatively objective, geographic, demographic, or material conditions of life in the New World
and, at the opposite pole, those that emphasize essentially mental, atti-
tudinal, or cultural formations.

The first category is dominated by explanations that point to one or
another aspect of the geopolitical good fortune of the white European
migrants to North America: the economic abundance that they and
their descendants have enjoyed; the "safety valve" for relieving the
pressure of socioeconomic discontent provided by "free land," or its
presumed availability, on the western frontier; and the existence of an
"internal colony" (the defeated slave states) that served, in effect, as a
more accessible and manageable equivalent of the overseas colonial empires of the European nations. All of these explanations point to the
economic well-being of Americans as counteracting the appeal of an
anticapitalist ideology. Among the demographic factors said to have
had a similar result, the most important probably is the presence of
Africans and other racial and ethnic minorities; the prejudice generated
against them has helped to establish and sustain the privileged status of
Anglo-Saxon whites, and it thus has served to impede the formation of
a shared working-class consciousness and political movement. Somewhere in the middle of this continuum we may locate those explanations that feature distinctive American institutions, especially the unusually successful constitutional system including, among other things,
the brilliant Madison–Hamilton strategy for inhibiting the formation of
political majorities.

At the other (cultural) pole the explanation for the imperviousness of
Americans to socialist ideology emphasize their distinctive habits of
mind. Material abundance is seen from this perspective as having been
less important in itself, as an economic fact of life, than in lending
credence to certain prevailing attitudes. (The same has been said about
the supposed availability of free land.) Whether people actually are

economically well-off or not, the important fact in this view is that they *believe* they have had a real chance to improve their lot. The nation's steadily rising productivity has encouraged the belief that equality of opportunity, or virtually unrestricted social mobility, is an American reality. (In its extreme form this idea shades into the illusion that the United States is a classless society.) All of these "land of opportunity" themes are traceable, historically, to the absence of a feudal past and its manifold political and ideological consequences: the fact, for one thing, that capitalism gained ascendancy without a revolutionary seizure of power, and without that heightened class consciousness that most often is generated by the presence of a landed aristocracy. (Hence the curious question that always has hovered over the use of the term "middle class"' in the American context: middle of what? In contemporary American usage, accordingly, the term "middle class" is almost indistinguishable from "middle income group.") An important result of this difference in the rigidity of class stratification is said to be the particularly strong hold of Lockean liberalism on the political thought and behavior of Americans. But there have been many other explanations for the exceptional failure of socialism in the United States based on the special favor that Americans ostensibly have granted to various other viewpoints: to Puritanism and its derivative, the Protestant work ethic; to Christian millennialism and the belief in a unique quasi-religious national mission; to pragmatism and an ostensible American matter-of-factness and imperviousness to all ideologies.[20]

Now, if these explanations seem less helpful than we might wish, it is because Professor Woodward's question, so far from being unanswerable, is all *too* answerable. Just about every imaginable difference between the United States and the prototypical bourgeois societies of western Europe has been advanced as *the* chief explanatory factor. Or, put differently, these ideas are somewhat disappointing because, like most historical explanations, they are so largely descriptive. What they reveal, taken together, is that the opposition to industrial capitalism in the United States has differed from the opposition in Europe because – well, because the society and the culture are different. When compared with Europeans in all of these ways, and despite all the manifest similarities, Americans, it turns out, have organized, thought about, and lived their lives differently. If this amounts to something like a giant tautology, it is nonetheless instructive. For one thing, it may lead us to recast the question. Instead of asking *why* the ideology of revolutionary socialism did not catch on with the American people in general, we might better be clear about *what* ideas actually did catch on with particular groups of disaffected Americans.

Pastoralism and Industrialization

Put in this way, the question leads back to pastoralism as the mentality of a small but highly influential, currently growing minority of dissident Americans. Even before colonialization of the New World began, as I tried to demonstrate in *The Machine in the Garden,* the pastoral ideal was used to define the meaning of America. One reason this mentality was particularly attractive to migratory Europeans is the emphasis it places on topography as the basis of belief or, to be more precise, the close connection it posits between place, a sense of place, and a view of the world. In the ancient Near East, as we have seen, each sector of the familiar tripartite landscape – urban, rural (or middle), and wild – was presumed to foster a different way of life, a different social structure and belief system. A similar assumption makes itself felt in the myth of American origins, with its stress on the redemptive possibilities opened up by the transit of civilization to the New World.

Before the onset of industrialization, the raw state of the continental terrain made it relatively easy for Americans to reconcile the idea of material progress with the ancient pastoral dream of regaining an ideal state of harmony with nature. To establish a society of the "middle landscape" it was first necessary to transform the wilderness into a garden. Unlike Europeans, in other words, Americans could proceed to execute their expansionary project, leveling the forests, building roads, houses, farms, and cities across the land and, at the very same time, could with some justice see themselves as engaged in the recovery of a simpler, more natural way of life – simpler and more natural, at least, as compared with the prototypical societies of the Old World. As long as the continent remained largely undeveloped, it was not implausible for Americans to embrace – simultaneously and as if perfectly compatible – both the progressive and the pastoral ideals. This bringing together of two potentially irreconcilable conceptions of the relations between society and nature was a distinctive feature of the emergent progressive ideology of democratic capitalism in the United States. It proposed an initial "conquest" of nature, as represented, say, by the building of railroads westward across the continent, in order to arrive at a more harmonious accommodation with nature.[21]

Before the new republic was established, however, at least one farsighted American had recognized the contradiction inherent in that ideology. When Thomas Jefferson first raised the issue in the early 1780s, the War of Independence had not yet been won, and even in England the new factory system had just begun to take hold. Would it be best, he asked with astonishing historical precocity, for America to remain an agricultural society, or to undertake the transfer of half its work force to manufactures? The point about his unequivocally negative answer – "let our work-shops remain in Europe" – that is not yet fully understood is the character of the vision that called it forth. It was not, as commonly believed, an agrarian vision. The characteristic agrarian doctrines of the late eighteenth century rested the case for the primacy of agriculture on economic grounds. They held that an agricultural economy is the best because it is potentially the basis for the wealthiest, most stable society. But in making his case against a policy of developing American manufactures, Jefferson categorically repudiated the priority of economic criteria. It would be better, he argued, to pay the extra cost of shipping raw materials to Europe and importing manufactures, than to develop an industrial capacity in the United States. "The loss by the transportation of commodities across the Atlantic," he wrote, "will be made up in happiness and permanence of government." Like some pastoralists of our time, especially the environmentalists, Jefferson explicitly rejected productivity, or the material standard of living, as the chief criterion in framing social policies; like them, also, he gave precedence to something like "quality of life" or, as he said, "It is the manners and spirit of a people which preserve a republic in vigor."

Jefferson's answer to this straightforward economic "policy question" was shaped by a pastoral, not an agrarian, vision. The famous tribute to the American husbandman that the question elicited from him ("Those who labor in the earth are the chosen people of God . . . whose breasts he has made his peculiar deposit for substantial and genuine virtue") rests on the allegedly superior moral integrity of people who live closer to the soil. But Jefferson's commitment to a pastoral viewpoint becomes more evident in the contrast he develops between farmers and their opposite numbers – the prototypical citizens of a commercial, manufacturing, urban society. Whereas there are no known instances of "the corruption of morals among the mass of cultivators," Jefferson argues, such corruption is the predictable moral condition of those who must adopt the ways of the new kind of society and its market economy. Such corruption, he contends, "is the mark set on those, who not looking up to heaven, to their own soil and industry, as does the husbandman, for their subsistence, depend for it on the casualties and caprice of customers. Dependence begets subservience and venality, suffocates the germ of virtue, and prepares fit tools for the designs of ambition." Such moral corruption, in other words, is the mark set on those who do not adequately mediate between the constraints of society and of nature. But in his self-sufficiency and independence, in his moral integrity and the metaphysical liminality of his position in the world, the American husbandman does just that. In doing so he bears a striking resemblance to the first known hero of pastoralism – the idealized shepherd of the ancient Near East.[22]

It is important to recognize the characteristically pliant, relativistic, or dialectical character of Jefferson's pastoralism. His tribute to the ideal husbandman and the *via media* he represents is called forth by the prospect of radical innovation, the introduction of a new system of production that he perceives as likely to create an imbalance on the side of urban, hierarchical, material development. Almost immediately after the passage in *Notes on Virginia* was published, Jefferson admitted to a correspondent that although it accurately represented his own preference, the idea of the new nation electing not to follow the obvious course of economic development, not to develop a manufacturing capability, was from a practical, political point of view simply untenable. It is, he said of the policy he himself had so recently advocated, "theory only, and a theory which the servants of America are not at liberty to follow." Why? Because Americans – he surely is thinking of his New England merchant compatriots – "have a decided taste for navigation and commerce." This means, in our language, that the germs of the oncoming industrial capitalist order already were deeply, ineradicably implanted in the culture. It also means that Jefferson understood that an ideal vision such as his own had to be set against, and periodically adjusted to, the imperatives rooted in the everyday, commonsense world of material needs and of practical activities, economic and technological, aimed at satisfying them. Hence there are no permanent or absolute cultural embodiments of the pastoral world view. (If in Jefferson's America the farmer represents the ideal *via media,* it is well to recall that in biblical times, as in the fable of Cain and Abel, the farmer represented the more worldly, aggressive, technologically sophisticated way of life – killer of his brother, Abel the herdsman.) In the extraordinary sequence of letters on the subject that Jefferson wrote in the next thirty years, he made it clear that in changing his judgment about the need for American manufactures, he was not abandoning the pastoral ideal, merely adapting it to changing circumstances. The problems that Jefferson wrestles with in these letters – the relationship between social ideals and the economic driving forces of history, the distinction between feasible and merely gratifying ideals – would prove to be central to the pastoral fables that occupy so prominent a place in classic American literature.

The "Classic" American Pastoral

For some time now it has been a commonplace to describe the literary works we have canonized as American "classics" as being, in a formal sense, hybrids. Thus such central nineteenth-century prose texts as the "Leatherstocking" tales, *The Scarlet Letter*, *Moby-Dick*, *Walden*, and *Adventures of Huckleberry Finn* combine features of the traditional English novel with features of the quest romance as well as Shakespearean tragedy, the sermon, the essay, the picaresque tale, the philosophic and scientific treatise, and so forth. In the mock-critical jargon of Polonius, *Moby-Dick* might be assigned to the category of romantical-cetological-tragical-novelistical. Literature in the modern era is still a messy business, and writers are as obstinate as ever in their unwillingness to confine their work to categories invented by scholars and critics.

As for the pastoral, it had lost its identity – disappeared – as a discrete literary form about a century before the great flowering of American letters. In an epoch of industrial and democratic revolution, when science was transforming the reigning conception of relations between mind and nature, when the idea of history as continuous progress was emerging as the crux of a telling secular world view – when all of these accelerating changes made what was current or "modern" seem wholly unrelated to what was ancient, the old pastoral had become fatally, ludicrously irrelevant. It therefore makes perfectly good sense to say, as Renato Poggioli did, that the modern world simply "destroyed" the traditional pastoral.[23] But it is important not to stop there, for in destroying the old form, modernity also had released pastoral motives from their bondage to the shepherd convention, and thereby had helped to set off a veritable explosion of those same motives. It was an explosion of such magnitude, however, and pastoral motives now were so widely diffused, so dressed up in the fashionable language of romanticism, which is to say invested in characters and situations so remote from those traditionally associated with the pastoral mode, as to make their identity all but unrecognizable.

The pastoral elements in the work of the classic American writers may be identified by looking closely at (1) the character and the situation of the protagonists, especially as they are initially established; (2) the setting, not so much what it *is* as what it *means*, especially the moral and metaphysical import of its various sectors; and (3) the complex interplay between protagonists and setting as revealed in the working out of the narrative. But it is important, first, to notice what is absent from this body of literature. It does not contain a single work that champions, or even for that matter lends much credence to, the progressive ideology adhered to by the nation's dominant elites. This is a cultural fact of cardinal importance. So far from affirming that optimistic belief in the United States as the global exemplar of material progress, our most gifted writers have consistently subverted it. It is only a slight exaggeration to say that in the work of Hawthorne and Melville, Mark Twain and Henry James, Faulkner and Hemingway, the characters who most explicitly endorse or embody that regnant viewpoint also tend to be narrow-minded, self-seeking, and, all in all, morally reprehensible. The primary emotional thrust of our major literature is generated by sympathy with protagonists who are at odds with the dominant culture, and by sympathy with their quest, however unsuccessful, for an alternative way of life.

"Are the green fields gone?" This question, asked by Melville's narrator at the beginning of *Moby-Dick,* exemplifies the pastoral impulse at the heart of many works in the canon. Here Ishmael is trying to explain why, some years before, he had decided to ship out on a whaler. At the time he was on Manhattan Island, broke, jobless, dispirited to the verge of being suicidal. (Because his current mood is so different, his tone in telling the story so casual, jocular, self-mocking, we may easily miss the point.) His discontent with the conditions of life in New York was closely bound up with his desire to go to sea, and he is at pains to explain that this was not an eccentric reaction. Almost all men, he says, cherish very nearly the same feelings for the ocean. Just think of Manhattan on a dreamy Sunday afternoon, how all around the island countless men stand, like so many silent sentinels, "fixed in ocean reveries." What most interests him is the strange pull exerted by unmodified nature, especially watery nature, upon the imagination. It is all the more strange when one considers that these others are landsmen, "of week days *pent up* in lath and plaster – *tied* to counters, *nailed* to benches, *clinched* to desks. How then is this? Are the green fields gone? What do they here?"[24] (Italics mine.)

Although these New Yorkers have jobs, and Ishmael is unemployed, their feelings about the society are similar to his. (Melville conveys this similarity in that remarkable series of verbs of unfreedom he uses – and that I have emphasized – to describe their unhappy relation to their work.) But if the behavior of these other men is partly attributable to the alienating character of the society, it also may be attributed to a less tangible psychological or metaphysical deprivation, the sort that might be explained by the disappearance of green fields. Not that Ishmael is suggesting that the fields literally have disappeared, only that these men are behaving *as if* they had, or put differently, *if* the fields had disap-

peared, that might constitute a plausible reason for their strange yearning – their ocean reveries. Whatever their motives, Ishmael surely
means to point up the similarity with his own disaffection, his own
desire. Except that what these other men merely dream, he enacts: His
voyage is at once a retreat from this constraining way of life and a quest
for an alternative.

Centrifugal motives such as the one Melville attributes to Ishmael
activate the dominant spirits throughout this body of writing. I am
thinking of such characters and voices as Cooper's Natty Bumppo and
Hawthorne's Hester Prynne; of the "I" of Emerson's *Nature* and Thoreau's *Walden* and Whitman's "Song of Myself"; of Mark Twain's
Huck Finn, Hemingway's Nick Adams, Fitzgerald's Jay Gatsby, and
Faulkner's Ike McCaslin; of the speaker of Robert Frost's lyrics and of
Wallace Stevens's cosmic poet and worldmaker – the list could be extended to the present with, say, Updike's Rabbit, Bellow's Henderson,
Kesey's Chief Broom, and many, many other characters and voices,
but here my only point is that all of them, whatever their differences,
tend like Ishmael to connect the recovery of self with the recovery of
the natural, and to represent their deepest longings in numinous visions
of landscape. In one way or another they all lend expression to what
may be called the pastoral impulse: a desire, in the face of the growing
power and complexity of organized society, to disengage from the
dominant culture and to seek out the basis for a simpler, more satisfying mode of life in a realm "closer," as we say, to nature.

A model, or ideal type, of the classic American fable would show the
playing out of this activating impulse in a symbolic terrain very much
like the terrain in which the mythical cult figure of the herdsman evidently had arisen some five thousand years before. The relatively constant features of pastoralism in this model text are figured forth by the
intricate interplay between the tripartite topography (urban, middle,
wild); the narrative or conceptual structure, and the sequence of the
protagonist's or speaker's states of mind and feeling. In explaining the
initial appeal of this ancient world view to white European migrants to
North America, it is easy to overemphasize the importance of the
merely external, topographical homology between the pastoral and the
American situations – the close resemblance, say, between the moral
geography inherent in the cult of the herdsman (as mediator between
civilization and raw nature) and the sectoring of Jefferson's characteristically American mental map: Old World – republican Virginia – savage
frontier. Telling as it is, this geographical homology is of relatively
superficial, necessarily transitory significance: to dwell upon it leads, as
in the Epilogue of *The Machine in the Garden,* to an underestimation of

the universality and adaptability of pastoralism, and to what now strikes me as the mistaken notion that this ancient world view will become increasingly irrelevant to the population of advanced industrial societies.

The continuing appeal of pastoralism in our time is attributable to its deeper, more nearly constant and universal features, especially the character and function of the pastoral figure. To establish this fact will be useful, among other things, as an antidote to the parochialism and presentism of American studies. According to the received academic wisdom, the viewpoint of the voyaging selves who dominate our literature, the heroes and heroines who disengage from organized social life in search of personal autonomy, is best elucidated by reference to the quasi-religious Emersonian ideal of "Self-Reliance," or to the socially and politically sanctioned behavior that led Alexis de Tocqueville to coin the word "individualism." These local nineteenth-century connections are of primary importance, to be sure, but their significance is immeasurably deepened when they are juxtaposed to the long history of thought and expression that is analogous to the idealization of the ancient Near Eastern herdsman as an embodiment of material self-sufficiency and spiritual autonomy. So far from having been generated by modern romanticism, the idea that the discontents and conflicts of society might be resolved by an act of disengagement – a movement in the direction of nature – had been implicit in the liminal function of the herdsman ever since the invention of that pastoral figure. It is tempting to make even more extravagant claims for the deep-structural, archetypal character of this pastoral dialectic when we consider, for example, the extent to which it prefigured the mediating role of the ego in its complex negotiations with the superego and the id in the spatial metaphor at the center of the Freudian metapsychology. Many features of that compelling Freudian landscape of the mind may be found, incidentally, in *The Scarlet Letter, Moby-Dick, Walden,* and other classic nineteenth-century American texts.

In the ideal type of this text the narrative structure is in large measure shaped by the mediating function of the protagonist. It begins with his or her disengagement from a social environment felt to be excessively constraining, complex, hierarchical, ordered, alienating. To be sure, there is more than a little escapist and nostalgic feeling to this pastoral impulse – the feeling Robert Frost compresses into the opening line of "Directive": "Back out of all this now too much for us." This impulse might stand condemned as mere psychological and historical regression if it did not also initiate a quest, the explanation of a realm "closer" to nature in search of freedom and independence or, in effect, the basis for a simpler, more natural way of life. This exploration comprises the second and central stage of the narrative. In the third and final stage we are made to feel the protagonist's need to effect something like a return to – or a coming to terms with – the established order. At every stage there is a complicated interaction between events, the implications of the familiar symbolic landscape, and the protagonist's shifting, all but irremediably ambivalent state of mind. The work of mediation enacted in the "plot" is even more strenuously undertaken within the protagonist's mind. In some cases – one thinks of Hester, Ishmael, the hero of *Walden* – the pastoral figures are themselves probing, original, philosophically inclined interpreters of that ambiguous middle state that is the crux of the pastoral vision and a primary fact of their own life histories.

What requires emphasis is the ineluctably "double" character of the pastoral figure's consciousness in these American fables. As in virtually all pastorals, the simple life is not his or her birthright but a desired alternative to complexity. The hero of *Walden,* for example, is an intellectual sophisticate, a Harvard graduate, heir of a complex urban civilization, who deliberately chooses to recover the natural. There is all the difference between the herdsman who lives the simple life because he knows no other way, and the courtier who voluntarily elects to imitate a simpler, shepherdlike existence – between Thoreau, who belongs to both worlds, and whose ambiguous "double consciousness" is a central fact of his life at the pond, and the merely simpleminded rustics he encounters. There is all the difference between a modern man's or woman's conscious renunciation of what counts as worldliness in a consumption-oriented capitalist culture, and a sentimentalized image of the simple, unworldly "common man." The pastoralism that emerges in American literature presents a vision of a disengaged, unworldly life, to be sure, but one that is entertained by a sophisticate.[25]

The liminal function of the pastoral figure may be illustrated by certain decisive and recurrent episodes in the central, exploratory stages of these fables. One such episode is a moment when the protagonist enjoys a sense of ecstatic fulfillment, a feeling of calm selfhood and integration with his or her surroundings sometimes including a lover or companion. These moments are linked to the old pastoral by a setting that often resembles the *locus amoenus* or pleasance: the lovely, peaceful shaded natural site that had figured prominently in the Arcadian mode since Virgil's first eclogue.[26] In the American texts this idyllic episode often brings in aspects of the Protestant conversion experience, and the blend of secular and religious implication imparts a moral and metaphysical authority to the protagonist, such as that imputed to the shepherds of old. As might be expected, however, this experience of transcendence is fleeting; it proves, in Frost's fine phrase, to be only "a momentary stay against confusion," and in the end that fact, along with others, constitutes a central criticism of the pastoral impulse and its consequences.

Another decisive episode is the protagonist's thrilling, tonic, but often traumatic and finally chastening encounter with wildness: some aspect, external or internal, of unmodified, intractable, seemingly hostile nature. The hero may meet a wild beast, a cannibal, a savage; in a storm or on a mountaintop he may be made aware of the brutal indifference and immensity of Not-Man. In these texts wildness also has its psychic counterpart: the potential loss of impulse control. The upshot of this episode, accordingly, also is to set limits to the initial, centrifugal impulse. To keep going in the direction of unmodified nature, the hero senses, is to risk another, more dire loss of selfhood: a merging with the nonhuman whose ultimate form is death. Here, as in that transitory idyllic moment, the narrative provides a motive for the change of direction that will constitute the concluding stage of the structure: a virtual "return" to society.

Of these recurrent episodes, however, the most important for a consideration of the ideological potential of pastoralism is the one alluded to in my earlier title, *The Machine in the Garden*: the "interrupted idyll." It often begins as another interlude of serenity, peace, and joy, but the mood in this case is abruptly transformed by the intrusion of a machine or some other manifest token of the dynamism of modern industrial society. This episode differs from the other two in that it has no obvious counterpart in the old pastoral; here, therefore, we may be said, in the language of structuralism, to be shifting from a *synchronic* to a *diachronic* mode of analysis. What this episode accomplishes, indeed, is to invert the "representative event" of the dominant, progressive ideology. So far from being an occasion for an optimistic vision of history, the sudden intrusion of the machine upon the native landscape evokes feelings of dislocation and anxiety. It reactivates the alienation that had initially provoked the pastoral impulse. It thus may seem to confirm the protagonist's original act of disengagement, but at the same time it helps to dispel the illusion that that act might have led to the immediate, practical, or political resolution of the complications and discontents that had provoked it. In the "interrupted idyll" the new machine technology is made to seem the irreversible motive force of history itself. "We have constructed a fate, an *Atropos,* that never turns aside. (Let that be the name of your engine),"[27] writes Thoreau of the railroad whose whistle disturbs his repose at Walden Pond. Like the other two recurrent episodes I have singled out, this one supports the logic of a final "return" or accomodation to society.

The machine-in-the-landscape episode marks the emergence of a distinctive industrial age variant of pastoralism. In the symbolic topography that had previously lent expression to that ancient world view, the locus of power, wealth, hierarchy, sophistication – of the complex world – had been fixed in space. It characteristically had been a city or royal court or aristocratic household, or at any rate a *place* unambiguously separated from the green world: the realm of urbane social life here, the countryside (and wilderness) there. But the new machine power figured forth a fundamental transformation in relations between society and nature – it introduced a vivid awareness of the unprecedented dynamism of industrial society into nineteenth-century conceptions of landscape. Power machinery, factories, steamboats, canals, railroads, telegraph lines, wherever they appeared, were perceived as extensions of urban power and complexity. Potential invaders of all sectors of the environment, the forces represented by the new technology necessarily blur (if they do not erase) the immemorial boundary lines between city, countryside, and wilderness. By threatening to take dominion everywhere, they intensify – at times to the point of apocalyptic stridency – the dissonance that pastoralism always had generated at the junction of civilization and nature.

But in American writing the ramifications of this inverted "representative event" are not confined to texts in which it is actually dramatized – enacted in a narrative episode. As it functions in the work of writers like Frost, Eliot, Faulkner, Hemingway, Fitzgerald, it is one of the great central figurative conceptions in our literature. Whether explicitly or by implication, this complex bipolar image, the machine-in-the-landscape, has served as a primary ordering principle in literature, painting, photography, film, music, and the like. It is a conceptual armature according to which the dominant culture and those who adhere to it are associated with the presumed attributes of a life closely bound up with machine technology (power, speed, rationality, efficiency, innovation, impersonality, productivity, organization), and much of what lies outside the dominant culture, especially the residual or past-oriented elements of culture and those who adhere to them, are associated with the presumed attributes of a life "closer" to the natural environment (spontaneity, simplicity, organic growth, freedom from society's constraints, erotic and sensual pleasure, intuitive or precognitive thought). It is important to emphasize the proximate character of the state of being "*closer* to nature" here, for this viewpoint rarely has issued in primitivist fantasies of regaining pure forms of the "natural" –

a return to some imagined state of unmodified nature. Writers and artists drawn to this new pastoralism have no wish to renounce the amenities of modern life. Nor do they necessarily have an attachment to any specific condition, wild or rural, of the actual environment. What matters most to them, as it had to Thomas Jefferson, is the proper subordination of material concerns to other, less tangible aspects of life – whether aesthetic, moral, political, or spiritual. This central figurative conception, in short, represents an adaptation of pastoralism to the novel conditions of life in a progressive, urban industrial society.

But how, it will be asked, in view of what eventually happens to the pastoral figures and motives in so many classic American literary texts, can they be said to cast favor upon pastoralism? The fact is, admittedly, that few if any of these "classic" fables are "pastorals of success" – works in which the protagonist's initial disengagement from complexity finally issues in what William James would call unequivocal "fruits for life."[28] *Walden* probably comes as close as any to being that, yet as compared with the Jeffersonian vision of an entire society dedicated to "the pursuit of happiness" – no doubt the most nearly official political declaration of pastoral intent in modern history – even Thoreau's self-transformation seems narrowly personal, anarchistic, which is to say, untranslatable into an effective ideology.

Far more typical, in any event, is an unmistakable "pastoral of failure" like *The Great Gatsby*. The direct cause of Gatsby's defeat and death is his stubborn refusal to let go of his distinctively American dream of green world felicity. Like Jefferson in his concessive letters, Fitzgerald conveys both the enormous appeal that this pastoral motive holds for him and, at the same time, his recognition of its utter infeasibility – its seemingly irremediable impotence in the face of the everyday, practical, material motives that ultimately determine what happens in a capitalist democracy. Yet *The Great Gatsby* nonetheless may be said to cast favor upon the pastoral view of life. If it reveals the incapacity of its adherents to cope with power, it absolutely repudiates the dominant culture and its obsession with material progress. That is why we are asked to believe that Gatsby, for all his fatal limitations, turned out all right in the end. The pastoral hope is indicted for its deadly falsity, but the man who clings to it is exonerated. By virtue of his fidelity to his ideal, however destructive that faith has proved to be, and by comparison with the "rotten crowd" of people who typify society, Gatsby is supposed to earn our approval. A similar point may be made about most of the pastoral figures in our literature. In *Moby-Dick, The Scarlet Letter, Huckleberry Finn, The Sun Also Rises*, "The Bear," *Miss Lonelyhearts*, and many other American fables, the essential vitality of the hero or heroine–of the work itself–derives from the pastoral vision the narrative condemns as illusory.

But finally there is an even more fundamental question to be asked about the justification for attaching so much importance to this minuscule, privileged literary canon. What warrant is there for taking these few texts seriously as an index of shared consciousness? An adequate answer would require another long essay, but this much seems clear: A large part of the case for their value as evidence of prevailing attitudes necessarily would rest upon the nature of the intricate, inadequately understood sociological and literary–critical process by which they have been canonized. In making that case one would not wish to deny that the canon embodies an ideological bias in favor of the most prosperous and influential (adult white male) group in the society. Yet the process of selecting these texts from among thousands of potential rivals has extended over so many decades; it has involved a continuing series of informal "elections" by such diverse groups of people (writers, publishers, editors, scholars, critics, teachers, librarians, and audiences); it has been informed by so many considerations–imaginative power; profitability; entertainment value; teachability; compatibility with class, nationalist, gender, regional biases–it is, in short, such a complicated impersonal, and uncontrolled process that it seems most unlikely to have been part of anything like a calculated program for realizing the hegemonic aspirations of a small, privileged class or group. This contention is borne out, I believe, by the consistency with which the texts in the canon have called into question the belief system favored by the nation's dominant elites. To be sure, one might counter by saying that a dissenting viewpoint that lends credence to pastoral ideals is by definition an elegiac, nonpolitical, hence pacifying, or at least diversionary, form of dissent. Perhaps. But it also should be noted that a century and a half ago the response to industrial capitalism embodied in the canon seemed to represent the outlook of a handful of eccentric, literary, and intellectual dissenters; in recent decades a similar set of attitudes toward the established system has been adopted by a sizable, growing, vocal, activist, dissident minority of Americans.

Pastoralism and the (New) American Left

William Empson is the first critic to concern himself with the political implications of literary pastoral and, more specifically, the subtle relationship between pastoral and twentieth-century left-wing ideology. In the opening chapter ("Proletarian Literature") of his idiosyncratic, inconsecutive, vividly illuminating 1935 study, *Some Versions of*

Pastoral, Empson demonstrates that the kind of writing favored by the Marxist aesthetic of that era, although professedly "proletarian," usually proves to be a disguised version of what he describes as a puzzling, old-fashioned form – the pastoral – "which looks proletarian but isn't."[29] As ideally conceived by critics close to the Communist left, "proletarian" art ought to be by, for, and about the working class; Empson curtly notes, however, that few if any writers or readers of texts carrying that ideological stamp of approval were members of the working class, and on inspection neither are the characters in "proletarian" novels, poems, films, and so on. They may be simple, "low" characters whose social significance is largely defined by their social distance from the rich and powerful, but in a few deft analyses Empson shows that in fact they have less in common with industrial workers than with that mythical cult figure of old: the self-contained herdsman. Strip the worker-heroes of their factory clothes, as it were, and you will see that what passed for "proletarian literature" in the 1930s usually was "Covert Pastoral."

But Empson's stunning insight had some far-reaching implications he could not have foreseen. For him the important point is what the falsity of this left-wing aesthetic reveals about the universal, possibly "permanent" sources of the pastoral mode. It is in his view a sentimental illusion to think that the artist and the factory worker could be "at one" or, for that matter, that there ever could be a complete identity of interests between the artists and *any* public. The insurmountable difference is more vocational or technical than political; the gulf in awareness that lies between the intellectually and aesthetically sophisticated artist and a relatively naïve audience is for Empson one of the more or less "permanent" sources of the complex–simple antinomy at the center of pastoral. (This antinomy is related to a vexed but habitually down-played problem of Marxist political practice: the degree of the radical left's reliance for its leaders upon recruits from the middle class and the intelligentsia.) Having exposed the illusory aspect of the left-wing literary aesthetic, Empson drops the political argument, apparently satisfied to leave the impression that the discrepancy between the pastoral mode and left radicalism would become obvious, and that intellectuals, artists, and writers on the left eventually would replace the idea of "proletarian" art with a more apt and feasible aesthetic. What did not occur to him, understandably enough, was the possibility of closing the gap in the other direction – the adoption of a political program closer in spirit to pastoral impulses and aspirations like those encoded in the classic American literary texts.

By the early 1960s the political and cultural situation in the United States was conducive to the emergence of a new kind of dissident movement. Since late antiquity, it should be noted, pastoralism – especially in its secular literary form – seems to have flourished within the orbit of world capitals in like situations: times when the pace of change had been quickening, cities growing, new technologies being introduced, and when (above all) political regimes or empires were close to the apex of their power. We think of Alexandria in the time of Theocritus and of Virgil's Rome, of Shakespeare's (or Wordsworth's) London, Rousseau's Paris and Tolstoy's Moscow, and of Washington, D.C., at the time of John F. Kennedy's inauguration as President of the United States. (That a pastoral poet, Robert Frost, was accorded a place of honor on that occasion is worth thinking about.) One common feature of these historical situations has been the presence of artists, writers, and intellectuals with an inherently ambiguous relationship to the system of power and wealth represented at the capital. They are likely to be affiliated with, and in some measure beholden to, those in power; yet at the same time they also are prone to a feeling of estrangement from the system – a feeling of moral disquiet or disapproval arising from the discrepancy between their principles and the prevailing mode of domination or, at any rate, and for whatever conscious or unconscious reasons, an ambivalence issuing in fantasies or (less often) acts of disengagement. It is hard to think of a time and place when the segment of a population susceptible to such ambivalence might have been larger than in the United States on the eve of the Vietnam War.

The unusual size and disposition of this privileged yet disaffected minority is attributable to a convergence of propitious economic, demographic, political, and cultural circumstances after World War II.[30] The great economic boom of that era increased the size and affluence of the well-educated, comfortable, socially and geographically mobile segment of the middle class made up of professionals, technicians, writers, students, and teachers – those who might be said to have, in the broad sense, intellectual vocations. They are people who tend to identify their interests neither with the most powerful financial and corporate elites nor with the workers who sell their labor by the hour, day, or week. Having rarely if ever experienced serious material deprivation, they are likely to take for granted the satisfaction of their basic needs, and may even regard the principled renunciation of some material advantages with relative equanimity. In spite of their good fortune, many of these liberally inclined people began to lose confidence in the dominant progressive belief system during the 1950s.[31] Among the factors contributing to this erosion of belief was a series of shocking public events, beginning with Hiroshima and including the accelerating nuclear arms race, the McCarthyite hysteria, and the Korean War; a widely felt sense that the nation may have reached the apex of its global economic and political power; and a heightened awareness of the unfulfilled promise of social justice, of democracy itself or, more specifically, of the unresponsiveness of the political system to the needs and rights of the poor and the powerless – especially the nonwhite poor and powerless. During those same years an increasingly strident, alienated, adversary youth culture was emerging, and many of its outspoken literary representatives, notably the Beat poets and novelists, had self-consciously set out to keep alive the legacy of radical dissidence deriving from the work of Emerson, Thoreau, and Whitman.

These large national trends coincided with the less obvious development of an ideological and organizational vacuum within the American left. The New Left of the 1960s was to be distinguished from the old orthodoxy by its ideological flexibility, especially in abandoning an entire set of doctrines based on Karl Marx's economic analysis of capitalism: the assumption that the left's primary aim is to replace the capitalistic system of ownership, hence its reliance on the industrial proletariat as the chief agent of change, on class struggle as the key to strategy, and on socialism – identified with the collective ownership of the means of production – its goal. Put in more positive terms, the demise of the old Communist left opened the way for a radical movement that was more hospitable to the aspirations of that stratum of relatively privileged dissidents less concerned with economic than with moral, political, and cultural issues.

In many respects the prototype of the movement was the coalition of Berkeley campus student groups known as the Free Speech Movement (FSM). It executed the first organized, large-scale act of civil disobedience by university students of that generation, and the first act of student rebellion to attract nationwide and, indeed, worldwide attention in the 1960s. On December 2, 1964, at the rally preceding the illegal occupation of the administration building, Mario Savio, a student leader, sounded the ideological keynote of the forthcoming movement. "There is a time," he said, "when the operation of the machine becomes so odious, makes you so sick at heart, that you can't take part; you can't even tacitly take part, and you've got to put your bodies upon the gears and upon the wheels, upon the levers, upon all the apparatus and you've got to make it stop. And you've got to indicate to the people who run it, to the people who own it, that unless you're free, the machine will be prevented from working at all."[32]

Savio's rhetoric exemplifies the continuity between the Berkeley students' response to organized power and that embodied in the work of the classic American writers. This brief, widely publicized speech is in essence a 1960s restatement of the great central figurative conception of our literature: the machine-in-the-landscape metaphor of contradiction. As Savio's large audience understood, the "machine" here is in the first instance the university administration, perceived by the rebellious students with good reason as having denied them their constitutional right of free speech; by extension, however, the "machine" brings in the larger interlocking bureaucratic network of universities, corporations, and government, in a word, the "system." The enormously effective figure transfers the attributes of modern industrial technology—efficiency, power, impersonality, rationality, productivity, organization, and so on—to the students' adversary, the university administration. The administrators, according to this figure, treat the students like so many IBM cards—like cogs in a vast machine.

To oppose this technocratic mentality—and it is important to notice that the target here is not technology per se, not technology in the common sense of useful apparatus, but rather as it makes itself felt in that debased form of progressive thought that takes the perfection of means as a sufficent end—to oppose their technocratic adversary, Savio calls upon the students to commit an act of civil disobedience. Like followers of Henry Thoreau or Martin Luther King, they will illegally defy authority, in this case by occupying the space reserved for that authority's official use. This is a political equivalent of the pastoral figure's act of disengagement—his move away from the complex world of organized power in the direction of nature. But "nature" here must not be taken too literally, as a thing or place, for it is primarily a set of antitechnocratic principles. To defend their freedom and resist illegitimate authority, they will risk arrest, beatings, jail sentences—all figured forth by the desperate image of throwing their bodies on the machine. This audacious if reckless image is a measure of their exasperation, their sense of their insignificance and powerlessness within the university. To defend freedom, they will mobilize a force of nature. But it is as if they had been thrown back on the last, the ultimate repository of the natural available to them in their struggle with organized power: their own bodies. Hence Savio's restatement of Thoreau's stern recommendation in "Civil Disobedience": "Let your life be a counter-friction to stop the machine."

Soon after the Berkeley student uprising, the escalation of the American war in Vietnam began, and the call to "stop the machine" took on a larger and more urgent meaning. But the depiction of the war in those figural terms, as an encounter between a superbly equipped military force and a technologically primitive, peasant people was not an invention of the antiwar movement. It was a conception unavoidably figured forth by the nightly television news, and its profoundly affective power surely had something to do with the speed and intensity of the popular reaction. Within two or three years the methods and spirit of the civil rights and student movements had enabled the dissident minority to mobilize an immense if ideologically amorphous protest movement whose chief focus was resistance to the war. As one historian puts it, the war had become the organizing principle around which all the doubts and disillusionments, and all the deeper discontents hidden beneath the glossy surface of American life, "coalesced into one great rebellion." The pressures of discontent grew and grew until, in the great schism of 1968–73, they had "polarized the country into two opposed camps, two mutually hostile cultures." It was a schism dividing the American people between those who clung to the old progressive faith, as embodied in the official rationale for the war, and those who did not.[33]

As for the latter, it is difficult to be sure what views they shared apart from their opposition to the war and their varying degrees of disillusionment with the dominant culture. The radical Movement of the 1960s was a loose coalition of protesting groups with a large following of unaffiliated individuals; it had no overall organization, no official leaders, no stated ideology. In their sharp recoil from the ideas and methods of the "old" Marxist left, its preoccupation with large structures of power and its traditional notions of ideological conformity, organizational hierarchy, and individual discipline, they had committed themselves to an opposed ideal of "participatory democracy." The movement was to consist of exemplary local communities whose purpose was to demonstrate the feasibility of–to actually realize–an alternative way of life. It was to be an egalitarian, noncompetitive, communal life aimed not at directly combating or seizing power, but rather at the creation of local enclaves that might constitute an entirely new, adversary culture within the old system. These "cultural revolutionaries" affirmed the values of spontaneity, solidarity, direct democracy, local self-sufficiency–the set of aspirations implied by Charles Reich's inspired title *The Greening of America*. If there was an incipient ideology with a wide popular appeal in the 1960s Movement, Reich's sentimental best seller of 1970 probably came as close to expressing it as any document of the period. What his book affirms is the possibility of a cultural revolution grounded in opposition to a technocratic idea of material progress, a "revolution" committed to the goal of material sufficiency rather than continuous growth, and to the recovery of "the natural."[34]

Since the Vietnam era most of the dissident movements and tendencies of thought in the United States have exhibited a similar shift away from a progressive – and toward a pastoral – world view. As a result of the heightened ecological awareness of recent years, the archetypal nineteenth-century image of the machine invading the landscape has been invested with a new, more literal meaning and credibility. Although it is a mistake to think of pastoralism as chiefly concerned with the defense of physical nature itself, the various threats to the environment seemingly inherent in advanced industrial societies have enhanced the appeal of programs aimed at achieving a way of life "closer" to nature.[35] Of all those threats – population growth, pollution, resource depletion – the one that makes the primary figural conception of classic American literature seem most prophetic is the menace of nuclear war. (It is a striking tribute to the hold of pastoralism on the native imagination that the most effective tract against the nuclear arms race, Jonathan Schell's *The Fate of the Earth,* is cast in that literary mode.) What the new consciousness has added to traditional pastoralism is a sense of the biophysical environment as a locus of meaning and value in the literal sense, at least, of setting limits within which social systems must operate.

But to come back, finally, to the initial question: Is it likely that pastoralism might yet provide the basis for an effective political ideology? If we rely on the evidence of the last twenty-five years in the United States, it would seem that the various dissident movements of the privileged white middle class are too unstable, too lacking in programmatic resources for coping with large-scale concentrations of political power, to make that a probability. On the other hand, the very conception of a left-tending ideology not based on a progressive world view is so novel, and it has so rapidly gained adherents in recent years, that we may be seeing the beginning of a major shift in modes of political thought and action. In the end, however, we come up against the difference between the prerequisites of a compelling literary view of life, which need not meet the test of feasibility, and those of a political ideology that must, in the long run, meet precisely such a test. Or, to invoke Raymond Williams's distinction between opposition to the dominant culture deriving from *residual* values and opposition embodied in *emergent* values, the appeal of pastoralism may be too exclusively confined to the relatively privileged groups that would defend (or regain) residual values.[36] To provide the basis for an effective ideology, in other words, adherents of pastoralism would have to form alliances with the hitherto disadvantaged carriers of emergent values – those for whom "the recovery of the natural" as yet has, in itself, little or no appeal.

Notes

1 Leo Marx, *The Machine in the Garden: Technology and the Pastoral Ideal in America* (New York: Oxford University Press, 1964).

2 For a penetrating criticism, from a Marxist viewpoint, of my use of the term "industrialism" and its implications, see Carolyn Porter, *Seeing and Being: The Plight of the Participant Observer in Emerson, James, Adams, and Faulkner* (Middletown, Conn.: Wesleyan University Press, 1981), pp. 69–82, and especially the long summary note, pp. 312–13.

3 "Representative event" is a modification of Kenneth Burke's ingenious concept of the "representative anecdote" that provides those who invoke the anecdote with a form with which to construct a vocabulary that "reflects" a larger reality. For Burke's definition, see *A Grammar of Motives* (Berkeley: University of California Press, 1969), p. 59.

4 By "dominant culture" I do not mean a culture that necessarily was adhered to by a majority of the people; rather, I mean one adhered to by the most powerful or influential social groups.

5 Thoreau relies heavily on the machine as a metaphor for the state in "Civil Disobedience" (1849), in *Walden and Other Writings* (New York: Random House, 1950), p. 644. For the relevant portion of Savio's speech, see *The Berkeley Student Revolt,* ed. Seymour Martin Lipsit and Sheldon S. Wolin (New York: Doubleday, 1965), p. 163.

6 For the alleged shift in the prevailing American ethos, or value system, see Daniel Yankelovich, *New Rules* (New York: Random House, 1981), and Peter Clecak, *America's Quest for the Ideal Self* (New York: Oxford University Press, 1981).

7 Alain Touraine, *The Voice and the Eye: An Analysis of Social Movements* (Cambridge University Press, 1981), pp. 6–7. See also A. Melucci, "The New Social Movements: A Theoretical Approach," *Social Science Information* 19, no. 2 (1980): 199–226; Claus Offe, "New Social Movements as a Metapolitical Challenge," mimeographed (Bielefeld, 1983), pp. 1–75.

8 Willard A. Mullins, "On the Concept of Ideology in Political Science," *American Political Science Review* 66 (1972): 498–510; Clifford Geertz, *The Interpretation of Cultures* (New York: Basic, 1973), pp. 87–141, 193–233; Edward Shils, "Ideology," *International Encyclopedia of the Social Sciences* (New York: Macmillan, 1968), 7: 66–75.

9 Geertz, *Interpretation of Cultures,* p. 127.

10 David M. Halperin, *Before Pastoral: Theocritus and the Ancient Tradition of Bucolic Poetry* (New Haven, Conn.: Yale University Press, 1983). For much of what follows, I am indebted to Halperin's summary chapter 6, "Pastoral Origins and the Ancient Near East," and to lengthy discussion of the issues with him. Some of the same ground is covered by William Berg, *Early Virgil* (London: Athlone Press, 1974).

11 Halperin, *Before Pastoral,* p. 95.

68 L. Marx

12 Ibid., pp. 91–5.

13 For a useful definition of ethos, see Geertz, *Interpretation of Cultures*, p. 127.

14 The part played by pastoral ideas and images in Judeo-Christian religious thought and expression is an immense subject, and although its exclusion here is somewhat arbitrary, it also is justified by the fact that my chief concern is the emergence of an essentially secular, latently political version of pastoralism in our time.

15 J. E. Congleton, *Theories of Pastoral Poetry in England, 1684–1798* (Gainesville: University of Florida Press, 1952).

16 Quite apart from the inherent good sense of the views Shakespeare attributes to Polonius, they comport with the serious regard for the mode implied by his own work in it, notably *As You Like It, The Winter's Tale,* and *The Tempest.* For a discussion of *The Tempest* as a version of pastoral that anticipates the character of "classic" American writing, see *The Machine in the Garden,* chapter 2.

17 William Empson, *Some Versions of Pastoral* (London: Chatto & Windus, 1935). Empson's chief contribution was to cut the idea of pastoral free of its ties to the old conventions, and to suggest that its essence is a "trick of thought" or the putting of the complex into the simple. Hence he indirectly opened the way for the historical views mentioned. For a somewhat closer approximation of those views, see Renato Poggioli, *The Oaten Flute: Essays on Pastoral Poetry and the Pastoral Ideal* (Cambridge, Mass.: Harvard University Press, 1975), pp. 1–41.

18 Karl Polanyi, *The Great Transformation* (New York: Rinehart, 1944).

19 C. Vann Woodward, *New York Review of Books,* April 5, 1979, p. 3.

20 The literature alluded to here is immense. A good starting point might be Werner Sombart, *Why Is There No Socialism in the United States?* trans. Patricia M. Hocking and C. T. Husbands (New York: M. E. Shappe, 1978). Sombart's book was first published in German in 1905. For an exhaustive review of the literature, see Seymour Martin Lipset, "Why No Socialism in the United States?" in Seweryn Bialer and Sophia Sluzar, eds., *Sources of Contemporary Radicalism* (New York: Westview Press, 1977.)

21 For a detailed discussion of this set of attitudes and the language in which they were conveyed, which I call the "rhetoric of the technological sublime," see *The Machine in the Garden,* pp. 190–209.

22 For a more detailed analysis of the passage, Query XIX of *Notes on Virginia,* and of Jefferson's subsequent letters on the subject, see *The Machine in the Garden,* pp. 116–41.

23 Poggioli, *The Oaten Flute,* p. 31.

24 Herman Melville, *Moby-Dick.* This discussion refers to the first three paragraphs of chap. 1.

25 For F. O. Matthiessen's view of the centrality of "double consciousness" in the work of the American Renaissance writers, see my essay, "Double Consciousness and the Cultural Politics of F. O. Matthiessen," in *Monthly Review* (February 1983): 34–55.

26 For an analysis of the *locus amoenus* in classical literature, see Thomas G. Rosenmeyer, *The Green Cabinet: Theocritus and the European Pastoral Lyric* (Berkeley: University of California Press, 1973), esp. pp. 186–203.

27 Thoreau, *Walden*, "Sounds," p. 107.

28 For the concept of pastorals of "success" and "failure," see Harold E. Toliver, *Marvell's Pastoral Vision* (New Haven, Conn.: Yale University Press, 1960), pp. 88–103. Toliver's test of "success" is more conservative than mine: In a pastoral of success, he says, the writer or the writer's representative "consolidates gains, becomes reoriented toward the world, and finally reenters society." Some conception of this sort is almost indispensable to the criticism of pastoral, and "pastorals of failure" also have been called "inverted pastorals" or "anti-pastorals."

29 Empson, *Some Versions*, p. 6.

30 Of the many historical surveys of the post–World War II era, the most reliable and useful for my purposes is Godfrey Hodgson, *America in Our Time* (New York: Random House, 1976).

31 Hodgson describes the specific postwar embodiment of the progressive belief system as "The Ideology of the Liberal Consensus" in chapter 4 of *America in Our Time*. Its most relevant items are the belief that the American "free enterprise system" is different from the old exploitative capitalism in that it is democratic, creates abundance, and therefore has a revolutionary potential for social justice. The key to that potential is the unprecedented capacity of the system for continuous economic growth, and that concept of material progress is the fulcrum of both this specific ideology and the larger progressive world view.

32 Lipset and Wolin, *Berkeley Student Revolt*, p. 163.

33 Hodgson, *America in Our Time*, p. 275.

34 The prominence accorded by the new left to this figurative conception, the mobilizing of "green" values against "the machine," may be said to bear out Clifford Geertz's contention that the essential structure of an ideology is to be found in its root metaphor. See Geertz, "Ideology as a Cultural System." For a discussion of a case example, see Leo Marx, "Susan Sontag's 'New Left' Pastoral: Notes on Revolutionary Pastoralism in America," *TriQuarterly* 23/24 (Spring 1972). Reprinted in George Abbott White and Charles Newman, eds., *Literature in Revolution* (New York: Holt, Rinehart & Winston, 1972), pp. 552–75.

35 I discuss the relationship between pastoralism and the ecological viewpoint in "American Institutions and Ecological Ideals," *Science* 170 (November 27, 1970): 945–52; and in "American Literary Culture and the Fatalistic View of Technology," *Alternative Futures* (Spring 1980): 45–70.

36 Raymond Williams, *Marxism and Literature* (New York: Oxford University Press, 1977), pp. 121–27.

4

Myth and the Production of History

RICHARD SLOTKIN

Myth is the primary language of historical memory: a body of traditional stories that have, over time, been used to summarize the course of our collective history and to assign ideological meanings to that history.

We tend to think of "myth" as the basis of someone else's religion – someone more primitive than ourselves; and we commonly use "ideology" to describe the premises of someone else's politics – our own are based on reason, logic, and realism. Such definitions reflect our ethnocentricity. In fact, the terms "myth" and "ideology" describe essential attributes of every human culture. Ideology is an abstraction of the system of beliefs, values, and institutional relationships that characterize a particular culture or society; mythology is the body of traditional narratives that exemplifies and historicizes ideology. Myths are stories, drawn from history, that have acquired through usage over many generations a symbolizing function central to the culture of the society that produces them. Through the processes of traditionalization historical narratives are conventionalized and abstracted, and their range of reference is extended so that they become structural metaphors containing all the essential elements of a culture's world view. The language of myth assimilates the peculiar and contingent phenomena of secular history to archetypal patterns of growth and decay, salvation and damnation, death and rebirth. So formulated, myths suggest that by understanding and imaginatively reenacting the conflict resolutions of the past, we can interpret and control the unresolved conflicts of the present.

The captain was taking his company out of Song Be for a search-and-destroy mission against the VC – one hundred infantrymen in full pack, with "rifles, heavy automatics, mortars, portable one-shot rocket launchers, radios, medics" and a helicopter gunship flying hover-cover–and he said to the reporter, "Come on . . . we'll take you out to play Cowboys and Indians." The war in Vietnam sometimes seemed so alien to American experience and expectations that it might have been happening on some other planet, and it had its own special lingo whose words and rhythm were native to its ordered lunacy. But even in that language the reporter knew what the captain meant, because they'd played that game as children back in "the World," and they knew how the rules worked. The rules were clear but flexible, adapting readily to shifts of mood that might be subtle or sudden, and might move from a mode in which the deployment of violence was so indirect or so absurdly motivated that it seemed almost playful, to another in which the war could only be fought with genocidal brutality, quarter neither expected nor given, torture for the captive and mutilation for the dead. It was the "Indian idea," one veteran said, "the only good gook is a dead gook." Taking the ears of dead VC was "Like scalps, you know, like from Indians. Some people were on an Indian trip over there."[1]

The language of the Cowboys and Indians "game" was one way to get a handle on experiences too terrible, too upsetting to be morally acceptable. The invocation of the game is a reaching for a rationale, a figurative mode of explanation that can at least give a precedent for what is happening, tie it to something familiar, normal, understood. We may be tempted to think of this "Indian trip" as the mythology only of badly educated "grunts," militarized versions of "drugstore cowboys" and "outlaw bikers" whose minds are filled with the gaudy cartoon violence of TV, movies, and comic books. But this falsifies not only the character of the soldier and citizen, but also the mind and character of the elites who presided over the army and the nation. In fact, the one language the grunts demonstrably shared with their military and bureaucratic superiors was this language of Cowboys and Indians. General and Ambassador Maxwell Taylor, testifying before Congress in an attempt to explain the difficulties of "pacification" in Vietnam, reached for a metaphor that would at once define the difficulty and suggest the likelihood of final success: "It is very hard," he said, "to plant corn outside the stockade when the Indians are still around. We have to get the Indians farther away . . . to make good progress." Senator Russell Long, rebuking his colleagues for criticizing the war effort, reached for a similar analogy: "If the men who came on the *Mayflower* were frightened to helplessness the first time they had to fight Indians, they would have gone back to England. . . . But they fought the Indians and won, meanwhile losing some fine Americans, until this Nation became great." Long's use of the metaphor is vulgarly self-serving, and he stumbles on the ambiguous identification of those "fine Americans" lost in the wars of English settlers and native Indians. But the same language could be deployed with a certain passionate elegance by John F. Kennedy, proclaiming his slogan of the "New Frontier" for a program of renewed economic expansion and forward movement on the borders of the American empire.[2]

Such metaphors are not merely ornamental. They invoke a tradition of discourse that has historical roots and referents, and carries with it a heavy and persistent ideological charge. All of these public figures and writers speak and think within that tradition of discourse, using a symbolic language that they acquired through the usual processes of acculturation and education. Tradition not only links them with each other as "natives" of the same culture, it associates them backward in time to earlier makers of American culture and ideology. Their association of the struggle against an ideological opposite with Indian wars, their belief that racially tinged wars provoke excessive violence, their linkage of such wars with the nation's rise to greatness, their identification with the figure planting corn (or rice) by the stockade would have been as intelligible to Andrew Jackson, or Thomas Jefferson, or General Custer as it is to us. On the other side, the readers of Fenimore Cooper in the 1830s, or of Helen Hunt Jackson in the 1890s, would have been as ready as the audience of *Little Big Man* or the "natives" of the Woodstock Nation to see in the Noble Savage an antidote to the discontents of that same triumphant civilization. The terminology of the Myth of the Frontier has become part of our common language, and we do not require an elaborate explanatory program to make it comprehensible.

These formulations not only define a situation for us, they prescribe our response to that situation. At the very least, they tell us how we ought to value the situation – whether we are to identify with it or against it, whether our attitude to "Indian country" or the "Lone Ranger" or the "cowboy economy" is hostile, friendly, or satirical. But they are also ideologically loaded formulations, which aim at affecting not only our perceptions but our behavior – by "enlisting," morally or physically, in the ideological program that the user of the language advocates.

Mythological statements always represent the ideology of the moment as if it were the embodiment of divine or natural law, or the reflection of a tradition so ancient that its origins are beyond historical ken. This sets the interests and attitudes of the ideology-producing group or class outside the purview of critical analysis. The interests and attitudes of the group take on the coloration of revelation *and science*. The moral political imperatives implicit in the myths are given as if they were the only possible choices for moral and intelligent beings; and, similarly, the set of choices confronted are limited to a few traditional either/or decisions. When we play the Cowboys and Indian game, only two or three human roles exist – aggressor, victim, avenger – and there are few options for moral choice: A man's *got* to do what a man's got to do.

The antidote to mythological thinking – or part of the antidote – may lie in rehistoricizing the myth. If we can understand where in history the rules of the "game" came from, what real human and social relationships the rules conceal or distort, and what the historical consequences of playing the game have been, we may be able to respond more intelligently when an infantry captain or a senator or a president asks us to come out and play it.

The central difficulty in myth study is the problem of *reification:* that is, the tendency to treat ideas, metaphors, and linguistic conventions as if they were palpable aspects of material reality. Mythmaking itself is a reifying process, through which metaphorical descriptions of reality come to substitute for an apprehension of reality. This is true whether the metaphor in question involves the sublimation of natural processes into a Deity who personifies natural and supernatural force, or the abstraction of nature into a tendentious system of "laws" like the Social-Darwinian equation of "survival of the fittest" with laissez-faire economics. But reification has also been the besetting sin of those who have made myth and ideology their field of study. The most radical critique of the field is that which regards the key concepts of "mind" and "culture" as the products of reification. The concept of mind is itself a metaphor for certain biological processes whose material form we cannot yet specify; and the concept of a "collective mentality" is an extrapolation from this metaphor, a more elaborate reification no less evasive of scientific testing. By assuming the existence of individual "mind" and collective "culture," students of myth and ideology have put their most fundamental assumptions beyond the reach of scientific disproof, and have thus made themselves guilty of the very error they note in primitive mythmakers: the resting of analysis on the authority of something that is "supernatural."[3]

Such a critique strikes me as too radical in its skepticism, and in its insistence on a certain kind of quantification that can deal only with the most concrete sorts of phenomena. The case against the theory that ideas influence behavior is strong enough, until we reverse the burden of proof and consider the alternative hypothesis: that ideas have *no* influence on behavior. Such an assertion belies our own experience of life, in which we are intensely aware of all sorts of mental phenomena that are responsive to experience and to pressures generated within our individual psychobiological systems.

The objections to theories of mentality are themselves a perverse affirmation of the real-world effects of the "unreal" and "immaterial" categories of metaphor and myth. The critique of myth study reflects an awareness that ideas – erroneous or valid – do indeed shape the behavior of one identifiable and not insignificant social entity: the community of writers, scholars, and historians whose work is in this "realm of ideas." And if ideas, false or true, can shape the work and social behavior of one class of humans, why not of others? It therefore seems more fruitful to me to accept, as the premise of study, the metaphorical character of our analytical processes and our tendency, as a species, to "reify" – to treat ideas as if they were real. We can then proceed to examine more closely the processes by which metaphors are generated and become reified – remaining aware, as we do this, that we ourselves share the projective and reifying propensities of the myths we study.

Myth is acquired and preserved as part of our language. We observe its operation in the quality of historical (or pseudohistorical) resonance that attaches to terms like "frontier," "Cowboys and Indians," or "Last Stand." That resonance derives less from the reality of the past than from the traditions of usage. It is not western history itself that shapes our sense of these terms, because we have not experienced that history – we know it at second or third hand, through the medium of our literary and historiographical traditions. Rather, our "memory" of the historical significance of these terms derives from the history of the language of the Frontier Myth – a history whose events are acts of imagination embodied in prose and set before the reading (or theatrical) public.

Myth is "fictional" in a double sense: It is an artifact of human intelligence and productive labor (although it may be made to appear as a "fact of nature"); and it is a "falsification" of experience – a partial representation masquerading as the whole truth. We are subjectively aware of the gap that exists on the level of individual psychology, between the perception of an event and its assimilation by the conscious mind; and of the ways in which our memory of past perception modifies the record of original experience, adapting it to preexisting memories, prejudices, and habits of thought. The ceremonies and artifacts of culture impose similar distortions on the historical experiences they mean to reproduce. As with historical events themselves, the production of works of art or history, of great public fairs or exhibitions, are overdetermined by the mixture of individual motives and limitations, of the differing imperatives of culture, politics, and economics and – not least – the special characteristics and generic forms of a given medium of expression. When we study a complex ceremonial like the centennial exposition or the journalistic responses to an event like the Tet offensive or Custer's Last Stand, or the literary fiction of a writer who works in the language of his society's preferred mythology, we engage ourselves with a complex reflecting mechanism whose special complications echo – in a special way – the complexities of history.[4]

Although the materials for a study of myth are necessarily "fictive," and in a modern culture, "literary," the study itself is historical in that it treats mythmaking as a human activity in the material world.

The media of literature, the public arts, and public ceremonies are given license by the culture to devote themselves explicitly and exclusively to creative development and even to play with the symbolic language of cultural values. The systematic language play that we observe in our literary culture has no necessary connection to the world of social action – it does not reflect that world one for one, its purpose is not always that of simple propaganda-making or moral suasion, and its fantasy projections of heroic action are not necessarily realized or acted out according to script by real actors on the stage of material history. The function of imaginative fiction (whether literary or folkloric) is to develop, elaborate, and bring to conscious expression the implicit logic of the culture's world view and sense of history, to play out more fully than life usually permits the consequences of the value system on which our mythic fantasies are based.

Cultural activity is an aspect of real-world behavior, and can be analyzed historically. The building blocks of cultural systems are the metaphor-generating processes inherent in individual human psychology. We apprehend the real world as much through linguistic and symbolizing acts as through physical interactions. As Wallace Stevens says, even "the senses paint by metaphor," refining the inarticulate perception by associating it with other objects in the field of sensation, and with memories of objects met with in the past. Clifford Geertz offers a less fanciful statement of a similar principle in his account of the basis of ideological thinking in human cultures. We apprehend and try to understand the world around us by projecting primitive hypotheses about the reality we encounter, and by attempting to "match . . . the states and processes of symbolic models against the states and processes of the wider world." We continually strive to resolve "the inherent contradictions between present circumstances and received wisdom," by testing remembered facts against present difficulties. The memory of similar past problems happily resolved proffers the metaphorical hypothesis we tentatively apply to the present. If the analogy works, our happiness persists; if it fails, then the complex work of finding a usable memory, adjusting memory to fact, and assimilating new facts to memory, begins again. On the social plane, the maker of metaphorical hypothesis becomes a human collectivity – tribe, clan, or class – whose projects for historical success are continually matched against a reality that sometimes rewards and sometimes rebuffs the projectors; and from the interacting pressures of fantasy, fact, and memory the direction of cultural development emerges.[5]

This process of primitive hypothesization involves the projection of immaterial elements of fantasy and memory onto the world; but these projections are so essential as instruments for apprehending reality that they are effectively a part of reality, and when we ignore them we ignore an aspect of the real. Even where the product of such activity is verbal or intellectual, it participates in material reality. Culture is an active process, not an abstract and timeless essence; and cultural activity is "symbolic action," the making of symbols, the conversion of sensory data into "fictions" that are simply images of reality linguistically endowed with significance. Paraphrasing Max Weber, Clifford Geertz sees man as "an animal suspended in webs of significance he himself has spun, [and we] take culture to be those webs." But cultural production so conceived is work, requiring energy and time, involving human choices and social consequences, engaging materials and labor, and connecting the producer with the network of relationships – social, political, economic – that constitute his society. Although cultural expressions are symbolic, they are not "occult." All of those manifold social actions that we regard as having or expressing meaning – glances, winks, speeches, credos, deeds – are the active constituents of social reality, and are at least as material as calculations of profit and loss.[6]

Similar theories are part of the new social history, as practiced by historians like Eric Foner, David Brion Davis, Herbert Gutman, E. P. Thompson, and Alan Dawley. For example, Thompson's *The Making of the English Working Class* emphasizes the role of preindustrial cultural influences, especially religion, in providing the language through which the emergent working class defined itself and its interests against those of its employers. In Thompson's view, to say that an idea or issue is "cultural" is "not to say that it [is] immaterial." Mental activity is also historically "real," because "historical actors give cultural significance to their material existence" when they verbally assign meanings to the material conditions in which they live. Material conditions may shape and limit their choices of meaning, but so too does the language of traditional meanings and forms of expression that are acquired through familial and social education. In this system, material and cultural real-

ity are not related deterministically, and neither are individual and collective psychology: Base does not *determine* superstructure, as in vulgar
Marxism; nor do ideas exert a supernatural force upon a plastic reality,
as in the idealist view. Rather, there is "a continuous interaction between ideology and the material forces of history," and the historical
process is shaped by "a field of mutually if also unevenly determining
forces." "Determination" in such a field takes the form of "setting
limits and exertion of pressure" rather than that of forceful direction.[7]
　　This account of ideological activity makes the process of symbolization sound like a variant of scientific method, with metaphor and myth
standing in the place of hypothesis. Geertz, for one, accepts this connection, insofar as both scientific and ideological discourse are to be
seen as "fictions" – that is, as artificial constructs of human imagination.
However, Geertz sees scientific discourse as a different sort of "fiction,"
whose motives are "diagnostic" and "critical"; whose methods of hy-
pothesizing are self-aware and self-correcting; and whose sphere of operation is restricted to a carefully bounded fraction of the culture. The
scientist recognizes the fact that metaphors are "treacherous" and "must
be watched," and therefore scientific metaphors receive a credulity that
is modified by skepticism – a conditional credulity that will become
complete only if certain systematic tests are met. The skeptic–scientist
is aware of the inherent tendency of metaphor to falsify what it represents. Metaphor establishes a linguistic relationship between two or
more different things, but does this indirectly and implicitly, omitting
those phrases that would specify the kind and degree of comparison
being made. Because it connects things by implication, metaphor relies
for its plausibility on our biases and habits of vision, and in effect reads
our prejudices into the interpretation of reality.[8] Such usage may be
harmless enough in the individual consciousness; but when we deal
with socialized metaphors – with myths – we confront a concept that has
the power to do harm.
　　When a metaphor is extended into a myth, its power to evade the
tests of reason is augmented by the authority of tradition, the power of
collective opinion, and the appeal of a well-told story. A myth makes a
single metaphor out of a large swath of history, and its implications
therefore invoke the authority of the dominant ideology, the givens
that shape cultural and political discourse. When societies adopt metaphors as ideological doctrine, those metaphors acquire a tyrannical
weight that does indeed restrain thought and behavior, binding them to
patterns that rationalize and reproduce the traditional order. The pretty
metaphor of cosmic spheres dancing to music was part of a myth –
ideological system whose safety required that Galileo be proscribed and

Bruno burnt. The metaphorical linkage of the Tonkin Gulf incident with Hitler's Anschluss or the Japanese invasion of Manchuria in 1931 invoked *as myth* the historical events that led up to the outbreak of World War II, and thus made escalation in Vietnam appear the only possible response to the situation in Southeast Asia.

Ideological discourse differs from scientific because the purposes for which it uses its metaphors are always "justificatory" and "apologetic," as Geertz says. François Jacob, in his essay on myth and science in *The Possible and the Actual* (1982), notes that both myth and science begin with the intention of explaining visible phenomena by invisible or un-seen forces, and both begin by "inventing a possible world." The dif-ference between them is that a myth is never just "a tale from which inferences can be drawn about the world" but "has a moral content" that converts inference into a set of imperatives for human action. Myth is always ideological, concerned with defining and defending "pattern of value" and not with facilitating the scientific verification of infer-ences drawn from observation. Within the sphere of ideological dis-course, there are two distinct modes of expression that we need to distinguish: the mode of ideology proper, and the mode of mythmak-ing. Our common notion of ideology is that it is the program or doctrine of a party, sect, class, or society, set out in discursive and schematic terms.[9] But ideology in the larger sense of a total abstraction of a society's values and beliefs is not only expressed in explicit and discursive manifestos and creeds. It is also voiced in fables and narra-tives, symbolic productions that exemplify ideological doctrine in the subtlest and most disarming way. Scientific discourse, ideology, and mythmaking have characteristic and different ways of organizing the apprehension of reality, the assertion of values, and the programming of behavior. They have been thought of as stages of intellectual growth, with mythology generally listed as the most primitive mode and scien-tific discourse as the most advanced. This view is flattering to our civilization, but it is more accurate to see science, ideology, and myth as representing a spectrum of intellectual responses to reality, which coexist both in individual minds and in the culture's battery of interpre-tive weapons.

Mythmaking may be the least analytical of these modes, and for this reason we have tended to associate it with primitive societies and our own prescientific past. The subject of myth is human history, but it is history processed in a "magical" or – to use Lévi-Strauss's analogy – a "musical" way. Whereas modern fictional narratives or historical accounts organize such experience sequentially, according to an analytically derived model of temporality, mythic accounts tend to be undifferentiated and "simultaneous." Although mythic accounts do recognize the elementary sequences of "before and after," their most meaningful units are not so organized. When a "before" event, such as the creation of the universe by the gods, is invoked in a mythic telling, it is rendered *as if* it were a "present" happening, an event that is somehow still going on. In this way myth registers the "presence" of those divine forces it aims to integrate in its account of reality and its prescription of ritual response. Like a metaphor or a page of a musical score, myth organizes its meanings into a simultaneous expression in which description and meaning are equated and fused. Thus, Lévi-Strauss speaks of the meaning of myth as residing in "bundles of meaning" rather than in a logically or temporally sequenced account.

Most cultural discourse, even among so-called primitives, is not purely "mythic." As soon as myths are deployed to account for contingent and historical phenomena, their character and function are modified. The coherence of the mythic "bundle of meaning" is retained in metaphor; but that metaphor is now employed in an account or explanation that is sequential and historical. Lévi-Strauss sees such contexts as symptomatic of "How Myths Die," that is, how they are transformed from myth proper into forms of expression that preserve mythic content in a new form. "Fictional elaboration" is one such form, and the genres of modern literary culture may be seen as bourgeois society's chosen means of transforming and representing its mythic heritage. With the exception of certain types of lyric poetry, these forms are built upon a narrative sequencing of experiences, which reflects an essentially historical conception of experience. Yet these genres also exhibit a tendency to replicate the "bundles of meaning" structure that characterizes myth. This is particularly the tendency when literary or historical narration is used for ideological purposes. In such cases, the account of the past is always rendered in such a way that it justifies the political and social arrangements of the present, and predicts the fulfillment of the society's program for the future. Thus the past/present/future distinction essential to historical narrative is, if not annihilated, at least severely compromised; and history approaches the character of pure myth.[10]

It is this modern form of mythmaking, in which myths are integrated with ideological discourse and historical narration, that concerns us here. There is a necessary tension in modern myth between the desire to render an account that stands up to rational analysis, that insists on differentiating past and present, intention and effect, assigned and objective meaning; and the desire to mythologize, to present a "bundle of meaning" that will be impervious to skepticism and powerfully evocative of belief. Thus, the accounts with which we have to deal continually beg the question of historical verification, while at the same time insisting that the *meanings* of the events (as distinct from the facts) are of timeless value. Myth gives us history impacted in a metaphor whose referents are (or are asserted to be) eternal and timeless. We must remember that, as Roland Barthes says, myth "can only have a historical foundation" because it is a human creation: "It cannot possibly evolve from the 'nature' of things," unless we wish to personify Nature or return to a theistic world view.

Myth is not truly "sacred" in origin – it is the work of men and women, not of gods – but the primary effect of mythmaking is to translate secular experience into sacred knowledge. Myth represents processes that are contingent and historical as if they were expressions of a divine will, or products of the operation of natural law. It is history successfully disguised as archetype. In a religious culture, the sacred account of cosmogony treats the origins of the world as if they were shaped by a different kind of power from that at work in ordinary physical processes; and they account for historical events by referring to a sacred paradigm or program set forth in the Word of God. In a more secular culture, similar effects are achieved by associating human actions with natural processes – for example, treating the "laws of economics" as if these were as universal and as mechanical as the law of gravity. We can only demystify our history by historicizing our myths – that is, by treating them as human creations, produced in a specific historical time and place, in response to the contingencies of social and personal life.[11]

Such demystification is difficult because "the very principle" of myth is that "it transforms history into nature." What "causes mythical speech to be uttered" is specificable in contingent terms, through analysis of the motives, methods, and political context in which the speech occurs. But because mythic language refers us to a prevalued picture of reality, and because that picture has been accepted by us as a traditional "given," the mythic statement "is immediately frozen into something natural; it is not read as a motive, but as a reason." Successful analysis depends on the recognition of human activity, which has a motive in responding to a situation, which has an implied politics – a wish to control the situation, if only conceptually. But in myth "things lose the memory that once they were made" and appear as if they were truly revelations or intuited truths. "Myth is constituted by the loss of the historical quality of things," the knowledge that things were made by people; hence myth can perform "the task of giving an historical intention a natural justification, and making contingency appear eternal."

Political conflict, clash of purposes, inconsistency of vision, are subsumed in a smooth narrative in which all difficulties are absorbed into
"a harmonious display of essences."[12]

Northrop Frye's *The Critical Path* offers an account that I find plausible. Frye's approach is based on that of Vico, and it sees culture as
beginning with the establishment in a society of "a framework of mythology," consisting of "canonical stories . . . true fables or myths."
These are narrative accounts of the creation of the cosmos and/or the
genesis of the particular society, which are accepted as true or valid
representations of something that really happened in natural and social
history. The notion of a "true fable" is paradoxical, but no more so
than the idea of a valid metaphor. If a true fable is not literally or
scientifically true, it nonetheless plays the role of hypothesis by making
possible a partial apprehension of something real. In Frye's scenario,
those fables whose applicability to reality is affirmed by continuing
experience become integrated into a system of beliefs, of mythology;
and this in turn provides the parameters from which "all [the society's]
verbal culture grows." The mythology draws "a *temenos* or magic
circle" around the culture, "and a literature develops within a limited
orbit of language, reference, allusion, belief, transmitted and shared
tradition." The system cannot, of course, be completely closed to new
inputs, as Frye sometimes seems to suggest. The original mythology is
a kind of net in which new materials will be caught; and when a fish
comes along too big for the net to comprehend, the net must either
stretch or break, be cast aside or repaired on a new scale.[13]

Frye calls these earliest mythological formulations the "myth of concern." Myths are stories, and however encyclopedic they may attempt
to be, they inevitably are selective in establishing the spectrum of available situations, conflicts, characters, deities, and natural settings. Thus
the central myths of a society will tend to be those that refer to issues
concerning that society most deeply, and most persistently over time.
Such myths will inevitably reflect archetypal patterns, not because such
patterns are induced by the gods or the laws of nature, but because
certain features of human experience are apparently inescapable. The
entire species must experience the cycle of birth, maturation, and death;
and the parallels between this cycle and that of the seasons is apparently
too obvious to be missed. The species is familial and social, and hence
the experiences of interpersonal bonding, tension, and separation are
recurrent story-subjects regardless of time or place. Since these elements are inescapable, we should not be surprised to find myths based
on them recurring throughout the spectrum of human cultures, nor to
find such myths clustering around the most sacred occasions and ritu-

als – their persistence through all historical changes marks them as of more than temporal significance. This is the way in which myth brings "natural law" to bear on the materials of history, and begins transforming "history" to "nature."

Nonetheless, the "myth of concern" does not stop with archetype. As societies change, developing new technologies or economic systems or moving to new territories, new issues arise that – if they persist – must be interpreted in the "myth of concern." A society of hunters may have mythology centered on the interaction of predator and prey; one of the farmers may see gods and men interacting primarily because of their concern with vegetative processes; a modern, industrial, and imperial society may see the basic concern or issue of human history as the struggle for class or racial hegemony in a secular world. "In every structured society," says Frye, "the ascendent class attempts to take over the myth of concern and make it . . . a rationalization of its ascendency." This activity is necessary because the "myth of concern" has been composed around the culture's central concerns, its interpretation of the central problem of human existence.[14]

It is on this level of "concern" that mythology and ideology form a "consensus": They agree on the terms in which the problem of existence and social survival will be stated; but they may disagree sharply as to programmatic solutions, as the Vietnam material cited earlier illustrates. It is at this point that the distinction between mythic and ideological elements in a belief system becomes crucial.

Myth and ideology share the function of expressing and enacting the values, the purposes, and the world views of the societies that produce them. However, ideological statement and mythological statement differ in form and in the kind of cultural discourse they involve. The preferred genres for ideological discourse are sermons, polemics, credos, manifestos, and the like – genres whose conventions derive from the tutelary or persuasive relationship between speaker and audience. Ideological statement as such is discursive and propositional in form, and is based on a deliberate abstraction of ideas from the field of cultural materials. The form of mythological statement is apparently metaphorical, but at the core of the mythic metaphor is a narrative structure. Mythic metaphors are condensed versions of cosmology and/or history – that is what gives them their meaning and their power as explanations and justifications of behavior. A mythic symbol such as the crucifix in a community of Christian believers, or a shot-torn American flag displayed at a patriotic gathering, has meaning and power because it refers to a history, a complete series of events, whose narrative structure is well known to that audience, and accepted by them as representing something both true and full of meaning. Because of that historical reference, and because of the narrative form in which history is represented, mythic metaphors are able to imply the existence and validity of a complete cosmology, a complete theory of historical cause-and-effect. Any narrative, however spare and summary it may be, automatically and implicitly invokes a theory of human behavior and historical causation. By incorporating a cosmological or historical narrative, mythic metaphor acquires this explanatory power. And since the historical–cosmological narratives it invokes are those that have been traditionally accepted, myth is able to invoke the meanings of the tales without having to repeat them in their entirety.

It is this reliance on traditional understandings that sets mythological narrative apart from historical narrative. As Louis Mink has argued, narrative can be a form of explanation that is not inferior to analytic approaches as a way of acquiring and representing knowledge of history: Indeed, narrative forms are better able to represent the historical reality of change over time, and the human experience of time, than purely analytical approaches to history. Modern narrative history overcomes the implicit biases of traditional narrative by incorporating analytical data, and by offering several different perspectives on the action being narrated. In this respect it copies modern fiction, which has generally abandoned the "omniscient narrator" of the nineteenth-century novel for fragmentary and partial perspectives rooted in the fictional actors themselves. In both fiction and historiography, this fragmenting of perspective implies a rejection not only of omniscience as a form or pose, but of the ideological premises that those omniscient narrators were so certain of.[15]

But mythological narrative does not admit a multiplicity of perspectives, and is not arranged to encourage questions – as a modern work of fiction or history does – about the values that shape history. Mythic narrative embodies tradition and invokes belief. Its primary appeal is to ritualized emotions, habitual associations, memory, nostalgia. Its representations are symbolic and metaphoric, depending for their force on an intuitive recognition and acceptance of the symbol by the audience. The purpose of myth is always ideological, never purely descriptive let alone analytic. It is invoked as a means of deriving usable values from history, and of putting those values beyond the reach of critical demystification. The language of myth reflects the conditioning of socialized minds to accept as true or valid certain metaphoric renderings of history. The vocabulary of myth is a lexicon of symbols in which contingent historical particularities become metaphoric carriers of eternal or sacred principles, embodiments of moral and natural laws. Myth organizes its metaphors synthetically and in narrative form, whereas science organizes metaphors analytically and ideology arranges them into an argument. When those laws themselves are known primarily through their embodiment in a store of remembered tales, we are in the presence of a mythology: a body of narrative material in which ideology, history, and human experience have been rendered as a sacred archetype.[16]

Myth does not argue its ideology, it exemplifies it. It projects models of good or heroic behavior that reinforce the values of ideology, and affirm as good the distribution of authority and power that ideology rationalizes. Myth uses the past as an "idealized example," in which "a heroic achievement in the past is linked to another in the future of which the reader is the potential hero." The invocation of Indian war precedents as a model for the Vietnam war was a mythological way of answering the question, *Why are we in Vietnam?* The answer implicit in the myth is, "We are there because our ancestors were heroes who fought the Indians." There is no logic to the connection, only the powerful force of tradition and habits of feeling and thought. It is this aspect of myth that Roland Barthes has in mind when he speaks of the "buttonholing" character of mythic discourse, its implicit demand that we make of the story a guide to perception and behavior, and its insistence that we acknowledge and affirm the social and political doctrines its terms imply.

Although it must address contradictions, a culture's mythology and ideology must be mutually compatible to a considerable degree, if the culture is to have any coherence. It often seems to be the case that in small relatively simple, preliterate societies myth and ideology are scarcely distinguishable aspects of a relatively homogeneous system of values and behaviors – legends reinforce rituals, rituals reinforce political authority, theology and politics appear to work in accordance with the scheme of cosmic organization. However, the continual agitation and disruption of social forms and systems of value appears to be the characteristic fate of modern and modernizing societies; and in these circumstances, the formal distinction between myth and ideology may become the basis of crucial distinctions. In such societies, the competition of different groups for power in a continually changing society forces the clear articulation of party or class ideology, in a form distinct from the half-spoken understandings of traditional society (as well as from the ideologies of competing groups). Myth, as the repository of reflexive symbolism and traditional emblems of value, may become the basis of a cultural resistance to the imperatives of ideology, exercising a "drag" on the swift alterations of course that political competition requires. There may be parties of ideology and parties of mythology – a variation on the parties of "hope" and "memory" that have been seen as the dialectical opposites of American literary and political culture. Or there may be attempts by opposing ideologies to claim for themselves the sanctifying connection to the traditions of myth by cloaking themselves in mythic symbolism.

The discursive–ideological and the fictive–mythological genres may become preferred vehicles of rather different social and political tendencies. For example, one of the central symbols of American political rhetoric and historiography in the nineteenth century was the identification of American ideology with the concepts of "agrarianism" and the figure of the "American farmer." However, the literary fiction of the same period – both popular and serious – accords no symbolic priority or heroic afflatus to the farmer. The representative male heroes of imaginative fiction in this period are wilderness hunters, virile young gentlemen, unjustly disinherited scions of wealthy houses: men of high status, earned or inherited, and men of adventure and exploit – not yeomen farmers laboriously cultivating the soil. The division suggests that although the agrarian was a real-life political factor whose vanity and self-interest required praise and cultivation, the life of the American farmer was not the pattern by which American writers and readers tended to cut their dreams. The personality types celebrated in fiction are close in spirit to those of the entrepreneurial go-getter and the captain of industry; and it is worth noting that, in this instance, the literary expression is more prophetic of future developments than are the agrarian panegyrics of Jefferson and his intellectual heirs.[17]

But myth also registers within itself the contradictions of the ideology that gives it direction. All ideological statements are, at bottom, representations about the nature, function, and distribution of political power; and the mythological symbolism projected from any ideological mind-set reproduces the definition of power in figurative language. Mythic fables identify heroes and classes of heroes; and in using myth to interpret reality, we transfer this identification to the class hierarchy that confronts us. We did not do this consistently or imitatively: Because modern society is ideologically and politically diverse, it was inevitable that opposing groups would identify (and identify with) different classes of heroes. Radicals have at times identified with the Indians of the myth or with classes of whites that a genteel audience might regard as marginal or antipathetic. Moreover, the response of a given audience to myth tends to reflect that group's ambivalence toward its own ideology: The genteel reader may, in his dismay with modern society, identify simultaneously with the primitive Indian of an idealized past and with the elite agents of modernity; the proletarian reader may identify his own suppressed rage with that of the defeated Red Man in certain moods, while in others his aspiration to power and respectability will be paradoxically invested in the conquering white man.

It is for this reason that the most potent recurring hero-figures in our mythologies are men in whom contradictory identities find expression: the white man with knowledge of the Indians, the outlaw who makes himself an agent of justice or even of law. Likewise, the most important myths are those that embody the central problems or "concerns" that agitate the collective conscience. As such, they will tend to embody in a single coherent fable moral and ideological perspectives that are logically and politically contradictory. The hunter-heroes of Frontier Myth embody both the progressive and order-loving values attributed to bourgeois civilization and the longing for escape from civilization and its discontents that is allegorically projected onto the "savage." The later heroes of the Frontier Myth tend to reflect the manners, values, and capacities of a managerial and genteel elite; but they are represented as having plebeian origins or an affinity with the humbler classes of frontiersmen – and an ability to sympathize with the Noble Savage.[18] Through myth we imaginatively hoard away the cake we have eaten and voice our affection for a precapitalist Eden even while we reaffirm our affiliation with the values and priorities of bourgeois society.

As the carrier of "received wisdom," myth is challenged by changes in material conditions or social arrangements. The smooth flow of a narrative in which values appear to be both sacred and self-evident is interrupted by questions arising from substantive changes in the social world. When myths prove inadequate as keys to interpreting and controlling the changing world, systematic ideologies are developed to reestablish the lost coherence between facts and values. As Geertz says, "It is in country unfamiliar emotionally or topographically that one needs poems and road maps." Ideology is the product of "discontent" with a world defined by myth; but the end of ideology is to reintegrate the cultural system, to generate a new narrative or myth that will account for and give value to reality, and so to create the basis for a new cultural consensus. Because even a shattered mythology preserves elements of the cultural past, the new mythology will inevitably find connection with the old; indeed, the readiest way to renew the force of a weakened mythology is to link new ideology to the traditional imagery of existing myth.

The classic instance of this in American cultural history is the takeover and transformation of the Myth of the Frontier, and its dependent literary and historical genres, by ideological "Progressives" in the 1890s and early 1900s. Theodore Roosevelt's enthusiasm for the West and pioneer history, and his linkage of Progressivism with the "strenuous life" of the Frontier, was the central formulation of this revised version of the myth; and Roosevelt himself was the center of a web of associations (community) of more or less like-minded men. The group included such political titans as Henry Cabot Lodge, the conservationist Gifford Pinchot, the historian Frederick Jackson Turner, novelists Owen Wister and S. E. White, racist–anthropologists Madison Grant and Henry Fairfield Osborn, and other business, political, and cultural magnates. These men identified their particular concerns – economic progress, political reform, literary "realism" – with the "frontier" virtues of "red-bloodedness," macho individualism, and heroic dominance that Roosevelt located in the personalities of frontier heroes. It was this group, working at the "end of the frontier," that formulated the myth–ideological system associated with that phase of American history into its most systematic form, and used it as the basis of a general theory of American history and politics. In so doing, they transformed the ambivalently democratic and agrarian materials of the original myth into a set of doctrines and fables suited to the ideological needs of an industrial economy and a managerial policy. Thus discontent breaks down the "harmonious display of essences," degrading sacred myth into secular ideology; and ideology, in the hands of a class-seeking hegemony, reaches out to co-opt myth.[19]

Notes

1 Michael Herr, *Dispatches* (New York: Knopf, 1977), p.61; Richard Drinnon, *Facing West: The Metaphysics of Indian-hating and Empire-building* (Minneapolis: University of Minnesota Press, 1980), pp. 456–57; Robert Jay Lifton, *Home From the War: Vietnam Veterans, Neither Victims nor Executioners* (New York: Simon & Schuster, 1975), esp. chap. 8; Mark Baker, *Nam* (New York: Morrow, 1982), pp. 21–23.
2 Drinnon, *Facing West*, p. 369; Long quoted in Marcus G. Raskin and Bernard B. Fall, eds., *The Viet-Nam Reader* (New York: Random House, 1967), p. 386; Frances Fitzgerald, *Fire in the Lake: The Vietnamese and the Americans in Vietnam* (Boston: Little, Brown, 1972), pp. 491–92.
3 Bruce A. Kuklik, "Myth and Symbol in American Studies," *American Quarterly* 24, no. 4 (October 1972): 29–30; Alan Trachtenberg, "Myth, History, and Literature in *Virgin Land,*" *Prospects,* 3 (1977): 125–34; Eugene Wise, "Paradigm Dramas in American Studies: A Cultural and Institutional History of the Movement," *American Quarterly* 31, no. 3 (Bibliography Issue): 295–96, 319–25; James A. Henretta, "Social History as Lived and Written," *American History Review* 84, no. 5 (December 1979): 1293–1322;

Carolyn Porter, *Seeing and Being: The Plight of the Participant Observer in Emerson, James, Adams and Faulkner* (Middletown, Conn.: Wesleyan University Press, 1981), chaps. 1 and 2, for the discussion of "reification"; William J. Bouwsma, "The Renaissance and the Drama of Western History," *American History Review* 84, no. 1 (February 1979): 1–15 and esp. 9.

4   Louis O. Mink, "History and Fiction as Modes of Comprehension," *New Literary History* 1, no. 3 (Spring 1970): 541–48; Henretta, "Social History as Lived and Written," 1303–4, 1315, 1318–22; Bill Nichols, *Ideology and the Image: Social Representation in the Cinema and Other Media* (Bloomington: Indiana University Press, 1981), esp. pp. 1–3; Todd Gitlin, *The Whole World Is Watching: Mass Media in the Making and Unmaking of the New Left* (Berkeley: University of California Press, 1980), pp. 1–20.

5   Clifford Geertz, *The Interpretation of Cultures* (New York: Basic, 1973), pp. 214, 211; Nichols, *Ideology and the Image,* pp. 1–3; Michael Rogin, *Fathers and Children: Andrew Jackson and the Subjugation of the American Indian* (New York: Knopf, 1975) and *Subversive Genealogy: Politics and Art of Herman Melville* (New York: Knopf, 1983) are useful case studies in the interpretation of the languages of individual psychology, family mystique, myth and ideology.

6   Geertz, *Interpretation of Cultures,* pp. 5, 17.

7   A good, concise definition of "ideology" is David Brion Davis, *The Problem of Slavery in the Age of Revolution, 1770–1823* (Ithaca, N.Y.: Cornell University Press, 1975), p. 14. Quotation is from Henretta, "Social History as Lived and Written," pp. 1303–4. See also Marshall Sahlins, *Historical Metaphors and Mythical Realities: Structure in the Early History of the Sandwich Islands Kingdom* (Ann Arbor: University of Michigan Press, 1981), p. 7, "Symbols are symptoms, direct or mystified, of the true force of things"; Alan Dawley, "E. P. Thompson and the Peculiarities of the Americans," *Radical History Review* 19 (March 1979: 35–59; E. P. Thompson, *The Making of the English Working Class* (London: Gollancz, 1963), pp. 9–11; Raymond Williams, *Marxism and Literature* (New York: Oxford University Press 1977), esp. pp. 75–89; Terence Eagleton, *Criticism and Ideology* (London: NLB, 1976); Thomas E. Lewis, "Notes Towards a Theory of the Referent," *PMLA* 94, no. 3 (May 1979): 459–75; Louis Chevalier, *Laboring Classes and Dangerous Classes in Paris During the First Half of the Nineteenth Century,* trans. Frank Jellinek (Princeton, N.J.: Princeton University Press, 1973), pp. 1–6, 19, 31, 41–2.

8   Geertz, *Interpretation of Cultures,* p. 231; Victor W. Turner, "Process, System, and Symbol: A New Anthropological Synthesis," *Daedalus* 1 (Summer 1977): 63–4, 74–5; Sahlins, *Historical Metaphors,* p.72; Robert Nisbet, "Genealogy, Growth, and Other Metaphors," *New Literary History* 1, no. 3 (Spring 1970): 350–52.

9   Geertz, *Interpretation of Cultures,* p. 231; François Jacob, "Science and Myth," in *The Possible and the Actual* (Seattle: University of Washington Press, 1980); Turner, "Process, System, and Symbol," p. 75; Sahlins, *His-*

torical Metaphors, p. 68; Raymond Williams, *Keywords: A Vocabulary of Culture and Society* (New York: Oxford University Press, 1976), pp. 176–77; Theodore M. Brown, "Putting Paradigms into History," *Modern Philology* 3, no. 1 (Spring 1980): 34–63.

10   Claude Lévi-Strauss, *Myth and Meaning: Five Talks for Radio* (Toronto: University of Toronto Press, 1978), pp. 42–43, 53–54; Lévi-Strauss, "How Myths Die," in T. Claire Jacobson and Brooke Grundfest, *Structural Anthropology* (New York: Basic, 1963–76),2: 256, 268 Alan Jenkins, *The Social Theory of Claude Lévi-Strauss* (New York: St. Martin's, 1978), pp. 88–155. On the ahistorical character of myth, see David Noble, *Historians Against History: The Frontier Thesis and the National Covenant in American Historical Writing Since 1830* (Minneapolis: University of Minnesota Press, 1965), chap. 1; Porter, *Seeing and Being,* chap. 1; Henry Nash Smith, *Virgin Land: The American West as Symbol and Myth* (Cambridge, Mass.: Harvard University Press, 1950; 1975).

11   Roland Barthes, "Mythology Today," in Annette Lavers, *Mythologies* (New York: Hill & Wang, 1972), p. 110; Sahlins, *Historical Metaphors,* pp. 68, 72.

12   Barthes, "Mythology Today," pp. 129, 142; Henry Glassie, "Meaningful Things and Appropriate Myths: The Artifact's Place in American Studies," *Prospects* 3 (1977); 1–51.

13   Northrop Frye, *The Critical Path: An Essay on the Social Context of Literary Criticism* (Bloomington: Indiana University Press, 1971), pp. 35–36, 107. See also Victor W. Turner, *The Ritual Process: Structure and Antistructure* (Hawthorn, N.Y.: Aldine, 1969), pp. 94–97, 102–11, and chap. 5; Turner, "Process, System, and Symbol," pp. 63–64, 72–73; Sahlins, *Historical Metaphors,* p. 68.

14   Frye, *Critical Path,* p.49; Frye, *The Secular Scripture: A Study of the Structure of Romance* (Cambridge, Mass.: Harvard University Press, 1976), chap. 6. See also Turner, *Ritual Process,* chap. 5; Sahlins, *Historical Metaphors,* chap.3. Thompson, *Making of the English Working Class,* studies the development of such myth–ideologies on the large level of the modern social class; Karen I. Blu, *The Lumbee Problem: The Making of an American Indian People* (Cambridge University Press, 1980), deals with a similar process on a smaller scale. Michael Grant, *Roman Myths* (New York: Scribner, 1972), pp. xiii–xiv, gives a classical instance of the seizure of a mythic tradition by a ruling "class" (or culture), its transformation into a cult, and its successful deployment as an instrument of hegemony.

15   Henretta, "Social History as Lived and Written," passim; Will Wright, *Six-Guns and Society: A Structural Study of the Western* (Berkeley: University of California Press, 1975), pp. 10–12, 124–29; Mink, "History and Fiction," pp. 541–48.

16   Frye, *Critical Path,* p. 115; Barthes, "Mythology Today."

17   Smith, *Virgin Land,* surveys the "agrarian" literary mythology in the period. The comparative cultural weight of "farmer" and "hunter" myths is

argued in Richard Slotkin, *Regeneration Through Violence: The Mythology of the American Frontier, 1600–1860* (Middletown, Conn.: Wesleyan University Press, 1973), and in the forthcoming *The Fatal Environment;* see also Richard Slotkin, "Nostalgia and Progress: Theodore Roosevelt's Myth of the Frontier," *American Quarterly* 33, no. 5 (Winter 1981): 608–38.

18   Slotkin, "Nostalgia and Progress," pp. 608–38.

19   Geertz, *Interpretation of Cultures*, pp. 218, 220; Sahlins, *Historical Metaphors,* pp. 64–66, chap. 4; Anthony F. C. Wallace, "Revitalization Movements," *American Anthropologist* 58 (April 1956): 265.

5

American Criticism
Left and Right

GERALD GRAFF

Much has been said lately about the omnipresence of power, politics, and ideology in the practice of literary criticism. It is pointed out that criticism is socially produced, that it arises out of political motivations and has political consequences, that no critical interpretation or theory is "innocent." One can hardly quarrel with tautologies, and I don't propose, in the following selective review of the ideological dimension of American literary criticism, to quarrel with the tautology that all criticism is necessarily political. Even tautologies can be forgotten or ignored, and this particular one has been reasserted at a time when many humanists had begun again to ignore the fact that criticism is a political activity. If I adopt a less than reverent tone toward the current reassertion of the politics of criticism, it is merely to underscore that its key proposition, that criticism has ideological motives and effects, is no more than a starting point, that *what* those ideological motives and effects *may be* is something we shouldn't assume we easily know. Motives and effects are disputable things, open as they are to the vicissitudes of inadequate evidence or interpretive bias. Even if the analyst of ideology were himself above suspicions of political bias, the fact would remain that the connections between ideas and their social uses are elusive.

History presents many instances in which the same idea or intellectual system has produced different or opposed social effects in different circumstances. In nineteenth-century Germany, for example, the same Hegelian ideas were invoked by Prussian nationalists and young Hegelian radicals. In American intellectual history, Puritan, transcendentalist, and pragmatic ideas have been similarly ambidextrous, lending themselves, at different times and places, to appropriation by Right, Left, and center. In the 1630s, New England Puritan dogmas of

91

grace, election, and covenant were subjected to both the authoritarian interpretation of John Winthrop and the antinomian interpretation of Anne Hutchinson. In 1750, Jonathan Mayhew's "Discourse Concerning Unlimited Submission" forged seemingly conservative Puritan doctrine into a justification of political revolt against the British. In the nineteenth century, the Emersonian philosophy of Self-Reliance functioned as a critique of conformist business values; yet the philosophy of Self-Reliance also served to deify the laissez-faire entrepreneur – a point not lost on Melville, who satirically exploited it in the Mark Winsome episode of *The Confidence-Man*. In the twentieth century, pragmatic philosophy has underwritten both Deweyite liberalism and America First jingoism. Most recently, the ideas of Nietzsche, long associated with the European Right, have reemerged on the French and Anglo-American critical scene in a poststructuralist textual Leftism. That these various ideas and systems could serve antagonistic social interests has to complicate, if it doesn't completely frustrate, attempts to specify their ideological implications.[1]

In fact, though we speak glibly about "ideological implications," just what kind of thing an ideological implication is remains a vexed question. If a distinction can be made between an idea and the way it is *used* or appropriated, then serious questions arise about the degree to which ideas control or predetermine their political uses. It seems desirable to strike a compromise somehow between the Hegelian idealist view that history conforms to the laws of reason and the more disenchanted modern view that historical consequences have no necessary relation to reason and logic. To suppose that history never obeys logic would release thought from any responsibility: We would not excuse a theory of white supremacy, for instance, on the ground that theory has no necessary consequence in the realm of action. On the other hand, the relation between a theory and its historical embodiments often does appear accidental. Ideas get used or appropriated for purposes very remote from anything seemingly implied or entailed by them, or from what their authors intended.

Such difficulties ensnare us when we try to assess the responsibility of thinkers for historical events. Apologists for John Dewey's theories, for example, long maintained that Dewey never intended the anti-intellectualism that came to be institutionalized in American schools in the name of progressive education. Yet it can also be argued – Christopher Lasch has in fact so argued in *The New Radicalism in America, 1889–1963* – that Dewey had plenty of opportunity to recognize what, given the context of American education, would likely happen to his ideas. Lasch concedes that Dewey didn't intend progressive education to be the vapidly permissive program it became, but he argues that the ambiguities of Dewey's exposition opened the way to that eventuality. Lasch puts the matter neatly:

> Dewey cannot be blamed for the perversion of his doctrines. It is curious, however, that although he repeatedly complained that his ideas were being distorted, the evident ease with which they were distorted did not cause him to reexamine the ideas themselves. He might at least have reflected that they contained ambiguities which made them peculiarly susceptible to misinterpretation, if misinterpretation was in fact what was taking place.[2]

This is an interesting observation because it suggests that one can be responsible for appropriations of one's thought that one abhors. But does it follow, then, that Nietzsche is liable for the criminal use made of his theories by the Third Reich? We know that Nietzsche detested German militarism. Yet his concept of the Will to Power theoretically justifies unlimited pursuit of power by cruelty and force, something Nietzsche might reasonably have been expected to foresee.

Perhaps we can say that thinkers (and creative artists) are responsible up to a point for the appropriations made of their doctrines, but that point is not theoretically definable. We can't make responsibility hinge on whatever we infer the writer to have *intended,* because writers, as we have just noted, can say things that conflict with their intentions, or can have conflicting intentions. Deconstructionist theorists have lately maintained that such conflicts exemplify a built-in aporia or "blindness" supposedly inherent in the nature of writing or thought. The aporias that deconstructionists have adduced are often interesting, but it seems a mystification to ascribe them to some inherent necessity of discourse.[3] It is preferable to attribute them less mysteriously to the fact that writing is situated amid contingencies that can be only imperfectly assessed. If the deconstructionists are right in maintaining that no writer can control the social uses of his or her text, the reason is probably that these possible uses are too diverse to be predicted. Furthermore, the contexts the writer addresses are always changing, so that what is written for one situation will be applied to more or less different ones. Nietzsche's Will to Power meant something more brutal in an age of extermination camps than it could have meant even in the age of nineteenth-century Prussian militarism, though how far that consideration absolves Nietzsche remains debatable.

It is often difficult to separate the *conceptual* problems attending the analysis of ideology (what political consequences follow logically from proposition A?) from the *historical* problems (what consequences followed in historical fact from proposition A?). The "conceptual" problems may themselves alter in character with changing historical circumstances. For example, when Marx and Engels formulated the classic theory of ideology in *The German Ideology,* the feudal and bourgeois societies they could study were arguably more coherent ideologically than the pluralistic mass culture of twentieth-century America. Later Marxists like Raymond Williams have thought there is something "mechanical" about Marx and Engels's "base"–"superstructure" relation between the means of production and culture.[4] Yet this base–superstructure model applies relatively well up to the later nineteenth century. It is chiefly for the late phases of capitalism that its conceptual inadequacy becomes obvious.

Indeed, one might argue that the base–superstructure correspondence is already implicitly called into question in Marx's analysis of the fetishism of commodities in volume 1 of *Capital.* There Marx characterizes the commodity as a volatile force. It tends to overturn preestablished correspondences and identities by leveling qualitative differences to the common measure of exchange value. Marx doesn't quite draw the conclusion himself, but if you follow what he says about the subversive effect of the commodity, you can infer that the commodity tends to dissolve fixed correspondences between the productive base and the cultural superstructure.

In this respect, Marx's account of the fetishism of commodities very much looks forward to twentieth-century consumerism, in which traditional alignments between class and ideology have been so radically overturned that would-be subversive ideas and imagery have themselves become fashionable commodities. Revolutionary ideas are picked up lightly, worn for a season, and disposed of when next season's models come in. The very profusion and confusion of ideas simultaneously competing for attention ensures that many, if not all, viewpoints will be tolerated while few have much impact. Only direct attacks on private control of production and on economic inequality appear resistant to easy "co-optation."

The muffling effect of this Intellectual Shopping Mall probably neutralizes social criticism and subversive art more effectively than either conservative argument or old-fashioned repression could do – something, to be sure, that doesn't discourage conservative politicians from engaging in both. To put the point more schematically, under the low-population, scarcity economy of the eighteenth and nineteenth centuries, ideologies of Protestant austerity were needed in order to stimulate production. Under the high-population, consumption economy of the twentieth century, Protestant austerity has to be actively rooted out and extirpated lest it serve as a drag on consumption. Early corporate apologists saw this change more clearly than current avant-gardists, who resist noticing anything that belies the myth of repressive establishment without which the avant-garde would have no reason for being. As one apologist, Edward Filene, put it in 1935, "In the old days, when capital was so sorely needed, it was right and proper that schoolchildren should be taught to save. In these days, when we are able to produce so much, and when the necessary saving can best be achieved by social co-operation, the masses should be educated to buy."[5]

A culture in which the masses have to be "educated to buy" must obviously be more "open" and "liberated" than one that educates them to save and produce. Such a culture must weaken older constraints on sensation, pleasure, and self-gratification; it must liberalize the range of permissible ideas and pluralize the self. To be sure, this pluralism has limits; certain positions, for example, attacks on private control of production, do not get a hearing. Nevertheless, such a society maintains stability not by enforcing a monolithic orthodoxy but by managing contradictory and incompatible impulses. Its ethos is no longer one of fixed, absolute principles but rather one of adapting to changing times – a rule of the market that conservatives oppose in theory but that all but the most backward accede to in practice. For it is only by systematic destruction of the past that the need for new markets and stepped-up consumption can be satisfied. This consumerist pluralism doesn't mean "the end of ideology" – pluralism itself being an ideology – but neither does it resemble the imperious ruling-class ideology posited by traditional radical theory.

Indeed, the "co-optation" of ostensibly radical culture has thrown the politics of the Left into confusion – a fact almost as important as the rise of the New Right in accounting for the late decline of radicalism. Whereas left-wing culture had earlier performed the heroic role of challenging the established ideology of production, it now finds itself unwillingly serving – indeed, panting to keep up with – the new ideology of consumption. With its glorification of the crossing of boundaries and the breaking of restraints, left-wing culture becomes merely one more exponent of what has been called (by Christopher Lasch) "the propaganda of commodities."[6] A further symptom results when those (like Lasch) who call attention to the self-defeating nature of radical strategy are written off as neoconservatives, which helps keep cultural strategy self-defeating.

In such circumstances, in which yesterday's apocalyptic imagery decorates todays T-shirt, boutique, or singles bar, trying to determine what counts as a truly "radical" or "conservative" idea becomes more difficult than before. Ideological criticism has been slow to adjust. The assertion that this or that aesthetic technique is "reactionary" or that this or that theory of art is "subversive" remains a familiar feature of critical writing. Although such assertions may refer only to the intra-mural spectrum of "traditional" versus "experimental" form, they often entail larger claims about the political effects of art. The usual assumption is that revolutions in artistic form disrupt orthodox modes of perception and thus carry an indirect but powerful challenge to the political status quo. This assumption becomes questionable when the political status quo is itself a commercial nihilism underwritten by the merchandising of "lifestyles."

If the concept of the Left has become problematic, that of the Right has been so for some time. Louis Hartz has pointed out in *The Liberal Tradition in America* that the United States differs from European coun-tries in lacking both a tradition of reaction and a genuine revolutionary tradition. "If the *ancien régime* is not present to begin with . . . it does not return in a blaze of glory."[7] Terms such as "aristocratic" and "pa-trician" are necessarily metaphors when applied to America. Still, mak-ing due allowances, we *can* speak of a quasi-aristocratic or patrician elite in America up to about World War I, when we still find men of letters who expressly conceive literature and criticism as reinforcements of existing class privilege. As William Charvat points out in *The Origins of American Critical Thought, 1810–1835,* through the changes of this pe-riod "one dominant and shaping critical principle persists: that literature is primarily social, and that the artist must adjust his work to the desires of established society."[8] The critics whom Charvat examines are open and unabashed in their allegiance to a hierarchical social ethic and their suspicion of egalitarian democracy. By contrast, it is difficult to think of a single influential critic after about 1915 who would assent to the proposition that "the artist must adjust his work to the desires of estab-lished society."

We can, to be sure, delineate a twentieth-century literary Right. It would include the New Humanism, Eliot's classical royalism, and the Southern Agrarian wing of the New Criticism. But these writers are "reactionary," not "conservative." They are almost as extreme in their opposition to the status quo as are their counterparts on the Left. Inso-far as they defend "established society," it is an established society that no longer exists. In this respect they could not be more remote from the so-called New Right of today's *National Review* and Moral Major-ity, who are unqualified apologists for the corporations. How different from such apologetics was the attitude of the self-styled reactionary

Allen Tate, for instance, who in 1939 noted "the iniquity of finance-capitalism" and proclaimed that "our social-economic system, with its decadent religion, depraved morals, and disorganized economics, is thoroughly rotten."[9] To be sure, the neoconservatism of such journals as *Commentary* and *The New Criterion* is markedly more benign toward capitalism than was Tate (or the editor of the original *Criterion*). Yet in their cultural judgments, if not their political ones, these neoconservatives tend to be more anti-Left than pro-American or procapitalist. And when they *are* pro-American and procapitalist, they ignore the inconvenient fact – which Tate had seen clearly – that capitalism has reduced literary and other high cultural traditionalisms to quaint survivals.[10]

In short, these complications disrupt attempts to map the history of American criticism in terms of such familiar oppositions as progressive versus retrograde, radical versus conservative, Left versus Right. Such oppositions were volatile in American culture to begin with, but it made sense to think in terms of them so long as the institutions of criticism defended the existing social order and saw literature as a means of socializing the citizenry. After World War I, this view of literature's socializing function ceased to be respectable within literary culture, if not outside. Although literature continued to be spoken of vaguely as an acculturating agent, the primary emphasis of modern literature and criticism, as Lionel Trilling points out, was "adversarial," seeking either to challenge the social order or to stand outside it entirely.

Ceasing to speak for an existing establishment, the literary Right came to share many of the countercultural characteristics of the Left. And after the exhaustion of the Popular Front at the end of the thirties, the Right and the Left of literary culture have been indistinguishable in many of their ideas, attitudes, and tastes. With the decay first of the genteel tradition and later of the thirties literary Left, culturally oriented criticism has perforce gravitated toward the various modes of the "alienated" avant-garde. In these modes, traditional Left- and Right-wing cultural ideas intermingle and become difficult to tell apart – just as in politics between the two wars the extreme Right and extreme Left become difficult to tell apart. The very integrity of "literary culture" as a distinct entity is tied to a commonly shared style of "apolitical politics" (in Irving Howe's strikingly apt phrase)[11] in which the forces of creativity, imagination and sensibility are set over against all organized systems, including the organized Left and Right. This apolitical politics of alienation, which in its highest expression defines for many critics the classic American literary tradition, shades imperceptibly into the therapeutic–escapist ideology of consumer society.

Let us begin our survey in the Revolutionary period, when aspirations for a national literary culture first became visible and literary opinion began to polarize in ideologically recognizable ways: on one side, liberal demands for cultural and political independence, on the other, loyalty to British and European supremacy. Guided by such works as Benjamin Spencer's *The Quest for Nationality* and Howard Mumford Jones's *The Theory of American Literature*, [12] we can trace this conflict through the nineteenth century, with the liberal impulse becoming embodied in the Transcendentalists and, after the Civil War, the proponents of naturalism and realism, while the conservative view is expounded by Federalists, patrician men of letters, and Anglophile professors. The conservative influence predominated, assisted by demographic conditions that permitted New England and Boston to think of themselves as representative of the national culture long after westward expansion. To quote Charvat once more, the critic in the early years of the century was frankly dedicated to the preservation of social order. He thought of himself, in Charvat's words, "as the watchdog of society," while the typical American journal in which he published his work – modeled on the great anti-Jacobin Scottish reviews – "felt it a duty to repress any writer who tended to disrupt the political, economic, and moral status quo. Its attitude was paternal: it thought of the public as a child who had to be educated along the proper lines and shielded from erroneous ideas."[13] Martin Green's *The Problem of Boston* shows this patrician criticism maintaining its dominance after the Civil War, though Green's book also suggests how fragile the dominance was and why it was vulnerable to the challenge of egalitarian ideas of literature and culture at the close of the century.[14]

As Howard Mumford Jones observes, "there is some reason to interpret the whole Anglophile tradition in the schools and colleges as a measure for cultural control on the part of 'Old Americans' over lesser breeds without the law." Jones cites Barrett Wendell's books of the first decade of the twentieth century, including *The Privileged Classes* (1908), as explicit statements of what was implicit in Wendell's *Literary History of America* (1900), "namely, his belief that a governing class of 'Old Americans,' the wise and good, should rule."[15] Jones is surely right about figures like Wendell, yet it is important to recognize that the ideas of such men were sometimes used for purposes they didn't intend.

An example is the American vogue of Scottish philosophers and rhetoricians such as Kames, Blair, and Alison, who were the chief models for critics in the 1820s and 1830s. Charvat observes that these Scottish thinkers and their American followers wished to restrict the standard of taste to "people of education, reflection, and experience." They agreed with Kames that "those who depend for food on bodily labor are totally devoid of taste." On the other hand, these critics believed that in theory "the standard of reason and taste is universal," a view with potentially democratic implications.[16] Universalism is often regarded today as a reactionary ideology: We feel that ruling classes invoke the supposed commonality of "human nature" in order to obscure the facts of domination and class-conflict. Such categorical distrust of universalism causes us to forget that appeals to a common human nature played a progressive role in undermining nineteenth-century class particularism. In propounding universalism, patrician men of letters popularized the ideas by which their own principles would be overthrown.

By the final decades of the century, a liberal intelligentsia, backed by the artistic accomplishments of realists, naturalists, and regionalists, and animated by the general spirit of an "Age of Reform," was eroding the assurance of genteel professors and men of letters. Henry May argues in *The End of American Innocence* that the decisive break with genteel culture occurred not after World War I but at least a decade before.[17] Henry Adams's idealizations of medieval unity and Charles Eliot Norton's sponsorship of a cult of Dante among Harvard undergraduates had been but two symptoms of an upper class that no longer felt in control.[18] This upper-class disaffection can be traced back to the first part of the century: Michael Rogin has found important elements of it in Melville's development.[19] But whereas previously such disaffection had coexisted with a more confident outlook, it increasingly became the dominant mood. After 1915, the patrician attitude is almost exclusively one of discontent and "alienation," and as such begins to assume interesting resemblances to the outlook of the literary Left.

Van Wyck Brooks's influential early writings, culminating in *The Wine of the Puritans* (1908) and *America's Coming-of-Age* (1915), helped shape the contours of radical opinion.[20] Brooks was impatient with the slow maturation of the national literature, but he was even more impatient with Anglophile professors who refused to take the national literature seriously. One of Brooks's chief targets was his former Harvard professor Wendell, whose aforementioned *Literary History of America* typified this academic condescension.[21] Like Randolph Bourne, his contemporary and friend, Brooks called himself a socialist and identified the prospects of an indigenous American culture with those of radical politics. Yet the union of cultural and political radicalism in critics such as Brooks and Bourne was never anything but tenuous, and it failed to survive World War I.

Writing of Greenwich Village in his "literary odyssey of the 1920's," *Exile's Return,* Malcolm Cowley commented on the fate of "two types

of revolt," cultural "bohemianism" and political "radicalism." Before
America's entry into the war, Cowley states, "the two currents were
hard to distinguish. Bohemians read Marx and all the radicals had a
touch of the bohemian: it seemed that both types were fighting in the
same cause. Socialism, free love, anarchism, syndicalism, free verse – all
these creeds were lumped together by the public and all were physically
dangerous to practice." The war changed all this, Cowley says; it

> separated the two currents. People were suddenly forced to
> decide what kind of rebels they were: if they were merely
> rebels against puritanism they could continue to exist safely in
> Mr. Wilson's world. The political rebels had no place in it. . . .
> Whatever course they followed, almost all the radicals of 1917
> were defeated by events. The bohemian tendency triumphed in
> the Village, and talk about revolution gave way to talk about
> psychoanalysis.[22]

History repeats itself as farce: a half-century later, talk about revolution
would give way to talk about expanding one's consciousness and getting one's head together. Cowley is criticizing the bohemians of the
twenties from the Marxist viewpoint of the thirties – *Exile's Return* was
first published in 1934. The 1951 revised edition, the one known to
most readers today, has had the explicit Marxism quietly deleted, so
one has the curious case of a narrative that remains arresting even after
its point has been surgically removed.

   Prominent in the conservative (more accurately, reactionary) opposition during the bohemian and radical decades was the New Humanism
of Irving Babbitt, Paul Elmer More, and Stuart P. Sherman, which first
achieved notoriety before the War and remained influential through the
thirties. The thirties also saw the emergence of Southern Agrarianism:
the Agrarian manifesto *I'll Take My Stand* and John Crowe Ransom's
God Without Thunder both appeared in 1930.[23] The New Humanists and
Agrarians were united in defending tradition against liberal individualism and industrialism, and both groups placed literature in a timeless
realm, above the political and historical concerns that preoccupied the
literary Left. Yet the literary programs of the two groups were at odds
in fundamental ways. Whereas the Agrarians embraced literary modernism as an antidote to romantic anarchy, the New Humanists saw
literary modernism as the culminating expression of that anarchy.
Whereas the Humanists invoked the "inner check" as the controlling
faculty of art, the Agrarians scorned such old-fashioned moralism, replacing it with a Coleridgean organic theory of art and an elaborate
method of explication designed to deal with complex artistic organ-

isms. As a political movement, Agrarianism expired before thirties Leftism, but Agrarian literary–critical and cultural ideas entered into the formation of the New Criticism. When literary fellow-traveling finally exhausted itself at the end of the thirties, it was the New Critical rather than the New Humanist alternative that won out.

What killed the literary Leftism of the thirties? To a large degree it was swept away in the reaction against the Moscow Trials, the Nazi– Soviet Pact, the Communist Party's repression of artistic and intellectual freedom, and the general Soviet regimentation of culture. But even without the help of Stalinism, literary Leftism would probably have expired from within. One need only look at Granville Hicks's *The Great Tradition* (1933), a doctrinaire history of American literature after the Civil War,[24] or at Cowley's conclusion to the 1934 edition of *Exile's Return* calling writers to arms in the proletarian cause (deleted without mention from the 1951 revised edition), or the copious documentation of radical polemic in Daniel Aaron's *Writers on the Left*,[25] to see why, when the recoil against Leftist criticism finally came, it was so devastating and final, and why the ostensibly apolitical theories of the New Criticism looked like just the antidote that was needed.

R. P. Blackmur's criticisms of Hicks's *The Great Tradition* in his 1935 essay, "A Critic's Job of Work," illustrate the way enlightened opinion was tending. Blackmur pointed up failings of the proletarian school that, in the succeeding decades, would be adduced by others to discourage *all* forms of political criticism. Blackmur begins with the obvious objection to Hicks's "tendentiousness," his "initial hortatory assumption that American literature ought to represent the class struggle from a Marxist viewpoint, and that it ought thus to be the spur and guide to political action." Blackmur then proceeds to the more subtle argument that Hicks's approach is "concerned with the separable content of literature, with what may be said without consideration of its specific setting and apparition in a form." For "the fine object of criticism," Blackmur argues, should be to "put us in direct possession of the principles whereby the works move without injuring or disintegrating the body of the works themselves." This "fine object" was to be secured by a procedure Blackmur found all too rarely exhibited in proletarian criticism, "sustained contact . . . with the works nominally in hand," in other words, what would soon be called "close reading."[26]

One can see in Blackmur's critique of Hicks how the New Criticism's preoccupation with the theoretical problem of form–content unity intersected with its evolving method of textual explication. And one can see how both these inclinations worked to discredit not only the Leftist school but the political approach to literature as such.

Among the things that made the New Critical complex of ideas attractive to the generation of critics that was coming to maturity just after World War II was the New Criticism's theoretical sophistication about problems of meaning and interpretation, its hostility to "message hunting" as an approach to literature. The principle of the inseparability of form and content tended to make the attribution of political "content" to a literary work seem a symptom either of the superficiality of the work or of the inexperience of its reader.

In theory, this conflict between the claims of political relevance and those of aesthetic integrity ought to have been reconcilable. After all, both aspects of literature can be acknowledged, even if it is difficult to say precisely how they coexist. Marxist critics as far back as Lenin, Engels, and Marx himself had deplored propagandistic conceptions of literature. For all his reductiveness, Hicks would have agreed in principle with Blackmur that literary form cannot be divorced from content. For their part, the New Critics in principle never denied that in some ultimate sense a literary work conveys a vision of the world beyond its aesthetic boundaries. In the heated climate of critical practice, however, critics tend to exaggerate in response to opposing exaggerations rather than look for areas of compromise. The Leftist critics *did* tend to reduce literature to extractable ideological premises, or at least they failed to show to their opponents' satisfaction how art and ideology could combine. And the New Critics *did* tend to see the principle of form–content unity as so restricting and qualifying the "vision" of a literary work that the vision virtually ceased to be classifiable in ideological terms.

New Critical doctrine drew a sharp line between literary works and those forms of discourse that make "statements" or are "about" something, and this Maginot Line of theoretically contrasting forms of discourse remains in force even among certain Leftist critics today. To be sure, if you look at what the New Critics *did* rather than what they said they were doing, you can see they ascribed their own kinds of statements to literature, however paradoxical and self-qualifying these statements may actually have been. Yet this recourse in practice to an idea of content did not stop them from holding in theory that literary discourse is uniquely impervious to any translatable ideological content. The thirties had so vulgarized the concept of "ideological content" that even a half-century later we don't feel comfortable without the quotation marks around the phrase. The question remains, though, whether criticism of any kind, much less political criticism, can do its work without employing some such concept.

I have mentioned that it was a new generation of critics that came to maturity after World War II. This generation marked a great change in the vocation of criticism at this time, a change resulting from the drying up of the market for literary journalism and the expansion of the universities into mass institutions. Before the thirties, "criticism" had with a few exceptions been the monopoly of journalists. What professors practiced was not criticism but "scholarship," a distinction that has recently become blurred but that as late as the fifties still inspired heated passions. After the thirties, although there still remained critics who supported themselves as independent journalists (Edmund Wilson's and Philip Rahv's names come to mind), the important critical voices were increasingly those of university professors, and critics began to occupy major academic positions like Ransom's at Kenyon, and his student Cleanth Brooks's at LSU.

The postwar generation of critics was academic in a new way. It was university-trained, depended on university positions for livelihood, and wrote largely for an audience of students and other professors. These facts help explain why the New Criticism flourished in the forties while the New Humanism expired. The New Humanism was "rearguard" not just in its politics but also in its hostility to professionalism and specialization. It upheld an Arnoldian liberal ideal of culture to which the university still gave lip service but which in practice (as the New Humanists perceived) it had long ago abandoned in favor of professionalized "research" and advancement of the various specialized "fields" and subindustries into which the world of scholarship was and still is divided. The countercultural attack on professionalism in the sixties and since owes an unwitting debt to the reactionary New Humanists.

The consequences of the absorption of criticism by the university remain an imponderable aspect of any examination of the ideology of American criticism. But it seems a safe conclusion that one consequence in the immediate postwar period was a marked lessening of the critic's sense of the social urgency of his enterprise. How much of that lessening was an effect of academicization per se, how much was part of the conservative drift of the whole country after the thirties and the war, is hard to assess. Whatever the cause, this is the period in which T. S. Eliot became, in Delmore Schwartz's phrase, a "literary dictator,"[27] Tory Anglo-Catholicism gained many followers, and the *Partisan Review* published a famous symposium, "Our Country and Our Culture" (1952), in which some contributors rejoiced that the intellectual's celebrated alienation from the American mainstream had come to an end. Critics were discouraged from examining history and society, now defined as "extrinsic" factors: A critic might choose to attend to them, but they were something other than "literary." The dominant schools of criticism saw literature in transhistorical terms, the embodiment

either of timeless verbal symbols or of the eternal recurrences of archetypal myths. In either version, the analogy between literature and
the Christian Incarnation was not hard to detect, and it might be explicitly stated, as in W. K. Wimsatt's conclusion to his and Cleanth
Brooks's *Literary Criticism: A Short History* (1957).[28]

Philip Rahv, in several essays of the late forties and early fifties (later
collected in *The Myth and the Powerhouse* [1965]), voiced what is still
perhaps the most eloquent critique of the politics of symbol and myth.
"The obsession with symbolization," Rahv wrote in 1950, "is at bottom expressive of the reactionary idealism that now afflicts our literary
life and that passes itself off as a strict concern with aesthetic form."
"The cultism of myth," Rahv added, betrays "the fear of history," and

> is patently a revival of romantic longings and attitudes. . . .
> The literary sensibility, disquieted by the effects of the growing
> division of labor and the differentiation of consciousness, is of
> course especially responsive to the vision of the lost unities and
> simplicities of times past. Now myth, the appeal of which lies
> precisely in its archaism, promises above all to heal the wounds
> of time. . . . Myth is reassuring in its stability, whereas history
> is that powerhouse of change which destroys custom and tradi-
> tion in producing the future.[29]

Rahv's point is hard to dispute, and it has been reinforced in copious
detail by subsequent left-wing historical critiques – works such as Richard Ohmann's *English in America* (1976), John Fekete's *The Critical Twilight* (1977), Frank Lentricchia's *After the New Criticism* (1980), and
Carolyn Porter's *Seeing and Being* (1981).[30] These writers concur in
making conservative "American ahistoricism," in Porter's phrase, as
the mark of fifties criticism. Marcus Klein, in *Foreigners: the Making of
American Literature, 1910–1940* (1981), a class analysis of the writings of
this period, points out how securely rooted in the leading families was
the modernist generation of Henry Adams, Eliot, Pound, and Stevens,
which conceived literature as an embodiment of tradition above and
beyond the conflicts of politics.[31] The link between modernism, New
Criticism, and fifties political retreat has become a given of literary
history.

I don't dispute this "given," which reinforces my argument that after
World War I, American criticism tends toward an "apolitical politics"
of alienation that distrusts political organization per se. What I think has
not been recognized is how this apolitical politics overrides boundaries
between reactionaries and radicals. Let's go back for a moment to the
battles of the twenties between New Humanists and young radicals. In

The Rediscovery of American Literature, Richard Ruland correctly points
out that the polemical violence of these battles obscured the fact that the
antagonists "shared a common enemy . . . America's Philistine culture
and the sentimental fiction it engendered." Ruland adds that the "black
and white opposition of 'young' to 'old' generation" in the period
created a "breakdown in communication" that left these parties "little
chance of making common cause against the common enemy."[32] Ruland is writing about an earlier time, but his point could be made
equally about conflicts between cultural radicals and reactionaries down
to the present moment. As we move farther into the twentieth century,
continued recourse to the Left–Right antithesis as a way of making
sense of the cultural situation blinds opposing factions to common attitudes and interests.

The increasingly marginal differentiation between Left and Right literary positions shows up in the convergence of their cultural programs.
Take the diagnosis of "dissociation of sensibility" and loss of unity that
we've just seen attacked by Rahv. This diagnosis was immensely influential in shaping the concept of literature of the postwar decades. It under-
lay the revision of taste promoted by Eliot and the New Critics and their
theory of poetry as a forcing into unity of disjunctive experience. Eliot's
idea of the poet as a person uniquely capable of fathoming a relation
between the smell of cooking, falling in love, and reading Spinoza followed directly from his analysis of the dissociation of sensibility as the
characteristic modern malady. Insofar as that analysis lay the blame for
the dissociation on liberal democracy and called for a restoration of traditional authority to cure it, it is fairly called reactionary. Yet there is an
alternative version of the analysis in which it is capitalism, not liberal
democracy, that is to blame for the dissociation. As a trained Marxist,
Rahv might have been expected to recognize that it wasn't only his
myth- and symbol-hunting contemporaries or their nostalgic romantic
predecessors who were "disquieted by the effects of the growing division
of labor." Marx and subsequent Marxists had been disquieted by them
too, and had indeed borrowed much of their critique of the industrial
split between work and leisure from the Right. Rahv might also have
noted that many of the Tory critics he was attacking found capitalism
almost as distasteful as did he and other democratic socialists, however
much these groups differed over what was the proper alternative. One
can find many passages in these Tory critics' writings (like the anticapitalist remarks I earlier quoted from Allen Tate) that could easily be
mistaken for Marxism.[33]

In fact, long before Eliot expounded the theory of dissociation of
sensibility, American radicals had advanced something very similar in

their views of American culture. Van Wyck Brooks (following George Santayana) had analyzed American culture as divided between "high-brow" and "lowbrow" extremes with no apparent middle ground. But it was Eliot's contemporary, F. O. Matthiessen, who most strenuously adapted the cultural myths of the Right to the purposes of the Left. In *American Renaissance* (1941), Matthiessen ingeniously blended the organicist poetics of Coleridge and Eliot with a homemade brand of Christian democratic socialism. Matthiessen opportunely perceived that there need be no necessary connection between the aesthetics of organic form and the politics of agrarianism or royalism, that the organic model of literature was equally compatible with a native egalitarian social vision. Who is to say, after all, that the organization of a growing plant is more hierarchical than democratic? Matthiessen could quote copiously from Emerson, Thoreau, Whitman, and Horatio Greenough to prove that organism was an appropriate metaphor for egalitarianism.

American Renaissance was one of the first in what would be a series of attempts to characterize the "Americanness" of American literature in terms of some single overriding theme or conflict, a project that appears to have no counterpart in other national literatures. For Matthiessen, what united his five major writers "was their devotion to the possibilities of democracy."[34] For subsequent critics, the common denominator would be found in a collision between Adamic innocence and experience (R. W. B. Lewis, *The American Adam* [1955]) or between the pastoral ideal and the industrial machine (Leo Marx *The Machine in the Garden* [1964]); in a confrontation with the frontier (Edwin Fussell, *Frontier* [1965]); or in an evasion of heterosexual relations and a consequent escape into male companionship (Leslie Fiedler, *Love and Death in the American Novel* [1960]). Alternatively, the specifically "American" quality was said to lie in a formal tendency – in Gothic romance and melodrama as opposed to social realism (Richard Chase, *The American Novel and Its Tradition* [1957]); in symbolism (Charles Feidelson, *Symbolism in American Literature* [1953]); or in the unfulfilled quest for a "world elsewhere" of style independent of the world as understood in collective social categories (Richard Poirier, *A World Elsewhere* [1966]).[35]

In one way or another, all these theories tend to see American literature in terms of some form of escape from social categories. As early as 1938, Yvor Winters advanced a searingly pejorative version of these "escape" theories in *Maule's Curse*. (It's probably because it was pejorative that Winters's book has never received the same attention as those it anticipated.) Winters describes the American legacy as one of "obscurantism," a self-alienation from a rationally intelligible world that produced a proliferation of literary "symbols" without the explicable meaning that we expect from symbols. Taken as a neutral description, what Winters calls obscurantist seems not very different from what Feidelson and Chase praise as symbolism or romance.[36]

Heterogeneous though they seem at first, these theories of the American element in American literature actually make many of the same points in different vocabularies. (Roughly, Adamic innocence equals pastoral equals frontier equals evasion of heterosexual love; over against which are the machine, coextensive with genteel society, coextensive with women and domestic love, etc. The collision results in tragedy, romance, symbolism, etc.) The overlap is not surprising when one considers that the theorists of Americanness tend to draw their generalizations from the same circumscribed body of data: Brockden Brown, Cooper, Emerson, Thoreau, Hawthorne, Melville, Twain, Dickinson, Whitman, James, and Faulkner, possibly West, Frost, Fitzgerald, and Hemingway. Usually excluded are Howells, Dreiser, Norris, Cather, Robinson, and Richard Wright, except in the rare case when one of them can be made to exemplify the thesis.

As we would expect, the overtly social tradition in American writing tends either to be excluded from the initial data of these thesis books, or else reinterpreted in asocial categories. Matthiessen tried resolutely to embrace the conflicting traditions, writing major studies of Dreiser as well as of James and Eliot, but the social novel was displaced from the canon with the same abruptness with which it had displaced the School-room Poets a generation before. With the exception of Matthiessen, the major critics shared the assumption that American literature stands apart from its British counterpart by its rejection of socially determined concepts of man. American literature as a whole was read in terms of the "apolitical politics" of literary modernism. To be sure, many of our literary classics invite just such a reading, yet that doesn't explain the rapidity or abjectness of the social tradition's eclipse, its prestige sinking so low in the fifties that to confess an admiration for Dreiser's novels within hearing of the literature faculty was to make oneself an object of ridicule and incredulity. (I still occasionally witness this derision today.)[37] Indeed, Lionel Trilling's merciless irony in his 1940 essay "Reality in America" seemed to be directed not only at V. L. Parrington's clumsy defense of the Dreiserian view of reality, but at Dreiser's novels themselves, without distinction.[38]

In defense of such preferences, it can always be argued that *The Scarlet Letter* is simply a better novel than *An American Tragedy* or *A Hazard of New Fortunes,* one that has spoken more vividly to readers, and that it therefore deserves the primacy accorded to it and its type.

To which it can be replied that such a statement begs the question of what standards should apply.

On the other hand, even if we grant the romance the primacy it has been accorded in the canon, we might argue that it is a more "social" genre than has been acknowledged. We need not take at face value the claims of Tocqueville, Cooper, Hawthorne, and James that American writers have had to work in a social vacuum. Michael Rogin seems right in arguing that "the critics most sensitive to the symbolic power of American fiction still separate it too far from American historical experience." It is against this tendency that Rogin, in *Subversive Genealogy: Politics and Art in Herman Melville,* relates Melville's work to "the distinctive American social facts of mobility, continental expansion, and racial conflict."[39] Rogin is a historian, but his work reflects a recent trend in literary scholarship to reverse the asocial readings of American romance that proliferated in the fifties.

With the tendency to see American literature as an escape from social experience into autonomous symbols, American criticism had seemingly come full circle from the nineteenth-century conservatives described by William Charvat for whom literature was "primarily social," and from the proletarian critics of the thirties. Oddly, however, the critics of the fifties strongly hinted that the impulse to evade social definition that they saw at the heart of so many American classics was itself socially motivated. Evidently the prevailing theory of the autonomy of literature discouraged critics from taking seriously the political significance they themselves ascribed to literary works.

Poirier, for instance, describes the American literary quest for a world elsewhere as "a way of preserving imaginatively those dreams about the continent that were systematically betrayed by the possession of it for economic and political advancement."[40] Though Poirier views American literature as a response to a massive political betrayal, reference to the betrayal is curiously absent from his account of the literature itself. Or is this betrayal only absent from the critic's interpretation, guided in this case by the theory that literary language is by definition not "about" material states of affairs? Poirier, to be sure, argues that American writers *failed* to purify their works of history and politics; they did not attain the "world elsewhere" they presumably sought. Material circumstances do thus intrude into the literature, in Poirier's account, but only as an extrinsic violation of an ideal purity. As Warner Berthoff pointed out in a review, "America" figures in Poirier's book "as an almost completely unanalyzed historical integer."[41]

It is harder to make the same criticism of Henry Nash Smith's *Virgin Land: The American West as Symbol and Myth.* Yet Smith, too, conjoined literature with politics in practice without quite acknowledging that he was doing so. Smith declared in the preface to the original 1950 edition of *Virgin Land* that though the symbols and myths of the West had exerted "a decided influence on practical affairs," he did not "mean to raise the question of whether such products of the imagination accurately reflect empirical fact. They exist on a different plane."[42] The disclaimer accorded with the theories of New Criticism and myth criticism, but it was contradicted by the book itself, which spends a good deal of time showing how the myths of Garden, Yeoman, and Agrarian Utopia repeatedly conflicted with the "empirical fact" of economic expansion. For example, Smith's chapter on "The Failure of the Agrarian Utopia" shows how the putatively democratic myth of the Garden was no sooner objectified in the Homestead Act than it was falsified by land speculation and railroad monopoly.

After reviewers (notably Barry Marks in his 1953 essay) pointed out the contradiction, Smith revised his principles, conceding in the 1970 preface that symbols and myths have to be seen in relation to "some process of verification" and acknowledging that *Virgin Land* had indeed been concerned with such a process.[43] It is tempting to conclude it was the literary theories of the forties that had led Smith to describe his own project inaccurately, and the shift in these theories, which had occurred by 1970, that led him to recognize the fact and revise his statement. Since the mid-sixties, in any case, the assumption that art and politics exist on a separate plane has been so widely challenged that, although it has not disappeared, it is now on the defensive and can no longer be taken for granted.

In the last decade, virtually every phase of American literature has been reinterpreted in political terms. Puritan studies, to take an example, have undergone a second revolution in which Perry Miller's pioneering intellectual and theological interpretations have been challenged – without, I think, having been superseded – by examinations of Puritan ideas as social productions and ideological rationalizations. Sacvan Bercovitch, in *The Puritan Origins of the American Self* (1975) and *The American Jeremiad* (1978), shows intricate connections between early Puritan ideas of corporate saintly destiny and subsequent American nationalism and exceptionalism. Larzer Ziff (*Puritanism in America* [1973]) connects such things as the seventeenth-century antinomian controversy with the transition from a feudal to a market economy.[44]

Comparable treatments of literature and ideas as social products could be listed for virtually every period and field – and these treatments have begun to call the concept of "period" and "field" themselves into question along with the canon of "classic" American works.[45] The new prominence of literary and cultural theory is implicitly political, in that it directs attention at founding assumptions and exposes their historically constructed rather than natural character. With this new theorization and politicization of criticism, a complex set of controversies has arisen in which Marxists (both old and new), feminists, and poststructuralists of several distinct varieties (some of them Marxist or feminist) oppose liberal and conservative "humanists" while debating among themselves the proper ways of specifying the political dimensions of culture.

It is difficult, in a short space, to reduce these new and complex trends to any simple pattern, but broadly, I think, certain general tendencies are evident. On the one hand, one can see an emerging agreement, across a variety of critical schools, that American literary criticism must attend to the influence of ideology and power not simply as aspects of literature and criticism but as forces that constitute them. On the other hand, there is a distinct lack of agreement over how this political analysis should proceed and particularly over the ways in which the political effects of literature and criticism can be calculated. Although it has become a commonplace that literary criticism itself is a political act and is inseparable from power, this view has arisen at a moment when criticism has become peculiarly closed off within the university, a fact that complicates further the problem of how the political effects of criticism should be measured.

The swift and spectacular emergence of feminist criticism in the late seventies has provoked a number of suggestive reinterpretations of American literature. It has also provoked vigorous debates over criteria of value as well as method. For example, in treating "the feminization of American culture" in the nineteenth century as an expression of a disabling sentimentalism, Ann Douglas opened herself to the charge of having merely reinforced an attitude of male condescension toward women. Jane P. Tompkins, arguing for a more positive view of sentimentalism as a politically subversive force, states that Douglas's view of most American literature written by women between 1820 and 1870 "is the one that the male-dominated scholarly tradition has always expressed – contempt."[46] It might have been fairer to say that Douglas's "contempt" was directed not at women but at debased conceptions of women's role that most feminists including Tompkins would object to.

In any case, whether nineteenth-century sentimentalism operated as a conservative or oppositional force, or perhaps as both at once in some dialectical fashion, is a complex question, and it is not clear that any one kind of answer to it is harmful or helpful to the interests of women. The censuring of Douglas for her critique of sentimental female stereotypes reflects the looseness with which accusatory ideological terminology is now used, as if criticism had become an arena where any position can be used against one by a critic purporting to be more "radical." This situation is in no way peculiar to feminist criticism, however. Indeed, one hears echoes in it of the quarrels of the twenties and thirties over proletarian culture, with "women" now substituted for *Proletkult* and "men" for decadent bourgeois.

Judith Fetterley's *The Resisting Reader* presents, as its subtitle proclaims, a "Feminist Approach to American Fiction." Asserting that American literature, as it has been conceived by the critical tradition, "is male," and that this literature "insists on its universality at the same time that it defines that universality in specifically male terms,"[47] Fetterley effectively uses the statements of male critics to hang them with. Thus she quotes Leslie Fiedler's remark that "the figure of Rip Van Winkle presides over the birth of the American imagination; and it is fitting that our first successful homegrown legend should memorialize, however playfully, the flight of the dreamer from the shrew."[48] Fetterley rightly argues that such a statement complacently assumes that "our" literature is naturally and exclusively what is defined from a male point of view.

Yet Fetterley is unfair to Fiedler in much the same way that Tompkins is unfair to Douglas: Fiedler was one of the first critics at least to see gender as an issue in American literature and he treated it as a historical rather than a universal problem. Like Douglas, Fiedler describes patterns without necessarily endorsing them – he is if anything critical of escapist "male bonding" – and if the pattern described is not flattering to women, that is hardly Fiedler's fault, unless one believes it is the obligation of feminists to write history that mythicizes women in flattering ways. Fetterley can be as peremptory with American writers as with their critics; her "resisting reader" does not always stop to read before resisting.[49] Many feminists have recoiled from such one-sidedness, however, and adopted more nuanced views that do not lend themselves to this sort of sweeping indictment.[50]

Poststructuralist criticism proceeds from the premise that all texts are rhetorical performances and as such must necessarily suppress some of the presuppositions and conditions that enable their operations and "valorizations." The implication is that texts are legitimated finally by arbitrary forms of power rather than by anything in the "reality" they purport to describe or the "self" they purport to express. Clearly, poststructuralism could hardly be farther from the literary Leftism of the thirties, with its naïvely realist view of literature, its Cartesian epistemology, and its reduction of cultural superstructures to an economic base – all of which constitute reactionary thinking from today's advanced standpoint. Thus an essentially Old Left·critic like Fetterley, radical though she may appear according to an earlier calculus, is being thoroughly retrograde from a poststructuralist reckoning when she declares that emasculation of women by men has been "the cultural reality."[51] To claim to designate "the cultural reality" as if it were "out there" prior to linguistic formulation is a logophallocentric mystification, regardless of what may have been intended by the claim. A feminist critic recently described to me her experience at a conference, where her work was denounced on the ground that no true feminist could believe in textual closure.

We come back again to tensions between "political" and "cultural" radicalisms that run throughout the modern period but have seemingly been exacerbated by the recent tendency of Left thinking to regard all vestiges of the Enlightenment as unredeemably reactionary. Followed to its extreme conclusions, this trend leads to a radicalism that views the traditional political Left as an avatar of the Right – a transposition all the easier to understand in Europe, where radicalism defines itself against not only bourgeois culture but the Communist Party. For the new radicalism, the project of cultural politics is to undermine all "bourgeois" perceptual, artistic, and philosophical categories, which allegedly prop up authoritarianism and patriarchy. It follows that formalist art and self-reflexive writing are more fundamentally subversive than the critical realisms promoted by Marx, Trotsky, and Lukács. The most oppositional criticism is that which demystifies mimetic views of art, the concept of the author and the unitary ego, the assumptions of genealogical history (which posit a logocentric endpoint and thus enforce authoritarian totalization), and the critical search for determinate or objective interpretations.

One outcome of this thinking is the view that the more "heterogeneous" and self-deconstructing literary language is (or can be made to appear), the more it will tend to overthrow "all accepted beliefs and significations."[52] By showing how texts "undo" the "logics of signification" on which they are founded, deconstructive readers of literature can claim to be destabilizing the conceptual hierarchies on which Western culture rests. There is a certain undeniable force in this argument when applied to such hierarchies as male–female, but it is not clear that all conceptual oppositions deconstruct themselves equally, or if they do, what this would mean. The very slipperiness of the notion of a conceptual hierarchy "undoing" itself, or "putting itself into question," whatever that may mean, makes it difficult to assess deconstructionist claims (or nonclaims). Nor is it clear that conceptual hierarchies must be coextensive with political and social ones, as deconstructionists sometimes assume.

It has taken little time for earlier theories of the Americanness of American literature to be rewritten in the deconstructionist register that many of them in fact anticipated, as Barbara Foley has noted.[53] It was only necessary to say that Americanness lay not in the romance of the symbol or the frontier but in reflexive awareness of the problematic of writing itself, which is to say, in the romance of self-deconstruction and of heterogeneity. Kenneth Dauber in *Diacritics* writes that

> American literature is a literature whose primary concern has always been its own nature. . . . To the poets and novelists of the classic period of American letters, the object of their work, inevitably, was its own process. Any "problem" they might address was incorporated, automatically, within their text as a "problematic," or principle inherent in the writing that embodied it. . . . Grounded in writing itself, American writing, in effect, *has* no ground, and until recently, with the turn of philosophy to an attack on the founding of (even philosophic) discourse on anything outside discourse we have had no language capable of dealing with it in any rigorous way.[54]

As Joseph Riddel puts the point, the " 'project' of 'American' poetry has always been anarchic rather than archeo-logical . . . a myth of origins that puts the myth of origins into question. It is a poetry of uprootedness, of radical origin, of the radical as origin – of the 'decentered image.' "[55]

There need not be anything *politically* subversive about decentered images, of course, but Riddel goes on to say that in deconstructing the nostalgia for lost origins American poetry questions "totalitarianism." Riddel praises Charles Olson for deconstructing a humanism whose "classic principle of totalization, of ideational centering, has displaced the coherence of the open or multicentered field . . ." and led to "ethnocentrism and thus authoritarianism." For Riddel, Olson's preoccupation with past cultures is a way of opening up "that 'play of creative accidents' which precedes all totalitarian cultures."[56] The implication is that by showing how language is always already decentered, heterogeneous, anarchic, deconstructive poetry (or poetry read as deconstructive) undermines the waning humanism that props up "authoritarianism."

Though not always explicitly stated, this attack on authoritarianism lies in the background of even the most "formalist" deconstructive criticism. The implication is that the humanist quest for interpretive "mastery" – a word that, in deconstructive writing, takes on the connotations of a Führer, or at least of whips and black stockings – constitutes a "policing" of language coextensive with social control. This analogical mode of argument neatly simplifies political critique, because it requires no analysis of social structures. The critic needs only to detect evidences in a textual field of closure, hierarchy, binaryism, appeal to origins, logocentrism, metaphysics of presence, and so on, in order to level charges of authoritarianism and totalitarianism.

There are already signs that poststructuralist politics is moving away from Derridean deconstruction in favor of the analysis of "discursive power" exemplified by the later work of Michel Foucault. The aim is not to reveal self-deconstructing oppositions in every text, but rather to locate the strategic operations performed by the text within a historically specific "discursive regime." Instead of hunting for predictable evidences of a metaphysics of presence that can be tarred with the brush of authoritarianism, the critic investigates the actual network of power and domination in which texts are implicated. All this is promising in principle and seems, at the moment, to have captured the enthusiasm of the most ambitious graduate students and younger faculty.[57]

Yet certain problems remain troublesome, particularly the ubiquitous conception of "power" (or "power/knowledge") promoted by Foucault's work. Rather like the asylum, the prison, the psychiatric clinic, and the confessional, as these institutions appear in Foucault's analysis, literature emerges as a form of disciplinary control and little else. The control is not "ideological" in the Marxist sense, since it is neither reducible to intersubjective interests nor open to criticism from some independent viewpoint. Though Foucault has identified himself with local, evidently anarchistic kinds of oppositon to disciplinary power, and has at times suggested that present forms of power can be detached from "hegemonic" uses and disposed to more just purposes,[58] he seems to disallow the possibility of any standpoint of reason or justice against which power can be measured. To think one can criticize power from the outside is merely to be co-opted by power. Thus the Left–Right opposition is finally overcome, but only to turn everything into the "Right," as it were, with disciplinary surveillance everywhere and complicitly universal. We have seen the enemy and he is us.

Viewed through Foucauldian lenses, literature ceases to be an innocent representation of reality and becomes a locus of discursive power that conceals its strategic operations. American realism comes to be seen, in Amy Kaplan's words, as "part of a broader cultural effort to fix and control a coherent representation of a reality that seems increasingly inaccessible, fragmented, and beyond control."[59] Though it seems an advance to treat realism as an "inscription" of social behavior rather than as a report from above on that behavior (I am not sure these views are incompatible), there remains the problem of how to characterize those moves and evaluate them politically. Although realistic representation may always be a politically constituted activity, it is not clear that its politics can always be reduced to the sinister modes of "normalization" that Foucaultians monotonously find everywhere.

Like the Derrideans, the Foucaultians are prone to facile analogies which conflate rhetorical and political terms, enabling them to write of the technique of narrative omniscience, say, as if it were a species of police surveillance or of the disciplinary "panopticism" of Jeremy Bentham's ideal prison. In a recent essay, Mark Seltzer sets out to counter "the depolitization of the text" of James's *The Princess of Casamassima.* This he does by reading the novel as "systematically the story of a criminal continuity between seeing and power" that James is trying to "disown."[60] James is not merely describing "policing" and "surveillance," he is in complicity with them! Of course, "seeing" has often been used for politically sinister purposes, but it is also obviously indispensible to anyone who opposed those purposes. One could use the same tactics with a similarly accusatory tone to "show" how Foucaultian investigations of specular imagery in fiction are just as deeply in complicity with disciplinary panopticism as any realistic novel is – perhaps some super-Foucaultian has already written the essay. One could perform such an exercise, but it is not clear what it would prove except that "power" loses its value as a term of analysis once it is stretched to cover everything.

Poststructuralist literary and cultural politics, whether of the Derridean or Foucaultian model (or the Lacanian, Althusserian, or Barthesian) represents a break with the liberal-democratic ideals that have informed most American literary radicalism up to recently. The current attack on academic humanism can certainly be justified by the complacency of established humanities departments in their sorry failure to provide a coherent education or to exemplify any cultural values at all. But poststructuralism does not indict the humanities for failing to live up to the ideals of liberal democracy; it indicts the humanities for living up to those ideals all too well. It is liberal-democratic idealism itself that is regarded as rotten.

How much of this hostility to liberalism should one believe? Now that radical cultural criticism has become a kind of "field" within the university, with its own self-promoting journals, conferences, and network of mutual backslappers just as in all the other fields, there is a consequent air of unreality about cultural–political talk. It is hard to know whether such rhetorical exaggeration and more-radical-than-thou posturing should be taken seriously. In their unofficial moments, one

gathers, most American poststructuralists still support liberal candidates
and policies, but their professional methodology requires a more flam-
boyant stance. Behind their insurrectionary rhetoric, one detects a
plaintive sign of the feeling that affects us all, as teachers and critics of
literature – the longing to recover a social function.

Notes

1 On the politics of poststructuralism and the politically "ambidextrous"
   aspect of ideas, see my "Textual Leftism," *Partisan Review* 49, no. 4 (1982):
   558–75, and "The Pseudopolitics of Interpretation," *Critical Inquiry* 9, no.
   3 (March 1983): 597–610 (reprinted in W. G. T. Mitchell, ed., *The Politics
   of Interpretation* [Chicago: University of Chicago Press, 1983], pp. 145–58).
2 Christopher Lasch, *The New Radicalism in America, 1889–1963: The Intellectual as a Social Type* (New York: Random House, 1965), p. 161.
3 Derrida states that "we are dispossessed of the longed-for presence in the
   gesture of language by which we attempt to seize it" (*Of Grammatology,*
   trans. Gayatri C. Spivak [Baltimore: Johns Hopkins University Press,
   1976], p. 141). Given Derrida's assumption that all language desires an
   originary "presence," and given the fact that language can never "seize"
   that presence, because language can never *be* whatever it expresses, any text
   can then be adduced as an instance of the self-undoing nature of language.
   Of course, if we argue that in at least some utterances there is no visible
   longing for presence from which to be dispossessed, then there will be
   nothing to be self-undone. Interpretations based on Derrida's premises will
   always "work" because their results are precontained in their axioms.
4 Raymond Williams, "Base and Superstructure," *Marxism and Literature*
   (New York: Oxford University Press, 1977), pp.75–82.
5 Edward A. Filene, *Speaking of Change: A Selection of Speeches and Articles*
   (Kingsport, Tenn.: Kingsport Press, 1939), p. 28. For an illuminating discussion of the attacks by Filene and other pioneers of consumerism on
   indigenous cultural traditions, see Stuart Ewen, *Captains of Consciousness:
   Advertising and the Social Roots of the Consumer Culture* (New York:
   McGraw-Hill, 1976). See also the discussion of "the propaganda of commodities" by Christopher Lasch in *Haven in a Heartless world: The Family
   Besieged* (New York: Basic, 1977), pp. 19–20, and *The Culture of Narcissism:
   American Life in an Age of Diminishing Expectations* (New York: Norton,
   1978), passim. Also the essays collected in Richard Wightman Fox and
   Jackson Lears, eds., *The Culture of Consumption: Critical Essays in American
   History, 1880–1980* (New York: Pantheon, 1983).
6 Lasch, *Haven in a Heartless World*, pp. 19–20.
7 Louis Hartz, *The Liberal Tradition in America* (New York: Harcourt Brace
   Jovanovich, 1955), pp. 6–32.
8 William Charvat, *The Origins of American Critical Thought, 1810–1835*
   (New York: Barnes, 1961; first published 1936), p. 58.

9   Allen Tate, unpublished letter to Malcolm Cowley, April 26, 1936. Mal-
    colm Cowley papers, Newberry Library, Chicago, Illinois.
10 I have been rebuked for a similar argument in *Literature Against Itself: Literary
    Ideas in Modern Society* (Chicago: University of Chicago Press, 1979), p. 8.
    Irvin Ehrenpreis quotes my statement that advanced capitalism has a "built-
    in need to destroy all vestiges of tradition" and comments as follows: "To
    anyone living a day's journey from Williamsburg, to anyone who knows the
    history of American art museums or of the launching of the New York
    Public Library, to anyone familiar with Harriet Monroe's method of launch-
    ing *Poetry Magazine,* this doctrine must sound like a comic defiance of real-
    ity" ("Lit in Trouble," *New York Review of Books,* 26, no. 11 [June 28, 1979]:
    41). It might have occurred to Ehrenpreis that if the past is available to him
    only through a good part of "a day's journey" to Williamsburg, there may
    be something to be said for my argument after all.
        On this point, if not on others, Ehrenpreis echoes the "neoconservative"
    position. And if the capitalist museumization of the past is judged against
    the outright destruction of the historical record by Communist dictator-
    ships, the neoconservatives are right to give capitalism high marks. The
    context of neoconservative argument is *always* a comparison with Com-
    munist dictatorships – reasonably enough, but not when it places capitalism
    above criticism.
11 Irving Howe, *Celebrations and Attacks: Thirty Years of Literary and Cultural
    Commentary* (New York: Horizon, 1979), p. 248.
12 Benjamin T. Spenser, *The Quest for Nationality: An American Campaign*
    (Syracuse, N.Y.: Syracuse University Press, 1957); Howard Mumford
    Jones, *The Theory of American Literature* (Ithaca, N.Y.: Cornell University
    Press, 1948).
13 Charvat, *Origins of American Critical Thought,* p. 37.
14 Martin Green, *The Problem of Boston: Some Readings in Cultural History*
    (New York: Norton, 1966).
15 Howard Mumford Jones, *Theory of American Literature,* p. 144.
16 Charvat, *Origins of American Critical Thought,* p. 42.
17 Henry May, *The End of American Innocence* (New York: Knopf, 1959).
18 See Martin Green's account of Norton and his Dante Circle at Harvard, in
    The Problem of Boston, pp. 122–41.
19 Michael Paul Rogin, *Subversive Genealogy: Politics and Art in Herman Mel-
    ville* (New York: Knopf, 1983).
20 Van Wyck Brooks, *The Wine of the Puritans: A Study of Present-Day Amer-
    ica* (London: Sisley's Ltd., 1908); *America's Coming-of-Age* (New York:
    Heubsch, 1915).
21 See Brooks's reminiscences of Wendell in *An Autobiography* (New York:
    Dutton, 1965), pp. 108–10.
22 Malcolm Cowley, *Exile's Return: A Literary Odyssey of the 1920's,* rev. ed.
    (New York: Viking, 1951), pp. 66–67.
23 Twelve Southerners, *I'll Take My Stand: The South and the Agrarian Tradi-*

tion (New York: Harper Torchbook, 1962). John Crowe Ransom, *God Without Thunder* (New York: Harcourt Brace, 1930).

24   Granville Hicks, *The Great Tradition: An Interpretation of American Literature since the Civil War* (Chicago: Quadrangle, 1969).

25   Daniel Aaron, *Writers on the Left* (New York: Avon, 1965).

26   R. P. Blackmur, *Language as Gesture: Essays in Poetry* (New York: Columbia University Press, 1980), pp. 384–85.

27   Delmore Schwartz, "The Literary Dictatorship of T. S. Eliot," in *Selected Essays,* ed. Donald A. Dike and David H. Zucker (Chicago: University of Chicago Press, 1970), pp. 312–31.

28   W. K. Wimsatt, "Epilogue," in W. K. Wimsatt and Cleanth Brooks, *Literary Criticism: A Short History* (New York: Knopf, 1957), pp. 724–55.

29   Philip Rahv, *The Myth and the Powerhouse: Essays in Literature and Ideas* (New York: New Directions, 1965), pp. 46, 6. Rahv's immediate targets included Ernst Cassirer, Suzanne Langer, and William Troy. Rahv also refers to R. W. Stallman's mythic interpretation of *The Red Badge of Courage.*

30   See John Fekete, *The Critical Twilight: Explorations in the Ideology of Anglo-American Literary Theory from Eliot to McLuhan* (New York: Routledge & Kegan Paul, 1977); Richard Ohmann, *English in America: A Radical View of the Profession* (New York: Oxford University Press, 1976), pp. 66–91; Frank Lentricchia, *After the New Criticism* (Chicago: University of Chicago Press, 1980); Carolyn Porter, *Seeing and Being: the Plight of the Participant Observer in Emerson, James, Adams, and Faulkner* (Middletown, Conn.: Wesleyan University Press, 1981), pp. 3–22. From a different viewpoint, see Grant Webster's treatment of the New Critics as "Tory Formalists," in *The Republic of Letters: A History of Postwar American Literary Opinion* (Baltimore: Johns Hopkins University Press, 1979), pp. 47–94.

31   Marcus Klein, *Foreigners: The Making of American Literature, 1910–1940* (Chicago: University of Chicago Press, 1981).

32   Richard Ruland, *The Rediscovery of American Literature: Premises of Critical Taste, 1900–1940* (Cambridge, Mass.: Harvard University Press, 1967), p. 56.

33   If you doubt the truth of this claim, then I challenge you to guess the political leanings of the writers of the following:

We are being made aware that the organization of society on the principle of private profit, as well as public destruction, is leading both to the deformation of humanity by unregulated industrialism, and to the exhaustion of natural resources.

Industrialism wants to take a short-cut to art. Seeing the world altogether in terms of commodities, it simply proposes to add one more commodity to the list, as a concession to humanity's unaccountable craving, or as just one more market – why not? And industrialism is quite unconscious that the bargain . . . involves the destruction of the thing bargained for. . . .

   Nor does the separation of our lives into two distinct parts, one of which is all labor – too often mechanical and deadening – and the other all play, undertaken as a nervous relief, seem to be conducive to a harmonious life.

Marx's *1844 Manuscripts?* Lukács? No. The first quotation is by T. S.
Eliot from *The Idea of a Christian Society* (1939), in *Christianity and Culture*
(New York: Harcourt Brace & World, 1949), p. 48. The second is by the
Agrarian Donald Davidson, from "A Mirror for Artists," in *I'll Take My
Stand*, pp. 30–31, 34.

34 F. O. Matthiessen, *American Renaissance: Art and Expression in the Age of
Emerson and Whitman* (New York: Oxford University Press, 1941), p. ix.

35 R. W. B. Lewis, *The American Adam: Innocence, Tragedy, and Tradition in
the Nineteenth Century* (Chicago: University of Chicago Press, 1955); Leo
Marx, *The Machine in the Garden: The Pastoral Ideal in America* (New York:
Oxford University Press, 1964); Edwin Fussell, *Frontier: American Literature
and the American West* (Princeton, N.J.: Princeton University Press, 1965);
Leslie Fiedler, *Love and Death in the American Novel*, rev. ed. (New York:
Dell, 1966; first published 1960); Richard Chase, *The American Novel and Its
Tradition* (New York: Doubleday, 1957); Charles Feidelson, *Symbolism and
American Literature* (Chicago: University of Chicago Press, 1953); Richard
Poirier, *A World Elsewhere: The Place of Style in American Literature* (New
York: Oxford University Press, 1966).

36 Yvor Winters, *Maule's Curse: Seven Studies in the History of American Obscurantism*, in *In Defense of Reason* (Denver: Alan Swallow, 1947).

37 See Ellen Moers's comment, in *Two Dreisers* (New York: Viking, 1969),
that her generation did not read Dreiser (p. vii); another symptom of the
turn away from social concerns is the relative neglect of Alfred Kazin's *On
Native Grounds* (1942), by comparison with the books advancing the "romance" thesis.

38 Lionel Trilling, *The Liberal Imagination: Essays on Literature and Society*
(New York: Doubleday, 1953), pp. 1–19.

39 Rogin, *Subversive Genealogy*, p. 38.

40 Poirier, *A World Elsewhere*, p. 51.

41 Warner Berthoff, "Ambitious Scheme," *Commentary* (October 1967): 111.

42 Henry Nash Smith, *Virgin Land: The American West as Symbol and Myth*,
(Cambridge, Mass.: Harvard University Press, 1950), p. v.

43 *Ibid.*, 2nd edition p. ix. Barry Marks's review "The Concept of Myth in
Virgin Land" appeared in *American Quarterly* 5 (Spring 1953): 71–76.

44 Sacvan Bercovitch, *The Puritan Origins of the American Self* (New Haven,
Conn.: Yale University Press, 1975); *The American Jeremiad* (Madison: Uni-
versity of Wisconsin Press, 1978); Larzer Ziff, *Puritanism in America: New
Culture in a New World* (New York: Viking, 1973); Ann Douglas, *The
Feminization of American Culture* (New York: Knopf, 1977); see also Darrett
B. Rutman, *Winthrop's Boston: A Portrait of a Puritan Town.* (Chapel Hill:
University of North Carolina Press, 1965.).

45 For some examples, see Myra Jehlen, *Class and Character in Faulkner's South*
(New York: Columbia University Press, 1976); Alan Trachtenberg, *The
Incorporation of America: Culture and Society in the Gilded Age* (New York:
Hill & Wang, 1982); on challenges to the canon, see Paul Lauter, ed.,

Reconstructing American Literature: Courses, Syllabi, Issues (Old Westbury, N.Y.: Feminist Press, 1983).

46 Jane P. Tompkins, "Sentimental Power: *Uncle Tom's Cabin* and the Politics of Literary History," *Glyph: Johns Hopkins Textual Studies* 8 (1981): 81. This discussion refers to an earlier version of Tompkins's essay, which dealt with Douglas more critically.

47 Judith Fetterley, *The Resisting Reader: A Feminist Approach to American Fiction* (Bloomington: Indiana University Press, 1978), p. xii.

48 *Ibid.*, p. 1.

49 Thus, Hawthorne is severely taken to task for "The Birthmark," even though his treatment of the aggressive delusions of his protagonist, Aylmer, which lead to the death of his wife, would seem cautionary enough. "Even so," Fetterley complains, Hawthorne "is unwilling to do more with the sickness than call it sick," obscuring "the issue of sexual politics behind a haze of 'universals . . .' " (*Ibid*, p. xv). This last charge is not quite true, since Hawthorne's story recognizes the messianic science symbolized by Aylmer as a historical phenomenon. In any case, calling a sickness sick is at least preferable to calling it healthy, even if Hawthorne did not yet understand that all issues between men and women can be reduced to issues of sexual politics. *The Great Gatsby* is described by Fetterley as "the quintessentially male drama of poor boy's becoming rich boy, ownership of women being invoked as the index of power" (Ibid., p. xvi). This may be partly right, but it essentially reduces Fitzgerald's perspective to that of Tom Buchanan, or at best Gatsby. On the other hand, James's *The Bostonians* and Mailer's *An American Dream* are unaccountably praised for providing what Fetterley calls, in connection with James, "the material for that analysis of American social reality which is the beginning of change" (Ibid., p. xvii).

50 See, for example, Nina Baym, *Woman's Fiction: A Guide to Novels by and about Women in America, 1820–1870* (Ithaca, N.Y.: Cornell University Press, 1978); on debates within American feminism, see Elizabeth Abel, ed. *Writing and Sexual Difference* (Chicago: University of Chicago Press, 1982), especially the critiques by Carolyn J. Allen and Carolyn G. Heilbrun. By comparison with its French counterpart, American feminist criticism is far less prone to see thought and writing as if they were simplistically gender-specific.

51 Fetterley, *The Resisting Reader,* p. xx.

52 Julia Kristeva, *Desire in Language: A Semiotic Approach to Literature and Art,* trans. Thomas Gora et. al., ed. Leon Roudiez (New York: Columbia University Press, 1980), p. 133. Quoted in an essay by T. H. Adamowski to appear in a forthcoming *Dalhousie Review*.

53 Barbara Foley, "From New Criticism to Deconstruction: The Example of Charles Feidelson's *Symbolism and American Literature,*" *American Quarterly* 36, no. 1 (Spring 1984): 43–64. See also the forthcoming study by Russell Reising *The Unusable Past*.

54 Kenneth Dauber, "Criticism of American Literature," *Diacritics* 7, no. 1 (Spring 1977): 55.
55 Joseph Riddell, "Decentering the Image: The 'Project' of 'American' Poetics?" in Josue Harari, ed., *Textual Strategies: Perspectives in Post-Structuralist Criticism* (Ithaca, N.Y.: Cornell University Press, 1979), p. 358. For a similar treatment in which "rhetoricity" and "tropes" subsume history, see Joseph G. Kronick, *American Poetics of History: From Emerson to the Moderns* (Baton Rouge: Louisiana State University Press, 1984): "History, I propose, is a rhetoric, for it consists of . . . tropological transformations. Hence, I find it characteristic of the American writer to treat history as a question of intertextuality, of reading and writing" (p. 6).
56 Ibid., pp. 355–56.
57 The influence of Foucault is prominent in the interesting collection *American Realism: New Essays,* ed. Eric J. Sundquist (Baltimore: Johns Hopkins University Press, 1982).
58 See, for example, the interview "Truth and Power," trans. Paul Patton and Meaghan Morris, in Foucault, *Power, Truth, Strategy,* ed. Patton and Morris (Sydney, Australia: Feral, 1979), p. 47; reprinted in a different translation in Foucault, *Power/Knowledge: Selected Interviews and Other Writings, 1972–1977* (New York: Pantheon, 1980).
59 Amy Kaplan, "Absent Things in American Life," *Yale Review* 72, no. 2 (Winter 1984).
60 Mark Seltzer, "*The Princess Casamassima:* Realism and the Fantasy of Surveillance," in *American Realism: New Essays,* pp. 97, 115.

II

Perspectives

6

The Novel and the
Middle Class in America

MYRA JEHLEN

The nineteenth-century novel is quintessentially the genre of the middle class. Yet in quintessentially middle-class America the major authors, except perhaps for Henry James who wrote mostly in England, seem not to have written novels at all. Our writers spun tales of extravagant individuals in flight to the wilderness and beyond while, until recently anyway, the novel has explored the everyday lives of ordinary people at home. There have been various reasons suggested for this lack of sociability in American fiction: the greater allure of an adventurous frontier or the lesser fictional interest of a primitive social scene, even the callowness of a young culture seeking, as one critic put it, "to avoid the facts of wooing, marriage and childbearing."[1] But underlying these explanations and comparisons of the realistic novel with the romance (the latter being a term used originally by Richard Chase to describe America's non-novelistic novels)[2] is a double assumption about the attitude to the real world that is implicit in each kind of fiction. It has seemed only logical to think that realism tends realistically to accept its material universe as given while the romance broods on metaphysical rebellion. But in fact the most characteristic examples of European realism are deeply, even radically critical of the world they depict, while however far away into the wilderness American romances take us, ultimately they find it an impossible situation and, whether out of commitment or by default, lead us back to society. For the self-reliant individuals, Natty Bumppo, Hester Prynne, Captain Ahab, Huck Finn or Isabel Archer all fail in the end to create their private worlds and their failure sounds dire warnings of the dangers of isolation and solipsism. Typically the American romance is the story of a *defeated*, a downed flight.

I use "flight" here in either or both its senses, as rising and as escaping. Both mean an attempt to transcend one's native condition and it is a remarkable irony that in the fiction of the New World such attempts are almost always stopped at an impassable frontier. Not that ambition is often successful in the English and French novel, but there the failure is of a different kind, not so automatic, more substantive. Julien Sorel and Emma Bovary, Dorothea Brooke or, for that matter, Clarissa Harlowe before them, are also downed but by real artillery, whereas the Americans must come down, as it were, just because they want up. Julien Sorel is broken by the power of an entrenched class and Clarissa by that of a rising class but when Ahab at last "strike(s) through the mask" he encounters – nothing. More precisely Melville stops writing about Ahab's thrust beyond this world at just the moment when it ostensibly happens. One minute Ahab, Melville and the reader press forward together on the threshold of knowledge. Ahab hurls his challenge: "*Thus* I give up the spear!" and:

> The harpoon was darted; the stricken whale flew forward; with igniting velocity the line ran through the groove; – ran afoul. Ahab stooped to clear it; he did clear it; but the flying turn caught him round the neck, and voicelessly as Turkish mutes bowstring their victim, he was shot out of the boat ere the crew knew he was gone.[3]

From the grandiloquent periods of the Captain's last defiance in the paragraph preceding the one just cited ("Ho, ho! from all your furthest bounds, pour ye now in, ye bold billows of my whole foregone life, and top this one piled comber of my death!")[4] the language itself retreats to the status of impartial recording, noting physical details with careful precision and quite declining to interpret anything. As for Ahab, why is it that in a book otherwise intoxicated with rhetoric and himself the greatest orator of all, he goes to his death mute?

On one level, of course, the answer is obvious. Melville could hardly follow his hero into the Other World. But the real point lies in the very locating of Ahab's goal, of his vision of freedom and self-realization in a realm that is not only unattainable but even inconceivable. In *Moby-Dick* one lives here or nowhere.[5] The Nantucket shore and the Pequod represent the concept of Society itself and the open sea its blank negation. Similarly Hester Prynne could choose in America only between Puritan Boston and the wild woods; and as he drifted down the Mississippi, steering clear of both its shores, Huck Finn would try to escape not only Hannibal but all Civilization. In contrast, as we will see a little later, the European novel more easily envisages alternative societies or

at least their theoretical possibilities. Other systems than the contemporary are not there so literally unthinkable.

The source of the difference lies, I think, in the different ways in which
the middle class achieved its hegemony in Europe and in America. This
issue of hegemony was discussed by Raymond Williams, who cites
Gramsci's stress on ideological hegemony as a totality "which is lived at
such a depth, which saturates the society to such an extent" that it "even
constitutes the limit of common sense for most people under its sway."[6]
But Williams himself wants to examine the inner complexity of hegemony and to describe the constant changes that it undergoes: its dynamic rather than static nature. To this end he distinguishes between
"the dominant culture" in the society and certain other "practices, experiences, meanings and values" which are "alternative" to the dominant
culture or even "oppositional" to it. He distinguishes further: "between
residual and *emergent* forms, both of alternative and of oppositional culture." One might put it another way, that the content of alternative or
oppositional cultural forms is lent by either residual or emergent ideologies. Now this is where the American experience has differed from the
European which in modern times became so charged by a sense of history that both residual and emergent cultures could achieve a remarkable
degree of immediacy. In America, on the other hand, at least through the
nineteenth century the dominant culture seems to have been able to
co-opt alternative and oppositional forms with unusual effectiveness, to
the point of appearing to preclude even their possibility. Residual values
here are associated with the Old World and thus rejected by the very
process of national emergence. As for notions of still further emergence,
these are also essentially precluded by that same peculiarly ideological
origin in America which identified nationhood itself with a specific vision of both nation and state.

America, in other words, was conceived not so much in liberty as
in liberalism. It was a new home that the middle class built for itself
according to a design it deemed not only desirable but natural. What
is generally recognized as a lack of historical sense in the national consciousness means just this, I think: the idea that the Founding Fathers,
building on the wisdom of the ages, erected a structure which was so
well suited to the basic needs of men and societies that with an addition here and there, it could accommodate all likely futures. Less
capable and well-destined peoples, of course, constantly had to redo
their societies, but not America which, having begun with a revolution, need never revolve again. History, in this view, is an affliction
brought on by a poor Constitution and America's growth is seen

instead as the unfolding realization of its inherent form and meaning. Paradoxically the middle class's faith in a progressive history had thus achieved an annihilating apotheosis in the conviction that all progress led to America. Indeed even those who have taken class struggles in this country seriously have usually shared in the millennial vision. As C. Vann Woodward observed, much of the persuasiveness of Southern populism, for example, derived from its claims to more truly represent the real America. The inherent fundamentalism of American dissenters is notorious; how else to explain the incomprehensible accusation of the trustbusters that monopolies are un-American?

In Europe, on the contrary, the rise of the there insurgent middle class is associated with an attack on such static absolutism, whether personal or social. Personality and history both come to be seen as continuous processes and capable therefore of only relative and mutable definition. And reflecting the individual's loss of given, a priori identity, his now problematic sense of self, the protagonist of the European novel is born already an existential outsider, self-generated in Georg Lukács' terms, as "the product of estrangement from the outside world."[7] For Lukács this condition reflected the personal alienation inevitably inflicted by bourgeois society. Unlike the members of older "integrated civilizations" each one of whom knew himself for a part of the organically cohesive whole, people were now thrown back on themselves, on "the autonomous life of interiority" for values and meaning in a universe become subjectively anomic. No longer able to identify *with* their society, in short, men and women in a bourgeois society identified themselves in terms of their existential distance from it. In an age "in which the extensive totality of life is no longer directly given," writes Lukács, "in which the immanence of meaning in life has become a problem yet which still thinks in terms of totality . . . the novel seeks, by giving form to uncover and construct the concealed totality of life." Quentin Anderson has put it with admirable brevity: "God dies and Stephen Dedalus goes to work."[8] Hence we note the novel's concern with plot continuity and development and with the inner coherence of its characters, all being structural components of the teleology it seeks to create. Or of its theology, as J. Hillis Miller thought, seeing "the fundamental theme" of Victorian fiction as "an exploration of the various ways in which a man may seek to make a god of another person in a world without God."[9]

The crux of the matter for these and other critics of the novel, the basic factor they have seen in its development, is the absence of transcendent order or unifying purpose in the novelist's bourgeois culture. (To use Williams' terms one might talk about a fatal relativism in the dominant culture which causes it to appear no longer so natural or common-sensical.) Taking this to be accurate, I would suggest that it was a contrary sense of order so pervasive as to seem inescapable that generated the American romance. Miller's thesis that the novel seeks God surrogates may be applied conversely to the romance: when God left Europe he came to America and went to work for Ben Franklin, which is why blasphemy is the darkest sin American fiction can envision. In Lukács' terms, middle-class America *was* an integrated society, I am suggesting, like Athens and Renaissance London, and very unlike nineteenth-century London and Paris.

But this integration was paradoxical. What American writers assumed by the terms "Human Nature" and "Society," those principles writ large in the New World cosmology, were nonetheless characteristically middle-class in describing the universe as essentially a natural market place. (Not that all writers sought to corner the market – Thoreau, for instance, wanted none of it – but they did take it for granted as the inevitable setting for the development of personal identity.) Indeed one has only to compare the Americas of Cooper, Hawthorne and Melville to Chaucer's or Shakespeare's Englands (the latter being comparably absolute paradigms), to see how ideologically particular American ideals really were. Even Cooper's fussy elitism does not make him an aristocrat but only a conservative burger; it is after all a natural, a competitively viable meritocracy that he envisages and that is not at all inconsistent with notions of equal opportunity. At the other end of the political spectrum, neither is the "Spirit of Equality" which inspires Melville to invest in "meanest mariners, and renegades and castaways . . . high qualities, though dark,"[10] in any sense proletarian. Its "august dignity" requires "no robed investiture" it is true, and it can be glimpsed radiating from "the arm that wields a pick or drives a spike," but it does not the less imply the transcendence of a unique Best One. "Thou great democratic God!" Melville intones,

> who didst not refuse to the swart convict, Bunyan, the pale poetic pearl; Thou who didst clothe with doubly hammered leaves of finest gold, the stumped and paupered arm of old Cervantes; Thou who didst pick up Andrew Jackson from the pebbles; who didst hurl him upon a warhorse; who didst thunder him higher than a throne! Thou who, in all Thy mighty, earthly marchings, ever cullest Thy selectest champions from the kingly commons . . .

Melville's democratic hero nurses at the common source of individualistic ambition only to rise the higher above his fellows.

Indeed one key middle-class assumption that Cooper, Melville and

their colleagues shared was of the naturalness of individualistic ambition. The self, in this view, is an autonomous entity one makes oneself
and therefore makes as powerful as possible. But here is the special
dilemma of American writers, and the source of tragedy in their works:
the self-made, self-regulated man is only viable in the context of an
open future, of an evolving social history that yields him the where-
withal to create. His identity is, precisely, a matter of "residual" or
"emergent" cultures. What happens when such an individualist inhabits
instead a world structured by the absolute necessities we associate with
theology or myth, is the story of Ahab. Or, if the individualist bows to
necessity, it is the story of Hester Prynne. It can also be the story of
Huck Finn, if he simply abandons the quest. But for any of these to
actually realize the power of their individualism is taboo, implying as it
would an un-American mutability. It is almost inevitable then that
however glorious the "Spirit of Equality," its incarnation in the Captain of the Pequod must become Satanic. I do not mean to interpret
Ahab simply as a heroic rebel. But for better and for worse the Captain
of the Pequod represents individualism and the assertion of total free
will. Indeed only in the context of possibility for substantive change
could the "Spirit" have taken a Promethean form.[11] But the myth that
American liberalism allows for all possible surface adjustments in the
system and thus obviates the need for basic ones, was too strong, even
for the national heroes, and especially for the historical dialectic they
would have energized.

   This is not the place for a discussion of philosophical dualism or its
absence in American thought but I want briefly to refer to Emerson as
highly representative in his urge to monistic resolutions of conflict and
his sense that the dualities which may arise at any stage of understanding are only apparent and thus capable of being transcended by rising
another level toward the ultimate abstract One. The concept of the
all-pervasive Oversoul in which oppositions and contradictions dissolve
is, of course, familiar. But more specific to my concerns here is Emerson's sense that there is no necessary contradiction either between the
individual and society. (He would have capitalized both and made the
principle absolute.) "Speak your latent conviction," he urged each fellow citizen, "and it shall be the universal sense."[12] And should society
seem for a time to have departed from this universal sense, then, it
would be due to a flagging "self-trust" among those who constitute its
"delegated intellect."[13] The difference between this "self-trust" as a
focus for individual political judgment and Lukács' previously cited
"autonomous life of interiority" is crucial. The latter is born of the
recognition that the individual is inevitably separate from society while

Emerson affirms their underlying identity of interest. Thus the latter's famed uncompromising individualism, his rejection of all external standards in order to be "doctrine, society, law"[14] unto himself never needed to place him in opposition to the doctrines and laws of a properly constituted society, as he thought America to be at bottom. If he proclaimed that "the only right is after my constitution; the only wrong what is against it,"[15] the point is that he considered the right defined by his constitution as really, objectively right. What was right for Emerson was happily right for the nation. And this because the world was made so, with individualism generating public morality as surely as free enterprise in the market place did the general welfare.[16] The neoclassical conservatism of this has been noted before but what I want to stress is Emerson's assumption of a snug at-oneness with the universe, and also with his local township. By this I do not mean, of course, that he necessarily approved of all its policies. "I know that the world I converse with in the city and in the farms, is not the world I *think*,"[17] he writes in the America of 1844–45.

> But I have not found that much was gained by manipular attempts to realize the world of thought. Many eager persons successively make an experiment in this way, and make themselves ridiculous. They acquire democratic manners, they foam at the mouth, they hate and deny. Worse, I observe that in the history of mankind there is never a solitary example of success, – taking their own tests of success. I say this polemically, or in reply to the inquiry, Why not realize your world? But far be from me the despair which prejudges the law by a paltry empiricism; – since there never was a right endeavor but it succeeded.

(This ultimate triumph of good is assured for him by the fact that "power is in nature the essential measure of right.")[18] He begins here with the recognition that the actual condition of the world is not what he thinks it should be. But he treats this as a pseudo-contradiction about which not only can nothing be done, and then not only *need* nothing be done but even nothing *should* be done lest the goal be lost in the attaining. For it is "in the solitude to which every man is always returning, [that] he has a sanity and revelations which in his passage into new worlds he will carry with him."[19] And in this last the contradictions of thought and action, of individual and society, and of ideal and reality have been resolved or, rather, dissolved in that single higher Reality which is already complete and will in its own time manifest itself.

Even Melville apparently came to feel that dualism was a wicked rationale for detaching oneself from the world with the intent to control it. Ahab's last speech bristles with dualities he has himself created out of his blasphemous ambition. In focusing on his monomania itself critics have overlooked its effect, which is to set up gratuitous oppositions between the self and the world. Insisting on his vision of such fatal contradictions, Ahab becomes a polarizing presence that threatens, if indeed he achieves his transcendence, a progressive dialectical episode. With his death, however, the dualities he has generated are rejoined. When finally the Pequod founders and the ocean rolls over the "Pole-pointed" ship which, in a last defiant affirmation of duality, has dragged down into the depths of the sea "a living part of heaven," Ishmael is left to reconcile land and ocean, man and society, and life and death, all of which, washed clean as lambs, we now recognize are one in the bosom of nature.[20]

It is worth comparing to Ahab's the last speech of Stendhal's Julien Sorel (about whom more later) who asserts his Napoleonic ambition to the last, drawing the lines of class conflict tight between himself and his persecutors.[21] But unlike Melville, Stendhal confirms his protagonist's vision of contradiction so that his execution in no way resolves the conflict but indeed affirms its inescapable reality. There is even something prophetic about Julien's last challenge suggesting the possibility of other outcomes sometime in the future. If other outcomes than defeat are ever projected in American fiction it is in the form of Hester's vision mentioned late in Hawthorne's book of "a new truth [which would] establish the whole relation between man and woman on a surer ground of mutual happiness."[22] But Hester learns Emerson's lesson: like his, her new world can be delivered only in the fullness of time, and then entirely from within the body of the old. Above all, she comes to understand, no one who has ever placed herself in radical opposition to her society can hope to assist in its transformation. For such a one has denied America, much, one feels, as Moses did God, for which, it will be recalled, he was barred from ever entering the Promised Land.

Emerson's version of better days coming is similarly apocalyptic. "There is victory yet for all justice" he proclaims, "and the true romance which the world exists to realize will be the transformation of genius into practical power." I hesitate to give much weight to his use of the term "romance" here, and yet it is suggestive. That "transformation" it will record is really the unfolding realization of an innate being: this is not an event about which one could write a history, for histories in the modern Hegelian sense focus on the creation of new conditions that negate the old. It needs "romance" to depict the timeless and agent-less comings-about that constitute Emerson's sense of the American future. Agent-less because as we noted earlier any attempt to enact the desired state hopelessy compromises it. Hence Emerson's notion of social responsibility which is fulfilled in the furtherance of one's own best interests; morality and identity, in short, are for him entirely intrinsic. Which is indeed how Richard Chase described the abstract characterizations of the "heroes, villains, victims [and] legendary types" who people American fiction and whose self-contained and self-defined careers led him to conclude, citing Henry James, that " 'the disconnected and uncontrolled experience' . . . is of the essence of the romance."[23] A central thesis of this chapter is that the anti-historicism and the disengaged, abstract concept of personal identity which characterize the romance, like those same aspects of Emerson's thinking, are ideological and ideally suited to the maintenance of a specific society, that individualistic "nation of men" which Emerson envisioned as America's special destiny. So that William Gilmore Simms' comparison of the romance to the epics of the ancient world was very precisely apt. Like the epics, the American romance makes heroic myth out of the ultimate efforts of characters to conquer structural constraints of a hermetic cosmos. No one in epic or romance believes he can overcome, but all have to try.

Still, if it ultimately generated the anomaly of a bourgeois yet tragic vision, the ideological triumph of America's middle class also had a positive, even an inspirational aspect. The task which Emerson set before American scholars (chiding that "events, actions arise, that must be sung, that will sing themselves")[24] was truly epic, at once elevating and celebrating a civilization with which the writer identified deeply. Even those American writers, perhaps the majority, who were less pleased with America than Emerson did feel privileged to be in at the second coming of Western Civilization and inspired to, god-like, create a new literature. The astonishing power and range of the best American writing was likely sparked by this, generated out of that terrible tension between imperial arrogance and the terror of blasphemy which also not infrequently drove American writers mad. And there is a sense in which the absolute hegemony that the middle class was able to claim in America, despite its paradoxical nature, also enabled a more complete ideological development than was attained in Europe. Perhaps it is to its American avatars that one should look for the real fulfillment of individualism – and therefore to such as Melville – for the most telling critiques, exposing at once the enormous creative potential and the appalling destructiveness it renders possible. So if Melville is less tolerant of romantic rebellion than his European counterparts he is also probably better aware than they of just what it can entail.

The contrast I have been sketching between the European novel and the American romance, whereby the former takes the internal organization of society as its "problem" and the latter, accepting the *status quo* as simply natural, focuses instead on the difficulties of individual conformity, may be clarified by more detailed examples of each genre. I want to stress again that basic assumptions are involved in creating the difference and not any conscious choices of subject. There is nice evidence for this basic divergence of vision in an introduction to *Madame Bovary* written by Henry James. This is his summary of the plot:

> A pretty young woman who lives, socially and morally speaking in a hole, and who is ignorant, foolish, flimsy, unhappy, takes a pair of lovers by whom she is successively deserted; in the midst of which, giving up her husband and her child, letting everything go, she sinks deeper into duplicity, debt, despair, and arrives on the spot, on the small scene of her poor depravities, at a pitiful, tragic end. She does those things above all, while remaining absorbed in the romantic vision, and she remains absorbed in the romantic vision while fairly rolling in the dust.[25]

For James who, ironically, criticizes his compatriots for their inadequate treatment of social experience, Emma Bovary is nevertheless to be understood in universal, abstract terms. She is thus merely an abject everywoman living anytime, anywhere. And since the predictable career of an ignorant, foolish, flimsy, unhappy, even if pretty housewife is of scant interest, James finds himself puzzled by the inconsequence of the novel and forced to conclude that it reveals a certain "defect of mind" in Flaubert himself. "Emma Bovary," James regretfully decides, "is really too small an affair." In France, of course, she was either a national scandal or an international triumph but no one seems to have doubted her significance. Indeed for one French critic writing at about the time James did, *Madame Bovary* said everything. But then he summed it up differently. "Trouver le moyen d'exhaler à la fois toutes les haines du romantisme contre le bourgeois et toutes les rancunes du bourgeois contre le romantisme," he noted with relish, "il y avait du ragoût."[26]

Instead of abstract romantic visions, the French critic sees nineteenth-century Romanticism embattled with the bourgeois ethos and perceives in Flaubert's small affair the representation of a very large social theme. Moreover it seems clear that for Flaubert himself, Emma's situation, which James passes over as merely the dust in which she rolls, is of paramount importance. Unlike the American who at once focuses on

Emma and then sees nothing but her, the French novelist opens his story with the supporting cast. We first meet a young school-boy who will someday be her husband, accompany him through his first marriage, the beginnings of his career as a country doctor, his loss of his first wife, and finally arrive at the eve of his second marriage where at last the heroine enters the story. It should be noted that she is in fact the third Madame Bovary to appear on the scene, and by the time we understand that it is she to whom the title refers, the stage is set and she can only assume a name and place she never made.

In this Flaubert is not so deterministic as pessimistic, for Emma's environment molds her less than it prevents her from molding herself, but even in the stuff of her most escapist fantasies, she remains inextricably involved with history and society. Madame Bovary's "self" is therefore more extensive, more socially encompassing than James, writing from within a social structure he tacitly approved, or anyway accepted, was prepared to see. The problems that essentially define her being were simply not problematical in his eyes; but neither did James quite acknowledge that, barring the rebel's engaged and thereby limited morality, the "finely civilized consciousness" which alone interested him could be developed only by someone who was very successful in just the civilization that made poor diminished Emma so boring.

One can imagine James comparing her deprecatingly to his own vibrant, perceptive Isable Archer; but unfairly, for the world is very good to Isabel, bestowing on her just what Emma dies for lack of, the financial means to "meet the requirements of [her] imagination."[27] If this bounty has unfortunate consequences, it is because Isabel herself is not wise enough to profit from it. Neither would Emma have been, of course, but the point is that she never has the chance to try, and this represents the great difference between the world of Flaubert and that of James. For the American writer's fictional universe is, especially by comparison to Yonville l'Abbaye, truly a land of opportunity where a woman may, and only therefore must, call her soul her own. James's America may not be altogether a free country but it is as free as any society can be. Flaubert's France is horrendously unfree: so much so that his villains can only just barely be blamed for their sins. Even the village usurer only acts out the logic of his social role. We can reproach him for personally accepting that role but not blame him for the very introduction of evil, as we can his counterpart in *Portrait of a Lady*, Madame Merle. When the romantic Isabel sees the world clearly, she acquires the freedom to choose on universal moral grounds; romantic Emma can come only to see that she has no choices. Ultimately it is her society we blame rather than any of its members and we readily imagine another society, drawn according to the precepts perhaps of the compassionate and aristocratic Docteur Larivière, in which Emma and her life would be entirely different.

That James should have missed the point of *Madame Bovary* is the more significant in that he and Flaubert were in other respects virtual counterparts. They would not have differed much about the politics of literature. Both cared most about form and language, and insisted that art be valued primarily for its own sake; both might well have been accused before the popular bar of a fastidious and most undemocratic snobbery. But while Flaubert despairingly viewed the French bourgeoisie as the most dire threat yet encountered by civilized values, James actually saw their best hope among the reigning elite of middle-class America. For Flaubert it was a historical catastrophe that France had become bourgeois. For James the coming of America offered at last the possibility of transcending both class and history.

Another illustration of the difference in world view that underlies the difference between the novel and the romance: both Melville and Balzac, as it happens, based characters explicitly on Shakespeare's Lear. That arch-individualist, of course, exaggerates both man's cosmic status and his domestic role as a father. Indicating no awareness that there was another side to his character, Melville and Balzac elaborated opposite facets of the king's fatal arrogance: Ahab acknowledges no mortal limits and the père Goriot aspires to ideal fatherhood. And the worlds each defines in his own image are also opposites. "La justice est pour moi, tout est pour moi, la nature, le code civil," the neglected Goriot protests. "La société, le monde roulent sur la paternité, tout croule si les enfants n'aiment pas leurs pères."[28] But Ahab cares nothing for the world: he aspires to the throne of heaven, or hell.

Thus Goriot, Lear's novelistic avatar, is realistically defined by a precise sociology and also by the details of a rich internal life that enables us not only to believe in him but also to feel that we know him personally. We know very little about Ahab personally and, if anything, less and less as the story progresses. He is mysterious, archetypal rather than socially typical, abstractly conceived, perhaps universal but certainly not of the everyday world. And the ideological assumptions which I suggested earlier were implied by each fictional form, are in fact evident in *Le Père Goriot* and *Moby-Dick:* the French novel enjoins defiance of a corrupt society while the American romance warns urgently that the wages of blasphemy are death. In short, judging by their respective interpretations of Lear, the American writer is, contrary to the usual expectations, *less* aggressively individualistic than the French.

For Melville, whose alienation from American society is only too painfully evident, still cannot reconcile himself to being alienated, while Balzac draws therefrom all his inspiration. Melville actually apologizes for conventional society through Starbuck, who is a man of delicate moral sensibility whose concern for the financial success of the whaling expedition expresses only devotion to his duty and not greed. Generally, indeed, the case for social constraints, for law and order, for conformity to conventional roles, is powerfully argued throughout American fiction, and particularly in those very works of the first part of the nineteenth century which are usually cited as evidence of America's intractable commitment to individual freedom. For it is in these writings, of Hawthorne and Melville especially, that the representation of such freedom is most tense and guilt-ridden, and its exercise most often sinful and/or fatal. Of course such freedom is also tantalizing. But like Milton who harbored passions that enkindled his Satan without therefore enlisting on the side of Hell, Melville never suggests that even the most limiting social compliance absolutely precludes personal integrity. And so Ishmael, the wisest character in *Moby-Dick,* who avoids institutional entanglements as scrupulously as cosmic confrontations, remains nevertheless on congenial terms with New England – and New England in turn readily accords him a reasonable degree of freedom, even, at intervals, to drop out. Moreover Ishmael's few active principles are more at variance with Ahab's behavior than with Starbuck's. For Ishmael believes in being companionable and survives largely for reasons embodied in his "marriage" to Queequeg, a relationship whose real interest has been unfortunately obscured. At the end, as we noted earlier, Ishmael sounds a last note of harmony with all of nature and with men too, represented by the whalers who rescue him. And the peace he has achieved is apparently attainable by anyone who can acknowledge the lure of total freedom yet recall that his mortal state requires that he still be social, even sociable.

This conclusion would have amazed Balzac who ends his novel with a declaration of war against a society he likens to an ocean of mud splattering one on mere proximity. Standing high on a hill overlooking Paris (as in the crow's nest which Ishmael warns us against for its dangerous isolation), Eugene Rastignac divorces himself from the "ruche bourdonnante" of the city below and vows to avenge the death of the old man who had tried to be something of a queen-bee. From the beginning Balzac juxtaposes the incipiently rebellious, ambitious Rastignac to the ultra-compliant and self-sacrificing Goriot (as Melville makes a reverse comparison between Ahab and Ishmael); and Goriot's final agony destroys Rastignac's last feelings of obligation to conventional values, exiling him in a moral autonomy that Cooper, Hawthorne, Melville, Howells, James and even, it can be argued,

Mark Twain would have deemed dangerously akin to blasphemy. But Balzac has few qualms, for Rastignac's ethics are at least superior to those of Paris, in all of which there is not one Starbuck. Thus the basic thrust of *Le Père Goriot,* which considers Lear's family to be the most problematical situation he faces, is just the opposite of *Moby-Dick's,* in which Melville depicts how cold and deadly can be the universe beyond the glow of the homefires.

The necessity therefore to live, as it were, within the city limits, is the recurrent motif of the work of Hawthorne. In fact in *The Scarlet Letter,* where he grants rebellion its strongest case by embodying it in his most compelling character and at the same time depicting society at its worst, the right and wrong of the matter are never even so much in doubt as they are for Melville. Hester Prynne presents a total contrast to Goriot, being initially as delinquent a wife and mother as he is the perfect *pater familias,* while in the end, when he dies disillusioned, she becomes not only personally reconciled to her role but its proselytizer toward other women. Of course her progress is not easy, nor is Hawthorne himself uninvolved in her trials. Her first appearance, cradling the innocent fruit of her sin, evokes disturbingly mingled associations: she is a madonna demanding sole custody. But all the more does it seem in the end, when she pledges her exceptional creativity to legitimacy and order, that she has reversed the course of the primordial rebellion.

Actually her whole career is relevant to this discussion. Before the start of the novel, Hawthorne tells us, she had lived in England as a seventeenth-century Lady Chatterley married to an aging scholar. She comes to the New World with the wrong expectations for, finding herself temporarily free of her husband, she defies all laws and commits adultery with the minister of her new community, subverting it to its very soul. By making the outlaw a woman who realizes the full implications of her sin when she bears a female child who could therefore continue to propagate anarchy, Hawthorne interprets Ahab's rather abstract defiance as an immediate threat to social order. For Hawthorne, the savage in man and especially in woman, is never noble, and individualistically to indulge it is to undermine at once civilization and one's own higher humanity. When the lovers meet in the forest to plan their escape somewhere they can live together openly, their child spurns them and, in pursuit of some wild fantasy, runs dangerously deeper into the woods. But later in the antithetical scene in the middle of town, she is said to weep her first human tears standing quietly between her humbled parents. For the minister, the adulteress and their child, at last a family and fully compliant to the will of the Protestant god and the laws of Boston, have become the real emblem of America's safe passage out of the wilderness.

It is a road traveled by most of the major American fictions, whose characters initially separate themselves from society but come back to it in the end. Even Huckleberry Finn's unique refusal sadly lacks conviction. But, as we saw earlier, Emma Bovary, Julien Sorel and Eugène Rastignac (whose stories are among the first to come to mind when one thinks of the French novel), sketch out a contrasting paradigm, trying first to realize themselves within society and failing, becoming outcasts and even subversives with the approval of their authors. Julien Sorel struggles from Verrières to Paris wanting only to become a man of the world. He will abide by its rules, adopt its priciples, adapt himself to its tastes, if only the world will have him. But when it won't, in pointed contrast to *Billy Budd,* for instance, he goes defiantly to a rebel's grave. American characters seldom die victorious, the deaths of such as Ahab and Hawthorne's Zenobia being used instead to prove a rightful subjection to higher laws.

It may be well to repeat that I do not claim that American writers were placid apologists for higher laws or for those of the state either, but that for a lack of a sense of a world elsewhere, this indeed being the world elsewhere, the malaise was guiltily exorcised; and once Hester Prynne voluntarily resumes the emblem of sin, once Melville consigns Ahab to the devil and Huck Finn drifts past Cairo, a certain imaginative vitality seems also extinguished. Indeed the frustratingly few real achievements which too early exhaust some of the greatest American writers may well represent their utmost attempt to establish an independently critical stance. It has been a persistent pattern, tracing a relatively rapid rise to a major defiant, sometimes demonic work and a subsequent painful retreat. At the end of *Absalom, Absalom!,* Faulkner's most critical and powerful work written midway in his career, a disillusioned Quentin Compson cries out in agonized denial, "I don't. I don't! I don't hate [the South]! I don't hate it!"[29] But of course he does, and also loves it too much or is too loyal, too frightened or too dependent to admit his revulsion. At any rate, it is not to society but at the possibility of active disssent that Quentin hurls the thunderous no. After this, Faulkner created more relaxed protagonists who confronted a less objectionable South and he found them easier to reconcile, but his writing suffered notably. A century before, Hawthorne also retreated after *The Scarlet Letter.* The descendants of the dangerously dualistic Hester come in allegorical pairs, a dark lady and a fair, a sexy one and a chaste, a rebel and a sweet conformist. The dark rebellious self need not be then overcome or absorbed: she can be exiled, excised. Only Melville tried to return to the fray in *Pierre,* albeit at the remove of an ambiguous irony.

Pierre's is probably the most radical critique in the contemporary literature. What he uncovers beneath the triumphant legitimacy of his family's social dominance, gnawing at the roots of his family tree, is a variant of Hester's subversion: a bastard child that his father never recognized. But whereas in Hawthorne's treatment legality and the definition of legitimacy are not at issue, only how an individual should relate to them, Melville questions the validity of both and, by extension, of the social order they preserve. Pierre's father who figures as a god of the ancestral estate and its ultimate law, had himself violated the most important law of all and the result has been potentially revolutionary. Instead of a legitimate heir, his eldest child is an illegitimate heiress; and thus personal morality and even the integrity of the law (of primogeniture) are hopelessly at odds with the preservation of the status quo. In contrast, Hester found her salvation in a right accommodation with a society whose shortcomings were stylistic rather than structural. And we need no political sociology to explain her temptation. Pierre's problems, on the other hand, are not properly his own but society's and society's not in manner but in substance. In short, Melville's is almost uniquely an internal political analysis. And, though he renders them abstractly, the structures of social life familiar in the European novel are for once at the center of an American work: the intricacies of the family, an urban setting (once Pierre realizes that life is not a pastoral idyl) and the rigors of economic survival. (It is interesting that one of the only two other similarly radical *and* novelistic works written by major American writers,[30] *Absalom, Absalom!,* has virtually the same plot as *Pierre*'s, the illegitimate eldest child whose existence must be denied being translated in Faulkner's southern idiom into a black son.)

It is worth explicating the plot of *Pierre* further to see how fundamental Melville's attack really was. The appearance of an illegitimate sister evokes for Pierre an alternate family shadowing his own: the cast-away mistress, the dark sister, Isabel, and the father whose alter-ego might quite overwhelm the super-ego he had always been to Pierre before. That family, Pierre now sees, has prior claim to all his worldly estate; he and his queenly mother are usurpers who can only atone by acknowledging the old injury and reinstating its surviving victim. Since his mother and the powers vested in her will never accede to this, Pierre must exile himself with his sister and suffer with her since she cannot rejoice with him. They will become outcasts together: might they not someday be guerrillas? Of course the good and the bad of the situation are not altogether as clear as I am suggesting. Just as toward the rebellious Ahab, Melville was ambivalent toward Pierre whose selflessness might well mask a towering, blasphemous egoism; we can never be sure. The angelic Isabel may be fallen; moreover legitimacy and convention have a powerful advocate in the unequivocally sainted Lucy, whose own attitude toward Pierre's sacrifice is finally undecipherable. Still, when they all three die (in the deepest dungeon of the dark city they fled to out of their Fallen Eden) leaving as heir a cousin whose very duplicity has been the key to both personal wealth and the preservation of the family, we have come very close to the state of mind with which Rastignac sets out to do subversive battle – only our battlers then commit suicide.

In this light, *Billy Budd* may be seen as the account of the suicide itself, a masochistic probing of the fatal wound, that irrevocable glimpse of a real opposition between the law (the structure, the institutions and the norms of society), and a true morality. Unable to imagine another world (the American blasphemy), Melville becomes both Captain Vere, representing the social order that can no more be set aside than that of God, and Billy Budd, the moral vision that is henceforth inarticulate except, in its agony, to praise its executioner. The impact of *Billy Budd,* as of *Moby-Dick* and of *Pierre,* may be to make *us* rebel (though only some of us) but it is against Melville's despair rather than in response to his vision. For even Melville had blinded himself rather than see beyond America.

Most American writers are at least reticent, and their allegiance, anomalous for the period and the hemisphere, was the main force shaping American fiction at least through the nineteenth century. The principles of the bourgeois family, as the heart of middle-class ethics, are consistently upheld in American writing and, not at all paradoxically, they have inspired the strident masculinity, even the celibacy of its heroes.

One of the important signs of the inadequacy of the unregenerate individualists in American fiction is their inability to form familial and social attachments. The significance of this should be clear: indeed in a middle-class society the family is the crucial institution that counters the disruptive and centrifugal potential of individualism. Hester Prynne's sins in this regard are evident as well as the source of her redemption, but Isabel Archer's recognition of the sacrosanct character of marriage, the doom inherent in Natty Bumppo's failure to marry and the moral triumph of Huck's filial relationship to Jim, not to mention the "marriage" of Ishmael and Queequeg, are all examples of an identification of family and social morality. The same ideology can be shown to have brought about that scarcity of adult women and of sexuality, the adolescent repression that worried Leslie Fiedler and appalled D. H. Lawrence and which Hawthorne explained clearly through Hester and Zenobia. Individualistic women were to him intolerably subversive because they undermined the very institution by which individualist men might yet cohere into a moral community. It was Hawthorne too who saw most clearly that sex is the wilderness within while American literature is a saga of colonization. American fiction has been willy-nilly an ally in that colonization. Indeed, it seems doubtful that a jury composed of American writers would have or could have been much more lenient with Stendhal's Julien Sorel than the "bourgeois indignés" who demand his head.

Notes

1   Leslie Fiedler, *Love and Death in the American Novel* (New York, 1966), p. 25.
2   Richard Chase, *The American Novel and Its Tradition* (Garden City, 1957).
3   Herman Melville, *Moby-Dick* (Indianapolis, 1964), pp. 721–22.
4   Ibid., p. 721.
5   The stark alternative has not always been clearly stated by Melville's critics.
6   Raymond Williams, "Base and Superstructure in Marxist Cultural Theory." *New Left Review*, 82 (November-December 1973), p. 8.
7   Georg Lukács, *The Theory of the Novel* (Cambridge, 1971), p. 66.
8   Quentin Anderson, *The Imperial Self* (New York, 1971), p. 167.
9   J. Hillis Miller, *The Form of Victorian Fiction* (Notre Dame, 1968), p. 96.
10 Melville, loc. cit., pp. 160–161.
11 Melville indeed toys with Promethean notion and abandons it in the character of Bulkington whose main value to the book may be to establish what Ahab is *not*.
12 Ralph Waldo Emerson, "Self-Reliance," *American Literature*, ed. Cleanth Brooks, R. W. B. Lewis, Robert Penn Warren (New York, 1973), Vol. 1, p. 712.
13 Emerson, "The American Scholar," ibid., p. 707.
14 Emerson, op. cit., p. 717.
15 Ibid., p. 713.
16 See "Discipline" section of *Nature* for Emerson's view of the association of a true morality with a particular kind of economy. E.g.:

[Instilling us with discipline] is performed by Property and its filial systems of debt and credit. Debt, grinding debt, whose iron face the widow, the orphan and the sons of genius fear and hate; – debt which consumes so much time, which so cripples and disheartens a great spirit with cares that seem so base, is a preceptor whose lessons cannot be foregone, and is needed most by those who suffer from it most. Moreover, property, which has been well compared to snow, – "if it fall today, it will be blown into drifts tomorrow," – is the surface action of internal machinery, like the index on the face of a clock. Whilst now it is the gymnastics of the understanding, it is hiving, in the foresight of the spirit, experience in profounder laws.

Nature, reprinted in *Selections form Ralph Waldo Emerson,* ed. Stephen E. Whicher (Cambridge, 1960), p. 37.

17   Emerson, "Experience," ibid., p. 273.
18   Emerson, "Self-Reliance," *American Literature,* ed. Cleanth Brooks, R. W. B. Lewis, Robert Penn Warren (New York), 1973, Vol. 1, p. 716.
19   Emerson, loc. cit.
20   Ahab's last is structured by imploding, collapsing dualities, these having been the very timbers of the Captain's distorted, unviable cosmos.

"Oh, lonely death on lonely life! Oh, now I feel my topmost greatness lies in my topmost grief. Ho, ho! from all your furthest bounds, pour ye now in, ye bold billows of my whole foregone life, and top this one piled comber of my death! Towards thee I roll, thou all-destroying but unconquering whale; to the last I grapple with thee; from hell's heart I stab at thee; for hate's sake I spit my last breath at thee. Sink all coffins and all hearses to one common pool! and since neither can be mine, let me then tow to pieces, while still chasing thee, though tied to thee, thou damned whale! *Thus,* I give up the spear!"

21   Here is Jùlien's speech to the jury:

. . . "Mon crime est atroce, et il fut *prémédité.* J'ai donc mérité la mort, Messieurs les jurés. Mais quand je serais moins coupable, je vois des hommes qui, sans s'arrêter a ce que ma jeunesse peut mériter de pitié, voudront punir en moi et décourager a jamais cette class de jeunes gens qui, nés dans une classe inférieure et en quelque sorte opprimés par la pauvreté, ont le bonheur de se procurer une bonne éducation, et l'audace de se meler a ce que l'orgeuil des gens riches appelle la société.
     Voilà mon crime, Messieurs, et il sera puni avec d'autant plus de severité que, dans le fait, je ne suis point jugé par mes pairs. Je ne vois point sur les bancs des jurés quelque paysan enrichi, mais uniquement des bourgeois indignés . . ."

Stendhal, *Le Rouge et le Noir* (Paris, 1964), p. 476.

22   And here is Hester's vision and her recognition that she is forever barred from participating in its realization:

She assured [women who came to her seeking comfort in unhappy marriages] of her firm belief, that, at some brighter period, when the world should have grown ripe for it, in Heaven's own time, a new truth would be revealed, in order to establish the whole relation between man and woman on a surer ground of mutual happiness. Earlier in life, Hester had vainly imagined that she herself might be the destined prophetess, but had long since recognized the impossibility that any mission of divine and mysterious truth should be confided to a woman stained with sin, bowed down with shame, or even burdened with a lifelong sorrow. The angel and apostle of the coming revelation must be a woman, indeed, but lofty, pure, and beautiful; and wise, moreover, not through dusky grief, but the ethereal medium of joy; and showing how sacred love should make us happy, by the truest test of a life successful to such an end!

Nathaniel Hawthorne, *The Scarlet Letter* (New York, 1959), p. 245. That last sentence is a veritable "catch-22" which ensures that whatever other world Hawthorne may envisage in the future, one certainly can't get there from here.

23 Chase, loc. cit. p. 25.
24 Emerson, "The American Scholar," op. cit., p. 703.
25 Gustave Flaubert, *Madame Bovary,* introduction by Henry James (London, 1904), pp. xviii–xix.
26 Emile Faguet, *Flaubert* (Paris, 1899), pp. 106–7.
27 Henry James, *The Portrait of a Lady* (Cambridge, 1956), p. 239. Ralph Touchett asks his father "to make Isabel rich" and thereby free.
28 Honoré de Balzac, *Le Père Goriot* (Paris, 1966), p. 239.
29 William Faulkner, *Absalom, Absalom!* (New York, 1951), p. 378.
30 The third being, in my view, *Sister Carrie.*

7

Figurations for a New American Literary History

HOUSTON A. BAKER, JR.

The old formulas had failed, and a new one had yet to be made, but, after all, the object was not extravagant or eccentric. One sought no absolute truth. One sought only a spool on which to wind the thread of history without breaking it.

Henry Adams,
The Education

Relics of by-gone instruments of labour possess the same importance for the investigation of extinct economic forms of society as do fossil bones for the determination of extinct species of animals.

Karl Marx,
Capital

(The bluesman Big Bill Broonzy sings:
I worked on a levee camp and the extra gangs too
Black man is a boy, I don't care what he can do.
I wonder when – I wonder when – I wonder when will
  I get to be called a man.

Big Bill's stanza signifies American meaning embedded in rocky places. Archaeology employs tropological energy to decode such meaning. In the foreground it places voices raised at the margin of civilization, at the very edge of the New World wilderness:

The first time I met the blues, mama, they came walking
  through the woods,
The first time I met the blues, baby, they came walking
  through the woods,
They stopped at my house first, mama, and done me all
  the harm they could.

Little Brother Montgomery's stanza implies harm's unequivocal conquest by a blues voice rising. From piney woods, sagging cabins, and settling levees vernacular tones rise, singing a different America. Archaeology foregrounds and deciphers this song, and when its work is finished what remains is not history as such, but a refigured knowledge. Louis Althusser makes explicit the distinction between history as such *and* historical knowledge.

> *We should have no illusions as to the incredible force of that prejudice, which still dominates us all, which is the very essence of contemporary historicity, and which attempts to make us confuse the object of knowledge with the real object, by affecting the object of knowledge with the very "qualities" of the real object of which it is knowledge. The knowledge of history is no more historical than the knowledge of sugar is sweet.*

The result of archaeology's endeavors is: "A mood blared by trumpets, trombones, saxophones and drums, a song with turgid, inadequate words." The song is a sign of an Afro-American discourse that strikingly refigures life on American shores.)

In 1822, Gideon Mantell, an English physician with a consuming interest in geology and paleontology, made a routine house call in Sussex.[1] On the visit, he discovered a fossilized tooth that seemed to be a vestige of a giant, herbivorous reptile. Since he had nothing in his own collection that was like his find, he traveled to the Hunterian Collection of the Royal College of Surgeons in London and spent hours searching drawers of fossil teeth attempting to find a comparable specimen. When he had nearly exhausted the possibilities, a young man who was also working at the Hunterian and who had heard of the Sussex physician's quest, presented him with the tooth of an iguana. The match was nearly perfect. On the basis of the similarity between the tooth of the living iguana and his own fossil discovery, Mantell named the bearer of the older tooth "Iguanodon" ("iguana tooth"). In 1825, his paper "Notice on the *Iguanodon,* a Newly-Discovered Fossil Reptile From the Sandstone of Tilgate Forest, in Sussex" appeared in the *Philosophical Transactions* of the Royal Society in London.

As the nineteenth century progressed and the fossil record expanded, it became apparent that Iguanodon was but one member of a family of reptiles that, in 1841, received the name "dinosaur" from Sir Richard Owen. By midcentury, it was possible to construct a feasible model of Iguanodon. Available evidence (including assumed homologies with living animals) indicated that the prehistoric creature was a giant, quadripedal reptile with a small triangular spike on his nose. The concrete and plaster model that was built on this plan in 1854 can be seen in England today.

The story of Iguanodon does not conclude at midcentury, however. The fossil record was substantially augmented later in the century by a splendid find of Iguanodon fossils at Bernissart, Belgium. Louis Dollo, the French paleontologist who oversaw the Bernissart site, was able to revise all existing models. Through cross-skeletal comparison and etho-logical inference, he concluded that Iguanodon was, in fact, bipedal. Moreover, he persuasively demonstrated that the triangular bone that had been taken for a nose spike was actually a horny thumb spike peculiar to dinosaurs.

The mode of thought implied by the Iguanodon example is similar to the mode of descriptive analysis designated by Michel Foucault the "archaeology of knowledge."[2] Foucault writes of his project: "[the 'ar-chaeology of knowledge'] does not imply the search for a beginning; it does not relate analysis to geological excavation. It designates the gen-eral theme of a description that questions the already-said [i.e., a family of concepts] at the level of its existence" (p. 131). He defines a family of concepts as a *discourse* (e.g. medicine, natural history, economics).

Explanatory models for any family of concepts, he insists, must be based on an analysis of its primary conceptual structures – what he terms the discourse's "governing statements."

> Archaeology, may . . . constitute the tree of derivation of a discourse. It will place at the root, as *governing statements,* those that concern the definition of observable structures and the field of possible objects, those that prescribe the forms of description and the perceptual codes that it can use, those that reveal the most general possibilities of characterization, and thus open up a whole domain of concepts to be constructed, and, lastly, those that, while constituting a strategic choice, leave room for the greatest number of subsequent options. (p. 147)

To survey the discursive family of "American history" from this perspective is to discover certain primary linguistic functions that serve as governing statements. "Religious man," "wilderness," "migratory errand," "increase in store," and "New Jerusalem" are prescriptive structures of a traditional American history.[3] "Religious man" signals a devout believer in God for whom matters of economics and wealth are minimal considerations. "Wilderness" refers to a savage territory de-void of human beings and institutions. "Migratory errand" announces a singular mission bestowed by God on religious man, prompting him to sail the Atlantic and settle the wilderness. The "New Jerusalem" is the promised end of the errand; it is the prospective city of God on earth. It represents the transformation of the wilderness into a community of believers who interpret an "increase in store" as secular evidence of an abiding spiritual faithfulness.

The graphics of most school history texts – with their portrayals of Pilgrims landing on bleak and barren New World shores and a subsequent "increase in store" and Thanksgiving – offer ample representations of these primary structures. The mode of dress, physiognomy, and bearing of the figures in the foreground of such graphics declare seventeenth-century European man as the epitome of religious man. Generally in such pictures non-Europeans are savagely clad, merging with the wilderness. The written accounts from which such graphics derive establish quite explicit boundaries of what might be called "ethnic exclusion." Describing the Pilgrims' arrival in the wilderness, William Bradford writes: "It is recorded in Scripture as a mercy to the Apostle and his shipwrecked company, that the barbarians showed them no small kindness in refreshing them, but these savage barbarians [Native Americans], when they met them . . . were readier to fill their sides full of arrows than otherwise."[4]

Traditional American literary history can be thought of as a branch of American history. As a kindred body of concepts, it reflects its parentage by reading the key statements of the larger discourse onto the ancestry of literary works of art. The texts included in Robert Spiller's influential model of American literary history,[5] for example, are arranged and explained in terms of an immigration-and-development pattern of events. And in a recent essay,[6] Spiller clearly implies that his literary-historical model, like the discursive family of which it forms a branch, is characterized by boundaries of ethnic exclusion:

> We can . . . distinguish three kinds of ethnic groups which were not parts of the main frontier movement. These are the immigrant groups which came to this country comparatively late; the blacks who were brought to this country under special circumstances; and the Jews who in all their history have mingled with, but rarely become totally absorbed into, any alien culture. All three are of great importance to the American identity today as expressed in its ever-changing literature, but only immigrations from European countries other than Great Britain followed a course close enough to our model to suggest inclusion here, even though the remarkable achievements of the Jews and the blacks in contemporary American literature suggest that – given a slightly different model – their

contributions to our culture would lend themselves to similar analyses. (p. 15)

If one were to produce a graphic representation of the literary history implied by this quotation, it would consist of a European author in the foreground (or a succession of such authors) turning out ever more sophisticated works of art. This "basic evolutionary development" (p. 15) is equivalent to the larger historical discourse's notion of European, or Euro-American, progress toward New Jerusalem. Within the larger discourse, God's plan is assumed to reveal (and, ultimately, to fulfill) itself only through the endeavors of religious, European men.[7] And just as such men are considered true builders of the New Jerusalem, so, too, they are considered exclusive chroniclers of their achievements in the evolutionary phases of an American national literature.

The exclusionist tendencies of Spiller are reinforced by the work of Cleanth Brooks, R. W. B. Lewis, and Robert Penn Warren in their giant anthology entitled *American Literature: The Makers and the Making*.[8] In an introductory "Letter to the Reader," the editors write:

> Since this book is, among other things, a history, it is only natural that its organization should be, in the main, chronological. But it is not strictly so; other considerations inevitably cross-hatch pure chronology. We have mentioned the two sections on southern writing, which overlap periods treated elsewhere. Similarly, the two sections on black literature together span many decades, for like Faulkner and other white southern writers, black writers in America, whether of the North or the South, have worked in terms of a special condition and cultural context. (p. xix)

In short, any verbal creativity that lies outside traditional, orthodox patterns of a spiritually evolving American literature is merely a shadow ("cross-hatch") on national history and literary history conceived as determinate "chronologies."

The "special condition and cultural context" of the editors' introductory "Letter" echo Spiller's "special circumstances." Brooks, Lewis, and Warren, like Spiller, begin with the Puritans and trace an evolutionary progression. But unlike Spiller, they find it necessary to ensure that shadows on an exalted past are not mistaken for acts of authentic literary creativity. "Literature of the Nonliterary World" is the title they provide for the concluding section of the first volume of their anthology. The section includes: David Walker, Frederick Douglass, Frederick Law Olmsted, "Folk Songs of the White People," Indian Oratory, "Folk Songs of the Black People," non-Puritan historians, southwest humorists, Abraham Lincoln, Davy Crockett, and so on. On the basis of definitions supplied by the editors, one must suppose that inclusions in this *category of the excluded* exist somewhere between secondary literature and *non*literature (p. xxi). The editors' definitions obviously conserve a Spiller orthodoxy.

When the discourses and practices contemporary with American history are brought to bear on this orthodoxy, the religious orientation, sites, and authorities are subject, like the Iguanodon, to radical reinterpretation. The savage barbarians of Bradford's earlier-cited passage manifest themselves not as scriptural reprobates but as negative functions of an ideology that classified European man as the acme of being. Similar revisions apply to both "religious man" and "increase in store." Euro-Americans who engaged in the transatlantic slave trade maintained a favorable balance of trade (both economic and spiritual) by defining Africans whom they loaded into ships' holds not only as heathens to be transported to Occidental salvation, but also as property, bullion, or real wealth. Africans thus deported from their homeland to the New World became, in a bizarre logic, spiritual revenue.[9] As West Indian author George Lamming puts it:

> The Americans took pleasure in their past because they were descended from men whose migration was a freely chosen act. They were descended from a history that was recorded, a history which was wholly contained in their own way of looking at the world . . . [but the history of African-descended black people] was a commercial deportation.[10]

"Commercial deportation" thus offers a new governing structure – one that dramatically alters the traditional discourse. The statement first signifies an involuntary transport of *human beings* as opposed to the export or import of will-less merchandise. And instead of bleak and barren beginnings on New World shores yet to be civilized, the history signified by commercial deportation implies European man as slave trader, divider of established civilizations, dealer in "hides of Fellatah/ Mandingo, Ibo, Kru."[11] The transportable stock on American vessels is no longer figured as a body of courageous Pilgrims, but as: "black gold" (p. 65). And providential history reveals itself as a spiritual discourse coextensive with economic practices of men who turned the middle passage to profit (p. 65).

The graphics accompanying this alternative historical formation are strikingly different from those accompanying traditional accounts. They evoke Armageddon rather than New Jerusalem.[12] And the shift effected by the governing structure "commercial deportation" opens the way for a corollary shift in perspective on "American literary history." What comes starkly to the foreground is the possibility of a new Afro-American historical and literary-historical discourse. That possibility is a function not only of an enlarged perspective, but also of the "method" of history itself. For if historical method consists in cataloguing elements, then all histories are, theoretically, open-ended – the possible inclusions, limitless. In practice, histories are always limited by ideology. Catalogues are constituted through principles of selection – on the basis of ideologies. In other words, a history is an ideologically governed catalogue of figurative elements. And a shift, or rupture, in ideological premises promotes strikingly new figurations.

The ideological orientation brought to the foreground under the prospect of the archaeology of knowledge is neither a vulgar Marxism nor a new "positivism." What I am interested in is a form of thought that grounds Afro-American discourse in concrete, historical situation. I hope to outline here a type of dialectical understanding that views a determinant ideology as something akin to Thomas Kuhn's "paradigm." Where Afro-American narratives derived from "commercial deportation" are concerned, the model that seems best suited to an analysis is not only an economic one but also one based on literary considerations. Let me call this ideological frame of reference the "economics of slavery." The phrase "economics of slavery," like "commercial deportation," stands as a governing statement in Afro-American discourse. In specifically Afro-American terms, the "economics of slavery" signifies the social system of the Old South that determined what, how, and for whom goods were produced to satisfy human wants. Now, the monographic histories of slavery reveal that this system evolved very differently in the Old South from the way it evolved in the Caribbean, and that, in each place, it involved a different dimension of experience. I propose here, however, that it is possible to telescope these dimensions, and to reveal others through a vertical, associative, metaphorical decoding of the phrase. Thus the diachrony of traditional historiography is complemented by a nonsuccessive, synchronic prospect. Hayden White defines this as a process of "tropological" understanding[13] – a discursive mode that employs unfamiliar terms to qualify what in a given discourse is considered traditional. It constitutes an effort to incorporate into "reality" phenomena that are generally refused the status "real," so as to alter "reality" itself. The end of such an enterprise is to release us from a tyranny of conceptual overdeterminations by the conscious employment of metaphor. Let me illustrate this briefly by surveying several representative images of Afro-American dwellings in terms of the "economics of slavery."

Africans aboard a slaver. (From Daniel P. Mannix and Malcolm Cowley: *A History of the Atlantic Slave Trade, 1518–1865.* New York: Viking, 1972.)

Inspection and sale of slaves. (From Malcolm Cowley, ed.: *Adventures of an African Slaver: Being a True Account of the Life of Captain Theodore Canot.* Garden City, New York: Garden City Publishing Company, 1928.)

In the Old South, according to John Blassingame, "The slaves often complained bitterly about what their masters described as 'adequate' housing. Most of the [slave] autobiographers reported that they lived in crudely built one-room log cabins with dirt floors and too many cracks in them to permit much comfort during the winter months."[14] After his own critical observation on the "size and arrangements" of a people's dwellings in *The Souls of Black Folk*, W. E. B. DuBois goes on to describe "Negro homes" in the "black belt" of Georgia at the turn of the century:

> All over the face of the land is the one-room cabin, –now standing in the shadow of the Big House, now staring at the dusty road, now rising dark and sombre amid the green of the cotton-fields. It is nearly always old and bare, built of rough boards and neither plastered nor ceiled.[15]

And a report on American working conditions in the late 1920s describes a black logging camp as follows: "Across the railroad track from the depot and company store were about one-hundred shacks for Negro workers. These are one room with a window at one end–not always glass but with a wood flap to let down."[16] I would suggest that the scant diachronic modification in "size and arrangements" of black dwellings allows them to stand as *signs* for the continuing impoverishment of blacks in the United States.

The places that Africans in America have lived (and continue to live) signify the "economics of slavery." An "army-style barracks" formed the home of Horace Taft of Philadelphia, for example, while he was in North Carolina engaged in an experience that he describes as follows:

> It was real slavery-time work I did down there. My first week's salary was $3. That was a week's pay. They kept all the rest. It was just horrible, the things I seen at those camps. I seen men beat with rubber hoses. I seen a woman beat. There was always someone guarding and watching you. You couldn't get away because they were sitting out there with guns.

Taft was kidnapped into a "migrant stream" of slave labor in 1979.

Yet, the dwellings of Africans in America cannot be confined exclusively to an economic signification. The nonmonetary, "mythical" dimensions that arise from the "size and arrangements" of black homes are supplied by a black expressiveness we have come to know as "the blues." Samuel Charters provides the following bleak description of a dwelling outside Brownsville, Tennessee:

About a mile and a half from the turnoff into Brownsville there is a sagging red cabin, the bare patch of, ground in front is littered with bits of clothing, dirty dishes, a broken chair. . . . The cabin has two rooms; one of them empty except for a few rags that lie in the filth of the floor. . . . In the other room is a chair, a rusted wood stove, and two dirty, unmade beds. In the heat of a summer afternoon it looks like the other empty buildings scattered along Winfield Lane.[17]

This sagging cabin is like all such dwellings in its dilapidatedness and overcrowding (a man, his wife, and five children inhabit it); but what we are presented with in Charter's passage is identity in difference. For the "sagging red cabin" is the home of Sleepy John Estes, one of the greatest of the traditional blues singers. The blues thereby serves to modify, ameliorate, order, and qualify the cabin's bleak "size and arrangements." John Estes's song arises from a "slave community" and it is fittingly designated as "blues."

The major mode of Afro-American literary discourse is the slave narrative. Appearing in England and America during the eighteenth and nineteenth centuries, the thousands of narratives produced by Africans in England and by fugitive slaves and freed black men and women in America constitute the first, literate manifestations of a tragic disruption in African cultural homogeneity. When the author of *The Life of Olaudah Equiano, or Gustavus Vassa, the African. Written by Himself* (1789) arrived at the African coast in the hands of his kidnappers, he had left behind the communal, familial ways sanctioned by his native village of Essaka in the province of Benin.[18] The last family member he embraces is a sister kidnapped in the same slave-trading raid that left him captive. His sibling serves as sign and source of familial, female love. And the nature of the final meeting is emblematic of the separations that a "commercial deportation" effected in the lives of Africans: "When these people [Africans carrying Vassa and his sister to the coast] knew we were brother and sister, they indulged us to be together; and the man, to whom I suppose we belonged, lay with us, he in the middle, while she and I held one another by the hands across his breast all night; and thus for a while we forgot our misfortunes, in the joy of being together" (p. 24). The phrase, "The man, to whom I supposed we belonged," signals a loss of self-possession. The man's position "in the middle" signals a corollary loss of familial (and, by implication, conjugal) relations. But the full import of loss comes to the African in a moment of terror, when, arrived at the coast, he encounters the full, objective reality of his commercially deportable status:

> The first object which saluted my eyes when I arrived on the coast, was the sea, and a *slave* ship, which was then riding at anchor, and waiting for its *cargo*. These filled me with astonishment, which was soon converted into terror, when I was carried on board. I was immediately handled, and tossed up to see if I were sound, by some of the crew; and I was now persuaded that I had gotten into a world of bad spirits, and that they were going to kill me. . . . When I looked round the ship too, and saw a large furnace of copper *boiling,* and a multitude of *black people* of every description *chained* together, every one of their countenances expressing dejection and sorrow, I no longer doubted my fate; and, quite overpowered with horror and anguish, I fell motionless on the deck and fainted. (My emphasis, p. 27)

His description captures, in graphic detail, the peremptory consignment of the African, chained body and soul, to the boiling hell of mercantilism.

At one interpretive level, the remainder of *The Life of Olaudah Equiano* is the story of a Christian convert who finds solace from bondage in the ministerings of a kind Providence. The Christian-missionary and civilizing effects of the slave trade that were so much vaunted by Europeans find an exemplary instance in the narrator's portrait of himself after a short sojourn in England: "I could now speak English tolerably well, and I perfectly understood everything that was said. . . . I no longer looked upon [Englishmen] as spirits, but as men superior to us [Africans]; and therefore I had the stronger desire to resemble them, to imbibe their spirit, and imitate their manners" (p. 48). Through the kindly instructions of "the Miss Guerins," Englishwomen who are friends of his master, the young Vassa learns to read and write. He is also baptized and received into St. Margaret's Church, Westminster, in February 1759 (p. 49). As a civilized, Christian subject, he is able to survive with equanimity the vagaries of servitude, the whims of fortune, and the cruelties of fate. After his manumission, he searches earnestly for the true, guiding light of salvation and achieves (in chapter 10) confirmation of his personal salvation in a vision of the crucified Christ:

> On the morning of the 6th October [1774], all that day, I thought I should either see or hear something supernatural. I

had a secret impulse on my mind of something that was to take place. . . . In the evening of the same day . . . the Lord was pleased to break in upon my soul with his bright beams of heavenly light; and in that instant, as it were, removing the veil, and letting light into a dark place, I saw clearly with an eye of faith, the crucified Saviour bleeding on the cross on Mount Calvary; the scriptures became an unsealed book. . . . Now every leading providential circumstance that happened to me, from the day I was taken from my parents to that hour, was then in my view, as if it had just occurred. I was sensible of the invisible hand of God, which guided and protected me, when in truth I knew it not. (Pp. 149–50)

The foregoing passage from *The Life* represents what might be termed the African's awakening and liberation from his coerced state of slavery. To the extent that the narrative reinforces a providential interpretation, the work seems coextensive with an "old" literary history that claims Africans as spiritual cargo delivered (under "special circumstances") unto God Himself.

If, however, one returns for a moment to the conditions of disruption that begin the narrator's passage into slavery, if one considers the truly "commercial" aspects of his deportation, a quite different perspective emerges. Further, an ideological analysis grounded in the economics (as opposed to the European-derived "ethics") of slavery allows us to perceive a quite different *awakening* on the part of the African. For the fact is that Vassa's status as "transportable property" is mediated as much by his canny mercantilism as by his pious toiling in the vineyards of Anglicanism. *The Life of Olaudah Equiano,* that is, considered in ideological terms, can be seen not only as a work whose protagonist masters the rudiments of economics that condition his life, but also as a narrative whose author creates a text that inscribes those very economics as a sign of its "social grounding." *The Life,* therefore, is less a passive "mirroring" of providential ascent than it is a literary work, or cultural object, that, in Fredric Jameson's phrase, "brings into being that situation to which it is also, at one and the same time, a reaction."[19] If there is a "new," or different, historical subtext distinguishing Vassa's narrative from traditional discourse, that subtext is in part a symbolic "invention" of the narrative itself. It is a text that becomes discernible only under an analysis that explores the relationship between *The Life* and the economics of slavery.

After a year's labor for Mr. Robert King, his new owner, Vassa writes: "I became very useful to my master, and saved him, as he used to acknowledge, above a hundred pounds a year" (p. 73). Thus begins a process of self-conscious, mercantile self-evaluation – that is, a meditation on the economics of African, or New World, black selfhood – that continues for the next two chapters of *The Life*. "I have sometimes heard it asserted," Vassa continues,

> that a negro cannot earn his master the first cost; but nothing can be further from the truth. . . . I have known many slaves whose masters would not take a thousand pounds current for them. . . . My master was several times offered, by different gentlemen, one hundred guineas for me, but he always told them he would not sell me, to my great joy. (p. 73)

These assertions of chapter 5 seem far more appropriate for a trader's secular diary than a devout acolyte's conversion journal.

Having gained the post of shipboard assistant, or "mate," to Captain Thomas Farmer, an Englishman who sails a Bermuda sloop for his new master, Vassa immediately thinks that he "might in time stand some chance by being on board to get a little money, or possibly make my escape if I should be used ill" (p. 83). This conflation of getting "a little money" and finding freedom sets the terms of narrative experience that lead to the African's receipt of a certificate of manumission in chapter 7. Describing his initial attempts at mercantilism, the narrator writes in ledgerlike detail:

> After I had been sailing for some time with this captain [Mr. Farmer], at length I endeavored to try my luck, and commence merchant. I had but very small capital to begin with; for one single half bit, which is equal to three pence in England, made up my whole stock. However, I trusted to the Lord to be with me; and at one of our trips to St. Eustatius, a Dutch island, I bought a glass tumbler with my half bit, and when I came to Montserrat, I sold it for a bit, or sixpence. Luckily we made several successive trips to St. Eustatius (which was a general mart for the West Indies, about twenty leagues from Montserrat), and in our next, finding my tumbler so profitable, with this one bit I bought two tumblers more; and when I came back, I sold them for two bits equal to a shilling sterling. When we went again, I bought with these two bits four more of these glasses, which I sold for four bits on our return to Montserrat. And in our next voyage to St. Eustatius, I bought two glasses with one bit, and with the other three I bought a jug of Geneva, nearly about three pints in measure. When we came to

Montserrat, I sold the gin for eight bits, and the tumblers for two, so that my capital now amounted in all to a dollar, well husbanded and acquired in space of a month or six weeks, when I blessed the Lord that I was so rich. (p. 84)

The ironies are manifold. Rather than a spiritual multiplication of "talents" the slave, on shipboard as "mate," selects transactions from his ledger and transcribes them, like any merchant autobiographer, into a narrative of his adventures. The pure product of trade (i.e., transportable property, chattel) has become the trader, with a well-husbanded store! Amid the lawless savagery visited upon blacks in the West Indies, Vassa calmly resolves to earn his freedom "by honest and honorable [read: mercantile] means" (p. 87). In order to achieve this end he redoubles his commercial efforts.

In its middle section, *The Life* almost entirely brackets the fact that a mercantile self's trans-Caribbean profit-making is a function of an egregious trade in slaves between the West Indies and South Carolina and Georgia. Having been reduced to *property* by a "commercial deportation," Vassa concludes during his West Indian captivity that neither sentiment nor spiritual sympathies can earn his liberation. He realizes, in effect, that only the *acquisition of property* will enable him to alter his designated status *as property*. With the blessings of his master, he sets out to make "money enough . . . to *purchase my freedom* . . . for forty pounds sterling money, which was only the same price he [Mr. King] gave for me" (my emphasis, pp. 93–94).By chapter 7, the slave's commercial venture is complete. Having entered the "West India trade," he has obtained "about forty-seven pounds." He offers the entire sum to Mr King, who "said he would not be worse than his promise; and taking the money, told me to go to the Secretary at the Register Office, and get my manumission drawn up" (pp. 101–102). Thus the West Indian slaveholder substitutes *one form of capital for another*. Presumably the merchant overcomes his initial reluctance to honor his promise by realizing that his "investment in black bodies" can be transformed easily enough into other forms of enterprise.

On Vassa's part, this entails a dramatic shift of voice – a shift that actually begins (in chapter 5), when he carefully transcribes his certificate of manumission. The certificate is, in effect, an economic sign that competes with and radically qualifies the ethical piousness of its enfolding text. The inscribed document is a token of mastery, signifying its recipient's successful negotiation of a deplorable system of exchange. The narrator of *The Life* (as distinguished from the author) is aware of both positive and negative implications of his certificate, and he self-consciously prevents his audience from bracketing his achievement of manumission as merely an act of virtuous perseverance in the face of adversity. "As the form of my manumission has something peculiar in it, and expresses the absolute power and dominion one man claims over his fellow, I shall beg leave to present it before my readers at full length" (p. 103).

The document – which grants to "the said Gustavus Vassa, all right, title, dominion, sovereignty, and property" that his "lord and master" Mr. King holds over him – signals the ironic transformation of property by property into humanity. Chattel has transformed itself into freeman through exchange of forty pounds sterling. The slave equates his elation on receiving freedom to the joys of conquering heroes, or to the contentment of mothers who have regained a "long lost infant," or to the gladness of the lover who once again embraces the mistress "ravished from his arms" or the "weary hungry mariner at the sight of the desired friendly port." (p. 103).

Two frames of mind are implied by the transcription of the certificate and the freeman's response. First, the narrator recognizes that the journey's end (i.e., the mariner's achievement of port) signaled by manumission provides enabling conditions for the kind of happy familial relations that seemed irrevocably lost with his departure from his sister. At the same time, he is aware that the evil of the economics he has "navigated" separated him from such relationships in the first instance. However, this seems to inspire no ambivalence in the *author* of *The Life of Olaudah Equiano*. For the structure of the text appears to reflect the author's conviction that it is absolutely necessary for the slave to negotiate the economics of slavery if he would be free. The mercantile endeavors of the autobiographical self in *The Life* occupy the very center of the narrative. Chapters 5, 6, and 7 mark an economic middle passage in a twelve-chapter account. They represent an active, inversive, ironically mercantile ascent by the propertied self from the hell of "commercial deportation." They are a graphic "reinvention" of the social grounding of the Afro-American symbolic act par excellence. For although they constitute a vivid delineation of the true character of Afro-America's historical origins in a slave economics, they also implicitly acknowledge that such economics *must be mastered* before liberation can be secured.

Ultimately it is Vassa's adept mercantilism that produces the conflation of a "theory" of trade, an abolitionist appeal, and a statement of conjugal union that conclude *The Life of Olaudah Equiano*. After attesting that "the manufactures of this country must and will, in the nature and reason of things, have a full and constant employ, by supplying the

African markets" (p. 190), the narrator depicts the commercial utopia that will result when the slave trade is abolished and a free mercantile commerce is established in which African raw materials are exchanged for British manufacture. The abolitionist intent of this "theory" of future commercial relationship is apparent. Equally apparent is the appeal for an economics of freedom that will produce a humane world in which slavery will be displaced by productive commerce. The African who successfully negotiaties his way through the dread exchanges of bondage to the type of expressive posture characterizing *The Life's* conclusion is surely a man who has *repossessed* himself and, hence, achieved the ability to reunite a severed African humanity.

The entire process is epitomized in the penultimate paragraph of Vassa's work. "I remained in London till I heard the debate in the House of Commons on the slave trade, April the 2nd and 3rd. I then went to Soham in Cambridgeshire, and was married on the 7th of April to Miss Cullen, daughter of James and Ann Cullen, late of Ely" (p. 192). The free, public African man, adept at the economics of his era, participating in the liberation of his people, and joined, with self-possessed calmness, in marriage – it is a signal image in a discourse born in "commercial deportation" and bred upon an "economics of slavery."

The ideological analysis I have applied to *The Life of Olaudah Equiano* has important implications for practical criticism because it discovers the social grounding of any genuinely Afro-American narrative. My claim here is that all Afro-American creativity is conditioned by (and part of) a historical discourse that privileges certain economic terms. The creative individual (the *black subject*) must perforce come to terms with "commercial deportation" and the "economics of slavery." His or her very inclusion in an *Afro-American* traditional discourse is contingent on an encounter with such priviliged economic signs. This is not to say, of course, that a randomly chosen black narrative will automatically confirm the well-worn notions about the relation between means of production and general cultural consciousness. My point is not that commerce determines consciousness. It is rather that ideological analysis yields certain recurrent, discursive patterns that in turn reveal a unified economic grounding for Afro-American narratives. Thus the locus classicus for the entire genre of slave narrative, the *Narrative of the Life of Frederick Douglass, An American Slave. Written by Himself* (1845), reads, ideologically, like a palimpsest of Vassa's "traditional" account.[20] Douglass's work, that is, constitutes a manuscript where the "already said" is clearly visible. Were it superimposed on Vassa's work, it would trace the eighteenth-century African's economic topography in all major details.

"My mother and I were separated when I was but an infant–before I knew her as my mother," writes Douglass's narrator (p. 22). "It is a common custom," he continues, "in the part of Maryland from which I ran away, to part children from their mothers at an early age. . . . I do not recollect of ever seeing my mother by the light of day. She was with me in the night. She would lie down with me, and get me to sleep, but long before I waked she was gone." The disruption of black familial relations signaled by the narrator's separation from his mother is equivalent to Vassa's kidnapping and severance from his sister. Douglass's narrator further announces that "it was rumored that my master [Captain Anthony] was my father," and he goes on to condemn unequivocally the "wicked desires," "lust," and "cunning" of slave-owners, traits that enable them to sustain a "double relation of master and father" to their mulatto children (p. 23).

These assertions of the *Narrative* in effect recapitulate the "man in the middle" first encountered in Vassa's account. In both narratives, the effect of "owners" destroying Afro-American familial bonds (mother–infant, lover–beloved) is forcefully represented. In a world where people are *property*, separation (physical and emotional) is the norm. The lengths to which the "man in the middle" will go to reinforce such norms is indicated not only by Vassa's account of the treatment of African women on trading sloops, but by Douglass's account of his Aunt Hester's fate:

> Aunt Hester went out one night–where or for what I do not know–and happened to be absent when my master desired her presence. He had ordered her not to go out evenings, and warned her that she must never let him catch her in company with a young man, who was paying attention to her belonging to Colonel Lloyd. The young man's name was Ned Roberts, generally called Lloyd's Ned. Why master was so careful of her, may be safely left to conjecture. (p. 24)

Discovering that Hester has, indeed, been in the company of Ned during her absence, the white owner strips her to the waist, binds her to a hook in the joist of the house, and flogs her until she is bloody. "I was so terrified and horror-stricken at the sight," Douglass reports, "that I hid myself in a closet, and dared not venture out" (p. 26).

The decisive delivery of the Afro-American into slavery takes place, however–as did Vassa's transport–by water. The "commercial deportation" of Douglass occurs when the young boy travels on the trading sloop *Sally Lloyd* to Baltimore to serve in the household of Mr. Hugh Auld. On the day that he is transported, the sloop, which normally transports tobacco, corn, and wheat (p. 27), carries "a large flock of sheep" bound for slaughter at "the slaughterhouse of Mr. Curtis on Louden Slater's Hill" (p. 46). The irrevocable break with beginnings, the helplessness of the young boy to determine his own destiny, the cargo status that marks his passage, and his immediately favorable response to the wonders of an alien world of experience – in all essentials the *Narrative* recalls Vassa's work.

A few pages after his account of a terrified response to the slave ship, Vassa describes his arrival at Barbados: "We were conducted immediately to the merchant's yard, where we were all pent together, like so many sheep in a fold, without regard to sex or age. As every object was new to me, everything I saw filled me with surprise" (p. 32). The mixed sense of powerlessness and inquisitive suspense foreshadows Douglass's reaction to Annapolis fifty years later: "It was the first large town that I had ever seen, and though it would look small compared with some of our New England factory villages, I thought it a wonderful place for its size – more imposing even than the Great House Farm!"(p. 46). Douglass's response also suggests a telling contrast between agrarian and industrial modes of existence. The capital of an industrially primitive southern slave state is less impressive than (in words that could only belong to a traveled narrator) some of "our New England factory villages." Vassa leaves an agrarian life devoid of "mechanics" (p. 27) only to encounter on shipboard the wonders of the quadrant, a world of "mechanical" invention at the farm of his first Virginia master, and, finally, the captains of industry of his day to whom the concluding remarks of his narrative are directed. Similarly, Douglass moves progressively beyond an agricultural landscape where slavery is omnipotent to the freedom of the "New England factory village." Mediating the progress of both narrators toward the economic sophistication implied by their privileging of industrial norms is their urban experience.

London, for Vassa, represents the most desirable mode of existence. The residents of the English metropole represent for the African occasions for understanding and self-improvement that he feels are available nowhere else. He even rejects, for example, an opportunity while at Guadeloupe to escape slavery because the fleet in which he would have served as a seaman is bound not for England but for "old France" (pp. 90–91). It is among Englishmen in London that Vassa comes to realize the "superiority" of Europeans to Africans and receives the kindly instructions of the Misses Guerin. Douglass's feelings toward Baltimore are scarcely as affectionate; still, the nineteenth-century author writes:

"Going to live at Baltimore laid the foundation, and opened the gateway, to all my subsequent prosperity" (pp. 46–47). And it is in Baltimore that Douglass (as does Vassa in London) discovers the "displaced" maternity of a kindly white womanhood. The familial affections blunted by the "man in the middle" in the feudal regions of slavery, find their rejuvenation in the ministrations of white urban women.

The women in both the *Narrative* and *The Life of Olaudah Equiano* are represented as examples of the best evangelical-missionary impulses of their day, fit vehicles for a kind Providence. Hence, in both cases, there is a convergence of literacy (through the white women's instructions) and Christianity (through the white women's desire to render such instruction.) An early result of Vassa's interaction with the Guerins is his baptism. Douglass ascribes his interactions with Sophia Auld to "divine Providence" (p. 47), but describes these interactions in Old Testament terms (p. 47).

Reflecting the slave's mastery of Christian instruction and comprehension of the ironies of his enslaved situation, Douglass represents his relationship with Sophia Auld as a symbolic inversion of the Fall of Man. On first view, the calm of the Auld household marked by "a white face beaming with the most kindly emotions" is disrupted by the entry of the slave (as serpent?). The slave's presence seems to convert the Edenic calm into a domain of "tiger-like fierceness" and calculated deception. Discovering that his wife has begun to instruct Douglass, Hugh Auld severely reprimands Sophia, prohibits future instructions, and lectures her on slaves and education. But in fact it is not the entry of the slave that precipitates Sophia's transformation. For if she stands in the role of Eve, it is in fact *the slave* who is her Adam, the subject of her providentially ordained instruction. The snake in this garden is Mr. Auld, who appears, ironically, in the guise of a chastising God rebuking the sinful "children."

In effect, Auld convicts himself as Satan, the old serpent successfully tempting Eve to perceive the Tree of Life (the bestowal of a *humanizing* instruction) as an interdicted Tree of Knowledge. Douglass listens with fascination. The *Narrative* portrays him in his encounter "in the garden" as a pristine innocent, amazed at the devious ways of the world. The words of Auld-as-serpent become for the narrator – in an enfoldingly ironic series of inversions – a "new and special revelation" of the source of slaveholders' power. Auld's words, like Providential instruction, lead the slave to realize that this is no Eden of urban benevolence, but a false paradise of white repression. He thus sets out to discover the true path to freedom. Like an allegorical pilgrim, he rejects soul-destroying ignorance and proceeds "with high hope, and a fixed purpose, at whatever cost or trouble, to learn how to read" (p. 49).

The symbolic inversion of the Fall attests the slave's mastery as a "reader." He refuses the role of hapless victim of texts (the slave-master's "false" moral rhetoric) and becomes instead an astute interpreter and creator of texts of his own. Hence, though Baltimore like Vassa's London bestows a traditional literacy and Christianity, Douglass's acquired skills *as reader* enable him to provide his own figurations. His ability ultimately results in a tension between two voices in the *Narrative*. The tones of a biblically oriented moral suasion eventually compete with the cadences of a secularly oriented economic voice.

This bifurcation of voices parallels the duality I have noted in *The Life of Olaudah Equiano*. One autobiographical self in the *Narrative* follows a developmental history that leads from Christian enlightenment, to the establishment of Sabbath schools for fellow slaves, to a career of messianic service on behalf of abolitionism. Of his address to a predominantly white audience at an abolitionist convention in Nantucket, Douglass says: "It was a severe cross, and I took it up reluctantly" (p. 119). The other self in the *Narrative,* one that contrasts with the cross-bearing pilgrim, follows a course dictated by the economics of slavery. It is this second, literate, secular self who produces inversions of received scripture such as that noted in the Auld encounter. It expresses itself sotto voce, subtextually, and, in a sense, "after the fact." It provides economic coding for what, on casual first view, appear simple descriptions in the service of moral suasion.

Let me illustrate the nature of that voice by returning for a moment to the first three chapters of the *Narrative*, where Douglass describes the wealthy slaveowner Colonel Lloyd's "finely cultivated garden, which afforded almost constant employment for four men, besides the chief gardener, (Mr. M'Durmond)" (p. 33). This garden prefigures the "false" Eden of Auld. Its description is coded in a manner that makes it the most significant economic sign in the initial chapters of the *Narrative*. The entire store of the slaveowner's "Job-like" (p. 35) riches are imaged by the garden, which was "probably the greatest attraction of the place [the Lloyd estate]" (p. 33). Abounding in "fruit of every description," the garden is "quite a temptation to the hungry swarms of boys, as well as the older slaves . . . few of whom had the virtue or the vice to resist it" (p. 33). In a brilliant reversal, this garden and its attendant temptations, a familiar Christian *topos,* images *all* the wealth of the "man in the middle," and serves Douglass as a wholly secular sign of surplus value. In Colonel Lloyd's garden the fruits of slave labor are *all* retained by the master. And any attempts by the slaves to share such fruits are not only dubbed "stealing" but are also "severely" punished. Even so, "the colonel had to resort to all kinds of stratagems [beyond mere flogging] to keep his slaves out of the garden" (p. 33).

The image of vast abundance produced by slaves but denied them through the owner's savagery transforms the garden and its temptations into a purely economic model. The narrator heightens the irony of this economic coding through implicit detailing of the process by which a cultural consciousness is determined *by commerce*. The folkloric aphorism that a single touch of the "tarbrush" defiles the whole is invoked in the *Narrative* as a humorous analogue for Colonel Lloyd's designation of those who are to be denied the fruits of the garden as unworthy. The colonel tars the fence around his garden, and any slave "caught with tar upon his person . . . was severely whipped by the chief gardener" (p. 33). It amounts to a symbolic use of *tar* (a *blackness* so sticky and entangling for American conscience that the Tar Baby story of African provenance has been an enduring cultural transplant) as a mark of deprivation and unworthiness, and Douglass comments: "The slaves became as fearful of tar as of the lash. They seemed to realize the impossibility of touching *tar* without being defiled" (p. 33). Through the *genetic* touch of the tarbrush that makes them "people of color," blacks become "guilty" of the paradoxically labeled "crime" of seeking to enjoy the fruits of their labor.

The "increase in store" of a traditional American history takes on quite other dimensions in this light. The keenly literate and secular self who so figures the economics of Lloyd's garden – summing in the process both the nil financial gain of blacks, and their placement in the left-hand, or debit, column of the ledgers of American status – is the same self encountered when the narrator describes the slaves on Auld's farm: "A great many times have we poor creatures been nearly perishing with hunger, when food in abundance lay mouldering in the safe and smoke-house, and our pious mistress was aware of the fact; and yet mistress and her husband would kneel every morning, and pray that God would bless them in basket and store!" (p. 66).

This is the same secular self, too, that returns as a teenager to southern, agrarian slavery. At the farm of Mr. Edward Covey, where he has been hired out for "breaking," the *Narrative* pictures four enslaved black men fanning wheat. Douglass constitutes one of their number, "carrying wheat to the fan" (p. 77). The sun proves too much for the unacclimatized Douglass, and he collapses, only to be beaten by Mr. Covey for his failure to serve effectively as a "mindless" cog in the machine of slave production. Seeking redress from his master (Auld), who hired him to Covey, Douglass finds that the profit motive drives all before it: "Master Thomas . . . said . . . that he could not think of taking me from . . . [Mr. Covey]; that should he do so, he would lose the whole year's wages" (p. 79).

The most bizzare profit accruing to the owners in the Covey episode, however, is not slave wages but slave offspring. If Colonel Lloyd takes the fruit of the slave's labor, Mr. Covey takes the fruit of the slave's very womb. He puts a black man "to stud" with one of his slave women and proclaims the children of this compelled union his property. This is a confiscation of surplus value with a vengeance! It manifests how aberrant relationships can become under the impress of a southern traffic in human "chattel." At Covey's farm, produce, labor, wages, and profit create a crisis that Douglass must negotiate as best he can. He resolves to fight Mr. Covey, the "man in the middle," physically.

In chapter 10, in contrast to a "resolved" young Douglass, stands Sandy Jenkins, the slave who is not allowed to live with his "free wife." Sandy offers Douglass a folk means of negotiating his crisis at Covey's, providing him with "a certain *root*," which, carried "*always on* . . . [the] *right side,* would render it impossible for Mr. Covey, or any other white man" to whip the slave (p. 80). This displacement of Christian metaphysics by Afro-American "superstition" ultimately denies the efficacy of trusting solely to supernatural aid for relief from slavery.

The root does not work. The physical confrontation does. By fighting, Douglass gains a measure of relief from Covey's harassments. Jenkins's mode of negotiating the economics of slavery, the *Narrative* implies, is not *a man's way,* since the narrator claims that his combat with Covey converted him, ipso facto, into *a man.* At this point, significantly, the text strongly suggests that Sandy is the traitor who reveals the escape plot of Douglass and fellow slaves at Mr. Freeland's estate. Sandy represents the inescapable limits of Afro-American slavery in the South; he is the pure negative product of an economics of slavery. Standing here in clear and monumentally *present* contrast to Douglass, Sandy reveals the virtual impossibility of achieving freedom on the terms implied by the attempted escape from Freeland's.

At its most developed, *southern* extension, the literate-abolitionist self of the *Narrative* engages in an act of physical revolt, forms a Christian brotherhood of fellow slaves through a Sabbath school, and formulates a plan for a *collective* escape from bondage. But this progress toward liberation in the agrarian South is betrayed by one whose mind is "tarred" by the economics of slavery. The possibility of collective freedom is foreclosed by treachery within the slave community. A communally dedicated Douglass ("The work of instructing my dear fellow-slaves was the sweetest engagement with which I was ever blessed" [p. 90]) finds that revolt, religion, and literacy *all* fail. The slave does, indeed, *write* his "own pass" and the passes of his fellows, but the Sabbath-school assembled group is no match for the enemy within.

What recourse, then, is available for the black man who would be free? The *Narrative* answers in an economic voice similar to that found in *The Life of Olaudah Equiano*. Returned to Baltimore and the home of Hugh Auld after a three-year absence, the teenage slave is hired out to "Mr. William Gardner, an extensive shipbuilder in Fell's Point. I was put there to learn how to calk" (p. 99). In a short space, Douglass is able "to command the highest wages given to the most experienced calkers" (p. 103). In lines that echo Vassa with resonant effect, he writes: "I was now of some importance to my master. I was bringing him from six to seven dollars per week. I sometimes brought him nine dollars per week: my wages were a dollar and a half a day" (p. 103). Having entered a world of real *wages,* Douglass sounds much like the Vassa who realized what a small "venture" could produce. And like Vassa, the nineteenth-century slave recognizes that the surplus value his master receives is stolen profit: "I was compelled to deliver every cent of that [money contracted for, earned, and paid for calking] to Master Auld. And why? Not because he earned it . . . but solely because he had the power to compel me to give it up" (p. 104).

Like Vassa, Douglass has arrived at a fully *commercial* view of his situation. He, too, enters into an agreement with his master that eventually results in freedom. Having gained, contractually, the right to hire his own time and to keep a portion of his wages, Douglass eventually converts property, through property, into humanity. Impelled by his commercial endeavors and the opportunities resulting from his *free commerce,* he takes leave of Mr. Auld. He, thus, removes (in his own person) the master's *property* and places it in the ranks of *humanity.* "According to my resolution, on the third day of September, 1838, I left my chains and succeeded in reaching New York" (p. 111). By "stealing away," Douglass not only steals the fruits of his own labor (not unlike the produce of Colonel Lloyd's garden) but also liberates the laborer (the "chattel" who works profitlessly in the garden).

That it is necessary for Douglass to effect his liberation through flight stands as a sign of the intransigence of southern patriarchs. As the young slave knows all too well, Auld cannot possibly conceive of the child of his "family," of the "nigger" fitted out to work for his master's profit, as a mere capital investment. Instead of exchanging capital, therefore, Douglass appropriates his own labor and flees to the camp of those who will eventually battle the Aulds of the South in civil war.

The inscribed document that effectively marks Douglass's liberation in the *Narrative* is, I think, no less an economic sign than Vassa's certificate of manumission:

> This may certify, that I joined together in holy matrimony Frederick Johnson and Anna Murray, as man and wife, in the presence of Mr. David Ruggles and Mrs. Michaels.
>
> James W. C. Pennington
> *New York, Sept.* 15, 1838.

Douglass's certificate of marriage, which he transcribes in full, signifies that the black man has *repossessed* himself in a manner that enables him to enter the type of relationship disrupted, or foreclosed, by the economics of slavery.

Unlike Sandy Jenkins – doomed forever to passive acquiescence and weekend visitation – Douglass enters a relationship that promises a new bonding of Afro-American humanity. As a married man, who understands the necessity for *individual* wage-earning (i.e., a mastery of the incumbencies of the economics of slavery), Douglass makes his way in the company of his new bride to a "New England factory village" where he quickly becomes a laborer at "the first work, the reward of which was to be entirely my own" (p. 116).

In fact, Douglass's representation of New Bedford seems closely akin to the economic, utopian vision that closes Vassa's account: "Everything looked clean, new, and beautiful. I saw few or no dilapidated houses, with poverty-stricken inmates, no half-naked children and bare-footed women, such as I had been accustomed to see in . . . [Maryland]" (p. 116). Ships of the best order and finest size, warehouses stowed to their utmost capacity, and ex-slaves "living in finer houses, and evidently enjoying more of the comforts of life, than the average slaveholders in Maryland" complete the splendid panorama. Such a landscape is gained by free, dignified, and individualistic labor – that is, the New England ideal that so frequently appears in Afro-American narratives. The equivalent vision for Vassa, of course, comprises ships of the finest size and best order plying their transatlantic trade between Africa and England. And presiding over the concluding vision in both narratives is the figure of the black abolitionist spokesman – the man who has arisen, found his "voice," and secured the confidence to address a "general public."

What one experiences in the conclusions of Vassa's and Douglass's narratives, however, is identity with a difference. For the expressive, married, economically astute self at the close of Douglass's work brings together the tensioned voices that mark the various autobiographical postures of the *Narrative* as a whole. The orator we see standing at a Nantucket convention at the close of Douglass's work is immediately to become a *salaried* spokesman, combining literacy, Christianity, and revolutionary zeal in an individual and economically profitable job of work. Douglass's authorship, oratory, and economics converge in the history of the *Narrative*'s publication and the course of action its appearance mandated in the life of the author.

The author's identity and place of residence were revealed in the *Narrative,* and Douglass, who was still a fugitive when his work appeared, was forced to flee to England, where he sold copies of his book for profit, earned lecture fees, and aroused sufficient sympathy and financial support to *purchase* his freedom with solid currency. Although his Garrisonian, abolitionist contemporaries were displeased by Douglass's commercial traffic with slaveholders, the act of purchase was simply the logical (and "traditionally" predictable) end of his negotiation of the economics of slavery.

Here, as elsewhere, I am arguing for the importance of what ideological analysis reveals about the black spokesperson's economic conditioning. In Douglass's *Narrative,* the commercial "voice"(and the narrative transaction it implies) shows how the nineteenth-century slave *publicly* sells his voice in order to secure *private* ownership of his voice–person. The ultimate convergence here is between money and the narrative sign. Exchanging words becomes a function of commerce and a commercial function, and what it reveals – through a blend of ideological analysis and the archaeology of knowledge – is nothing less than the fundamental, "subtextual" dimension of Afro-American discourse.

I believe that this sort of analysis supports the recent dramatic shifts in the ordering principles of American historical and American literary-historical discourse. At the level of practical criticism, such shifts have offered "revised" readings of traditional texts. At a more global level, reconceptualizations of historical discourse have led to the laying bare, the surfacing and recognition, of myriad unofficial American histories . . . *until we are left with a song known at the outset. A traditional American history and literary history give way, for example, before the blues artist's restless, troping mind:*

> You know I laid down last night,
> You know I laid down last night, and tried to take me
>   some rest,
> But my mind got to ramblin' like wild geese from
>   the west.
>
>   Skip James

The "rambling" is significance in rocky places. Its discovery creates a vastly enlarged perspective. Indeed, if one were to put forward a model of American literary history to represent our present knowledge, it would be far more akin to Dollo's accounts than the prosaic quadripedalism of the English 1850s.

Notes

1   The story of Gideon Mantell and Iguanodon is captivatingly recorded in Edwin H. Colbert's *Men and Dinosaurs* (New York: Dutton, 1968). I want to thank Professor Alan Mann for introducing me to both the story and the reference.

2   Michel Foucault, *The Archaeology of Knowledge,* trans. A. M. Sheridan Smith (New York: Harper & Row, 1972). All citations from the text refer to this edition and are marked by page numbers in parentheses.

3   The classic statement of this construction of American history is, of course, Perry Miller's *Errand into the Wilderness* (Cambridge, Mass.: Harvard University Press, 1956).

4   William Bradford, "Of Plymouth Plantation," in *American Poetry and Prose,* ed. Norman Foerster (Boston: Houghton Mifflin, 1957), pp. 20–21.

5   Robert Spiller, et al., eds., *A Literary History of the United States,* 4th rev. ed., (New York: Macmillan, 1974).

6   Robert E. Spiller, "The Cycle and the Roots: National Identity in American Literature." In *Toward A New American Literary History,* eds. Louis J. Budd, Edwin H. Cady, and Carol L. Anderson (Durham, N.C.: Duke University Press, 1980). All citations from the text refer to this edition and are marked by page numbers in parentheses.

7   In *Literature and the American Tradition* (New York: Doubleday, 1970), Leon Howard details the conviction held by Puritans and Pilgrims alike that their signal task was to establish New World communities that would facilitate God's plan to constitute the earthly paradise in America.

8   (New York: St. Martin's Press, 1973). All citations are hereafter marked by page numbers in parentheses.

9   One suspects it was this type of "spiritual revenue" that D. H. Lawrence had in mind when he described the God of eighteenth-century America as "the supreme servant of men who want to get on, to *produce.* Providence. The provider. The heavenly store-keeper. The everlasting Wanamaker. And this is all the God the grandsons of the Pilgrim Fathers had left. Aloft on a pillar of dollars . . . He is head of nothing except a vast heavenly store that keeps every imaginable line of goods, from victrolas to cat-o-nine-tails." *Studies in Classic American Literature* (New York: Thomas Seltzer, 1923), pp. 15, 27.

10   George Lamming, *Season of Adventure* (London: Allison and Busby, 1979), p. 93.

11   Robert Hayden, *Selected Poems,* (New York: October House, 1966), p. 67.

12   I have chosen to employ graphics because they seemed to make the point so

effectively in an earlier version of this chapter presented as a lecture. The Miguel Covarrubias illustration of the inspection and sale of slaves is drawn from Malcolm Cowley, ed., *Adventures of an African Slaver: Being a True Account of the Life of Captain Theodore Canot* (Garden City, N.Y.: Garden City Publishing, 1928). The picture of the "cargo" of an African slaver is drawn from Daniel P. Mannix and Malcolm Cowley, *Black Cargoes: A History of the Atlantic Slave Trade, 1518–1865* (New York: Viking, 1972).

13 Hayden White, in *Tropics of Discourse: Essays in Cultural Criticism* (Baltimore: Johns Hopkins University Press, 1978), p. 5. Subsequent citations are marked by page numbers in parentheses.

14 John Blassingame, *The Slave Community* (New York: Oxford University Press, 1972), p. 159.

15 W. E. B. DuBois, *The Souls of Black Folk*, in *Three Negro Classics*, ed. John Hope Franklin (New York: Avon, 1965), p. 304.

16 Quoted from Paul Oliver, *The Story of the Blues* (London: Chilton, 1969), p. 79.

17 Samuel Charters, "Sleepy John Estes," *Saturday Review*, November 10, 1962, p. 57.

18 In *Great Slave Narratives*, ed. Arna Bontemps (Boston: Beacon, 1969), pp. 4–192. Subsequent citations refer to this edition and are marked by page numbers in parentheses.

19 Fredric Jameson, "The Symbolic Inference; or, Kenneth Burke and Ideological Analysis," *Critical Inquiry* 4 (1978): 504.

20 Frederick Douglass, *Narrative of the Life of Frederick Douglass, An American Slave. Written by Himself.* (New York: New American Library, 1968). All citations refer to this edition and are hereafter marked by page numbers in parentheses.

8

American Studies as a Cultural Program

ALAN TRACHTENBERG

I begin with a rather remarkable coincidence of voices, each speaking within a few years of one another, and speaking in a distinctive way ostensibly about the same subject: the word "culture." In that coincidence lies a revealing passage in cross-cultural intellectual history, as well as a formative moment in the evolution of an idea of the uniqueness, the exceptional character of America itself.

Here is Matthew Arnold in 1869: "I have been trying to show that culture is, or ought to be, the study and pursuit of perfection: and that of perfection as pursued by culture, beauty and intelligence, or, in other words, sweetness and light, are the main characters." That pursuit, Arnold explained, entailed "getting to know, on all the matters which most concern us, the best which has been thought and said in the world," a process, he was at pains to make clear in *Culture and Anarchy*, that represented the author's own best answer to a question he had posed some eight years earlier in a report to the government on education: "What influence may help us to prevent the English people from becoming, with the growth of democracy, *Americanised?*"[1]

Two years later, in 1871, Walt Whitman had this to say, in *Democratic Vistas*:

America has as yet morally and artistically originated nothing. She seems singularly unaware that the models of persons, books, manners, etc., appropriate for former conditions and for European lands, are but exiles and exotics here. No current of her life, as shown on the surfaces of what is authoritatively called her society, accepts or runs into social or esthetic democracy; but all the currents set squarely against it. Never, in the Old World, was thoroughly upholster'd exterior appearance and show, mental and other, built entirely on the idea of caste, and on the sufficiency of mere outside acquisition – never were glibness, verbal intellect, more the test, the emulation – more loftily elevated as head and sample – then they are on the surface of our republican States this day. The writers of a time hint the mottoes of its gods. The word of the modern, say these voices, is the word Culture.

We find ourselves abruptly in close quarters with the enemy. This word Culture, or what it has come to represent, involves, by contrast, our whole theme.[2]

In the same year, 1871, probably unbeknowst to either Arnold or Whitman, Edward B. Tylor published the work that would earn him the title of "father of British anthropology." And in *Primitive Culture*, in a voice notably less embattled and without reference to the term that raised the fever of both Arnold's and Whitman's prose, the term "democracy," Tylor issued his contribution to the convoluted modern history of this term, which Raymond Williams calls, in *Keywords*, "one of the two or three most complicated words in the English language,"[3] a contribution not only calm and even-tempered, but with a claim to definitive certitude: not what culture "ought to be," not a "Word of the modern," but what it *is*: "that complex whole which includes knowledge, beliefs, art, morals, laws, customs and any other capabilities and habits acquired by man as a member of society." According to authorities, this opening sentence of *Primitive Culture* established "the word culture with its modern technical or anthropological meaning . . . in English" (Kroeber and Kluckhohn), though significantly not until its supplement of 1933 did the Oxford English Dictionary add Tylor's definition to Anold's "sweetness and light," which had already been inscribed as authoritative in the 1893 edition.[4]

Certainly an eloquently disequilibrious triad of utterances. Although between Arnold and Whitman we have what seems a neatly symmetrical difference, Tylor seems apart, detached from the passions that burn through the respective essays by the two poets, his insistence upon a technical, a comprehensively descriptive and morally neutral definition, thus creating an asymmetrical design among the three voices, precisely that oddness of pattern in which lies the chief point of interest in bringing them together. At the very least we can identify two key vectors of difference: the line between what we can for the moment call "English" and "American," the crux of difference between the two lying as much in the point of view toward the word "democracy" as the meaning of the word "culture," and then, slanting across this difference, as if mindless of the great issues at stake for the two embattled advocates, the other vector shaping the emergent historical debate in yet another way, along the axis of "science" and "humanism" – the one detached, descriptive, analytical; the other engaged, political, and adversarial.

To be sure, such a diagram rather ruthlessly simplifies the relations between the anthropological and the literary senses of culture in the past hundred years. But the simplification serves at least to locate a point, to provide a nexus for the problem I want to discuss: the ambiguous status of the word "culture" in the academic enterprise we call American Studies. I have in mind ambiguities following from the uneasy and frequently unacknowledged relations between the politically charged and the apparently neutral or merely heuristic uses of the term: ambiguities so deeply entrenched that it may take the kind of dissonance generated by the conjunction of Arnold, Whitman, and Tylor to shake them loose. That disharmony reminds us of what we have taken perhaps too much for granted since the eye-opening work of Raymond Williams in *Culture and Society*,[5] that culture has accumulated varied meanings in its relatively brief career as a keyword in modern thought, a variety of conceptual differences signifying differences in moral, political, and social perspective. The particular configuration of dissonance we have here underscores what is perhaps not so well or so actively known: that the national difference – the very fact of there being a difference expressible by both Arnold and Whitman in national terms – is of no small moment in the English-speaking career of this most complicated of words. One looks in vain in Raymond Williams's studies of that career, however, for any hint of this fact: an absence all the more extraordinary in light of how consequential to Arnold's thinking about culture is the counterinstance of America or "Americanizing." Of course it needs to be said that Williams also ignores Tylor, allowing no voice (at least in his first book) to the envolving culture-concept in what were beginning to call themselves the "social sciences." E.P. Thompson observed this omission in his lengthy review of *The Long Revolution* in 1961, where he commented on the failure of *Culture and Society* to register any "frontal encounter with an historian, an anthropologist, a sociologist of major stature," thus calling into question the likelihood of achieving from a study of the literary "tradition" alone an "adequate theory of culture." One major test of adequacy for Thompson is the extent to which the theory takes account of culture's relation to that which it is not: "Any theory of culture must include the concept of the dialectical interaction between culture and something that is *not* culture." The something else Thompson has in mind is, of course, "society." The notion of culture as the "whole way of life," – a notion Williams credits as a precipitate of the nineteenth-century "tradition" – tends to embrace the social as inseparable from the cultural, to efface distinctions, and thus to stress the cohesive, the consensual features of any historical community, rather than elements of conflict, of division and divisiveness. To subsume the social within the cultural is thus to lose a sense of culture as process – in Thompson's emendation, as "a whole way of conflict. . . . a way of struggle." Not Tylor's own voice as such – a voice that embodied as much a vocational agenda for a fledgling discipline as an effort to enunciate a "law" – but the collective voice of the social studies, especially that of Karl Marx, Thompson implies (and Williams in his more recent work seems to agree) is wanting in order for "culture" to serve at once as a principle of historical explanation and as an image of integration and interrelatedness, of a feasible social and political goal. [6]

The pressure upon the term to serve both ends – as method, let us say, and as politics – represents exactly that ambiguity I want to explore as an element within American Studies itself. We need first to clarify yet another shift and slippage in meaning. As Williams shows, culture came to mean for early nineteenth-century English critics of modernity a perceived "wholeness" rapidly receding before the engines of industry. Then culture accrued further meanings, further particularizations as *certain* values, certain inward possessions and accomplishments. In the first sense the term implied a social cohesion; in the second, a private possession.

It is this second sense, of culture as mere cultivation, that Whitman seems especially to rail against. What makes his animus interesting and worth looking into is not its surface of resentment and outrage but the depth at which it is linked to a positive argument. Whitman's ulterior purpose is to win culture away from gentility; and the animus measures his sense of the stakes involved in the question who will say what constitutes culture? Who will decide its priorities and write its "programme"? Whitman assumes nothing less intense and consequential than a class war over such keywords as culture, democracy, and America: interchangeable terms for him, and all open for definition. His rage against "the word Culture" is a rage against what he considers a fatal flaw in the prevailing definition, especially with its colonial mentality, its self-abasement before a sanctified Old World tradition. The valuation Arnold places upon culture as sweetness and light flowing from the best that has been thought and said is precisely Whitman's negative starting point; he begins by disgorging just what Arnold cherishes.

The heart of the issue for Whitman, what sets his version of culture decisively apart from the tradition charted by Williams, is exactly that convertibility of terms, for it lays the ground for a historically new relation of culture to its society or polity. The key to Whitman's method in the remarkable and difficult essay is the absence of fixed and determinate meanings. The terms signify potentiality; their meaning is always becoming and thus always doubled: something visibly manifest, and something latent, on the edge of visibility. Vision itself serves as the essay's dominant trope, vision ranging in focus from a microscopic scrutiny – the "moral microscope" in which the author sees the present as "a sort of dry and flat Sahara . . . crowded with petty grotesques, malformations, phantoms"(p. 205) – to the panoramic prophecy of the final paragraphs that begins "prospecting thus the coming unsped days" and concludes: "We see our land, America, her literature, esthetics, etc., as, substantially, the getting in form, or effusement and statement, of deepest basic elements and loftiest final meanings, of history and man." (pp. 249–250).

In light of this structure of becoming mediated by vision, Whitman's assertion early in the essay that he "shall use the words America and Democracy as convertible terms" takes on a pointed significance. The nub of the argument lies in a parallel unfolding disclosure of potential meaning at odds with manifest meaning in each of the terms. America may appear a dry and flat Sahara, yet it is really the home of mankind, a promised land; democracy may seem to be "only for elections, for politics, and for a party name," yet it is really for "the highest forms of interaction," for "all public and private life." In each case the achievement of what is latent depends upon the convertibility of the terms: Only by becoming democracy will America realize itself as the "getting in form . . . of deepest basic elements"; only by becoming America will democracy transcend its merely political forms of elections and parties, and realize itself in manners, in all forms of public and private life. Rather than strictly parallel, then, the terms cross over and sustain each other, becoming each other's occasion for realization. And this dependency, this mutuality, is absolute. The words are as if nothing without each other.

In their mutuality, then, the terms hold an implied theory of history; they suggest transactions in historical time, a process of becoming that is also a fusion, an interpenetration. The terms name the historical givens of the American situation: a place presently given over to material progress and well-being (the moral Sahara), and a polity fastened on electoral politics alone. What is vested in the process of becoming, of interpenetration, is the highest. When Whitman writes, in one of his best-known sentences, that "the United States are destined either to surmount the gorgeous history of feudalism, or else prove the most

tremendous failure of time," he means that the destiny of the United
States is either to become America—the materialization of spiritual
democracy—or to remain merely a country, a nation like any other.

Here we have, of course, American exceptionalism in crystalline
form: the belief in a special providence, a destiny that is simultaneously
America's utopia and its nightmare. Sacvan Bercovitch is surely correct
in reading *Democratic Vistas* as an American Jeremiad, a "state-of-the-
covenant address" whose terms are "doomsday or millennium," and
whose "political or social commentary" is thus disappointing.[7] True
enough, but Whitman's exceptionalism cannot be traced only to a reflex
of belated Puritan rhetoric, a rhetoric of covenant, of errand, of jeremiad, as resonant as the sounds of such patterns may be in the text. The
view of America here is founded as well upon a theory of history and of
culture in which political democracy, the principle of equality, plays the
central, the most noteworthy role. For the convertibility of America
and democracy represents for Whitman a definite (though not an inevitable) historical process. It also represents, that mutuality of terms, a
role for culture, a role Whitman is able to articulate as a distinct "programme," a "programme of culture" (as he calls it) based upon "a
radical change of category," "in the distribution of precedence." He
would redeem the word by purging it of its discriminations, its class
distinctions, its disdain for the low and vulgar.

Here again is Arnold in *Culture and Anarchy* in 1869:

> Culture says: "Consider these people, then, their way of life,
> their habits, their manners, the very tones of their voice; look
> at them attentively; observe the literature they read, the things
> which give them pleasure, the words which come forth out of
> their mouths, the thoughts which make the furniture of their
> minds; would any amount of wealth be worth having with the
> condition that one was to become like these people by having
> it?" (pp. 40–41)

Curiously, the attentiveness and closeness of observation here sound
strikingly like those of an ethnographer, a field-worker armed with
some definition of culture derived from Tylor. But neutrality of observation and description is not Arnold's purpose. He continues: "And
thus culture begets a dissatisfaction which is of the highest possible
value in stemming the common tide of men's thoughts in a wealthy and
industrial community, and which saves the future, as one may hope,
from being vulgarized. even if it cannot save the present." (p. 41). It is
not difficult to imagine Whitman's reaction to such a passage, for it
seems full of just that superciliousness he identified with "the word

Culture." And indeed a good many of Arnold's followers in America might well have taken just this passage as sanction for the kind of snobbery and exclusiveness Whitman disdained.

But in fact if we listen closely we hear a more complex voice, one less at odds with Whitman's own contempt for "thoroughly upholstered exterior appearance and show, mental and otherwise, built entirely on the idea of caste, and on the sufficiency of mere outside acquisition." Arnold expected that the dissatisfaction begun by culture would produce "a certain number of *aliens*," aliens in that a revulsion from vulgarity results in an inward break with the "stock notions" of conventional thinking, with worldly wealth, power, and the "machinery" of everyday life. Out of dissatisfaction they pursue inward perfection; they seek their "best selves" hidden within their "ordinary selves." They become ardent critics of ordinariness in all forms, and thus prepare themselves as "sovereign educators," men of culture who belong to no class but owe their sole allegiance to sweetness and light. And as educators (not in the ordinary sense but virtually as priests) Arnold's aliens bear a compelling resemblance to Whitman's democratic bards, the literati whose role will be to transform political democracy into a religious belief in equality. Indeed, Arnold insists that the "social idea" in culture is to do away with classes; to make the best that has been thought and known in the world current everywhere; to make all men live in an atmosphere of sweetness and light. This is not mere beneficence, moreover, but an organic feature of culture: "Perfection, as culture conceives it, is not possible while the individual remains isolated. The individual is required, under pain of being stunted and enfeebled in his own development if he disobeys, to carry others along with him in his march towards perfection." Thus, "the men of culture are the true apostles of equality."

There is, then, a radical element in Arnold's culture; it derives in all likelihood from evangelical Prostestantism and its assertion of a "kingdom of God within you," a universalizing kingdom of spirit. Arnold translated the sacred process into a secular experience, and his stress on *inwardness* led him logically to the principle of equality in culture. Though this principle existed in culture alone, it does suggest an ideal political state. Here, too, the implications of Arnold's reasoning are surprisingly radical. Within the notion of the "best self" lies the corollary of a best "state." Just as in our ordinary, everyday selves we confront all other ordinary selves in that state of antagonism, which threatens "anarchy," so we habitually think of the state as partial, "as something equivalent to the class in occupation of the executive government, and are afraid of that class abusing power to its own purposes." By our "best selves," on the other hand, "we are united, impersonal, at harmony." Thus does culture suggest "the idea of *the State,*" an imagined idea of unity and social cohesion.

Arnold, to be sure, withdraws from the antinomian implications of this vision. He offered *Culture and Anarchy,* we must remember, explicitly in response to middle-class fears of impending disorder following the 1867 Reform Act. Among the vulgar notions disdained by the aliens is that freedom consists in "doing as one likes." Order, authority, stability: These are very ordinary values, associated with the ordinary state, much appreciated by those aliens, whose very alienation encourages respect for the necessity of external authority. And so, in their "disinterested pursuit of perfect," the aliens come to appreciate "that profound sense of settled order and security, without which a society like ours cannot live and grow at all." "For us," Arnold reminded his readers, "who believe in right reason, in the duty and possibility of extricating and elevating our best self, in the progress of humanity towards perfection, – for us the framework of society, that theatre on which this august drama has to unroll itself is sacred."

We can better understand, then, the full range of Whitman's negative response to "the word Culture." Arnold assumed a society of contending classes ruled over by an ordinary state representing partial interests. His sovereign educators opposed their sovereignty – that of culture – to the existing state and social order. But their opposition remained benign; they wished not to overthrow but to meliorate the ordinary polity, to convert it to its own better possibilities. "Settled order and security" were positive factors, and culture too, Arnold admitted, played its "weighty part" in the defense of order, security, and property. This contradictory association between culture and the status quo may well be a rather vague and unclear feature of Arnold's thought, as commentators have remarked, but in Whitman's eyes the association between culture and the rule of privilege seemed unequivocal. Thus "the word Culture" seemed ridden with political interest, "for a single class alone." Thus the call for a "radical change of category," for a new "programme of culture."

> I should demand a programme of culture drawn out, not for a single class alone, or for the parlors or lecture-rooms, but with an eye to practical life, the west, workingmen, the facts of farms and jack-planes and engineers, and of the broad range of women also of the middle and working strata. . . . I should demand of this programme or theory a scope generous enough to include the widest human area. It must have for its spinal

meaning the formation of a typical personality of character,
eligible to the uses of the high average of men—and *not* restricted by conditions ineligible to the masses. (pp. 224–25)

Whitman here invites direct comparison with Arnold. The most obvious and, of course, most telling differences are rhetorical: Compare
the voice that asks "Would any amount of wealth be worth having with
the condition that one was to become like these people by having it,"
with the voice that speaks with ease of farms and jack-planes and engi-
neers, of spinal meanings, and of the masses. The egalitarianism proposed by Whitman in his programme is already present, prefigured as a
social and cultural fact, in his speech. Although Arnold's voice may
well be that of an "apostle of equality," equality itself remains a principle, outside the voice that utters it, a condition the voice contemplates
rather than exemplifies. Moreover, on the level of doctrine, Whitman's
insistence on a culture "drawn out" (the image is of a draftsman, of a
plan for a construction) for common life, with special stress on the life
of labor, calls attention to the exact opposite in Arnold's account of the
process of culture, from dissatisfaction to the quest for a "best self."
Arnold seems imprisoned by the following paradox: In order to preserve culture as a realm of the sweetness and light of human perfection,
he must detach it from the common life, from practical affairs. He must
see it as an alien force, standing in opposition to the "machinery" of
society. Culture begets its antagonism thus from without. It produces
aliens because it itself is alien to its society and its polity. Indeed,
estrangement from the ordinary is the very condition of its origin. Thus
when culture intervenes in everyday life, as the voice that says "consider these people," what it proposes is even further alienation in the
form of an imagined equality in an imagined state. Arnold's aliens, his
sovereign educators, seem able only to criticize from without, rather
than to transform from within.

The difficulty I am attempting to formulate in Arnold's vision of
culture can be stated in yet another way: How might the alien apostle
overcome the contemplative stance that is the sign of culture within
him, his origin as an alien in the first place, and perform an act, a
political act, to restore culture to society, not as a critical voice but as an
existential condition? How might the actual state be transformed in real
history to "the idea of *the State*," that state of a unifying universality?
Arnold provides tactical answers—improvement of public education,
for example. Whitman, however, has no need to pose the question, and
this is the most consequential of the differences of his culture from
Arnold's. Whitman believes he already inhabits a state whose ideal

character, its commitment to universal equality, is a fact of history. Thus the call for a "radical change of category" urges not revolution, or overthrow, but an awakening of America to the fact that, with democratic institutions and sufficient material well-being to dispel want and need, only "Religious Democracy" is needed to realize the full meaning of the nation, of the convertible terms "America" and "democracy." The fact of America, in short, changes the entire set of relations between culture and politics.

We can better gauge the force of this change, the difference to the word "culture" made by the word "America," by taking up yet another line of thought, another set of voices. In 1795 the German philosopher Friedrich Schiller spoke of a "wound" inflicted on humankind by the divisions of modern life, the separation from each other of the realms of politics and religion, law and custom, work and play, necessity and enjoyment. "Eternally chained to only one single little fragment of the whole, Man himself grew to be only a fragment. With the monstrous noise of the wheel he drives everlastingly in his ears," Schiller wrote in *On the Aesthetic Education of Man*, "he never develops the harmony of his being, and instead of imprinting humanity upon his nature he becomes merely the imprint of his occupation." It will thus be the task of culture "to restore the unity of mankind," a task best performed by an '"aesthetic education" that will reconcile "the receptive faculty" of play with the "determining faculty" of work. Such an education will then have a political consequence in the formation of an "aesthetic State," similar to Arnold's ideal State: both instances registering the dawning paradoxical recognition in nineteenth-century Europe that although a stateless culture, a culture without politics, could not survive, by its character as the realm of the universal, of the unity and equality of mankind, culture must always stand in opposition to existing states.[8]

Following Schiller, Hegel developed further the connection between culture and universality, identifying it in *The Phenomenology of Mind* (1807) as a phase in the evolution of consciousness, that phase when the mind steps out of itself and "puts itself in the position of something universal." In such a moment the person comes to see his or her "equality . . . with all selves," an equality that is something more than the "spiritless formal" equality of legal systems. Moreover culture proceeds by opposition and negation, for example, by "cancelling and transcending both the natural self" and the social self. Culture represents both reality and power in the individual consciousness, and it does so by an absolute inversion of statepower, worldly wealth, mundane moral distinctions. Hegel calls such inversions "pure culture," and takes

Rameau's nephew, Diderot's classic figure of total estrangement, as its instance, his corrosive wit representing the absoluteness of his revolt and thus his culture. "In such utterances this *self*– in the form of a pure self not associated with or bound by determinations derived either from reality or thought – comes consciously to be a spiritual entity having a truly universal significance and value. It is the condition in which the nature of all relationships is rent asunder, and it is the conscious rending of them all."[9] Thus culture reveals itself to Hegel as fundamentally antinomian, an utter negation, defining and constructing itself in direct opposition to civil and political society. And in Marx we hear of a recovery of "species being," of that universality riven and fragmented by commodity production and the social relations of bourgeois society: a recovery that Marx sees as a function only of a material revolution that will reconnect culture and its image of wholeness with a new classless society.

Now, in this German line of thought, culture represents opposition and negation, a radicalism rather muted in the British tradition traced by Williams, where culture seemed often attached to the past, to a passing rural order, and to a fundamentally conservative outlook. Significantly, Whitman associates "the word Culture" with the British line, at least in the anglophile versions becoming prominent in genteel circles in the United States, and evokes what he calls the "Hegelian formulas" to recover culture's more radical meanings, meanings Emerson had already explored in relation to another radical concept, that of America itself. In 1836, in *Nature,* Emerson sounded a Hegelian note linking culture with the idealist notion of nature as appearance: "Culture inverts the vulgar views of nature, and brings the mind to call that apparent which it used to call real, and that real which it used to call visionary." The following year, in the Phi Beta Kappa address known as "The American Scholar," Emerson allowed the notion to blossom in all its negativity:

> Men, such as they are, very naturally seek money or power; and power because it is as good as money, – the "spoils," so called, "of office." And why not? for they aspire to the highest, and this, in their sleep-walking they dream is the highest. Wake them and they shall quit the false good and leap to the true, and leave governments to clerks and desks. The revolution is to be wrought by the gradual domestication of the idea of Culture.[10]

The very idea of a *domestication* seems an oxymoron, yet this paradox is only apparent, for if we attend with care to Emerson's voice in the famous passage to follow, it is no ordinary nationalism or patriotism that fires his rejection of exactly that tradition upon which Arnold would found his culture a generation later: "We have listened too long to the courtly muses of Europe." A specifically *American* literature is wanted, not for the sake of celebrating the native, but for the domestication of an idea without political domicile abroad, the idea of Culture. It is for the sake of a home for culture, a home in ordinary experience, that he issues his famous call:

> I ask not for the great, the remote, the romantic; what is doing in Italy or Arabia; what is Greek art, or provencal minstrelsey; I embrace the common, I explore and sit at the feet of the familiar, the low. Give me insight into today, and you may have the antique and future worlds. What would we really know the meaning of? The meal in the firkin; the milk in the pan; the ballad in the street; the news of the boat; the glance of the eye; the form and gait of the body; – show me the ultimate reason of these matters.

Here, too, as in Arnold's inventory of what culture considers and observes, we recognize an ethnological element, a prefiguration of the culture-concept of Tylor – with, of course, the difference that Emerson does not, like Arnold, seek grounds of discrimination, nor like Tylor, a model for study. Emerson seeks instead a connectedness, a perspective – literally an insight, a way of seeing – through which the ordinary discloses its extraordinariness: "Let me see every trifle bristling with the polarity that ranges it instantly on an eternal law; and the shop, the plough, and the ledger referred to the like cause by which light undulates and poets sing; – and the world no longer lies a dull miscellany and lumber-room, but has form and order." America *is,* then, its own ordinary experience, the details of its collective social existence viewed as a whole, as "one design" that "united and animates the farthest pinnacle and lowest trench."

Here is a vision of what Emerson in the same lecture called "the conversion of the world," a vision clearly touched with the evangelical and millennialist fervor Sacvan Bercovitch has shown to be a formative power in American rhetoric. And what gives the vision focus and credibility, for Emerson in 1837 and for Whitman a generation later, is *America,* a political entity founded on the inner principle of culture itself: absolute existential equality. "A nation of men will for the first time exist," Emerson foretells, "because each believes himself inspired by the Divine Soul which also inspires all men."

So it was believed, and so the belief produced an idea of culture convertible with an idea of America: a culture whose politics seemed no more than a matter of the eyesight, of prospects, visions, and vistas, of right seeing. Thirty years later, in 1867, Emerson returned to Harvard for another Phi Beta Kappa address. Under the promising title "The Progress of Culture" he paid tribute still to the inversions of culture: "culture alters the political status of an individual. It raises a rival royalty in a monarchy. . . . It creates a personal independence which the monarch cannot look down." But why now this talk of monarchy, as if the politics of culture were an old-world issue, as if the issue were already settled in the new? Writing in the aftermath of the Northern victory in perhaps the bloodiest war yet fought on earth, Emerson seemed not in the mood to unsettle his audience. He speaks now of "the power of minorities," of the "few superior and attractive men" who constitute a "knighthood of virtue." It was their victory, he explained, their program for industry and science, for reform. Their victory, Emerson must have pleased his audience by saying, represented "the progress of culture." Much has changed in thirty years, for now Emerson rests his hopes as much on a Brahmin Knighthood of virtue as would Arnold in the same years on his apostles of culture:

> Here you are set down, scholars and idealists, in a barbarous age; amidst insanity, to calm and guide it; amidst fools and the blind, to see the right done; among violent proprietors, to check self-interest, stone-blind and stone-deaf, by considerations of humanity to the workman and to his child; amongst angry politicians swelling with self-esteem, pledged to parties, pledged to clients, you are to make valid the large considerations of equity and good sense; under bad government to force on them, by your persistence, good laws. Around that immovable persistency of yours, statesmen, legislators, must revolve, denying you, but not less forced to obey.[11]

We can see, then, even more vividly what predicament Whitman faced in "the word Culture," what difficulties confronted his "programme." Emerson's retreat to calm, to guidance, to "considerations of humanity," measured his perception of the change in era, his sense of the actual America having fallen on barbarous times. Whitman's insistence on a "programme," implying advocacy, a plan of action, even belligerency, also registers at least a covert recognition that in the present social and political universe culture can no longer be counted on to realize itself. A programme represents a need for action in the historical world: for ideology. True, Whitman imagined poetry rather than politics as the mode of implementation – which is to say that in the largest sense he imagined poetry as performing a political, an ideological, function: as certainly "Song of Myself," by articulating a myth of an American way of being, offers, in Kenneth Burke's terminology, an ideological statement of the "culture's essence in narrative terms." Indeed, the high priestly–which is again to say ideological–role of the poet in Whitman's vistas strikes another unexpectedly harmonious note with Arnold. "The priest departs, the divine literatus comes." Whitman places all his political hope on this, that "a great original literature is surely to become the justification and reliance, (in some respects the sole reliance,) of American democracy." Still, the radical change of category sets Whitman resolutely against any notion of culture tinged with "the gorgeous history of feudalism." "The great poems," he writes, "Shakespeare included, are poisonous to the idea of the pride and dignity of the common people, the life-blood of democracy."

Whitman's programme represents the realm of historical action in which the conversion of America to democracy might occur. Culture provides the instruments of change; it is through culture that democracy will flower into manners, and that flowering of the dry Sahara will be America, will be Religious Democracy, will be culture in its political essence. "Culture" thus provides the ideological term to the mythic and utopian aspects of the linked pair, the convertible term "America" and "Democracy." If existential equality represents the utopia hidden from view within the manifest America, rife with fraud, corruption, and cynicism as it is, then culture is the vehicle of realization, of making utopia palpable, bringing it into history. "The great word Solidarity has arisen," Whitman proclaims, and it is the business of culture to transform the body politic in the image of that great word: another link in the chain that signifies America.

Whitman's essay, then, registers the difference certain words make for others. Clearly it is the difference of "America" by which Whitman's culture differs from Arnold's. The term "America" promised a positive political destiny for culture, a domestication. That failed, as we see in the retreat of the 1867 Emerson–although why remains a question to be explored. And Whitman's programme, although kept alive at least rhetorically by critics of culture such as Van Wyck Brooks and Lewis Mumford, came to rest as soon as it was promulgated safely on the margins of American life. Assuming a politics, Whitman in fact failed to examine the political terrain in terms themselves political or ideological. The hold of the myth of America on his imagination was such that the actual terrain hardly appears in his "vista": the character of American civil society (its structure of classes, its institutional networks, its rapid bureaucratization); the character of the state, then undergoing major changes and expansions. The dry Sahara is a potent image, yet what it leaves unsaid may be the most important features of the American scene in 1870: the new configurations of economic forces consolidating their power over the state.

"I can conceive a community, to-day and here, in which, on a sufficient scale, the perfect personalities, without noise meet." When Whitman paused in *Democratic Vistas* to imagine the actual look and shape of a democratic community, of America in realized form, this is what appeared:

> Say in some pleasant western settlement or town, where a couple of hundred of best men and women, of ordinary worldly status have by luck been together, with nothing extra of genius or wealth, but virtuous, chaste, industrious, cheerful, resolute, friendly and devout. I can conceive such a community organized in running order, powers judiciously delegated – farming, building, trade, courts, mails, schools, elections, all attended to; and then the rest of life, the main thing, freely branching and blossoming in each individual, and bearing golden fruit. (p. 229)

The golden apples of the sun, in Whitman's version of the myth of the garden: a magical western commune, in good running order, no factory or railroad in sight, no bosses, no workers or ethnic or racial or religious difference. And all by luck drawn together.

The communal utopia seems a concession of marginality. Still, successive generations of readers of *Democratic Vistas,* including many practioners of American Studies, have been haunted by the essay, by just this mythic vision, and also by its failures. Where America assumed the guise of an actual society, there Whitman found Sahara. In the essay's final prophecy – "prospecting thus the coming unsped days" – we cannot help overhearing a lament, an elegiac note; for the prophecy, Whitman may have belatedly realized, as did Fitzgerald in the closing lines of *The Great Gatsby,* was already past. It may once have seemed to Brooks and Mumford and Waldo Frank, to V. L. Parrington and to F. O. Matthiessen – progenitors of the idea that American Studies by its making of a usable past might itself perform a politics of culture – that the idea of America might still serve as a focus. Matthiessen prefaces *American Renaissance,* the establishing text of academic American Studies, with a tribute to Whitman and an acceptance of an obligation to be answerable to his standard (as restated by Louis Sullivan): "Are you using such gifts as you possess for or against the People?" Such standards are, writes Matthiessen. "the inevitable and right extension of Emerson's demands in The American Scholar," adding that his own work "has value only to the extent that it comes anywhere near measuring up to them."[12] Although it may be difficult to know exactly what this means, or how we might go about taking such a measurement, the words serve as a reminder that American Studies, too, has been steeped in the politics of culture and all the ambiguities thereof.

Notes

1 Matthew Arnold, *Culture and Anarchy* (Indianapolis: Bobbs-Merrill, 1971), pp. 58, 5; "Democracy," *Portable Matthew Arnold,* ed. Lionell Trilling (New York: Viking, 1949), p. 452.

2 Walt Whitman, *Democratic Vistas, Complete Prose Works* (Boston: Small, Maynard, 1901), p. 224.

3 Raymond Williams, *Keywords* (New York: Oxford University Press, 1976).

4 A. L. Kroeber and Clyde Kluckhohn, *Culture: A Critical Review of Concepts and Definitions* (New York: Random House, 1952), p. 11.

5 Raymond Williams, *Culture and Society* (New York: Doubleday, 1960).

6 E. P. Thompson, "The Long Revolution," *New Left Review* 9 (1961): 24–39.

7 Sacvan Bercovitch, *American Jeremiad* (Madison: University of Wisconsin Press, 1978), pp. 198–99.

8 Friedrich Schiller, *On the Aesthetic Education of Man* (New York: Ungar, 1965), p. 40 and passim.

9 G. W. F. Hegel, "Culture and Its Realm of Actual Reality," in *The Phenomenology of Mind,* trans. G. B. Baillie (New York: Harper Torchbook, 1967), pp. 514–48.

10 Ralph Waldo Emerson, *Selections from Ralph Waldo Emerson,* ed. Stephen Whicher (Boston: Houghton Mifflin, 1957): "Nature," p. 48' "The American Scholar," pp. 76,78.

11 Ralph Waldo Emerson, *Letters and Social Aims* (Boston: Houghton Mifflin, 1904), pp. 230–31.

12 F. O. Matthiessen, *American Renaissance* (New York: Oxford University Press, 1941), pp. 15–16.

9

Reification and American Literature

CAROLYN PORTER

> The detached observer is as much entangled as the active participant.
>
> Theodor Adorno

It is a critical commonplace that American literature's classic tradition lacks the social and historical density of its European counterparts. Henry James's famous list of "the items of high civilization . . . absent from the texture of American life" in his little book on Hawthorne is only one of the earliest attempts to explain what has become virtually an unquestioned assumption not merely about Hawthorne or the American novel, but about major American writers from Ralph Waldo Emerson to Wallace Stevens – that American literature, whether it turns inward on the self, downward toward metaphysical darkness, or backward on its own language, typically turns away from social reality. I wish to question this assumption by suggesting that if we approach major American writers not by comparison with their European contemporaries, but in relation to the social reality they actually inhabited – a social reality formed by the relatively unimpeded development of capitalism from the beginning of the nineteenth century on – we will find inscribed in their work as deep a response to social reality as any to be found in the work of a Balzac or a George Eliot. In other words, we should focus not on the lack of a monarchical state or a feudal society to be overthrown in American history, but instead on what the absence of such obstacles to capitalist expansion has fostered in that history, a social reality breeding an extreme form of alienation. In reacting critically to that alienation, American writers have produced texts that can be understood, if we only bring to bear the proper tools, as social to the core.[1]

What follows is an attempt to outline such an approach and, more specifically, to suggest how an analysis of major works by Emerson, Henry Adams, Henry James, and William Faulkner can enable us to identify a developing pattern in American literary history, a pattern that emerges from, and constitutes a revelatory response to, that feature of capitalist society to which Georg Lukács gave the name "reification."

In the broadest sense, reification refers to a process in the course of which man becomes alienated from himself. This process is generated by the developing autonomy of a commodified world of objects that confronts man as a mystery "simply because," as Marx put it, "in it the social character of men's labour appears to them as an objective character stamped upon the product of that labour." The effects of this process as Lukács describes them, however, are by no means limited to the experience of the laborer, but in fact infiltrate the consciousness of everyone living in a society driven by capitalist growth. The reifying process endemic to capitalism produces a new kind of world and a new kind of person. It generates, on the one hand, a "new objectivity," a "second nature" in which people's own productive activity is obscured, so that what they have made appears to them as a given, an external and objective reality operating according to its own immutable laws. On the other hand, it generates people who assume a passive and "contemplative" stance in the face of that objectified and rationalized reality – people who seem to themselves to stand outside that reality because their own participation in producing it is mystified. I want first to specify more precisely these two aspects of reification, and then to focus attention on the contradiction, and finally on the kind of crisis, to which it leads.[2]

As a result of the commodity structure informing capitalist society, a new world of objects "springs into being" in which the material and substantial qualities of things as things are hidden beneath their status as commodities. Marx dramatizes this myserious development at one point by giving the commodity its own voice: "If commodities could speak, they would say this: our use-value may interest men, but it does not belong to us as objects. What does belong to us as objects, however, is our value. Our own intercourse as commodities proves it. We relate to each other merely as exchange-values." Notice that these commodities do not address us, but seem to be agreeing among themselves. Marx's rhetorical strategy underlines how autonomous is the realm in which commodities live and move and have their being. We become alienated observers of this bizarre theatrical performance in which objects have "intercourse" with each other without the slightest concern for, or relation to, our illusory belief that they exist for our use.[3]

Not only does one confront an alien world of commodified objects, according to Lukács, but one's own activity becomes a "commodity which, subject to the non-human objectivity of the natural laws of society, must go its own way independently of man just like any consumer article." For the factory worker, this is nothing more (and nothing less) than the experience of daily life. The worker finds himself or herself in the position of a "mechanical part incorporated into a mechanical system," and the more mechanized the labor process, the more the worker's "lack of will is reinforced by the way in which his activity becomes less and less active and more and more *contemplative*." Workers thus confront their own activity in the form of an alien process they themselves do not set in motion, but merely contemplate. As the commodification of society proceeds with the expansion of capital, "the fate of the worker becomes the fate of society as a whole." Thus, both aspects of reification – an alien world of commodities with a life of their own, and an alienated consciousness that can only contemplate this independent and autonomous process, moving in accord with its own "natural laws" – are repeated in bourgeois consciousness as a whole. Not only does man "become the passive observer of society; he also lapses into a contemplative attitude vis-à-vis the workings of his own objectified and reified faculties." In other words, as a result of the reifying process, not only does the worker contemplate his or her own activity in the alienated form of commodities interacting in accord with their own laws of motion, but so does the bureaucrat, the technologist, the scientist, each of whom assumes a detached contemplative stance not only toward an objective external world, but toward the objectified constructs of his or her own mind, which he or she takes to be incorporated in the external world: "Just as the capitalist system continuously produces and reproduces itself economically on higher and higher levels, the structure of reification progressively sinks more deeply, more fatefully and more definitively into the consciousness of man." What needs to be stressed is the "artificially abstract" nature of this "new objectivity," this "second nature" people inhabit in modern capitalism. Nowhere is this artificiality more apparent than in the scientist's laboratory.

> The experimenter creates an artificial, abstract milieu in order to be able to *observe,* undisturbed the untrammeled workings of the laws under examination, eliminating all irrational factors both of the subject and the object. He strives as far as possible to reduce the material substratum of his observation to the purely rational "product," to the "intelligible matter" of mathematics.

Furthermore, the intelligible matter is reduced finally to that "supreme scientific concept which is no longer the name of anything real . . . like money, e.g., the concept of an atom, or of energy."[4]

In the posture of the scientist for whom, in the words of Marx's first thesis on Ludwig Feuerbach, "reality, what we apprehend through our senses, is understood only in the form of the object of contemplation, but not as sensuous human activity," reification takes a materialist form. The idealist's oposition to this situation, however, does not overcome reification, but only reveals more pointedly what has been submerged by it—"sensuous human activity." In Raymond Williams's terms, it is "the exclusion of activity, of making, from the category of 'objective relality'," an exclusion already evident in the scientist's posture as neutral observer, which leads the idealist to invest the transcendent subject with the active dimension lost from the objectified reality he confronts. But since, according to Marx, idealism "does not know real sensuous activity as such," the active, creative subject of idealist thought is necessarily an abstraction. In short, both the neutral observer and the transcendent seer occupy the same contemplative stance, rooted in reification. The "sensuous human activity" drained out of the objectified reality observed by the scientist is only abstractly projected onto the creative, active subject of romantic idealism.[5]

One could describe reification, then, in straightforward terms such as this: Man makes his world but then it takes on the appearance of an alien, autonomous, given world. Further, as the idealist response demonstrates, we cannot, simply by taking thought, reclaim this alien world as the product of human labor, any more than the worker, by taking thought, can reclaim his or her commodified activity. Although there comes a point, and an important one for Lukács, when this analogy between the proletariat and the bourgeois breaks down, at this stage it holds true that, for both, the reifying process is irreversible.

As a result of the suppression of "sensuous human activity," the reifying process generates conditions in which a contradiction comes into view, the contradiction between "details which are subject to laws and a totality ruled by chance." For example, the "strictly rational organization of work on the basis of rational technology," which Max Weber found "specific to modern capitalism" requires "rational laws" if it is to function at all. The judge in a bureaucratic state, to quote Weber's apt phrase, is "an automatic statute-dispensing machine." Capitalist society requires, in short, that the businessman and the bureaucrat be able to calculate and predict, and thus requires a "unified system of general 'laws.'" Yet because this system disregards "the concrete aspects of the subject matter of these laws," it is and must be incoherent. One sign of this "incoherence" is the unceasing flow of conflicts that develop between the legal system and an expanding capitalist economy. In periods of crisis the system's incoherence manifests itself dramatically, for then it becomes clear that the " 'eternal, iron' laws" are mere pretenses, that the system has no real coherence at all. Lukács is not talking about a crisis which merely exposes the hypocrisy of a legal system's claim to dispense justice; he is talking about a crisis that exposes how untenable is its claim to coherence. A depression, for example, may expose the pretense of the claim of classical economics to comprehend the economic system. The point is that the reifying process yields a world that is presented to us as operating according to known or knowable laws, but which in fact operates irrationally.[6]

In its materialist form, then, reification harbors a contradiction that exposes the rationalized reality of postivism as a "second nature." But the exclusion of "sensuous human activity" that generates this contradiction resurfaces abstractly in the idealist's response to it, as we find when we examine Kant's rationalism. Kant reintroduces the hypothesis that "objects must conform to our knowledge," contrary to the empiricist claim that "all our knowledge must conform to the objects." The irony of the Kantian revolution, however, is that ultimately, whatever it may or may not conform to, our knowledge becomes objectified. Kant's rationalism differs from its predecessors primarily in that it "undertakes to confer universal significance on rational categories," whereas all earlier forms of rationalism accorded such categories only a limited scope, acknowledging a realm of the irrational presided over by God or some other mythic presence. In Kant's system, this limit is marked by the thing-in-itself, but such a limit has the effect of driving underground the irrational – both the "content" of the forms by which we know the world and the "ultimate substance" of that knowledge. The problem posed by the thing-in-itself, as Lukács's rehearsal of subsequent German philosophy through Hegel makes abundantly evident, is insoluble; it is, in effect, the perfect expression of reified consciousness, for it defines an artifical limit to knowledge that constitutes the limit of the thinkable. Henceforth, all that lies beyond the thing-in-itself, the formalized barrier of rationalist thought, closes itself off to human cognition.[7]

On the one hand, a "methodologically purified world" emerges in which the specialized sciences may become "exact" precisely *because* of the "recognition that this problem of the thing-in-itself is insoluble." Philosophy narrows its focus to a concern with the "formal presuppositions of the special sciences which it neither corrects nor interferes with." So the same contradiction arises: Our knowledge of and control over "the details of social existence" allow us to subject them to our needs to some extent, while we progressively lose "intellectual control of society as a whole." On the other hand, idealist philosophy generally and romantic aesthetics in particular struggle to rescue the subject from his or her alienated condition as the victim of an objectified reality whose active dimension has been excluded by being pushed into the realm of the irrational behind the iron wall of the thing-in-itself. Johann Fichte describes this *"projectio per hiatum irrationalem"* definitively when he explains the problem as "the absolute projection of an object *of the origin of which no account can be given* with the result that *the space between projection and thing projected is dark and void."* The romantic effort to restore man's active participation in making the objectified world he confronts can only reconstitute his activity on a nonsensuous, idealist ground. Ferdinand Schiller, for example, makes of the play-instinct an aesthetic principle, arguing that "man only plays when he is man in the full meaning of the world, and he is fully human only when he plays." Realizing that "man as man" has been destroyed, Schiller tries to make *"man whole again in thought."* But the dogma of rationality, as we know from the results of the New Criticism, remains "unimpaired" and "by no means superseded" when the active material substratum of life is rescued through its aesthetic transformation in art. Hegel realizes that the solution to the problem must be sought in history, but as an idealist, Hegel could not locate the subject of history within history itself, and had to "go out beyond history itself, and, there to establish the empire of Reason which has discovered itself."[8]

The solution to reification for Lukács, of course, resides in proletarian consciousness. Lukács develops an identity theory, in which the proletariat is the identical subject–object of history. However, we do not need to enter these troubled waters further than to say that the recognition of history's primacy as "sensuous human activity" can only occur from a vantage point within that activity. For Lukács, that vantage point can belong only to proletarian consciousness, understood not in any immediate and empirical form, but as an imputed recognition of the mediations hidden behind the reified, immediate appearance of the world. According to Lukács, such a vantage point must be ascribed exclusively to proletarian class consciousness because it experiences its own objectification differently than does the bourgeois, as instrument rather than essence, to oversimplify grossly a complex and problematical argument. For our purposes, it suffices to note that one of the limitations of reified thought that Lukács describes at some length here is its incapacity to conceptualize change.[9]

Reified bourgeois consciousness inhabits an illusory world "where the immediately given form of the objects, the fact'of their existing here and now and in this particular way appears to be primary, real, and objective, whereas their 'relations' seem to be secondary and subjective." Marx's critique of Feuerbach in *The German Ideology* provides the most straightforward, not to mention comic, refutation of the mistaken notion, itself a result of reification, that the "sensuous world" is "a thing given direct from all eternity." Feuerbach does not inhabit the given world he presumes to live in, Marx explains, because

> even the objects of the simplest "sensuous certainty" are only given him through social development, industry and commercial intercourse. The cherry-tree, like almost all fruit-trees, was, as is well known, only a few centuries ago transplanted by *commerce* into our zone, and therefore only by this action of a definite society in a definite age it has become "sensuous certainty" for Feuerbach. . . . So much is this activity, this unceasing sensuous labour and creation, this production, the basis of the whole sensuous world as it now exists, that, were it interrupted only for a year, Feruerbach would not only find an enormous change in the natural world, but would very soon find that the whole world of men and his own perceptive faculty, nay his own existence, were missing.

Only when the apparently stable and given world is understood as already mediated can it be understood as the realm of change, of what Marx called "sensuous human activity." When reified consciousness tries to apprehend change, however, it simply reifies it, as Bergson does in the form of the eternal flux. As Lukács puts it, such a flux "is and does not become, . . . it is just a becoming that confronts the rigid existence of the individual objects." An analogous chasm opens before reified consciousness when it tries to apprehend a relation between the past and the present. Here the contemplative attitude is "polarized into two extremes": On the one hand, historical change is produced by "great individuals," and on the other hand, it is the result of "natural laws." Neither interpretation can account for the present "in all its radical novelty." Any significant change, in short, appears to be "a sudden, unexpected turn of events that comes from outside and eliminates all mediations."[10]

Reification, then, is a process in the course of which man becomes alienated from himself. But we may also speak of both a reified consciousness, marked by its contemplative stance, and of a reified world, that "second nature" which reified consciousness experiences as already given. (For reified consciousness, "objective reality has the character of a thing-in-itself.") If we turn the question around to ask what has been reified, the answer is neither man per se nor a primary nature out there beyond the objectivized world of immediacy, but rather that "sensuous human activity" encompassing both, which we shall hereafter take as the referent for "history." From this point of view, then, bourgeois man does not deny history, but rather is incapable of apprehending it at all, except in reified forms. Yet at moments of crisis, the contradictions inherent in bourgeois society surface, seem to break through the reified patina of the objectified world, revealing the incoherence of the rational systems by which its actual sensuous activity has been obscured, as well as the historically mediated nature of "objectivity."[11]

We can now leave Lukács's account of reification in order to focus on two moments of crisis in which reified consciousness confronts activity beneath the hardened surface of its reified world.

One such moment occurs when Werner Heisenberg "discovers" the uncertainty principle, a concept that seems to have provided the philosophy of science with its own private version of the thing-in-itself. The uncertainty principle is designed to recognize the interference of our instruments of observation in the behavior of the phenomena being observed, and not merely in the degree of necessary error in our measurements. In his own account of indeterminacy, Heisenberg tries in effect to recontain the problems his discovery poses for scientific method, but he cannot obscure its radical content. For indeterminacy introduces, in Heisenberg's words, "the concept of probability into the definition of state of the object of scientific knowledge in quantum mechanics," and thus "rules out . . . the satisfying of the condition that the object of the physicist's knowledge is an isolated system." If the system cannot be isolated, then the objective reality of classical physics is punctured by the emergence of the subject. For, as Heisenberg notes, "classical physics may be said to be just that idealization in which we can speak about parts of the world without any reference to ourselves." This idealization is implicit in the Cartesian split between subject and object, a split that relies heavily on the privileged status accorded sight by natural science. Seventeenth-century science gave "sight . . . an almost exclusive privilege," as Foucault points out, "not . . . because men looked harder and more closely," but because sight is "the sense by which we perceive extent and establish proof." Other senses are either excluded or downgraded so that the natural scientist is "content with seeing – with seeing a few things systematically." But eventually, on the level of the atomic event, the scientist's observational instrument betrays the purpose for which it was designed; that is, it undermines the measurable and systematic picture of nature it is supposed to disclose. In the realm of the atomic event, at least, the observational instrument apparently participates, and with effects that cannot themselves be strictly measured. The segment of the world we had presumed to isolate for observation proves to be related to the observer. We might say, then, that if Cartesian dualism formally acknowledged the claim that we are separate from the world we examine, the uncertainty principle acknowledges the rediscovery of our inseparability from it.[12]

Such a crisis in natural science momentarily tears the fabric of a reified objectivity, not only revealing an irrational void beyond the limits of cognition but also resituating the detached observer as a participant within the carefully framed picture he confronts. This irrationality resides not in some noumenal reality whose penetration challenges us onward in our work, for indeterminacy inheres not in the "objective" world, but rather in the very act of examining it. Indeterminacy constitutes a scandal for science precisely because it reconstitutes the objective world as one including the subject. In other words, any epistemology entails an ontology, at least since Kant, and the ontology necessitated by indeterminacy defines reality as activity. As Heisenberg puts it, "quantum mechanics has brought the concept of potentiality back into physical science." As the observer faces the fact that he stands within the world he observes, he comes to recognize a moving world in which his observation constitutes an act.[13]

A similar rupture occurs at what John Berger calls "the moment of cubism." Berger analyzes the experience of a person viewing a cubist painting in terms of a contrast between the cubist's use of space and the illusionist space of Renaissance perspective. In the cubist painting, he says, "the viewing point of Renaissance perspective, fixed and outside the picture, but to which everything within the picture was drawn, has become a field of vision that is the picture itself." Consequently, when we view a cubist painting, we observe spaces defined between objects, but the relation defined between any two objects "does not, as it does in illusionist space, establish the rule for all spatial relationships between all the forms portrayed in the picture." Berger depicts the viewer's eye as moving into the picture and back to its surface repeatedly, depositing each time the newly acquired knowledge before returning to discover another relation. Thus, the cubist painting acts as "an expression of the relation between viewer and subject," and the evaluative question appropriate to it is not "Is it true?" or "Is it sincere?" but "Does it continue?" Berger concludes that the content of a cubist painting is "the relation between the seer and the seen," and that the works of Pablo

Picasso, George Braque, Juan Gris, and Fernand Léger from 1907 to 1914 "do not illustrate a human or social situation, they posit" one. The situation such paintings posit is one that radically redefines the epistemological relationship between perceiving subject and perceived object as interaction rather than confrontation. The detached viewer of an illusionist space in the Renaissance painting becomes the active participant in a process of vision inaugurated by the cubist painting.[14]

In both "moments," that of indeterminacy and cubism alike, relations overtake isolated objects in a field itself constituted by events. We can examine neither the atomic event nor the cubist painting without participating in its activity. The shock to reified consciousness first created by these ruptures in "objectivity" has long since been recontained, incorporated, that is, within the given world of "fact." Yet if one reads Heisenberg's account of his work, it remains possible to appreciate the genuine agony with which he and Niels Bohr brought themselves to accept the results of their own experiments. We need to be able to reinhabit such moments in order to comprehend the phenomenon of reification at all, so accustomed have we grown to incoherence. Lukács's account, first published in 1923, is outdated in one major respect: It does not fully appreciate the extent to which capitalist society can tolerate incoherence. *The Education of Henry Adams,* written some fifteen years before Lukács's essay, can serve as an example of how the threshold of tolerance has risen. For Adams the twentieth century is to be so incoherent as to be unimaginable; it must therefore cease to exist.[15]

If we try to reinhabit these moments of indeterminacy and cubism, they can serve to identify a particular result of reification and its contradictions. For in these moments, the relation between the contemplative observer and the objectified world undergoes a momentary transformation. Rather than confronting a static object, the observer finds himself participating in a process. In a Marxist perspective, the shock of such an experience results from the inability of reified consciousness to comprehend "reality . . . as sensuous human activity." Historical materialism, as Marx developed and applied it to political economy, constitutes a critical and revolutionary method precisely because it takes the interaction of man and nature through time as its subject and its ground observation, establishing its point of view of necessity within the process it studies, thereby voiding all escape hatches not only into detached objectivity, but also into idealized subjectivity. But in the daily life of reified consciousness, these moments of crisis come as a shock. Not only is the objectified surface of rationalization torn, revealing the irrational void lying beyond the limit of the thing-in-itself, but once admit that observation of the world constitutes a form of participation in its activity, and you experience a curious modern version of the Fall, for you become at least theoretically implicated and complicit in events you presume merely to watch, analyze, and interpret.[16]

Both the moral and epistemological implications of a presumed detachment on the part of an observer become clear in Henry James's *The Sacred Fount,* a work in which very little else becomes clear. The narrator of this novella devotes himself to observing his fellow guests during a weekend visit at a country home aptly called "Newmarch" in honor of the new march of society toward sham values and deceitful relations. The narrator, whose detachment is underscored by the fact that he remains nameless in a world of Lord Lutleys and Lady Froomes, observes among the couples assembled what he takes to be an alarming array of evidence suggesting vampirism; wives, husbands, and lovers seem to be sucking their partners dry of their youth or intelligence or beauty. But as the narrator's observations carry him on in the development of his theory, the reader is forced to abandon all hope of sharing his vision because here the Jamesian lucid reflector has become opaque. When the novel reaches its climactic concluding scene – the confrontation between the narrator and Mrs. Brissenden – the narrator's theory crumbles into a "pile of ruins." And the dialogue that takes place suggests not only that the narrator has allowed his theory to run away with him, but that his constant spying is itself a supreme instance of vampirism.[17]

Read as a kind of botched parable about the perils of vampirism for the artist who assumes a cold and detached posture toward his fellow creatures, pouring his passion into the effort to arrange them according to the needs of his own design, *The Sacred Fount* illustrates the well-known concern James shared with Hawthorne about the responsibilities of the artist. But when we recall that Mrs. Brissenden's explanation of people's behavior is no more reliable than the narrator's, such a reading becomes inadequate. For if *The Sacred Fount* were merely this, merely a parable, the narrator's theory would have to be exploded by a verifiable explanation, and it is not. Instead, the final dialogue presents us with a bewildering scene in which we can form no judgment at all about the observations we have been offered, because Mrs. Brissenden is no more reliable than the narrator. The scene thus calls attention not only to the inadequacies of the narrator's theory and the limitations of his subjective perspective, but also to the circumstance that dictates these problems – the narrator, while observing with such vengeance, has also been observed, a fact he is forced to realized for the first time when

Mrs. Brissenden demands to know his purposes. The closing scene reveals, in short, that he has been a participant in the events he has presented himself as merely observing. The entire narrative framework of the novel is called into question by this scene because the narrator's status as observer is undermined. Once afforded a view of him as a participant in the events he has been describing, we are faced with the realization that the narrator is a character who, like everyone else at Newmarch, has put on a mask to hide his peculiar passion. His unreliability is exposed on terms that not only destroy his theory but, more importantly, implicate him in the scene he observes in a wholly undetermined and undeterminable way. The closing scene of *The Sacred Fount* constitutes a moment of crisis not only for the narrator but for the reader as well. Mrs. Brissenden tells the narrator he's mad, and we are inclined to accept that judgment, because it allows us to retreat in safety from the fissure opened here – not that between the world "as it is" and the narrator's fabricated house of cards, but that within our own faith in the world as "objectively" accessible to cognition.

The cognitive abyss exposed in *The Sacred Fount's* concluding scene, only to be obscured by an appeal to the irrational, reflects a disjunction inherent in a reified social world, the disjunction between an immediate rationalized objectivity and an actual "sensuous human activity." The scandal surfaces, as in the case of indeterminacy, when the contemplative posture of the observer becomes so entrenched as to seem to constitute his identity. When observarion is carried to this point, reified consciousness behaves as if it were a disembodied eye, only to be faced with its own presence in the world it presumes to observe. That is, the contemplative stance of the detached observer, by virtue of the extreme to which it is taken, is undermined from within, and the observer of an immediately given world is exposed as a participant in the mediated activity of which that world is constituted. It is this scandal, I wish to argue, that haunts the worlds of Emerson, Adams, James, and Faulkner.

These are different worlds, to be sure. Ralph Waldo Emerson was born at the beginning of the nineteenth century (1803) into a family long associated with New England's religious tradition; Henry Adams, born close to midcentury (1838), grew up in a different Boston, one whose political heritage was inscribed in his family's history; Henry James, Adams's contemporary (1843), escaped his father's New England to become an expatriate, but by no means escaped America as a fictional subject; William Faulkner, born at century's end (1897), was the product of a fallen South and a frontier tradition. Emerson, the secular minister, Adams, the historian, and the novelists James and

Faulkner, emerge from different social and historical circumstances – which makes their shared concerns the more significant. Each of them responds critically to his society, and the related terms in which these several radical critiques take shape reveal at once the deepening structure of reification in American sociey as it moves from the nineteenth century into the twentieth, and the exemplary efforts of four of America's most formidable critical minds to overcome and resist that reification. According to Sartre, "Man is characterized above all by his going beyond a situation, and by what he succeeds in making of what he had been made – even if he never recognizes himself in his objectification." It is this "project," as Sartre calls it, to which Emerson, Adams, James, and Faulkner are committed, and in their attempts to go beyond the situation in which they find themselves, they all exhibit the effects of that reification for which they are trying to compensate.[18]

By examining these projects, we may trace a development in which both the contemplative stance of reified consciousness and the rationalized objectivity of a reifined world, while sinking deeper into the structure of social reality, are subjected to increasingly complex critical strategies. Emerson's critical reaction to rationalization yields an idealist version of the contemplative stance whose inherent contradiction resurfaces in *The Sacred Fount*. The later James tries to recontain this crisis in *The Golden Bowl*, by means of an aesthetic theory and practice designed to account for the detached seer's complicity as participant. The materialist version of reified consciousness, repressed but by no means escaped in Emerson's strategy, resurfaces in *The Education of Henry Adams*, where the contradiction inherent in the neutral observer's detached contemplation of a rationalized objectivity is exposed. James expands the role of the visionary seer to its critical limits, as he struggles to account for the complicity of the detached seer in the world he confronts, while Adams takes rationalization to its limits, revealing the more vividly as he struggles to comprehend it, the incoherence of the vision afforded the neutral observer. In the work of James and Adams, the contemplative stance of reified consciousness comes into view in an increasingly critical light, revealing both the impotence of the neutral observer's intellectual control of society as a whole, and the complicity of the observer's companion in reification, the visionary seer, as a participant in the world beyond which he or she presumes to stand. It is this combined impotence and complicity that we not only find fused in the figure of Thomas Sutpen, but also must find ways of defending ourselves against as readers of *Absalom, Absalom!* Rejoining neutral observer and visionary seer as victims of the same reified consciousness, Faulkner devises a narrative strategy that reveals the source of the contradiction that had first surfaced for Emerson – the exclusion of "sensuous human activity" from the objectified world. The inability of reified consciousness to apprehend history as sensuous human activity is here revealed as rooted in a specific historical process, one dominated by the unimpeded capitalist development that both made America, and made it "innocent."

In the course of the progression traceable in these projects, detached seers and observers are increasingly threatened with the recognition forced on Heisenberg – the recognition of the seer's participation in an active reality whose status as an "object of contemplation" is undermined. Because reification operates to exclude sensuous human activity from the objective reality the observer confronts, that activity erupts in a kind of return of the repressed. It is not, however, until Faulkner's response to this crisis that its actual sources are revealed, for Emerson's initial diagnosis enables him finally to evade the contradictions he bequeaths to James and Adams. They, in their turn, develop strategies designed to save the detached observer, to recontain the crisis to which his contemplative stance makes him vulnerable. If we trace this developing struggle in outline, we can see why Faulkner's treatment of the detached observer yields such explosive results.[19]

Emerson's opposition to the "mechanical powers and the mechanical philosophy" of his time stems from his disaffection with a society that is turning man "into a thing, into many things," as its faith in the "goddess of Reason" leads it to contrive systems in which man is "pedled out" and reduced to an aggregate of atomized beings making up " 'the mass' and 'the herd.' " In his attempt to compensate for this degradation by speaking in the name of the whole man, and in the service of his salvation from alienation, Emerson attacks the most evident feature of reification in his day – rationalization, or the tendency to mechanize man in the service of profit-making enterprises requiring calculation and measurable risks. But Emerson's critical revolt ultimately reveals the penetrating force of reification, for inherent in his resistance to rationalization is the detached contemplative stance of reified consciousness.[20]

The conviction at the heart of Emerson's career is that "the reason why the world lacks unity, and lies broken and in heaps, is because man is disunited with himself." When he set out in *Nature* to forge an "original relation" between the me and the "Not Me," he did so in the faith that within the reified objectivity confronting him as alien spectator lay "imbedded" his essential selfhood. Thus the issue in *Nature* is the same issue to which Emerson referred in a journal entry of 1839 – whether "the world is not a dualism, is not a bipolar unity, but is two, is Me and It." If this is the case, "then there is the alien, the unknown, and all we have believed and chanted out of our deep instinctive hope is a pretty dream." If man's self-alienation is a given, eternal, immutable condition, then Emerson's entire project proves a fool's game.[21]

So much must be grasped in order to appreciate the purpose of Emerson's procedure in *Nature,* where he establishes the opposition between the me and the "Not Me" at the outset as a given in order to transform it into an illusion. His method is based on the conviction he shared with Fichte, that the reunion of subject and object required a translation of facts into events, of substance into act. On an epistemological level, Emerson succeeded in reunifying the subject and the object within an act – an act of signification authorized by and grounded in Spirit. By the essay's end, the "Not Me" – the "involuntary," the given and opaque "objectivity" of the world – has been dissolved and transformed into an illusion. Emerson's method is designed to serve a rhetorical purpose: to provide a vantage point from which the world can be seen as fluid, volatile, and obedient to man's will. As he put it in a journal entry of Februry 1836, "I do not dispute" the "absolute being" of "a field of corn or a rich pasture," but "point out the just way of viewing them." In his effort to arrive at this "just way of viewing" a reified objectivity, Emerson constructed a method whose genuis lay in its power to penetrate the immediate and show it to be mediated.[22]

Both the power and the limitations of that method are apparent in Emerson's summary statement: "Nature from an immoveable God . . . on which as reptiles we creep, & to which we must conform our being, becomes an instrument, & serves us with all her kingdoms. Then becomes a spectacle." Emerson saw clearly enough that "man is not what man should be," and that bourgeois society had made him so. Further, he understood that this society was the product of human agency, that it was historically mediated. Yet his attempt to overcome immediacy, to reconstruct the "original relation" of man to his world led finally to a metaphysics of vision. Emerson was virtually unable to conceptualize the self except in the form of an eye. Man was for him a "subject-lens," whose self-alienation is indicated by the distorted vision resulting from a kind of false correction in that lens. Even when he tried to conceive of nonalienation, to imagine the reunion of man and nature, he could only do so by turning man into a transparent eyeball, a procedure that merely reconstitutes alienation in a different guise. The transparent eyeball is an attempt to fuse epistemological detachment with ontological participation, to project as image the active relation between man and nature, between seer and seen, that *Nature* as a whole aims to establish. Yet when, as transparent eyeball, Emerson says, "I am nothing: I see all," the split temporarily obscured in the eyeball image reemerges. The rhetorical emphasis falls on the predicates, distracting us from the miraculous return in the second clause of the "I" who has just been voided by the first. Swallowed up by its role as seer, the material self disappears. Thus the problem raised by Hegel's somewhat similar attempt to unify the subject and the object within a process emerges, for Emerson's Spirit, like Hegel's Absolute Reason, comes to the rescue as the missing subject of historical mediation. And Lukács's remark about the freedom of man in Hegel's history applies to Emersonian freedom as well: It is the "freedom to reflect upon laws – which themselves govern man, a freedom which in Spinoza a thrown stone would possess if it had consciousness."[23]

Yet as Newton Arvin points out, "it is a paradox that the writer who most perfectly expressed the aspirations of the America middle-class . . . also, more than almost any other . . . anticipated its passing." Arvin calls this a "vital" paradox, and so indeed it is. For Emerson's attempt to reunite man with himself led on the one hand to a faith in Spirit's benevolence in history so total as to sanctify the contemplative stance of the most ardent capitalist entrepreneur, and to a rhetorical program, on the other, designed to persuade people that the world they confronted as given was made by men and women and could be radically changed by them. The same paradox emerges when Emerson says, "Speak your latent conviction, and it shall be the universal sense." This is a flat statement of Emerson's deepest faith in the power of people to shape their destinies, and as such may indicate his "underlying identity of interest" with a society whose creed was individualism. Yet one must remember that the statement was delivered in "Self-Reliance" not as a calm philosophical doctrine, but as both a charge to the reader to change society and a firm assurance that he or she could do so. Emerson's own struggle to speak his latent conviction is in retrospect belied by the degree to which it became the universal sense. Finally, however, the paradox is inscribed within the method he developed for overcoming alienation. "Cannot I conceive the Universe without a contradiction?" he asked himself. The answer was no, but his effort to do so led him to expose the sources of the contradiction he could not override, the contradiction between a desire to "be" and to "see my being, at the same time."[24]

Perhaps the most energetic and sustained development of Emerson's program for the visionary seer as poet is to be found in Henry

James's career as a novelist. In his third-person center of consciousness, James exploited the transparent eyeball as a lucid reflector, but as we have already noted, the lucid reflector serving as a narrative lens is not transparent and cannot blithely float in the "currents of Universal Being." As *The Sacred Fount* demonstrates, the detached seer whom James invests with the role of visionary artist is also a participant in the world he confronts, and is thus potentially implicated in the events he watches, a point by no means lost on James. Sharing Emerson's conviction that the visionary seer is intensely active, James attempted to account for the seer's agency without forfeiting his status as seer. The final result of that effort is Maggie Verver, who acts on the Emersonian belief that, having made his world, man can remake it in accord with his dreams. But Maggie's career at the same time serves in one sense to de-mystify the transparent eyeball, demonstrating how the creative subject "in action," as Lukács describes the capitalist, is "transformed into a receptive organ ready to pounce," a subject, that is, whose "activity will narrow itself down to the adoption of a vantage point" from which the world is reshaped in accord with "his best interests," and who thereby assumes a "purely contemplative" attitude. Maggie, in short, is at once the visionary poet and the capitalist entrepreneur.[25]

It is this identity, implicit in Emerson's own program, which helps to account for the contradictory response which *The Golden Bowl* has always evoked. With characteristic lucidity, F. R. Leavis stated the issue when he said that although we are meant "to watch with intense sympathy Maggie's victorious struggle to break the clandestine relation between her husband and Charlotte," it remains the case that "our sympathies . . . are with Charlotte and (a little) the Prince." The contradiction to which Leavis points is unmistakably present in the novel, although it need not lead us to agree with Leavis's diagnosis that the later James had somehow "lost his full sense of life and let his moral taste slip into abeyance." I would propose a different diagnosis, that the logic of James's career as a devotee of the Imagination led him to produce a work in which the visionary seer's valorization is achieved on the basis of a narrative that exposes the crack, the something "terrible at the heart of man," as the Prince calls it, which must be there, and yet be concealed, if the redemptive project is to succeed, if what Maggie calls a "distinctly bourgeois" world is to be secure. Our conflicting responses to Maggie's career, as at once miraculous and monstrous, derive from the scrupulous logic of James's procedure, which goes beyond Maggie's in exposing the commodified society whose values are adumbrated by her redemptive project.[26]

That procedure stems from James's effort to recontain the crisis erupting in *The Sacred Fount* by means of a strategy that allows him to acknowledge the seer's complicity without sacrificing his detached contemplative stance. The success of this strategy depends on a world constituted exclusively of and by seers who are also seen. In effect, James is led to solve the problems attendant upon reified consciousness by conceiving a completely reified society. The finally exposed condition of *The Sacred Fount's* narrator becomes essentially the condition of everyone in *The Golden Bowl,* insofar as everyone here is simultaneously both a detached seer and a complicit participant. It is only in a world made up entirely of people constituted as seers and seen that the activity of the visionary artist can proceed without her abandoning her detached contemplative stance. Maggie is a visionary seer whose innocence consists in her failure to recognize her complicity as participant in the creation of her peculiar world. In acting to redeem that world, she takes responsibility for her complicity, thereby meeting the moral dilemma implicit in the epistemological rupture that concludes *The Sacred Fount.* But far from abandoning her detached posture as seer, she exploits and solidifies it. Thus, although Maggie's career serves to acknowledge the seer's complicity, her success both presupposes and exposes a world in which man's reified status is confirmed. At the novel's end, that is, we have a world in which man has become, in Lukács's words, at once "an element in the movement of commodities" and the "impotent observer of that movement."[27]

   Such is the fate of Charlotte and the Prince, whose destiny is to be initiated into a fully capitalist world as commodities. Both purchased by Adam Verver, Charlotte and Amerigo are to fulfill their roles as commodities in significantly different ways, but their fate as pieces of "human furniture" is prophetically evident at the novel's outset. Here the Prince surveys objects perhaps more "massive and lumpish" than the "*morceau de musée*" which he constitutes, but since they reside behind "plate glass," and are soon to be confined within "the iron shutter of a shop" like the one in which he is similarly to be put on display, it is not surprising that his gaze is troubled. He is confronted with his own image in the marketplace world he is about to join, not as the prospective capitalist adventurer he hopes to become, but as the commodity he has already unwittingly consented to be.[28]

   What is essential to an understanding of *The Golden Bowl* is the recognition that its world is in fact commodified from the beginning, for Maggie's redemptive action presupposes a marketplace world, and she succeeds by acting in accord with its laws. Thus, although her career valorizes the visionary artist's redemptive role, it ends by solidifying a world now thoroughly reified. By standing outside the "funny form" of her marriage as spectator, while playing an improvised role in the play she is watching, Maggie fulfills Emerson's desire to "be and see my being at the same time." But her success as transcendent seer is ironic, for it leaves her bifurcated in these very terms, doomed to be split permanently into the detached seer and the observed actress she has had to become. Her world is remade, to be sure, but it is remade on the basis of the "sublime economy of art" which, as we shall see, emulates the sublime economy of Capital.[29]

Emerson's desire to "be and see my being at the same time" assumes a rather different ironic form in Henry Adams's reputed capacity to "sit on a fence and watch himself go by." Alienated early from a society whose contradictions came almost to hypnotize him. Adams turned detached contemplation into a profession; while James exploited the spectator's role in his development of the third-person center of consciousness, Adams fetishized it. Adams had little patience for Emersonian idealism, much less for the complexities it had generated in the later novels of his friend James. But Adams was far from escaping his own Emersonian heritage. Struggling to maintain a materialist position, Adams was finally to expose the contradictions attendant upon his faith in a rationalized objectivity, just as James was forced to expose a reified world in his effort to recontain the contradiction implicit in Emerson's idealized version of reified vision.[30]

Like Emerson, Adams questioned the solidity of a society driven forward by forces that made its faith in Reason and Progress the more untenable with every passing year. Adams sought to comprehend the contradiction between the advance of scientific reason and the spread of social chaos, and did so with a logical rigor conspicuously absent from Emerson's thinking. Marshaling all the available intellectual resources for calculation and prediction, Adams demonstrated their inadequacy, but never suspended his effort to comprehend history within some intelligible framework.

At the outset of their careers, Emerson and Adams occupied opposite ends of the spectrum as far as reified thought's effort to apprehend history is concerned. Emerson appealed to great men, and Adams, to "natural laws." But eventually, Emerson was saying prayers to "Beautiful Necessity," and Adams was inquiring whether men might after all be able to "react, not at haphazard, but by choice on the lines of force that attract their world." Both oscillated between the two extremes of the contemplative attitude toward history, although they moved in opposite directions.[31]

Early in life, Emerson found confirmation of his belief in the social structure's mediated status when a crisis occurred. During the panic of 1837 we find him remarking, "when these full measures come, it then stands confessed – Society has played out its last stake; it is check-mated." There is a distinct glee in the following response to the "black times": "What was, ever since my memory, solid continent, now yawns apart and discloses its composition and genesis. I learn geology the morning after an earthquake. . . . I see the natural fracture of the stone. I see the tearing of the tree & learn its fibre & its rooting. The Artificial is rent from the Eternal." At this stage, Emerson was grateful for such evidence that the world had "failed," because it confirmed his faith in the power of man to make and remake that world. Eventually, however, reified objectivity was to take on a more powerful aspect, and the "torrents of tendency" to acquire the status of a metaphysical prin-ciple. Adams's early efforts, on the other hand, to trace the sequence of history within the terms dictated by his eighteenth-century belief in progress, led him to regard men as "mere grasshoppers kicking and gesticulating on the middle of the Mississippi River." When the panic of 1893 broke out, it confirmed Adams's belief that society had failed, but the spectator here had grown nervous in his seat. Writing to John Hay, Adams exclaimed,

> For a thorough chaos I have seen nothing since the war to compare with it. The world surely cannot long remain as mad as it is, without breaking into acute mania. . . . I'm mad. I'm madder than ever. . . . I am seriously speculating whether I shall have a better view of the *fin-de-siècle* circus in England, Germany, France, or India, and whether I should engage seats to view the debacle in London, Paris, Berlin or Calcutta.

He went on to say, "My dear democracy is all in pieces." Such ruptures were to occupy Adams's attention for the rest of his productive life, as he tried to comprehend them within a rational scheme. Adams had begun with the conviction that "if anything universal was unreal . . . it was his own thought, and not the thing that moved it." Yet he ended by trying to measure the "sequence of force" by reference to its "attrac-tion on thought."[32]

Henry Adams enjoyed the freedom to reflect upon laws for many years, and he reached the conclusion that the laws did not bear reflect-ing upon; science itself had revealed their inadequacy by exploding them one after another. When "Madame Curie threw on his desk the metaphysical bomb she called radium," the scientist, Adams remarks, had "no hole to hide in – no one could longer hope to bar out the unknowable, for the unknowable was known." Thus when Adams hypothesized that history was a sequence of forces, and set about trying to order that sequence, his purpose was to discover whether man might after all play some role in directing history's course. Adopting the attitude of the scientist, he decided that if man is to control such forces, he must be able to measure them. Only then could he hope to "react . . . by choice" and not involuntarily. Adams's effort to measure force in terms of its "attraction on thought" had the advantage of reinserting man within the historical process to be apprehended, but the man reinserted remained an observer, and Adams became an observer twice removed. For now he set about observing the reactions of "great men before great monuments," and devising a "dynamic theory" of history based on the "law of reaction between force and force – between mind and nature – the law of progress."[33]

That Adams's procedure is "unscientific" in conventional terms, no one would question. Yet in a sense, this is precisely its value. In his effort to abide by the premises of Newtonian physics – to speak about parts of the world without reference to himself – Adams was forced to violate those premises. Because the picture of history he confronted failed to cohere, he was compelled to reinsert a neutralized self into that picture, a "manikin" designed to serve the purposes of measurement. By carrying rational observation to this point, along with his other scientific paraphernalia, Adams simulateously carries out the program of scientific progress, and shows that program's incoherence. The problem Adams always presents to us as critical readers is that of irony. We find it impossible to take seriously his analogy between the mind and a comet, except as simply that, an analogy with no cognitive foundation. Yet Adams's endeavor to treat himself as a "barometer, pedometer, radiometer" reflects at once a bitter irony and a genuinely serious enterprise. Adams *was* the *"type-bourgeois-bostonian"* for which he took himself, and he could not help trying to carry out the rational program of the eighteenth century, to whose ideal of enlightenment he remained, like Gatsby, true to the end. It was precisely because of his struggle to remain true to these ideals that he was forced again and again to confront the contradictions in that program. Adams's fatalism, in other words, is an exemplary one, for his effort to discover whether men or women might have some part to play in history's direction reflects a genuine desire to disprove his own suspicion that they were atoms pushed and pulled by forces of which they were wholly ignorant. His fatalism results from the intellectual honesty with which he confronted the evidence before him.[34]

Adams's was perhaps the last great mind in America capable of following current developments in geology, physics, economics, politics, literature, philosophy, and historical research on anything approaching a global scale. The picture presented to him by this assemblage of evidence forced the question that he posed and reposed from 1893 until the end of his life, the question that *The Education of Henry Adams* was designed to raise for its reader: Can man control the direction of history? *The Education*'s peculiar contradictions derive from the fact that it poses for bourgeois society the question of its own survival. *The Education* is an attempt to educate, "to fit young men in universities and elsewhere, to be men of the world, equipped for any emergency." As such, *The Education* is not a wholly futilitarian document, for it records the heroic struggle of the reified bourgeois mind to formulate a coherent basis for the future of its society. Yet its didactic purpose is inscribed upon a narrative that tells the story of that society's self-destruction. In his effort to face squarely the multiple contradictions thrown up by his didactic pursuit, Adams dismantles, step by step, in his narrative, the complacent assumptions of that society, exposing the impotence of its systems of thought in the face of the energies it has itself unleashed. It is this contradiction between the desire to educate, stemming from Adams's unregenerate reformist tendencies, and the desire to tell a story whose moral could not but reveal the futility of that "heavy dissertation on modern education" for which it was intended as a vehicle, which undermines Adams's attempt to make *The Education* cohere. But the contradiction between what Adams described as his "narrative and didactic purpose and style" makes for more than a formal problem. It generates an ethical dilemma as well.[35]

Adams is given to making pronouncements throughout *The Education* about his absolute lack of responsibility, only to find himself eventually asking "where his responsibility began or ended." Here the contradiction between the individual's imputed freedom to shape – and his consequent responsibility for – his world, and his actual freedom in capitalist society merely to reflect upon "natural laws" manifests itself most dramatically. For if the Adams whose recorded life is that of a mere "bystander," the man on the fence, observing a drama for which he takes no responsibility, the Adams who writes *The Education* with a didactic purpose thereby inadvertently reveals his status as a member of the procession going by. In other words, by pursuing his didactic goal, to "encourage foresight and to economize waste of mind," Adams betrays and undermines his contemplative stance, revealing his own participation in the spectacle he repeatedly insists he is merely watching. By the end of *The Education,* he partly admits to the contradiction in assuming the role of an "umpire," whose "attitude is apt to infuriate the spectators," but whose duty is fulfilled. The narrative strategy of *The Educa-*

tion, in other words, is designed primarily to deny what the act of writing it demonstrates – that Adams was a participant in the social process he presumed merely to observe.[36]

The contradictions Adams keeps confronting in *The Education* reveal the irrationality he seeks to expose and to remedy; America has rarely had a more brilliant and incisive critic. Yet the more radical Adams's critical responses become, the more evident is the reified consciousness that delivers the judgment. For instance, Adams cannot quit blaming his age's problems on the stupidity of it's men, while all the time describing their impotence. More significantly, he cannot stop trying to affect history even though he insists that he is a mere observer of it. He is after all a bit like James's Fanny Assingham, always pronouncing that he is not responsible, but never able to escape completely his sense of complicity. It is this combination of complicity and impotence whose sources Faulkner exposes.

Like Emerson, Faulkner revolts against a stolid adherence to tradition; like Adams, Faulkner brings to bear the full weight of a historical imagination on his critique of modern society; like James, he works out his critical response in terms of a complex narrative strategy. But Faulkner cuts deeper, and exposes the roots of reification from which his own critical interpretation grows. Each of these writers exhibits a deep-seated ambivalence toward his society, but in Faulkner that ambivalence achieves a certain purity, a kind of stoic and open-faced acceptance of despair in comparison with which Hemingway's concept of courageous honesty, for example, looks irremediably sentimental. Faulkner's despair, I suggest, grows out of a recognition, registered in his greatest work, that the very project he himself pursues in his fiction, the drive to go beyond one's situation, is both irresistible and doomed.

In *Absalom, Absalom!* and *Light in August,* Faulkner developed a narrative strategy designed to undermine the reader's detachment so as to implicate him in a "stream of event" that he presumes merely to witness. The complex demands Faulkner makes on the reader, particularly in these two novels where the moral implications of detachment are so powerfully demonstrated, stem from a strategy that undermines the reader's compulsion to contain the moving flow of narrative within some ordering frame, to remain the fixed, detached spectator of a given and preformed fictional world. *Light in August* already undermines any effort on the reader's part to maintain a secure vantage point, and does so in terms that make clear why such a vantage point is illegitimate; to order the flow of time, one must presume to stand outside it, as does

Gail Hightower. *Light in August* resists our desire for the fixed perspective of illusionist space by refusing to allow us to follow any single action through to its completion. Each story necessitates another, until plot lines seem to spread out indefinitely. Moreover, we are set down *in medias res,* so that as we move forward in time, we double back farther and farther into the past. Faulkner denies not merely the validity of a detached perspective, but the very possibility of one. Any fixed perspective we may hope to gain is disrupted by time's unceasing flow. In other words, the reader is compelled to order time while it is moving, a task at which he is doomed to fail. In short, the novel frustrates the reader's desire to frame a coherent picture by means of a narrative structure that enforces the rule that time's flow outstrips all attempts to order it.[37]

In *Absalom, Absalom!,* however, Faulkner went further. What was demonstrated in *Light in August* is now enacted. Quentin Compson comes to us as an auditor who is forced to listen to Rosa Coldfield, to his father, and to his roommate, but who struggles to resist a narrative pull that threatens to engulf him. By refusing to speak while watching static pictures of Sutpen and his family resolve out of nothing into "painted portraits hung in a vacuum," Quentin tries to maintain a detached perspective on the story of Sutpen, and so to free himself not only from the weight of the past but from his involvement in the "stream of event" itself. But he is forced eventually to participate in the telling of Sutpen's story, a process that undermines his effort to see it as an assembled totality distinct from himself. The very endeavor to secure and maintain a detached perspective on history by imposing narrative coherence on it leads inexorably to Quentin's participation in it. Furthermore, readers' detachment is undermined in the same way, for like Quentin, we struggle to confront a story that insists on engulfing us. The reader can no more succeed in securing a fixed point of view from which to confront the novel as a discrete totality than Quentin can find a position outside the tale of Sutpen. In *Absalom, Absalom!,* as in life itself, by the time we find out what's going on, we are already implicated in it.[38]

We have been too much concerned with the fact that Rosa, Mr. Compson, and Quentin/Shreve produce different versions of Sutpen's story to pay sufficient attention to the medium out of which we extract these versions, the medium of conversation. For *Absalom, Absalom!* does not simply conduct us through a series of perspectives, calling attention to the limitations of each; it implicates the reader in the collective act of narrative construction of which it is constituted. By making conversation the vehicle for the novel's central action, the telling of a

story, and by reiterating the physical and material substratum of conversation – breathing, air – Fraulkner exploits the radical potential of
speech as social act. The halting yet persistent voice of Byron Bunch
that drew Gail Hightower temporarily into the moving world outside
his window in *Light in August* becomes in *Absalom, Absalom!* the relent-
less insistence not only of Shreve's voice drawing Quentin into a conversation, but of Faulkner's voice struggling to draw the reader into
one as well.

Needless to say, Faulkner cannot finally succeed at making the reader
a participant. To do so would entail actually bridging the gap between
words and deeds, the gap to which Addie Bundren refers in *As I Lay
Dying* when she laments how "words go straight up in a thin line . . .
and how terribly doing goes along the earth." Yet what Faulkner can
and does achieve, is a resolution to the novel that contaminates what it
cannot undercut – the reader's inherently contemplative position. At the
novel's end, we have only two places to stand – within the picture with
Quentin, or outside it with Shreve. I do not mean that we must "identify" with one or the other of these two characters, but rather that
between them they exhaust all the available epistemological positions.
We cannot accept Quentin's position, for in telling and hearing Sutpen's
story, Quentin has in effect fallen into history. He has become a blood
relation of Charles Bon's, and thus of Sutpen's. There are a host of
reasons why Quentin's position is closed to us, not the least of which is
that we cannot afford to know history as Quentin knows it at the
novel's end. The point is that it is not a question of choice; we could
not adopt Quentin's position even if we wanted to, and given his fate,
we certainly do not want to. Our position must be that of Shreve, who
is once again fixed and outside the picture, and as such, our position is
contaminated. For when Shreve turns on Quentin in the last chapter to
draw a conclusion to the story, he no longer sounds like Quentin's
father, but like Sutpen himself. The conclusion he draws is that "it
takes two niggers to get rid of one Sutpen." This "clears the whole
ledger," he thinks, except that "you've got one nigger left" whom you
can't "catch" and "don't even always see," but you still "hear." While
Quentin indeed continues to "hear" Jim Bond's voice, Shreve pursues a
different course; he finds a "use" for this dangling fraction by issuing a
prophecy – "the Jim Bonds are going to conquer the western hemisphere." Whatever accuracy may be attributed to Shreve's prediction,
the significant point is that his resolution provokes the question of
accuracy in the first place. For Shreve has become not only the detached
observer, confronting and assembling the story of Sutpen, but a parodic
case of the scientist who quantifies and predicts. He thereby mimics the

Sutpen who searches for his "mistake" at the end of a life conducted as an experiment designed to prove his immortality.[39]

Behind this ending to *Absalom, Absalom!* lies a series of resolutions-by-schizophrenia in Faulkner's fiction. Quentin's conversation with Shreve actually begins in the novel's first chapter as a dialogue between "two separate Quentins," a dialogue whose two voices are, in as literal a sense as possible, materialized later at Harvard. The quantum leap in Faulkner's narrative strategy that *Absalom, Absalom!* represents may be indicated by looking at a similar splitting-up of a single identity in the closing pages of *As I Lay Dying*. In this novel, Faulkner uses multiple perspective to present events as constituted by subjects and objects interacting in a flux presided over by no single and detached perspective. Subjects are constituted in this novel by other subjects' objectification of them. Everyone is both a subject and an object, but no one is both at once; herein lies their alienation from each other and themselves. The reader relies most heavily on Addie and Darl for his knowledge of events. In these two characters, however, the epistemological dilemma is resolved in two equally scandalous ways; Addie's death resolves her alienation, and Darl's madness resolves his. Until he splits apart, Darl serves as a transparent eyeball. Indeed, his problem is precisely that he is nothing and he sees all. It is only when he splits in two and confronts himself as "Darl" that he knows, for the first time, that he exists. The "I" who sees the world, long since alienated from the "I" who inhabits it by Emerson's transparent eyeball, now confronts itself across the chasm of self-alienation and responds with the hysterical laughter of madness.

The advance marked by *Absalom, Absalom!*'s analogous resolution derives from Faulkner's translation of the issue from visual terms into auditory ones. Dialogue replaces sight as the means by which present events are constituted. This shift enables Faulkner to translate the epistemological dilemma from the context of reified flux to that of history as "sensuous human activity." The fact reiterated throughout the novel, that Quentin and Shreve breathe and speak through the same air breathed by those whom they try to confront as static figures in a picture, makes of dialogue a physical act whose active material substratum cannot be denied. This unwitting exploitation of Marx's remark that language is "agitated layers of air, sound" enables Faulkner to reconstitute the isolated case of Darl's self-alienation as the social condition of man in modern history. For what is severed at the end of *Absalom, Absalom!* is the bond between Quentin and Shreve formed by the "happy marriage of speaking and hearing" in chapter 8; when that bond is cut in chapter 9, Quentin is left in the realm of sound, hearing Jim Bond's howling, while Shreve retreats to the realm of sight.[40]

By exploiting the potential of speech as social act – a potential already implicit in the projects of Emerson, James, and Adams – and by undercutting the privileged status of sight, *Absalom, Absalom!* undermines both the active self of subjectivist idealism and the neutral observer of objectivist materialism. In other words, it is not only Sutpen's attempt to transcend history, but also Quentin's effort to escape it, which is doomed, and for the same reason. It is not difficult to see that Sutpen's fate gives the lie to the Emersonian project of self-reliance. Sutpen's story exposes the consequences of the Emersonian denial of the flesh, the family, and the social relatedness of every individual in the human community, past, present, and future. But what dooms Sutpen's effort át transcedence is also what undermines Quentin's effort at detachment – the fact, as Marx put it in *The German Ideology,* that "as soon as this active life process is described history ceases to be a collection of dead facts as it is with the empiricists (themselves still abstract), or an imagined activity of imagined subjects, as with the idealists." History becomes, in short, "sensuous human activity."[41]

Each of these writers struggles to overcome immediacy by reconstituting an active and dynamic realm in which man can truly be at home. Each one also fails to gain access to that reality, and yet in their effort to reconstitute it, the scandal we saw first in James surfaces. The contemplative stance of the detached observer, by virtue of the extreme to which it is taken, is undermined from within. The observer becomes a participant. Of course, the scandal must then be recontained, for reified consciousness cannot apprehend history as active life process without, as Lukács puts it, confronting its own suicide. Yet, with Faulkner, this is precisely the conclusion at which the romantic tradition in American literature arrives. At least one detached observer in *Absalom, Absalom!* falls into the picture he tries merely to observe, and the consequence of his fall is death.[42]

Lukács identified the heroic quality in classical German philosophy in just this ability "to think the deepest and most fundamental problems of the development of bourgeois society through to the very end . . . to take all the paradoxes of its position to the point where the necessity of going beyond this historical state . . . can at least be seen as a problem," and thus "in thought . . . complete the evolution of class." If, as Lukács claims, "the *developing tendencies of history constitute a higher reality than the empirical 'facts',*" then perhaps the formal, stylistic, and thematic extremities to which American literature has resorted reflect not a flight from the constraints of civilized life, but a radical understanding of the mediated nature of the given social world. In any case, one is forced to consider this possibility after examining the projects of Emerson, James, Adams, and Faulkner in the light of Lukács's formulation of reification. For here we find a repeated struggle to overcome the immediacy of a reified bourgeois society in the course of which the limits of reified thought are not only repeatedly demonstrated but ultimately confronted and exposed.[43]

Notes

1 Henry James, *Hawthorne* (New York: Macmillan, 1967), p. 55. The critical commonplace in question is rooted in views going back to Tocqueville. In our century, it has been elaborated most notably in works familiar to all students of American literature by D. H. Lawrence, R. W. B. Lewis, Richard Chase, and Richard Poirier. More recently, it has been reiterated in more politicized terms in Quentin Anderson, *The Imperial Self* (New York: Knopf, 1971), and in Myra Jehlen, "New World Epics: The Middle Class Novel in America," *Salmagundi* 36 (Winter 1977): 49–68.

2 In his essay in *History and Class Consciousness,* "Reification and the Consciousness of the Proletariat," Lukács applies to the realm of classical German philosophy the methods Marx used to analyze classical economics. Divided into three sections, the essay first formulates "structural analogues" between the situation of the worker and that of the bureaucrat, the technologist, indeed of all who inhabit capitalist society; second, focuses on the "antimonies of bourgeois thought," specifically those evident in German philosophy from Kant to Hegel; and finally, outlines a resolution of these contradictions that depends on the self-consciousness of the proletariat. I am drawing on Lukács's essay for a formulation of the concept of reification and do not pretend to address the many issues it has raised for Marxist theorists, particularly those generated by Lukács's identity theory.

   Karl Marx, *Capital,* trans. Ben Fowkes (New York: Random House, 1977), 1:164, quoted in Georg Lukács, *History and Class Consciousness,* trans. Rodney Livingstone (Cambridge, Mass.: MIT Press, 1971), p. 86; Lukács, *History,* pp. 86–87, 97.

3 Lukács, *History,* p. 87; Marx, *Capital,* 1:176–77.

4 Lukács, *History,* pp. 87, 89, 91–92, 100, 93, 132, 131.

5 Karl Marx and Friedrich Engels, *The German Ideology,* trans. Salo Ryanaskaya (London: Laurence & Wishart, 1965), p. 645; Raymond Williams, *Marxism and Literature* (New York: Oxford University Press, 1977), p. 32.

6 Lukács, *History,* pp. 102, 96, 100.

7 Ibid., pp. 111, 116.

8 Ibid., pp. 120, 121, 119, 139, 147.

9 For a basic history of identity theory as an issue in subsequent Marxist debate, see Martin Jay's history of the Frankfurt School, *The Dialectical Imagination* (Boston: Little, Brown, 1973).

10 Lukács, *History*, pp. 154, 158; Marx and Engels, *German Ideology*, pp. 57–58, 645.

11 Lukács, *History*, p. 150; Marx and Engels, *German Ideology*, p. 645.

12 Werner Heisenberg, *Physics and Philosophy* (New York: Harper & Row, 1962), pp. 24, 25; Michel Foucault, *The Order of Things* (New York: Random House, 1970), pp. 133–34.

13 Heisenberg, *Physics and Philosophy*, p. 4.

14 John Berger, "The Moment of Cubism," in *The Look of Things*, ed. Nokos Strangos (New York: Viking, 1971), pp. 150–59.

15 During the autumn of 1926, when he was in Copenhagen working on the problems of quantum theory with Erwin Schrodinger and Niels Bohr, Heisenberg recalls, there were "discussions with Bohr which went through many hours till very late at night and ended almost in despair: and when at the end of the discussion I went alone for a walk in the neighboring park I repeated to myself again and again the question: Can nature possibly be as absurd as it seemed to us in these atomic experiments?" See Heisenberg, *Physics and Philosophy*, p. 42.

16 Marx and Engels, *German Ideology*, p. 645.

17 Henry James, *The Sacred Fount*, ed. Leon Edel (New York: Grove, 1953), p. 312.

18 Jean-Paul Sartre, *Search for a Method*, trans. Hazel E. Barnes (New York: Random House, 1968), p. 91.

19 Lukács, *History*, p. 121.

20 Ralph Waldo Emerson, *The Journals and Miscellaneous Notebooks of Ralph Waldo Emerson*, ed. William A. Gilman, Alfred R. Ferguson, et al. (Cambridge: Mass.: Harvard University Press, 1960–). 7:271 (hereafter cited as *Journals*); Emerson, *The Collected Works of Ralph Waldo Emerson*, ed. Alfred R. Ferguson, William H. Gilman, Robert E. Spiller, and Carl F. Strauch (Cambridge, Mass.: Harvard University Press, 1971—), 1:53, 65, 92 (hereafter cited as *Collected Works*).

21 Emerson, *Collected Works*, 1:43, 7–8.

22 "The kingdom of the involuntary, of the not me." Emerson, *Journals*, 5:333, 123–4.

23 Emerson, *Journals*, 5:125, 333; Emerson, *Collected Works*, 1:10; Lukács, *History*, p. 146.

24 Newton Arvin, *American Pantheon*, ed. Daniel Aaron and Sylvan Schendler (New York: Delacorte, 1966), p. 13; Emerson, *The Complete Works of Ralph Waldo Emerson*, ed. Edward Waldo Emerson, 12 vols. (Boston: Houghton Mifflin, 1904), 2:45 (hereafter cited as *Complete Works*); Emerson, *Journals*, 5:337; 4:278.

25 Lukács, *History*, p. 166.

26 F. R. Leavis, *The Great Tradition* (New York: New York University Press, 197), pp. 160–61; Henry James, *The Golden Bowl* (New York: Penguin, 1966), p. 537.

27 Lukács, *History*, p. 166.

28 James, *The Golden Bowl,* pp. 541, 29, 35, 39.
29 Ibid., p. 316: Emerson, *Journals,* 4:278; Henry James, *The Art of the Novel: Critical Prefaces,* ed. R. P. Blackmur (New York: Scribner, 1934), p. 120.
30 Emerson, *Journals,* 4:278. The remark about Adams's fence-sitting was made by Ed Howe. See Ernest Samuels, *Henry Adams: The Middle Years* (Cambridge, Mass.: Harvard University Press, 1958), p. 96.
31 Emerson, *Complete Works,* 6:31; Henry Adams, *The Education of Henry Adams,* ed. Ernst Samuels (Boston: Houghton Mifflin, 1973), p. 314.
32 Emerson, *Journals,* 5:333; "To Samuel Jones Tilden," January 24, 1883, "To John Hay," 21, September 1893, in *Henry Adams and His Friends,* ed. Harold Dean Cater (Boston: Houghton Mifflin, 1947), pp. 126, 289–90; Adams, *The Education,* pp. 452, 493.
33 Adams, *The Education,* pp. 452, 493.
34 Ibid., p. 456; "To Henry James," November 18, 1903, in *Letters of Henry Adams,* ed. Worthington Chauncey Ford (Boston: Houghton Mifflin, 1938), 2:414.
35 Adams, *The Education,* p. xxx; "To Whitelaw Reid," September 13, 1908, "To Barrett Wendell," March 12, 1909, in Cater, *Henry Adams,* pp. 623, 645.
36 Adams, *The Education,* pp. 458, 346, 501.
37 William Faulkner, *Absalom, Absalom!* (New York: Random House, 1936), p. 158
38 Ibid., p. 75.
39 William Faulkner, *As I Lay Dying* (New York: Random Houses, 1932), p. 165; Faulkner, *Absalom, Absalom!,* p. 378.
40 Marx and Engels, *German Ideology,* pp. 645, 37; Faulkner, *Absalom, Absalom!,* p. 316.
41 Marx and Engels, *German Ideology,* pp. 41–42, 38.
42 See Lukács, *History,* p. 181.
43 Ibid., pp. 121, 181.

III
Texts

10

Mysteries of the City:
A Reading of Poe's
"The Man of the Crowd"

ROBERT H. BYER

> For it is often a dreary thing to be an observer, it makes one as
> melancholy as being a detective on the police force; and when an
> observer performs well the duties of his calling he is to be regarded as
> a police spy in a higher service, for the art of the observer is to bring
> hidden things to light.
>
> Kierkegaard,
Repetition

> The pleasure of being in crowds is a mysterious expression of sensual
> joy in the multiplication of Number.
>
> Baudelaire

"The Man of the Crowd" is one of Poe's major achievements
as a literary artist.[1] It also provides a text in which certain seminal
explorations of "modernity" have taken their bearings, as we learn
from Baudelaire's essay "The Painter of Modern Life" and from
Walter Benjamin's remarkable interpretation of Baudelaire's work.
Poe's story forms a point of origins for many of the imaginative and
social preoccupations of these later explorations of modernity and its
ideology: the developing image of the crowd as a "spectacle of nature," the figure of the *flâneur,* the urban context of capitalism, the
world of the private citizen, the poetry of material life, the social
production of the "uncanny."[2]

The mid-nineteenth-century city and its crowds seemed to countless
observers the incarnation of unprecedented incoherence and disorder,
"a landscape whose human, social and natural parts" appeared "related
simply by accidents, a random agglomeration."[3] Having recently returned from a trip to New York in 1842, Emerson noted in his journal
that "In New York City lately, as in cities generally, one seems to lose

all substance, and become surface in a world of surfaces. Everything is external, and I remember my hat and coat, and all my other surfaces, and nothing else."[4] Like Emerson, Poe's contemporaries saw this world of strange and estranging surfaces, of unrelieved materiality, as revealing what in their culture posed a threat to their Providential and Republican dreams of the New World.[5] What might be described as the wish to "naturalize" the city guided the imaginative strategies of writers as well as social thinkers in their encounters with its perplexing and threatening, if fascinating, spectacle. These efforts to recover the recognizably natural or the naturally recognizable in the city, to discover a "natural perspective" for it, are recurrently marked by the convergence and confusion of aesthetic, moral, and ideological purposes. Thus, representing the city "naturalistically" could mean exposing the uncanny or alien character of society's so-called natural arrangements, but it could also form part of an ideological adaptation to, or justification of, the authority of those arrangements as "natural" responses to a world projected as dangerous, foreign, or barbarous. In this way, the literary effort to conventionalize the city, whether by inventing new forms of drama and description or by revising traditional ones, unavoidably implicated aesthetic questions in social ones.[6]

That the representation of the city in nineteenth-century literature constituted a problematic or became an occasion for the "slippage" of artistic control in the face of social and cultural disorder, begins to suggest how as a *condition* as well as an object of representation, the metropolis and its crowds confronted the writer's imagination with an uncanny, mysterious double. I take such perplexities of representation to be the central concern of Poe's "The Man of the Crowd." In undertaking to explore Poe's tale in light of its significant connections to these artistic and ideological questions of modernity, I hope to begin to indicate some further prospects for reading Poe's work and to provide some preliminary direction for a fuller investigation of what remains largely unexplored about Poe's imagination, namely, the character and depth of its engagement with his culture.[7]

At the outset of Poe's story, we find the narrator seated next to the window of a London coffeehouse on one of the city's busiest streets as evening settles in. Returning to strength after a long illness, the narrator's mood is "the converse of *ennui*," a mood of "the keenest appetency," that finds pleasure in any or all of the details that catch his attention in this commonplace setting. At the crucial juncture of the story, he is struck by the "absolute idiosyncrasy" of an old man's countenance, a sight that arouses in him a "craving desire to keep the man in view – to know more of him." The narrator then rushes out into the crowd and into the night in order to satisfy this desire. Like the old man's physiognomy, the diamond and the dagger that the narrator glimpses portend a gothic tale of crime and concealed identity. "These observations heightened my curiosity, and I resolved to follow the stranger whithersoever he should go." Through the night and the next day, the narrator follows the man through the city's streets and various neighborhoods. In the process, his effort at detection enacts for the reader the same mysterious concealment that the old man's anonymity represents to him. The mystery of the old man is, then, compounded by the mystery of the narrator and his "craving desire" to have a special kind of view of the city in his pursuit of the old man. The relationships among his convalescent idleness, his leisurely fancy, his shock of encounter with the old man, his tracking and spying, and his final and inconclusive exhaustion, are as enigmatic as the old man.

Moreover, this narrative pattern is made more enigmatic by the numerous ironic and suggestive allusions to it that the narrator's speculations about his several views of the world seem to provide. His descriptions of the crowd often seem mysteriously to offer the precise words by which we might want to describe his own act of storytelling. For example, the narrator describes men in the crowd who "were restless in their movements, had flushed faces, and talked and gesticulated to themselves, as if feeling in solitude on account of the very denseness of the company around"; or "feeble and ghastly invalids, upon whom death had placed a sure hand, and who sidled and tottered through the mob, looking everyone beseechingly in the face, as if in search of some chance consolation, some lost hope"; or "men [drunkards] who walked with a more than naturally firm and springy step, but whose countenances were fearfully pale, whose eyes hideously wild and red, and who clutched with quivering fingers, as they strode through the crowd, at every object which came within their reach." All of these descriptions mirror the narrator's own actions and anticipate his identification with the old man.

Returning at the end to the geographical starting point of the narrative, the narrator confronts the old man, desiring some communication of meaning from him. The old man, however, does not even know he is being confronted, and the narrator withdraws from his pursuit. In this as well, the old man's case is his. Equally frustrated are the narrator's desires for a communication and for communicating: His act of following achieves neither. At the story's end, the narrator has grown "wearied unto death," his situation echoing and his actions seeming to illustrate or comment upon those of whom the story's first paragraph speaks:

> There are some secrets which do not permit themselves to be told. Men die nightly in their beds, wringing the hands of ghostly confessors, and looking them piteously in the eyes – die with despair of heart and convulsion of throat, on account of the hideousness of mysteries which will not *suffer themselves* to be revealed.

But the structure of the story does not indicate how we are to chart the passages from such "darker and deeper themes for speculation" to the narrator's actions, and back again. As readers, we are in the position of "ghostly confessors" who encounter the narrator's act of storytelling as a text presenting an unreadable physiognomy, as a "convulsion of throat" that struggles between speech and perverse "circumlocution."[8]

The narrator's hesitating, circular utterance itself mirrors the crowd, whose form and genius occasion a mysteriously inconclusive recognition. This pattern of ironic doubling turns, at the story's conclusion, both farther inward and outward, the "objective" or social mystery of the crowd inextricably knotted with the textual or psychological mystery of the narrator's representation of it. Both the object and subjective condition of the narrator's actions and desire, the crowd is a sort of two-way mirror.

The most explicit source of the vision of the crowd's sublime mystery that opens Poe's story is a passage from Bulwer-Lytton's *Eugene Aram,* a narrative of crime set in modern London, which Poe admired as one of the "master novels" of the age:

> What an incalculable field of dread and sombre contemplation is opened to every man who, with his heart disengaged from himself, and his eyes accustomed to the sharp observance of his tribe, walks through the streets of a great city! What a world of dark and troubled secrets in the breast of everyone who hurries by you! Goethe has said somewhere that each of us, the best as the worst, hides within him something, – some feeling, some remembrance that, if known, would make you hate him. No doubt the saying is exaggerated; but still, what a gloomy and profound sublimity in the idea! – what a new insight it gives into the hearts of the common herd, – with what a strange interest it may inspire us for the humblest, the tritest passenger that shoulders us in the great thoroughfare of life![9]

Bulwer claims to be writing "a romance of real life," as filled with the "homely" as with the "epic," with the ordinary "wants of the daily world" as "with its loftier sorrows and its grander crimes."[10] In his night vision of the crowd, however, it is precisely the details and weight of the ordinary that are invisible. Poe's tale of mystery might be thought of as an ironic commentary on the metaphysical or "Germanic" manner of Bulwer's "endless, various meditation," which mystifies and conceals the very details of urban life he claims to be fascinated with.[11]

By contrast, the mystery of Poe's tale inheres in the very surface of the city's daily life. Though brief and schematic, Poe's descriptions of the crowd and of the city are remarkably exact and comprehensive in the detail of their social observation. He catalogues the crowd's descending order of class and status, progressing from the businessmen through the levels of "gentility" to society's underclasses. With nightfall, these "darker and deeper themes" of the boulevard's crowd come more sharply into focus as "the more orderly portion of the people" withdraw into the security of their private lives. The streets, then, disclose a harsh world of dangers in the form of a lumpen proletariat of criminals, con men, gamblers, dandies, street vendors, beggars, lonely working women, prostitutes, and drunkards, and of the class of "ragged artizans and exhausted laborers." When the narrator later pursues the old man through the city's various districts, they wander from the grand boulevard of their encounter, through other crowded streets, to a "large and busy bazaar," then to a theater, then to the city's "most noisome quarter" of poverty and crime, then to the further desolation of a gin "palace," and finally back to the boulevard of the story's opening. In quick but precise strokes, Poe has sketched the form and the most prominent details of the public life of bourgeois society.

The old man's descent into the underworld of the city's "most deplorable poverty, and . . . most desperate crime" bring the narrator a view of the social landscape whose fearful physiognomy is that of the uncontrollable wildness lying at the margins of the bourgeoisie's "orderly" and controlling vision of social life. Each of the places traversed by the old man's wandering can be thought of as a sight epitomizing the social imagination of the bourgeoisie, now in its dream of a universal order and rationality, now in its phantasmagoria of fear. In following the old man through this landscape, the narrator's gaze passes through the phases and sensations, the archaeology, of the bourgeoisie's consciousness of the world it has made in its own image. The narrator, however, finds all these locales equally tinged by the uncanny physiognomy of the old man, whose mysterious story as the man of the crowd is inscribed in and expresses the elusive and fateful connection among these social realities.

In his richly suggestive reading of the "poetic realism" of Poe's story in the context of his study of Baudelaire, Walter Benjamin associates Poe's depiction of the "uncanny elements" of the big-city crowd, of its grotesque "wildness and discipline," with the ever-increasing mechanization of everyday life brought about by industrial capitalism. Poe's pedestrians act, Benjamin writes, "as if they had adapted themselves to . . . machines and could express themselves only automatically. Their behavior is a reaction to shocks."[12]

A somewhat different orientation to understanding the crowd as both a spiritual reflection and a social form mediating the material basis of capitalist society, one that comes closer to suggesting the specific surface of Poe's story, is provided by a line of thought in Marx's *The Eighteenth Brumaire*. Marx notes that in America "the feverish, youthful movement of material production, which has to make a new world its own, has left neither time nor opportunity for abolishing the old spirit world."[13] For Marx, the coexistence in America's republic of "political emancipation" with the alienation and spiritual enslavement signified by a pervasive "religiosity" constituted the most developed moment of contradiction between political and human emancipation, between the freedoms of civil society and the interests of "material life." "Where the political state has achieved its full development, man leads a double life, a heavenly and an earthly life, not only in thought or consciousness but in *actuality*."[14] The "imaginary universality" of republican citizenship stands opposed to the mutal isolation of "egoistic" interest that dominates the material life of capitalism.[15] "In the *political* community he regards himself as a *communal being;* but in *civil society* he is active as a *private individual,* treats other men as means, reduces himself to a means, and becomes the plaything of alien powers."[16] The "religiosity" of the Americans is the reflection, in both the actuality and consciousness of everyday life, of the "imaginary universality" and "spiritualism," the haunting doubleness, of democratic political community.[17]

Poe's image of the crowd in "The Man of the Crowd" bears striking resemblances to this view of the "double life" of community and privacy of America's republic. Each pedestrian bears the haunting, almost erotic interest of community, of common destiny, and, at the same time, is unreadable in the privacy of his interests, potentially dangerous and anticommunal.

The "feverish," haunted movement of Poe's crowd is a characteristic "result of the immediate process of production," as Marx called it,[18] disclosing the impact of its material interests on the forms of daily bourgeois social life. The structure and animation of the crowd are determined not by machinery but rather by the social relations and temporal

organization of production as a whole.[19] Existing in the transitions between the social world of work and the private world of the home, the
crowd is literally the institution or process in which social and private
life, communal and egoistic interests, are connected. The crowd's demonic and threatening physiognomy measures the wild incoherence and
irrationality of this everyday "integration" of material and civil life, of
this effort to "naturalize" the contradictory social relations of bourgeois
society. The crowd is the domain or process within which the uncanny
takes on a socially concrete form: It is the place where the rationality of
social existence encounters its "perverse" double.

Arguing that *"the production of the city* was the end, the objective and
meaning of *industrial* production,"* Henri Lefebvre views the mystery of
the modern city as the culminating form taken by the mystery of the
commodity, reproducing in the domain of everyday life the fetishistic
aura in which commodity production cloaks itself and which it produces as a way of seeing.[20] Following Lefebvre, we might say that
everyday life in the modern city constitutes itself as a theater compelling certain characteristic or "natural" ways of viewing and being
viewed: Society appears as an epic spectacle of commodities and abstract humanity.[21]

Like the commodity, the crowd is a hieroglyph whose mystery arises
from its concealment of the social relations that produced it. With the
exchange of commodities, the abstract mediation of money creates the
illusion of equality among things and of free and equal commerce between buyer and seller. The mutually isolating anonymity of the
crowd, expressed in the exchange of gazes to which all seems equally
and freely visible, conceals the privacy of self-interest and creates the
illusory picture of a homogeneous, even organic mass of humanity that
mediates, and seems to mirror, the consciousness and self-consciousness
of its members. The mystery of the crowd derives from the fact that
the forces animating it lie beyond and contradict the interest circum-
scribing the perceptual horizons of its members. Imagining his "membership" in the crowd to be merely an extension of his privacy and his
political equality into the realm of everyday life, the urban pedestrian
views the crowd as another form of market, as a place of free and equal
exchange, of imagined and imaginary universality. But the random
encounters with and revelations of strangers, the danger and wildness
of the street, the differences between businessmen and wanderers, resist
assimilation to such a picturing of social life that would regard everyone
in the crowd with the equanimity (and equal "affectionateness") of a
customer or a friend.

In part, the dramatic setting of Poe's story might be likened to, though it inverts, the window gazing and endless appetency that define the perspective of the commodity shopper. Here, the viewer (the narrator) himself sits in the window while his viewed objects (the men and women of the crowd) are displayed to him "outside" in the street, where the viewer of the kaleidoscopic world of commodities would "naturally" place himself. The initially idle gaze of the narrator focuses on the individuals of the crowd as if they were merely pleasurable objects in a spectacle, as if they existed only for the aesthetic delight of viewing. Just before plunging into the crowd, however, the narrator is described as having his "brow to the glass" as he peers intently into the street. As if dissatisfied with the merely aesthetic value of the crowd as spectacle, the narrator seeks to appropriate, to use, to comprehend it, by following the traces that seem to reveal its origins. His effort to penetrate and read the secret of the crowd's mysterious physiognomy ultimately fails, as the crowd (its process/procession) comes instead to possess him.

In its very depiction of the uncanny spectacle of the crowd, Poe's story destroys the picture of social life as the product of, or the motion imparted by, the activity of mutually free and openly communicating, and exchanging, private citizens. A hieroglyph of the mysterious social conditions facing the private citizen, the crowd was both means and end, subject and object of his destiny. Neither freedom nor progress, but the circularity and doubleness of everyday life was its secret.

Poe's story of the urban crowd evokes in mood and structure a world in which the needs and satisfactions of everyday life are subject to "uninterrupted disturbance," to "everlasting uncertainty and agitation," in which the commonplace situation or ordinary moment can be transformed into the shocking, can erupt with the promise of transcendent satisfaction or verge on the abyss of frustration and disillusionment.[22] Lefebvre draws a suggestive connection between the "uncanny" in everyday life and in the unconscious, seeing the former as a condition signified by the recurrent, if chance, eruption of desire into, and subsidence of desire from, the commonplace material world.[23] Like Benjamin, Lefebvre aims to historicize the concept of everyday life. He argues that, as it refers to the mode of social existence and destiny specific to industrial capitalism, certain kinds of societies "illustrate the *total absence of everyday life.*" In such societies, "every detail (gestures, words, tools, utensils, costumes, etc.) bears the imprint of a *style;* nothing had as yet become prosaic, not even the quotidian; the prose and the poetry of life were still identical. Our own everyday life is typical for its yearning and quest for a style that obstinately eludes it."[24]

The "yearning and quest" for style and the conspicuous idleness of the Baudelairean *flâneur,* whom Benjamin sees as the descendant of Poe's old man of the crowd, sought to negate the "everlasting uncertainty and agitation" of everyday life in the modern city and to turn back, or against, the clock of daily affairs.[25] "Time *is* money – to an American at least," remarked Poe, taking up the stance of the *flâneur* in an article on "Street Paving" in the *Broadway Journal.*[26] Poe satirizes the method of the businessman that sought to impose a clockwork rigidity on daily life. Turning on its head the businessman's civic-minded, utilitarian economy and devotion to Progress, Poe notes the physiological discomfort and practical inconvenience, the "loss of time" and "temper," resulting from the literal procession on (and of) the surface of the city's daily life.[27] The *flâneur* seeks to recapture the heroic sense of public spectacle. "Ancient life was a great *parade,"* wrote Baudelaire in 1846, describing how the poetic dignity and splendor of public life was reflected in the movements and attitudes of each individual.[28]

Baudelaire's dandy, like Poe's man of the crowd, is a kind of social outlaw, but unlike the old man, the dandy is a "virtuoso of nonutilitarianism," a figure who seeks to overcome the fragmentation and shocks of everyday life not only in its objects and pursuits, but in its capacity for expressiveness and integrity. The *flâneur* at once embraces and opposes the uncanny life of the crowd: "To be away from home and yet to feel [him]self everywhere at home," is his "joy" in the crowd. Through the detachment of style, he seeks to affront the restless methodicalness of the daily life of bourgeois society, transvaluing the "electrical energy" of the crowd's "multiplicity" and "flickering grace" into "pictures more living than life itself."[29] In contrast to this sublime picturesqueness, Poe's old man represents to the narrator the crowd's capacity to shock and unsettle him, a power epitomized by the "absolute idiosyncracy" of the old man's *physiognomy* that "arrests and absorbs" the narrator's "whole attention." Unlike the *flâneur,* Poe's man of the crowd expresses the demonic methodicalness of the crowd itself. Rather than being antiutilitarian, the old man's actions, "the type and genius of deep crime," are a perverse mimicry of the rationality and routine, the need and the utility, of the crowd. The *flâneur* was one for whom the crowd was the object of his pleasure, but not the subjective field of his desire. Poe's old man is less the type of the *flâneur* than of the democrat: The crowd is both object and subject of his desire, the form of both his pleasure and his need.

Although the narrator also synchronizes his actions and desires with the crowd, at least for a time, the dialectic of his equally mysterious dissociation from and need for it comes closer to Baudelaire's dandy.

Yet, whereas for the dandy such a dialectic defines an aesthetic occupation and profession, Poe's narrator derives "positive pleasure even from many of the legitimate sources of pain."[30] Originating in illness and convalescence and ending in exhaustion, the narrator's pedestrian adventures, his activities of pursuit and spying, suggest no sequel. This differs sharply both from the self-conscious social posturing of the *flâneur* and from Poe's later creation, Dupin, in whom these occupations have become a profession.

Central to the dandy's posturing is the appropriation of the street with the intimacy and individuality of a private interior. For the bourgeoisie, the interior had come to signify its safety from the street. Having created the crowd as the image of a social destiny, the bourgeoisie sought to escape that destiny in an interior world of possessions that provided a "casing" of experiential insulation.[31] In Poe's story, such gestures of separation and insulation are linked to the theater and shown to be themselves part of the crowd experience. One detail vividly captures this. At a certain point in his wanderings, the old man rushes to the theater district and hurls himself into the departing crowd. Unknown to them, these spectators have once again become an audience or, rather, in their self-absorbed privacy, have become actors for this strange audience of one (or two). The old man's viewing of them transforms their commonplace sense of privacy into an uncanny theater.

The dramatic turning point of "The Man of the Crowd" occurs when the narrator's perception of the "absolute idiosyncracy" of the old man dissolves whatever residual "film" of sensory insulation and prosaic perception continues to separate him from the crowd. For the duration of the story, the narrator is infected with the old man's incapacity to be alone, to have privacy. This ultimate violation of the narrator's capacity for self-containment is one way of understanding the old man's "crime." Dragged from his privacy by his fascination with the old man, the narrator can imagine him only as something lurid and sensational, like a criminal (or "the fiend") – as if the magnitude of the shock that has disrupted his detached reverie can only be explained by referring it to the actions of a criminal; as if the eruption of metaphysical desire into the everyday, of the "poetic" into the commonplace, could only be understood as a crime.

If the crowd is portrayed in Poe's story as an arena of such wildness, both socially and as sensory stimulation, what is anterior to the crowd, the interior and its privacy, is also pictured as the opposite of tranquil, healthful existence. The narrator's initial insulation from the crowd is described as the lingering effect of an illness that had literally confined him (at home). Nor, at the end, does the narrator's exhaustion and perplexity indicate any condition or place to which he can escape in order to free himself from the destiny of "crime," which the crowd imposes. In other stories, particularly "The Fall of the House of Usher" and the Dupin tales, Poe is, in Benjamin's phrase, the "physiognomist of the interior" as he is here the physiognomist of the crowd.[32] As an asylum providing anonymity for "criminals," the crowd discloses the same destiny that the phantasmagoric interior of the private citizen inscribes: escape, illness, wildness, confinement, observation, the discipline of invisible authority.

A brief comparison of Poe's description of the "crowded" spectacle of wildness at Prince Prospero's in "The Masque of the Red Death" with his account of the perverse "interiority" and uncanny pageantry of the urban crowd helps clarify how Poe's representation of the latter assimilates its meaning to such materialized environments of *dis*eased spirit. At Prospero's, "There were delirious fancies such as the madman fashions. There were much of the beautiful, much of the wanton, much of the *bizarre,* something of the terrible, and not a little of that which might have excited disgust." The ebony clock's hourly reminder of death brings Prospero's revelers to a stop, the masks of their suddenly "stiff-frozen" dreams become grotesque portraits of terror.[33] Unlike Prospero's masque, the physiognomy of Poe's crowd is continually "stiff-frozen," testimony to the discipline of daily affairs rather than to the shock of periodic reminders of mortality: the crowd's physiognomy is not just another version of Prospero's *danse macabre* in modern dress.[34] Whereas Prospero's revel discloses the grinning face of death lurking beneath the masks of the living, the grimly ironic reminder of the eternal order underlying society's order, Poe's crowd instead reveals the restless automatism of daily affairs that offers neither the promise nor the threat of surcease. In Benjamin's striking phrase, these fixed physiognomies are "mimetic shock absorbers."[35] The crowd's unhealthy vitality mirrors, and is imparted by, the circulation of commodities: It is the vitality of a grotesquely partial humanity in which things have come to represent people. In the crowd's uncanny choreography, each member seems to have been robbed of the capacity for a fully human expressiveness in the absorbing gestures, countenance, gait, or clothing that constitute his social identity. Each seems at once the victim and potential agent of such a crime. As the expression or threat of a kind of demonic possession, the dance of dailiness of Poe's crowd resembles less a Dance of Death than a St. Vitus's dance.

Evincing no impatience in this bustle and quickly adjusting to any disturbance of their methodical hurry, the "business-like" class receives virtually no comment in Poe's story. Lords of the daylight, they are the very essence of the socially commonplace, those who impart the "natural" rhythms of the crowd's movement. The relationship institutionalized in the crowd between the daylight methodicalness of the businessman and the dangerously perverse, nighttime mimicry of this rationality by the crowd's criminal "genius" is illuminated by a somewhat jesting remark of Marx's on the social value and productive labor of the criminal:

> The criminal produces an impression, partly moral and partly tragic, as the case may be, and in this way renders a "service" by arousing the moral and aesthetic feelings of the public. . . . The criminal breaks the monotony and everyday security of bourgeois life. In this way he keeps it from stagnation, and gives rise to that uneasy tension and agility without which even the spur of competition would get blunted. Thus he gives a stimulus to the productive forces.[36]

The first half of this remark cogently summarizes the ritual use and ideological value of the sensational, popular literature of crime through which Poe's contemporaries sought to renew their sense of community.[37]

The second half of the remark suggests the specific social form of the businessman's peculiar gait in the crowd that Poe describes. The discipline of the crowd follows both from the businessman's "Protestant ethic" and, for the crowd's underclasses, from the direct and coercive control over their labor that is essential to capitalist production. The criminal—that is, anyone refusing to obey the laws (in the largest sense) of bourgeois life, to consent to the "imaginary universality" of its enterprise—provides the bourgeoisie with a visible rationale for, and a symbolic reminder of, the quotidian necessity of its law, both in the street and in the workplace. Thus the criminal, as much as the Puritan, is the key to the "spirit of capitalism."[38]

I turn now to more specific questions about Poe's representation of the crowd that are raised by the narrator's attraction to and participation in it. In this aspect, the crowd's mysterious animation appears as the universalized condition of the "craving desire" the narrator has for the old man and the old man has for the crowd. This desire seems to oscillate between the need to belong to the crowd, which is socially organized as the uncanny world of commodities, and the natural "craving" of desire as such. Just what sort of grotesque "spectacle of nature" the crowd presented, is suggested in a remarkable passage in Ruskin. Thinking about drawing, thus about the physiognomy of the natural world, he imagines mass society as one "in which every soul would be as the syllable of a stammerer instead of the word of a speaker, in which every man would walk as in a frightful dream, seeing spectres of himself, in everlasting multiplication, gliding helplessly around him in a speechless darkness."[39]

The social vision most immediately figured by Poe's story is suggested by its very title. The narrator's and the old man's relations to the crowd can be thought of as two versions of the individual's relation to the mass in a democratic society. In these terms, "The Man of the Crowd" dramatizes tensions at the heart of democratic culture, developing motifs about the fate of romantic individualism explored by Poe in two other stories written during the preceding year.

In "William Wilson," the two Wilsons, among other things, represent the antagonism between the haughty, aristocratic values of the narrator and his "plebeian" double. That the "similarity" between them had never "been made a subject, or even observed at all by our schoolfellows" but rather "was noticed by myself alone" implies that what the narrator is obsessed by is precisely what Karl Mannheim has termed the premise of "the ontological equality of all men" in a democracy.[40] The narrator describes Wilson's doubling of him as the latter's ability "to perfect an imitation of myself . . . both in words and action . . . even my voice did not escape him." What most galls the narrator about "this most exquisite portraiture" is Wilson's "most unwelcome *affectionateness.*" It is the almost erotic sympathy, attraction, and goodwill of the other Wilson that drives the narrator to his moral and social lawlessness. As in "The Man of the Crowd," the narrator in "William Wilson" is obsessed by his double who mimics his "gait and general manner" and feels this other to be a kind of criminal, though the pursuit and mimicry are reversed in the two stories. Yet, in each story, the double, and the obsession and mystery surrounding his appearance, has a clearly specified social character that is a crucial determinant of the psychological relationship between the two protagonists.[41]

The social milieu of "William Wilson" is, however, much less specifically a matter of the narrative's foreground than in "The Man of the Crowd." In "The Fall of the House of Usher," the image of a man inextricably and mysteriously embedded in an environment that, in its inanimateness, still animates his destiny, is fully realized, though here the environment is not socially specified but, rather, a gothic world particular to Usher's strange privacy of desire and experience.[42] Dramatically, however, this story bears a closer similarity than "William Wilson" does to "The Man of the Crowd." The narrator in "Usher" is, like the narrator in "The Man of the Crowd," simultaneously dissociated from and drawn into the confining, haunting milieu of its obsessed "genius" or poet. To be so completely an expression of one's milieu is in both stories a symptom of unhealth, even an intimation of catastrophe. It is also a dangerously compelling and implicating mystery for the observer of such a scene. The narrator of "Usher" observes Usher throughout the story at a diminishing distance from the latter's increasing animation and disorder. In "The Man of the Crowd" the narrator's mystery is not only in his need for proximity to the old man, but in his obsessive, seemingly endless pursuit. Both stories end with their narrators preserving their individual identities by narrowly escaping from the influence of these mysterious environments.

Poe's well-known strictures against "the mob," in valuing individualism, are, above all, expressions of his awareness of the danger (psychological and erotic, at the same time as social) of the affective bonding requisite to democratic society, of the "oceanic feeling" that transforms all others into one's intimate doubles.[43] It is this erotic motion, rather than an aristocratic posturing or ideology, that shapes the dramas of these three stories. To be drawn (or to have been drawn) obsessively into the mysterious, material milieu possessed by and possessing another's spirit, be it Usher's house, or Wilson's image of his double, or the crowd, is a recurrent if variously rendered motif in Poe's fiction.[44] Only in "The Man of the Crowd" do the social implications of this narrative structure receive primary emphasis and become fully thematic.

Poe's story gives form to the narrator's desire in two primary ways. First, his pursuit of the old man, as well as the old man's wanderings themselves, are constituted by a temporal pattern that echoes the diurnal rhythm of nature. It is important, however, to notice how this natural cycle differs from the temporal patterns of the actions of the crowd, the old man, and the narrator. Although the crowd's ebbing and flowing continues ceaselessly, its specific pattern of shifting densities and locales is socially determined. The old man's restless actions and transient satisfaction are a corollary of this.

The narrator's story follows a somewhat different time scheme. Although he follows the old man through the cycle of a day, he stops at the end in a gesture of concluding wisdom, whereas the old man moves on. Furthermore, the narrator's pursuit of the old man begins only after a "long" but unspecified period of illness and idleness. Thus, the narrator's day of pursuit is framed on both sides by this other, indeterminate temporal sequence. The narrator's abandonment of pursuit in his final gesture of puzzlement not only makes explicit this other temporal sequence but also acknowledges the inaccessibility of the crowd through such a frame of natural, cyclical time. Although the crowd and the old man suggest the diurnal pattern of nature, their secrets resist the narrator's metaphysical speculation in part because these are the irreducible residue of the mute materiality of the specific details of the city's life. The crowd appears as the perverse double of nature, following the pattern of a collective, unconscious desire, which both is and is not synchronized to the objects of nature. The mystery of the crowd's uncanny dèsire resides in its origins. As both an object and process of desire, the crowd shapes the narrator's effort to know it: It refuses access to, and creates a way of seeing that is in some sense incapable of, purely metaphysical speculation. Against this urban background of everyday life that mysteriously inscribes his destiny, the narrator pursues some magic that will make it readable.

The second way in which the narrative figures this "craving desire" is in terms of the shock that transforms the narrator from an initially detached observer of the crowd to a participant in it, from one whose detachment is associated with his recovering health to one whose exhaustion is the consequence of the crowd's contagious energy. Noting the crowd's "noisy and inordinate vivacity which jarred discordantly upon the ear, and gave an aching sensation to the eye," the narrator represents the crowd as constituting a crisis of his own capacity for perception, a crisis made fully explicit by the eruption of "craving desire" accompanying his unsettling chance encounter with the old man. The mystery of the narrator's desire for the crowd is inextricably linked to the drama of his viewing it. Thus, a more detailed account of the nature and form of the narrator's activity of observation or perception will further characterize the crowd as such a condition of subjectivity.

The narrator initially describes his leisurely observation of his surroundings as "a calm but inquisitive interest" that follows the leisurely rhythms of a distracted and distracting idleness. Finding equal pleasure in everything, the narrator has spent the afternoon gazing aimlessly, but "with a delicious novelty of emotion," over the endless and changing field of things that pass before him. The distractions of his eye define a way of reading the world, "now in poring over advertisements, now in observing the promiscuous company in the room, and now in peering through the smoky panes into the street." As his narrative unfolds, describing the story of this "interest in everything," we are confronted with "darker and deeper" implications of his gaze than are suggested by this "calm but inquisitive" collection of impressions.

As an object of contemplation, the crowd at first seems to offer "naturally" two ways of viewing it. "At first my observations took an abstract and generalizing turn. I looked at the passengers in masses, and thought of them in their aggregate relations. Soon however, I descended to details, and regarded with minute interest the innumerable varieties of figure, dress, air, gait, visage, and expression of countenance." The descent "to details" defines a significant shift in the narrator's relation to the crowd.

The shift in the intensity and focus of the narrator's gaze is marked by a shift in light away from the natural illumination of daylight. As night falls, the crowd's demonic physiognomy is revealed in the "wild effects" of the gas lamps that seem to project a "fitful and garish lustre" over everything and that, the narrator says, "enchained me to an examination of individual faces." The "aching sensation" imparted by the crowd to the narrator's eyes is a consequence of the shift in his gaze from a kind of casual detachment that composes the crowd to a wild discipline that seeks to identify with it and is captivated by its motions. Rather than providing distracted pleasure, the crowd, in this second view, compels the narrator with a series of physiognomies that he strains after: "Although the rapidity with which the world of light flitted before the window, prevented me from casting more than a glance upon each visage, still it seemed that, in my then peculiar mental state, I could frequently read, even in that brief interval of a glance, the history of long years." No longer subsumed in a picturesque spectacle, the members of the crowd appear to the narrator as types, as a series of portraits that seem to offer stories to the imagination, as do characters in a novel or faces in anonymous photographs.

It is at this point that the narrator catches sight of the old man and leaves his box seat behind, initiating an action that problematizes those previous perspectives from which the crowd could be coherently or intelligibly represented in its wholeness, that is, as an object "outside" the coffeehouse or as a social typology whose meaning or spirit is somehow epitomized by its procession of uncanny physiognomies. The sighting of the old man leads to a third way of looking at the crowd, one that comes from being a part of it, in the grip of its secret, rather than an interested observer of it. The old man's "countenance" arrests and absorbs the narrator's "whole attention, on account of the absolute idiosyncracy of its expression." Not a type, the old man seems a confusing and paradoxical revelation of all the meanings of the crowd's life. Thus, his physiognomy appears to the narrator as a singular occasion for identification and understanding, for "some analysis of the meaning [it] conveyed." That is, the old man seems to provide the narrator with an image of his own destiny and makes explicit what had previously remained latent about the crowd, namely, that each man of the crowd is an analogue for the others (and for the narrator), that each is a clue to the organism that contains them all (and all their meanings), and that the (narrator's) gaze that sees them with an equal interest is thus implicitly a wish for identification and self-identification.

The implications of this kind of gaze are fully unlocked only with the sighting of the old man, only when the narrator's "aroused, startled, fascinated" interest in what he views takes on the urgency of action, the same urgency and intensity as the questions he asks himself about the "meanings" of (his) life. That is, his gaze at another becomes an encounter and revelation (albeit of a finally inaccessible enigma) only when it is a vision that doubles, that reflects back to the viewer an image of both himself and the viewed. It is the vision of a doubleness that looks back (in some way) at the viewer, who can glimpse, in the specular mystery of the other, the image of himself therein contained.

The narrator's initial view of the old man thus produces in him an almost erotic intimation of a destiny both personal and social. His pursuit is an effort to catch another view of the old man that will transform this intimation into an understanding or reading of the specific character of that destiny. Like the detective or the photographer, the narrator attempts to find in the traces of the old man's peregrinations an inscription that will be a clue to this larger disclosure. The narrator is first led to a confused and paradoxical series of ideas about the range of human emotions and the vivid history inscribed in the old man's face, but is not satisfied that these intense but enigmatic impressions answer to his desire to read what he imagines is written there. Unwilling to lose sight of that physiognomy as it disappears into the crowd's rapid bustle, the narrator rushes out into the crowd "to know more of him," "to keep" him "in view," to read the "wild history" he imagines is "written within that bosom," as he suggestively, and alternatively, characterizes the need of his "craving desire."

As both concluding and precipitating certain of the narrator's actions, this "craving desire" climaxes the appetency of his increasingly intense and detailed gazing at the crowd. At the same time, this desire transforms the need satisfied by the narrator's gazing at the crowd into the unappeasable hunger to read the man's physiognomy, to penetrate the physiognomy of the crowd in order to discover an "absolute idiosyncracy" of meaning, to abandon and get beyond his own fanciful impressions of the "stories" of the passersby, to find a reality in the crowd that he can have access to only by becoming part of it.

The initial sighting of the old man thus divides the narrative into two almost equal parts. The first, in depicting the crowd and the relation of the narrator's gaze to it, constitutes a history of the narrator's gaze into which the old man intrudes as an "absolute idiosyncracy." Thus it also constitutes a prehistory of the narrator's desire to capture the old man as the object of his speculations about the "meaning" of the crowd's wholeness. The second half of the narrative follows the narrator's pursuit of some further encounter with (or view of) the old man that will unlock the secret of his physiognomy. The narrative traces the narrator's actions in trying to "know," to "view," to "read" in a way that will answer the "craving desire" that has been aroused in him. In the social landscape and in the temporality disclosed by the old man's mysterious wanderings, the narrator seeks to capture a glimpse of the history immanent and unfolding in that physiognomy. In the end, the narrator finds the man's apparent "absolute idiosyncracy" merely to be a personification of the crowd itself.

Although the circularity or tautology of the old man's actions proves no less enigmatic than the world he is embedded in and epitomizes, he does bring the city into view for the narrator in a way that seems to order and mark it as a "text" fraught with significance. Though the narrator is finally unable either to recognize or to read the "text" the old man's movements seem to inscribe (i.e., as a vision or dream or allegory or epigram or hieroglyph or story or poem), these movements nonetheless provide a *formal* ordering of the city, in three ways. First, in passing through the entirety of the city's diverse districts during the course of the night, and day, the old man enables the narrator to encompass the wholeness of the city, to experience its unity in space and time by a sort of compression or condensation. Second, the old man's circulation through the city seems to create meaning by connecting these diverse districts in a sequence. The progression or directedness (if not the direction) of his movements seems to provide a kind of narrative syntax or order to the city. Finally, the old man provides for the narrator a conjunction between the crowd and the city, signifying the wholeness of the former and being what is signified by the mysterious, labyrinthine connectedness of the latter. This formal, quasi-linguistic integration of the city provides, if not precisely a "meaning," the occasion for an unparaphrasable, lyric apprehension of the city's presence as a sort of destiny.

At the dawning of the next day, the old man and the narrator return to the place of their meeting and again walk "to and fro" amid the "turmoil" of "that most thronged mart of the populous town." This new day brings no encouragement for the narrator's resoluteness, and, encountering only the endless repetitiveness of the old man's behavior, he abandons his "scrutiny" of the other, "wearied unto death." Feeling his single day of accompanying the old man in the crowd as a lifetime of such days, the narrator has literally experienced the completeness of the duration of the city's round of daily activity and, in this single moment of an endlessly repeated cycle, has encountered the totality of the city's social life as if simultaneously. For this day of being always in the midst of the crowd with the old man, the narrator has been continuously present at the common places where the city's populace most "naturally" gathers. The narrator's experience of viewing the crowd takes the form, we might want to say, of a dream or nightmare of the city's everyday life, a dream that is the life of the old man. It is a dream the narrator enters into by way of a feverishly enhanced appetite for the world and from which he reawakens to the mysterious conditions of his own mortality.

It is tempting to pursue a bit further this analogy between the narrator's vision of the city, which projects it as a mysterious hieroglyph of destiny, and a dream. Like an apparition in a dream, the old man seems to inhabit a world other than the narrator's, one that the narrator cannot communicate with in ordinary ways yet that is "all-absorbing" to him. The analogy to dreams also provides a way of grasping the indeterminacy framed by the story as to whether or not, or to what degree, the narrator is "conscious" of the pattern of observation he is enacting. Futhermore, the crowd itself may at first glance seem to share leading features of Poe's dreamworlds of doomed, poetic timelessness. The crowd is an "interior place, circumscribed, independent of all other places," possessing its "own time . . . a perpetual present," as Georges Poulet has characterized these worlds. Yet, if Poe's crowd establishes a perspective in which the hours of the city "indefinitely protract themselves into each other, without showing any evidence of a real succession in their passage," it is no "land of dream." Rather than measuring a time that is "always the same . . . *sheltered* from diurnal duration," the crowd's endlessly repeated "diurnal duration" is its mode of a "perpetual present." Unlike the dreamer's "interior place . . . independent of all other places," the crowd is *the* common place.[45]

To be more precise, then, we might describe the narrator's vision of the city not so much as a dream itself but in terms of one of its typical components. "Every dream," according to Freud, has "some link with a recent daytime impression – often of the most insignificant sort." Although such trivial, quotidian material is one of the many means by which unconscious wishes disguise themselves, Freud notes as more significant the fact of the *recentness* of such daily material, which marks the point at which consciousness allows the influx of the dream's repressed "instinctual force."[46] The vision of the city's daily life in Poe's story suggests such a collectively imprinted "day's residue," that is, a sort of preconscious memory trace of the city as a shared domain of the familiar and the proximate that is charged with (the potential for) an indeterminate (or unreadable) content of deeper wishes.[47]

The narrator's vision of the urban crowd thus records a version of one of modern man's most powerful and bottomless dreams of the wholeness or communion of social life. Baudelaire paraphrased it as a heroic image of the natural milieu of the "lover of universal life."[48] At the end of Poe's story, however, the narrator comes to see the old man simply as "the man of the crowd," thereby reconnecting the latter's mysterious "criminal" agency to the commonplace as its "poetic" expression. If the old man seems for a period to express a destiny that is not commonplace (the dream of such a world, if not precisely a dreamworld), in the end, it is precisely the "genius" of the commonplace to signify its opposite, the restless desire for transcendence, the haunting residue of its surface. In occasioning the eruption in the narrator, at least for a season, of a sense of larger fulfillments and meanings, the old man signifies to the narrator the conditions of his own narration and communicates to him the possibilities of his own story as the enactment of a kind of communion.

"We walk about, amid the destinies of our world existence," wrote Poe in *Eureka,* "encompassed by dim but ever-present Memories of a Destiny more vast."[49] But in contrast to *Eureka* and to Poe's other depictions of dreamworlds, in which such shadowy memories are said to be things that are known with certainty, if intuitively, the city's quotidian ordinariness in "The Man of the Crowd" does not reveal such dreams of a "vast Destiny," either private or collective. Beyond the unities of space and time that form the mysterious "plot" of the city's daily life, the crowd begins and ends in an abyss that prohibits metaphysical, or narrative, revelation. That the crowd's "film" of quotidian perception makes these "vast," metaphysical destinies of others as impenetrable and mysterious as a closed book is, the narrator reminds us at the end, a merciful fate.

Earlier, I sketched three modes or phases of the narrator's viewing of the crowd. Poe characterizes each of these in terms of certain paradigmatic visual or pictorial experiences. Just before taking his "abstract and generalizing" view of the crowd, which is organized within the field defined by the coffeehouse window, the narrator is described as engaged in two other activities that aim to recover the world (as he seeks to recover his health). Both by reading the newspaper and by observing the "promiscuous company" within the confines of the coffeehouse, the narrator tries to contain the life of the city within a *frame* (of cultural convention). In his "descent to details," the framing of the window, which offers to the eye a continual if changing panoramic view that orders the crowd, gives way to a direct gaze (mediated only by the transparent surface of the window) in which the wholeness of the crowd no longer appears metaphorically but rather synecdochically. This, in turn, leads to the narrator's fixation on the detail of the old man's physiognomy, which not only seems to contain the inwardness or meaning of the entirety of the crowd, but which draws the narrator into the crowd, making his eye part of the kaleidoscope it mirrors. Contained by the crowd he seeks to contain, the narrator's grasp of its wholeness resides in this last view in the duration of his motion within it. Here, the crowd is contained as a kind of simultaneity not in the form of a spatial or pictorial framing (or encounter) but in the form of the narrator's desire for an endless presence to it.

The narrator's desire to recover the wholeness of the crowd spreads, as if by contagion, from his eye to his whole body. This movement from seeing as framing or reading to seeing as immediate proximity or absolute presence is described in the story by a pattern of physiological detail (illness, recovery, exhaustion, infection, shock) rather than in moral terms. The story characterizes its psychological drama of recognizing the human in others in terms of a dialectic of the "surface" rather than between "surface" and "depth."[50] The cyclical or recurrent "craving desire" figured by Poe's crowd cannot be cured or, as we might say, known or redeemed, by seeing it as a ritual or metaphor or form of the moral life.[51] The contagious spreading and contracting of the crowd's disease, of its diurnal pattern of eruption and subsiding, defines the narrator's inability to contain it, to bring to it the sense or form of an ending (or beginning). In the idea of contagion, then, we capture the identity in Poe's story between the *formal* aspect of the crowd as the object of a mysterious contiguity observed by the narrator and the *energy* of the crowd as it enters into and transforms his mode of viewing it.

While Poe's psychology of the crowd lies at the borders of the moral, the sociological, and the metaphysical, his representation of it is framed by a dialectic of seeing and reading. If the narrator's dominant and guiding response to the crowd is visual, it should be recalled that his effort to "read" the meaning of the crowd, which arises from his observing it, also continues and finally leads back to the thematics of reading introduced by the story's very first sentence, as if confirming the portent of "it does not permit itself to be read." This interplay between reading and seeing does not come to a resolution but enacts a kind of circular pattern. In its figuration of the crowd, Poe's story represents social life neither as a readable text nor as a recognizable structure of the visible, but as an inescapable condition of everydayness, a condition of origins and destinations shaping both reading and seeing.

Notes

I would like to thank Alan Trachtenberg, who encouraged this project and saw it through its initial versions, and the editors of this volume, who provided timely and valuable advice about its revision.

1 All quotations, unless otherwise noted, are from *The Complete Works of Edgar Allan Poe,* ed. James A. Harrison (New York, 1902), 17 vols., hereafter cited as *Works.* "The Man of the Crowd" is at 4: 134–45. I will also refer to the newer Harvard edition of Poe's works, *The Collected Works of Edgar Allan Poe,* ed. Thomas Olive Mabbott (Cambridge, Mass.: Harvard University Press, 1969–1978), vols. 1–3, as *Collected Works.* The story, along with valuable notes and suggestions about sources, is at 2: 505–18.

2 Walter Benjamin, "On Some Motifs in Baudelaire," in *Illuminations,* ed. Hannah Arendt, trans. Harry Zohn (New York: Schocken, 1969), pp. 155–200. The first draft of this essay, "The Paris of the Second Empire in Baudelaire," and "Paris–The Capital of the Nineteenth Century" are collected with it in Benjamin's *Charles Baudelaire: A Lyric Poet in the Era of High Capitalism* (London: New Left Books, 1973). Baudelaire's "The Painter of Modern Life" is collected in *The Painter of Modern Life and Other Essays,* ed. Jonathan Mayne (London: Phaidon, 1964). Also of importance is the section of his 1846 Salon called "The Heroism of Modern Life," which is collected in *Art in Paris 1845–1862,* ed. Jonathan Mayne (London: Phaidon, 1964). On the crowd as a "spectacle of nature," see *Charles Baudelaire,* p. 62. A recent study of these issues of "modernity" is Marshall Berman, *All That Is Solid Melts into Air: The Experience of Modernity* (New York: Simon & Schuster, 1982).

3 Steven Marcus, *Engels, Manchester, and the Working Class* (New York: Random House, 1975), p. 98.

4 *The Journals of Ralph Waldo Emerson,* 10 vols., ed. Edward Waldo Emerson and Waldo Emerson Forbes (Boston and New York, 1909–14), 6:165.

5 On the contemporaneous attitudes about the New World's historical destiny, see Fred Somkin, *Unquiet Eagle: Memory and Desire in the Idea of American Freedom, 1815–1860* (Ithaca, N.Y.: Cornell University Press, 1967), pp. 55–90. Traditional attitudes toward the city in Jacksonian America were dominated by Protestant and Jeffersonian fears of corruption. Valuable studies of these attitudes can be found in Morton and Lucia White, *The Intellectual Versus the City* (New York: New American Library, 1967), Neil Harris, *The Artist in American Society: The Formative Years 1790–1860* (New York: Braziller, 1966), pp. 107–22, and, most recently, Thomas Bender, *Toward an Urban Vision: Ideas and Institutions in Nineteenth-Century America* (Lexington: University Press of Kentucky, 1975), pp. 1–51.

6   My effort to formulate these extremely general ideas about the relation of
    Poe's story to certain preoccupations of nineteenth-century literature is
    indebted to Raymond Williams, *The Country and the City* (New York:
    Oxford University Press, 1973), esp. chaps. 14–16, and 19–20, and most
    immediately provoked by the interpretive schemes proposed by two recent
    studies: Edwin M. Eigner, *The Metaphysical Novel in England and America:
    Dickens, Bulwer, Hawthorne, Melville* (Berkeley: University of California
    Press, 1978); and Jonathan Arac, *Commissioned Spirits: The Shaping of Social
    Motion in Dickens, Carlyle, Melville, and Hawthorne* (New Brunswick, N.J.:
    Rutgers University Press, 1979). It is the character of what I call in the next
    paragraph the "slippage" between the social and the metaphysical (or psy-
    chological) modes of this fiction that seems to me to be most deeply at
    issue in the relations of Poe's work to the narrative problematics investi-
    gated by Eigner and Arac. On the effort to locate the natural in the city,
    see Alexander Welsh, *The City of Dickens* (New York: Oxford University
    Press, 1971).

7   I endeavor to do this in my forthcoming *The Man of the Crowd: Edgar Allan
    Poe in His Culture*. Stuart Levine's recent "Poe and American Society" (*The
    Canadian Review of American Studies* 9, no. 1 [Spring 1978]: 16–33) is, at
    best, sketchy. The starting point for any such exploration of Poe's work
    should be the extraordinary, and extraordinarily neglected, essay on Poe by
    William Carlos Williams in *In the American Grain* (1925);

8   See "The Imp of the Perverse," *Works*, 6:147–8.

9   Edward Bulwer-Lytton, *Eugene Aram* (Boston, 1893), pp. 342–43. So far
    as I know, this has not previously been recognized as a source for Poe's
    story. Poe's comment on the novel is from *Works*, 8:95.

10 Bulwer-Lytton, *Eugene Aram*, p. 350.

11 In the Preface to his *Tales of the Grotesque and Arabesque* published earlier in
    1840, Poe had declared as a guiding purpose of his fiction that "terror was
    not of Germany, but of the soul" (*Collected Works*, 2:473). Eigner, *Meta-
    physical Novel*, pp. 1–12, 56–57, offers a somewhat different view of the
    seriousness of Bulwer's philosophical motives, in particular, of his opposi-
    tion to materialism. The best study of Poe's complex relation to gothicism
    in fiction is G. R. Thompson, *Poe's Fiction: Romantic Irony in the Gothic
    Tales* (Madison: University of Wisconsin Press, 1973).

12 Benjamin, *Illuminations*, pp. 175–76. On Poe's "poetic realism," see p. 171.
    The important exchange between Benjamin and Theodor Adorno on these
    theoretical issues is collected in *Aesthetics and Politics* (NLB, London, 1977),
    pp. 110–41. See also the afterword by Fredric Jameson. Jameson develops
    these issues about "mediation" at greater length in *The Political Unconscious:
    Narrative as a Socially Symbolic Act* (Ithaca, N.Y.: Cornell University Press,
    1981), esp. pp. 17–102, the essay "On Interpretation: Literature as a So-
    cially Symbolic Act."

13 Karl Marx, *The Eighteenth Brumaire of Louis Bonaparte* (New York: Interna-
    tional Publishers, 1963), p. 25.

14 *The Writings of the Young Marx on Philosophy and Society*, eds. Lloyd D.
    Easton and Kurt H. Guddat (Garden City, N.Y.: Doubleday, 1976), pp.
    222–23, 225. See also Alexis de Tocqueville, *Democracy in America*, 2 vols.
    (New York: Random House, 1945), 1:283ff.

15 *The Young Marx*, p. 184.

16. *Ibid.*, p. 225.

17 *Ibid.*, p. 186.

18 Karl Marx, *Capital*, trans. Ben Fowkes (New York: Random House,
    1977), 1:948–1084, esp. pp. 1060–65.

19 On the labor process and the social organization of time, see E. P. Thomp-
    son, "Time, Work-Discipline, and Industrial Capitalism," *Past and Present*
    50 (1971): 76–136.

20 Henri Lefebvre, *Everyday Life in the Modern World*, trans. Sacha Rabino-
    vitch (New York: Harper & Row 1971), pp. 195–97 and passim. On the
    fetishism of commodities, see Marx, *Capital*, 1:163–77.

21 See also Guy Debord, *Society of the Spectacle*, trans. anon. (Detroit: Black &
    Red, 1970).

22 The quotes are from Karl Marx and Friedrich Engels, *The Communist
    Manifesto*, ed. A. J. P. Taylor (New York: Penguin, 1967), p. 83.

23 Lefebvre, *Everyday Life*, pp. 117–18. See also pp. 5–6, 18–19. See Sigmund
    Freud, "The Uncanny," in *Studies in Parapsychology* (New York: Macmil-
    lan, 1971), pp. 19–60.

24 Lefebvre, *Everyday Life*, p. 29.

25 Benjamin, *Illuminations*, pp. 172–73. On the *flâneur*, see also Benjamin,
    Charles Baudelaire, pp. 170–71, and César Graña, *Modernity and Its Discon-
    tents* (New York: Harper & Row 1967), pp. 148–54, 192. Baudelaire's most
    famous account of the dandy is in "The Painter of Modern Life," in
    Mayne, ed., *The Painter of Modern Life*, pp. 5–12.

26 *Works*, 14:166.

27 *Ibid*. See also "The Business Man" and "Devil in the Belfry," both pub-
    lished in the year preceding "The Man of the Crowd."

28 Baudelaire, *Art in Paris*, p. 117.

29 Graña, *Modernity and Its Discontents*, p. 192; Baudelaire, "The Painter of
    Modern Life," pp. 9–10.

30 For a related exploration of some of these connected themes and of the
    dialectic of pleasure shaping the dandy's relation to the crowd, see Leo
    Bersani, *Baudelaire and Freud* (Berkeley: University of California Press,
    1977).

31 See Benjamin, *Charles Baudelaire*, pp. 54, 169–71. The quote is from p.
    169.

32 *Ibid.*, p. 169. See in particular the interiors described in "The Fall of the
    House of Usher," "Ligeia," and "The Assignation."

33 *Works*, 4:254.

34 See James M. Clark, *The Dance of Death in the Middle Ages and the Renais-
    sance* (Glasgow: Jackson, 1950), esp. pp. 1–6, 90–111, and Leonard P.

Kurtz, *The Dance of Death and the Macabre Spirit in European Literature* (New York: Gordian Press, 1975; rpt. of 1934 ed.), pp. 246–70. Kurtz considers Poe at pp. 263–65.

35 Benjamin, *Illuminations*, p. 176.

36 Karl Marx and Friedrich Engels, *On Literature and Art* (Moscow: Progress Publishers, 1976), p. 155.

37 See David Brion Davis, "Some Themes of Countersubversion: An Analysis of Anti-Masonic, Anti-Catholic, and Anti-Mormon Literature," *Mississippi Valley Historical Review* 47 (September 1960): 205–24.

38 See Harry Braverman, *Labor and Monopoly Capital: The Degradation of Work in the Twentieth Century* (New York & London: Monthly Review Press, 1974), pp. 59–69 and *passim,* on coercion in capitalist society, and Max Weber, *The Protestant Ethic and the Spirit of Capitalism,* trans. Talcott Parsons (New York: Scribner, 1958), esp. pp. 47–78.

39 Quoted in Eve Kosofsky Sedgwick, "The Character in the Veil: Imagery of the Surface in the Gothic Novel," *PMLA* 96, no. 2 (March 1981): 263–64.

40 Karl Mannheim, "The Democratization of Culture," in *Essays on the Sociology of Culture,* ed. Ernest Mannheim (London: Routledge & Kegan Paul, 1956), esp. pp. 180–88.

41 The quotations from "William Wilson" are from *Works,* 3:305–6, 308–9.

42 See especially *Works,* 3:280–81.

43 For Poe's views on the "mob," see *Works,* 16:160, 161; 6:207–9, 136. On the "oceanic feeling," see Sigmund Freud, *Civilization and Its Discontents,* trans. and ed. James Strachey (New York: Norton, 1962), pp. 1–2. On the narcissistic character of doubleness, see Otto Rank, *The Double: A Psychoanalytic Study* (New York: New American Library, 1979), pp. 69–86. Walt Whitman could be seen as the greatest exponent of this particular conception of democracy.

44 See Poe's letter of July 2, 1844, to James Russell Lowell for his view of the spiritual as the material, in *The Letters of Edgar Allan Poe,* ed. John Ward Ostrom, 2 vols. (New York: Gordian Press, 1966), 1:257. On the role of such a "material milieu" in Poe's fiction, see Leo Spitzer, "A Reinterpretation of 'The Fall of the House of Usher,' " in *Essays on English and American Literature* (Princeton, N.J.: Princeton University Press, 1962), pp. 51–66.

45 Georges Poulet, *Studies in Human Time* (Baltimore: Johns Hopkins University Press, 1956), pp. 330–34. See also Poulet, *The Metamorphoses of the Circle* (Baltimore: Johns Hopkins University Press, 1966), pp. 182–202.

46 Sigmund Freud, *The Interpretation of Dreams* (New York: Avon, 1965), pp. 591–603, for his discussion of "day's residue." Quotes are from pp. 601 and 603. Interestingly, Freud also draws an analogy between the role of the "day's residue" as an "instigator" of dreams and the economic activity of the "entrepreneur."

47 One likely source for the dreamlike aspects of Poe's description of the narrator's experience of the London streets is a passage from the chapter "The Pleasures of Opium" in Thomas De Quincey's *Confessions of an English*

Opium-Eater, in which he remarks that "the human face tyrannized over my dreams," the haunting residue of "the perplexities of my [drugged] steps in London." As with the passage from Bulwer, De Quincey's work is not postulated by Mabbot as a source for Poe's story.

48 Baudelaire, "The Painter of Modern Life," p. 9.

49 *Works,* 16:311–12.

50 It may not be quite accurate to characterize this process as a "dialectic," as the "surface" remains radically unreadable in terms of any sort of code, however attenuated. The old man's physiognomy is characterized precisely by its "absolute idiosyncracy" or, finally, by its absolute typicalness. See Sedgwick, "The Character in the Veil."

51 Nor can "contagious disease" in Poe be understood as a version of the theories of social ecology that many of his contemporaries evoked in order to explain urban crime. See Welsh, *The City of Dickens,* pp. 24–28; Yi-Fu Tuan, *Landscapes of Fear* (Minneapolis: University of Minnesota Press, 1979), pp. 168, 102–3; and Asa Briggs, "Cholera and Society in the Nineteenth Century," in Eugene C. Black, ed., *European Political History, 1815–1870: Aspects of Liberalism* (New York: Harper Torchbook, 1967), pp. 45–68.

11

The Politics of *The Scarlet Letter*

JONATHAN ARAC

If the study of American literature is not merely to reproduce the American ideology, it must engage directly with the debates of literary theory, which allow us to raise basic questions about the values and practices at stake in reading, studying, and teaching American literature and culture. Thus far, however, Americanists have left such engagements to writers from Comparative Literature, New Criticism, and Composition.[1] My attempt to understand *The Scarlet Letter* begins from the recent debate over "indeterminacy" in interpretation. Such repositioning of a classic text will reduce the privilege usually accorded the study of American literature in the United States, where of all the literary curriculum it has at once the greatest continuing appeal to students and the least commitment to self-questioning. Especially now, when the centralizing of left and right achieved after World War II yields to pulls in both directions, we must ask again what we are doing.

I find exemplary the interpretive premises formulated by Walter Benjamin early in World War II: "Whoever has emerged victorious participates to this day in the triumphal procession in which the present rulers step over those who are lying prostrate. According to traditional practice, the spoils are carried along in the procession. They are called cultural treasures." Such treasures, Benjamin asserts, have an origin that one "cannot contemplate without horror," for "They owe their existence not only to the efforts of the great minds who have created them, but also to the anonymous toil of their contemporaries." Benjamin's genealogical understanding challenges those of us professionally devoted to transmitting a culture: "There is no document of civilization which is not at the same time a document of barbarism. and just as such a document is not free of barbarism, barbarism taints also the manner in which it was transmitted from one owner to another." Benjamin's ideal figure of the "historical materialist" is obligated to "brush history against the grain."[2]

The reproduction of the American ideology I am taking in Benjamin's terms as the transmission of certain spoils, the canonized texts, and a complacency in that transmission that continues to neglect or depreciate the anonymous toil of the losers and thus prolongs specific conditions of domination.

What will it mean to "brush history against the grain"? To raise up to prominence what is usually smoothed over will include the correlative features of barbarism and anonymous toil. *The Scarlet Letter* addresses the anonymous toil of women under the barbarism of patriarchy, but we must go farther to understand its immediate and continuing power long before feminism became an unavoidable presence. Slavery was the issue that agitated American politics most deeply in Hawthorne's time, and abolitionism made the young Henry Adams feel that Boston in 1850 was once again revolutionary. I propose, then, to define a relation between *The Scarlet Letter* and the political response to masters' barbarism and slaves' anonymous toil.

Studies of local politics help us to understand the genesis of Hawthorne's work, but only national concerns account for its powerful reception and effect. Firmly entrenched in American economic, social, and moral life, slavery was contested through political, legal, and cultural means – all of which I shall have something to say about. Yet even the profession of history has recently diverted attention from this historical "horror" except as an isolated subfield.[3] In literary studies the diversion has been much easier, and the reason for this defines the second feature I want to raise to prominence: the very status of his writing as art, of his identity as an artist, that Hawthorne established to defend himself against implication in the political embroilments of Salem.[4] Poe may have preceded Hawthorne in the attempt to establish such an artistic space, but Hawthorne was the first to do it effectively, to make it stick, in a way recognized by his contemporaries and for the future.

The immunity Hawthorne won has protected very different kinds of writers, such as Mark Twain. *Huckleberry Finn* has been much in the news recently as school boards try to restrict it for compliance with, and fueling of, American racism. Because of this controversy, the *New York Times* interviewed a woman prominent on the liberal side in a dispute over school libraries. She was asked, "Can you think of any materials that might legitimately be ke[pt] out of school libraries?" She replied, "I don't see the need for girlie magazines. I don't see the need for a political-type magazine unless they were going to be used in a curriculum to show all views. (But) I can't see any harm in anything classified as literature" (June 27, 1982, E8).

The traditional claim for the innocence of art, most explicitly since Kant and Schiller, warrants both this civil rights activist and the more theoretically elaborate "hermeneutics of indeterminacy" in current criticism. Through this principle, Geoffrey Hartman tries to protect art from the domination of politics and the economy alike, from "technocratic, predictive, and authoritarian formulas," from the exploitive utilitarianism that would "resolve it into available meanings."[5] By protecting art in this way, Hartman hopes to protect its readers as well, to leave a portion of our capacities and experience free from the marketplace, the cold war, and whatever else is inhumane in our surroundings. Yet decades earlier, in "The Affirmative Character of Culture" (1937), Herbert Marcuse had already historically analyzed this aesthetic strategy and shown the dangers that lurk within the protections.

It may be necessary to forgo protection entirely, for in *The Scarlet Letter,* as in some current criticism, "indeterminacy" functions as a closure. Paradoxes abound here, for I would want to say of my own enterprise that by venturing a specific interpretation within historical process, I am *opening* the work and opening criticism to political engagements. If we could truly escape such engagements, there might be some point in doing so, but they press upon us in any case. To ignore these possibilities for the sake of art is simply to make decisions that are less aware and responsible than they should be.

In standing for interpretive specificity against a hermeneutics of indeterminacy, I want to differentiate myself from some who abstractly – in favoring specificity over indeterminacy – share my position. A striking instance of this abstractly similar position appeared in *Commentary,* the leading ideological organ of American neoconservatism. Perhaps my disagreement here is part of the splitting I earlier mentioned, with the "Yale Critics," once seen as avant-garde, occupying a new center.

Confusion has arisen in the recent use of the term "interpretation." In the work that inaugurated the American boom in theory of criticism, *Validity in Interpretation* (1967), E. D. Hirsch distinguished between "interpretation" and "criticism" as parallel to his famous distinction between "meaning" and "significance." That is, interpretation is concerned with meaning and criticism with significance. In *Commentary,* however, a self-proclaimed follower of Hirsch, Frederick Crews, supports a definition of criticism "as it is still widely conceived," namely, "the pursuit of meaning that authors presumably impart to their works in creating them."[6] Despite the reassuring rhetoric of long-standing consensus, this definition is not how Samuel Johnson or Coleridge or Arnold or Eliot or Leavis or Lionel Trilling or Northrop Frye "conceived" of criticism; it is, however, just what Hirsch calls interpretation. The essay goes on to combat "indeterminists" on the grounds that they are "Luddites[7] in the factories of meaning production" (p. 70). This metaphoric link between critical theory and the "machine-breakers" of the early English Industrial Revolution makes clear why a national organ of opinion should bother about a specialized technicality within professional literary study. Powerful interests require the smooth functioning of knowledge mills. Thought, debate, or criticism within the universities might impede "production."

Now the story is further complicated by the work of Fredric Jameson, who in *The Political Unconscious* argues against the anti-interpretive stands associated with French structuralist and poststructuralist theory. As a Marxist, Jameson does not share the factory manager's fear of Luddites. From that point of view, indeed, he too falls among the "indeterminists," despite his commitment to interpretation, because he does not give unique and complete authority to the author. But what are the grounds for the author? Crews faults indeterminists for "dependence on empirically dubious sources of authority" (p. 68) such as Marx, Nietzsche, Freud, Saussure, and Jakobson, and he also deplores their "renunciation of rationally based choice between competing theories" (p. 71), but he has himself acted neither empirically nor rationally, by his own acknowledgment: "The decision to say that texts do or don't bear authorially determined meaning is not an empirical matter, but one of methodological and even temperamental convenience. . . . If we want to believe that a work's meaning became fixed forever in the act of its creation, all we need to do is say so. Then, following E. D. Hirsch" (p. 65) – all good things will follow. I think on the contrary that such desperate throwing away of intelligence, such decapitation of literary studies by a debased pragmatism will only ensure their demise.

In arguing for a specific interpretation of *The Scarlet Letter* that is neither authorial in the "interpretationist" sense nor mystifying, as I find indeterminism, I begin from several concrete problems in our received understanding of Hawthorne. Arlin Turner's standard biography finds Hawthorne almost unique among major American writers in the degree to which he is "extensively and significantly involved" in "the affairs of his time."[8] The chapters on this involvement, however, do little more than detail Hawthorne's role in allocating patronage for Pierce's presidency. The problem is, what state of American politics allows such patronage brokering to count as "significant"?

Patronage haunts my next problem as well. Students marvel that the author of "The Custom-House" was in less than three years to write *The Life of Franklin Pierce* – that in the decade following publication of *Mosses from an Old Manse* (1846), Hawthorne held patronage positions for seven years, interrupted by a three-year career as a romancer. The problem is to determine a relation, perhaps even a common ground, between the writing of *The Scarlet Letter* and that of the *Life of Pierce*.

The next related problems also arise from the classroom. Students judge *The Scarlet Letter* an intransitive "work of art," unlike, say, *Uncle Tom's Cabin,* which is "propaganda" rather than "art," for it aims to change your life.[9] If recent revaluation has shown that *Uncle Tom's Cabin* is also art, may it not be equally important to show that *The Scarlet Letter* is also propaganda – *not* to change your life?[10] I at once draw back from the extremity of this last suggestion. *The Scarlet Letter* aims to produce an invisible change, an internal deepening like that which transforms the letter even as its form remains identical. Stowe, too, aims at an internal change, but she holds that this change would visibly affect your outer actions as well. Both Hawthorne and Stowe situate their work as cultural – not political or legal – but they differ on the relation of culture to the other activities of life. It was not yet taken for granted that literature must be intransitive, useless as well as harmless.

My final problem is that a standard classroom text of *The Scarlet Letter* includes "historical background" materials, but they all relate to the seventeenth century, not to the nineteenth. Has Hawthorne's art truly achieved a timeless escape from his age? I would expect that even if *The Scarlet Letter* is an antithesis to the frustrations of contemporary political life, an escape from that life in the custom house, compensation for those frustrations, nonetheless the situation being turned from should leave some traces, through which to read a relation between the fiction of the 1640s and the history of around 1850. Such reading starts from the relation of "The Custom-House" to "The Scarlet Letter."

There is always some doubt what we mean when we say, "The Scarlet Letter." Do we mean the book that includes "The Custom-House," or do we mean only the twenty-four chapters that follow "The Custom-House"? *The Scarlet Letter* names both the whole book and one of its parts – as well as the colored work of printer's art on the title page of the first edition and a major element within the fiction. "The Custom-House" holds a supplementary position, occupying a space that in its absence would not be recognized as vacant; it adds something gratuitous that was not required and thus destabilizes what it claims to support.[11] So it offers to prove the "authenticity" (p. 85) of the narrative to follow but does so in terms of "literary propriety," an appeal to convention rather than a warrant of authenticity.[12] By taking possession through "The Custom-House" of the (physical) scarlet letter as his property, the author of "The Custom-House" personalizes the narrative. The many correspondences between the authorial figure of "The Custom-House" and the characters of "The Scarlet Letter" – for example, the disapproval shown to both Hester and Hawthorne by an imagined crowd of Puritan authorities, the dual status Dimmesdale and Hawthorne share of a passionate inner life wholly at odds with their "official" public position, the work both author and Chillingworth do as analysts of character – allow us to naturalize the presence of "The Custom-House" and justify its excess. But they also undermine the self-sufficiency of "The Scarlet Letter" – making it an allegory of the writer's situation in 1850. We could say that Hester emerges from the Custom House as much as she issues from prison; we may even argue that "The Custom-House" – as the prehistory of the scarlet letter (the thing itself) – stands in lieu of narrating the love affair between Hester and Dimmesdale.[13] Either would suffice to explain how Hester came to stand marked on the scaffold. "The Custom-House" concludes that the public character of the "decapitated surveyor" – Hawthorne in the newspapers – is only "figurative" and that Hawthorne's "real human being" is a "literary man" (pp. 109–10). By the same logic, we may conclude that the public life of Hester – in the novel – is also only figurative, and its reality is Hawthorne's literary life.

A recurrent mood of "The Custom-House," emphatic near its end, is harried dejection – like that which sends Ishmael off whaling – which leads Hawthorne to welcome his "execution" in the change of administrations, as if a man planning suicide had "the good hap to be murdered" (p. 109). From this mood issues forth "The Scarlet Letter," only to end where it began, in the mood of the questions the heartsick women of Massachusetts ask Hester: "why they were so wretched and what the remedy" (p. 240). From the man alone in 1850 to the women together in the seventeenth century, there is nothing to *do* to become happy: With luck you'll be decapitated, or else "the angel and apostle of the coming revelation" (p. 240) will appear. The only remedy is patient trust in the future. "The Scarlet Letter" does, however, propose a specific source for the misery: Hester once *did* something, which both found her a child and lost its father – a situation like that of Hawthorne's own family as he grew up with his widowed mother. *The Scarlet Letter* ends with the death of Hester, and its writing began with the death of Hawthorne's own mother. The difference is that Mrs. Hawthorne committed no crime in marrying a mariner who then happened to die in Surinam of yellow fever.[14] Hawthorne's novel transforms his life situation by adding accountable guilt. A complex social fact–involving American trade relations in the Caribbean, the inadequacy of mosquito control, the conditions of medical knowledge–is turned into a crime. Something that might require political action–as it did to empower public health undertaking in the nineteenth century–becomes a matter for ethical judgment and psychological reflection.

A comparable personalization is crucial for the politics of *The Scarlet Letter*. The attempt to separate the artwork from pragmatic concerns, the programmatically willed alienation of the artist that Hawthorne achieved, function within a political world that allowed *issues* no part in the discourse of the two established parties. Hawthorne's criticism of the "official" life of the Custom House, its distance from any concerns that could be considered real, is accurate.

Consider a major rhetorical motif in "The Custom-House," the insistence that "The Scarlet Letter" arises in all its gloom from an act of revolutionary victimization, the decapitation of the headless surveyor, who now writes as a "politically dead man" (p. 110). This joke hinges on a common hyperbole, that of likening patronage dismissals to acts of French revolutionary terror. Franklin Pierce, a man of no linguistic originality, used the figure in a speech of 1841 that Hawthorne quotes,[15] and Turner suggests that Hawthorne himself adapted the figure from an article in the news (p. 181). The particular wit of the joke is that patronage changes are not "revolution" (p. 110) but carry out the etymologically related action of "rotation" in office: Revolutionary principle has become rotatory patronage. Whether one is in office or out, one is as good as politically dead, for the officeholder, Hawthorne argues, "does not share in the united effort of mankind" (p. 107). Paradoxically, then, public office is private. In a polity that allows for no significant action, politics can only be the corrupting hunt for spoils.

As politics became merely officeholding and patronage brokering, articulated, speculative, passionate intelligence had withdrawn from the ranks of the Democrats and Whigs. The sketches of "official" character that occupy Hawthorne in the avowedly antipolitical literary practice of "The Custom-House" correspond to his occupation during his maximal political involvement. Turner specifies Hawthorne's political prowess as "manipulation" and "understanding of the men involved" (p. 254). In the *Life of Pierce,* Hawthorne's claim to authority is knowledge of "the individual," his capacity to read Pierce's "character" and judge his "motives" (p. 349). This emphasis on character is not the idiosyncrasy of a "literary man"; the Whigs ran exactly the same campaign on their side. The 1852 campaign allowed no issue but personality.[16]

We know the 1850s as a turning point in American political history:

The Whig Party was about to disappear; the long Democratic majority, to become a sectionalized and ethnicized minority; and the Republicans were about to emerge and rule for three generations. The Union was about to split and be reunited by bloody conquest. And in all this, slavery was crucial. All this, however, was unthinkable to the still dominant established parties, especially between the Compromise of 1850 and the Kansas–Nebraska troubles of 1854, an interlude of paralytic calm that seemed to mark the extinction of abolitionist and free-soil possibilities for transforming the national polity. When Charles Sumner entered the Senate in 1851, old Thomas Hart Benton took him aside and explained that he had "come up on the stage too late, sir. Not only have our great men passed away, but the great issues have been settled also. The last of these was the National Bank."[17]

Consensus reigned between the two established parties. The *Life of Pierce* declared that no "great and radical principles are at present in dispute" between the Democrats and Whigs, but both are "united in one common purpose"–that of "preserving our sacred Union" (p. 436). The reason for choosing Pierce is that Pierce is younger, a "new man" (p. 436) to lead us into the future. In the politics of the 1850s, character offered a ground for choice when there were no issues at stake, no policy plans. For Pierce did not undertake to do anything if elected.

Hawthorne recognized slavery as potentially divisive, and he did not favor slavery; he only urged that nothing be done about it. Slavery is "one of those evils which divine Providence does not leave to be remedied by human contrivances, but which, in its own good time, by some means impossible to be anticipated, but of the simplest and easiest operation, when all its uses shall have been fulfilled, it causes to vanish like a dream" (p. 417).[18]

Such a fantasy of evanescence recalls not only Chillingworth's extinction after Dimmesdale's confession, but even more the death of Jaffrey Pyncheon in *The House of the Seven Gables,* like a "defunct nightmare" (p. 394). The key to redemption in that book is replacing all human action, which is guilt-ridden, with the beneficent process of nature. The dreadful pattern of stasis in the house and repetition in the crimes of its inhabitants is undone by the natural development of Phoebe at her moment of transition from girl to woman (a positive contrast to the degenerate mixture of senility and puerility in the ruined Clifford).

The point of the plot in *The House of the Seven Gables* is to erase and undo all action. Just as Holgrave is about to repeat his ancestor's mesmeric possession of a Pyncheon woman, he holds back, and it will be through the natural course of love that he and Phoebe are united instead. So, too, the apparent murder of Jaffrey proves to be death by natural causes, and so likewise the death thirty years earlier for which Clifford had been imprisoned. Even Jaffrey, we learn, had not actively committed any crime in allowing Clifford to be convicted. (This passivity reminds us that even in death he remains a respectable, conservative Whig and has not joined the "Free-Soilers" as a Conscience Whig – see p. 408.) The long-standing class conflict of owners and workers, Pyncheons and Maules, is mediated through modest marriage: The daughter of the Pyncheons is a housewife herself rather than a lady waited upon by servants; the son of the Maules is both a radical and an entrepreneur. Together they embody a country where a cent shop may lose you five dollars or gain you a million – all without government interference, social motion regulated by Providence alone.

This logic of romance Hawthorne envisaged for America in politics as well. As late as 1863, he wrote to Elizabeth Peabody that the Civil War would only achieve "by a horrible convulsion" what might have come by "a gradual and peaceful change," and Mrs. Hawthorne echoes this judgment to a Union general, agreeing with his conviction that "God's law" would surely have removed slavery "without this dreadful convulsive action."[19]

Action is intolerable; character takes its place. We recognize the Romantic reinterpretation of *Hamlet,* and this move in the American politics of the 1850s and in Hawthorne's writing echoes earlier English experience.[20] Wordsworth's disillusion with the French Revolution, the English anti-French consensus politics that marginalized any attempt at change such as the French example had first promised – all these go into his famous lines:

> Action is transitory – a step, a blow,
> The motion of a muscle – this way or that –
> 'Tis done, and in the after-vacancy
> We wonder at ourselves like men betrayed:
> Suffering is permanent, obscure and dark,
> And shares the nature of infinity.[21]

Contemporary with Goethe's *Wilhelm Meister,* which drew on *Hamlet* to inaugurate the tradition of the *Bildungsroman,* these lines signal a change in the status of literary character. No longer the traditional Aristotelian one who acts, nor, as in many great nineteenth-century novels, one who speaks, a character becomes one who is known. Coming from tale-writing, Hawthorne maintains in his longer works an extremely high proportion of narration to dialogue, while at the same time abandoning most of the traditional materials – that is, actions – of traditional narration. His fiction in certain ways thus technically anticipates that of Flaubert or Henry James in the emphasis it places on its characters, as narrated. Michel Foucault in *Discipline and Punish* has done the most to help us understand the social basis and political implications of such inquisitorial knowledge.

Within *The Scarlet Letter*, Chillingworth, the knower of Dimmesdale (we do not penetrate the "interior" of Dimmesdale's "heart" until Chillingworth has led us there), represents the processes of social knowing that Foucault argues have come to produce the "post-Christian" soul. But personalization is again at work: In projecting the methods of the nineteenth century back into the seventeenth century (which in fact initiated some of them), Hawthorne has transformed anonymous impersonality into a pseudonymous personality, whose relation with Dimmesdale rather anticipates psychoanalysis than corresponds to any actual medical practice from the 1640s or 1850s. Thus, in Chillingworth, Hawthorne focuses the full ambivalence of a fantasy of being personally known: the dream of intimacy, the nightmare of violation.

Such extremes are no greater than those in "The Custom-House" between the wish for "some true relation with his audience" in literature (p. 85) and its demonic counterpart in official life – the stenciled and black-painted name of Hawthorne that circulates the world on "all kinds of dutiable merchandise" (p. 100). The characters of the name are known and effective, but through no action of Hawthorne's. Yet even as that of a writer, Hawthorne's signature in the Democratic press was valuable to his party, and appearing where it did, converted book reviews into political capital. Hawthorne's name circulated as a sign in a complex system of exchange that made it worth the party's while to provide him a livelihood, and that gave him the character of a Democrat, without requiring action.[22] Wordworth's lines questioning action are the words of a successful tempter, who turned out to speak for a whole culture. Evert Duyckinck of the New York *Literary World* alluded to these lines in his review of *The Scarlet Letter*, although without touching on the political implications. Hawthorne had been writing this way for some twenty years; his literary mode did not suddenly change in response to politics, but at this point there was a sudden change in his popularity. The official "end of ideology" in the 1850s took to Hawthorne, just as it did again in the 1950s. Even now in American political life we displace politics into personality when fundamental debate is marginalized. We assess the reliability of character among the candidates competing to control the nuclear holocaust button. To dismantle that monstrous apparatus is still as unthinkable to major parties now as in Hawthorne's time was dismantling slavery or the Union.

Might the Freeze movement have the same catalytic power of political realignment that Free Soil had for the Republicans?

A politics of issueless patience causes rhetorical confusion in a party that aims to the future and claims responsibility for the "destinies, not of America alone, but of mankind at large" as they are "carried upward and consummated" (*Life of Pierce,* p. 436). The *Life of Pierce* early identifies Hawthorne and Pierce with the "progressive or democratic" political stance, as opposed to the "respectable conservative" (p. 357). But on slavery, Hawthorne judges that "the statesman of practical sagacity – who loves his country as it is, and evolves good from things as they exist . . . will be likely . . . to stand in the attitude of a conservative" (p. 416). So the Democrats become progressive conservatives.[23]

Similar blurring marked legislative activity in the period. David Potter argues that the Abolititonists were hated "because they insisted upon the necessity to choose" and were dangerous because they converted "resolvable disputes" into "questions of principle," giving a polemical "false clarity and simplicity" to issues better left "qualified and diffuse." Potter is not so happy, however, with the results of his recommended politics of indeterminacy when Congress actually followed such a course. Avoiding both clarity and principle, Congress could no longer agree on anything that both sides understood in the same way, but could pass only "measures ambiguous enough in their meaning or uncertain enough in their operation to gain support from men who hoped for opposite results."[24]

Such a politics of Freudian compromise-formation has, according to Sacvan Bercovitch, persisted in American life since its Puritan origins. The "paranosic gain" is large. Such "both – and" rhetoric offers America an ambiguity that denies contradictions, encouraging a "multiplicity of meanings" while "precluding contradiction in fact." This is a "mythical mode of cultural continuity" that contrasts with, and prevents, any possible "historical gesture at cultural discontinuity." Setting aside their contrasting evaluations, Bercovitch shares this understanding of American Democracy with Arthur Schlesinger, Jr., who claimed, "Democracy . . . suspends in solution logical antinomies which work out more or less harmoniously in practice."[25]

Given a political rhetoric, and a national identity, that depend on blurring together what are ordinarily taken as contraries, we may find in Hawthorne's style a response to this situation. His prose negotiates the conflicting realities of past and present, the overlays of Puritan, agrarian, commercial, and industrial ways of life that he encountered in New England, as well as the tension between American politics as a

continuing revolution and politics as patronage, mere "rotation."
Hawthorne's derealizing style represents objects so that we doubt their
reality, yet while thus questioning what offers itself as our world, he
refuses to commit himself to the authenticity of any other world or way
of seeing.[26]

Antinomies may be suspended not only in local stylistic practice but also
over the course of a narrative. Claude Lévi-Strauss has defined "myth" as
the narrative mode that so negotiates the fundamental antinomies of a
culture, and Fredric Jameson has elaborated a model for analyzing such
ideological compromise formations in modern literature.[27]

As in Hawthorne's uncertainty between "progressive" and "conservative," the contradictory wish of the Democrats in the early 1850s was to
go ahead into the future without losing control of what they had established: Let us call this the tension between motion and regulation.[28] In the
Life of Pierce this determines the contradiction between the *future* we wish
to gain and the *stability* we fear to lose. In *The Scarlet Letter* the turn from
action to character means that we should find the terms of our contradiction in Hawthorne's analysis of what prevents a character from acting –
as when Hester tempts Dimmesdale in the forest. Hester's "intellect and
heart had their home . . . in desert places, where they roamed as freely as
the wild Indian."[29] In contrast, Dimmesdale "had never gone through an
experience calculated to lead him beyond the scope of generally received
laws; although in a single instance" he had transgressed one. Hawthorne
elaborates: "But this had been a sin of passion, not of principle, nor even
purpose. . . . At the head of the social system . . . he was only the more
trammelled by its regulations, its principles, and even its prejudices. . . .
The framework of his order inevitably hemmed him in" (pp. 202–3).
Dimmesdale's emotional wavering is structured like Pierce's political
trimming: The tension of regulation versus motion that determined the
contradiction between stability and the future in the *Life of Pierce* here
determines the contradiction of "principle" versus "passion" (e-motion).

From the contradictory pair of terms we may logically generate a
further pair – the negation of each of the contradictory pair, giving us a
four-part matrix in terms of which we may align the characters of a
work. This scheme offers a way of interpreting characters as projections
of ideological possibilities, given a literature that suppresses the overtly
ideological plotting of action and prefers investment in character.

Dimmesdale is the character defined by passion and no principle; opposed to him is the "iron framework" (pp. 156, 180) of Puritanism,
defined by principle without passion. In the double negative place, possessing neither passion nor principle, is Chillingworth. He "violated, in
cold blood, the sanctity of a human heart" (p. 200) – violation negating
principle and cold blood negating passion. At times, however, the text

marks Chillingworth with "dark passion" (e.g., p. 200), thus making him a double of Dimmesdale (and after all, they are identified as the two men with claims upon Hester). Thus "Chillingworth," the proper name, covers both these narrative functions. Finally, the double positive, uniting passion and principle,[30] projects the ideal Hester. We all construct this figure in our readings and then must confront Hawthorne's failure to actualize her in his text. Almost the whole history of interpreting Hawthorne may be charted here: praise for his realism; condemnation for the failure of his imaginative energy; understanding the glimmering half-existence of the ideal Hester as proof of Hawthorne's duplicitous negotiation with his external audience or internal self-censor. Just as Chillingworth's passion when present displaces his significance, so in Hester the usual preponderance of ascetic principle and burial of passion make her a double of the Puritan establishment. Only to the extent that the ideal Hester exists can Hawthorne be considered a fundamentally subversive writer; otherwise, we must value the hope he offers in his openness to our interpretive energies but must recognize his own limitations within a "framework."

The *Life of Pierce* does not hesitate to offer Pierce as the imaginary mediating figure who combines the future with stability. The campaign-biography genre of annunciatory historical fiction saves Hawthorne the need actually to specify the works of such a figure. Pierce's Whig opponent, Scott, shares the value of stability, but he has done his work; he does not belong to the future. Slavery negates stability, for it threatens the Union, and because slavery is also providentially doomed, the slave South combines the two negatives – instability and no future. Free Soilers and Abolitionists point toward the future without slavery, but no less than the slavery they oppose, they threaten stability.

Thus the organization of (in)action in both books works through a structure of conflicting values related to the political impasse of the 1850s. In American legal practice and theory at about this time, a characteristic array of dualisms (comparable to those of motion and regulation) came into use to negotiate the separation of a legal area of competence distinct from that of politics.[31] The predominance of legal interpretive problems and methods in the middle nineteenth century suggests that more than theology (which had predominated in the seventeenth century), American legal experience may cast light on the hermeneutics of the scarlet letter itself.[32]

Consider the problems of reading the letter in relation to the fundamental debates in the 1850s over the meaning of such documents of American life as the Declaration of Independence and the Constitution. As America left behind the directly "political" statements and actions of the Founders, the age of Clay, Webster, and Calhoun made "constitu-

tional" questions a matter of "exegesis."[33] All the fundamental questions of interpretation arose around these no less than around Hester's
letter. Recall particularly that "adulterer" (or "adultery"?) is nowhere
spelled out in Hawthorne's text, just as "slavery" is nowhere present in
the Declaration or the Constitution. The authorial meaning of the Constitution, in particular, was deliberately "indeterminate" on the question of slavery, yet at a certain moment in American life a decision, and
so a violation, was necessary.[34]

In *The Scarlet Letter,* adultery, unnamed, begins as the "self-evident"
meaning of a woman alone with a child exposed to public scorn. As the
letter leaves its original context, however, it takes on new meanings:
"Many people refused to interpret the scarlet A by its original significance" (p. 179). Hester plans never to abandon the letter, for while it
endures, it will be "transformed into something that should speak a
different purport" (p. 184). Early in the nineteenth century, Joseph
Hopkinson had opposed statutes "expressed in black and white" and
defended common law: "Consider the dictionary: scarcely a word in
the language has a single, fixed, determinate meaning."[35] Exploiting
such indeterminacy, Hester's letter combines without contradiction the
celebratory communal hopes of A for Angel in the sky, together with
the anguished solitary pain of Dimmesdale's A in his flesh. John Picker-
ing argues that the "ambiguity of language," especially in a "community where every man has an equal right to decide the construction,"
requires the "positive decision of a tribunal" in order to give "doubtful
words a determinate signification."[36] If law moves toward this desired
scene of authoritative judgment, literature moves toward a community
of readers. Hawthorne details a judgment's aftermath, and not only
"every man" but also a woman claims the right of construction. The
identification of Pearl with the letter further emphasizes that its meaning must be understood historically, through experience, growth, and
development, not as a "declaration" expressed "in black and white."
Taken back into politics, such a Burkean emphasis would protect the
Constitution against Abolitionists: It denies the need for any tampering
innovation and denies also the value of any reductive fixation on the
original meaning or intention. Chillingworth's quest of this sort is dis-
gusting and damaging; it makes him the book's villain. So much for
genealogy as demystification!

The Scarlet Letter does, however, consider an alternative status for the
letter, for its embroidery manifests Hester's will and not only that of
the public. Perhaps, then, it might be better understood as a contract.
The authoritative *Commentaries* of Chancellor Kent had defined contract
law through the intention of the parties, which should prevail even

"over the strict letter of the contract." In this area, the law "will control even the literal terms of the contract, if they manifestly contravene the purpose."[37] Hawthorne, however, deprecates such a line of analysis. Hester is described as not true to the letter when she analyzes it contractually, as the mark of her meeting with the black man in the woods. Nor did Hawthorne think William Lloyd Garrison was true to the Constitution when the Abolitionist leader proclaimed it "a covenant with death and an agreement with hell."[38] More in keeping with Hawthorne's analysis was the new understanding of contract promulgated by Theophilus Parsons in 1855. The "intent of the parties" becomes subject to powers beyond it, including not only the rules of law, but also "the rules of language."[39]

Yet whether on the model of constitutional law or of contract law, the temporal hermeneutics of the Jacksonian Democrats wanted things both ways. The Constitution was a document appropriate to guide our better future, since it did not mention slavery, yet one must also in our bad present recognize the original constitutional "guarantees" of slavery (*Life of Pierce,* p. 433). This double vision allowed them to deny the need for present action, but in refusing to open itself to the new issues of the day, Jacksonian Democracy became a dead letter.

This context allows us to reread the halfhearted wishfulness of Miles Coverdale's finale in *The Blithedale Romance:* "Were there any cause . . . worth a sane man's dying for . . . provided, however, the effort did not involve an unreasonable amount of trouble – methinks I might be bold to offer up my life . . . if Kossuth . . . would pitch the battlefield of Hungarian rights within an easy ride of my abode" (p. 584). Typically, critics who have commented on Hawthorne's piercing exposure of Coverdale have failed to remark that he is a representative man. All America offered Kossuth great enthusiasm and no substantial aid. Even the supposed interventionists of "Young America" treated Kossuth's appeal as an opportunity for sympathetic involvement without any active commitment.[40] The wish for a happy rather than melancholy outcome to a world in which action is not to be taken differentiates the *Life of Pierce* from its predecessors among Hawthorne's romances, but we must remember at last Hawthorne's abject identity with Coverdale. In the *Life of Pierce* he recognizes the possibility that "the work of antislavery agitation . . . must be done," but since it costs one's love for the Union, he can only pray, "Let others do it" (p. 416).

My argument has tried to show that Hawthorne's own authorial meaning establishes an "indeterminacy" that is not merely a modern critical aberration. I have further assayed a critical evaluation of that indeterminacy in Hawthorne's time and ours, for it still remains effective both in literature and in politics. This act of historical interpretation runs strongly against any "hermeneutics of indeterminacy," although it has much in common with the claims of Fredric Jameson, upon whom I have drawn. I want to conclude, however, with some arguments against Jameson's notion of the "political unconscious," for I think it does not offer enough "grain" to suit Benjamin's historical materialist. No less than Derridean "textuality," insistence on an unconscious may too quickly curtail the scope of knowledge and specificity. We all recognize the problem of an analyst who *already knows* what is being repressed and what must be uncovered.

The notion of a "political unconscious" depends on conceptualizing the social totality as a whole implicit in each of its parts. Any aspects of the whole not immediately visible in a part must be latent in it, repressed or unconscious within it. The model of "production," however, may work much better than the model of "repression." Marx, for example, may be better understood as arguing that capitalism *produces* the proletariat than that it represses it (except through a wordplay that assimilates political domination to erasure from consciousness). So in their very different ways Michel Foucault in *The Order of Things* and Raymond Williams in *Culture and Society* have analyzed the production of "literature" as a particular social and linguistic space in the nineteenth century, achieved through a series of separations and purifications. Likewise in this period, legal discourse was produced in a much greater autonomy. I would argue then that literature and politics, or law and politics, were not superimposed one upon the other (politics "relentlessly driven underground," in Jameson's phrase) but rather *juxtaposed* to one another. To conceptualize such affiliation does not, as Jameson fears, require us to "imagine" that "sheltered from the omnipresence of history and the implacable influences of the social, there already exists a realm of freedom."[41] It does suggest, however, that the relations of politics and literature are different from what he understands them to be. It also serves to disqualify the exclusive delving into literary texts as an authentically political activity – a sore matter for the literary academic who might rather hold with Jameson that "everything is 'in the last analysis' political." Against this metaphoric model of identification, stands the metonymic model: "Everything is *connected with* the political."[42]

In juxtaposing the *Life of Pierce* and *The Scarlet Letter* I have operated by adjacency, rather than trusting that I could uncover within *The Scarlet Letter* alone all that I needed for its interpretation. Although the two works could be analyzed as *narratives* together, the *Life* was "closed" in its unequivocal endorsement of Pierce as representing the ideal combination of future and stability; *The Scarlet Letter,* by contrast, was "open" in its refusal to make similarly absolute claims for Hester's transcendence of the contradiction between passion and principle, and also in the overall mobility among the ideological positions that its characters were granted. That very openness, however, mystified as the value of "art," has encouraged neglect of the ideological limits on the "positions" themselves. Perhaps only in the last fifty years has the fundamental opposition of motion versus regulation been sufficiently overcome in America's conception of its economy, polity, and society to allow us from the standpoint of our new social and political contradictions a sharp sense of this earlier phase.

Notes

1 Carol Kay's very different work in progress on political philosophy and the novel inspired this chapter. In 1981, Donald Pease and Chaviva Hošek offered a forum to try out my ideas, as did Edward Said and Marie-Rose Logan in 1982. The critical encouragement of Sacvan Bercovitch and Myra Jehlen made this final version possible. I thank them all. On the disciplinary structure of American literary studies, see my Afterword to *The Yale Critics: Deconstruction in America,* which I edited with Wlad Godzich and Wallace Martin (Minneapolis: University of Minnesota Press, 1983), especially pp. 185–86. Part of my present point is that when Americanists such as Joseph Riddel or Frank Lentricchia join the debate, they are at once perceived as in "theory" and no longer "American."

2 "Theses on the Philosophy of History," in *Illuminations,* trans. Harry Zohn (1968; rpt. New York: Schocken, 1969), pp. 256–57.

3 Eric Foner, Introduction to *Politics and Ideology in the Age of the Civil War* (New York: Oxford University Press, 1980), esp. p. 11. More broadly, see Elizabeth Fox-Genovese and Eugene D. Genovese, "The Political Crisis of Social History," in *Fruits of Merchant Capital* (New York: Oxford University Press, 1983), pp. 179–212.

4 The best analysis of those embroilments is Stephen Nissenbaum, "The Firing of Nathaniel Hawthorne," *Essex Institute Historical Collections* 114 (April 1978): 57–86.

5 Geoffrey H. Hartman, *Criticism in the Wilderness* (New Haven, Conn.: Yale University Press, 1980), pp. 41, 274.

6 "Criticism without Constraint," *Commentary* 73 (January 1982): 65. Further citations follow parenthetically. Students of American literature know Crews as the author of *The Sins of the Fathers* (1966), an important psychoanalytic study of Hawthorne, the principles of which he no longer accepts; but more relevant to his attack on Hartman is Crews's authorship of the composition text, *The Random House Handbook* (New York: Knopf, 1974; 4th ed. 1984), which, according to its publisher, was a "best seller since its

first edition" (*PMLA* 99 [1984]: 1326). More philosophically precise, but without concrete institutional focus, is Charles Altieri, "The Hermeneutics of Literary Indeterminacy: A Dissent from the New Orthodoxy," *New Literary History* 9 (1978): 71–98. See now also Gerald Graff, "The Pseudo-Politics of Interpretation," *Critical Inquiry* 9 (1983): 597–610.

7   First C. P. Snow in the "two cultures" debate and then Zbigniew Brzezin-ski assailing students of the later 1960s for their resistance to the "techne-tronic" age are responsible for popularizing this term from English labor history of the early nineteenth century. Even the new supplement to the *OED* fails to register this metaphoric sense, and those who use it have apparently failed to register the revisionary historiography that has given cogency and dignity to the actual Luddites. See notably E. P. Thompson, *The Making of the English Working Class* (1963).

8   *Nathaniel Hawthorne* (New York: Oxford University Press, 1980), p. v. James R. Mellow, *Nathaniel Hawthorne in His Time* (Boston: Houghton Mifflin, 1980), is more satisfactory on Hawthorne's political relations but has less authoritative standing in the discipline.

9   On the affront Stowe's book offers to our authorized principles of study, see Jane P. Tompkins, "Sentimental Power: *Uncle Tom's Cabin* and the Politics of Literary History," *Glyph,* no. 8 (1981): 79–102. Tompkins and I have reached similar conclusions while both teaching in massive urban, public, commuter universities.

10   I cannot accept the claims of Henry Nash Smith in *Democracy and the Novel* (New York: Oxford University Press, 1978) for the "challenge to all insti-tutions" implicit in Hawthorne's romance (p. 18), any more than I can those of the French *Tel Quel* group for the decisively subversive "textual practice" of contemporary avant-garde works. Those who, like Smith, set their hearts on a "guerrilla campaign" (p. 15) often neglect the endurance and effectivity of institutions, which allow them to thrive on what imag-ines itself hostile to them.

11   On the logic of supplementarity, see Jacques Derrida, *On Grammatology,* trans. Gayatri C. Spivak (Baltimore: Johns Hopkins University Press, 1976).

12   For ease of reference I cite what remains the best single-volume anthology of Hawthorne, the Modern Library Giant edited by Norman Holmes Pear-son (New York: Random House, 1937).

13   See James M. Cox, "*The Scarlet Letter:* Through the Old Manse and the Custom House," *Virginia Quarterly Review* 51 (1975): 431–47.

14   For evidence, however, of sexual irregularity on her part, see Nina Baym, "Hawthorne and His Mother," *American Literature* 54 (1982): esp. 9–10.

15   *Life of Franklin Pierce,* in *Works,* ed. G. P. Lathrop (Boston: Houghton Mifflin, 1883), 12:381. Further references to this text follow parenthetically.

16   Roy Franklin Nichols, *The Democratic Machine: 1850–1854* (New York: Longmans, 1923), p. 225; and *Franklin Pierce* (Philadelphia: University of Pennsylvania Press, 1931), p. 209. On the role of issues in 1848, consider

the observation of Don E. Fehrenbacher: "Each of the two major parties claimed in each section that its own candidate was the more reliably pro-slavery or antislavery, as the case required. Their success in this strategy of dualism was roughly equal" (*Slavery, Law, and Politics* [New York: Oxford Univ. Press, 1981], p. 75). In trying to unite Barnburner Democrats with Conscience Whigs, the Free Soil Party forged the "honestly equivocal" slogan "Van Buren and Free Soil, Adams and Liberty." See Harold M. Hyman and William M. Wiecek, *Equal Justice Under Law* (New York: Harper & Row, 1982), p. 142.

17 Cited in Louis M. Filler, *The Crusade Against Slavery* (New York: Harper & Row, 1969), p. 216.

18 On a similar national rhetoric celebrating the annihilation of Native Americans by "natural causes," see Michael Paul Rogin, *Fathers and Children: Andrew Jackson and the Subjugation of the American Indians* (1975: rpt. New York: Random House, 1976), p. 247.

19 Mellow, *Nathaniel Hawthorne,* p. 567; Turner, *Hawthorne in His Time,* p. 373.

20 My analysis of character versus action largely concurs with that of George B. Forgie, *Patricide in the House Divided* (New York: Norton, 1979), but I stronly differ on its uniquely American status. Even a book so strongly demystificatory as Forgie's can only forge yet another American mythology if it refuses to engage in concrete comparative analysis. Thus, he accepts on authority the claim that Romanticism in America was "thin and marginal" (p. 106) and does not recognize that one of his fundamental topics is precisely part of Romanticism. Even in the America of Forgie's "post-heroic generation," French revolutionary experiences could still be decisive. Chief Justice Roger Taney, the exact contemporary of Henry Clay at the older extreme of Forgie's generational cohort, wrote in fear of racial violence at Lincoln's election, "I am old enough to remember the horrors of St. Domingo." See Fehrenbacher, *Slavery, Law, and Politics,* pp. 284–85.

21 *The Borderers* (1797), lines 1539–44. For more on the Romantic Hamlet and the novel, see my "Romanticism, the Self, and the City," *boundary 2,* 9 (Fall 1980): esp. 86–87.

22 See Nissenbaum ("The Firing of Nathaniel Hawthorne," p. 80), who also analyzes the political function for the Salem Democrats of Hawthorne's name on lists of committee members and convention delegates, even when he did not attend the events.

23 On the complexities of the term "conservative" in this period, see Perry Miller, *The Life of the Mind in America from the Revolution to the Civil War* (New York: Harcourt Brace & World, 1965), pp. 69, 154, 213.

24 David Potter, *The Impending Crisis* (New York: Harper & Row, 1976), pp. 43, 47, 74.

25 Sacvan Bercovitch, *The American Jeremiad* (Madison: University of Wisconsin Press, 1978), pp. 12, 170; and *The Puritan Origins of the American Self*

(New Haven, Conn.: Yale University Press, 1975), p. 143; Arthur M. Schlesinger, Jr., *The Age of Jackson* (Boston: Little, Brown, 1945), p. 421. "Paranosic gain" is standard psychoanalytic discourse for the primary advantage(s) gained from illness. See the case history of "Dora" in the *Standard Edition of the Complete Psychological Works of Sigmund Freud*, trans. and ed. James Strachey (London: Hogarth Press, 1953–1973), 7:43.

26   On nineteenth-century characterizations and judgments of this style, see my "Reading the Letter," *Diacritics* 9 (Summer 1979): 42–52.

27   See Claude Lévi-Strauss, "The Structural Study of Myth," in *Structural Anthropology* (New York: Basic, 1963), and Fredric Jameson, *The Political Unconscious* (Ithaca: Cornell University Press, 1981), pp. 46–49, 165–69, 253–56.

28   On the "shaping of social motion" in this period, see my *Commissioned Spirits* (New Brunswick, N.J.: Rutgers University Press, 1979).

29   To guard against reading this as primitivist approbation, the context offered by Roy Harvey Pearce, *Savagism and Civilization* (Baltimore: Johns Hopkins University Press, 1966), remains fundamental.

30   On the complexity of the term "principle," see Michael Davitt Bell, *Nathaniel Hawthorne and the Historical Romance of New England* (Princeton, N.J.: Princeton University Press, 1971), p. 182; and for a challenging commentary on passion, principle, and purpose, see Bell, *The Development of American Romance* (Chicago: University of Chicago Press, 1980), p. 178. I find, however, that Bell's analysis repeats Hawthorne's impasse.

31   Morton J. Horwitz, *The Transformation of American Law, 1780–1860* (Cambridge, Mass.: Harvard University Press, 1977), p. 256. I thank Brook Thomas for discussing with me his work in progress on American law and literature.

32   On the predominance of legal over theological hermeneutics in the American nineteenth century, see Miller, *Life of the Mind*, p. 24; also p. 217.

33   Fehrenbacher, *Slavery, Law, and Politics*, p. 50.

34   Fehrenbacher, *Slavery, Law, and Politics*, chap. 1, surveys some sixty years of interpretive grappling with this indeterminacy.

35   Miller, *Life of the Mind*, p. 132.

36   Ibid., p. 162.

37   Horwitz, *The Transformation of American Law*, pp. 197–98, 200.

38   Filler, *Crusade Against Slavery*, p. 205.

39   Horwitz, *The Transformation of American Law*, pp. 197–98.

40   Rush Welter (*The Mind of America: 1820–1860* [New York: Columbia University Press, 1975], p. 55), goes so far as to compare this with our attitude toward "spectator sports."

41   Jameson, *The Political Unconscious*, p. 20.

42   I develop this argument more fully in "Nietzsche, Theology, the Political Unconscious," *Union Seminary Quarterly Review* 37 (1983): 273–81.

12

Sentimental Power: *Uncle Tom's Cabin* and the Politics of Literary History

JANE TOMPKINS

Once, during a difficult period of my life, I lived in the basement of a house on Forest Street in Hartford, Connecticut, which had belonged to Isabella Beecher Hooker—Harriet Beecher Stowe's half-sister. This woman at one time in her life had believed that the millennium was at hand and that she was destined to be the leader of a new matriarchy.[1] When I lived in that basement, however, I knew nothing of Stowe, or of the Beechers, or of the utopian visions of nineteen-century American women. I made a reverential visit to the Mark Twain house a few blocks away, took photographs of his study, and completely ignored Stowe's own house—also open to the public—which stood across the lawn. Why should I go? Neither I nor anyone I knew regarded Stowe as a serious writer. At the time, I was giving my first lecture course in the American Renaissance—concentrated exclusively on Hawthorne, Melville, Poe, Emerson, Thoreau, and Whitman—and although *Uncle Tom's Cabin* was written in exactly the same period, and although it is probably the most influential book ever written by an American, I would never have dreamed of including it on my reading list. To begin with, its very popularity would have militated against it; as everybody knew, the classics of American fiction were, with a few exceptions, all *succès d'estime*.

In 1969, when I lived on Forest Street, the women's movement was just under way. It was several years before Chopin's *The Awakening* and Gilman's "The Yellow Wallpaper" would make it onto college reading lists, sandwiched in between Theodore Dreiser and Frank Norris. These women, like some of their male counterparts, had been unpopular in their own time and owed their reputations to the discernment of latter-day critics. Because of their work, it is now respectable to read these writers, who, unlike Nathaniel Hawthorne, had to wait

several generations for their champions to appear in the literary establishment. But despite the influence of the women's movement, and
despite the explosion of work in nineteenth-century American social
history, and despite the new historicism infiltrating literary studies, the
women, like Harriet Beecher Stowe, whose names were household
words in the nineteenth century – women like Susan Warner, Sarah J.
Hale, Augusta Evans, Elizabeth Stuart Phelps, her daughter Mary, who
took the same name, and Frances Hodgson Burnett – these women remain excluded from the literary canon. And while it has recently become fashionable to study their works as examples of cultural deformation, even critics who have invested their professional careers in that
study and who declare themselves feminists still refer to their novels as
trash.[2]

My principal target of concern, however, is not feminists who have
written on popular women novelists of the nineteenth century, but the
male-dominated scholarly tradition that controls both the canon of
American literature (from which these novelists are excluded) and the
critical perspective that interprets the canon for society. For the tradition
of Perry Miller, F. O. Matthiessen, Harry Levin, Richard Chase, R. W. B.
Lewis, and Yvor Winters has prevented even committed feminists from
recognizing and asserting the *value* of a powerful and specifically female
novelist tradition. The very grounds on which sentimental fiction has
been dismissed by its detractors, grounds that have come to seem universal standards of aesthetic judgment, were established in a struggle to
supplant the tradition of evangelical piety and moral commitment these
novelists represent. In reaction against their world view, and perhaps
even more against their success, twentieth-century critics have taught
generations of students to equate popularity with debasement, emotion-
ality with ineffectiveness, religiosity with fakery, domesticity with trivi-
ality, and all of these, implicitly, with womanly inferiority.

In this view, sentimental novels written by women in the nineteenth
century were responsible for a series of cultural evils whose effects still
plague us: the degeneration of American religion from theological rigor
to anti-intellectual consumerism, the rationalization of an unjust economic order, the propagation of the debased images of modern mass
culture, and the encouragement of self-indulgence and narcissism in literature's most avid readers – women.[3] To the extent that they protested
the evils of society, their protest is seen as duplicitous – the product and
expression of the very values they pretended to condemn. Unwittingly
or not, so the story goes, they were apologists for an oppresive social
order. In contrast to male authors like Thoreau, Whitman, and Melville,
who are celebrated as models of intellectual daring and honesty, these

women are generally thought to have traded in false stereotypes, dishing out weak-minded pap to nourish the prejudices of an ill-educated and underemployed female readership. Self-deluded and unable to face the harsh facts of a competitive society, they are portrayed as manipulators of a gullible public who kept their readers imprisoned in a dreamworld of self-justifying clichés. Their fight against the evils of their society was a fixed match from the start.[4]

The thesis I will argue in this chapter is diametrically opposed to these portrayals. It holds that the popular domestic novel of the nineteenth century represents a monumental effort to reorganize culture from the woman's point of view, that this body of work is remarkable for its intellectual complexity, ambition, and resourcefulness, and that, in certain cases, it offers a critique of American society far more devastating than any delivered by better-known critics such as Hawthorne and Melville. Finally, it suggests that the enormous popularity of these novels, which has been cause for suspicion bordering on disgust, is a reason for paying close attention to them. *Uncle Tom's Cabin* was, in almost any terms one can think of, the most important book of the century. It was the first American novel ever to sell over a million copies and its impact is generally thought to have been incalculable. Expressive of and responsible for the values of its time, it also belongs to a genre, the sentimental novel, whose chief characteristic is that it is written by, for, and about women. In this respect, *Uncle Tom's Cabin* is not exceptional but representative. It is the *summa theologica* of nineteenth-century America's religion of domesticity, a brilliant redaction of the culture's favorite story about itself – the story of salvation through motherly love. Out of the ideological materials they had at their disposal, the sentimental novelists elaborated a myth that gave women the central position of power and authority in the culture; and of these efforts *Uncle Tom's Cabin* is the most dazzling exemplar.

I have used words like "monumental" and "dazzling" to describe Stowe's novel and the tradition of which it is a part because they have for too long been the casualties of a set of critical attitudes which equate intellectual merit with a certain kind of argumentative discourse and certain kinds of subject matter. A long tradition of academic parochialism has enforced this sort of discourse through a series of cultural contrasts: light "feminine" novels versus tough-minded intellectual treatises; domestic "chattiness" versus serious thinking; and, summarily, the "damned mco of scribbling women" versus a few giant intellects, unappreciated and misunderstood in their time, struggling manfully against a flood of sentimental rubbish.[5]

The inability of twentieth-century critics either to appreciate the complexity and scope of a novel like Stowe's, or to account for its enormous popular success, stems from their assumptions about the nature and function of literature. In modernist thinking, literature is by definition a form of discourse that has no designs on the world. It does not attempt to change things but merely to represent them, and it does so in a specifically literary language whose claim to value lies in its uniqueness. Consequently, works whose stated purpose is to influence the course of history, and which therefore employ a language that is not only not unique but common and accessible to everyone, do not qualify as works of art. Literary texts, such as the sentimental novel, which make continual and obvious appeals to the reader's emotions and use technical devices that are distinguished by their utter conventionality, epitomize the opposite of everything that good literature is supposed to be. "For the literary critic," writes J. W. Ward, summing up the dilemma posed by *Uncle Tom's Cabin,* "the problem is how a book so seemingly artless, so lacking in apparent literary talent, was not only an immediate success but has endured."[6]

How deep the problem goes it illustrated dramatically by George F. Whicher's discussion of Stowe's novel in *The Literary History of the United States.* Reflecting the consensus view on what good novels are made of, Whicher writes: "Nothing attributable to Mrs. Stowe or her handiwork can account for the novel's enormous vogue; its author's resources as a purveyor of Sunday-school fiction were not remarkable. She had at most a ready command of broadly conceived melodrama, humor, and pathos, and of these popular elements she compounded her book."[7] At a loss to understand how a book so compounded was able to "convulse a mighty nation," Whicher concludes – incredibly – that Stowe's own explanation, that "God wrote it," "solved the paradox." Rather than give up his bias against "melodrama," "pathos," and "Sunday-school fiction," Whicher takes refuge in a solution which, even according to his lights, is patently absurd.[8] And no wonder. The modernist literary aesthetic cannot account for the unprecedented and persistent popularity of a book like *Uncle Tom's Cabin,* for this novel operates according to principles quite other than those which have been responsible for determining the currently sanctified American literary classics.

It is not my purpose, however, to drag Hawthorne and Melville from their pedestals, nor to claim that the novels of Harriet Beecher Stowe, Fanny Fern, and Elizabeth Stuart Phelps are good in the same way that *Moby-Dick* and *The Scarlet Letter* are; rather, I will argue that the work of the sentimental writers is complex and significant in ways *other than* those which characterize the established masterpieces. I will ask the reader to set aside some familiar categories for evaluating fiction – stylistic intricacy, psychological subtlety, epistemological complexity – and to see the sentimental novel not as an artifice of eternity answerable to certain formal criteria and to certain psychological and philosophical concerns, but as a political enterprise, halfway between sermon and social theory, that both codifies and attempts to mold the values of its time.

The power of a sentimental novel to move its audience depends upon the audience's being in possession of the conceptual categories that constitute character and event. The storehouse of assumptions includes attitudes toward the family and toward social institutions, a definition of power and its relation to individual human feeling, notions of political and social equality, and above all, a set of religious beliefs which organize and sustain the rest. Once in possession of the system of beliefs that undergirds the patterns of sentimental fiction, it is possible for modern readers to see how its tearful espisodes and frequent violations of probability were invested with a structure of meanings that fixed these works, for nineteenth-century readers, not in the realm of fairy tale or escapist fantasy, but in the very bedrock of reality. I do not say that we can read sentimental fiction exactly as Stowe's audience did – that would be impossible – but that we can and should set aside the modernist prejudices which consign this fiction to oblivion, in order to see how and why it worked for its readers, in its time, with such unexampled effect.

Let us consider the episode in *Uncle Tom's Cabin* most often cited as the epitome of Victorian sentimentalism – the death of little Eva – because it is the kind of incident most offensive to the sensibilities of twentieth-century academic critics. It is on the belief that this incident is nothing more than a sob story that the whole case against sentimentalism rests. Little Eva's death, so the argument goes, like every other sentimental tale, is awash with emotion but does nothing to remedy the evils it deplores. Essentially, it leaves the slave system and the other characters unchanged. This trivializing view of the episode is grounded in assumptions about power and reality so common that we are not even aware they are in force. Thus, generations of critics have commented with condescending irony on little Eva's death. But in the system of belief which undergirds Stowe's eterprise, dying is the supreme form of heroism. In *Uncle Tom's Cabin,* death is the equivalent not of defeat but of victory; it brings an access of power, not a loss of it; it is not only the crowning achievement of life, it *is* life, and Stowe's entire presentation of little Eva is designed to dramatize this fact.

Stories like the death of little Eva are compelling for the same reason that the story of Christ's death is compelling: They enact a philosophy, as much political as religious, in which the pure and powerless die to save the powerful and corrupt, and thereby show themselves more powerful than those they save. They enact, in short, a *theory* of power in which the ordinary or "commonsense" view of what is efficacious and what is not (a view to which most modern critics are committed) is simply reversed, as the very possibility of social action is made dependent on the action taking place in individual hearts. Little Eva's death enacts the drama of which all the major episodes of the novel are transformations, the idea, central to Christian soteriology, that the highest human calling is to give one's life for another. It presents one version of the ethic of sacrifice on which the entire novel is based and contains in some form all of the motifs that, by their frequent recurrence, constitute the novel's ideological framework.

Little Eva's death, moreover, is also a transformation of a story circulating in the culture at large. It may be found, for example, in a dozen or more versions in the evangelical sermons of the Reverend Dwight Lyman Moody which he preached in Great Britian and Ireland in 1875. In one version it is called "The Child Angel" and it concerns a beautiful golden-haired girl of seven, her father's pride and joy, who dies and, by appearing to him in a dream in which she calls to him from heaven, brings him salvation.[9] The tale shows that by dying even a child can be the instrument of redemption for others, since in death she acquires a spiritual power over those who loved her beyond what she possessed in life.

The power of the dead or the dying to redeem the unregenerate is a major theme of nineteenth-century popular fiction and religious literature. Mothers and children are thought to be uniquely capable of this work. In a sketch entitled "Children" published the year after *Uncle Tom* came out Stowe writes: "Wouldst thou know, o parent, what is that faith which unlocks heaven? Go not to wrangling polemics, or creeds and forms of theology, but draw to thy bosom thy little one, and read in that clear trusting eye the lesson of eternal life."[10] If children because of their purity and innocence can lead adults to God while living, their spirtual power when they are dead is greater still. Death, Stowe argues in a pamphlet, entitled "Ministration of Departed Spirits," enables the Christian to begin his "real work." God takes people from us sometimes so that their "ministry can act upon us more powerfully from the unseen world."[11]

> The mother would fain electrify the heart of her child. She yearns and burns in vain to make her soul effective on its soul, and to inspire it with a spiritual and holy life; but all her own

weaknesses, faults and mortal cares, cramp and confine her till death breaks all fetters; and then, first truly alive, risen, purified, and at rest, she may do calmly, sweetly, and certainly, what, amid the tempest and tossings of her life, she labored for painfully and fitfully.[12]

When the spiritual power of death is combined with the natural sanctity of childhood, the child becomes an angel endowed with salvific force.

Most often, it is the moment of death that saves, when the dying child, glimpsing for a moment the glory of heaven, testifies to the reality of the life to come. Uncle Tom knows that this will happen when little Eva dies, and explains it to Miss Ophelia as follows:

> "You know it says in Scripture, 'At midnight there was a great cry made. Behold the bridgegroom cometh.' That's what I'm spectin' now, every night, Miss Feely, – and I couldn't sleep out o' hearin' no ways."
>
> "Why, Uncle Tom, what makes you think so?"
>
> "Miss Eva, she talks to me. The Lord, he sends his messenger in the soul. I must be thar, Miss Feely; for when that ar blessed child goes into the kingdom, they'll open the door so wide, we'll all get a look in at the glory, Miss Feely."[13]

Little Eva does not disappoint them. She exclaims at the moment when she passes "from death unto life," "O, love! – joy! – peace!" And her exclamation echoes those of scores of children who die in Victorian fiction and sermon literature with heaven in their eyes. Dickens's Paul Dombey, seeing the face of his dead mother, dies with the words, "The light about the head is shining on me as I go!" The fair, blue-eyed young girl in Lydia Sigourney's *Letters to Mothers*, "death's purple tinge upon her brow," when implored by her mother to utter one last word, whispers "Praise!"[14]

Of course, it could be argued by critics of sentimentalism that the prominence of stories about the deaths of children is precisely what is wrong with the literature of the period; rather than being cited as a source of strength, the presence of such stories in *Uncle Tom's Cabin* should be regarded as an unfortunate concession to the age's fondness for lachrymose scenes. But to dismiss such scenes as "all tears and flapdoodle" is to leave unexplained the popularity of the novels and sermons that are filled with them, unless we choose to believe that a generation of readers was unaccountably moved to tears by matters that are intrinsically silly and trivial. That popularity is better explained, I believe, by the relationship of these scenes to a pervasive cultural myth which invests the suffering and death of an innocent victim with just the kind of power that critics deny to Stowe's novel: the power to work in, and change, the world.

This is the kind of action which little Eva's death in fact performs. It proves its efficacy not through the sudden collapse of the slave system but through the conversion of Topsy, a motherless, godless black child who has up until that point successfully resisted all attempts to make her "good." Topsy will not be "good" because, never having had a mother's love, she believes that no one can love her. When Eva suggests that Miss Ophelia would love her if only she were good, Topsy cries out: "No; she can't bar me, 'cause I'm a nigger! – she'd soon have a toad touch her! Ther can't nobody love niggers, and niggers can't do nothin'! *I* don't care."

> "O, Topsy, poor child, *I* love you!" said Eva, with a sudden burst of feeling, and laying her little thin, white hand on Topsy's shoulder; "I love you, because you haven't had any father, or mother, or friends; – because you've been a poor, abused child! I love you, and I want you to be good. I am very unwell, Topsy, and I think I shan't live a great while; and it really grieves me, to have you be so naughty. I wish you would try to be good, for my sake; – it's only a little while I shall be with you."
>
> The round, keen eyes of the black child were overcast with tears; – large, bright drops rolled heavily down one by one, and fell on the little white hand. Yes, in that moment, a ray of real belief, a ray of heavenly love, had penetrated the darkness of her heathen soul! She laid her head down between her knees, and wept and sobbed, – while the beautiful child, bending over her, looked like the picture of some bright angel stooping to reclaim a sinner. (p. 283)

The rhetoric and imagery of this passage – its little white hand, its ray from heaven, bending angel, and plentiful tears – suggest a literary version of the kind of polychrome religious picture that hangs on Sunday-school walls. Words like "kitsch," "camp," and "corny" come to mind. But what is being dramatized here bears no relation to these designations. By giving Topsy her love, Eva initiates a process of redemption whose power, transmitted from heart to heart, can change the entire world. And indeed the process has begun. From that time on Topsy is "different from what she used to be" (eventually she will go to Africa and become a missionary to her entire race), and Miss Ophelia, who overhears the conversation, is different, too. When little Eva is

dead and Topsy cries out "ther an't *nobody* left now," Miss Ophelia
answers her in Eva's place:

> "Topsy, you poor child," she said, as she led her into her
> room, "don't give up! *I* can love you, though I am not like that
> dear little child. I hope I've learnt something of the love of
> Christ from her. I can love you; I do, and I'll try to help you to
> grow up a good Christian girl."
> Miss Ophelia's voice was more than her words, and more
> ‚than that were the honest tears that fell down her face. From
> that hour, she acquired an influence over the mind of the desti-
> tute child that she never lost. (p. 300)

The tears of Topsy and of Miss Ophelia, which we find easy to
ridicule, are the sign of redemption in *Uncle Tom's Cabin;* not words
but the emotions of the heart bespeak a state of grace, and these are
known by the sound of a voice, the touch of a hand, but chiefly, in
moments of greatest importance, by tears. When Tom lies dying on the
plantation on the Red River, the disciples to whom he has preached
testify to their conversion by weeping: "Tears had fallen on that honest,
insensible face, – tears of late repentance in the poor, ignorant heathen,
whom his dying love and patience had awakened to repentance"(p.
420). Even the bitter and unregenerate Cassy, "moved by the sacrifice
that had been made for her," breaks down; "moved by the few last
words which the affectionate soul had yet strength to breath, . . . the
dark, despairing woman had wept and prayed" (p. 420). When George
Shelby, the son of Tom's old master, arrives too late to free him, "tears
which did honor to his manly heart fell from the young man's eyes as
he bent over his poor friend." And when Tom realizes who is there,
"the whole face lighted up, the hard hands clasped, and tears ran down
the cheeks" (p. 420). The vocabulary of clasping hands and falling tears
is one we associate with emotional exhibitionism, with the overacting
that kills true feeling off through exaggeration. But the tears and gestures of Stowe's characters are not in excess of what they feel; if anything, they fall short of expressing the experiences they point to –
salvation, communion, reconciliation.

If the language of tears seems maudlin and little Eva's death ineffec-
tual, it is because both the tears and the redemption they signify belong
to a conception of the world now generally regarded as naïve and
unrealistic. Topsy's salvation and Miss Ophelia's do not alter the anti-
abolitionist majority in the Senate or prevent southern plantation
owners and northern investment bankers from doing business to their
mutual advantage. Because most modern readers regard such political

and economic facts as final, it is difficult for them to take seriously a novel that insists on religious conversion as the necessary precondition for sweeping social change. But in Stowe's understanding of what such change requires, it is the *modern* view that is naïve. The political and economic measures that constitute effective action for us, she regards as superficial, mere extensions of the worldly policies that produced the slave system in the first place. Therefore, when Stowe asks the question that is in every reader's mind at the end of the novel – namely, "What can any individual do?" – she recommends not specific alterations in the current and political and economic arrangements but rather a change of heart.

> There is one thing that every individual can do – they can see to it that *they feel right*. An atmosphere of sympathetic influence encircles every human being; and the man or woman who *feels* strongly, healthily and justly, on the great interests of human-ity, is a constant benefactor to the human race. See, then, to your sympathies in this matter! Are they in harmony with the sympathies of Christ? or are they swayed and perverted by the sophistries of worldly policy? (p. 448).

Stowe is not opposed to concrete measures such as the passage of laws or the formation of political pressure groups; it is just that, by them-selves, such actions would be useless. For if slavery *were* to be abolished by these means, the moral conditions that produced slavery in the first place would continue in force. The choice is not between action and inaction, programs and feelings; the choice is between actions that spring from the "sophistries of worldly policy" and those inspired by the "sympathies of Christ." Reality, in Stowe's view, cannot be changed by manipulating the physical environment; it can only be changed by conversion in the spirit, because it is the spirit alone that is finally real.

The notion that historical change takes place only through religious conversion, which is a theory of power as old as Christianity itself, is dramatized and vindicated in *Uncle Tom's Cabin* by the novel's insis-tence that all human events are organized, clarified, and made meaning-ful by the existence of spiritual realities.[15] The novel is packed with references to the four last things – Heaven, Hell, Death, and Judgment – references which remind the reader constantly that historical events can only be seen for what they are in the light of eternal truths. When St. Clare stands over the grave of little Eva, unable to realize "that it was his Eva that they were hiding from his sight," Stowe interjects, "Nor was it! – not Eva, but only the frail seed of that bright immortal form in with which she shall yet come forth, in the day of the Lord Jesus!" (p. 300). And when Legree expresses satisfaction that Tom is dead, she turns to him and says: "Yes, Legree; but who shall shut up that voice in thy soul? that soul, past repentence, past prayer, past hope, in whom the fire that never shall be quenched is already burning?" (p. 416). These reminders come thick and fast; they are present in Stowe's countless quotations from Scripture – introduced at every possible opportunity, in the narrative, in dialogue, in epigraphs, in quotations from other authors; they are present in the Protestant hymns that thread their way through scene after scene, in asides to the reader, apostrophes to the characters, in quotations from religious poetry, sermons, and prayers, and in long stretches of dialogue and narrative devoted to the discussion of religious matters. Stowe's narrative stipulates a world in which the facts of Christ's death and resurrection and coming day of judgment are never far from our minds because it is only within this frame of reference that she can legitimately have Tom claim, as he dies, "I've got the victory."

The eschatological vision, by putting all individual events in relation to an order that is unchanging, collapses the distinctions among them so that they become interchangeable representations of a single timeless reality. Groups of characters blend into the same character, while the plot abounds in incidents that mirror one another. These are the features not of classical nineteenth-century fiction but of typological narrative. It is this tradition rather than that of the English novel which *Uncle Tom's Cabin* reproduces and extends; for this novel does not simply quote the Bible, it rewrites the Bible as the story of a Negro slave. Formally and philosophically, it stands opposed to works like *Middlemarch* and *The Portrait of a Lady* in which everything depends on human action and decision unfolding in a temporal sequence that withholds revelation until the final moment. The truths that Stowe's narrative conveys can only be reembodied, never discovered, because they are already revealed from the beginning. Therefore, what seem from a modernist point of view to be gross stereotypes in characterization and a needless proliferation of incident are essential properties of a narrative aimed at demonstrating that human history is a continual reenactment of the sacred drama of redemption. It is the novel's reenactment of this drama that made it irresistible in its day.

Uncle Tom's Cabin retells the culture's central religious myth – the story of the crucifixion – in terms of the nation's political conflict – slavery – and of its most cherished social beliefs – the sanctity of motherhood and the family. It is because Stowe is able to combine so many of the culture's central concerns in a narrative that is immediately accessible to the general population that she is able to move so many people so deeply. The novel's typological organization allows her to present political and social situations both as themselves and as transformations of a religious paradigm which interprets them in a way that readers can both understand and respond to emotionally. For the novel functions both as a means of describing the social world and as a means of changing it. It not only offers an interpretive framework for understanding the culture, and, through the reinforcement of a particular code of values, recommends a strategy for dealing with cultural conflict, but it is itself an agent of that strategy, putting into practice the measures it prescribes. As the religious stereotypes of "Sunday-school fiction" define and organize the elements of social and political life, so the "melodrama" and "pathos" associated with the underlying myth of the crucifixion put the reader's heart in the right place with respect to the problems the narrative defines. Hence, rather than making the enduring success of *Uncle Tom's Cabin* inexplicable, these popular elements that puzzled Whicher and have puzzled so many modern scholars – melodrama, pathos, Sunday-school fiction – are the *only* terms in which the book's success can be explained.

The nature of these popular elements also dictates the terms in which any full-scale analysis of *Uncle Tom's Cabin* must be carried out. As I have suggested, its distinguishing features, generically speaking, are those not of the realistic novel but of typological narrative. Its characters, like the figures in an allegory, do not change or develop but reveal themselves in response to the demands of a situation. They are not defined primarily by their mental and emotional characteristics – that is to say, psychologically – but soteriologically, according to whether they are saved or damned. The plot likewise unfolds not according to Aristotelian standards of probability but in keeping with the logic of a preordained design, a design that every incident is intended, in one way or another, to enforce.[16] The setting does not so much describe the features of a particular time and place as point to positions on a spiritual map. In *Uncle Tom's Cabin* the presence of realistic detail tends to obscure its highly programmatic nature and to lull readers into thinking that they are in an everyday world of material cause and effect. But what pass for realistic details – the use of dialect, the minute descriptions of domestic activity – are in fact performing a rhetorical function dictated by the novel's ruling paradigm; once that paradigm is perceived, even the homeliest details show up not as the empirically observed facts of human existence but as the expression of a highly schematic intent.[17]

This schematization has what one might call a totalizing effect on the particulars of the narrative, so that every character in the novel, every scene, and every incident, comes to be apprehended in terms of every *other* character, scene, and incident: All are caught up in a system of endless cross-references in which it is impossible to refer to one without referring to all the rest. To demonstrate what I mean by this kind of narrative organization–a demonstration which will have to stand in lieu of a full-scale reading of the novel–let me show how it works in relation to a single scene. Eva and Tom are seated in the garden of St. Clare's house on the shores of Lake Pontchartrain.

> It was Sunday evening, and Eva's Bible lay open on her knee, she read, – "And I saw a sea of glass, mingled with fire."
> "Tom," said Eva, suddenly stopping, and pointing to the lake, "there 't is."
> "What, Miss Eva?"
> "Don't you see, – there?" said the child, pointing to the glassy water, which, as it rose and fell, reflected the golden glow of the sky. "There's a 'sea of glass, mingled with fire.' "
> "True enough, Miss Eva," said Tom; and Tom sang –
>> "O, had I the wings of the morning,
>> I'd fly away to Canaan's shore;
>> Bright angels should convey me home,
>> To the new Jerusalem."
> "Where do you suppose new Jerusalem is, Uncle Tom?" said Eva.
> "O, up in the clouds, Miss Eva."
> "Then I think I see it," said Eva. "Look in those clouds!– they look like great gates of pearl; and you can see beyond them–far, far off–it's all gold. Tom, sing about 'spirits bright.' "
> Tom sung the words of a well-known Methodist hymn,
>> "I see a band of spirits bright,
>> That taste the glories there;
>> They are all robed in spotless white,
>> And conquering palms they bear."
> "Uncle Tom, I've seen *them*," said Eva. . . .
> "They come to me sometimes in my sleep, those spirits;" and Eva's eyes grew dreamy, and she hummed in a low voice.
>> "They are all robed in spotless white,
>> And conquering palms, they bear."
> "Uncle Tom," said Eva, "I'm going there."
> "Where, Miss Eva?"

The child rose, and pointed her little hand to the sky; the glow of the evening lit her golden hair and flushed cheek with a kind of unearthly radiance, and her eyes were bent earnestly on the skies.

"I'm going *there,*" she said, "to the spirits bright, Tom; *I'm going, before long.*"(pp. 261–62)

The iterative nature of this scene presents in miniature the structure of the whole novel. Eva reads from her Bible about a "sea of glass, mingled with fire," then looks up to find one before her. She reads the words aloud a second time. They remind Tom of a hymn which describes the same vision in a slightly different form (Lake Ponchartrain and the sea of glass become "Canaan's shore" and the "new Jerusalem) and Eva sees what he has sung, this time in the clouds, and offers her own description. Eva asks Tom to sing again and his hymn presents yet another form of the same vision, which Eva again says she has seen: The spirits bright come to her in her sleep. Finally, Eva repeats the last two lines of the hymn and declares that she is going "there" – to the place which has now been referred to a dozen times in this passage. Stowe follows with another description of the golden skies and then with a description of Eva as a spirit bright, and closes the passage with Eva's double reiteration that she is going "there."

The entire scene itself is a re-presentation of others that come before and after. When Eva looks over Lake Pontchartrain, she sees the "Canaan of liberty" which Eliza saw on the other side of the Ohio River, and the "eternal shores" Eliza and George Harris will reach when they cross Lake Erie in the end. Bodies of water mediate between worlds: The Ohio runs between the slave states and the free; Lake Erie divides the United States from Canada, where runaway slaves cannot be returned to their masters; the Atlantic Ocean divides the North American continent from Africa, where Negroes will have a nation of their own; Lake Pontchatrain shows Eva the heavenly home to which she is going soon; the Mississippi River carries slaves from the relative ease of the middle states to the grinding toil of the southern plantations; the Red River carries Tom to the infernal regions ruled over by Simon Legree. The correspondences between the episodes I have mentioned are themselves based on correspondences between earth and heaven (or hell). Ohio, Canada, and Liberia are related to one another by virtue of their relationship to the one "bright Canaan" for which they stand; the Mississippi River and the Ohio are linked by the Jordan. (Ultimately, there are only three places to be in this story: heaven, hell, or Kentucky, which represents the earthly middle ground in Stowe's geography.)

Characters in the novel are linked to each other in exactly the same way that places are – with reference to a third term that is the source of their identity. The figure of Christ is the common term which unites all of the novel's good characters, who are good precisely in proportion as they are imitations of him. Eva and Tom head the list (she reenacts the Last Supper and he the crucifixion), but they are also linked to most of the slaves, women, and children in the novel by characteristics they all share: piety, impressionability, spontaneous affection – and victimization.[18] In this scene, Eva is linked with the "spirits bright" (she later becomes a "bright immortal form") both because she can see them and is soon to join them, and because she, too, always wears white and is elsewhere several times referred to as an "angel." When Eva dies, she will join her father's mother, who was also named Evangeline, and who herself always wore white, and who, like Eva, is said to be " 'the direct embodiment and personification of the New Testament.' " And this identification, in its turn, refers back to Uncle Tom, who is " 'all the moral and Christian virtues bound in black morocco complete.' " The circularity of this train of association is typical of the way the narrative doubles back on itself: Later on, Cassy, impersonating the ghost of Legree's saintly mother, will wrap herself in a white sheet.[19]

The scene I have been describing is a node with a network of allusion in which every character and event in the novel has a place. The narrative's rhetorical strength derives in part from the impression it gives of taking every kind of detail in the world into account, from the preparation of breakfast to the orders of the angels, and investing those details with a purpose and a meaning which are both immediately apprehensible and finally significant. The novel reaches out into the reader's world and colonizes it for its own eschatology: that is, it not only incorporates the homely particulars of "Life among the Lowly" into its universal scheme, but it gives them a power and a centrality in that scheme thereby turning the sociopolitical order upside down. The totalizing effect of the novel's iterative organization and its doctrine of spiritual redemption are inseparably bound to its political purpose – which is to bring in the day when the meek – which is to say, women – will inherit the earth.

The specifically political intent of the novel is apparent in its forms of address. Stowe addresses her readers not simply as individuals but as citizens of the United States: "to you, generous, noble-minded men and women of the South," "farmers of Massachusetts, of New Hampshire, of Vermont," "brave and generous men of New York," "and you, mothers of America." She speaks to her audience directly in the way the Old Testament prophets spoke to Israel, exhorting, praising, blaming, warning of the wrath to come. "This is an age of the world when nations are trembling and convulsed. Almighty influence is abroad, surging and heaving the world, as with an earthquake. And is America safe? . . . O, Church of Christ, read the signs of the times!" (p. 451). Passages like these, descended from the revivalist rhetoric of "Sinners in the Hands of any Angry God," are intended, in the words of a noted scholar, "to direct an imperiled people toward the fulfillment of their destiny, to guide them individually toward salvation, and collectively toward the American city of God."[20]

These sentences are from Sacvan Bercovitch's *The American Jeremiad,* an influential work of modern scholarship which, although it completely ignores Stowe's novel, makes us aware that *Uncle Tom's Cabin* is a jeremiad in the fullest and truest sense. A jeremiad, in Bercovitch's definition, is "a mode of public exhortation . . . designed to join social criticism to spiritual renewal, public to private identity, the shifting 'signs of the times' to certain traditional metaphors, themes, and symbols."[21] Stowe's novel provides the most obvious and compelling instance of the jeremiad since the Great Awakening, and its exclusion from Bercovitch's book is a striking instance of how totally academic criticism has foreclosed on sentimental fiction; for, because *Uncle Tom's Cabin* is absent from the canon, it isn't "there" to be referred to even when it fulfills a man's theory to perfection. Hence its exclusion from critical discourse is perpetuated automatically, and absence begets itself in a self-confirming cycle of neglect. Nonetheless, Bercovitch's characterization of the jeremiad provides an excellent account of how *Uncle Tom's Cabin* actually worked: Among its characters, settings, situations, symbols, and doctrines, the novel establishes a set of correspondences which untie the disparate realms of experience Bercovitch names – social and spiritual, public and private, theological and political – *and,* through the vigor of its representations, attempts to move the nation as a whole toward the vision it proclaims.

The tradition of the jeremiad throws light on *Uncle Tom's Cabin* because Stowe's novel was political in exactly the same way the jeremiad was: Both were forms of discourse in which "theology was wedded to politics and politics to the progress of the kingdom of God."[22] The jeremiad strives to persuade its listeners to a providential view of human history which serves, among other things, to maintain the Puritan theocracy in power. Its fusion of theology and politics is not only doctrinal – in that it ties the salvation of the individual to the community's historical enterprise – it is practical as well, for it reflects the interests of Puritan ministers in their bid to retain spiritual and secular authority. The sentimental novel, too, is an act of persuasion aimed at defining social reality;

the difference is that the jeremiad represents the interests of Puritan ministers, while the sentimental novel represents the interests of middle-class women. But the relationship between rhetoric and history in both cases is the same. In both cases it is not as if rhetoric and history stand opposed, with rhetoric made up of wish-fulfillment and history made up of recalcitrant facts that resist rhetoric's onslaught. Rhetoric *makes* history by shaping reality to the dictates of its political design; it makes history by convincing the people of the world that its description of the world is the true one. The sentimental novelists make their bid for power by positing the kingdom of heaven on earth as a world over which women exercise ultimate control. If history did not take the course these writers recommended, it is not because they were not political, but because they were insufficiently persuasive.

Uncle Tom's Cabin, however, unlike its counterparts in the sentimental tradition, was spectacularly persuasive in conventional political terms: It helped convince a nation to go to war and to free its slaves. But in terms of its own conception of power, a conception it shares with other sentimental fiction, the novel was a political failure. Stowe conceived her book as an instrument for bringing about the day when the world would be ruled not by force but by Christian love. The novel's deepest political aspirations are expressed only secondarily in its devastating attack on the slave system; the true goal of Stowe's rhetorical undertaking is nothing less than the institution of the kingdom of heaven on earth. Embedded in the world of *Uncle Tom's Cabin,* which is the fallen world of slavery, there appears an idyllic picture, both utopian and Arcadian, of the form human life would assume if Stowe's readers were to heed her moral lesson. In this vision, described in the chapter entitled "The Quaker Settlement," Christian love fulfills itself not in war but in daily living, and the principle of sacrifice is revealed not in crucifixion but in motherhood. The form that society takes bears no resemblance to the current social order. Man-made institutions – the church, the courts of law, the legislatures, the economic system – are nowhere in sight. The home is the center of all meaningful activity, women perform the most important tasks, work is carried on in a spirit of mutual cooperation, and the whole is guided by a Christian woman who, through the influence of her "loving words," "gentle moralities," and "motherly loving kindness," rules the world.

Stowe locates her domestic Eden in the center of the American continent – Indiana – and in a rural environment, for not the commercial or industrial but the agricultural mode of life is her economic model. The Quaker community which surrounds and mirrors the home is specifically religious, pacifist, and egalitarian. As the home is the center of the community and the community of the nation, so the kitchen is the center of the home, and at *its* center Stowe locates the symbol of maternal comfort, the rocking chair, throne of the presiding deity. The rocking chair is "motherly and old," its "wide arms breathed hospitable invitation, seconded by the solicitation of its feather cushions, – a real comfortable, persuasive old chair, and worth, in the way of honest, homely enjoyment, a dozen of your plush or brochetelle drawing-room gentry." (p. 185). The image is ideologically charged in a manner typical of Stowe's narrative. Metonymically, the rocking chair stands for the mother and therefore gathers to itself the cluster of associations that the novel has already established around the maternal figure. Ontologically, it represents the "real" thing, as opposed to gaudier versions of itself that, with their plush and brochetelle, exist for appearance's sake. By contrast with the drawing room "gentry," the rocking chair, "old" and "homely," is identified with the lower social orders, but despite this association (though in fact because of it) the rocking chair is morally superior because its wide arms and feather cushions offer comfort and "hospitable invitation." And finally, toward the end of the description, the chair attains the status of a mystical object; its "creechy crawchy" sounds are "music": "For why? for twenty years or more, nothing but loving words, and gentle moralities, and motherly loving kindness, had come from that chair; – head-aches and heart-aches innumerable had been cured there, – difficulties spiritual and temporal solved there, – all by one good, loving woman, God bless her!" (p. 136).

The woman in question *is* God in human form. Seated in her kitchen at the head of her table, passing out coffee and cake for breakfast, Rachel Halliday, the millenarian counterpart of little Eva, enacts the redeemed form of the Last Supper. This is Holy Communion as it will be under the new dispensation: instead of the breaking of bones, the breaking of bread. The preparation of breakfast exemplifies the way people will work in the ideal society; there will be no competition, no exploitation, no commands. Motivated by self-sacrificing love, and joined to one another by its cohesive power, people will perform their duties willingly and with pleasure: Moral suasion will take the place of force. "All moved obediently to Rachel's gentle 'Thee had better,' or more gentle 'Hadn't thee better?' in the work of getting breakfast. . . . Everything went on sociably, so quietly, so harmoniously, in the great kitchen, – it seemed so pleasant to everyone to do just what they were doing, there was an atmosphere of mutual confidence and good fellowship everywhere." (pp. 141–42).

The new matriarchy which Isabella Beecher Hooker had dreamed of leading, pictured here in the Indiana kitchen ("for a breakfast in the luxurious valleys of Indiana is . . . like picking up the rose-leaves and trimming the bushes in Paradise"), constitutes the most politically sub-versive dimension of Stowe's novel, more disruptive and far-reaching in its potential consequences than even the starting of a war or the freeing of slaves. Nor is the ideal of matriarchy simply a daydream; Catherine Beecher, Stowe's elder sister, had offered a ground plan for the realization of such a vision in her *Treatise on Domestic Economy* (1841), which the two sisters republished in an enlarged version entitled *The American Woman's Home* in 1869.[23] Dedicated "To the Women of America, in whose hands rest the real destinies of the republic," this is an instructional book on homemaking in which a wealth of scientific information and practical advice is pointed toward a millenarian goal. Centering on the home, for these women, is not a way of indulging in narcissistic fantasy, as critics have argued, or a turning away from the world into self-absorption and idle reverie, it is the prerequisite of world conquest – defined as the reformation of the human race through the proper care and nuturing of its young. Like *Uncle Tom's Cabin, The American Woman's Home* situates the minutiae of domestic life in relation to their soteriological function: "What, then is the end designed by the family state which Jesus Christ came into this world to secure? It is to provide for the training of our race . . . by means of the self-sacrificing labors of the wise and good . . . with chief reference to a future immor-tal existence."[24] "The family state," the authors announce at the begin-ning, "is the aptest earthly illustration of the heavenly kingdom, and . . . woman is its chief minister."[25] In the body of the text the authors provide women with everything they need to know for the proper establishment and maintenance of home and family, from the construction of furniture ("The [bed] frame is to be fourteen inches [wide], and three inches in thickness. At the head, and at the foot, is to be screwed a notched two-inch board, three inches wide, as in Fig. 8"), to architectural plans, to chapters of instruction on heating, ventilation, lighting, healthful diet, preparation of food, cleanliness, the making and mending of clothes, the care of the sick, the organization of routines, financial managements, psychological health, the care of infants, the managing of young children, home amusement, the care of furniture, planting of gardens, the care of domestic animals, the disposal of waste, the cultivation of fruit, and providing for the "Helpless, the Homeless, and the Vicious." After each of these activities has been treated in detail, they conclude by describing the ultimate aim of the domestic enterprise. The founding of a "truly 'Christian family' " will lead to the gathering of a "Christian neighborhood." This "cheering example," they continue, would soon spread, and ere long colonies from these prosperous and Christian communities would go forth to shine as "lights of the world" in all the now darkened nations. Thus the "Christian family" and "Christian neighborhood" would become the grand ministry, as they were designed to be, in training our whole race for heaven.[26]

The imperialistic drive behind the encyclopedism and determined practicality of this household manual flatly contradicts the traditional derogations of the American cult of domesticity ("mirror-phenomenon," "self-immersed," "self-congratulatory").[27] *The American Woman's Home* is a blueprint for colonizing the world in the name of the "family state" (p. 19) under the leadership of Christian women. What is more, people like Stowe and Catherine Beecher were speaking not simply for a set of moral and religious values. In speaking for the home, they speak for an economy – a household economy – which had supported New England since its inception. The home, rather than representing a retreat or a refuge from a crass industrial–commercial world, offers an economic *alternative* to that world, one which calls into question the whole structure of American society growing up in response to the increase in trade and manufacturing.[28] Stowe's image of a utopian community as presented in Rachel Halliday's kitchen is not simply a Christian dream of communitarian cooperation and harmony; it is a reflection of the real communitarian practices of village life, practices which had depended on cooperation, trust, and a spirit of mutual supportiveness that characterize the Quaker community of Stowe's novel.

One could argue, then, that for all its revolutionary fervor, *Uncle Tom's Cabin* is a conservative book because it advocates a return to an older way of life – household economy – in the name of the nation's most cherished social and religious beliefs. Even the woman's centrality might be seen as harking back to the "age of homespun," when the essential goods were manufactured in the home and their production was carried out and guided by women. But Stowe's very conservatism – her reliance on established patterns of living and traditional beliefs – is precisely what gives her novel its revolutionary potential. By pushing those beliefs to an extreme and by insisting that they be applied universally, not just to one segregated corner of civil life but to the conduct of all human affairs, Stowe means to effect a radical transformation of her society. The brilliance of the strategy is that it puts the central affirmations of a culture into the service of a vision that would destroy the present economic and social institutions; by resting her case, absolutely, on the saving power of Christian love and on the sanctity of motherhood and the family, Stowe relocates the center of power in American life, placing it not in the government, nor in the courts of law, nor in the factories, nor in the marketplace, but in the kitchen. And that means that the new society will be controlled not by men but by women. The image of the home created by Stowe and Catherine Beecher in their treatise on domestic science is in no sense a shelter from the stormy blast of economic and political life, a haven from reality divorced from fact that allows the machinery of industrial capitalism to grind on; it is conceived as a dynamic center of activity, physical and spirtual, economic and moral, whose influence spreads out in ever-widening circles. To this activity – and this is the crucial innovation – men are incidental. Although the Beecher sisters pay lip service on occasion to male supremacy, women's roles occupy virtually the whole of their attention and dominate the scene. Male provender is deemphasized in favor of female processing. Men provide the seed, but women bear and raise the children. Men provide the flour, but women bake the bread and get the breakfast. The removal of the male from the center to the periphery of the human sphere is the most radical component of this millenarian scheme, which is rooted so solidly in the most traditional values – religion, motherhood, home, and family. Exactly what position men will occupy in the millennium is specified by a detail inserted casually into Stowe's description of the Indiana kitchen. While the women and children are busy preparing breakfast, Simeon Halliday, the husband and father, stands "in his shirt-sleeves before a little looking-glass in the corner, engaged in the anti-partriarchal activity of shaving" (pp. 141–42).

With this detail, so innocently placed, Stowe reconceives the role of men in human history: While Negroes, children, mothers, and grand-mothers do the world's primary work, men groom themselves content-edly in a corner. The scene, as critics have noted is often the case in sentimental fiction, is "intimate," the backdrop is "domestic," the tone at times is even "chatty"; but the import, as critics have failed to recognize, is world-shaking. The enterprise of sentimental fiction, as Stowe's novel attests, is anything but domestic, in the sense of being limited to purely personal concerns. Its mission, on the contrary, is global and its interests indentical with the interests of the race. If the fiction written in the nineteenth century by women whose works sold in the hundreds of thousands has seemed narrow and parochial to the critics of the twentieth century, that narrowness and parochialism be-long not to these works nor to the women who wrote them; they are the beholders' share.[29]

Notes

1 Johanna Johnston, *Runaway to Heaven* (New York: Doubleday, 1963).
2 Edward Halsey Foster, for example, prefaces his book-length study of the work of Susan and Anna Warner by saying: "If one searches nineteenth century popular fiction for something that has literary value, one searches, by and large, in vain" (*Susan and Anna Warner* [Boston: Twayne, n.d.], p. 9). At the other end of the spectrum stands a critic like Sally Mitchell, whose excellent studies of Victorian women's fiction contain statements that, intentionally or not, condescend to the subject matter: for example, "Thus, we should see popular novels as emotional analyses, rather than intellectual analyses, of a particular society" ("Sentiment and Suffering: Women's Recreational Reading in the 1860's," *Victorian Studies* 21, no. 1 [Autumn 1977]: 34). The most typical move, however, is to apologize for the poor literary quality of the novels in a concessive clause, and then to assert that these texts are valuable on historical grounds.
3 Ann Douglas is the foremost of the feminist critics who have accepted this characterization of the sentimental writers, and it is to her formulation of the antisentimentalist position that my arguments throughout are principally addressed (*The Feminization of American Culture* [New York: Knopf, 1977]). Although her attitude toward the vast quantity of literature written by women between 1820 and 1870 is the one that the male-dominated tradition has always expressed – contempt – Douglas's book is nevertheless extremely important because of its powerful and sustained consideration of this long-neglected body of work. Because Douglas successfully focused critical attention on the cultural centrality of sentimental fiction, forcing the realization that it can no longer be ignored, it is now possible for other critics to put forward a new characterization of these novels and not be dismissed. For these reasons, it seems to me, her work is invaluable.
4 These attitudes are forcefully articulated by Douglas, *Feminization*, p. 9.
5 The phrase "a damned mob of scribbling women," coined by Hawthorne in a letter he wrote to his publisher in 1855, and clearly the product of Hawthorne's own feelings of frustration and envy, comes embedded in a much quoted passage that has set the tone for criticism of sentimental fiction ever since: "America [he wrote] is now wholly given over to a d****d mob of scribbling women, and I should have no chance of success while the public taste is occupied with their trash – and should be ashamed of myself if I did succeed. What is the mystery of these innumerable editions of *The Lamplighter,* and other books neither better nor worse? Worse they could not be, and better they need not be, when they sell by the hundred thousand." As quoted by Fred Lewis Pattee, *The Feminine Fifties* (New York: Appleton-Century, 1940), p. 110.
6 J. W. Ward, *Red, White, and Blue; Men, Books, and Ideas in American Culture* (New York: Oxford University Press, 1961), p. 75.

7 George F. Whicher, "Literature and Conflict," in *The Literary History of the United States,* ed. Robert E. Spiller et al., 3d ed., rev. (New York: Macmillan, 1963), p. 583.

8 Ibid., p. 586. Edmund Wilson, despite his somewhat sympathetic treatment of Stowe in *Patriotic Gore,* seems to concur in this opinion, reflecting a characteristic tendency of commentators on the most popular works of sentimental fiction to regard the success of these women as some sort of mysterious eruption, inexplicable by natural causes (*Patriotic Gore: Studies in the Literature of the American Civil War* [New York: Oxford University Press, 1966], pp. 5, 32). Henry James gives this attitude its most articulate, though perhaps least defensible, expression in a remarkable passage from *A Small Boy and Others* (New York: Scribners, 1913), pp. 159–60, where he describes Stowe's book as really not a book at all but "a fish, a wonderful, leaping, fish" – the point being to deny Stowe any role in the process that produced such a wonder:

> Appreciation and judgment, the whole impression, were thus an effect for which there had been no process – any process so related having in other cases *had* to be at some point or other critical; nothing in the guise of a written book, therefore, a book printed, published, sold, bought and "noticed," probably ever reached its mark, the mark of exciting interest, without having at least groped for that goal *as a book* or by the exposure of some literary side. Letters, here, languished unconscious, and Uncle Tom, instead of making even one of the cheap short cuts through the medium in which books breathe, even as fishes in water, went gaily roundabout it altogether, as if a fish, a wonderful "leaping" fish, had simply flown in through the air.

9 Reverend Dwight Lyman Moody, *Sermons and Addresses,* in *Narrative of Messrs. Moody and Sankey's Labors in Great Britain and Ireland with Eleven Addresses and Lectures in Full* (New York: Anson D. F. Randolph, 1875).

10 Harriet Beecher Stowe, "Children," in *Uncle Sam's Emancipation; Earthly Care, a Heavenly Discipline; and Other Sketches* (Philadelphia: W. P. Hazard, 1853), p. 83.

11 Harriet Beecher Stowe, *Ministration of Departed Spirits* (Boston: American Tract Society, n.d.), pp. 4, 3.

12 Ibid., p. 3.

13 Harriet Beecher Stowe, *Uncle Tom's Cabin; or, Life Among the Lowly* (New York: Harper & Row, 1965), pp. 295–96. This Harper Classic gives the text of the first edition originally published in 1852 by John P. Jewett and Company of Boston and Cleveland. All references to *Uncle Tom's Cabin* will be to this edition; page numbers are given in parentheses in the text.

14 Charles Dickens, *Dombey and Son* (Boston: Estes & Lauriat, 1882), p. 278; Lydia H. Sigourney, *Letters to Mothers* (Hartford: Hudson & Skinner, 1838).

15 Religious conversion as the basis for a new social order was the mainspring of the Christian evangelical movement of the mid-nineteenth century. The emphasis on "feeling," which seems to modern readers to provide no basis

whatever for the organization of society, was the key factor in the evangelical theory of reform. See Sandra Sizer's discussions of this phenomenon
in *Gospel Hymns and Social Religion* (Philadelphia: Temple University Press,
1979). "It is clear from the available literature that prayer, testimony, and
exhortation were employed to create a *community* of intense *feeling,* in
which individuals underwent similar experiences (centering on conversion)
and would thenceforth unite with others in matters of moral decision and
social behavior" (p. 52). "People in similar states of feeling, in short,
would 'walk together,' would be agreed" (p. 59). "Conversion established
individuals in a particular kind of relationship with God, by virtue of
which they were automatically members of a social company, alike in
interests and feelings" (pp. 70–71). Good order would be preserved by
"relying on the spiritual and moral discipline provided by conversion, and
on the company of fellow Christians, operating without the coercive force
of government" (p. 72).

16   Angus Fletcher's *Allegory, The Theory of a Symbolic Mode* (Ithaca, N.Y.:
Cornell University Press, 1964) discusses the characteristic features of allegory in such a way as to make clear the family resemblance between
sentimental fiction and the allegorical mode. See particularly, his analysis
of character (pp. 35, 60), symbolic action (pp. 150 ff., 178, 180, 182), and
imagery (p. 171).

17   Fletcher's comment in *Allegory* on the presence of naturalistic detail in
allegory is pertinent here:

> The apparent surface realism of an allegorical agent will recede in importance, as
> soon as he is felt to take part in a magical plot, as soon as his causal reltions to others
> in that plot are seen to be magically based. This is an important point because there
> has often been confusion as to the function of the naturalist detail of so much
> allegory. In terms I have been outlining, this detail now appears not to have a
> journalistic function; it is more than mere record of observed facts. It serves instead
> the purposes of magical containment, since the more the allegorist can circumscribe
> the attributes, metonymic and synecdochic, of his personae, the better he can shape
> their fictional destiny. Naturalist detail is "cosmic," universalizing, not accidental as
> it would be in straight journalism. (pp. 189–99)

18   The associations that link slaves, women, and children are ubiquitous and
operate on several levels. Besides being described in the same set of terms,
these characters occupy parallel structural positions in the plot. They function chiefly as mediators between God and the unredeemed, so that, for
example, Mrs. Shelby intercedes for Mr. Shelby, Mrs. Bird for Senator
Bird, Simon Legree's mother (unsuccessfully) for Simon Legree, Little Eva
and St. Clare's mother for St. Clare, Tom Loker's mother for Tom Loker,
Eliza for George Harris (spiritually, she is the agent of his conversion), and
for Harry Harris (physically, she saves him from being sold down the
river), and Tom for all the slaves on the Legree plantation (spiritually, he
converts them) and for all the slaves on the Shelby plantation (physically,
he is the cause of their being set free).

19   For a parallel example, see Alice Crozier's analysis of the way the lock of hair that Little Eva gives Tom becomes transformed into the lock of hair that Simon Legree's mother sent to Simon Legree, in *The Novels of Harriet Beecher Stowe* (New York: Oxford University Press, 1969), pp. 29–31.

20   Sacvan Bercovitch, *The American Jeremiad* (Madison: University of Wisconsin Press, 1978), p. 9.

21   Ibid., p. xi.

22   Ibid., p. xiv.

23   For an excellent discussion of Beecher's *Treatise* and of the entire cult of domesticity as well, see Kathryn Kish Sklar, *Catherine Beecher, A Study in American Domesticity* (New York: Norton, 1976. Copyright 1973 by Yale University). For other helpful discussions of the topic, see Barbara G. Berg, *The Remembered Gate: Origins of American Feminism, The Woman and the City, 1800–1860* (New York: Oxford University Press, 1978); Ronald G. Walters, *The Antislavery Appeal, American Abolitionism After 1830* (Baltimore: Johns Hopkins University Press, 1976); and Barbara Welter, "The Cult of True Womanhood, 1820–1860," *American Quarterly* 18 (1966): 151–74.

24   Catherine Beecher and Harriet Beecher Stowe, *The American Woman's Home: or, Principles of Domestic Science; Being a Guide to the Formation and Maintenance of Economical, Healthful, Beautiful, and Christian Homes* (New York: J. B. Ford, 1869), p. 18.

25   Ibid., p. 19.

26   Ibid., pp. 458–59.

27   These are Douglas's epithets, *Feminization of American Culture*, p. 307.

28   For a detailed discussion of the changes referred to here, see Christopher Clark, "Household Economy, Market Exchange and the Rise of Capitalism in the Connecticut Valley, 1800–1860," *Journal of Social History* 13, no. 2 (Winter 1979): 169–89, and Nancy F. Cott, *The Bonds of Womanhood: "Woman's Sphere" in New England, 1780–1835* (New Haven, Conn.: Yale University Press, 1977).

29   In a recent article, "The Sentimentalists: Promise and Betrayal in the Home" (*Signs* 4, no. 3 [Spring 1979]: pp. 434–46), Mary Kelley characterizes the main positions in the debate over the significance of sentimental fiction as follows: (1) the Cowie-Welter thesis, which holds that women's fiction expresses an "ethics of conformity" and accepts the stereotype of the woman as pious, pure, submissive, and dedicated to the home; and (2) the Papashvily–Garrison thesis, which sees sentimental fiction as profoundly subversive of traditional ideas of male authority and female subservience. Kelley locates herself somewhere in between, holding that sentimental novels convey a "contradictory message": "they tried to project an Edenic image," Kelley writes, but their own tales "subverted their intentions," by showing how often women were frustrated and defeated in the performance of their heroic roles. My own position is that the sentimental novelists are both conformist and subversive, but not, as Kelley believes,

in a self-contradictory way. They used the central myth of their culture – the story of Christ's death for the sins of mankind – as the basis for a new myth that reflected their own interests. They regarded their vision of the Christian home as God's kingdom on earth as the fulfillment of the gospel, "the end . . . which Jesus Christ came into this world to secure," in exactly the same way that the Puritans believed their mission was to found the "American city of God," and that Christians believe the New Testament to be a fulfillment of the Old. Revolutionary ideologies typically announce themselves as the fulfillment of old promises or as a return to a golden age. What I am suggesting here, in short, is that the argument over whether the sentimental novelists were radical or conservative is a false issue. The real problem is how we, in the light of everything that has happened since they wrote, can understand and appreciate their work. See Mary Kelley, "The Sentimentalists"; Alexander Cowie, "The Vogue of the Domestic Novel, 1850–1870," *South Atlantic Quarterly* 41 (October 1942): 420; Barbara Welter, "The Cult of True Womanhood: 1820–1860," *American Quarterly* 18 (Summer 1966): 151–74; Helen Waite Papashvily, *All the Happy Endings: A Study of the Domestic Novel in America, the Women Who Wrote It, the Women Who Read It, in the Nineteenth Century* (New York: Harper Bros., 1956); Dee Garrison, "Immoral Fiction in the Late Victorian Library," *American Quarterly* 28 (Spring 1976): 71–80.

13

Walden and the "Curse of Trade"

MICHAEL T. GILMORE

Among the many paradoxes of *Walden* perhaps none is more ironic than the fact that this modernist text – modernist in its celebration of private consciousness, its aestheticizing of experience, its demands upon the reader – starts out as a denunciation of modernity. It is inspired by the agrarian ideals of the past, yet in making a metaphor of those ideals it fails as a rejoinder to the nineteenth century and creates as many problems as it lays to rest. Personal and historical disappointment determines the shape of Thoreau's masterpiece. In important ways it is a defeated text. Although Thoreau begins with the conviction that literature can change the world, the aesthetic strategies he adopts to accomplish political objectives involve him in a series of withdrawals from history; in each case the ahistorical maneuver disables the political and is compromised by the very historical moment it seeks to repudiate.

This is not to deny *Walden*'s greatness, but is rather to emphasize the cost of Thoreau's achievement and to begin to specify its limits. No reader of the book can fail to notice the exultant tone of the "Conclusion"; the impression it leaves is of an author who has made good on his promise not to write "an ode to dejection" (p. 84).[1] But one might say, in another paradox, that *Walden*'s triumphant success is precisely what constitutes its defeat. For underlying that triumph is a forsaking of civic aspirations for an exclusive concern with "the art of living well" (in Emerson's phrase about his former disciple).[2] And to say this is to suggest that *Walden* is a book at odds with its own beliefs; it is to point out Thoreau's complicity in the ideological universe he abhors.

At the heart of Thoreau's dissent from modernity is a profound hostility to the process of exchange, to what he calls the "curse of trade" (p. 70). He pictures a contemporary Concord where everyone is

293

implicated in the market, and he mounts a critique of that society as antithetical to independence, to identity, and to life itself. His antimarket attitude, although it has similarities to pastoralism,[3] is more properly understood as a nineteenth-century revision of the agrarian or civic humanist tradition. Civic humanists regarded the economic autonomy of the individual as the basis for his membership in the polis. The self-sufficient owner of the soil, in their view, was the ideal citizen because he relied on his own property and exertions for his livelihood and was virtually immune to compromising pressures. Commercial enterprise, in contrast, endangered liberty because it fostered dependence on others and, by legitimating the pursuit of private interest, undermined devotion to the common good. Jeffersonian agrarianism, the American development of this tradition, retained its antimarket bias and its stress on freedom from the wills of others. In Jefferson's own formulation from the *Notes on the State of Virginia,* commerce is productive of subservience, and the independent husbandman uniquely capable of civic virtue.[4]

Thoreau, writing some sixty years after Jefferson, shows a similar antipathy to exchange but entertains no illusions about either the present-day husbandman or the benefits conferred by real property. Several pages into *Walden* appears his well-known indictment of the various forms of ingratiation and venality practiced by his neighbors in order to make money – an indictment that applies to the farmer as much as to the tradesman.

> It is very evident what mean and sneaking lives many of you live . . . always promising to pay, promising to pay, to-morrow, and dying to-day, insolvent; seeking to curry favor, to get custom, by how many modes, only not state-prison offences; lying, flattering, voting [cf. Thoreau's attack on democracy in "Civil Disobedience"], contracting yourselves into a nutshell of civility, or dilating into an atmosphere of thin and vaporous generosity, that you may persuade your neighbor to let you make his shoes, or his hat, or his coat, or import his groceries for him. (pp. 6–7)

Thoreau's position in this passage is directly opposed to the laissez-faire ideology gaining in popularity among his contemporaries. He sees the marketplace not as a discipline in self-reliance, an arena where the man of enterprise can prove his worth, but rather as a site of humiliation where the seller has to court and · conciliate potential buyers to gain their custom. The interactions of exchange, in his view, breed not independence but servility. Nor, insists Thoreau, does nineteenth-century agriculture offer an exemption from the abasements and dependencies of the exchange process. The land has become an investment like any other and the farmer a willing participant in the marketplace. The husbandmen of Concord, immortalized by Emerson for their stand "by the rude bridge that arched the flood," are now "serfs of the soil" who spend their lives "buying and selling" and have forgotten the meaning of self-reliance (pp. 5, 208). Thoreau envisions them, in a celebrated image, "creeping down the road of life," each pushing before him "a barn seventy-five feet by forty . . . and one hundred acres of land, tillage, mowing, pasture, and wood-lot!" (p. 5).

For Thoreau, commercial agriculture has an impact on the physical world that is just as devastating as its effect on the farmer. In the chapter "The Ponds" he describes an agricultural entrepreneur named Flint, for whom nature exists solely as commodity. Indeed, on Flint's farm the use value of natural objects has been consumed by their exchange value; their abstract character as potential money has completely obliterated their "sensuous" reality (to use a favorite adjective of Marx's in this connection) as fruits and vegetables. The result is an impoverishment of the thing, an alteration of its very nature. "I respect not his labors," Thoreau writes of Flint,

> his farm where every thing has its price; who would carry the landscape, who would carry his God, to market, if he could get any thing for him; . . . on whose farm nothing grows free, whose fields bear no crops, whose meadows no flowers, whose trees no fruits, but dollars; who loves not the beauty of his fruits, whose fruits are not ripe for him till they are turned to dollars. (p. 196)

A companion chapter, "The Pond in Winter," shows this destruction of nature actually coming to pass through the speculations of "a gentleman farmer" who carries the landscape off to market. Wanting "to cover each one of his dollars with another," the farmer has hired a crew of laborers to strip Walden of its ice. Thoreau treats the entire operation as though the ice-cutters were "busy husbandmen" engaged in skimming the land: "They went to work at once, ploughing, harrowing, rolling, furrowing [and] suddenly began to hook up the virgin mould itself, with a peculiar jerk, clear down to the sand, or rather the water, . . . all the *terra firma* there was, and haul it away on sleds" (pp. 294–95).

As Thoreau's denunciation of Flint makes clear, his quarrel with the marketplace is in large measure ontological. He sees the exchange process as emptying the world of its concrete reality and not only converting objects into dollars but causing their "it-ness" or being to disappear. A particularly powerful statement of this idea occurs at the beginning of "The Ponds," where Thoreau condemns the marketing of huckleberries. He argues that nature's fruits "do not yield their true flavor" either to the man who raises them commercially or to their urban purchasers. Depleted of their essence en route to the customer, they cannot be tasted or even said to exist outside their native habitat: "A huckleberry never reaches Boston; they have not been known there since they grew on her three hills. The ambrosial and essential part of the fruit is lost with the bloom which is rubbed off in the market cart, and they become mere provender. As long as eternal Justice reigns, not one innocent huckleberry can be transported thither from the country's hills" (p. 173).

Thoreau believes that along with the degradation of the physical object in exchange there occurs a shriveling of the individual. Men in the marketplace, according to *Walden,* relate not as persons but as something less than human; they commit violence against their own natures in their incessant anxiety to induce others to buy their products or their labor. "The finest qualities of our nature," Thoreau says in a passage paralleling his discussion of the huckleberry, "like the bloom of fruits, can be preserved only by the most delicate handling. Yet we do not treat ourselves or one another thus tenderly" (p. 6). The laborer's self, his authentic being, has as little chance to survive the exchange process as a genuine huckleberry. To satisfy his employer, he has to suppress his individuality and become a mechanical thing: "Actually, the laboring man has not leisure for a true integrity day by day; he cannot afford to sustain the manliest relations to men; his labor would be depreciated in the market. He has no time to be anything but a machine" (p. 6). The final disappearance of the person, the most extreme form of absence, would be death, and Thoreau does in fact equate exchange with the deprivation of life. "The cost of a thing," he writes, "is the amount of what I will call life which is required to be exchanged for it, immediately or in the long run" (p. 31). Exchange brings about the ultimate alienation of man from himself; to engage in buying and selling is not merely to debase the self but to extinguish it, to hurry into death.

Thoreau's analysis of commodification has certain affinities with the Marxist critique of capitalism. His comments on the erosion of human presence in exchange evoke the notion of reification, a concept developed in the twentieth century by the Marxist philosopher Georg Lukács. Reification refers to the phenomenon whereby a social relation between men assumes the character of a relation between things. Because they interact through the commodities they exchange, including the commodity of labor, individuals in the capitalist market confront each other not as human beings but as objectified, nonhuman entities. They lose sight altogether of the subjective element in their activity. An important corollary to this loss of the person is a confusion of history with nature. By mystifying or obscuring man's involvement in the production of his social reality, reification leads him to apprehend that reality as a "second nature." He perceives the social realm as an immutable and universal order over which he exerts no control. The result is greatly to diminish the possibility of human freedom.[5]

Thoreau reaches a similar conclusion about the decline of liberty under capitalism: He portrays his townsmen as the slave drivers of themselves. The weakness of his position, a weakness to which we shall return, is that he launches his attack against history rather than in its name, with the result that he mystifies the temporality of his own experience, presenting it as natural or removed from social time. He is outspoken in debunking such "naturalization" when it functions as a way of legitimating social codes. In his disquisition on clothing, for example, he points out how the fetishism of fashion invests the merely whimsical with the prestige of inevitability. "When I ask for a garment of a particular form," he explains, "my tailoress tells me gravely, 'They do not make them so now,' not emphasizing the 'They' at all, as if she quoted an authority as impersonal as the Fates. . . . We worship not the Graces, nor the Parcae, but Fashion" (p. 25).

Thoreau constantly challenges the false identification of what "They" say or do with the course of nature. He maintains that social reality, to which men submit as though to "a seeming fate" (p. 5), is in fact made by men and subject to their revision. His neighbors, whose resignation only masks their desperation, do not adopt the customary modes of living out of preference but "honestly think there is no choice left" (p. 8). Although they deny the possibility of change and say, "This is the only way," Thoreau insists that they are mistaken, that "there are as many ways" to live as "can be drawn radii from one centre" (p. 11). His lack of deference toward his elders stems from the same impatience with a reified social reality. Old people, he finds, regard their own experience as exemplary and refuse even to contemplate alternatives to the existing order of things. But "what old people say you cannot do you try and find that you can" (p. 8). What they fail to realize, what Thoreau feels all neighbors are unable to see, is that "their daily life of routine and habit . . . is built on purely illusory foundations." They "think that *is* which *appears* to be" (p. 96).

To negate the "curse of trade" during his stay in the woods, Thoreau supports himself by farming. This is the occupation followed by the majority of his neighbors, but his own experiment in husbandry differs significantly from the commercial agriculture prevalent in Concord. By building his own house and growing his own food, by concentrating on the necessaries of life and renouncing luxuries, he minimizes his dependency on others and removes himself as far as possible from the market economy. In keeping with his precept "Enjoy the land, but own it not" (p. 207), he squats on soil belonging to someone else (Emerson, as it happens) and endeavors to "avoid all trade and barter" (p. 64). "More independent than any farmer in Concord," he claims to have learned from his experience that something approaching self-sufficiency is still practicable in mid-nineteenth-century America, if only "one would live simply and eat only the crop which he raised, and raise no more than he ate, and not exchange it for an insufficient quantity of more luxurious and expensive things" (pp. 55–56).

Something *approaching* self-sufficiency: Thoreau makes no attempt to disguise the fact that he is unable to emancipate himself completely from exchange relations. He freely "publishes his guilt," as he puts it (p. 59), that his venture at subsistence farming is not, strictly speaking, an economic success. He raises a cash crop of beans and uses the proceeds to give variety to his diet, and he is forced to supplement his income from farming by hiring himself out as a day laborer, the employment he finds "the most independent of any, especially as it required only thirty to forty days in a year to support one" (p. 70). He recognizes, in other words, the obsolescence of his program as a *literal* antidote to the ills of market civilization.

What Thoreau does affirm, and affirm consistently, is the possibility even in the nineteenth century of a way of life characterized by self-reliance and minimal involvement in exchange. Following the civic humanist tradition, he identifies this ideal with husbandry, and husbandry in turn supplies him with a metaphoric solution to the problems of the marketplace. Agriculture, he states, "was once a sacred art; but it is pursued with irreverent haste and heedlessness by us, our object being to have large farms and large crops merely" (p. 165). Thoreau makes a point of actually farming in the traditional way,[6] going down to the woods and living by himself, because he refuses to sacrifice the use value of husbandry to its symbolic value in the manner of Flint. He wants to earn his metaphor by dwelling "near enough to Nature and Truth to borrow a trope from them" (p. 245).

Thoreau has an acute sense of the relationship between commodity and symbolism – or rather of the commodified thinking concealed in symbolization. The commodity, like the symbol, is both what it is and the token of something else (i.e., money); on Flint's farm, the something else has totally displaced the concrete reality. To use farming as a trope for self-sufficiency without literally farming would be to perform in thought the same violation Flint commits on his land. Thoreau finds this commodified habit of mind to be the common practice of his contemporaries. "Our lives," he complains, "pass at such remoteness from its symbols, and its metaphors and tropes are so far fetched" (pp. 244–45). At Walden he redeems his own life from such distancing and loss of the real; he farms the land, as he says in "The Bean-Field," "for the sake of tropes and expression, to serve a parable-maker one day" (p. 162).[7]

Thoreau suggests that the values formerly associated with farming are available to all men, in all pursuits. "Labor of the hands," as he describes his hoeing, "has a constant and imperishable moral, and to the scholar it yields a classic result" (p. 157). The moral yielded by *Walden* is that virtually any kind of workman can be a figurative farmer and any kind of work independent "labor of the hands." The centrality of this phrase to Thoreau's undertaking is suggested by its position at the very outset of the book; it appears in the opening sentence: "When I wrote the following pages, or rather the bulk of them, I lived alone, in the woods, a mile from any neighbor, in a house which I had built myself, on the shore of Walden Pond, in Concord, Massachusetts, and earned my living by the labor of my hands only" (p. 3). Labor of the hands is clearly meant to encompass intellectual as well as manual work. As Thoreau says in explaining what he lived for, "My head is hands and feet. I feel all my best faculties concentrated in it" (p. 98).

A difficulty that arises immediately with Thoreau's metaphoric solution to exchange is that it has the effect of privatizing a civic virtue. Farming as a way of life enjoyed the high standing it did in civic humanist thought because it was a training for participation in the public or political sphere. In *Walden,* as a figure for self-reliant labor, it has become a private virtue – a virtue without civic consequences. And there is no doubt that Thoreau hoped his text would result in some form of political awakening. Indeed, one of his principal objectives in writing *Walden* is to restore his countrymen to the freedom they have lost under the market system. He moves to the woods on "Independence Day, or the fourth of July, 1845," because he considers this a civic enterprise, requiring a reformation or new foundation of American liberty (p. 84). A close connection can be seen here between the project of *Walden* and Thoreau's appeal at the end of "Civil Disobedience" for a founder or reformer whose eloquence will revive the polity.

In the essay, which he wrote while working on the early drafts of the book, he criticizes the country's lawmakers for their failure to "speak with authority" about the government. Implicitly he projects a role for himself as a model legislator, one whose effectiveness will lie in his ability to inspire others through his words:

> No man with a genius for legislation has appeared in America. They are rare in the history of the world. There are orators, politicians, and eloquent men, by the thousand; but the speaker has not yet opened his mouth to speak, who is capable of settling the much-vexed questions of the day. We love elo-quence for its own sake, and not for any truth which it may utter, or any heroism it may inspire.[8]

In *Walden* Thoreau assumes the duties of this reformer–legislator as a writer rather than a speaker because of the greater range and authority of literature. The orator, he says in the chapter "Reading," addresses the mob on the transitory issues of the moment, but the author "speaks to the heart and intellect of mankind, to all in any age who can *under-stand* him" (p. 102). Great writers, he adds, "are a natural and irresist-ible aristocracy in every society, and, more than kings or emperors, exert an influence on mankind" (p. 103). Twentieth-century readers, with their very different ideas about the functions of texts and the role of the writer, may find it difficult to take these statements seriously. But it is a mistake to treat *Walden* as though it were imbued with the modernist sentiment (to paraphrase W. H. Auden) that literature makes nothing happen. This kind of accommodation with "reality" – of reified consciousness – is precisely what Thoreau is arguing against in the book. Nor for the time and place is there anything especially unusual about his civic ambitions; on the contrary, they are perfectly consistent with the New England ideal of the literary vocation.

Lewis P. Simpson has shown that a conception of the writer as a spiritual and intellectual authority was particularly strong around Bos-ton and Concord during the early decades of the nineteenth century. Simpson uses the term "clerisy," a borrowing from Coleridge, to des-ignate the literary community that emerged at this time and sought to claim for men of letters the influence formerly exercised by the minis-try. The wise and learned, it was felt, had a special obligation to edu-cate the nation; through the practice of literature, they were to provide moral guidance and enlightenment.[9] Although Thoreau was hardly a conventional member of the New England elite, he shared his culture's emphasis on the usefulness of the literary calling. He conceives *Walden* as a reforming text meant to produce results in the world, and hopes to be remembered, like the heroic writers whom he so admires, as a "messenger from heaven, [a] bearer of divine gifts to man" (p. 36). But in this respect *Walden* is a notably different text from "Civil Disobedience": Although both works begin, as it were, in the social world, *Walden* retreats into the self whereas "Civil Disobedience" calls for resistance to the government. This change can be seen in *Walden*'s very structure, its transition from "Economy" to "Conclusion," from Concord and Thoreau's neighbors to the inwardness of self-discovery. A mood of withdrawal totally dominates the final pages, as Thoreau urges his readers to turn their backs on society and look inside themselves. "Be a Columbus to whole new continents and worlds within you," he exhorts, "opening new channels, not of trade, but of thought. . . . [E]xplore the private sea, the Atlantic and Pacific Ocean of [your] being alone" (p. 321). The ending contains some of the book's best-known aphorisms, most of which revolve around the sentiment that "every one [should] mind his own business, and endeavor to be what he was made" (p. 326). The image left is of a solitary individual pursuing his own development, cultivating his own consciousness, in utter indifference to the common good. Such an image is not only radically at odds with the tone of *Walden*'s beginning; it also amounts to a distorted – and reified – reflection of the laissez-faire individualist pursuing his private economic interest at the expense of the public welfare.

Thoreau's unwitting kinship with social behavior he deplores can also be seen in his effort to create a myth of his experience. As the narrative progresses, he seems to grow intent on suppressing all traces of autobiography and treating his two years at the pond as a timeless and universal experience. The patterning of the book after the cycle of the seasons contributes to this sense of the mythological, as does perhaps even more strongly the almost purely metaphorical character of the "Conclusion." In contrast to the specificity of the opening chapter, which takes place in Concord, Massachusetts, in the year 1845, the ending is situated in no time and no physical location. Thoreau declares open war on history: After ridiculing the "transient and fleeting" doings of his contemporaries, he vows "not to live in this restless, nervous, bustling, trivial Nineteenth Century, but stand or sit thoughtfully while it goes by" (pp. 329–30). The text's denial of history, its flight from Jacksonian America, paradoxically resembles the commodified mode of thought that Thoreau charges against his countrymen and that permits a Flint to perceive his fruits and vegetables as dollars. In an analogous way, Thoreau allows the symbolic value of his Walden experiment as myth to all but wipe out the actual circumstances of its occurrence. Moreover, his determination to empty his adventure of historical content replicates a basic feature of reified consciousness. As he himself has pointed out repeatedly, market society engenders a conflation of history with nature. By presenting its limited, time-bound conventions as eternal, the existing order in effect places itself outside time and beyond the possibility of change. Although Thoreau rigorously condemns his society's "naturalizing" of itself in this fashion, he can be charged with performing a version of the same process on his own life by erasing history from *Walden* and mythologizing his experiment at the pond.[10]

The privatizing and antihistorical tendencies that blunt *Walden*'s critical edge reappear in Thoreau's attempt to devise a conception of reading and writing as unalienated labor. He is obliged to seek such a formulation because as a maker of texts, a would-be reformer in literature, he encounters the same problem his neighbors experience in their daily transactions as farmers, merchants, and workmen: He has to confront the specter of the marketplace. In this area, too, Thoreau's rebuttal to exchange embroils him in difficulties he is unable to overcome. Indeed, the two goals he sets himself as an author, to initiate civic reformation while resisting the exchange process, turn out to be so incompatible by the mid-nineteenth century as to render their attainment mutually exclusive.

Trade, Thoreau keeps insisting, "curses every thing it handles; and though you trade in messages from heaven, the whole curse of trade attaches to the business" (p. 70). Anything that is done for money, including the effort to instruct mankind, to be a "messenger from heaven" as Thoreau desires, is compromised by that very fact. Of his brief experience as a schoolteacher, he observes: "As I did not teach for the good of my fellow-men, but simply for a livelihood, this was a failure" (p. 69). In *Walden* he regularly refers to his readers as students – "Perhaps these pages are more particularly addressed to poor students," he says as early as the second paragraph (p. 4) – and he clearly sees the threat of failure hanging over his writing unless he can circumvent exchange in his dealings with his audience.

Thoreau regards life and presence, two qualities nullified by the capitalist market, as fundamental to his efficacy as an author–legislator. In censuring philanthropists, he says that their error is distributing money rather than spending themselves. "Be sure to give the poor [i.e., poor students] the aid they most need, though it be your example which leaves them far behind" (p. 75). When he introduces himself on the first page as *Walden*'s narrator, he emphasizes his own determination to retain the "I" or the self in his writing, to speak in the first person, and he adds that he requires of every writer "a simple and sincere amount of his own life, and not merely what he has heard of other men's lives" (p. 3). This conception of literature as synonymous with life and the person recurs throughout the book, for example, when Thoreau states of the written word that it "is the work of art nearest to life itself. It may be translated into every language, and not only be read but actually breathed from all human lips" (p. 102). But if words have to be alive to "inspire" the reader, there are two senses in which exchange turns them into dead letters and kills the text. Because the cost of a thing is the amount of life expended for it, the book as commodity becomes an instrument of death, as does any item sold on the market. It also suffers an internal demise, commodification destroying literature's "bloom" just as surely as it blights the fruits and flowers on Flint's farm.

The literary work as article of exchange and the author as tradesman was the accepted state of affairs when Thoreau wrote *Walden*. As Tocqueville noted after his visit to America, the aristocratic domain of letters had become in democratic-capitalist society "the trade of litera- ture."[11] Thoreau, who claims to want "the flower and fruit of a man, that some fragrance be wafted from him to me, and some ripeness flavor our intercourse" (p. 77), views the situation of literary culture with dismay. The books read and written by his countrymen, he feels, are not literature at all but commodities with the impoverished nature of commodities. Singularly lacking in either fragrance or flavor, they are fit only to be consumed by "those who, like cormorants and ostriches, can digest" any sort of foodstuff (p. 104). To Thoreau, they are simply one more piece of merchandise in the unending stream of commerce that connects "the desperate city" to "the desperate coun- try" (p. 8); and as do the huckleberries transported to the Boston market from the country's hills, they lose their most essential qualities in transit. "Up comes the cotton, down does the woven cloth; up comes the silk, down goes the woolen; up comes the books, but down goes the wit that writes them" (p. 116). Popular writers are "the machines to provide this provender," Thoreau contends, evoking his characterizations of both the huckleberry and the laboring man, and his neighbors are "the machines to read it" (pp. 104–5). He pro- ceeds to deliver a lengthy diatribe against fashionable literature and the public that devours it "with unwearied gizzard," concluding with the statement that "this sort of gingerbread is baked daily and more sedu- lously than pure wheat or rye-and-Indian in almost every oven, and finds a surer market" (p. 105).[12]

In addition to changing the text into a commodity, and taking away its life and essence, the marketplace endangers Thoreau's literary-civic en- terprise because it encourages the reader in his addiction to mediation.

Mediation, the substitution or replacement of one thing or person by another, is the heart and soul of the exchange process. In "Civil Disobedience," Thoreau disapproves of money, the medium of exchange, on precisely the grounds that it "comes between a man and his objects, and obtains them for him," thereby reducing his capacity for self-reliance.[13] In *Walden* he states repeatedly that he wants the reader to obtain his objects by his own exertions (see his definition of a "*necessary of life*," p. 12). To allow the reader to accept Thoreau's experience as a substitute for his own would be the literary equivalent of the use of money. "I would not have any one adopt *my* mode of living on any account," he declares; rather, "I would have each one be very careful to find out and pursue *his own* way" (p. 71). Reading or studying something should never become a substitute for doing it, according to Thoreau, who expresses disdain for the "common course" of instruction whereby the student (or reader) is required "to study chemistry, and not learn how his bread is made, or mechanics, and not learn how it is earned." " 'But,' " he continues, anticipating a probable critic,

> "you do not mean that the students should go to work with their hands instead of their heads?" I do not mean that exactly, but I mean something which he might think a good deal like that; I mean that they should not *play* life, or *study* it merely, while the community supports them at this expensive game, but earnestly *live* it from beginning to end. How could youths better learn to live than by at once trying the experiment of living? (p. 51)

As Thoreau also points out, those who make a habit of depending on others through exchange and the division of labor court the risk of not being able to use their heads at all. "No doubt another *may* also think for me; but it is not therefore desirable that he should do so to the exclusion of my thinking for myself" (p. 46).

The reader who lets another do his thinking or his acting for him is a reader whose consciousness has been reified. He reacts to the words on the printed page with the same passivity and sense of noninvolvement as he feels in bowing to social reality. Most readers, in Thoreau's view, are in exactly this position; they limit themselves to books meant for deficient intellects and children and so "dissipate their faculties in what is called easy reading" (p. 104). To read in this feeble way, without exerting one's mind or relying on oneself, is merely to be confirmed in one's present condition. "Easy reading," like the writing that elicits it, obviously cannot promote the spirit of independence Thoreau seeks to nurture as the author of *Walden*.

Thoreau's task as a writer–reformer accordingly requires him to make a book that is not a commodity. To spare *Walden* the fate of the huckleberry, he has to ensure that, like the pond, it contains "no muck" and is "too pure to have a market value" (p. 199). He also has to find a way for the reader to eliminate mediation and achieve independence in his own right. And here again he has recourse to the civic humanist ideal of husbandry for his solution. He links authorship and agriculture and portrays both artist and audience as figurative husbandmen, extricating *Walden* from the marketplace by means of a metaphor.

In "The Bean-Field," Thoreau draws a sustained comparison between composing a text and planting a crop. He likens himself at his hoe to "a plastic artist in the dewy and crumbling sand," and he speaks of "making the yellow soil express its summer thought in bean leaves and blossoms rather than in wormwood and piper and millet grass, making the earth say beans instead of grass" (pp. 156–57). The writer as metaphorical farmer remains outside the exchange process and never deals in commodities because he never sells his crop for money. His text, which never reaches the Boston market, preserves its effectiveness as a living expression of his individuality.

Thoreau also depicts the reader as a laborer "of the hands" and contrasts the toil of reading *Walden* with the "easy reading" suitable to popular literature. He claims that the diligent student who sits alone with his books throughout the day and late into the night is "at work in *his* field, and chopping in *his* woods, as the farmer is in his" (p. 136). Such strenuous intellectual exertion is the price of comprehending *Walden,* which requires a "heroic reader" to emulate its heroic author (p. 106). "The heroic books, even if printed in the character of our mother tongue, will always be in a language dead to degenerate times; and we must *laboriously* seek the meaning of each word and line, conjecturing a larger sense than common use permits out of what wisdom and valor and generosity we have" (p. 100, italics addded). The reader as symbolic farmer, tasked more by *Walden*'s intricacies than by "any exercise which the customs of the day esteem" (p. 101), triumphs over mediation by having the same "laborious" experience at his desk that Thoreau has at the pond. Reading *Walden* becomes figuratively identical with being at Walden, a discipline in the mental self-reliance that enables one, or so Thoreau believes, to penetrate the "veil of reification."[14]

The qualification is in order because in metaphorizing reading and writing as activities outside history and the marketplace, Thoreau disregards the realities of the text's evolution and his relation to the public. History forcibly enters *Walden* in the changes and additions made between the first draft and the published version, changes stretching over a period of nearly ten years. J. Lyndon Shanley, who has done the most thorough study of the original draft, finds that Thoreau enlarged the second half of the manuscript far more than the first, adding "more to the account of his life in the woods than to his criticism of contemporary ways," and that his major revisions were intended to emphasize the cycle of the seasons.[15] The development *within* the text, in other words, corresponds to a development *outside* the text, a shift in attitude suggesting a deepening estrangement from the social realm. Thoreau seems to have suffered a crisis of confidence in the likelihood of civic reform and the idea of his writing as a means of instigating it. Besides the addition of the "Conclusion," none of which appeared in the first draft, one change in particular is unequivocal in suggesting his disenchantment with the role of educator–legislator. In both versions he speaks of planting in his readers the seeds of sincerity, truth, and simplicity, to "see if they will not grow in this soil." But missing from the original manuscript is the sentence that comes next in the book: "Alas! I said this to myself; but now another summer is gone, and another, and another, and I am obliged to say to you, Reader, that the seeds which I planted, if indeed they *were* the seeds of those virtues, were wormeaten or had lost their vitality, and so did not come up" (p. 164).[16]

Between 1846, when he began *Walden,* and 1854, when he completed it, Thoreau had good reason to lose confidence in the viability of his civic aspirations. "Civil Disobedience" (1849) and *A Week on the Concord and Merrimack Rivers* (1849) had been published in that time; the first elicited no reaction whatsoever from the public, and the second has been described as "one of the most complete failures in literary history."[17] In the final version of *Walden,* Thoreau himself alludes to the discouraging reception of his earlier work. He tells the story of an Indian who came to Concord to sell baskets but learned to his chagrin that the inhabitants did not want to buy any. The Indian wrongly supposed that he had done his part by making the baskets, "and then it would be the white man's to buy them. He had not discovered," comments Thoreau,

> that it was necessary for him to make it worth the other's while to buy them, or at least to make him think that it was so, or to make something else which it would be worth his while to buy. I too had woven a kind of basket of delicate texture, but I had not made it worth any one's while to buy them. Yet not the less, in my case, did I think it worth my while to weave them, and instead of studying how to make it worth men's

while to buy my baskets, I studied rather how to avoid the necessity of selling them. (p. 19)

The "kind of basket" woven by Thoreau before *Walden* was, of course, *A Week,* a book that sold so poorly, as he reveals in a journal entry for 1853, that he was obligated to take possession of "706 copies out of an edition of 1000." He confides to the journal (and the bravado does not hide his feelings of hurt and vexation), "I believe that this result is more inspiring and better for me than if a thousand had bought my wares. It affects my privacy less and leaves me freer."[18]

Under the market system, there is no way for an author to exert influence to a significant degree without attracting a popular audience. If a book never reaches Boston, it is not likely to have much impact there. The influential writers praised by Thoreau enjoyed an "advantage" that was unavailable to him in the United States in the middle of the nineteenth century: the advantage of patronage by kings, noblemen, and warriors. Thoreau is caught in a contradiction of his own and history's devising: Although he craves the authority of a founder, he refuses to view his text as a commodity and to accept "the necessity of selling" it. The failures of "Civil Disobedience" and *A Week* strengthen his antimarket resolution, but at the same time they force him to retreat from his ambition to reform the polity. Since he cannot shape popular opinion without large sales, he effectively abandons his civic project by striving to make *Walden* a difficult text at which the reader has to labor – hence a text that is inaccessible to the great majority of the public. "It is a ridiculous demand which England and America make," he writes in the "Conclusion," "that you shall speak so that they can understand you." And he goes on to voice defiant satisfaction that his own pages "admit of more than one interpretation," approximating the obscurity of the Walden ice (pp. 324–25). At this point Thoreau's celebration of figurative husbandry has become indistinguishable from the modernist credo of textual complexity, even incomprehensibility. The first draft of *Walden* was "Addressed to my Townsmen," but the last, colored by disappointment, seeks to exclude the many and narrow its appeal to a "fit audience, though few."[19]

Thoreau worked five years longer on *Walden* than he had originally intended. Expecting a success with his first book, he hoped to bring out the second as early as 1849; copies of *A Week* included the announcement that *Walden* would be published shortly.[20] But when it became evident that *A Week* was not selling, his publishers refused to issue *Walden,* and Thoreau spent five additional years revising and refining it. Because neither *A Week* nor the first draft of *Walden* is a masterpiece, this brief account of Thoreau's publishing difficulties suggests some final ironies of history. Insofar as *Walden* does "transcend" the Age of Jackson, does rise above its historical moment as a consequence of its excellence as an artwork, it does so precisely because of the particular nineteenth-century circumstances under which it reached print. Its transcendence of history is rooted in the conditions of its production – its *belated* production – as a commodity to be marketed by publishers. And still more: There is the additional irony that *Walden* is its own most effective reply to Thoreau's denigrations of commercial enterprise. One need not even point out that the values of brotherhood and love, values conspicuously absent from *Walden,* are inextricably bound up with the principle of "exchange." On strictly aesthetic grounds, the text disputes the contention that "trade curses every thing it handles." Far from impairing the quality of *Walden,* commercial considerations conspired to make it a better work. *Walden* is the one undeniably great book Thoreau ever wrote, thanks in part to the operations of the marketplace.

Notes

1   Henry D. Thoreau, *Walden,* ed. J. Lyndon Shanley (Princeton, N.J.: Princeton University Press, 1971). Page numbers included in the text refer to this edition.
2   Ralph Waldo Emerson, "Thoreau," in *The Selected Writings of Ralph Waldo Emerson,* ed. Brooks Atkinson (New York: Random House, 1950), p. 896. The standard view of *Walden's* development is given by Walter Harding and Michael Meyer in their edition of *The New Thoreau Handbook* (New York: New York University Press, 1980), p. 51: "*Walden* may seem to begin in despair, but it ends in ecstasy."
3   Leo Marx has explored *Walden* from the perspective of pastoralism in *The Machine in the Garden: Technology and the Pastoral Ideal in America* (New York: Oxford University Press, 1964), pp. 242-65. Marx sees Thoreau's great foe as technology, the railroad in particular; I regard technology as simply one aspect of the market society that is his real adversary.
4   On the civic humanist tradition, see J. G. A. Pocock, *The Machiavellian Moment: Florentine Political Thought and the Atlantic Republican Tradition* (Princeton, N.J.: Princeton University Press, 1975).
5   See Lukács's *History and Class Consciousness: Studies in Marxist Dialectics* (Cambridge, Mass.: MIT Press, 1971), pp. 83–222. Also relevant is Roland Barthes, *Mythologies,* trans. Annette Lavers (New York: Hill & Wang, 1972), esp. pp. 109–59. A valuable discussion of reification and American literature appears in Carolyn Porter, *Seeing and Being: The Plight of the Participant Observer in Emerson, James, Adams, and Faulkner* (Middletown, Conn.: Wesleyan University Press, 1981), pp. 23–53, passim. On reifica-

tion in Thoreau, the best treatment is John P. Diggins, "Thoreau, Marx, and the 'Riddle' of Alienation," *Social Research* 39, (1972): 571–98.

6 The question of whether American farmers were ever really self-sufficient is obviously beyond the scope of this essay. Clarence H. Danhof, for one, has argued that the market orientation deplored by Thoreau did not come to dominate American agriculture until the nineteenth century. See Danhof's *Change in Agriculture: The Northern United States, 1820–1870* (Cambridge, Mass.: Harvard University Press, 1969).

7 Compare Thoreau's question in *A Week on the Concord and Merrimack Rivers,* ed. Carl F. Hovde, William L. Howarth, and Elizabeth Hall Witherell (Princeton, N.J.: Princeton University Press, 1980), p. 382: "Is not Nature, rightly read, that of which she is commonly taken to be the symbol merely?" It is no accident that symbolism emerges as the dominant mode in American writing during a period when the United States transformed itself into a market society.

8 Henry D. Thoreau, *Reform Papers,* ed. Wendell Glick (Princeton, N.J.: Princeton University Press, 1973), p. 88. For a reading of *Walden* as a heroic text, see Stanley Cavell, *The Senses of Walden* (New York: Viking, 1972).

9 See Lewis P. Simpson, *The Man of Letters in New England and the South: Essays on the History of the Literary Vocation in America* (Baton Rouge: Louisiana State University Press, 1973), esp. pp. 3–31.

10 Compare Roland Barthes, *Mythologies,* p. 141: "The status of the bourgeoisie is particular, historical: man as represented by it is universal, eternal."

11 Alexis de Tocqueville, *Democracy in America,* ed. Phillips Bradley (New York: Random House, 1945), 2:64. On this development generally, see the essays by William Charvat collected in Matthew J. Bruccoli, ed., *The Profession of Authorship in America, 1800–1870: The Papers of William Charvat* (Columbus: Ohio State University Press, 1968).

12 Thoreau's outburst here brings to mind another prominent American author who was for a time his townsman: Nathaniel Hawthorne. In *The House of the Seven Gables* (1851), Hawthorne takes an equally dim – if rather more bemused – view of his potential audience. His image for the undiscriminating public, eager to devour whatever is available (including the latest literature) and always hungry for more, is little Ned Higgins, the Yankee schoolboy who patronizes Hepzibah's cent shop and feasts on gingerbread figures of everything from men to locomotives.

13 Thoreau, *Reform Papers,* p. 77.

14 Lukács, *History and Class Consciousness,* p. 86.

15 J. Lyndon Shanley, *The Making of Walden: With the Text of the First Version* (Chicago: University of Chicago Press, 1957), pp. 57, 87; see also Lawrence Buell, *Literary Transcendentalism: Style and Vision in the American Renaissance* (Ithaca, N.Y.: Cornell University Press, 1973), pp. 309–10.

16 Compare Shanley, *The Making of Walden,* p. 182.

17 Harding and Meyer, *The New Thoreau Handbook,* p. 11.

18   Laurence Stapleton, ed., *H. D. Thoreau: A Writer's Journal* (Mineola, N.Y.: Dover, 1960), p. 107. Walter Harding discerns a strain of despair in Thoreau's journal for 1853–54 and speculates that he was discouraged because "his literary career seemed to have reached a stalemate." See Harding's *The Days of Henry Thoreau* (New York: Knopf, 1965), p. 329.

19   Shanley, *The Making of Walden*, p. 11. I am suggesting that at least at the beginning of his literary career, Thoreau was more ambivalent about popular success than has commonly been supposed. Thoreau the alienated artist is a partial portrait to which he himself contributed. Emerson's remark in the memorial address is usually taken to be definitive on this score: He quotes Thoreau as saying that "whatever succeeded with an audience was bad" (*Selected Writings*, p. 898). But the Concord sage had a very different impression of his young friend's wishes when Thoreau was seeking a publisher for *A Week*. He stated in a letter of 1847, "Thoreau is mainly bent on having it printed in a cheap form for large circulation" (cited in the "Historical Introduction" to the Princeton edition of *A Week*, p. 462). One might also consult the letters Thoreau exchanged with Horace Greeley, the resourceful New York editor who served him for several years as a kind of informal literary agent. And after *Walden*, it should be remembered, Thoreau continued to speak out on public issues, obviously hoping to affect the thinking of his countrymen.

20   See Shanley's "Historical Introduction" to the Princeton edition of *Walden*, p. 363.

IV

The Example of Melville

14

Melville's Economy of Language

PAUL ROYSTER

No other novel of the nineteenth century is so concerned with the actions and relations of the workplace or so committed to describing the processes of production as *Moby-Dick*. Yet *Moby-Dick* is no ordinary industrial novel, because of its conscious attention to the task of constructing itself as language. The interaction of these two processes – industrial production and literary construction – produces a work rich in the metaphorical interplay of language and labor. In *Pierre; or, the Ambiguities*, the novel that followed, Melville abandoned this sense of language's connection to the world and the multiple assurances that natural signs and economic symbols had formerly provided. In these two novels Melville traveled from one extreme to the other: from endorsing language as the world's perfect counterpart to exposing it as a shadow without corresponding substance. In the same process, Melville also moved from a deep commitment to the capitalist economy to an outright condemnation of it, both as a means of life and as a mode of representation.

Moby-Dick is an exuberant paean to labor, an elaborate celebration of the human energy and industry of nineteenth-century America. Yet what it converts to metaphor is a particular set of economic relations: Whaling is a capitalist enterprise, an industry that produces commodities for a market and employs labor to return a profit on investment. Ishmael's advocacy of "the honor and glory of whaling" does not separate labor from capital, as being distinct parts of the industry. He is as proud of the number, size, and efficiency of the American whaling fleet as of the skill, productivity, and dedication of its seamen. Both the labor and the physical means of production emerge from Ishmael's account in favorable colors. Meanwhile, he invests the process of producing whale oil with additional symbolic meanings, which make it an extended metaphor for various social and metaphysical referents. Ishmael is never so happy as when he is finding in some dull, arduous, or onerous task an allegory of universal truth. Work takes on extra value when Ishmael can interpret it symbolically, when it assumes the pattern of some larger structure or condition of human life.

With Ishmael, this rhetoric of labor is in part a defensive strategy, an ideology that allows him to cope with the embarrassments or unpleasantness of his working-class position. For example, he dexterously explains away the kick administered by Captain Peleg as a sample of "the universal thump," passed the whole world round and imaginatively linking the entire race of men in the vast circuit of taking one's lumps. Ishmael's rhetoric transforms this striking example of class relations (owner/employee) into an illustration of higher democracy. Of course, the incident need not have been mentioned at all, and Ishmael's explication of it is noticeably ironic. Nonetheless, it supports his construction of whaling as an occupation representative of the universal human condition, even if this blurs the distinction between industrial discipline and human equality.

In general, Ishmael's rhetoric of labor does not dwell on such relations of production or on the social structure of the workplace. Most often it finds in some feature of the job at hand analogies for the universe of absolutes. In the chapter "The Mat-Maker," the job of weaving mats figures as an explanation of metaphysics: "It seemed as if this were the Loom of Time, and I myself were a shuttle mechanically weaving and weaving away at the Fates."[1] Ishmael analogizes the fixed threads of the warp as necessity or fate, the threads of the woof that he weaves with his own hand as free will, and the wooden sword with which Queegueg drives home the yarns as chance:

> The straight warp of necessity, not to be swerved from its ultimate course – its every alternating vibration, indeed, only tending to that; free will still free to ply her shuttle between given threads; and chance, though restrained in its play within the right lines of necessity, and sideways in its motions directed by free will, though thus prescribed to by both, chance by turns rules either, and has the last featuring blow at events. (pp. 1021–22)

Necessity, free will, and chance – Ishmael's labor contains these elements even as it represents them: Weaving mats participates in the structure of metaphysics that it signifies. This works out very neatly: Ishmael's understanding of his task illuminates the larger process of events – the parameters of human history brought together on the Loom of Time. The metaphor rests not on the product (the mat) but on the process, the labor, the weaving, the act of production. Ishmael's labor partakes of the historical process it represents, as Ishmael's labor both produces the symbol and is produced in turn by the things it signifies – necessity, free will, and chance.

In a later chapter, "The Monkey-Rope," Ishmael again introduces labor as a symbolic reproduction; this time when he finds in the work of "cutting-in" (or stripping the layers of blubber from the dead whale) an emblem of the social networks of human interdependence. The "monkey-rope," tied around the waists of Queequeg on the slippery back of the whale and Ishmael on the ship's deck, forces Ishmael to realize "that my own individuality was now merged in a joint stock company of two: that my free will had received a mortal wound; and that another's mistake or misfortune might plunge innocent me into unmerited disaster and death" (p. 1135). In this case, the rope serves as the figure, representing the ties among men because it *is* one – an outward and visible sign of the mutual dependence and linked fates of men. The monkey-rope is a material example of what it represents; it simply conforms (in a remarkable degree) to the pattern of other social relations. Its bond is an economic relation, dictated by the process of production. The structure of interdependence it stands for is also a set of economic relations: Ishmael suggests that the failure of one's banker or apothecary would be as disastrous as if Queequeg should slip and fall off the whale. Here again the figure represents by synecdoche rather than pure metaphor; the rope's extended meaning is produced by universalizing it, by identifying one particular economic relation with the total structure of relations in society. At bottom Ishmael insists, his situation is no different from any other: "I saw that this situation of mine was the precise situation of every mortal that breathes; only, in most cases, he, one way or other, has this Siamese connexion with a plurality of other mortals" (p. 1135). In Ishmael's case, his connections are concentrated and made symbolically manifest through the act of production.

On another occasion, in the chapter "A Bower in the Arsacides," Ishmael employs industrial labor as a metaphor for the natural world, comparing the growth and intermixture of living things in a tropical glade to a vast textile factory, so that he represents nature as the ongoing production of an industrious weaver-god:

> The wood was green as the mosses of the Icy Glen; the trees stood high and haughty, feeling their living sap; the industri-

ous earth beneath was as a weaver's loom, with a gorgeous
carpet on it, whereof the ground-vine tendrils formed the
warp and woof, and the living flowers the figures. All the
trees, with all their laden branches, all the shrubs, and ferns,
and grasses; the message-carrying air; all these unceasingly
were active. Through the lacings of the leaves, the great sun
seemed a flying shuttle weaving the unwearied verdure. Oh,
busy weaver! unseen weaver! – pause! – one word! – whither
flows the fabric? what palace may it deck? Speak, weaver! –
stay thy hand! – but one single word with thee! Nay – the
shuttle flies – the figures float from forth the loom; the freshet-
rushing carpet for ever slides away. The weaver-god, he
weaves; and by that weaving is he deafened, that he hears no
mortal voice; and by that humming, we, too, who look on
the loom are deafened; and only when we escape it shall we
hear the thousand voices that speak through it. For even so it
is in all material factories. The spoken words that are inaudi-
ble among the flying spindles; those same words are plainly
heard without the walls, bursting from the opened casements.
(pp. 1272–73).

Ishmael constructs this trope on a different model from the two
preceding ones: The two halves of the figure (textile factory and tropical nature) are not conflatable; they stand in the relation of analogy. The
natural world in certain features resembles a carpet factory; but this
simile is built on another, prior level of signification. If the weaver-god
is busy weaving living figures into his vast carpet that is the world,
then one of those figures must be this same one of the weaver-god at
his loom. The figure describes its own genesis or origin, and it recalls
the system of correspondences and meanings already woven into nature, which makes Ishmael's system of references possible. The figure
of the weaver-god is represented as being woven by the weaver-god
himself, and Ishmael shows us a symbol hard at work on its own
production.

In *Moby-Dick,* labor represents and becomes part of nature; whereas
the other side of economy – money – represents and becomes part of
language. Ishmael repairs this division in economy (and in semantics)
by unfolding correspondences that reinstate the symbolic unity of the
experienced world and authorize language and money as representatives
of a single integrated whole, consisting of man and nature. Money and
language become authentic signs by virtue of their multivocalness and
their ability to mediate between a singular objective world and a diver-

sity of imaginative ones. In a central chapter that dramatizes this theory of signs, all the various characters confront a talismanic object and read themselves in a piece of money – "The Doubloon" – the Spanish-American gold piece that Ahab nails to the mast as the reward for the first to sight the white whale. All the major characters (except Ishmael) attempt to interpret the doubloon's significance, and this progression of imaginative encounters centralizes the issues of perception and motivation that so concern the novel. The chapter arrays a multiplicity of meanings around a central sign or text, and the pattern of the different readings illuminates the differences among the observers and suggests the semi-magical properties that adhere to the sign of money.

The coin described by Ishmael is an eight escudo gold piece (or doubloon) actually minted in Ecuador from 1838 through 1843. The obverse, showing a "Liberty" head, is nailed toward the mast, so that it is never seen. But the reverse, showing a sun flanked by the zodiac over three mountains, capped by a tower, fowl, and volcanic cloud, proves a fertile text. Ahab, Starbuck, Stubb, Flask, the Manxman, Queequeg, Fedallah, and Pip, each sees his own portrait on the coin and constructs his own particular relation to the value it represents. To Ahab the coin is a mirror of Ahab himself; for Starbuck it is a reflection of his own religious faith and doubt, cast in lights and shadows, heights and depths; to Stubb it represents the biography of man in one round chapter, the sequence of events that define the cycles of life and death; for Flask it stands for 960 cigars, or his own particular form of desire, and an incentive to forward Ahab's design; to the Manxman it is a prophecy, a link to a future event; for Queequeg it refers to his own body, perhaps especially to its sexual functions; to Fedallah it is a sign or icon or idol – he "makes a sign to the sign" – worshiping not the coin but the fire it represents; and finally, to Pip the doubloon "means" its series of onlookers, all illuminated by the one central symbol. The doubloon's manifold uses as a figure derive from its doubleness, or reflective function, its separation of individualized meanings, so that no one reading excludes or impinges on another, and its accumulation of significance from the procession of observers. The coin multiplies the fetish quality of money by making many different systems of value reside in a single material object.

The doubloon is ultimately a fit symbol of symbols – its worth proves its significance, while its value is defined through its symbolic meanings. The coin is not involved in any transaction; it is not the product of labor, nor part of the system of capital that commissioned the ship. Of "purest, virgin gold . . . untouchable and immaculate to any foulness," the *Pequod*'s doubloon "was set apart and sanctified to one awe-striking end; . . . the mariners revered it as the white whale's talisman." Through various tropes (synecdoche, metonymy, typology, symbolism) the doubloon's system of representation expands to include the entire world: from Ahab to Moby Dick, from the trinity to the zodiac, from cigars to signs and wonders, from the life of man to the language of interpretation. As money and as symbol the doubloon serves as a pledge of Ahab's will; it represents the debt he owes Moby Dick. The coin also seals Ahab's unholy bargain with the crew; it represents the abrogation of the social contract expressed in the ship's articles; it is the token of the diabolical covenant to hunt the white whale.

The doubloon presents a reflective surface to each observer. Ahab declares: "This round gold is but an image of the rounder globe, which, like a magician's glass, to each and every man in turn but mirrors back his own mysterious self." Queequeg's perspective (like Stubb's and Starbuck's) is much the same: He sees his identity with the coin – its value is representative of himself; the coin is his own reflected double. Perhaps this is why Melville chose the "doubloon" as his figure, for its doubling effect is its most characteristic function. The coin is a figure that both divides and reunites, bifurcating the world and reintegrating it by reflective correspondences. Pip, the last speaker, must recognize something of this, for his jingle implies that reality resides not in the coin but in the progression of its observers: "I look, you look, he looks; we look, ye look, they look." Not the thing that is seen, but the ways of seeing it and the connections among the observers determine for Pip the doubloon's value or significance. "I, you, he, we, ye, they" imply a range of human relations, relations, moreover, that are mediated by language. Pip's conjugation of looking brings together the different readings just as the coin itself does, except that Pip's emphasis is on the human subjects and not, like the coin's, on the reflective world of signs. Pip looks, so to speak, on the other side of the coin, the obverse side, which is never seen, and from that perspective he announces the identity of all the observers.

The different values that Pip, Ahab, Starbuck, and the others place on the doubloon become in some sense equivalent, being mutually represented by the same thing. The chorus of readings locates the doubloon's meaning not in the coin but in the different observers; the doubloon's abundance of signs accommodates all interpretations and offers a language to each understanding. But even though the coin eventually conflates all these meanings, it does not work, as currency should, to mediate the relations among its human observers. None of the interpreters speaks to another. Each has a separate encounter with the substance of value and a different reading of its nature. Stubb, who overhears them all musing aloud, narrates the episode and allows each reader to take away his own proper meaning without impinging on the meanings attributed by the others. As Stubb says, "There's another rendering now; but still one text. All sorts of men in one kind of world, you see." Eight ways of looking at a gold coin (nine if we count Ishmael's, ten if we count the crew's) do not upset its reality; no one questions the coin's value or authenticity. The doubloon remains a substantial and definite object; its multiplicity, although ambiguous, is cumulative and reassuring; its value is not neutralized by contradictory appraisals. The meanings that are concentrated in the coin can coexist without conflict because the doubloon itself is fixed and static, never becoming part of the system of exchanges or a token of men's economic relations. The coin's elaborate dual structure of supply and demand, of desire and object, of man and his reflections, refers each observer in turn to an alternate version of himself. The value of the coin is achieved in each case only by way of an imaginative exchange or symbolic transaction.

Moby-Dick grounds its entire system of metaphor in economy: Money initiates a chain of representation that binds men to their natural, social, and metaphysical states; labor provides images of nature, Providence, and society. Melville's symbolic economy usually suggests the *structure* of the visible or invisible world. His extended figures invoke elaborate analogies between economic "facts" and formal organizations that might properly be called ideological. The doubloon, for example, recalls the organization of the ship, of human society, of the stars, of the body, and of language. Significantly, labor also shares this same representative system, illustrating by turns social structure, universal laws, and moral bonds and conditions. Yet Melville at times employs a different mode of symbolism for labor, one that presents it as ritual rather than analogy. In this mode, labor expresses substance rather than structure; it incorporates the material process of life's production and reproduction, rather than merely referring to its form or organization. This happens particularly in the chapter "A Squeeze of the Hand," where the labor of squeezing sperm represents neither a structure external to itself nor even its own redoubled reflection as activity or as figure. Where labor had been illustrative, this now becomes transformative. Ishmael's work dissolves him into his most generalized human identity, reconstitutes or re-creates him, and then relocates him in the world of men. Labor's value here exceeds its productive and representative qualities; it evolves into an expression of the universal life of the species, "Man":

Squeeze! squeeze! squeeze! all the morning long; I squeezed that
sperm till I myself almost melted into it; I squeezed that sperm
till a strange sort of insanity came over me; and I found myself
unwittingly squeezing my co-laborers' hands in it, mistaking
their hands for all the gentle globules. Such an abounding,
affectionate, friendly, loving feeling did this avocation beget;
that at last I was continually squeezing their hands, and looking
up into their eyes sentimentally; as much as to say, – Oh! my
dear fellow beings, why should we longer cherish any social
acerbities, or know the slightest ill-humor or envy! Come; let
us squeeze hands all round; nay, let us all squeeze ourselves into
each other; let us squeeze ourselves universally into the very
milk and sperm of kindness. (p. 1239)

Such a universal communion of labor is what Marx would have called
"species-being" – the "conscious life-activity" of the living for the production of the species itself. Ishmael's work, it is true, banishes his
alienation and wipes away all memory of social divisions, acerbities,
petulance, ill will, ill humor, and envy. Its summons to the climactic
vast human union and dissolution of laborers – "let us squeeze ourselves
universally into the very milk and sperm of kindness" – appeals to an
undifferentiated and unstructured nature of the human "kind."

This episode of "A Squeeze of the Hand" expresses what the anthropologist Victor Turner has called "anti-structure." Turner describes a
phase in rituals of acculturation or rites of passage, known as "liminality," during which initiates are symbolically separated from the ordinary
roles and norms of social life. This period or phase enforces a mystical
solidarity or *communitas* and is marked by the initiates' abstraction from
their cultural milieu, by the rejection of settled definitions of relations,
and by the implantation of ultimate standards of reference in some version of universal, pan-human values. In effect, this phase of the ritual
process strips away all partial and particular definitions of identity, leveling the initiates to the stark and fundamental equality of the essentially
human. On this level the sole authoritative group that remains is the
species itself. The experience of liminality, of being or feeling totally
outside social ties, and the experience of *communitas*, the shared identity
of the initiates, make up what Turner calls "anti-structure." Subsequently, as the initiates are ritually resocialized to assume new roles and
relations, the social world is reconstituted for them *ab ovo*, symbolically
rebuilt out of a generatively central experience.[2]

Ishmael's account of squeezing sperm follows a parallel process. His
vision of unbounded human kindness must be reintegrated into the

structured roles of the social world, while he retains the mystical affirmation of human identity as an absolute but irrecoverable value:

> Would that I could keep squeezing that sperm for ever! For now, since by many prolonged, repeated experiences, I have perceived that in all cases man must eventually lower, or at least shift, his conceit of attainable felicity; not placing it anywhere in the intellect or the fancy; but in the wife, the heart, the bed, the table, the saddle, the fire-side, the country; now that I have perceived all this, I am ready to squeeze case eternally. In thoughts of the visions of the night, I saw long rows of angels in paradise, each with his hands in a jar of spermaceti. (p. 1239)

Ishmael's ritualized process of labor, however, contradicts its own social context. Although set within the specifically capitalist process of production, squeezing sperm suggests not structure but the breakdown of structure. Labor here expresses liminality and *communitas,* anti-structure rather than social structure. Labor in this ritual mode also induces an absolute identification with its product, and through this identification Ishmael's work emerges as a universal communion of human laborers. What Ishmael experiences might even be described as a loss of difference – a loss of selfhood or subjectivity, a condition of unmediated union and unbounded creation. And yet (to recall), Ishmael is confined within a specific economic structure. He is subject to the relations of labor and capital and to the specific hierarchy of power these entail. Nonetheless, the production process accommodates Ishmael's universal self through these gaps or inversions in the power structure that allow (mythically) for the continuing flow of essential human forces. Couching this mystical affirmation of humankindness within an activity engineered for the production of capital separates labor from the system of wealth and identifies work with the essential nature of the species – "man." Ishmael recognizes labor as the objective form of his common, human life. His moment of species-identity (symbolically reinforced by all the sexual references of "sperm") occurs within the whaleship's manufacturing process, but is not represented as part of the economic structure. The mystical quality of the sperm allows Ishmael to transcend the relations of production. His labor is conceived not as an exchange of value, involving some commodity-form of capital, but as an elaboration or manipulation of the vital fluid or essence of humanity. Ishmael knows no alienation from his product, his labor, or his fellow workers; his is a labor of unbounded potential, an evocation of the largest unity of humankind.

The crucial thing about this universalizing ritual of labor is that it is in no sense an indictment of the system of economic relations. Indictments there are in *Moby-Dick,* to be sure. One follows this passage almost immediately, as Ishmael gives an account of the Infernolike blubber room, where men's alienation from themselves is graphically figured by their cutting off their own toes. Yet the criticisms of America, of industrialism, commercial society, or the system of capital never obscure Ishmael's ideological loyalties. In fact, the rhetoric of these values – equality, productivity, individualism – actually provides the language for Ishmael's objections to the economic order. Although he often takes an ironic tone in describing the economic system, Ishmael is never ironic about the value of labor and production. In the case of squeezing sperm in particular, the accommodation of a mystical species-unity within the basically nonhuman system of capitalist production redeems (albeit symbolically) that organization of labor.

Viewing *Moby-Dick* as a less than radical critique of American capitalism coincides with one of the plot's central features: Ahab's rebellion against God, economy, and nature. Ahab has no respect for the commercial purposes of the *Pequod*'s voyage, yet the form of his opposition to the system of economic relations serves ultimately to reinforce the values of the bourgeois order. Ahab's madness, his usurpation of power, and his rigid authoritarianism all deflect criticism away from the economic system that launched the *Pequod*. Ahab is more dangerous than the ship's owners; and although he is also more sympathetic and even admirable in his grand self-reliance, it is a self-reliance run amok. Ahab sets up a false opposition – between his own wild romanticism and the commercial values of the Starbuck and the owners. These emerge as the two formal choices; while Ishmael, who, if anyone, would seem to represent an alternative to this dichotomy of capitalism straight or capitalism perverted, declines to choose and so serves both sides. Ahab radiates the grandeur of the heroic individual; Starbuck, the conventional values of business, family, and home. Ahab, with his demonic power and enormous attractiveness, is represented as a demagogue who usurps the system of production for his own private mission of vengeance. His revolt against the system of profit diverts Ishmael's criticism away from the whaling industry itself, which in its pristine form regularly sacrifices human life to the production of capital.

Ishmael's ideology of labor offers no effective antithesis to the system of production; the novel is balanced rather than dialectical. Ishmael's ideology combines comic resignation with democratic rhetoric; his perspective on events is emphatically not subversive of whaling as a capitalist industry. Ishmael often has his reveries and epiphanies of mystical transcendence – not only squeezing sperm, but also at the masthead, or floating serenely among schools of whales. But while each of these occurs in a social context – that is, during some form of labor – the content of Ishmael's meditations is distinctly asocial, concerning not the relations among men but those imaginary relations between the individual mind and the universe at large. The rhetoric of labor and the types and figures through which production corresponds to its universal referents make Ishmael's work inseparable from what it represents. The relations of production are sanctioned by their symbolic qualities. Ishmael is reminded of nature, Providence, time, society, and human life processes because they are both symbolized and literalized in his labor. This redoubling or inner reflection characterizes all his tropes: Each illuminates itself and effectively eliminates the distance between the sign (labor) and whatever it signifies.

Melville remained enthusiastic about his practice of representation in *Moby-Dick*, even though he was fast becoming aware of its potential limitations. His representations are generally achieved at the price of stasis, by abstraction from process, by the suspension of time or history. Squeezing sperm is set apart from the system of capital and the economic process of labor, just as the doubloon is separated from the active commerce of the world. Both are symbolic structures that somehow evade the category of history – the coin by becoming eternally fixed, labor by self-generation or self-reflection, by carrying out its own origin. In this fashion, representation manages to comprise both repetition and difference: The symbol encompasses the nonsymbolic to which it refers; it includes its own outside. Meaning is organized in terms of signs – naturally occuring figures whose structures suggest an overall design – rather than as a product of motivated human actions. By pondering the different possible meanings of the coin, the whale, or the labor, Melville emphasizes the man-made or artificial quality of his signs. Yet the central symbol always predates any of its interpretations, each of which is incomplete and inferior insofar as it is partial or personal. The signs themselves remain seemingly unmotivated, though displayed within a structure of motivated meanings. There is clearly a sense in which Ahab invents Moby Dick, even though, significantly, Moby Dick is already there, ubiquitous in space and time. In much the same way, Ishmael does not merely invent any of the labor he finds so meaningful. It awaits his discovery, and its independence from himself lends additional authority to his symbolic readings. This is also true more generally of Ishmael's relation to language (his other means of production); for he is ever protesting that he has found, and not originated, such arcane whaling terms as "squilgee," "specksynder," "white-horse," "plum-pudding," or "slobgollion." The things and the words for them are always there, but signification awaits the conception that links the object or person to its name, a situation emphasized from the novel's very beginning – "Call me Ishmael" – where the symbol ("Ishmael") applies to the self ("me") in a relation produced by an act of language. The ambiguity of symbols such as money and labor revolves around this question of whether signs are discovered or invented, whether economy is natural or artificial. Ishmael's discovery of chains of analogies throughout the economic process must always be balanced against competing interpretations. The signs themselves, however, are solid, definite, unmistakable, and authoritative in their own right. Upon this literal level of economic fact Ishmael rests with confidence, doubting neither the material world nor its connection to other worlds beyond. Similarly, Ishmael's philosophy, his irony, and his vision of human and cosmic nature depend on the values of a certain way of life – American democratic free enterprise. This ideology gives substance to Ishmael's language, and he benefits from going with rather than against the grain of his rhetoric.

After *Moby-Dick,* Melville's methods of economic symbolism became more complicated. His rhetoric of labor acquired an ironic edge, and his disaffection with the system of economic relations became more conscious and more explicit. In his later works Melville showed an increasing tendency to distrust language, to undercut and conflate systems of representation, and to highlight the separation of words or signs from what they purport to represent. *Pierre; or, The Ambiguities* is the turning point in this development, a deconstruction of the elaborate system of natural analogies. It presents a negative version of the symbolic language of correspondence between man, nature, and the invisible world that makes *Moby-Dick* so rich in meaningful detail. The symbolic language of *Pierre* distorts the rhetoric of economy to expose its contradictions, inconsistencies, and ideological motives. The novel is as critical of language, society, and economy as *Moby-Dick* is celebratory. To account for Melville's startling reversal of method, let me suggest that in *Moby-Dick* he pushed a rhetoric to its limits, and in *Pierre,* for personal, political, and intellectual reasons, he took one further step, moved beyond that rhetoric, and turned it upside down and inside out. Here, as in *Moby-Dick,* mythological connections between men and things provide structures for meaning that resonate on various levels (economic, natural, social, or metaphysical), but *Pierre* offers us a look at the other side of the coin. Language has now lost its affinity to experience; the correspondence between the inner world of feeling and the outer world of nature no longer obtains. The rich significance that *Moby-Dick* had placed in words is inverted in *Pierre* to alienate the work of literature from what it presumes to represent. As *Pierre* describes the imaginative labor of literary production, it also explores the imaginary relations of production that are represented by ideology. These imaginary relations – of Pierre to his book, his audience, his critics, his publishers, and to himself – form the backdrop against which Pierre's economic and social conflicts are played.

Writing, not whaling, is the industry that provides metaphors in *Pierre*. Literature here describes its own production and confronts its own status as commodity, so that the writing fashions a new relation to its subject and reference, stamping a particular interest, bias, or hidden motivation on its field of possible meanings. In *Moby-Dick*, Melville had not been constrained to establish a direct agreement between the described labor of whaling and his own literary product. Certainly, he made occasional gestures in this direction: the division of whales into categories of folio, octavo, and duodecimo, for example; or, more generally, Ishmael's penchant for reading the world as hieroglyphic, in which the reader of the novel is urged to participate. But in *Pierre* the hero is himself a writer – first a juvenile author of popular verse and devotee of classical literature (Dante, Shakespeare), and then, fully and explicitly in the novel's second half, a professional author – a would-be creator of a book of world-shaking import. Literature exists in *Pierre* both as sign and as product; literature is the figure or image of whatever is to be represented by metaphor and also the record or repetition of that representation. Writing, having become in this sense self-reflexive, must now sustain its own authority and elaborate its own significance in order to survive as an adequate model of all that whaling had stood for in *Moby-Dick* – time, nature, society, Providence, the eternal verities. This is a ponderous responsibility to rest on any rhetoric of labor, even one as highly developed as that of writing. Yet Pierre clearly intends to meet such expectations: "I will gospelize the world anew," he cries, "and show them deeper secrets than the Apocalypse! – I will write it, I will write it."[3]

In *Pierre*, Melville's economic rhetoric shifts from the notion of labor as a source of value (economic or universal) toward a conception of labor as a system of constraints or a settled structure of power relations. Work becomes a form of self-denial – not merely in the sense of diligence and industry, but as an actual self-immolation and a sacrifice of common humankindness. Pierre's work isolates him from community, family, and even the women with whom he lives. It becomes effectually a labor that entails not the production of value but the negation of human life. *Pierre* does not rely on writing in quite the same way that *Moby-Dick* relies on whaling; it addresses the production of literature in only five of the novel's twenty-six chapters.[4] But for Pierre, authorship represents an alternative to the class-structured society he formally renounces; although he finally discovers that literature serves as an alternate version of that very same social system. Writing appears as Pierre's way out; and he stakes everything on his literary career only to find his writing constrained by the same forces he had planned to escape. In *Pierre,* Melville's critique of the work of writing applies as well to political economy in general, and is dramatized by the transition of his author-hero from a practitioner of this seemingly freest of all free enterprises into a forlorn, oppressed "states-prisoner of letters" (p. 340).

The novel begins in the summer of Pierre's twenty-first year, when he is on the verge of marrying his fiancée, Lucy Tartan, and inheriting the family estate, Saddle Meadows, from his widowed and domineering mother. But the discovery of an illegitimate half sister, Isabel, the supposed child of his father's wayward youth, intervenes between Pierre and the happy enjoyment of his inheritance. The complex developments that set Pierre at odds with the world he has known have been described as psychological, philosophical, metaphysical, aesthetic, or religious – and they are all these things. But Pierre's problem also concerns social structure: Isabel's illegitimacy excludes her from her proper place in Saddle Meadows. Pierre is rich and she is poor; he is the heir, she is the orphan. There is no way they could share their common father's estate. Class boundaries are rigidly fixed, and reinforced by a rural economy of landlords and tenants. Saddle Meadows is a static culture, stratified, repressive, and (as Melville repeatedly underlines) thriving in the bosom of American democracy. To rescue Isabel from her false position at Saddle Meadows, Pierre pretends to marry her, and they elope to New York City, passing by stagecoach from their pseudo-Arcadia to the Jacksonian commercial metropolis.

Isabel's violation of family, social, and symbolic boundaries is formally indicated in the text by names (Isabel *Banford*), chapter titles ("He Crosses the Rubicon"), and a predilection for certain physical sites (doors, thresholds, gates, crossroads, and windows) where separate spaces meet and merge. Isabel causes Pierre to reject his patrimony and adopt literature as a profession. Dislocated within the structured society at Saddle Meadows, she opens up for Pierre a vaster and more mysterious world of the passions and the unconscious. Pierre transfers his ideal of virtue to that alternate inner world, a world subversive of the conventional definitions of family and culture, an antinomian world that values feeling and intuition over experience and law. Pierre attempts to describe this inner world in literature. He intends his writing to behold the truths of the heart through introspection and then to project them into the world of culture and forms against which the self is strategically set. Pierre envisions his labor as an emanation of value from a divine inner source, which the text compares to a mine, or well, or fountain. Pierre's relations of literary production consistently reflect his relations with Isabel. She is (he believes) his half sister, both the same and different from himself, his own image and his own perfect opposite. Pierre's book occupies the same kind of polar relation to him, and his alternating identification with and alienation from the product of his labor suggests a violation of the crucial boundary between the "me" and the "not-me":

> Two books are being writ; of which the world will only see one, and that the bungled one. The larger book, and the infinitely better, is for Pierre's own private shelf. That it is, whose unfathomable cravings drink his blood; the other only demands his ink. But circumstances have so decreed, that the one cannot be composed on the paper, but only as the other is writ down in his soul. And the one of the soul is elephantinely sluggish, and will not budge at a breath. (p. 304)

This redoubled production isolates Pierre from the product of his labor, from his activity of producing, and from his common humanity. It is an example of alienation in its classic Marxian form. Pierre is intent first of all on the production of a commodity – of "such matters as publishers would pay something for in the way of a mere business transaction which they thought would prove profitable" (p. 260). He is induced by the success of his juvenile attempts at literature to equate writing with money, and to invest "the dollars derived from his ditties," like Flask, in Havana cigars. When Pierre takes up writing as a profession, he approaches his labor with what will prove to be contradictory motives:

> Pierre was now engaged in a comprehensive compacted work, to whose speedy completion two tremendous motives unitedly impelled; – the burning desire to deliver what he thought to be new, or at least miserably neglected Truth to the world; and the prospective menace of being absolutely penniless, unless by the sale of his book, he could realize money. (p. 283)

Pierre's divided enterprise can create no product to satisfy both desires. Labor cannot transform his soul's experience into a marketable commodity. Any salable product will necessarily be some exterior thing, something renounced, cast off, and alienable, a commodity separate from himself. Nonetheless, Pierre's persistent identification with his book reveals his contradictory notions of labor: He so closely associates his outward product's reception with the inner experience of writing that his book's failure to represent value in the marketplace convinces him of his own failure to represent himself. The public abuse of his book proves it (and himself) to be counterfeit: "Now, then, where is this swindler's, this coiner's book? Here, on this vile counter [his desk], over which the coiner thought to pass it to the world, here will I nail it fast, for a detected cheat!" (p. 357). This writing alienates Pierre not only from his product but from himself as well. Pierre's process of labor, his attempt to produce a marketable book, forces him to negate himself and his own experience: "With the soul of an Atheist, he wrote down the godliest things; with the feeling of misery and death in him, he created forms of gladness and life. For the pangs in his heart, he put down hoots on the paper" (p. 330).

Pierre experiences the otherness of his book to such an extent that it eventually confronts him as a hostile thing. The final worthlessness of his product in the literary market forces Pierre to abandon writing entirely, and so removes his potential threat to the existing order of literature. But even before this, the self-negation involved in his writing carries over into the actual labor itself, so that Pierre at work cannot even identify himself as the person actively writing what he writes: "Sometimes he blindly wrote with his eyes turned away from the paper; – thus unconsciously symbolizing the hostile necessity and distaste, the former whereof made him this most unwilling states-prisoner of letters" (p. 340). This "hostile necessity" represents a need that Pierre attempts to fill through language. In identifying himself by language, he finds that the symbolic relations it imposes are not his to command absolutely. His writing remains alien from him, constraining him by codes and symbolic forms that implicitly deny his unique and anomalous desires. This otherness of language extends even to Pierre's unconscious, to his actions in an "unwilling" state. Suppressing his consciousness of labor, Pierre had hoped to open up a channel through which an unconscious genius would flow. The genius of the unconscious, however, is simply a ready-made rhetoric: Pierre's automatic writing only shows that his unconscious is coded by ideology in much the same way that his language is.

Pierre's alienating labor even isolates him from his own species. He walks the crowded streets of Manhattan, "that so, the utter isolation of his soul, might feel itself the more intensely from the incessant jogglings of his body against the bodies of the hurrying thousands" (p. 340). Pierre later wanders New York's deserted back streets and alleys, until one desolate evening he is seized by a fit of vertigo, so that "he did not have any ordinary life-feeling at all." This rebellion of "the very blood in his body," and the subsequent treason of his eyes, which "absolutely refused to look on paper," warn him of the alienation of his own physical humanity. Pierre, however, persists in his writing at the expense of his mortal life.

The climax of Pierre's labor comes when he is no longer able to work, when a trance or "state of semi-unconsciousness" steals upon him while he attempts to write; so that his actual labor gives way to a remarkable oneiric labor that reconstitutes the process of his work in a symbolic or mythological form. This dream unfolds as an image of Pierre's literary labor, and for the scene of writing it substitutes a scene from nature: "The actual artificial objects around him slid from him, and were replaced by a baseless yet most imposing spectacle of natural scenery" (p. 342). Pierre's dream transposes the site of labor onto a scene of nature – a landscape of violence and destruction, which becomes the symbol of a "natural" state of war. The symbol itself (Nature), so conceived, has two poles around which meanings cluster: one physiological (or orectic), suggesting the parts and functions of the body; the other ideological (or normative), suggesting the patterns of social organization.[5]

Pierre dreams of the Mount of Titans, "a singular height standing quite detached in a wide solitude not far from the grand range of dark blue hills encircling his ancestral manor" (p. 342). Formerly called (after Bunyan) the "Delectable Mountain," it owed its more Romantic name to the moody fancy of a wandering, disappointed poet. The lower parts of this mountain consist of sloping terraces or hillside pastures, belonging to the manor of Saddle Meadows, and rented out to tenants in exchange for a portion of their dairy products. Now, these hillside pastures had become covered with a small white flower, the amaranth, which, being distasteful to the cattle, greatly diminished the productivity of the fields and caused economic hardships among the tenants. The first action in Pierre's dream is the appeal of these tenants to the lady of the manor "for some abatement in their annual tribute":

> "The small white flower, it is our bane!" the imploring tenants cried. "The aspiring amaranth, every year it climbs and adds new terraces to its sway! The immortal amaranth, it will not die, but last year's flowers survive to this! The terraced pastures grow glittering white, and in warm June still show like banks of snow: – fit token of the sterileness the amaranth begets! Then free us from the amaranth, good lady, or be pleased to abate our rent!" (p. 343)

This part of Pierre's vision renders very clearly the social structure of the manor at Saddle Meadows. Pierre's mother – the "good lady" – sits atop a stratified system of land tenure, controlling her tenants as she does her son by the exercise of economic power. Two points of interest emerge from this part of the dream. First, the narrator allegorizes the dream, converting its class confrontation into a moral illustration or "family romance"; and second, he subsequently disguises its economic structure or its conflict of social forces as a competition of natural powers. The amaranth is no ordinary weed or wildflower; it is named for the amaranth of mythology, a white flower that blooms perpetually. It also, in its whiteness, is associated with milk (the dairy product), with the "good lady," and with a sterile, cold, and heavenly purity. All symbols in *Pierre* represent contradictory things – the amaranth represents purity and incest, sterility and immortality. Turner has shown that symbols in ritual contexts do this regularly – that they concentrate, make palpable, and charge with emotion the various conflicts and tensions that animate the social structure. The symbolic readings of the amaranth change on each level: Economically it represents oppression (of the tenants); in a personal sense it means dependence (Pierre's); on a religious level it refers to purity and immortality; and for the human race as a biological species it omens sterility and extinction. Of the earth, the amaranth is a heavenly flower; a perpetual celestial bloom, it is rooted in the desolation of the domestic hearth.[6]

In Pierre's vision, the tenants' appeal for rent relief receives no answer. Instead the dream moves on to the precipice of cliffs surrounding the summit of the mountain, returning several paragraphs later to brood over the ruined foundations of abandoned cottages still marked by the remnants of patches of the domestic herb catnip, planted by the departed tenants and slowly giving way before the incessant inroads of the aspiring amaranth: "For every spring the amaranthine and celestial flower gained on the mortal household herb; for every autumn the catnip dies, but never an autumn made the amaranth to wane. The catnip and the amaranth! – man's earthly household peace, and the ever-enroaching appetite for God" (pp. 344–45). "Appetite" is surely significant, reinforcing as it does the associations of the amaranth in a symbolic cluster that brings together a variety of different and irreconcilable images – God, mother, milk, flower, heaven, and earth. Tenants and lady give way to the catnip and amaranth and to the conflict of domestic peace and heavenly appetite. What begins as an illustration of economic relations concludes in the vegetable world as an eternal, metaphysical dualism.[7]

The amaranth and rent question may be termed the first part of

Pierre's dream. The second part displaces the revolt of the tenants with the revolt of the Titans, chief among them one called Enceladus, an armless stone giant who rises out of the earth, shakes off the soil that holds him imprisoned, and leads the other recumbent rocks and boulders in an assault against the precipitous wall of the mountain's summit. These giant stones, long since fallen from the mountain's heights, are transformed into an army of Titans, who now seek to recapture their original lofty position atop the mountain only to be violently repulsed and cast down again. The Titans' impotent offensive represents Pierre's own labor and desire; and Enceladus is explicitly revealed as the personal double of Pierre (whose name, of course, means "stone"):

> Foremost among them all, he saw a moss-turbaned, armless giant, who despairing of any other mode of wreaking his immitigable hate, turned his vast trunk into a battering-ram, and hurled his own arched-out ribs again and yet again against the invulnerable steep.
>
> "Enceladus! it is Enceladus!" – Pierre cried out in his sleep. That moment the phantom faced him; and Pierre saw Enceladus no more; but on the Titan's armless trunk, his own duplicate face and features magnifiedly gleamed upon him with prophetic discomfiture and woe. With trembling frame he started from his chair, and woke from that ideal horror to all his actual grief. (p. 346)

Pierre becomes Sisyphus and the rock rolled into one. His vision imitates his own baffled desires – his hopeless and unceasing efforts to reclaim something originally lost: father, sister, birthright, mother, or Lucy. Pierre's reading of the dream sees truth and virtue frustrated by their natural earthly ties and ignored by an impassive, idealized heaven. Pierre treats the dream as prophecy, but the narrator, in an alternate reading, understands it as myth. This second interpretation is more hopeful because its incestuous cosmogony places Pierre's condition in a universal or cosmic context:

> Old Titan's self was the son of incestuous Coelus and Terra, the son of incestuous Heaven and Earth. And Titan married his mother Terra, another and accumulatively incestuous match. And thereof Enceladus was one issue. So Enceladus was both the son and grandson of an incest; and even thus, there had been born from the organic blended heavenliness and earthliness of Pierre, another unmixed, uncertain, heaven-aspiring, but still not wholly earth-emancipated mood; which again, by

its terrestrial taint held down to its terrestrial mother, generated there the present doubly-incestuous Enceladus within him; so that the present mood of Pierre – that reckless sky-assaulting mood of his, was nevertheless on one side the grandson of the sky. For it is according to eternal fitness, that the precipitated Titan should seek to regain his paternal birthright even by fierce escalade. Wherefore who storms the sky gives best proof he came he came from thither! But whatso crawls contented in the moat before that crystal fort, shows it was born within that slime, and there forever will abide. (p. 347)

Melville's narrator completes the movement of deferral in the interpretation of the dream from social and psychological conflicts to the opposition of natural forces. What began with the tenants as an economic structure of class relations becomes in this last analysis an illustration of cosmic structure, a myth of eternal oppositions – natural, elemental, and static. By tracing them back to the origin of nature, the narrator can speak of the "eternal fitness" of Pierre's agonies, which serve as proof of noble lineage. He neither attributes fault nor offers any possible solution, because Pierre's problems inhere in the cosmic order of things. His mythological reading, moreover, suppresses the first part of Pierre's dream, obscuring the parallelism between the Titans and the tenants, a similarity that evidently escapes Pierre as well. What is elided, of course, is the political dimension of Pierre's vision – what I would call its mythically disguised social landscape. Unlike the meeker tenants, the Titans are social climbers, not content with their lowly position, and convinced that the summit of success belongs to them by right. Their upward struggle represents a middle-class image of the social process: Individuals rise and fall, but the social hierarchy is immutable. Ambition is, as it were, deified; and success is seen strictly in terms of personal struggle. Enceladus (or Pierre) is held back by his earthly origins and impelled forward by his celestial lineage. Pierre does not finally achieve the status of the self-reliant hero because he cannot accomplish the necessary union of opposites in himself, cannot wed the contradictions of "high" and "low" in a way that would make the self representative of the whole society. In some sense, Pierre's dream is a distorted version of the class struggle: Enceladus reflects the anxieties inherent in the "natural" ambition of the bourgeoisie. The myths that infect Pierre's dream represent social conflicts as emblems of natural order and render his personal failure into universal terms.[8]

This conceit of the Mount of Titans may well have been inspired by Shakespeare, in a passage marked by Melville in his copy of *Timon of*

Athens.[9] In the first scene of the play, a poet and a painter are discussing the aesthetic conceits they have brought (as commodities) to offer the rich and noble Timon:

> *Poet.* Sir, I have upon a high and pleasant hill
> Feign'd Fortune to be thron'd. The base o' th' mount
> Is ranked with all deserts, all kinds of natures,
> That labor on the bosom of this sphere
> To propagate their states. Amongst them all,
> Whose eyes are on this sovereign lady fix'd,
> One do I personate of Timon's frame,
> Whom Fortune with her ivory hand wafts to her,
> Whose present grace to present slaves and servants
> Translates his rivals.
>
> *Painter.* 'Tis conceived to scope.
> This throne, this Fortune, and this hill, methinks,
> With one man beckon'd from the rest below,
> Bowing his head against the steepy mount
> To climb his happiness, would be well express'd
> In our condition.

These sycophantic vendors of conceits have translated Lord Timon into the emblem of success, making him a caricature and exaggeration of Fortune's darling. The high and pleasant hill where Fortune sits enthroned represents the social world of Elizabethan England, with the lower orders ranged around its base and a select class designated to attain its eminence. Some differences from Melville's Mount of Titans are obvious: Fortune's hill is transparently allegorical, whereas the Mount of Titans is apparently natural; Fortune is a notoriously changeable lady, always rotating her wheel of favor, whereas the summit of the Mount of Titans seems to promise security; Timon and his rivals for Fortune's favor are recognized as men, whereas those who would climb Melville's mountain are romanticized into Titans. These symbolic features outline the critical ideological differences between the Elizabethan and the nineteenth-century American notions of success. Melville's debt here to Shakespeare (which is minor at most) is less interesting than the imprint of ideology on these two complementary visions of the social landscape.

As an example of ideology, Pierre's dream is an alternative version of his alienated labor. The dream-text reflects Pierre's labor of writing; but it inverts in the process of this reflection the relations of men to their social conditions. Pierre's labor commits him to a deterministic universe: His work is not creative, merely reproductive. Pierre's literary work generates a world of constraints and necessities, rather than one of open possibilities. The ideology of romantic literature is hostile to his experience, and the task of converting his life into that standard coin becomes eventually a process of denying himself. Pierre's labor produces a negative form of identity, an estrangement of the product, activity, and common interest of literature. The vision of Enceladus "naturalizes" and masks this alienation. The dream and its interpretations trace Pierre's problems back to the original constitution of the world. Enceladus is an exemplum of ideology: He expresses Pierre's imaginary relationship to his real conditions of existence. For, in fact, the Mount of Titans is not "natural" at all; it only represents the unnatural "nature" of the bourgeois ideology.[10]

In *Moby-Dick,* ideologies are Ishmael's playthings; each lends an added set of meanings to a world rich in analogies of its own natural order. Those significances are not necessarily in ideological conflict (with the one exception of Ahab's truncated argument with Starbuck, in which the system of capital emerges on the humane side of the debate). Industrialism, capitalism, and many sorts of economic chicanery come under Ishmael's critical fire; but the work ethic, the democratic dignity of labor, and the common production of life represented by work remain Ishmael's ideological base. *Pierre,* on the other hand, is a bitter invective against literary, economic, and social ambition. Pierre is essentially committed to the middle-class terms of success. Robbed of his paternal birthright, he looks to his labor to regain his heritage, seeking to make it on his own by individual and inward struggle. Separated from its active, productive funcion, labor is represented as an upward climb, a myth of ascent. When Pierre sees himself as Enceladus, the social universe of the novel is distorted to represent the order of nature. This sort of distortion is not unique to *Pierre;* indeed, in American literature generally, the word "nature" often serves as a more or less innocent disguise for the values of the middle class. Melville, however, offers a startling variation on the theme. His nature is a battlefield of cosmic forces; its universal order is exposed as a form of oppression and alienation. This image of nature makes it an unflattering figure of the middle class, even though the narrator employs it to sanction the social order. In this sense, many of the symbols in *Pierre* are self-effacing: They are terms borrowed from ideology that render meanings "outside" that ideology incomprehensible or ineffable. *Pierre* is unusual in the extent to which this normally unconscious borrowing is made explicit and problematic. Pierre believes that all signs refer to him; as he discovers their ambiguity, and as they decompose under his critical scrutiny, he is carried along in their disintegration. Melville's critique in *Pierre* centers on the extent to which a dominant ideology controls the lives not only of those who believe in it, but also of those, like Pierre, who stand in opposition.

Melville's discomfort with the dominant ideology arose from being simultaneously its adherent and its opponent. The middle-class mythology of Jacksonian America furnished him with an inventory of signs and a supply of symbolic language that he was constrained to use and distrust at the same time. Melville never completely escaped this mythology or its concurrent rhetoric of economy, but in the inverted and alienated language of *Pierre* he immobilized its symbols, nullified its system of representation, and made explicit its subtle and pervasive hegemony.

Notes

1   Herman Melville, *Moby-Dick* (New York: The Library of America, 1983), p. 1021. Subsequent references are to this edition, which is based on the forthcoming Northwestern–Newberry text.

2   Victor Turner, *Dramas, Fields, and Metaphors: Symbolic Action in Human Society* (Ithaca, N.Y.: Cornell University Press, 1975), p. 273.

3   *Pierre; or, The Ambiguities* (Evanston, Ill.: Northwestern University Press, 1971), p. 273. Subsequent references are to this edition.

4   Hershel Parker has argued that the attention to writing was added by Melville in the later stages of the novel's composition, largely in reaction to the critical reception of *Moby-Dick*. Parker divides the novel roughly into halves: the first a parody of romantic pastoral, the second a vituperative attack on American letters. See his "Historical Note" in *Pierre* (Evanston, Ill.: Northwestern University Press, 1971) and "Why *Pierre* Went Wrong," *Studies in the Novel* 8 (1976): 7–23.

5   The terms are Victor Turner's; see *The Forest of Symbols* (Ithaca, N.Y.: Cornell University Press, 1967), p. 54.

6   Interestingly, the amaranth is mentioned in the title-page motto of James Fenimore Cooper's Littlepage trilogy, as an image of the perpetuity of families and their estates. These three novels – *Satanstoe, The Chainbearer, The Redskins* – narrate the lineage and fortunes of the Littlepage family from the settlement of their Hudson River manor through the anti-rent uprising of their tenants in the 1840's.

7   Some commentators do not admit the episode of the lady and tenants as part of the dream per se, confining this last to the scene of the rocks assaulting the mountain. This does not necessarily argue against my reading, which emphasizes (as Melville does) the loss of distinction between dream and consciousness.

8   I rely here on Roland Barthes's assessment of the bourgeois ideology as a

form of myth – as a system of "depoliticized speech" (*Mythologies,* trans. Annette Lavers [New York: Hill & Wang, 1972], pp. 109–59).

10 "Ideology represents the imaginary relationship of individuals to their real conditions of existence." Louis Althusser, *Lenin and Philosophy,* trans. Ben Brewster (New York: Monthly Review Press, 1971), p. 162.

15

Art, Religion, and the Problem of Authority in *Pierre*

EMORY ELLIOTT

In recent years considerable scholarly attention has been directed to the question of the continuity of American intellectual history from the Puritans to the nineteenth century. The works of the cultural and intellectual historians have convinced many students of American literature that thought and writing in early nineteenth-century America owes much to the early Puritan divines and to the ministers, writers, and intellectuals of the American Enlightenment and the Revolution.[1] Perhaps the most sensible resolution of the debate over the relative importance of American versus European influences on American writers in the Jacksonian period is the conclusion that nineteenth-century American writers possessed two cultural legacies: one temporally immediate but geographically distant in the romantic revolution abroad, and one more historically remote but readily available in the histories, sermons, pamphlets, diaries, and biographies that filled the shelves of local libraries.

Composing in this American context, the classic American writers created literary works that internalized, quarreled with, but invariably preserved the values, myths, and beliefs that constituted an American ideological consensus.[2] The term "ideology" here describes a shared "system of meanings" that are held in common by the members of the dominant culture and that constitute the set of values encompassed by the phrase "the American way of life." Implicit in this definition of ideology is a conviction that in the United States in the mid-nineteenth century the dominant classes embraced political and social ideas that were not imposed by the coercive power of the nation's leaders but sprang from the religious idiom and nationalistic myths that constituted an internal system of beliefs for the majority of the American people. Generations of fervent preachers and thumping orators had so thoroughly established certain notions, such as liberty, equality, freedom, geographic expansion, and manifest destiny, that most Americans believed such ideals described present realities or future achievements.[3]

For serious writers in the 1830s and 1840s one of the most disconcerting aspects of the kind of society and culture this ideology had fostered was the trivializing and commercializing of the role of the artist. In this rising middle-class nation the position of the artist was devalued to that of the outsider whose labors were irrelevant or even threatening to the ongoing democratic–capitalistic errand. The obsessions with commerce, expansion, manufacture, and masculinity that characterized the middle-class values and that would drive Americans to remarkable practical achievements in the nineteenth century seemed to leave the populace with little time or inclination for aesthetic pleasures or flights of fancy. From the time of the Revolution, perceptive observers such as Philip Freneau, Hugh Henry Brackenridge, and Charles Brockden Brown realized that changes of attitude had occurred that were a part of a major reassignment of values. As the familiar religious rhetoric and Protestant values were being appropriated into political formulas to advance the national mission, the American people began to accept and internalize this ideological consensus of what it meant to be part of the American enterprise. In this process traditional forms of authority were threatened, especially that of the clergy and men of learning and letters. Whatever did not contribute directly to the commercial enterprises of the new nation was identified as frivolous, or "feminine," an inferior kind of activity for idle moments or idle people. The frustrations and failures of the first generation of serious authors in the new republic provide a useful context for understanding some of our later writers, for those who defined themselves as writers of imaginative literature had to contend with this popular image.[4] The artist was considered a weak and peripheral member of the community.

Two nineteenth-century writers who felt this isolation keenly and who recognized its sources in the cultural legacy of seventeenth- and eighteenth-century America were Nathaniel Hawthorne and Herman Melville. Although Hawthorne and Melville were not long deceived by such a public consensus, they nevertheless possessed, as their verbal legacies, the clusters of symbols, the elaborations of the myths, and the assertions of the dream through which this powerful national ideology had been formulated. Both writers recognized that too often the pervasive American ideology inhibited both the culture's positive valuation of art and even the very production of serious literature. It is the main purpose of this essay to suggest some of the ways this complicated literary-historical situation is expressed in Melville's *Pierre,* perhaps the most intriguing exploration of the role of the artist in mid-nineteenth-century America.[5] But in order to set Melville's achievement in perspective, I want first to discuss Hawthorne's response to that situation in *The Scarlet Letter*.

When Hawthorne composed *The Scarlet Letter,* he had little doubt that the social attitudes and values that constituted the American middle-class ideology of his generation had evolved from the Puritan heritage.[6] In particular, the juxtaposition of "The Custom-House" sketch with the Puritan romance draws attention to the relationship between the repression of two forms of emotional and imaginative experience, writing and sex, and suggests several connections between Hawthorne's self-reflexive introduction on the problem of the writer in Jacksonian America and the plight of Hester and Dimmesdale. The sexual sin for which the Puritan fathers stigmatize and isolate Hester and that torments Dimmesdale to death parallels the violation of the Puritan code of duty committed by the narrator–author – let us call him Nathaniel Hawthorne – the modern resident of Salem who labors under a deep sense of guilt for the sin of pursuing his artistic vocation.[7] Ironically, Hawthorne depicts the Puritans as at least providing the literary and social forms that permit repressed feelings to be channeled into other socially acceptable modes of artistic expression: Dimmesdale's jeremiads and Hester's embroidery. In his own nineteenth-century society, the pressure toward ideological conformity and economic productivity had become so discouraging to imaginative production that even the artist with the strength to overcome the practical barriers – such as having to work in a Custom House – may still succumb to the psychological controls of guilt, self-doubt, and isolation.

To put it another way, by the 1830s the screws had been tightened so that the imaginative outlets that had enabled Hester and Dimmesdale to become productive and respected artists were no longer condoned. Dimmesdale the preacher could command a Puritan audience with his eloquence in religious expression, but in Jacksonian America the artist in the Custom House (or the Old Manse) would best serve his society by remaining silent, performing bureaucratic duties, or perhaps producing a practical campaign biography.[8] These connections between historical past and present, between the Puritan family romance and the modern writer, imply thematic dimensions that go far beyond the political satire of "The Custom-House." By the nineteenth century both the minister and the artist, like Hawthorne himself, had become victims of an increasingly dominant ideology that undermined their authority to be public spokesmen through their respective callings. Hawthorne's linking of Hester and Dimmesdale, as types of artists, to the narrator of

"The Custom-House" illuminates a historical continuity that ties his own situation to theirs.[9]

Obviously, Dimmesdale represents the overly self-conscious minister of the seventeenth century. His sermons give eloquent expression to public ideals. But because he must maintain a strictly pure and moral image before his congregation, he represses his normal desires to the point of obliterating his physical self to become pure spirit, and at his death becomes a mythic hero of his culture, his life another chapter in the ' volumes of hagiography about the glories of New England.[10] He is the establishment artist destroyed by his desire for public renown. In contrast, Hester is the outcast artist whose salvation is her detachment from those who first scorn her and then come to cherish her work. In this she bears a striking resemblance to the hermit–philosopher portrayed in the literature of the postrevolutionary period. When the first writers of the republic were struggling to establish their authority as keepers of the American conscience, some poets like Philip Freneau, turned to the persona of the hermit or the philosopher in the forest, as a fitting type of the American artist – a voice crying in a moral wilderness. In these early writings the character of the hermit–pilgrim is a wise and learned but humble man who has withdrawn to the forest because he is aware that his ideas are subversive and threatening to those in power. Still, he remains accessible to those who seek him out, and occasionally, significant public events provoke him to send his thoughts to newspapers and magazines for publication. When at the end of the tale Hester returns to take up a lifetime residence as a prophetess and counselor, she may be said to blend the roles of the hermit–philosopher with that of the Romantic poet–priestess.[11]

To perceive the connection between this Puritan family romance and Hawthorne's quarrel with nineteenth-century American ideology, one must return to the speaker of "The Custom-House." Like Dimmesdale, the speaker of "The Custom-House" has tried to play a public role his Puritan ancestors would have approved. His desire to become a public official, his inbred sense of duty, and his guilt over his artistic impulses have led him to join the ranks of the patriarchy of government officials. Thus, he is not unlike Dimmesdale in risking his life – his imaginative and intellectual life – in pursuit of success in the public domain. He must struggle not only against repressive society but against his own self-destructive impulse to conform to its expectations. In order to survive psychologically, however, he retreats into an inner imaginative world and clings to a hope for future freedom: He says, "There was always a prophetic instinct, a low whisper in my ear, that, within no long period, and whenever a new change of custom should be essential to my good, a change would come" (p. 26). In fact, he later realizes that had he not been expelled from office, he might have lost his artistic power completely.[12] Unlike Dimmesdale, who lives too long under the scrutiny of the public and his superiors and thereby loses his capacity for rejuvenation, Hawthorne escapes with his powers intact.

The connection between Dimmesdale and his Custom-House counterpart calls attention to the effect of a national ideology not only on the artist but on the sense of self and personal identity of all Americans, especially sexual identity. In fact, the narrator often speaks of his literary capacity in terms of manhood. This association of sexual and artistic anxiety implies an important connection between Puritanism and the emergent middle-class ideology of Hawthorne's America. As Carroll Smith-Rosenberg suggests, "what we chose to call 'Puritanism' began in America during the last stages of preindustrial commercial capitalism," because Puritan modes of repression were secularized and internalized over time to form the system of sexual and psychological repression that characterized American Victorianism.[13] She describes the sense of guilt, doubt, failure, and personal self-loathing instilled in those whose lives did not conform to ideological expectations.[14]

In exposing these Puritan–Victorian continuities and contrasts, *The Scarlet Letter* can provide a foreground to Melville's probing and severe critique of the psychological power of the emergent ideology in *Pierre*. In many respects, Melville's portrait of the struggles and torments of a failed American author seems on its surface to defy any attempt to read the work as cultural expression. Since the time of its publication, Melville's parodies of Christian allegory, the popular romance, and the *Bildungsroman* and his satiric treatment of Pierre's literary failure have convinced many readers that the book reveals more about Melville's disturbed psyche than about his insights into his society. Yet if the reader can separate the image of Pierre's shielding his eyes from his own pages even as he writes them from the image of Melville's facing his own disappointments in the 1850s with publishers and the reading public, he may discover a searing cultural critique.[15]

As a descendant of the Puritans and the grandson of a Revolutionary War hero, young Pierre grows up secured in the enclosed sacred garden of the family estate of Saddle Meadows. Through the civil leadership of Pierre's mother, Mary Glendinning, and the religious guidance of the pastor Reverend Falsgrave, the Calvinist legacy of duty, sanctity, and submission to authority is preserved. Surrounded by symbols of his national and religious heritage, Pierre feels that life is to be a text written by others, an "illuminated scroll," a "sweetly-writ manuscript" that ordained for him a course of comfort and docility.[16] Recalling a pattern of generational decline precedented in the Old Testament, however, the narrator wonders if "that blessing pass from him as did the divine blessing from the Hebrews" (p. 14).

Not surprisingly, then, just as the third generation Hebrews backslid from their faith, so Pierre becomes a rebellious youth. The change, which has strong religious overtones, comes with two events: a revelation of a purported secret sin on the part of his father; and Pierre's dedication of his life to right the wrong. After Isabel asserts her identity as Pierre's sister and persuades Pierre that his father was a sinner, Pierre is set on a course of rebellion that leads to his destruction. The action that follows depicting Pierre's moral outrage, his psychological torment, his bohemian life in the city, and his pathetic attempts to become an artist does not mark this work as peculiarly American. Indeed, references to Dante, Shakespeare, Milton, Wordsworth, and Byron delineate a European literary continuity that gives the book its narrative frame and much of its allusive richness. At the same time, however, the complex details of Pierre's experience convey the significance of the legacy of New England Calvinism and the American Revolution as cultural facts that have helped to shape his individual identity, foster his ideological inflexibility, and thereby profoundly affect his ability to become a successful artist.

For example, one of Pierre's first expressions of his unrest is in a theological conflict between himself on one side and his mother and pastor on the other, involving scriptural interpretation. When Mary Glendinning is deciding whether she should allow her servant Delly and Delly's illegitimate child to remain on her estate, Mrs. Glendinning resorts, as did the early Puritans and the Whig preachers of the Revolution, to the Old Testament to buttress her wrathful judgment against the sinner. To support her opinion that "no such profligate should pollute this place" and that the child shall be cast out with the mother, Mary turns to her minister: "Reverend sir, what are the words of the Bible?" Because he favors New Testament charity over Mary's harsh justice, Falsgrave reluctantly answers, "The sins of the father shall be visited upon the children of the third generation" (p. 100). On the issue of Delly's child, this text has powerful meaning for Pierre, who now thinks of himself as bearing the burden of his father's sin. Opposing his mother on this issue, Pierre proposes that true Christian love and charity dictate mercy. When mother and son press their clergyman to resolve the debate, Falsgrave, who fears offending his patroness, equivocates that "millions of circumstances modify all moral questions" (p. 102). As the pastor evades the issue, the narrator reveals an "exquisitely cut cameo, representing the allegorical union of the serpent and dove" (p. 102) that Mr. Falsgrave wears beneath his surplice, symbolizing for the reader the minister's readiness to compromise his Christian principles for self interest. Pierre's perception of this hypocrisy and his inability to accept the moral complexity behind the symbol deepen his personal self-doubt and heighten his anxiety. From the outset Pierre's psychic conflict within himself and his relationships with others are intertwined with his inherited religious beliefs, which form the foundations of his cultural ideology and deeply affect his understanding of himself and of others.

In describing the moral and psychological transformation that follows Pierre's disillusionment, Melville draws ironically and pointedly upon the terminology of religious conversion experience, and he depicts Pierre's commitment to a life of sacrifice for the sake of his beloved "sister" Isabel in terms of a religious rebirth. "For two days Pierre wrestled with his own haunted spirit" like "Fortune's Knight" in the "ever-primeval wilderness" (p. 175) until, as if by "sacred providence," his old life is dissolved in a flash, and the light of "truth" breaks upon his heart "like electricity suddenly received into any sultry atmosphere of the dark" (p. 88). These "flashing revelations" both "purge the soul of gay-hearted errors and replenish it with a saddened truth"; that "holy office" is performed by a "purifying light" (p. 88). Having left the old life of corruption and error behind him, Pierre joins Isabel in a communion supper and dedicates himself to follow pure, uncompromised Christian principles (p. 162). Appropriately, he embarks on his new errand with a prayer: "Now, thank God, thought Pierre, the night is past – the night of Chaos and Doom. . . . May heaven new-string my soul, and confirm me in the Christ-like feeling I first felt. . . . Let no unmanly, mean temptation cross my path this day" (p. 106). During his entire crisis Isabel guides, one might even say prepares his heart for, his passage with the expertness of a New Light preacher.

Throughout this process of the preparation and conversion of Pierre, Melville keeps before the reader the question of Pierre's calling. In his well-established American society of the eastern seaboard no longer fraught with revolution or Indian wars, an angry young man has few creative outlets for his righteous indignation. Filled with the passion to bring justice to Isabel and thereby reform the past, Pierre wanders through an actual woods and an inner wilderness in search of some sense of self-direction, but he remains lost: "Even in the most withdrawn and subtlest region of his own essential spirit, Pierre could not now find one single agreeable twig of thought where on to perch his weary soul" (p. 136). The central questions here are why Pierre is unable to create a new self, to find a role in the world, and to discover in himself imaginative powers to match his reformist zeal, and what forces have "fated" him to fail, as the narrator frequently foreshadows, in his attempts at reform and creativity. Clearly one of the reasons Pierre remains intellectually paralyzed is that he is so burdened with a sense of guilt that he lacks the self-esteem needed to break the unconscious psychological bonds that tie him to his mother, his colonial ancestors, and his old religion. The narrator attributes Pierre's lack of inner strength and sense of self-worth directly to the Calvinist doctrine of justification by faith alone: The narrator says that Pierre is one of those men with "self-disdainful spirits, in whose chosen souls heaven itself hath by a primitive persuasion unindoctrinally fixed that most true Christian doctrine of the utter nothingness of good works; the casual remembrance of their benevolent well-doings, does never distill one drop of comfort for them" (p. 137). Throughout his attempts Pierre remains trapped between Jonathan Edward's doctrine of divine sovereignty and Emerson's declaration of self-reliance, unable to believe in a higher authority and incapable of trusting himself.

The inescapable hold that Pierre's religious and moral education has on him is more evident in the key scene in which Isabel attempts to move him from their platonic "sibling" relationship to a sexual relationship. Significantly, she picks the moment when Pierre declares that he has achieved intellectual transcendence and is now ready to become a true artist. He claims to have seen through the sham of moral systems that attach mere value-laden words to deeds and thereby inhibit mankind from discovering real truth: "Virtue and Vice are trash! Isabel, I will write such things – I will gospelize the world anew, and show them deeper secrets than the Apocalypse – I will write it, I will write it" (p. 273). To determine whether Pierre is really free to join her in a new relationship, Isabel formulates a test for membership in her liberated society: "Speakest of Virtue and Vice . . . Pierre? Tell me first what is Virtue: – begin!" Isabel insists that Vice and Virtue are nothing but words describing nothing, but Pierre finds that he cannot agree. When she says "Virtue is nothing," he replies "Not that!" But Isabel pushes forward: "Why torment thyself so, dearest Pierre?" Pierre moves closer to her nihilistic vision of freedom when he asserts, "It is all a dream – we dream that we dreamed we dream." Gaining confidence, Isabel proclaims, "Yes. It is all a dream!" Suddenly, the crisis of passion is upon him: "Swiftly he caught her in his arms: – 'From nothing proceeds nothing Isabel! How can one sin in a dream?' " Isabel agrees, but she must be sure that Pierre is now a true skeptic, for she knows that were he to backslide into guilt later, that would bring a tragic end to their affair. So she resumes her query:

"First, what is sin, Pierre?"
"Another name for the other name, Isabel."
"For Virtue, Pierre?"
"No, for Vice."

This however, is the wrong answer, and Isabel ceases the questioning by saying "Let us sit down again, my brother."

What Isabel recognizes is that Pierre continues to cling to his inherited values. Had Pierre said that "virtue is another name for nothing," he would have proved that he was free. When he simply exchanges the meanings of the words, he reveals that he is still thinking within the terms of his moral training; he cannot reject these terms as meaningless. Melville underscores the central importance of this dialogue to Pierre's artistic and intellectual limitations when he has Pierre conclude the examination by saying, "I am Pierre." Pierre cannot commit what he believes to be incest with Isabel because his sense of guilt and his moral values are too much a part of his individual identity. Although he may rebel against his old beliefs, Pierre cannot escape them, lest he completely lose his sense of self. If Pierre could follow Isabel's imagination, reject the taboo of incest, and leave behind all sense of guilt, he would both satisfy his passionate yearning for her and leave behind his old American Protestant self, but he cannot.

Throughout the work Pierre's powerlessness to escape his bonds of his own predispositions are intricately intertwined with his failed literary attempts. Just as Pierre's mother and the Reverend Falsgrave represent the social, religious, moral, and political authority of Pierre's world, they also typify the aesthetic values of the culture against which Pierre tries to define himself. Falsgrave is not only a minister; he is also the type of the clergyman–poet. The narrator describes him as "a splendid example of the polishing and gentlemanizing influences of Christianity upon the mind and manners," who represents the sort of writer who pursues style and grace of execution instead of truth: "Besides his eloquent persuasiveness in the pulpit, various fugitive papers upon subjects of nature, art, and literature, attested [that] he possessed a genius for celebrating such things, which in a less indolent and more ambitious nature, would have been sure to have gained a fair poet's name ere now" (p. 98). Just as Pierre sets out to destroy the hypocrisy, injustice, and corruption by returning to an earlier Christian purity, he also seeks to supplant the literary authority of "the Dilettante in literature," like Falsgrave, by restoring the tradition of Dante and Shakespeare (p. 169). Before his conversion to the quest Pierre has been an avid reader of the novels of his day, but now he sees through the fraud of these productions: "Their false inverted attempts at systematizing eternally unsystemizable elements; their audacious, intermeddling impotency; . . . these things over Pierre had no power now" (p. 141). But although Pierre seems to have escaped these external bonds, he still fails miserably as a writer, for more powerful internal restraints hold his imagination in check.

In the final chapter, Melville exposes Pierre's inability to transform his personal longings into artistic expression. His attempts are pathetic, unshaped, and uncontrolled outbursts of his own narcissistic obsession with his fate. The passages from Pierre's autobiographical novel included by the narrator expose important weaknesses in Pierre's fictional persona, Vivia, that help to explain Pierre's failure. For one thing, Vivia declares that he rejects all humor and all attempts to separate his own thoughts and feelings from those of his own fictional character: "Now I drop all humorous or indifferent disguises . . . Oh God, that men that call themselves men should still insist on a laugh!" (pp. 302–03). Pierre's complete lack of humor and his incapacity to distance himself from his situation are direct results of the same intellectual inflexibility that prevents him from freeing himself from the Saddle Meadows prison house of ideas and culture inherited from his American forefathers. Unlike Melville himself, who writes a very funny book in *Pierre*, Pierre is a humorless Puritan, locked in an either/or, saint/sinner, Ramisitic logic. In the brief passages of Vivia's commentary included, Pierre does present one accurate metaphor to describe his own situation: "Cast thy eye in there on Vivia; tell me why those four limbs should be clapped in a dismal jail – day out, day in – week out, week in – month out, month in – and himself the voluntary jailer!" In this image of Vivia locked in prison, Pierre depicts his own fate as an individual and as a writer bound and blinded by fixed ideas.

The reason Pierre is unable to laugh at the joke that life has played on him, to learn from his experience, and to become a wiser young man and perhaps a better writer is that he takes himself and his American heritage too seriously. He has believed so fervently in the myth of the greatness of the fathers and the glory of their achievement that he misses the human comedy in his own past; absorbed by the horrors of *Hamlet* and Dante's *Inferno*, he shuts out the implications of *A Midsummer Night's Dream* and the larger *Divine Comedy*.

Melville deftly links this grand flaw in Pierre's character to a weakness in Melville's own generation of Americans in the opening pages of the book where he recounts both the actual history and the idealized myth of the great-grandfather's establishment of Saddle Meadows. The fact is that the "green and golden world" of Saddle Meadows took its name from the common memory of the image of

Pierre's great-grandfather sitting "unhorsed on his saddle in the grass . . . still cheering his men on into the fray" (p. 26). This image is morally ambiguous: Even though the great-grandfather may be admired for his courage and ardor in urging his men forward with his "dying voice," the ludicrous image of the unhorsed cavalryman and the naming of the place "Saddle Meadows" to memorialize his fate is not without a comic dimension. In addition, Melville draws attention to the fact that the white great-grandfather is battling to take land, yet to be renamed, from the "aboriginal" owners who are "the only conveyancers of those noble woods and plains." Knowledge of this history should teach young Pierre something about the moral complexity of his legacy. But since Pierre is blind to the irony and humor of this history, the tale is soon transformed into myth for him through the addition of the "golden humanities of religion." Because Pierre's father insists that no man is a gentleman unless he "assume the meek, but kingly style of Christian," Pierre "partook with his mother of the Holy Sacraments" at the age of sixteen. From this interweaving of history and religion he derives a sense of his sacred purpose and chosenness, developing a mystified image of his family's glory and a misleading assurance about his own predestined fate. Although the narrator is necessarily vague about how exactly this generational transmission of attitudes occurs, he assures the reader that this nineteenth-century youth is intellectually, culturally, and spiritually linked even to his earliest Puritan ancestors:

> It were needless, and more difficult, perhaps to trace out precisely the absolute motives which prompted these youthful vows. Enough, that as to Pierre had descended the numerous other noble qualities of his ancestor; and as he now stood heir to their forests and farms; so by the same insensible sliding process, he seemed to have inherited their docile homage to a venerable Faith, which the first Glendinning had brought over sea, from beneath the shadow of an English minister. Thus in Pierre was the complete polished steel of the gentleman, girded with Religion's silken sash; and his great-grandfather's soldierly fate had taught him that the generous sash should, in the last bitter trial, furnish its wearer with Glory's shroud; so that what through life had been worn for Grace's sake, in death might safely hold the man. But while thus all alive to the beauty and poesy of his father's faith, Pierre little foresaw that this world hath a secret deeper than beauty, and Life some burdens heavier than death. (p. 7)

For Pierre the interweaving of history and religious imagery transforms the brutal and comic details of his family heritage into a romanticized tale, which distorts his view of reality, creates his sense of inadequacy and guilt, and leads to his extreme form of disillusionment and rebellion.

Ironically, through all of his bitter experience of the burdens of life, Pierre learns nothing. When he stands in his physical cell at the end, Pierre can still only see his life in terms of salvation versus damnation, good versus evil, heaven versus hell, docile acceptance versus defiant rejection: "Had I been heartless now, disowned, and spurningly portioned off the girl in Saddle Meadows, then had I been happy through a long life on earth, and perchance through a long eternity in heaven! Now, 'tis merely hell in both worlds. Well, be it hell. I will mold a trumpet of the flames, and with my breath of flame, breathe back my defiance!" (p. 360). But instead of the heavenly silken sash of his grandfather to shield him in death, Pierre perishes in his prison covered with the earthly "ebon vines" of Isabel's hair.

Both *Pierre* and *The Scarlet Letter* depict Americans as people committed to certain national, religiously buttressed, ideals that constitute the individual's identity as an acceptable and successful member of the community. For those who become obsessive in proving their faith in these beliefs and their worthiness for membership in society, dedication can be destructive of individual identity, as in the case of Dimmesdale. For those who refuse to accept the identification of themselves as individuals with the accepted beliefs of the society, rebellion can bring disaster, as in the case of Pierre, who lacks the power and imagination to escape the bonds of the established ideology. At either extreme this tension between the individual and the cultural heritage can be destructive to originality, imagination, love, and art. In both Pierre and Dimmesdale, pride and ambition are combined with an incapacity to define themselves apart from the values of their culture, and these inner forces set them on a disastrous course that can only end in self-annihilation. Interestingly enough, in both cases there stand ready bold antinomian women in the form of Hester and Isabel who possess radical new visions of what may still be humanly possible. But like the speaker of Frost's "Mending Wall," who must wait for a change of mind in a neighbor who moves in darkness like an old stone savage, these women must wait until their male companions are ready to go beyond their fathers' sayings. As Hawthorne and Melville knew, for the individual and the artist to go beyond the sayings of the Revolutionary or the Puritan fathers required intellectual flexibility and artistic power that few of their countrymen had been able to manifest.

Notes

1 For a current reappraisal of the issues, see the special issue on "The Puritan Imagination in 19th Century America," ed. James McIntosh, *Texas Studies in Literature and Language* 25 (Spring 1983): ii, 1–178.

2 Setting his own work in the context of definitions advanced by the cultural studies of Clifford Geertz, Antonio Gramsci, and Raymond Williams, Sacvan Bercovitch traces the transmission and evolution of values and myths in public rhetoric from the seventeenth to the nineteenth century in *The American Jeremiad* (Madison, 1978), pp. xii–xiii and passim.

3 I have made this argument in detail in *Revolutionary Writers: Literature and Authority in the New Republic, 1725–1810* (New York, 1982) and even more specifically in articles cited in that volume.

4 See *Revolutionary Writers* and the important essays of William L. Hedges, "Toward a Theory of American Literature, 1765–1800," *Early American Literature* 6 (1972): 26–38; and Hedges, "The Myth of the Republic and the Theory of American Literature," *Prospects* 4 (1979): 101–20.

5 The purpose of this essay is not to prove that Hawthorne and Melville were obsessed with the American past or even that the cultural legacy was the primary thematic material of *The Scarlet Letter* and *Pierre;* thus, I have made no attempt to bring to bear the ample biographical and literary materials that demonstrate this aspect of their interests. T. Walter Herbert's *Moby-Dick and Calvinsim: A World Dismantled* (New Brunswick, 1977) and Michael Colacurcio's essays on Hawthorne (see esp. "Parson Hooper's Power of Blackness: Sin and Self in 'The Minister's Black Veil.' " *Prospects* 4 [1979]: 331–411) may serve as beginning references to the issues of Puritan continuities.

6 *The Scarlet Letter, The Centenary Edition of the Works of Nathaniel Hawthorne* (Columbus, Ohio, 1962), 1: 10. Hereafter cited in the text. A deft survey of recent Hawthorne research and criticism is Michael J. Colacurcio's "The Sense of an Author: The Familiar Life and Strange Imaginings of Nathaniel Hawthorne," *Emerson Society Quarterly* 27 (1981): 108–33.

7 The narrator reflects: "Doubtless, however, either of these stern and black-browed Puritans would have thought it quite a sufficient retribution for his sins, that after so long a lapse of years, the trunk of the family tree . . . would have borne, at its topmost bough, an idler like myself. . . . A writer of story-books! What kind of business in life, – what mode of glorifying God, or being serviceable to mankind in his day and generation, – may that be?" (p. 10). Hawthorne recognized a connection between the Puritan rejection of art as a wasteful distraction from divinely ordained activities and his own society's benign neglect of the serious writer. In neither world was art considered part of the "business of life"; in one case it was a sin against theology and in the other a frivolous distraction from capitalist enterprise.

Further evidence of Hawthorne's recognition of the ministerial heritage of the artist's role in the mid-nineteenth century is contained in his introductory sketch to *Mosses from an Old Manse* (1846). He stresses that before he occupied the manse it had long been the sacred abode of generations of clergymen. For general considerations of "The Custom-House," see Dan McCall, "The Design of Hawthorne's 'Custom-House,' " *Nineteenth Century Fiction* 21 (1967): 349–58; Nina Baym, "The Romantic *Malgré Lui*," *Emerson Society Quaterly* 19 (1973): 14–25; and the articles cited in the notes to the latter. I am also indebted to Michael Kramer's argument for Hawthorne's awareness of the close relationship between himself as artist and the former role of the Puritan clergyman; see his dissertation "Language and Liberty in America: 1830–1860" (Columbia University, 1983), pp. 211–22.

8   Thus, the description of Dimmesdale at the pinnacle of his public prominence: "There has come to the Reverend Mr. Dimmesdale . . . an epoch of life more brilliant and full of triumph than any previous one, or than any which could hereafter be. He stood, at this moment, on the very proudest eminence of superiority, to which the gifts of intellect, rich lore, prevailing eloquence, and a reputation of whitest sanctity could exalt a clergyman in New England's earliest days, when the professional character was itself a lofty pedestal. Such was the position which the minister occupied, and he bowed his head forward on the cushions of the pulpit, at the close of his election sermon" (pp. 249–50). Of course, in Hawthorne's time there were still popular preachers, but the romantic artist and man of letters has surpassed the minister in intellectual respectability.

9   Whereas Dimmesdale's rhetorical art is a successful form for communal expression, Hester's more private art, typified in the intricate embroidery of her "A," ultimately conveys the deeper yearnings of her society. Because Dimmesdale practices his socially approved art within the community, he must live up to a public image his role demands. Meanwhile, Hester, who is first a social outcast, finds in her isolation the freedom to surpass her contemporaries in imaginative power (p. 263). Through this interplay of the roles of the artist and the spiritual leader, Hawthorne exposes the uneasy relationship between the roles of the artist and clergyman that had its American beginnings in Puritan New England.

10 Even his confession of his adultery is transformed into a symbolic act through which he is to have proven his greater piety by disparaging his spotless life: "He had made the manner of his death a parable, in order to impress on his admirers the mighty and mournful lesson, that, in the view of Infinite Purity, we are sinners all alike" (p. 259).

11 Although Hester herself is unable to become the true prophetess of her society, she plays a role as adviser and guide that anticipates the role of the poet–priest in the nineteenth century. She offers encouragement by looking forward to a day when "the whole relation between man and woman [would be established] on a surer ground of mutual happiness" (p. 263).

Although Hawthorne's biography points to his belief in community, order, and moral restraint, his text suggests a more radical vision of freedom and equality for women.

12   A "wretched numbness held possession" of him, affecting, most significantly, not only his ability to create but his capacity for appreciating the natural world around him: "It went with me on my sea-shore walks and rambles into the country, whenever – which was seldom and reluctantly – I bestirred myself to seek that invigorating charm of Nature, which used to give me such freshness and activity of thought, the moment that I stepped across the threshold of the Old Manse. The same torpor, as regarded the capacitiy for intellectual effort, accompanied me home, and weighted upon me in the chamber which I most absurdly termed my study" (p. 35).

13   Carroll Smith-Rosenberg, "Sex as Symbol in Victorian America," in Jack Salzman, ed., *Prospects: An Annual of American Cultural Studies,* (New York, 1980), 5: 52. And she adds, "At no other period in American history has such a sexually repressive belief system been so elaborately delineated. Appearing suddenly in the 1830s and 1840s, it contrasts sharply with the sexual permissiveness of either the eighteenth or the twentieth century."

14   For the fullest examination of these connections, see Martha Banta, *Failure and Success in America* (Princeton, N.J., 1978).

15   Compare Michael Paul Rogin, *Subversive Genealogy: Politics and Art in Herman Melville* (New York, 1983), pp. 160–86. On reevaluations of Melville and the problem of the artist in the nineteenth-century American culture, see Larzer Ziff, *Literary Democracy* (New York, 1982); Michael Bell, *The Development of the American Romance: A Sacrifice of Relation* (Chicago, 1980); Henry Nash Smith, *Democracy and the Novel: Popular Resistance to Classic American Writers* (New York, 1978); and Myra Jehlen, "The Novel and the Middle Class in America," *Salmagundi* 36 (Winter 1977): 3–22. My own reading of *Pierre* stands in contrast to those that take the collapse of Pierre himself and the apparent narrative chaos at the end of the novel as resulting from Melville's own deteriorating psychological state. The present interpretation views these seemingly compulsive elements as the product of a comic vision that challenges reader expectations and denies traditional closure for thematic purposes.

16   *Pierre or The Ambiguities* (Northwestern–Newberry Edition), ed. Harrison Hayford et al. (Evanston and Chicago, 1971), p. 7. Pages numbers cited in parentheses in text hereafter.

16

That Hive of Subtlety: "Benito Cereno" and the Liberal Hero

JAMES H. KAVANAGH

> It is with fiction as with religion: it should present another world, and yet one to which we feel the tie.
>
> Melville, The Confidence-Man

It is worth remembering that critical approval of Herman Melville was belated and sporadic. Only after World War II did the short fiction of the 1852–56 period gain widespread critical acceptance, and then only with sharp disagreement over the relative success of the various stories. In a comment on *Pierre,* George Washington Peck succinctly expressed the annoyance of many contemporary reviewers with Melville's post–Moby-Dick fiction:

> We can afford Melville full license to do what he likes with "Omoo" and its inhabitants: it is only when he presumes to thrust his tragic *Fantocinni* upon us, as representatives of our own race, that we feel compelled to turn our critical Aegis upon him and freeze him into silence . . . he strikes with an impious, though, happily, weak hand at the very foundations of our society.
>
> Let him continue, then, if he must write, his pleasant sea and island tales. We will always be happy to hear Mr. Melville discourse about savages.[1]

If Peck's discourse can be taken as typical of a critical strategy that consigned Melville to a rather severe literary oblivion,[2] the twentieth century has seen quite a change in the dominant appraisal of Melville's literary "value" – a transformation from the *eccentric* to the *aesthetic* aptly

352

signified, for example, by the Yale University Library's reclassification (ca. 1930) of *Moby-Dick* from "Cetology" to "American Literature."[3] Such radical shifts in critical designation make Melville a particularly strong example of what we can call the ideological constitution of the aesthetic (or the literary).[4]

My concept of "ideology" here derives from Althusserian Marxism, where the word signifies not a set of explicit political ideas but a "'lived' relation to the real" determined by a matrix of psychosexual and social investments.[5] This relation is supported less by ideas than by preconscious images that "show" the subject a self-evident version of the social world and his or her place in it. "A society," Karl Mannheim says, "is possible in the last analysis because the individuals in it carry around in their heads some sort of picture of that society."[6] To which Althusserian theory would add, with some elaboration, "and of one's self."

Because ideology works most effectively through its *unconscious* hold on the subject, it resists being made conscious or explicit. An ideology structures "seeing" and "feeling" before it structures "thinking," and appears to have no historical or social specificity but to be simply the *natural* way of perceiving reality. Explicitly political ideas are anchored in this preconscious "'lived' relation to the real" that is ideology, and seem forced by the structure of the "real itself." Ideological conflicts can be deadly because at stake in them are not different *opinions,* but different *realities.* The ideological, in this sense, is not some mental sphere of dogma or doctrine[7] that one can embrace or reject at will (and that afflicts only *others,* who try to "impose" it on reality), but an unavoidable terrain of social practice, where collective imaginations are fabricated, where the social construction of reality is continually articulated with the constitution of the self.

Literature is a specific field of symbolic practice that works on these whole modes of imaging, living, and feeling the "reality" of a self and a social universe. It is as "'lived' relations to the real" that literature puts ideologies into play; literary work disassembles ideologies, breaking them from their former "natural" reality, fixing and displaying them on the stage of the text.[8] With this staging, the literary text *allows* a reader to see, and question, the historical and social specificity of one's assumed sense of self and social reality, to understand it *as* ideology. Whether a reader actually does deconstruct his or her ideological "reality," or whether she or he returns to it even more comforted, depends very much on how readings are directed by the social practice of literary criticism, whose function is to manage precisely this problem.

We can easily see how Peck's literary-critical practice explicitly judges a text's *literary* value in direct proportion to the permissibility of its ideological effects, defined within quite narrow limits; his criticism can only designate the "Herman Melville" of the late fiction as *unacceptable* for a canon that must, to be "literary," ratify the dominant mid-nineteenth-century bourgeois sense of coherent self and social order. A more flexible modern criticism has generated new and positive readings of Melville's entire corpus, based on another critical paradigm that seems to embrace even a text that, like "Benito Cereno," operates a critical irony against a representative of "our own race" and civilization. Yet, I should argue, this modern critical embrace often covers an equally tenacious ideological grip, in effect a more subtle rejection of the late Melville; this critical discourse recuperates his text as safe for "our" civilization's new ideological and literary-ideological values and self-images, in ways that actually deflect the irony that such criticism explicitly claims to identify and affirm.[9]

F. O. Matthiessen, for example, established a reading of "Benito Cereno" as a kind of gothic melodrama, whose portrayal of "evil" black mutineers betrays an insensitivity to the realities of slavery:

> In "Benito Cereno" . . . the embodiment of good in the pale Spanish captain and of evil in the mutinied African crew, though pictorially and theatrically effective, was unfortunate in raising unanswered questions. Although the Negroes were savagely vindictive and drove a terror of blackness into Cereno's heart, the fact remains that they were slaves and that evil had thus originally been done to them. Melville's failure to reckon with this fact within the limits of the narrative makes its tragedy, for all its prolonged suspense, comparatively superficial.[10]

Leslie Fiedler also found "Benito Cereno" confused and insensitive about black slavery, a conclusion he derived from identifying the innocent but befuddled mind of the "good" Captain Delano with Melville's own mind and the voice of the text. Thus could be ratified the metamorphosis of a Melville whom a conservative Peck found too critical into a Melville whom a liberal criticism now understands as not critical enough:

> Captain Amasa Delano fails to recognize the rebellion on a Spanish slave ship which he encounters, precisely because he is a good American. He is endowed, that is to say, with an "undistrustful good nature" and will not credit "the imputation of malign evil in man." . . . Though the fact of slavery, out of which all the violence and deceit aboard the Spanish ship had been bred, re-

mains a part of his own democratic world as well as Don Benito's aristocratic one, Amasa Delano is undismayed. . . . Indeed, Melville seems to share the bafflement of his American protagonist; a Northerner like Captain Delano, Melville finds the problem of slavery and the Negro a little exotic, a gothic horror in an almost theatrical sense of the word.[11]

Modern critical strategy, then, seems to promote readings of "Benito Cereno" as allegorizing the failure of innocence and perception – with Babo and the slaves representing a "terror of blackness" whose pervasive "Gothic horror" the "good American" (Delano) in his unfortunate "naïveté" fails to perceive, even as he is enmeshed in its complex layers of violence and deception. More complex critical elaborations construe the text as leading the reader into an infinite maze of irony and ambiguity, if not moral and epistemological uncertainty, until the story becomes a "paradigm of the secret ambiguity of appearances." These constructions are then implicitly ratified by recourse to Melville's own sense of cynicism, doubt, and confusion in a world unsure of its God or its truth.[12] The literary value of "Benito Cereno" is found, after all, in its irony and ambiguity, which more than compensate for its insufficient criticism of slavery.

"Benito Cereno" and "Herman Melville" have come to signify the sophisticated doubt and ambivalence now found everywhere in a literary canon redefined in the terms of a twentieth-century, postexistential liberal ideology. The point here is not to deny the irony and ambiguity in "Benito Cereno" but to question how critical suggestions for reading – for resolving or not resolving – such textual ambiguity necessarily situate the ambiguity, the text, and the criticism in some specific relation to extant ideological discourses and practices. If ideology is an "imaginary relationship . . . to [the] real conditions of [one's] existence,"[13] then one version of modern American bourgeois ideology (adopted, with pitifully different effects, by the bourgeoisie and all who come under its ideological domination) is to fail to imagine *any* relation to the real conditions of one's social existence. Any emphasis on Melvillean ambiguity must beware of the tendency to be drawn into this ideological gambit.

Along with these opposed evaluations given by successive paradigmatic readings of the literary "Herman Melville," we can find a set of what we might call insurgent readings, which find "Benito Cereno" expressing a radical or even revolutionary "ideology" (as "set of ideas"). These versions of ideological analysis tend also to appeal for justification to the "real" author, as the locus of a coherent opinion, formed prior to and represented *just as it is* in the text.[14] Thus, these very different conclusions proceed from the same critical problematic, governed by a shared ideology of the literary that takes for granted the terms ("author," "text," etc.) within which problems are invoked and resolved (or not resolved). This ideology defends itself as staunchly empiricist, insisting that the text is grounded in a toe-stubbing "reality"; but its empiricism tends to dissolve when the hard reality that ostensibly serves as the ground of text and meaning turns out to be some version of the authorial "mind." Thus, this problematic begs all questions, since *every* such reading tends to justify itself by conjuring into visibility, as a necessary effect of its own rhetoric and procedures, the appropriate "real" Herman Melville, anterior to the text and guarantor of its meaning.

My point is not to deny that there are "realities" on which what we commonly call the literary text depends, and that offer resistance to "just any" interpretation; my point is that the first reality we confront, stumble over, and cannot get behind, is the historically and ideologically overdetermined ensemble of procedures that determine the ways in which significance can be attributed to a literary text. This process of determination neither fixes a single essential meaning, nor remains equally indifferent to an infinitude of possible meanings, but typically unfolds as a struggle among a few interpretive tendencies, associated with definite, extra-literary, socio-ideological locations, that vie for predominance. It is the historical and social pressures on this process, transmitted (directly or indirectly) through literary institutions themselves, that both open and close possibilities of meaning in the literary text.

This is the strong sense in which the discrepant readings of Melville, and of "Benito Cereno," are determined more by critical ideologies working through readers than by any intentions of the "real" Herman Melville. The modern reader's relation to, or understanding of, this text cannot be judged by its *proximity* to Melville's opinions,[15] but by the force with which it operates theoretical investigations whose results and purposes Melville cannot be asked to ratify. Melville's political or philosophical purposes in writing "Benito Cereno" cannot determine what the modern critic can, or should, do or promote in reading the text, nor can they determine how to analyze the text's ideological effect—its effect, that is, on the dominant mode of "lived" social subjectivity among an audience of his contemporaries, *or* ours, or that of some other specific historical–ideological conjuncture.

Even if we could know exactly what the author *intended,* we would have to decide, using our own critical procedures, whether he *succeeded.*

Between authorial intention and textual effect are encountered the complex resistances of a specific literary practice: publishers, styles, audiences, events, critics, institutions. These determinations are necessarily
worked into the text, both at its moment of composition and in the
continuing process of its reconstruction, pulling it out of the control of
a single author-itative consciousness. Melville's authorial work involved more than simply *transferring,* as it was, some finished ideological formation from one place (the "real" – i.e., his "mind") to another
(the "text," now implicitly "unreal"); this work involved *producing* a
specifically differentiated ideological formation *that was not there before,*
and whose potential significance he could not entirely determine.[16] The
difference between intention and effect, then, results from the transformative labor involved in the production of any text *as* literary, as offering itself for a constitutive reading by an always-already-formed audience and an always-already-formed critical practice. It is a difference
that should be especially clear with Melville, who constantly complained (as noted later in this chapter) about the pressures that prevented him from presenting his ideas even "in the form" he preferred.

"Benito Cereno" is particularly provocative ideologically because it
does not remain a "discourse about savages," and the primitive "terror
of blackness" they supposedly represent. It becomes, rather, a discourse
that parodies the "civilized" mind itself, the mind of a specific social
formation: the "straight-thinking" Yankee mind with whose image our
culture is so familiar. In this sense, "Benito Cereno" can be read as a
discourse about discourse, about how the mind of a certain type of social
subject *talks to itself,* giving itself the evidence with which to feel and live
its own ruthlessness as "innocence" and "moral simplicity."[17] "Benito
Cereno" appears, then, to take as both its form of presentation and object
of critique a peculiar American ideology that sets an imaginary relation
to the world in which one can "feel" comfortable and innocent even
while one is actively working to reproduce repressive social relations.

"Benito Cereno," like much of Melville's late fiction, has been a
charged and controversial text for dominant critical ideologies because
it effects what Althusser calls an "internal distantiation" of an ideology, requiring us, through its principal character, "to 'perceive' . . .
from the inside, by an *internal distance,* the ideology in which it is
held."[18] This close insinuation of the reader into an ideology makes
the text available for readings whose ostensible criticisms of Delano
are framed in terms that, ironically, implicate the criticisms themselves
in the ideology Delano inhabits; such readings follow the paths of his
ideology that lead toward a kind of metaphysical speculation, slipping
into the presuppositions *of* his discourse in the same movement that

generates a "corrected" ironic reading of the character as too "naïve" or "good-natured." Yet the "internal distantiation" of "Benito Cereno" can also support another reading of the text's ideological effect, one that breaks definitively from the ideology of bourgeois innocence that holds Delano, Melville, and many of the text's American readers.

Like other Melville texts, "Benito Cereno" presents this double image of itself through an ironic narration, which establishes at once the "lived experience" of, and the "internal distance" from, a specific ideological "lived relation to the real." "Benito Cereno's" peculiar third-person, determinate point-of-view, quasi-stream-of-consciousness narration ironizes the "real" Amasa Delano's discourse from the *Narrative of Voyages and Travels*[19] with subtle, often minute, syntactical changes and framing devices; this narration *is* Melville's textualizing of the ideology, allowing the reader either to identify with the experience of the fictionalized American Captain, or to take a critical distance from it. The reader can, and indeed must (up to a point), "live" the textual experience from within Delano's peculiar subject position; but the text, in maintaining the difference between Delano's "eye" and its own "I," also allows the reader to see, this time as an object, "the way Delano sees."

That same syntax of long, complex-compound sentences within which Delano tries forever to bury the knowledge of his real activities within social relations, can be used by the critical reader as a map to extricate himself or herself from Delano's ideological maze, and discover its displayed but denied political significance. Because the reader is usually "deceived" along with Delano on first reading, this extrication requires a second reading that is not so much a rereading of the text "itself" as a reading of one's first spontaneous *relation to* the text. This second reading must be no less than an ideological analysis of one's relation to the text, and to the ideology it puts into production – a reading that indicates how the preconscious ideological matrix in which the reader is held (the "shifts and side-slippings" of even the twentieth-century reader's "ordinary consciousness")[20] is enough like that of Amasa Delano that we can be "fooled" into identifying with his "deception." By making us "follow the leader" through the ironic unfolding of Delano's ideology, the text becomes that ideology's immanent critique, bringing us up against the complex of violence and death that subvene the ideology, and allowing us to break from it.

This formal complexity can be read as resuming an anterior ideology of the "real" Melville in the sense that it textualizes his contradictory *relation to* – not his "ideas about" – the prevailing ideological sense of self and reality persistently reproduced by the system of social relations and literary practices in which he lived and worked. Melville, along with his contemporaries, certainly "bathed" in an ideology much like that of Amasa Delano. That he knew, or at least "saw" this somewhat differently did not mean he could escape it, and his literary practice was formed under its pressure. He lived this contradiction so acutely that the implicit force of this ideology, inhering in the apparatuses and practices of literary production, became for him an explicit form of censorship, as real and oppressive as that operated by any commissar: "Dollars damn me," he wrote to Hawthorne. "What I feel most moved to write, that is banned – it will not pay. Yet altogether write the *other* way I cannot."[21]

Although we do not claim that Melville would specify the "what" and "that" of his complaint with the same terms that will supply our reading of his text, it seems clear that Melville was working at once to conceal and to preserve a radical distance from dominant general and literary ideologies.[22] There are many ways of being "frozen into silence," and the ironic characterization of Delano in "Benito Cereno" could be read as an imaginary working up of Melville's own lived contradiction precisely in its determinate, critical "fixing" of this paralysis, of the inability to remain at ease within, or get definitively out of, a stifling ideology. Perhaps, indeed, we are using Melville's text to effect a more irreversible break from an ideology than he could.

Like any literary text, then, "Benito Cereno" is ambiguous and open because it has to be; its indeterminacy of meaning is real and forced – a condition to which the text is condemned by severe and specific forces, not a sign of some essential, metaphysical freedom lurking in language. The text eludes univocity only by being ensnared in a net of contradictory ideological demands. This determinate freedom of the text derives first from the conditions of its production – its emergence from the labor of an author working within/against bourgeois ideological practices that prevent the formulation of radical critique, save as double-edged irony or "anti-literary" silence. And the text cannot then escape the critical apparatus that makes it "literary" and renders its gaps and silences eloquent with ideologemes[23] carefully chosen to enlist the text for specific ideological strategies, specific modes of living the relation between self and social order. In both cases, the text becomes an instantiation of contradictions whose precise and final significance Melville cannot supply.

But *this* "ambiguity" is a *condition* of the text's existence in history and ideological practice, not its substantive or intrinsic *meaning*. Meaning is assigned to the text through a naïve or critical reading practice that provisionally fixes the text in relation to a given universe of ideological possibilities. To recognize the structural "ambiguity" of "Benito Cereno" as a field of ideological contention in no way demands, or even sanctions, construing its meaning in terms of the "ambiguity of appearances" – a meaning that in fact enlists the text for a particular ideological position far less radical than others to which it is open. The same word ("ambiguity") appears here, but in two entirely different problematics.[24]

Far from any New Critical autonomization of the "text-itself" with its "intrinsic" meaning, I intend to suggest that the text has *no* "meaning," except as it comes to instantiate some specific set of relations among dominant and insurgent, general and literary ideologies (including ideologies of "author," "text" "form," etc.). The meaning of the text is nothing but the history of such instantiations, of its successive re-construal/construction in changing literary and literary-critical practices. This reading of "Benito Cereno," like any other, attempts a transformative instantiation or enactment of the text, in order to inscribe it in new relations to dominant literary and general ideologies, and to make it effectively available for a certain form of teaching practice. As does any reading, it encourages certain specific meanings and excludes others, for reasons that derive not from Melville, or from the "text itself," but from a need provisionally to resolve the ongoing struggle over the ideological significance that will be associated with a text now recognized as having literary – that is, a kind of social – "value." Rather than autonomizing text or criticism, this view forces the critical reader to take responsibility for understanding how his or her work might help to reproduce or challenge a dominant ideology, and for consciously developing an appropriate theoretical and rhetorical strategy to intervene in that profoundly political, unceasing and unavoidable, struggle over the meaning of words, and of those peculiarly effective word-systems we call literary texts.

In this reading of "Benito Cereno," everything hinges on the character of that irony through which the text establishes an internal distance from a dominant ideology. The analysis of "Benito Cereno" must begin by breaking absolutely the seductive grip of identification between the reader and Amasa Delano, a grip not even loosened by the seemingly negative judgments of the American Captain carried in phrases like "moral simplicity" and "weak-wittedness."[25] Indeed, such a language remains perfectly consistent with Delano's own form of self-understanding – a semblance of critique that actually absolves him of all responsibility. A criticism that takes the grammar of Delano's ideological self-consciousness as its own is bound to reproduce his strategy of evasion through perplexity. It is not sufficient to understand the text's ironic critical distance from Delano as evoking an epistemological problem of knowledge and ignorance; this textual gap also opens the political–ethical question of Delano's implicit disavowal of an active responsibility within a set of social relations.

One should not have to belabor the text's careful internal historical framing of events. We can surely read as significant the setting of this story of a rebellion in 1799, a period flush with the triumphant victories of the American and French revolutions, a period whose "momentousness," as Melville elsewhere remarks, is unexceeded "by any other era of which there is record."[26] These victories promised a new social and political order, whose rational, democratic slogan of "liberty, equality, fraternity" (or "life, liberty, and the pursuit of happiness") was heard as the death knell of decadence, superstition, and arbitrary feudal privilege – as the "rectification of the Old World's hereditary wrongs"[27] – of which no country provided a more regressive example than Spain. The tension between the American and Spanish captains is heavily laden with these contrasts, as indicated in Delano's condescending, moralizing judgment of the "Spanish spite" that he thinks impels Cereno to punish Babo: "Ah," Delano sighs, "this slavery breeds ugly passions in man. – Poor fellow!"[28]

And this story is being written, of course, in 1855, at a time when the hypocrisy of that bourgeois democratic ideology had just been challenged (in Europe if not in America) by the revolutions of 1848; the repressive possibilities of that ideology had now become visible, including even the restoration of monarchist politics for the purposes of bourgeois reaction. In the United States at this time, the institution of chattel slavery that had for so long not only coexisted with but materially supported North American capitalist democracy was coming under direct attack in incidents like the *Amistad* rebellion – incidents that shook Northerners as well as Southerners.[29]

This is the frame in which one must read Captain Delano's inability to understand what he sees aboard the *San Dominick*. It is in this frame that one must register the deep, bitter irony with which the narration follows the intricate contours of Delano's mind, a mind the text describes as itself "incapable of satire or irony" (p. 75). There is no such thing as "ideology in general," and this text takes as its object not just any ideology but the specific form of bourgeois ideology exuding from the social relations of the more liberal sectors of a relatively advanced bourgeois society. At stake in this text is not the "problem of evil" as figured in the blacks, nor even the problem of precapitalist forms of social relations as figured in Cereno and Aranda, but the problem of

362 J. H. Kavanagh

ideology as figured in Delano; at stake is how a man like Delano –
neither a decadent aristocrat, nor even a Southern slaveholding American, but a "Northerner" from the most radical and abolitionist of states
(Massachusetts) – can think of himself as liberal, progressive, and char-
itable while staring in the face of his own racism, paranoia, and authoritarianism. At issue in "Benito Cereno" is how, for a man immersed in
Delano's ideology, a belief in one's own "goodness" and "moral simplicity" is not just "naïveté," but a necessary condition for the violent,
sometimes vicious, defense of privilege, power, and self-image.

Such sharp conclusions can be supported by a careful reading of how
the text's ironic narration superimposes what Delano thinks and says
over what he *does*. It is a mistake – it is *the* mistake – to read this text for
the ambiguous knowledge it gives at any moment of "events aboard
the San Dominick"; one must rather read the text for the unambiguous
knowledge it gives at every moment about Delano's ideological construction of, and self-insertion into, that situation. The text becomes
eminently readable once we assume *that* as what it seeks to communicate. As is generally recognized, the ironic stance toward Delano is
quickly and firmly established with his initial reaction to the sight of the
San Dominick:

> To Captain Delano's surprise, the stranger, viewed through the
> glass, showed no colors; though to do so was the custom
> among peaceful seamen of all nations. . . . Captain Delano's
> surprise might have deepened into some uneasiness had he not
> been a person of a singularly undistrustful good nature, not
> liable . . . to indulge in personal alarms, any way involving the
> imputation of malign evil in man. Whether, in view of what
> humanity is capable, such a trait implies, along with a benevo-
> lent heart, more than ordinary quickness and accuracy of intel-
> lectual perception, may be left to the wise to determine. (p. 55)

The ironic distancing of Delano's perceptions here is more severe
than one would expect for a character with whom the text supposedly
identifies more strongly than others, whose "bafflement" Melville
"seems to share." With the last sentence of this paragraph, the text
makes Delano an object of criticism bordering on derision, saying definitely, if indirectly, that he is stupid. Nor does the text unambiguously
associate his "undistrustful good nature" with any sense of moral virtue. Many critics take this formulation at face value as the text's precise
definition of Delano's "problem," but I should claim that the sentence
can be read with the "whether" governing the phrase about a "benevolent heart," as well as that concerning Delano's "intellectual percep-

tion," leaving it uncertain "whether . . . such a trait implies . . . a benevolent heart."[30] Thus, the language of the text begins on the first page of the story as a complicated discourse of formal deference to Delano, a discourse that actually squirrels away – conceals *and* preserves – radically negative judgments about him. The reader might *feel* that he or she has read something positive about Delano in this sentence ("benevolent heart") but the one characterization most clearly communicated is: "Delano is thickheaded." This characteristically Melvillean prose makes the text "difficult" for many readers and "flawed" for many critics, but it is not some kind of fault that can be dispensed with; it is a necessary condition of a textual production that distantiates an ideology within the discourse of that ideology itself.

Indeed, criticism has at times pondered Delano's "bafflement" with a humourlessness similar to his, often ignoring passages where the text becomes unmistakably *comic,* and dissolves Delano's sense of self-importance by making him a butt of its humor. In the scene, for example, where the "not unbewildered" Delano falls through the *San Dominick's* railing, a reader with the least pictorial imagination might find it difficult to keep from laughing *at* Delano:

> As with some eagerness he bent forward, . . . the balustrade gave way before him like charcoal. Had he not clutched an outreaching rope he would have fallen into the sea. The crash, though feeble, and the fall, though hollow, of the rotten fragments, must have been overheard. He glanced up. With sober curiosity peering down upon him was one of the old oakum-pickers. (p. 89)

And in the scene when an old sailor surreptitiously hands Delano a knotted rope, the text characterizes Delano's reaction with withering irony: "For a moment, knot in hand, and knot in head, Captain Delano stood mute" (p. 91). A critical reading should treat Delano's "bafflement" as he cannot treat the knot: "Undo it. Cut it. Quick." Otherwise, like him, it will prevent itself from seeing what *is* serious: in this instance, the fact that the old man's life is at stake.[31]

Given this kind of textual ridicule, which occurs as Delano cogitates on Cereno's puzzling behavior, it would seem consistent to find the text framing his thoughts about Cereno with equally severe irony. And, indeed, Delano's ruminations shift in a near schizophrenic pattern from a belief that everyone is conspiring to kill him to a satisfied certainty that everyone loves him too much to do him any harm. The following passage can be read as a kind of case study in megalomania, paranoia, and racism:

From something suddenly suggested by the man's air, the mad idea now darted into Captain Delano's mind, that Don Benito's plea of indisposition, in withdrawing below, was but a pretense: that he was engaged there maturing his plot, of which the sailor by some means gaining an inkling had a mind to warn the stranger against; incited, it may be, by gratitude for a kind word on first boarding the ship. Was it from foreseeing some possible interference like this, that Don Benito had, beforehand, given such bad character of his sailors, while praising the negroes; though, indeed, the former seemed as docile as the latter the contrary? The whites, too, by nature, were the shrewder race. A man with some evil design, would he not be likely to speak well of that stupidity which was blind to his depravity, and malign that intelligence from which it might not be hidden? Not unlikely, perhaps. But if the whites had dark secrets concerning Don Benito, could then Don Benito be any way in complicity with the blacks? But they were too stupid. Besides, who ever heard of a white so far a renegade as to apostatize from his very species almost, by leaguing in against it with negroes? These difficulties recalled former ones. Lost in their maze, Captain Delano . . . had now regained the deck. (pp. 89–90)

With this passage, one can give a truly "symptomatic" reading of Delano:[32] megalomania – Delano feels he is at the center of everyone's attention, not because of what he has done or might do, but because of what he *is;* thus, Delano thinks that the lowly sailor risks his own life to save Delano out of "gratitude for a kind word"; paranoia – everyone, under the control of the mirror-image figure of authority (Cereno), is plotting against him, plotting to take away *his* power; racism – Delano puts every possible construction on the evidence before him except the correct and most obvious one, and this possibility he refuses to consider because the blacks are "too stupid."

Delano's misrecognition here exemplifies the "overdetermination of the real by the imaginary" in ideology.[33] There is a real enough sense in which Delano is the center of everyone's attention and in mortal danger, but this sense is not congruent with the "reality" he perceives. Delano *sees* as "real" only the situation that conforms to his imaginary struggle with his sole "equal" in rank, race, class, power, and therefore (for Delano) intelligence – Cereno. Cereno functions as a kind of mirror for Delano in the text: The similarity of their names and their tendency always to confront each other face-to-face suggest Cereno's "imaginary" status. The puzzle of Cereno, then, becomes the puzzle of what Delano sees in his mirror, how it reflects his own image back to him; and Delano sees many disturbing things: arbitrary cruelty, decadence, weak-mindedness, and so on. But most disturbing, he sees his own ultimate vulnerability, an image that seems to be dissolving before his eyes – a nightmare image for Delano indeed. Delano wants Cereno to be a mirror in which his own image of power and security is confirmed and justified, and when Cereno fails to play that role appropriately, Delano then "sees" him as a figure of evil, plotting against Delano's own power.

Delano, then, can be read as a textual figure of an ideology in crisis. For Delano, the crucial task is to reconstruct a confirming "reality" of power and authority – the "natural" authority of racial superiors (whites), and the political authority of social superiors (captains, "gentle-men"). The whole scene aboard the *San Dominick* appears as unsettlingly *unreal* to Delano because it presents an image of social power relations that lacks the appropriate reference points for any reality he can construct. Thus, Delano's anxieties center on loss of control – either his own possible loss of the *Bachelor's Delight,* or his perception of Cereno's loss of control of the *San Dominick.* What most confuses Delano about the scene aboard the *San Dominick* is the absence of the familiar network of repressive practices and apparatuses that would ratify his own heavily imaginary sense of himself and of reality, that would reproduce the ideology, the "lived relation to the real," which would make his world *look* as it should:

> At bottom it was Don Benito's reserve which displeased him. . . . So that to have beheld this undemonstrative invalid gliding about, apathetic and mute, no landsman could have dreamed that in him was lodged a dictatorship beyond which, while at sea, there was no earthly appeal.
> . . . Some prominent breaches, not only of discipline but of decency, were observed. These Captain Delano could not but ascribe, in the main, to the absence of those subordinate deck-officers to whom, along with higher duties, is intrusted what may be styled the police department of a populous ship. (pp. 63–64)[34]

What most calms Delano, then, is the image of restored authority, an image that alternates between the megalomaniac project of restoring the "weak" Cereno to his command, and the paranoid project of heading off the "evil" Cereno's plot against Delano's own command. The text makes explicit Delano's fantastic version of aid to the foreigner as counterplot:

Evidently, for the present, the man [Cereno] was not fit to be intrusted with the ship. On some benevolent plea withdrawing her command from him, Captain Delano would yet have to send her to Conception, in charge of his second mate. . . .

Such were the American's thoughts. They were tranquilizing. There was a difference between the idea of Don Benito's darkly pre-ordaining Captain Delano's fate, and Captain Delano's lightly arranging Don Benito's. (p. 83)

In this story about the suppression of a revolt off the coast of Chile, can modern criticism read the text as sharing Delano's self-serving idea of this "difference"? We shall see how Delano goes about "lightly arranging" the fate of the *San Dominick*.

Given the text's consistently critical and ironic fixing of Delano, notions of "moral simplicity" or of a "bafflement . . . Melville seems to share" with his "good American" protagonist about "the problem of slavery and the Negro" seem entirely inadequate to describe how the text projects a Delano who muses thus:

There is something about the negro which, in a peculiar way, fits him for avocations about one's person. Most negroes are natural valets and hair-dressers; taking to the comb and brush congenially as to the castinets, and flourishing them apparently with almost equal satisfaction. There is, too, a smooth tact about them in this employment, with a marvellous, noiseless, gliding briskness, not ungraceful in its way, singularly pleasing to behold, and still more so to be the manipulated subject of. And above all is the great gift of good-humor. Not the mere grin or laugh is here meant. Those were unsuitable. But a certain easy cheerfulness, harmonious in every glance and gesture; as though God had set the whole negro to some pleasant tune.

When to this is added the docility arising from the unaspiring contentment of a limited mind, and that susceptibility of blind attachment sometimes inhering in indisputable inferiors, one readily perceives why those hypochondriacs, Johnson and Byron – it may be, something like the hypochondriac Benito Cereno – took to their hearts, almost to the exclusion of the entire negro race, their serving men, the negroes, Barber and Fletcher. But if there be that in the negro which exempts him from the inflicted sourness of the morbid or cynical mind, how, in his most prepossessing aspects, must he appear to a benevolent one? Captain Delano's nature was not only benign, but familiarly and humorously so. At home, he had often taken rare satisfaction in sitting in his door, watching some free man of color at work or play. If on a voyage he chanced to have a black sailor, invariably he was on chatty and half-gamesome terms with him. In fact, like most men with a good, blithe heart, Captain Delano took to negroes, not philanthropically, but genially, just as other men to Newfoundland dogs. (pp. 99–100)

The text certainly "knows" what is going on here.[35] The critical reader knows, even if she or he did not on *first* reading, that Delano is himself the "manipulated subject of" a rebellious black man threatening to slit his captive white master's throat. With this assumption, it is impossible to read this text as identifying with Delano's ideological perception of the blacks; it is impossible not to read this text as fixing for a scathing ironic gaze the preconscious mind-set of a character whose ignorance of his own mortal danger derives precisely from his *seeing* blacks as equivalent to "Newfoundland dogs." Nor, again, is there any reason to assume that the textual discourse is more ironic about the "limitation" of Babo's mind than about the "benevolence" of Delano's. The text, furthermore, painstakingly frames in this scene, as sharing the attitudes of paternalism and condescension toward blacks, two pillars of English literary culture – Johnson and Byron. This scene, then, unites in a unique literary tableau the Spanish aristocrat, the liberal-minded American Yankee, and the Tory and "revolutionary" literati – diverse instantiations of general and literary ideologies – under the sign of shared delusions about "inferior" people, about servitude, power, and the security of privilege. All of these men remain unable, literally, to *see* the reality of the hatred and incipient rebellion that stares them in the face, because ideology constructs for them a "reality" upon which their eyes (and their "I's") can rest with comfort, finding a reassuring reflection of their own essential innocence, self-satisfaction, and power.

It would be no less ideologically imposing to read this scene in any other way, and certainly to read it as anything like, as Matthiessen would have it, a symptom of "Melville's failure to reckon with the injustice of slavery within the limits of the narrative [which] makes its tragedy . . . comparatively superficial."[36] "Benito Cereno" can be read this way only from within an ideology similar to that suggested by the text's evocation of Johnson and Byron; the text can be read this way, that is, only from within a lived relation to a literary canon that would limit the range of possible meanings for this text of a "great American author" in the same way Delano's ideology limited his perception of the possible meanings of the actions of "Don Benito" aboard the *San*

Dominick – an ideology that would make it impossible to conceive that Melville's text might be so radically "in complicity with the blacks." Such a discourse finds in every possible meaning of this text ratification of its own image of the world, of literature, and of itself: Either Melville is to be slapped on the wrist for being a little racist and corrected with a moderate dose of liberal humanism, or (sometimes "and") he is to be congratulated for showing us once again (what all "great literature" shows us) that evil and ambiguity are everywhere, if only we would see them, and that the only (regrettably imperfect) choice an intelligent person can make is for the "benevolent" and "genial" mind itself. Such a critical ideology hardly imagines that this text might be read "with" the blacks, nor even that it might be read irrevocably *against* the "good American," let alone that reading it might rudely force the reader to choose between accepting or refusing Delano's ideological "lived relation to the real," "undistrustful good nature" and all. In my view, Melville's narrative gives the reader just this choice, just this opportunity, with more discomfiting force than most explicitly political critiques of ideology.

Lest the reader register the paternalism of Delano's ideology as referring only to "inferior" *races,* the text describes Delano's thrill at the sight of his own sailors approaching in the small boat:

> The sensation here experienced, after at first relieving his uneasiness, with unforeseen efficacy soon began to remove it. The less distant sight of that well-known boat – showing it, not as before, half-blended with the haze, but with outline defined, so that its individuality, like a man's, was manifest; that boat, *Rover* by name, which, though now in strange seas, had often pressed the beach of Captain Delano's home, and brought to its threshold for repairs, had familiarly lain there, as a Newfoundland dog; the sight of that household boat evoked a thousand trustful associations, which, contrasted with previous suspicions, filled him not only with lightsome confidence, but somehow with half humorous self-reproaches at his former lack of it. (pp. 91–92)

Ideology is precisely that network of "a thousand trustful associations" upon which Delano seizes with glee at the sight of his boat. The boat and the associations it evokes are singularly comforting reminders of the relationships of power and authority that encode the social universe of a man like Delano, and secure his position as "master," this time over social inferiors of his own race but of a different class, to be treated – like the Negro – with the condescension and paternalism normally reserved for a "Newfoundland dog." And the simple textual movement of the set-off adjectival phrase "like a man's," indicates with subtle but definite emphasis that, for someone immersed in Delano's ideology, every man's individuality functions as a reminder of his own power. Indeed, so inflated is Delano with the impending verification of the natural social order promised by the arrival of "his men," that he virtually dissolves in regression, assuring himself that nobody can hurt him because he is innocent (Who accuses him? Of what?) and God watches over him:

> "What I, Amasa Delano – Jack of the Beach, as they called me when a lad – I, Amasa . . . to be murdered here at the ends of the earth, on board a haunted pirate ship by a horrible Spaniard? Too nonsensical to think of! Who would murder Amasa Delano? His conscience is clean. There is someone above. Fie, Fie, Jack of the Beach! you are a child indeed; a child of the second childhood, old boy; you are beginning to dote and drule, I'm afraid." (p. 92)

When a text has a character warning himself that he is "beginning to dote and drule," the critical reader might legitimately read the ironic distance signified as insufficiently measured by notions of "naïveté," or "undistrustful good nature." And when the text, a few sentences later, puts in Delano's head the words: "Ha! glancing towards the boat; there's *Rover;* good dog; a white bone in her mouth. A pretty big bone though, seems to me," one can easily read an association between Delano's vision of the surf as a "bone" in the mouth of his boat and the text's image of the skeleton affixed to the prow of the *San Dominick* – a bone on which this ideology will have to choke. Captain Delano of the *Bachelor's Delight* seems to have a "good nature" much like that of those other Melvillean bachelors:

> For these men of wealth, pain and trouble simply do not exist: the thing called pain, the bugbear called trouble – those two legends seemed preposterous to their bachelor imaginations. How could men of liberal sense, ripe scholarship in the world, and capacious philosophical and convivial understandings – how could they suffer themselves to be imposed upon by such monkish fables? Pain! Trouble! As well talk of Catholic miracles. No such thing. – Pass the sherry, sir. – Pooh, pooh! Can't be![37]

If ideology is a kind of preconscious grid that prestructures all experience (and any idea) in a form tending to validate those held within the
ideology, a certain Yankee bourgeois ideology confirms just this social
self-perception as "men of liberal sense." It has been something of an
ironic fate for "Benito Cereno" that its simultaneous internalization of
and distantiation from this ideology have allowed critical readings to
mis-take for their object, rather than ideology, the "problem of the
blacks" or "the problem of evil" – thereby "drowning criticism in com-
passion" (p. 69), and presenting this text as safe for all "men of liberal
sense." Take the following excerpt from a criticism that sincerely tries
to account for the text's ironic distance from Delano's attitude toward
the blacks:

> The fascinating enigma of *Benito Cereno* revolves around the
> question of what Melville intended his blacks to be. . . .
>   *Benito Cereno* is neither an abolitionist tract nor a condemna-
> tion of the Negro race. Evil and ferocity are not confined to the
> blacks; heroism and virtue are not the exclusive trait of the
> whites. Both blacks and whites are part of the humanity whose
> dark side Melville will not deny. Babo is part man, part
> beast. . . . But the white man, who ironically espouses a reli-
> gion of . . . brotherhood, is also a beast. Who can say where
> the blame rests for the carnage unleashed aboard the flaming
> coffin? The untamed and daemonic forces rampant on the *San
> Dominick* characterize . . . all of mankind.[38]

By taking as its starting point that Melville's text is about "his"
blacks rather than "about" ideology because "of" ideology, this reading
follows the road of good intentions into a familiar humanist ideological
cul-de-sac. We can almost see Delano and his confreres of "liberal sense
and ripe scholarship" nodding with approval at hearing that everyone
has a dark side and a light side, is half man and half beast; and we can
hear the whispered "Not I!" in response to the comforting rhetorical
query: "Who can say where the blame rests?" For "men of liberal
sense," the "carnage" and "daemonic forces" that provide the conditions of their own social possibility remain unspoken problems in a
moralizing discourse about the problem of the blacks or the problem of
evil.

But "Benito Cereno" tenaciously refuses to let Delano's ideology off
its ironic hook. In fact, the text explicitly presents Delano's misrecognition of himself and his situation not just as naïveté (that is, a mistake
based on an assumed *innocence*), but as the condition of a deliberate,
unnecessary, and massively lethal violence. Such a sharp assertion takes

strong evidence from that textual moment when, after realizing that he has been fooled to the last minute and beyond by the blacks' manipulation of his ideology, Delano orders his men to attack the *San Dominick* and recover control from the rebellious slaves:

> Upon inquiring of Don Benito what firearms they had on board the *San Dominick,* Captain Delano was answered that they had none that could be used; because, in the earlier stages of the mutiny, a cabin-passenger, since dead, had secretly put out of order the locks of what few muskets there were. But with all his remaining strength, Don Benito entreated the American not to give chase, either with ship or boat; for . . . , in the case of a present assault, nothing but a total massacre of the whites could be looked for. But, regarding this warning as coming from one whose spirit had been crushed by misery, the American did not give up his design.
>
> The boats were got ready and armed. . . .
>
> The officers . . . , for reasons connected with their interests and those of the voyage, and a duty owing to the owners, strongly objected against their commander's going. Weighing their remonstrances a moment, Captain Delano felt bound to remain; appointing his chief mate – an athletic and resolute man, who had been a privateer's-man – to head the party. The more to encourage the sailors, they were told, that the Spanish captain considered this ship good as lost; that she and her cargo, including some gold and silver, were worth more than a thousand doubloons. Take her, and no small part should be theirs. The sailors replied with a shout. (p. 120)[39]

This passage gives the reader some definite textual characterizations of Delano: (1) Delano knows that the blacks are effectively unarmed, *and* that they are unaware of this disadvantage, because the firearms have been "secretly put out of order." (Indeed, heroism is "not the exclusive trait of the whites"); (2) Delano is unconcerned about the possible mass slaughter of blacks *and* whites; he insists on pursuing his scheme forcibly to restore the proper image and order of the "real," despite the impassioned ("with all his remaining strength") plea of Cereno, who has the only semblance of "real" interest in recapturing the *San Dominick;* Delano, because of his class-political position as the representative of the interests of the officers and owners as a whole,[40] piously refrains from going, sending instead his chief mate, an ex-pirate (the kind of subordinate whom men like Delano often keep around to do their "police" work), to lead the charge; and (3) again, the simple textual movement of a phrase set off by commas – "they were told" – suggests subtly but definitely that Delano lies to his own men, provoking their greed in order to encourage their participation in a deadly expedition in which they have no real interest. "They were told," "the more to encourage them," that the *San Dominick* contained gold and silver; but the text gives two inventories of the ship's cargo, and in neither is there any mention of this inspirational gold and silver.[41] The communicative effect here, what the text tells the reader, is not that there *was* gold, but that Delano *said* there was, and why he said it. The text again communicates that Delano's discourse is the "subject" of its own, that his ideology is its "problem."

Delano's ideology reveals, at the core of its innocence and "whiteness," a skeletal infrastructure that is death and violence. Not only does the *San Dominick* have "death for the figurehead, in a human skeleton; chalky comment on the chalked words below, '*Follow Your Leader*'" (p. 119), it also has death for its avenging angel – death in the form of a fleshed-out whiteness sent by Delano through the agency of his first mate. If the reader but recall the text's rendering of Delano's early spontaneous perception of the blacks:

> There's naked nature, now; pure tenderness and love, thought Captain Delano, well pleased.
> This incident prompted him to remark the other negresses more particularly than before. He was gratified with their manners: like most uncivilized women, they seemed at once tender of heart and tough of constitution; equally ready to die for their infants or fight for them. Unsophisticated as leopardesses; loving as doves. Ah! thought Captain Delano . . . (p. 87)

– if the reader but *read* Delano's pleasure and gratification at this "primitive" tenderness and strength, under the text's rendering of the following scene of attack on the *San Dominick,* then "Benito Cereno" will register all its scathing ironic effect, irrevocably displaying the cruelty and hypocrisy of Delano's "lived relation to the real." This scene, at once lyrical and cynical in its evocation of the desperate but futile struggle of the blacks, and the text in which it is set, can be read as achieving at least one aspect of authorial intention with unanticipated force, presenting "another world, and yet one to which we feel the tie":

> With creaking masts, she came heavily round to the wind; the prow slowly swinging into view of the boats, its skeleton gleaming in the horizontal moonlight, and casting a gigantic

ribbed shadow upon the water. One extended arm of the ghost seemed beckoning the whites to avenge it.

"Follow your leader!" cried the mate; and, one on each bow, the boats boarded. Sealing spears and cutlasses crossed hatchets and handspikes. Huddled among the longboat amidships, the negresses raised a wailing chant, whose chorus was the clash of the steel.

For a time, the attack wavered; the negroes wedging themselves to beat it back; the half-repelled sailors, as yet unable to gain a footing, fighting as troopers in the saddle, one leg sideways flung over the bulwarks, and one without, plying their cutlasses like carters' whips. But in vain. They were almost overborne, when, rallying themselves into a squad as one man, with a huzza, they sprang inboard, where, entangled, they involuntarily separated again. For a few breaths' space, there was a vague, muffled, inner sound, as of submerged sword-fish rushing hither and thither through shoals of black-fish. Soon, in a reunited band, and joined by the Spanish seamen, the whites came to the surface, irresistibly driving the negroes toward the stern. But a barricade of casks and sacks, from side to side, had been thrown up by the mainmast. Here the negroes faced about, and though scorning peace or truce, yet fain would have had respite. But, without pause, overleaping the barrier, the unflagging sailors again closed. Exhausted, the blacks now fought in despair. Their red tongues lolled, wolflike, from their black mouths. But the pale sailors' teeth were set; not a word was spoken; and, in five minutes more, the ship was won. (p. 122)[42]

This rendering of the personal courage of black men and women is a remarkable achievement in American literature for any year, let alone 1855. Even the white sailors' courage stands as an implicit indictment of Delano, the absent author of this slaughter, who can rely on others to enforce his peculiar sense of justice. And the simple textual movement of "as troopers in the saddle" and "like carters' whips" marks this text as, indeed, no mere "abolitionist tract" but a resonant gloss on the history of a civilization. In a characteristic Melvillean trope, the scene closes where the literary ends, in a space where words cannot be spoken.[43]

Certainly, Melville's text gives us the blacks as uncompromising in their use of force, deception (but not self-deception), and courage to resist enslavement; and then it gives us Delano (not "the whites")[44] as ruthless in his use of violence, deception, and the manipulation of the greed and strength of others to annihilate any challenge to his self-deceiving "reality" of power, authority, and superiority. And if one is to choose how to *read* this çarefully specified situation (as the reader must, and does), it is of no help for criticism to translate the text into a metaphysics of light versus dark, or man versus beast, terms whose only possible function is to make a choice seem impossible by offering ambivalence as the only possible choice.

Delano's violent repression of the blacks, against Cereno's own entreaties, seeks to reconstruct that comforting order of things in which other men assume their proper relation to him, a relation like that of "Newfoundland dogs." Delano wants to believe – wants really to *see* – this order, not as constructed by his own egotistical and violent practices, but as justified by his own essential innocence. Cereno's deposition, forming a separate part of the narrative, serves only to underscore Delano's bad faith. The repeated phrase "the noble Captain Amasa Delano" forms part of a ritual courtroom litany, and the critical reader can take it less as a sincere expression of Cereno's respect than an ironic interpellation of the Yankee trader as the kind of "gentleman" whom the decadent Spanish aristocracy recognizes as one of its own.[45] And Delano's assertion of a moral distance from the actions of his subordinates, in stopping "with his own hand" sailors' attempts to kill "shackled negroes," must be understood in relation to his responsibility for instigating the slaughter. For Delano, the American, the sense of his own innocence and goodwill serves as a condition for the forcible maintenance of political and social relations that support his privilege. In the ideological discourse of a man like Delano, of the "civilization" that produces such men, the use of armed force must never be understood for what it is (the social equivalent of the class-interested violence of aristocrats and slaveowners), but as a mistake resulting from an excess of goodness, a mistake to be abolished from memory and history as quickly as possible. If this is naïveté, it is *imperial* naïveté – one of the specific conditions of a peculiarly *American* imperialism.

But Cereno, the European, knows better. And whereas Delano restores the order of his world, with his own "good nature" as its imaginary linchpin, Cereno finds himself unable to continue in self-deception, unable to ignore that death-dealing which is the real lynchpin of the social order, unable, it seems, even to exist as he was before. In the last section of the narrative, we find a final, telling exchange between Cereno and Delano. Both now possess full knowledge of the events aboard the *San Dominick*, but only one has been dislodged from his ideological lived relation to a specular, self-justifying "real." The American's desperate, insane plea for the saving power of his own innocence and closeness to Providence now rings especially hollow against the Spaniard's polite but definite charge of responsibility, and against Cereno's own profound self-transformation, even self-dissolution:

> "You have saved my life, Don Benito, more than I yours; saved it, too, against my knowledge and will."
>
> "Nay, my friend," rejoined the Spaniard, courteous even to the point of religion, "God charmed your life, but you saved mine. To think of some of the things you did – those smilings and chattings, rash pointings and gesturings. For less than these, they slew my mate, Raneds; but you had the Prince of Heaven's safe conduct. . . ."
>
> "Yes, all is owing to Providence, I know: but the temper of my mind that morning was more than commonly pleasant, while the sight of so much suffering, more apparent than real, added to my good-nature, compassion, and charity, happily interweaving the three. Had it been otherwise, doubtless, as you hint, some of my interferences might have ended unhappily enough. . . . Only at the end, did my suspicions get the better of me, and you know how wide of the mark they then proved."
>
> "Wide, indeed," said Don Benito sadly; "you were with me all day; stood with me, looked at me, ate with me, drank with me; and yet, your last act was to clutch for a monster, not only an innocent man but the most pitiable of all men. To such degree may malign machinations and deceptions impose. So far may even the best men err in judging the conduct of one with the recesses of whose condition he is not acquainted." (pp. 138–39)[46]

Cereno, "courteous even to the point of religion," speaks in a discourse informed by the ironic nuance of the text. He speaks of Delano's protection by "the Prince of Heaven": The reader might easily infer that the text means Christ, but is not Christ a king?[47] And what was Delano's "last act"? When he lashed out at Cereno, was that the *last* time he lashed out at "the most pitiable of all men," the kind of man "with the recesses of whose condition he is not acquainted"? Does the text here mean Christ or Satan, Aristocrat or Slave? Do these phrases speak for themselves? For Melville? For us? The textual ambiguity cannot be resolved by peering into the blinding light of the words "themselves," but only in that shadow cast upon them by an unspoken relation to an ideology.

So Cereno, in the shadow of ideology, wastes away and dies, know-ing without illusion what he was and is, but unable to communicate why "the negro" still haunts him, and why it might come back to haunt the Yankee himself. "Slowly and unconsciously gathering his mantle about him, as if it were a pall," Cereno falls deadly silent: "There was no more conversation that day" (p. 139). Again, the text marks a space where words must end. Cereno remains unable to speak of the empty inscriptions of his rank and command – the ceremonial dress, sword, and scabbard he was forced to don for Delano; he refuses to confirm Babo's identity as the accused.[48] Having been made to oc-cupy the position of the slave – having been forced to choke on the ideology of the master – Cereno, like Babo, stands mute, knowing the futility of speech in the face of an infinite, closed ideological discourse whose only pronouncement can be, whose every pronouncement is, death.

In death, Babo's decapitated gaze forms a circuit of silent communi-cation with Cereno and Aranda, a circuit of complicity in which each acknowledges the shared burden of death, violence, and oppression, and a circuit from which Amasa Delano is excluded, not – as he might like to believe – because he is any better or more innocent than they are, but because he thinks that he is. In the final scene of the text, the characters fall on either side of a divide, not of race or even of slavery, but of ideology – of the ability to continue living within social relations whose precondition is the discourse of self-deception:

> Some months after, dragged to the gibbet at the tail of a mule, the black met his voiceless end. The body was burned to ashes; but for many days, the head, that hive of subtlety, fixed on a pole in the Plaza, met, unabashed, the gaze of the whites; and across the Plaza looked towards St. Bartholomew's church, in whose vaults slept then, as now, the recovered bones of Aranda; and across the Rimac bridge looked towards the mon-astery, on Mount Agonia without; where, three months after being dismissed by the court, Benito Cereno, borne on the bier, did, indeed, follow his leader. (p. 140)

The text here is not quite "frozen into silence" but has written its way into that final, voiceless space where words no longer rule. This laden silence is a characteristic Melvillean ending, invoking a sense of futile defiance in the face of an ideological, "literary," discursivity that often pronounces the text's decapitation in order to immortalize, uni-versalize, and enshrine it as an object of specular fascination for a domi-nant "lived relation to the real":

The primary theme of "Benito Cereno," determined by Melville's emphasis, is Delano's struggle to comprehend the action. . . . At the end two conclusions are made about the meaning of the facts: first, that reality is a mystery and hard to read, and second, that evil is real and must be reckoned with. To which should perhaps be added, there are some evils cureless and some mysteries insoluble to man. . . . The mystery of "Benito Cereno" is a mystery of evil, contrived by an evil will [Babo's]. . . . Delano has one vital disability. . . . He does not comprehend "of what humanity is capable." Beyond this, the problem is real. It is the creation of a complex and malignant mind [Babo's], a "hive of subtlety," which has deliberately contrived its own confusions.[49]

Such a reading ignores all the incisive ideological effect of a text that evokes with ironic precision the first triumphal period of bourgeois revolutionary ideals, even while written as the bankruptcy of those ideals is being seriously challenged by popular struggles. Such a reading can only dilute the power of a text that, written on the eve of a civil war over slavery, speaks beyond the issue of slavery to racial oppression as a constant shadow within larger questions of political and social relations – questions to which even the "Northerner" is blind. Such a reading dispels all the formal tension of a work that strains implicitly to enunciate a radical, devastating critique of an ideology that it is constrained explicitly to enter. Indeed, such a reading, with its "reality is a mystery" and "evil is real," marks the passage of "Benito Cereno" into the court of a "literary" ideological apparatus – its self-anticipated fate, for which it prepared its own ambiguous silences.

But our historical and ideological conjecture allows us to restore the strong voice of this text's irony, encouraging it to give, not cringing witness against itself, but compelling testimony that its prosecutors – who for the moment must listen – may not want to hear. We can hear "Benito Cereno" say that the "mystery" of violence and social oppression can only be disclosed through analysis and dissolution of that even more complex and malignant "hive of subtlety," which deliberately contrives its own confusions: the ideology of men like the "good American," Amasa Delano.

Notes

1 George Washington Peck, in *Melville: The Critical Heritage,* ed. Watson G. Branch (New York: Routledge & Kegan Paul, 1974), pp. 316–17, 321.

378   J. H. Kavanagh

2   Between 1863 and 1887, an average of twenty-three copies of *Moby-Dick*
    were sold in the United States each year; after the first Melville "revival"
    (centering on *Moby-Dick*), between 1921 and 1947, the book sold more
    than one million copies. See H. Hetherington, *Melville's Reviewers: British
    and American, 1846–1971* (Chapel Hill: University of North Carolina Press,
    1961), p. 221. George Thomas Tanselle notes that, of the fifty-six editions
    of *Moby-Dick,* half have been published during the last twenty-five years,
    and all but six after 1920, with many more copies of the book sold each
    year now than the total sold in the nineteenth century. See Tanselle, *A
    Checklist of Editions of Moby-Dick, 1851–1976* (Evanston, Ill.: Northwestern
    University Press and the Newberry Library, 1976).
3   According to F. O. Matthiessen, in *From the Heart of Europe* (New York:
    Oxford University Press, 1948), p. 45, *Moby-Dick* was still catalogued
    under "Cetology" in 1930.
4   See my essay "To the Same Defect: Toward a Critique of the Ideology of
    the Aesthetic," *The Bucknell Review* 27, no. 1, (Fall 1982): 102–123, for a
    more complete discussion of this ideological constitution of the aesthetic.
5   Louis Althusser, *For Marx* (New York: Random House, 1970), pp. 232–
    33.
6   Karl Mannheim, *Ideology and Utopia,* trans. Louis Wirth & Edward Shils
    (New York: Harcourt Brace, 1964), p. xxiii. I have commented on the
    usefulness of Mannheim's remark for understanding the Althusserian the-
    ory of ideology in "'Marks of Weakness': Ideology, Science, and Textual
    Criticism," *Praxis,* no. 5 (1980): 23–38.
7   Under the entry for "ideology" in the most recent *MLA Bibliography,* one
    finds "*See also related term:* Doctrines" (Modern Language Association,
    *1981 MLA International Bibliography of Books and Articles on the Modern
    Languages and Literatures,* vol. 1: British American, Australian, English-Cana-
    dian, New Zealand, and English-Caribbean Literatures [New York: Modern
    Language Association, 1983], p. A168).
8   Louis Althusser, *Lenin and Philosophy and Other Essays* (New York:
    Monthly Review Press, 1971), pp. 222–23.
9   I make no claim to account for any representative cross section of the
    voluminous Melville criticism. I consider as constituting a kind of critical
    "paradigm" those readings that have set the terms for critical debate over a
    long period, and that have been the most widely anthologized. In Richard
    Chase, ed., *Melville: Twentieth-Century Views* (Englewood Cliffs, N.J.:
    Prentice-Hall, 1972), for example, we find articles by Matthiessen, Arvin,
    Fogle, and Chase himself. These readings have formed a kind of unavoid-
    able threshold for Melville readers.
10 F. O. Matthiessen, *American Renaissance* (New York: Oxford University
    Press, 1941), p. 508. For analysis of the ideological and critical tensions in
    Matthiessen's "Christian socialism," see: Giles B. Gunn, *F. O. Matthiessen,
    The Critical Achievement* (Seattle: University of Washington Press, 1975);
    Fredrick Stern, *F. O. Matthiessen: Christian Socialist as Critic* (Chapel Hill:

University of North Carolina Press, 1981); George Abbott White, "Ideology and Literature: *American Renaissance* and F. O. Matthiessen," in George Abbott White and Charles Newman, eds., *Literature and Revolution* (New York: Holt, Rinehart & Winston, 1972), pp. 430–50; and Leo Marx, "Double Consciousness and the Cultural Politics of F. O. Matthiessen, *Monthly Review*, 34, no. 9 (February 1983): 34–56.

11 Leslie Fiedler, *Love and Death in the American Novel* (Cleveland: Meridian Books, 1962), pp. 400–401. See also Chase's *Herman Melville: A Critical Study* (New York: Macmillan, 1949), p. 157, where he asserts that Captain Delano is "a benevolent and courageous man."

12 See Warner Berthoff, *The Example of Melville* (Princeton, N.J.: Princeton University Press, 1962), p. 153. See also Lawrance Thompson, *Melville's Quarrel with God* (Princeton, N.J.: Princeton University Press, 1952), passim. Interesting, too, is the chapter on "Benito Cereno" in William B. Dillingham, *Melville's Short Fiction, 1853–1856* (Athens: University of Georgia Press, 1977), pp. 227–70. Note also the argument Fiedler implies above: that Melville's attitudes toward slavery are the same as Delano's because they are both from the same region.

13 Althusser's definition of ideology in his essay on "Ideology and Ideological State Apparatuses," in *Lenin and Philosophy*, pp. 162–65.

14 H. Bruce Franklin's work, asserting that Melville was a "consciously proletarian writer," provides the best example of this implicit justification. See H. Bruce Franklin, "Herman Melville: Artist of the Worker's World," in Norman Rudich, ed., *Weapons of Criticism: Marxism in America and the Literary Tradition* (Palo Alto, Calif.: Ramparts Press, 1976), pp. 287–310; "On the Teaching of Literature in the Highest Academies of the Empire," in Louis Kampf and Paul Lauter, eds., *The Politics of Literature: Dissenting Essays in the Teaching of English* (New York: Pantheon, 1972), pp. 101–29; and *The Victim as Criminal and Artist* (New York: Oxford University Press, 1978), pp. 31–72. See also Marvin Fisher's strong treatment in *Going Under: Melville's Short Fiction and the American 1850s* (Baton Rouge: Louisiana State University Press, 1977). Many readings of "Benito Cereno" have strayed outside the dominant critical paradigms, and are as a result much less widely known; examples include: E. F. Carlisle, "Captain Amasa Delano: Melville's American Fool," *Criticism* 7, no. 4 (Fall 1965): 349–62; Joseph Schiffman, "Critical Problems in 'Benito Cereno,'" *Modern Language Quarterly* 11, no. 3 (September 1950): 317–24; Jean Fagin Yellin, "Black Masks: Melville's 'Benito Cereno,'" *American Quarterly* 22, no. 3 (Fall 1970): 678–89; Jack Matlack, "Attica and Melville's 'Benito Cereno,'" *American Transcendental Quarterly*, no. 26 (supplement; Spring 1975): 18–23; Glenn C. Altschuler, "Whose Foot on Whose Throat? A Re-examination of 'Benito Cereno,'" *College Language Association Journal* 18, no. 3 (March 1975): 383–92. Theoretical differences notwithstanding, I find all these readings cogent, and support their political effect; they also highlight in various ways much of what I emphasize in Melville's text.

15 A reading is only constrained by Melville's intentions insofar as its purpose is explicitly to reconstruct those intentions – and even then the procedures followed would be determined by the reader. But this is not what is usually understood by, or done in, the process of construing a text's "meaning." It is precisely the conflation of meaning and intention that is at issue. I can only allude here to the insufficient hyperrationalism, posing as historicism, in counterarguments, such as those of E. D. Hirsch in *Validity in Interpretation* (New Haven, Conn.: Yale University Press, 1967), that insist on authorial intention as the ground of critical interpretation.

16 See Terry Eagleton, *Criticism and Ideology* (London: New Left Books, 1976), especially chapters 2 and 3 on the literary text as putting ideology into production.

17 Newton Arvin, *Herman Melville* (New York: Sloane, 1950), pp. 239–40.

18 Althusser, *Lenin and Philosophy*, p. 223.

19 Amasa Delano, *Narrative of Voyages and Travels in the Northern and Southern Hemispheres Comprising Three Voyages Around the World Together with a Voyage of Survey and Discovery in the Pacific and Oriental Islands* (Boston: E. G. House, 1817), privately printed for the author. This edition bears the seal of William S. Shaw, District Clerk of Massachusetts, probably related to Lemuel Shaw, the Chief Justice of Massachusetts and Melville's father-in-law. See also the excellent article by Brook Thomas, "The Legal Fictions of Herman Melville and Lemuel Shaw," *Critical Inquiry* 11, no. 3 (September 1984): 24–51.

20 Berthoff, *The Example of Melville*, p. 153.

21 Jay Leyda, ed., *The Portable Melville* (New York: Penguin, 1976), p. 430.

22 Fisher, in *Going Under*, gives a strong account of Melville as a writer who "went underground." See Eagleton, *Criticism and Ideology*, chapter 2, for the categories of "general" and "literary" ideology.

23 Fredric Jameson coins this word to refer to "the smallest intelligible unit of the essentially antagonistic collective discourses of social classes." See *The Political Unconscious: Narrative as a Socially Symbolic Act* (Ithaca, N.Y.: Cornell University Press, 1981), p. 76.

24 For a more rigorous distinction between literary theory, a practice oriented to analyzing the text's determinate structural openness to various ideological ensembles, and literary criticism, a practice oriented toward a provisional fixing of a meaning for the text in ongoing ideological contention, see my "Marxism's Althusser: Toward a Politics of Literary Theory," *Diacritics* 12, no. 1 (Spring 1982): 43–44.

25 Arvin, *Herman Melville*, p. 239.

26 Preface to "Billy Budd," in Leyda, *The Portable Melville*, p. 637.

27 Ibid., p. 637.

28 Herman Melville, "Benito Cereno," in *The Piazza Tales* (New York: Hendricks House, Farrar, Straus, 1948), p. 105. This text is an exact copy of the first edition of *The Piazza Tales*, which Melville himself prepared from the original *Putnam's Monthly Magazine* version of the story, making some

changes. Further citations are referenced in my essay by page numbers from the Hendricks House edition, with footnotes clarifying any of Melville's changes from the *Putnam's* version.

29 The *Amistad* rebellion (in which Spaniards and Americans fought over captured slaves) had a progressive denouement, with the Supreme Court freeing the insurgent slaves rather than sending them back. (See J. Q. Adams, *Arguments of John Quincy Adams before the Supreme Court of the United States, in the case of the United States, Apellants, vs. Cinque, and others, Africans, Captured in the Schooner Amistad* [New York, 1841]. But this trend was reversed near the time Melville wrote "Benito Cereno," with the Supreme Court decision to return fugitive slaves Thomas Sims and Anthony Burns. The *Creole* incident, the Nat Turner rebellion, and the Toussaint L'Ouverture uprising have all been mentioned as possible historical raw materials for Melville's text. See Altschuler, "Whose Foot on Whose Throat?," pp. 388–89, and Fisher, *Going Under,* pp. 109, 116.

30 If this seems a convoluted reading of the sentence, the syntax, I believe, allows it. The aptness of such a reading would depend on how one construes the point the sentence is trying to make, and one's spontaneous construal of that point is exactly what the critical reader cannot take for granted. In general, moreover, *any* reading of a sentence in this text is somewhat convoluted. Rather than seeing this problem in terms of an infinitely repeating hermeneutic circularity, I suggest seeing these sentences as determinately undecidable – undecidable, that is, except on taking up one of the finite number of determinate positions that would decide a meaning.

31 The reader does not learn of the old man's death until p. 135.

32 A *loose* reference to the Althusserian concept of "symptomatic reading." See *For Marx,* pp. 69–70, and Althusser and Etienne Balibar, *Reading Capital* (London: New Left Books, 1975), pp. 32–33.

33 Althusser, *For Marx,* p. 234.

34 This passage also explicity alludes to the need for such "police officers" on an "emigrant ship"; in his *Narrative,* the real Captain Delano worries about a possible mutiny on his own ship when he comes upon the Spanish slaver.

35 Strictly speaking, one should say that the text "knows" nothing, but that in giving a reading, criticism must construct either a text that operates *as if* it knows what is going on here, or one that operates as if it does not, and that the latter construction would require a critical labor at least as peculiar, controverted, and heavily ideologically determined as the former.

36 Matthiessen, *American Renaissance,* p. 508.

37 Herman Melville, "The Paradise of Bachelors and the Tartarus of Maids," in Warner Berthoff, ed., *The Great Short Works of Herman Melville* (New York: Harper & Row, 1969), p. 209.

38 Edward S. Grejda, *The Common Continent of Man: Racial Equality in the Writings of Herman Melville* (Port Washington, N.Y.: Kennikat Press, 1974), pp. 136, 147. For a view that finds Melville regressively reproducing

racist stereotypes, see Sidney Kaplan, "Herman Melville and the American National Sin," in Seymour L. Gross and John Edward Hardy, eds., *Images of the Negro in American Literature* (Chicago: University of Chicago Press, 1966; fourth printing, 1972), pp. 135–62; this article first appeared in the *Journal of Negro History* 41 (1956): 311–38; 42 (1957): 11–37. Its inclusion, along with Fiedler's section on "Benito Cereno," in a 1972 anthology underscores my point about the tenacity of "paradigmatic readings" within the ideological practice of literary criticism.

39   The original text in *Putnam's Monthly Magazine of American Literature, Science, and Arts* (July–December, 1855), p. 636, reads "a privateer's man, and, as his enemies whispered, a pirate."

40   This straight Marxist gloss on Melville's phrase beginning "for reasons connected with their interests," suggests some of the problems in attempting to have the "real" Herman Melville ratify a textual reading. Whether the "real" Herman Melville would have made or would have agreed with such a similar yet significantly different restatement himself (knowing all its theoretical and political implications) is, strictly speaking, irrelevant; it remains a fair reading of the sentence in the text, as "close" as any that could be given. Matthiessen's tendency to recuperate social analyses within metaphysical categories leads him to assert that Melville saw "an incurable antagonism . . . where two classes, the officers and the men, are in perpetual conflict, and where the smaller of the two groups is backed by all the controls of power" (*American Renaissance,* p. 402), and then to use this assertion to make the point that Melville "arrived at a more thoroughgoing conception of human evil than Hawthorne" (p. 404).

41   Cereno gives the first inventory on p. 65: "a general cargo, hardware, Paraguay tea and the like – and . . . that parcel of negroes"; the *Putnam's* text (p. 358) omits "hardware." Melville's deliberate additions to the cargo inventories for the *Piazza Tales* edition can give an "intentional" *defense* (not positive support) for reading the omission of the gold and silver (which Delano's 1818 *Narrative* does not mention explicitly) as a significant absence. Characteristically, too, the text never tells us that the sailors *got* any gold or silver, only that Delano, in typically evasive fashion, *promised* them "no small amount"; since "nothing" is indeed "no small amount," Delano's discourse, even here, constructs itself so as to avoid any kind of positive, unambiguous self-definition for which he could be held accountable.

42   The *Putnam's* text (p. 637) includes a comma after "swinging."

43   I find that this recurrent Melvillean gesture of ending in silence symptomatizes a suspicion, even a refusal, of the mode in which further literary discourse would recuperate the text. It is almost as if Melville's texts were signaling: "This is where *literary* analysis must stop" – a silent signal, obscured just enough so that a garrulous critical practice can take it as an occasion for endless literary commentary.

44   The white American sailors, as indicated, are deceived into jeopardizing their lives for no interest of their own; two of the white Spanish sailors are

deliberately killed by the boarding party on the suspicion that they "favored the cause of the negroes" (p. 136).

45 "Interpellation" is Althusser's word for the "hailing" process through which ideologies at once address and constitute subjects. It is taken, in fact, from legal and judicial practice, where it means something like "summons" or "subpoena" – "calling one before the court to identify one's self and testify." See the essay "Ideology and Ideological State Apparatuses," in *Lenin and Philosophy*.

46 The *Putnam's* text reads "clutch for a villain." This again indicates the problem with searching for authorial ratification for a reading. Although we can probably never know Melville's reason for this seemingly minute revision, his deliberate replacement of "villain" with "monster" gives a connotation and an objective indeterminacy of meaning that supports the Cereno/Babo ambivalence I suggest we can read in the word.

47 A well-known (certainly to Melville) literary allusion to Satan as "Prince of Heaven" is in Beelzebub's speech to Satan in *Paradise Lost* 1:128–32: "O Prince, O Chief of many throned Powers/That led the embattled Seraphim to war/Under thy conduct, and, in dreadful deeds/Fearless, endangered Heaven's perpetual King,/And put to proof his high supremacy."

48 "Before the tribunal he refused. When pressed by the judges he fainted. On the testimony of the sailors alone rested the legal identity of Babo" (p. 140).

49 Richard Harter Fogle, *Melville's Shorter Tales* (Norman: University of Oklahoma Press, 1960), pp. 121–22, 124–25.

17

Melville and
Cultural Persuasion

DONALD E. PEASE

The broad topic of this discussion will be the scene of cultural persuasion at the time of the publication of *Moby-Dick*. Some of the more powerful moments in literature occur when characters are persuaded to see reality in a form they would otherwise reject, as when Othello is persuaded by Iago to distrust Desdemona; when the serpent persuades Eve that God has denied her knowledge; or when Ahab persuades the crew to embark on a mission unlike any they had signed on for. And in each of these moments, the means of persuasion involves terms crucial to the organization and maintenance of the differing cultures. The famous quarterdeck scene in *Moby-Dick* exemplifies the dynamics of cultural persuasion in mid-nineteenth-century America, and I begin accordingly with an analysis of Ahab's means of persuasion in that scene.

As it happened, Ahab's first mate voices the only opposition, pointing out, with a sure sense of the persuasive power of marketplace rationality, that he has signed on to hunt whales for the Nantucket market and not to hunt them for his captain's vengeance. Vengeance on a dumb brute motivated only by instinct, Starbuck righteously concludes, constitutes a form of blasphemy. The terms of Starbuck's dissent, grounded as they are in a strong faith in the American system of free enterprise, with the religious piety in that common ground underscored by the accusation of blasphemy, a designation usually reserved for religious controversy, could, out of their own persuasive power, initiate a mutiny. But they do not.

An understanding of why they do not requires an analysis of Ahab's response:

"Hark ye yet again – the little lower layer. All visible objects, man, are but as pasteboard masks. But in each event – in the living act, the undoubted deed – there, some unknown but still reasoning thing puts forth the mouldings of its features from behind the unreasoning mask. If man will strike, strike through the mask! How can the prisoner reach outside except by thrusting through the wall? To me, the white whale is that wall, shoved near to me. Sometimes I think there's nought beyond. But 'tis enough. He tasks me; he heaps me; I see in him outrageous strength, with an inscrutable malice sinewing it. That inscrutable thing is chiefly what I hate; and be the white whale agent; or be the white whale principal, I will wreak that hate upon him. Talk not to me of blasphemy, man. I'd strike the sun if it insulted me. For could the sun do that, then could I do the other; since there is ever a sort of free play herein, jealously presiding over all creations. But not my master, man, is even that fair play. Who's over me? Truth hath no confines. Take off thine eye! more intolerable than friend's glarings is a doltish stare."[1]

In responding in this way, Ahab does not so much answer Starbuck's charges as he invests those charges with a power Starbuck is unable to command. Starbuck's words resound with righteous indignation; Ahab relocates righteous indignation in a context capable of converting it into the full-fledged wrath of a prophet. In taking Starbuck down a little lower layer, in other words, Ahab also deepens the context for Starbuck's indignation. Implicitly, however, Ahab in this dive also chastens Starbuck for the shallow purposes to which he puts his religion. If Starbuck is willing to kill whales for the capital their oil will bring in Nantucket, he is not willing to see them as representative of any purpose other than his need for capital. His profit motive makes it necessary for him to see the whales as dumb brutes. Ahab's vengeance, in informing the whale with a deeper cosmic design, turns Starbuck into the blasphemer. In treating the whale as a pasteboard mask for his profit motive, Starbuck necessarily confirms the other alternative in Ahab's apocalyptic either/or. For the Christian whose rationality is equiprimordial with the profit motive, there is indeed "nought beyond" this market context. Ahab speaks with all the rage of a man who can no longer be satisfied with this conception. So instead of responding in the terms sanctioned by Starbuck's context, Ahab declaims with all the rage of a man who experiences Starbuck's context as a further source for his sense of lost freedom.

In other words, Ahab does not respond either in or to the terms of Starbuck's argument; rather, he displaces Starbuck as well as the terms of his argument onto another scene. On this other scene, however, Starbuck cannot continue his argument with Ahab. For Ahab has cast the terms (the profit motive, the Nantucket market, the instrumental reason) informing Starbuck's argument into the role of oppressive agents. Ahab's recasting of the terms of his argument with Starbuck from a marketplace context into an apocalyptic realm, converts his public argument with Starbuck into Ahab's private argument with the cosmic plan. And this *conversion,* in its turn, reverses the positions of the combatants. Instead of remaining the cruel captain whose exploitation of his crew would justify Starbuck's mutiny, Ahab, in turning into the enraged victim of a cruel cosmic design, lays claim to the right to mutiny. In taking Starbuck down onto *his* little lower layer, he *acts out* Starbuck's motive for mutiny, but does so on a *scene* that has at once co-opted the terms of Starbuck's potential mutiny but also virtually eliminated any part for Starbuck to play. On this other scene, in other words, Ahab idealizes the impulse to mutiny. By elevating defiance onto an apocalyptic scene where it appears utterly coincident with his character, Ahab, instead of remaining a force to be defied, gives defiance its most noble expression.

In laying prior claim to Starbuck's defiance, however, Ahab does not lessen Starbuck's anger. In bringing Starbuck up against his own rage, Ahab further exploits the resources in this other scene. As an enraged man who now feels all the rage he needs to kill Ahab, Starbuck no longer can claim the character of a rational, Christian man. Whereas formerly he could oppose Ahab precisely because of the clear distinction between Ahab's rage and his own moral identity, Starbuck now knows a state of mind enabling him to identify Ahab's rage with an impulse of his own inner life.

After provoking Starbuck to "anger-glow," Ahab, in the most remarkable move in this extraordinary scene, does not bring Starbuck up against his apocalyptic rage but gently chides Starbuck to let go of the anger Ahab *has agreed to embody alone.*

> "So, so, thou reddenest and palest; my heat has melted thee to anger-glow. But look ye, Starbuck, what is said in heat, that thing unsays itself. There are men from whom warm words are small indignity. I meant not to incense thee. Let it go. Look! see yonder Turkish cheeks of spotted tawn – living, breathing pictures painted by the sun. The pagan leopards – the unrecking and unworshipping things, that live; and seek, and give no

reasons for the torrid life they feel! The crew, man, the crew!
Are they not one and all with Ahab, in this matter of the
whale? See Stubb! he laughs! See yonder Chilean! he snorts to
think of it. Stand up amid the general hurricane thy one tost
sapling cannot, Starbuck. And what is it? Reckon it. 'Tis but to
help strike a fin; no wondrous feat for Starbuck. What is it
more? From this one poor hunt, the best lance out of all Nantucket, surely he will not hang back, when every foremast-
hand has clutched a whetstone? Ah! constrainings seize thee; I
see! the billow lifts thee! Speak, but speak! – Aye, aye! thy silence, then, *that* voices thee." (p. 144)

In this passage Ahab completes his elimination of Starbuck from the
scene of persuasion in which the motives for action are determined.
Earlier, Ahab provoked his own reaction to the universe, a defiance
grown out of rage, in Starbuck. In this passage he recovers defiance as
his trial and not the burden of a man who can now recover his rightful
place – not in Ahab's world but with the rest of the crew.

In his encounter with Starbuck, Ahab has elicited his inner life, the
rage against a potentially nihilistic universe, which Starbuck must
deny in order to remain himself. And Ahab acts out that inner life as
his means of dominating the Starbuck who can *free himself from rage* by
finding it thoroughly perfected in Ahab's extraordinary character.
Once located on his scene of persuasion, Ahab ceases to be a locus for
Starbuck's dissent; instead, he elevates Starbuck's dissent into apocalyptic status where dissent and a final reckoning become indistinguishable from each other. In this elevation, however, Ahab also utterly
separates what we might call the *ideological motives for action,* the
struggle between an utterly self-reliant man and oppressive cosmic
forces, from the individual's action. Once he has voiced *his* rationale
for hunting the whale, Ahab does not expect Starbuck to hunt for the
same reasons alluded to on Ahab's scene, but expects him to return to
a scene more in keeping with his character. After revealing the powerful forces at work in his inner world, Ahab releases Starbuck from the
need to "stand up amid the general hurricane" and enables him to
return to his appropriate position with the crew, where instead of
hunting whales for either cosmic revenge or for the profit motive he
will merely "help strike a fin." Having established the world of motives onto the scene where he will control the resolution, Ahab converts the crew into a realm *informed* and *determined* by this other scene
but, as is the case with the world of the pagan leopards, living and
seeking without the need to understand the motives for their actions.

Ahab's scene of persuasion collapses the space of argument, where dissent would otherwise be acknowledged, into an opposition – that between him and cosmic forces – whose terms carry the conclusion within their organization.

That Ahab manages all this in cadences borrowed from Shakespeare only underscores the "scenic" character of his separation from the crew. If he talks to the men at all, he talks to them in a language that immediately encloses him in a theatrical frame: a theatrical frame, moreover, claiming all the "unapproachable" cultural power that Melville, in his review of Hawthorne's *Mosses from an Old Manse,* claimed Shakespeare's wielded over the mob.[2] Thus, Ahab not only "acts out" and "ideally resolves" the principle of rebellion he evokes in the crew, but he does so in a language so invested with cultural power that they can only be inspired by the cultural heights to which Ahab elevates their will to rebel. In short, Ahab embodies not only the crew's inner life but also the best means of articulating it.

In transforming Starbuck's dissent into a pretext for the demonstration of the force of his character, Ahab effectively silenced any opposition from the crew. As if to supply the opposition the crew did not, the formulators of the American canon, from F. O. Matthiessen to the present, have set the freedom they find displayed not in Starbuck's dissent but in Ishmael's narrative against the totalitarian will at work in Ahab's polity. Now, although I began by claiming the broad topic for this discussion would be the scene of cultural persuasion at the time of *Moby-Dick,* I must confess to a more personal motive – a failure to remain persuaded by the reading of *Moby-Dick* that has become canonical, the one in which Ishmael proves his freedom by opposing Ahab's totalitarian will. In this chapter I do not wish merely to prove the superiority of an alternative reading but to argue that the reading to which I was not persuaded appropriated *Moby-Dick* to quite a different scene of cultural persuasion, the global scenario popularly designated as the "Cold War." The Cold War may initially seem an unfit context for a discussion of *Moby-Dick,* but I shall argue that the Cold War is crucial both for the canonical reading of that narrative and for its ongoing placement within the rationalist context F. O. Matthiessen called the "American Renaissance."

Unlike other paradigms in the American sphere of political discussion, but like Ahab in his "dialogue" with Starbuck, the Cold War scenario does not mediate or adjudicate discussion, but in recasting the terms of the discussion into the opposition (between the United States and the Soviet Union) organizing its scenario, it derives all of its explanatory force by simply being the fundamental ground for political persuasion. It is persuasive, that is to say, without either having resulted *from* discussion among individuals with differing opinions or having persuaded a liberal nation *to* any action other than the acceptance of the scenario.

The best way to ascertain the compelling force of its persuasiveness is to attempt to locate any geographical territory or political question that could not be accommodated by the Cold War frame. In totalizing the globe into a super opposition between the two superpowers – the free world supervised by the United States and the totalitarian countries under Soviet domination – the Cold War can recast all conflicts anyplace in the world in terms of this pervasive opposition. So inclusive is this frame and so pervasive is its control of the interpretation of world events that there appear to be no alternatives to it. Because this scenario co-opts the universe of argumentation, there is no moving outside its frame. As soon as we might believe we have moved outside this area, we discover we still must use its terms and their accompanying fore-gone conclusion. And anyone wishing to question this frame rather than to oppose the two superpowers elementing it can witness, on the world stage, this opposition already acted out, as it were, in the interna-tional arena called the "third world." For whatever the specifics of third-world conflicts, whether in El Salvador, Chile, or Chad, and however alien they may appear to first-world concerns, in fact they are assimilated to the ideological opposition between the United States and the Soviet Union.[3]

What we understand through this paradigm are not historical facts or specific historical events but a way of organizing their relationship. The organization of the opposition provides the conclusive formulation for every political opponent. And as the explanation for every argument, the Cold War scenario appears persuasive without having undergone the work of persuasion. Because the terms of the opposition already carry the conclusion within their organization, the space of argument has been collapsed. In positing the conclusion rather than arriving at it through argument, the Cold War scenario renders implicit what never has to become explicit. And in translating explicit political argument into the implicit resolution of that argument,[4] the Cold War scenario silences dissent as effectively as did Ahab in the quarterdeck scene.

Now, in what follows I wish to use the term "scene of cultural persuasion" to designate the ideological work performed in two differ-ent cultural contexts: that at work in the culture of the time of *Moby-Dick*'s publication and that at work in the culture that has elevated *Moby-Dick* into a masterwork of the American canon. The conception of the difference in the ideological work performed by these two different scenes releases a context sufficiently alienated from the Cold War to make *Moby-Dick* susceptible to another reading.

The scenes of cultural persuasion generated by the Cold War and by Captain Ahab both work through a form of radical displacement – one in which the specific terms of conflict or dissent are recast in other terms and on another scene. Captain Ahab, when confronted with Starbuck's commonsense argument against his revenge quest, converts the commonsense opposition into a scenario in which Ahab's belief in his right to utter self-reliance has been violated by cosmic design. Ahab, in other words, embodies nineteenth-century faith in the self-made, self-reliant man. And in embodying this faith, the ideological ground for Starbuck's right to dissent, Ahab cannot be perceived as opposing Starbuck's right to dissent. Instead he speaks *as* the ideological principle, the belief in absolute freedom, justifying Starbuck's right to dissent. As the enabling ground for Starbuck's dissent, Ahab cannot be responsive to the specific terms of Starbuck's dissent; instead he provides Starbuck with an occasion to witness what sanctions this right: Ahab's embodiment of *absolute freedom.*

Ahab's displacement of the terms of Starbuck's dissent onto another scene *resolves* the implicit contradiction between Starbuck's rights and Ahab's demands by elevating that contradiction into an ideal, *revolutionary* opposition between a free Ahab and a tyrannical universe. With an even greater display of efficiency, the Cold War scene can displace any opposition against the scene itself into one of the agencies of the opposition. So when a political analyst as astute as, say, Noam Chomsky writes about the distortions of the Cold War frame, he can find himself pictured, in the reviews of his work, as the dupe of a totalitarian power. In short, the Cold War scenario manages to control, in advance, all the positions the opposition can occupy. And all the oppositions, whether of the Batista regime against Cuban rebels, the Israelis against the Palestinians, or Ishmael against Ahab, can be read in terms of "our" freedom versus their totalitarianism.

Both scenes of cultural persuasion put into words the same fundamental operation: the displacement of potentially disorienting political arguments into a context where the unquestioned ground, the ideological subtext justifying political dissent, can empty the terms of the political argument of their historical specificity and replace them with abstract ideological principles – Ahab's absolute freedom in the case of *Moby-Dick,* America's freedom as opposed to Soviet totalitarianism in the case of the Cold War.

But the problem with the appropriation of *Moby-Dick* by critics who have written with a Cold War consensus is that they have converted

Ahab into a figure whose totalitarian will opposed the freedom displayed in Ishmael's narrative formulations, rather than, as we suggested in our discussion of the quarterdeck scene, the figure whose belief in absolute freedom constituted the basis for any of his crew's – whether Starbuck's or Ishmael's – exercise of freedom. The Cold War frame, in other words, flatttens into an opposition between two different characters, a contradiction between absolute and individual freedom, displayed in Ahab. In Melville's time, Ahab's need for absolute power over the crew was interpreted in the psychological terms of *monomania*[5] rather than the political term "totalitarianism." And, as I will suggest, it is not at all clear that for Melville, Ishmael was any more immune to the contradictory pulls between individual and absolute freedom than was Ahab. Although they represented two different rhetorical traditions, neither these traditions nor the characters representing them quite contradicted so much as they complemented one another in the formation of a national character quite different from that of postwar America.

In coming to terms with the difference between these two cultural periods, it is best to begin with a document on the American Renaissance written in 1941, the year of America's entrance into a world war that would make necessary the Cold War scenario as a means of postwar containment.[6] I refer to the criticism of F. O. Matthiessen, whose work on the cultural period in which Melville wrote *Moby-Dick* would establish American literature as a discipline and America as a culture, at a time America needed such a self-consensus to acknowledge the great tradition it stood to lose to a totalitarian power as different from the Soviet Union as Nazism was from Communism. At a time when America needed to be educated to the global duties of renaissance men whose loyalty was to America as a nation with a national tradition great enough to enable it to take its place as a free nation among free nations, Matthiessen would meet what he called the need of every great civilization, "like the Renaissance," to create "its own heritage out of everything in the past that helps it to transcend itself,"[7] with the publication of *American Renaissance: Art and Expression in the Age of Emerson and Whitman.* His choice of an age was timely. For those were the years when the United States, in confronting the issue of slavery, union, and expansionism, would decide to wage a just war destined to establish her identity as a nation among nations.

Curiously, however, as if not to threaten the coherence of the cultural space called the *American Renaissance,* Matthiessen, although he did not completely eliminate them, at least discounted such political questions informing his own earlier work as class inequality and the extension of democracy to economic as well as political levels, even as he reduced the political questions informing the age he called the American Renaissance to the opposition between what he called the Emersonian will to virtue and Ahab's will to power. Yet in 1941 Matthiessen could exclude certain political issues, for the political questions were as clearly defined then by the international arena as the Cold War claims to define them today: in both cases, as the struggle of the free world against a totalitarian power. What was needed was what *American Renaissance* provided: the designation of a cultural power morally superior to that of any totalitarian power with which the free world was then at war. And not the least sign of that cultural power was the American Renaissance's claim for a canonical place among the American masterworks for a work that had only recently been discovered: a survivor from the period of greatness in America's past, and a text that in its plot enacted the survival by a free man of the destructive actions of a totalitarian figure. *Moby-Dick,* in getting into the *American Renaissance,* seemed to prefigure America's power to get the free world through a war.

Acting as a means of consensus formation as well as canon definition, Matthiessen's American Renaissance *displaced* the need to acknowledge dissenting political opinions from the past onto the power to discover an unrecognized masterwork that guaranteed a future for a free world. Among the dissenting opinions *American Renaissance* silenced was Matthiessen's own, for, in returning to the time of Whitman and Emerson, his political aspirations for a democracy free of class division could be treated as already achieved – in the past. But with the return, after World War II, of political opinions – most specifically the anticapitalism of *From the Heart of Europe* – to his literary work, the progenitor of the American Renaissance became, in the recasting of him in the position of "fellow-traveller"[8] rather than cultural hero, the sign of the cultural power of another consensus formation. In reading Matthiessen's dissenting opinions as the discourse of the enemy within, the Cold War paradigm turned him into one of its first victims.

As we have seen, Matthiessen anticipates this repressive activity in his own work of consensus formation, silencing not only his own potentially disruptive political opinions but those of the other politicians and orators he simply excluded from the American Renaissance. More precisely, Matthiessen did not quite leave them out altogether but consigned them to a subordinate context, one easily assimilated by the cultural consensus he formulated through Emerson and Whitman. In the years after the war, with the disappearance of the need for a united cultural front, we might say that another F. O. Matthiessen, unpersuaded by the consensus formation underwritten by the American Renaissance, appeared. Before we can hear this other Matthiessen, however, we have to locate for him a context other than the *American Renaissance,* that, like the Cold War, silenced his dissent.

Writing as he did at a time in the international political arena marked by Nazi hegemony, when national self-consciousness could not appear merely locally political, Matthiessen separated politics from a cultural politics indistinguishable from consensus formation. But, writing in the years when the Vietnamese War made national self-consciousness appear indistinguishable from the political rhetoric of the Cold War, Sacvan Bercovitch found the Cold War rhetoric supported by another tradition that he called the tradition of the American jeremiad.[9] And he found a broad-based locus for this form precisely in the rhetoric Emerson and Whitman shared with the orators and politicians of the American Renaissance. If for F. O. Matthiessen the American Renaissance proved its power as a cultural consensus by silencing dissenting political opinions, for Bercovitch the American jeremiad derived all its cultural force at precisely that moment in the nation's history when dissenting *political* opinions over such explosive issues as union, slavery, and expansionism would make a difference in the very form of the nation handed over from the past.

But, like the Cold War paradigm it prefigures, the American jeremiad did not quite come to terms with these explosive issues. Rather, it put them into other terms: other terms, moreover, that made these issues indistinguishable from those surrounding the single event – the American Revolution – that, once resolved, seemed to have made up the nation's mind once and for all. Seeing issues in terms of the American Revolution, that is, precluded them from becoming explosive political issues. For the Revolution, in its office as the fulfillment of the Puritan Divine Mission, lost its status as a historical event that took place and turned into a perpetual national resource, a rhetorical means for making up the nation's mind over whatever issue presented itself. Displaying the same power to *alienate opposition* we found at work in the Cold War scenario, the jeremiad compels any listener intent on issuing his own dissenting opinion to discover that his dissent has, in the American Revolution, already achieved its ideal form. So dissent becomes indistinguishable from a national revolutionary ideal, which, Bercovitch argues, has in its turn become the ideological representation of the free enterprise system.

When translated into the form of the American jeremiad, political issues become occasions for Scripture lessons like the one Theodore Parker attached to his 1848 "sermon" on the Mexican War. In this sermon, America's war with Mexico turned into the "lesson" of King Ahab, who coveted Naboth's vineyard.[10] Now, whatever may be obscure in the lesson, what remains clear is that it was not an occasion for persuading a group of individuals to perform an action by presenting an argument about a complex issue. If the Mexican War embroiled the American people in an anxious political conjuncture involving debates over slavery and national identity, in Parker's lesson that war and all the anxiety surrounding the issues that gave rise to it give way to another scene, a calm and secure one. Writ seems to have already adjudicated these as well as all other matters.

Despite the clarity of the security-inducing effect of Parker's sermon, it nevertheless should serve as an occasion to complicate Bercovitch's model. For Parker does not directly discuss the Mexican War in terms of the American Revolution. He does, however, borrow on that power to discuss political events in religious terms, a power authorized by the revolutionary moment in which God's will and the nation's will become one, secured by the American jeremiad. And Bercovitch needs some explanation for the willingness of the American public to cede him this power. Such an explanation cannot simply posit the power of the jeremiad to constrain public opinion but must demonstrate how, given the cultural variations and violent dislocations of American life, it could continue to attract public attention at all. Why, for example, given Bercovitch's terms, isn't the very form of the American jeremiad, a form in which figures from the past reappear, an occasion for anxiety over the loss of relation with those figures?

A consideration of Parker's sermon in terms borrowed from our earlier discussion of the conditions overdetermining the acceptance of the Cold War paradigm could begin to provide an explanation. For in this oratorical scene Parker depends on his audience's anxiety and doubt over the issues surrounding the Mexican War for his very authority to invoke his other scene. Once these anxiety-provoking issues are replaced by figures like King Ahab, the issues disappear, for such figures seem already to have acted out the present dilemma in the past, thereby relieving the American public of the need to let the issues enter its consciousness at all. Or, if they must enter the consciousness, they do so precisely in another scene, one, as was the case with the Cold War opposition, in which all the issues have, in their very presentation within the language of Divine Writ, already received definitive judgment. In Parker's sermon, then, King Ahab, the very figure designating the figure of the Mexican War, turns out to have already resolved it.

So political issues turn into great public occasions for displacement of scenes of present troubles by scenes in which those troubles have already been solved. And the same figures who made up the public's mind for it in the past, in acting out potentially divisive public issues, can in the present separate the issue from the anxiety attending it. In place of the anxiety over political events in the present, these figures foreground a threat that seems to have a greater claim to public attention: the loss of a relation with a past. These same figures then allay the anxiety they have aroused by returning from a past, a past become all the more gratifying because of its claim to fulfill all present political aspirations.

The "other scene" does not utterly displace any political issue, but works as a background scene, one capable of relieving the explicit political questions of their anxiety, by relocating them in a scene in which the issues have already been resolved. This relocation so economizes on any individual exertion of will that the "mental work" that might otherwise have been expended in resolving a political question gets released from the doubts, second thoughts, calculations, and judgments informing any political decision.[11] It gets released, moreover, in a discourse that, if it ever became conscious, might have been called inspired – the discovery that the political issue troubling the mind has already been solved by the very rhetorical figures used to articulate the problem. Perhaps we should pause over this discovery to register one more observation. The very wording of the political issue excludes the question of individual freedom. More precisely, the jeremiad identifies individual freedom not with the freedom *to* perform an action, but with the freedom *from* the doubts, decisions, and judgments leading to action. Which is to say that this other scene depoliticizes freedom, exempts it from political questions. Because the very words used to articulate political questions have already resolved them, the individual's *freedom* moves elsewhere, into a realm emptied of actantial, judgmental, *determinate* energies: but with the foreknowledge that the sheer freedom and sheer chanciness of this potentially "free" realm will be returned to security once the need for security overdetermines the need to return to the other scene.

Obviously the "other scene" did not limit its power to the listeners. For the orators, in their abilities to transcribe everyday events into a form that interwove them with inspired words of the God of the Revolutionary Father, turned into the figural effects of these words. When perceived as the effects rather than the proponents of the words that seemed to utter them, such orators became indistinguishable from those rhetorical figures appearing *within* their discourse. In their office as realized effects of the Revolutionary Fathers, these orators gave the American people still another opportunity. For in their sermons, the American people did not quite hear the whispered word of God but witnessed the ways in which their own historical lives had become inspirations *for* God's words. And in their office as present occasions for the Divine Inspiration, the American people did not feel compelled to hear God's word so much as to conceive themselves as His means of representing it. Consequently, such scenes of public persuasion as that performed by Theodore Parker became occasions in which the public idealized the most basic form of acknowledgment. Instead of turning a listener toward a neighbor, the need for mutual recognition turned him toward the orator, in whose "inspired" figure he was to recognize what he, in his everyday life, had become.

As the prophetic fulfillment of both speaker and listener, the jeremiad does not really represent their differing positions but, as does the scene of persuasion in the Cold War paradigm it might now be said to prefigure, the jeremiad assimilates both speaker and listener into the means of articulating its form. Moreover, although, unlike the Cold War paradigm, the jeremiad presents its *pre*mediation of all positions as if it were an *un*mediated vision, nonetheless the effect of both paradigms remains the same. Either you come to your decision in their terms or you cannot decide. The same all-or-nothing logic was at work then as now: Either you use the terms sanctioned by the form or, as a person, literally outside of the shared language of the American people, you lose the possibility for representation in the scene of public persuasion altogether.

Although the concept of the American jeremiad is quite resourceful in disclosing the way in which the distinction between consensus and compulsion, always a difficult one to maintain, disappears altogether, nevertheless it cannot quite account for what we might call crises in coercion occasioned by those moments in American cultural history when identical figures in nearly identical forms of the jeremiad were used to represent opposing opinions on related questions. When scenes of cultural persuasion work, they are able to return all the potentially disruptive contradictions in political debate to their ideological ground, which, as we have seen, is capable of functioning as the ideal resolution for these contradictions. But the scenes of cultural persuasion became themselves a source of contradiction at times, and a threat to the ideological ground could result. Such a threat clearly appeared when Theodore Parker, speaking against slavery, John Calhoun, speaking against Union, and David Lee Childs, speaking against expansionism, could all write variations on the same line: "If I am rightly informed, King Ahab made a law that all the Hebrews serve the idol Baal."[12] When this same line could be used by different orators to represent such violently opposed views on such explosive issues, King Ahab could not be said to have made up his mind on these matters. And with the recognition of

Ahab's confusion, Americans lost their traditional way of feeling compelled about what to do.

Given our analysis of the unique cultural apparatus brought into existence by the consensus formations we have by turns called the American jeremiad and the Cold War, we cannot simply dismiss such moments as manifestations of cognitive dissonance on a massive scale. In the national economy of the representation of dissent we have been describing, the figures who idealized dissent into final, resolved form existed in a world we called the other scene, in which everyday dissenting opinions, doubts, and contradictions existed only in a fully resolved state. And the relation between the everyday world of indecision and the other scene of *The Decision* was an overdetermined and compensatory one. This everyday world could function precisely because that other world hedged its bet, converting all of its irresolution into a resolved form. It is not simply that doubts and indecisions do exist in local, contingent form, but that they exist *free from the need for decisive resolution* precisely because this other world exists as *The Resolution*.[13] Dissent exists free from the need for resolution in the everyday world because the jeremiad can resolve dissent of its indecision by wording it into an indubitable final reckoning on the other scene. Not only does the other scene permit indecision and doubts; it demands them as ongoing proof of its authoritative power to judge.

Now, with this relation between words as a context, imagine one of the rhetorical figures used to free the individual of the consequences of doubt (that is, the need to decide on a course of action) – such as Ahab in Parker's sermon – himself become human enough to experience indecision. What results is a confusion of realms on an apocalyptic scale. When the Ahab who exists to absolve this world of its conflicts himself experiences on that other scene the irresolvable doubts of this world, the other scene reverses its relation to this world. Whereas before, actual indecision discharged itself through symbolic resolution in the other scene, now a form of symbolic resolution from the other scene demands actualization of its indecision in the everyday world. Whereas before, *The Decision* in the other scene was an overdetermined form of the indecisions of everyday life, with this confusion of realms everyday decisions get invested with the overdetermined energy of decision.

Unless one were an orator who actually experienced himself as a figure brought into existence by the words uttered in that other scene, it is difficult to imagine a rhetorical figure (like the Ahab used by different orators to justify expansionism, slavery, and union) who can come into the actual world full of the conflicting demands the other scene can no longer resolve. If Ahab, who was formerly used as an ideal resolution of conflicting demands in the public sphere, now appears in his multiple representations as an ideal expression of the conflicting demands in that same public sphere, it might be said that Ahab, as a means of making up the mind of the public sphere, has come to life as the "character" of that mind. As the "lived experience" of its *betrayed* resolution, he expresses what we call the "national character" as a desperate need to convert conflicting demands back into a decisive form.

As the force released by the loss of authority for the American jeremiad, Ahab the tortured national character discloses the prior form of the American jeremiad's power. It generated and contained two different worlds. But the relation between these two worlds was not that of a "type" *fulfilled* by an "antitype" in the typological model Bercovitch offers. Instead, the one world (we have called the Other Scene) definitively separated the doubts and indecisions of the other world (we have called everyday life) from the need for resolution. Existing as a colossal estrangement effect, the Other Scene provided the occasion for individuals to reexperience their personal failures to decide as freedom from the need to decide. The Other Scene provided other "personal" benefits as well. As the Source World of primary action, the Other Scene relegated authenticity not to the activities of individuals in the everyday world, but to the action performed by such gigantic rhetorical figures as Ahab in Parker's sermon. Consequently, those "persons" who sensed the disconnection between the individual as effective cause and agent and the individual as an effect of forces beyond any individual's control could, with the relocation of "personal" authenticity in the "national character" acting on the Other Scene, reexperience alienation from an authentic self as freedom to perform a multiplicity of roles.

And the loss of Ahab's power on the Other Scene we might say brought about a reversal in the national relation to "act" and "action." Although I do not want to reduce the national motives for the Civil War to the terms of this reversal, I do want to note that this crisis in the nation's means of self-representation or its rhetoric of consensus could no longer, as Kenneth Burke suggests rhetoric should, purify the motives that made war necessary. And the failure of the scene of cultural persuasion accompanied the other forces, economic and political, leading to the Civil War. When the form of the jeremiad no longer could contain and actualize national conflicts in the Final Reckoning acted out on the Other Scene, this *undecided* conflict demanded not a symbolic but an actual war in order to become a decisive opposition once again. Without eliminating the other factors, we might say that from a rhetorical perspective the Civil War became a means of recovering in the everyday world the *stability* and *force* of *containment* lost by the rhetorical figures in the Other Scene. If before, the staging of the Other Scene was all the persuasion there was, the Civil War exposed that persuasion as merely staged. And this exposure became the occasion for individuals no longer merely to be content to "act out" but to *need to actualize* those dissenting opinions the American jeremiad, in its ideal resolution of the "national character," has formally alienated from them.

The Ahab in Parker's sermon was the figure of the "national character" who impersonated the American jeremiad's forces of containment. But the conflicting Ahabs in Calhoun's and Childs's orations released an Ahab who could no longer feel persuaded by the form of the American jeremiad. If Sacvan Bercovitch feels, as do the other Americans in his text, the need to recover the form of the American jeremiad at moments, like that of the Civil War, when it loses all of its effective historical force, he recovers the jeremiad at the expense of the character of Ahab, who no longer feels persuaded by it. If, in the perhaps excessive characterization of our discussion, Ahab was said to impersonate the power of the jeremiad to persuade, he now impersonates the felt loss of the authority of that power.

The Ahab who feels the compulsive need to persuade utterly separated from the form sanctioning persuasion appears not in anyone's jeremiad but in Melville's novel *Moby-Dick*. And should we follow Melville's lead and remain attentive to the demands not of the American jeremiad but of the figure who is not persuaded by it, we can turn to another American Renaissance. This time, however, we should not be guided by the figure who organized it into an ideal consensus formation. Rather, we should be prepared (by the figure of Ahab) to hear what we called that other F. O. Matthiessen, whose own dissenting opinions were silenced by what we can now recognize as the jeremiad force of *American Renaissance: Art and Expression in the Age of Emerson and Whitman*.

When guided by Matthiessen's opinions in conflict with the consensus formed by the *American Renaissance*, we can revalue the use of Whitman and Emerson. In using Coleridge's organicist aesthetic to distinguish the political rhetoric of such orators as Parker from what he called the "vitally" aesthetic writings of Emerson and Whitman, *American Renaissance* (as a consensus formed at the expense of Matthiessen's own dissenting position) strategically promotes Whitman's and Emerson's rhetoric, in which national self-consciousness becomes indistinguishable from personal self-consciousness, into a cultural asset. Moreover, this act of promotion constitutes the historical power of consensus formation in 1941. For in order to sanction America's national right to a free culture at a time when that right was threatened less by national than international politics, *American Renaissance* locates a cultural past so united that even the political issues surrounding the Civil War seem petty. When viewed in this context, Whitman and Emerson perform the same function for Matthiessen, in his politics of consensus formation, that they performed for the politicians used to the consensus formed by the American jeremiad in their time. They silence the conflicting claims in that form by replacing the politicians' forensic motives with motives open to the more rarified concerns of aesthetics. Seeming, then, to distinguish Emerson and Whitman from the politicians, *American Renaissance* in fact locates in their writings an organicist aesthetic justification for the rhetoric of national individualism at precisely the moment when the politicians seem to be losing the Divine justification for that rhetoric. As we have seen, this bracketing out of politics through a turn to aesthetic questions in fact served Matthiessen's "higher" political purpose – to devise a national consensus. Now we might best sense the cultural power of his "higher" purpose if we imagine F. O. Matthiessen coming after Sacvan Bercovitch to convert the "mere rhetoric' of the American jeremiad into the achieved art of the American Renaissance.

When conceived in terms of this "higher" purpose, however, Emerson and Whitman lose their purely aesthetic characters and reveal the explicitly rhetorical use to which *American Renaissance* put them. Nowhere does Emerson lose this character and Matthiessen lose control of the working of his consensus formation more definitely than in the midst of an analysis of the tyranny of Captain Ahab in the quarterdeck scene in *Moby-Dick*. Curiously, Matthiessen presents this analysis in what we could call a scene of critical persuasion. When considering Ahab's compelling domination of the men in the quarterdeck scene, Matthiessen pays no attention to specific lines but reads the compulsion in Ahab's language as a "sign" of Shakespeare's "power over" Melville. Then, in a monodrama intended ultimately to reveal Melville's artistic power, he transcribes lines exchanged by Ahab and Starbuck into their blank-verse form and observes that "the danger of such unconsciously compelled verse is always evident. As it wavers and breaks down into ejaculatory prose, it seems never to have belonged to the speakers but to have been at best a ventriloquist's trick."[14] Having first *posited* Shakespeare's language as the rhetorical power informing Ahab's exchanges, Matthiessen then rediscovers this power Shakespeare wields *through* Ahab at work in the spell Shakespeare cast *over* Melville's prose. This dramatic conflict ends only after Melville "masters" the power Shakespeare's rhetoric wields over him by discovering the secret of his own dramatic power.

Of course, all the power in this drama inheres less in Melville's discovery than in the dramatic use to which Matthiessen puts it. When Matthiessen's drama, which should have concluded with an example of Melville's triumphant "mastery" of Shakespeare, comes to its close, Melville's "mastery" of Shakespeare neither reveals itself through one of Melville's own characters nor represents one of Melville's own themes. Instead, Melville's "vital rhetoric" is said to "build up a defense of one of the chief doctrines of the age, the splendor of the single personality."[15] In other words, Melville's recovery from Shakespeare's rhetoric becomes a means for Emerson to defend his doctrine of self-reliance.

That Matthiessen sees the need for this defense gives pause. But the cause for the defense is implicit in the drama that builds up to it. Although he mentions Hitler only in his account of Chillingworth, the figure whose totalitarian position Matthiessen wrote *American Renaissance* to oppose is everywhere present in his discussion of Ahab. By staging the textual appearance of the doctrine of self-reliance within the scenes of Melville's recovery from a compulsive rhetorical principle, Matthiessen defends its rhetoric in advance from the charge that it may be as compelling in its excesses as Hitler was in his. When Matthiessen writes, "living in the age of Hitler, even the least religious can know and be terrified by what it is for a man to be possessed,"[16] it is clear that compulsive rhetoric, in all of its forms, is what figures from Matthiessen's *American Renaissance* exist to oppose. Consequently, when Melville dramatically achieves independence from the compulsive hold of Shakespeare's rhetoric, in the eyes trained to see by the *American Renaissance,* he earns the *authenticity* of the doctrine of self-reliance by literally realizing its *doctrine* as his defining aesthetic action.

The compelling logic of this dramatic sequence is clear. Matthiessen wants to *see* the doctrine of self-reliance at work, but when Matthiessen "hears" this doctrine enunciated by Ahab, he loses all the benefits accrued by the rest of his drama. Indeed, Matthiessen's own earlier treatment of Ahab as the "dummy" through whom Melville performs ventriloquist's tricks with Shakespeare's language posits Ahab as the principle of mere rhetoric rather than authentic art. And this earlier treatment releases troubling questions. If Ahab served as the dummy figure through whom Matthiessen could reveal Melville's act of "working through" his possession by Shakespeare's rhetoric, does he not, once Matthiessen hears him speaking Emerson's rhetoric of self-reliance, disclose Matthiessen's unstated fear that compulsion might be at work in the doctrine of self-reliance? In short, doesn't the quarter-deck scene become Matthiessen's pretext for the articulation of a felt need – not the need to defend but the need to defend himself against Emerson's ideology of self-reliance, which informs the consensus formation he called the American Renaissance?

Instead of revealing an instance of self-reliance at work, this scene releases (as two Matthiessens) the conflicts Matthiessen experienced in relation to the doctrine of self-reliance but which the American Renaissance made it impossible for him to state. Although Matthiessen wished to affirm Emerson's essays as liberating rather than disabling rhetoric, the moment Emerson appears within the context of *Moby-Dick* his doctrine appears least *vital* because most coercive. Moreover, the moment Matthiessen would defend this doctrine, he becomes, according to the logic of his own dramatic metaphor, less himself than an occasion for self-division in which *through* the figure of Ahab one Matthiessen doubts what the other Matthiessen affirms: that is, the liberating power of Emerson' rhetoric.

As we have seen, Melville's Ahab discloses the conflicts the American jeremiad could no longer silence. When Matthiessen attempts to speak the doctrine of his jeremiad through the figure of Ahab, the other Matthiessen, the Matthiessen whose dissenting opinions *American Renaissance* existed to silence, the Matthiessen who fears the doctrine of individualism may deny rights to "all the people" begins to speak instead. This doubling is crucial. For it indicates not only Matthiessen's understanding of the conflict between absolute freedom and individual rights and duties in Melville's time; it also articulates the presence within Ahab of the principle of freedom, or the "Ishmael figure" the Cold War scenario sets in opposition to Ahab. *American Renaissance,* in its most telling moment, acts out the different crises in consensus formation in Melville's as well as Matthiessen's time.

Matthiessen found self-reliance to be not only the chief ethical doctrine of the age but the ethical principle of the work, *American Renaissance,* earning for that age a cultural power that, in organizing the American canon, has itself become canonical. But despite *Moby-Dick*'s power to reduce the doctrine of self-reliance once it appears within its context – to reduce, in fact, both it and the canon of the American Renaissance that it informs – to the status of a ventriloquist's figure, I should consider the persuasive power of this doctrine before turning again to *Moby-Dick,* the book that I will argue is not persuaded by it.

Emerson states the doctrine with a simplicity that almost conceals its power. "Self-reliance is precisely that secret," he writes, "to make your supposed deficiency redundancy. If I am true, the theory is, the very want of action, my very impotency, shall become a greater excellency than all skill and toil."[17] When revealed, the secret is as simple as the doctrine; it makes a promise to convert powerlessness into a form of power. Before the reader can wish to find this doctrine appealing, however, he needs as his prior experience to feel powerless. The doctrine, in other words, presupposes a disproportion between a secret inner man and an outer world that it works to maintain. Actually, the doctrine of self-reliance doesn't simply presuppose such a disproportion between inner man and outer world but demands it as the context for its display of power.

By definition, a self-reliant man cannot rely on an outer world but only on an inner self, experienced as superior to the external world. But he can create this inner self only by first reducing the outer world to the level of an abstract externality, as arbitrary as it is merely contingent. Such a reduction cuts two ways. A world that is viewed as *arbitrary at best* allows for a retreat from it without too much regret. And this separation from the mere contingencies of the external world can, out of sheer contrast, be experienced from *within* as the first *authentic* choice in an otherwise arbitrary world.

But at least two problems attend the appearance of this inner self. If its authenticity is derived from a prior experience of contingency, then the inner self has not replaced but only internalized the contingency of an outer world. What results, moreover, is what Ishmael, at the beginning of *Moby-Dick,* calls a bad case of the hypos: that is, a wish for intense action but, given the contingency of internal as well as external worlds, without any incitement to act. The self-reliant man, then, feels empowered to act but has disconnected himself from any world that can validate his action.

In addressing these two problems, Emerson devised two distinct roles for self-reliance to perform. In its role as a doctrine, self-reliance encouraged a sense of withdrawal from the world; but in its role as an address, self-reliance converted this withdrawal into the appearance of a power. In this second role, self-reliance acts less like a doctrine corroborating any particular inner self and more like one of those rhetorical figures of will we saw at work on the Other Scene of the American jeremiad, capable of providing the private person with the freedom in relation to the external world denied him by the doctrine. We begin to understand the power inherent in this division better when we discover what happens when Emerson declares this doctrine as an address. As a figure of address effected by the self-reliance he evokes, Emerson can presume to speak to another individual, not from a position external to him but with all the power of that individual's "secret" inner life to which each self-reliant individual aspires. And so effective is this power to speak the inner life that such public figures as John Jay Chapman,

James Garfield, and Moncure Conway will declare after listening that Emerson's words have become their "secret" character.[18]

When speaking *as* what we might call the sovereign figure of the will released by the doctrine of self-reliance, however, Emerson does not encourage the individual either to act in the world or to will action. Instead he encourages the individual to discover his power in his inability to act: "If I am true, . . . my very impotency shall secure a greater excellency than any skill and toil." In what we could call a compensatory unconscious, the inability to perform any particular action recovers the sovereign *capability* to perform *all* actions. And through this remarkable turn, the sovereign will can recover the motivation lost after the devaluation of the external world. The individual will recovers its motivation, however, not by bridging the gap between motive and action but by enlarging it to the point where the motivating power, the sheer impulse to action, assumes priority over any particular action.

Thus the doctrine of self-reliance fulfilled the private will, but only through an address by a figure effected by a sovereign will, who relocates *within the abstract capability of the alienated individual* the Other Scene of *Final Reckoning* we discovered in the form of the American jeremiad. If the jeremiad separated the individual from the need for political decision by providing the scene on which everything had already been decided, self-reliance alienated individual action from individual motives for action by providing an internal sovereign will whose abstract capability to do what "might be done" was all the action there could be. When addressed by a spokesman, like Emerson, for this sovereign, the private person could feel persuaded not to perform any particular action but to experience the sheer force of the motivation to act – resounding in such imperatives as "trust thyself, every heart vibrates to that iron string" – as if it were already the only fulfillment needed.

If the doctrine of self-reliance justified the individual's alienation from a world of action, the power of address it made possible justified the separation of self-reliant individuals from one another. In replacing the merely private will with the "sovereign will," self-reliance also allowed for a great economy of discussion in the public sphere. For it eliminated first and third persons altogether and turned everyone into representations of what we could call a national "second person," an empty discursive slot to be filled in by a figure addressing the nation. Although this second person seems to address "you," he derives all of his power by presuming to speak *as* "your" inner life. Thus, in listening to him, "you" can believe you are investing yourself with executive power. But some pathos should return when "you," perhaps as a "second thought," recognize that this second person alone possesses the only self-reliant inner life in the nation.

Thus, the status of this national and sovereign second person must also give pause. For he is not only composed of and as "compensation" for the powerlessness of first persons, but he is empowered, as it were, out of a sensed disconnection between persons. In a nation of second persons, individuals do not discuss matters with other individuals but "address" or, better, "move" one another with inspirational apostrophes and imperatives. In inspiring one another, however, a nation of second persons need not listen to or even recognize one another but can, in moving another, look forward to being unmoved in return; or, if moved at all, be moved by the sheer power of moving called the "sovereign will." And here, again, we see not consensus but a kind of compulsion in its place. The work of compulsion performed by the figure of address we have called the sovereign will of the self-reliant man faces none of the conflicts that tore apart the form of the American jeremiad. There, as we saw in the person of Ahab, the conflicting claims (which the form of the jeremiad was used to sanction) internalized rather than silenced the conflicts. But because the figure of sovereign will *can* perform any action, no *particular position* can lay claim to his power to sanction. As the capability to perform all actions, the sovereign will need not experience the conflicts endemic to any *particular* expression of will. Without the possibility for conflict, the sovereign will need not negotiate conflicts among separate individuals. Instead it demands the separation of individuals as the only appropriate effect of the sovereign will.

Although it is everywhere present in Emerson's theory of friendship, Thoreau elevates disconnection into a national ideological value when he writes, "When they say farewell then indeed we begin to keep them company. [For just as] I always assign to him a nobler employment in my absence than I ever find him engaged in, so I value and trust those who love and praise my aspiration rather than my performance."[19] In these lines Thoreau etherealizes friendship to the status of mutual evanescence, as the sheer potential to be an inspiring friend replaces the need for any actual friendship and sheer motivation replaces action.

But an even clearer sense of the cultural value of this doctrine of friendship arises when we juxtapose it to the doctrine of self-reliance. That doctrine, as we recall, separated the inner self from a devalued because external world. But the address of the sovereign will, to the internal world from a position external to it, revalued, if not the external world, at least an external field of force: a second person capable of addressing private individuals with all the force of his or her inner life. This second person, less a person than an abstraction of other persons to the position of addressee, in belonging to nobody in particular provided a platform of address for everyone in general. And as the sheer capability of address, belonging to everybody in general and no one in particular, this sovereign will, through Thoreau's doctrine of the Friend, could as the means of mutual inspiration function as the very principle of community. In other words, this sovereign will could, despite its origin in the sensed disconnection of self-reliant individuals from one another, represent itself, in its capacity to speak for everybody and nobody, as the general will of the people. When speaking from this position, an individual could, through the fiction of the sovereign will, claim to address the people from the position not of their will or his will but (with all the force of a second person) *thy* will.

As was the case with the witnesses of the scene of persuasion in the American jeremiad, however, the "general will" of the people did not originate from discussions among themselves. Instead, the people could only hearken to the inner life as it addressed them from the position of that irresistible field of force resulting from the sensed disconnection of individuals both from the world and from each other: a force we have called the national second person.

In its role as the spokesman for the sovereign will of the people, Emerson's doctrine of self-reliance obviously provided politicians and orators with a tremendous practical advantage. For in self-reliance the public found a way not to be persuaded by any particular action but instead, in what we would call the turn to a rhetoric of pure persuasion, to be inspired by the felt sense of the motive to act purified of any specific action to be performed. In valuing motive over action, listeners need not question the acts to which orators would persuade them. Perhaps here we have the reason such public figures as Garfield, Conway, and Chapman felt so empowered by Emerson. Aspiring as they did to speak for the will of the people, they found in the person of Emerson's self-reliant or sovereign will the people's consent. In listening to an orator, a self-reliant man *need* not question what was said, for he was not being addressed as a figure *other* than the figure addressing him. In a relentlessly closed communication circuit, self-reliance addressed that figure of will Emerson called self-reliance. On these occasions, the individual could witness his own independence coming to him, as it were, in the person of the nation's second person. Most importantly, however, Emerson's conversion of the politician's purposive rhetoric into pure persuasion had the effect of purifying that rhetoric of the confusions we saw at work when King Ahab was used to sanction three conflicting attitudes toward national politics. Because pure persuasion turned purpose into a purposiveness without purpose, it became a means of receiving the inspirational power of political rhetoric when conflicting political demands were breaking apart its form.

When observing what he called the resultant American pleniloquence from the detached position of a third rather than second person, Alexis de Tocqueville did not, as did Matthiessen and Bercovitch, use it as an occasion either to describe or to engage in consensus formation. Instead he recovered the first-person privileges of the humorist:

> Debating clubs in America are to a certain extent a substitute for theatrical entertainment: [for] an American *cannot converse* . . . [instead] his talk falls into a dissertation. He speaks to you as if he were addressing a meeting, and if he should chance to become warm in the discussion, he will say "Gentlemen" to the person with whom he is conversing.[20]

Since de Tocqueville, in his outsider's account, seems to have achieved a position enabling him to recover a first person capable of poking fun at what I have called the scene of cultural persuasion, I want to take this opportunity to distinguish his outsider's narrative not only from the forms of address called the jeremiad and the sovereign will, but also from those insiders' narratives – the legends and tall tales – written by Americans as means of remaining within the address of the national second person.

In order to understand how this inside narrative works, we need to return to the scene of pure persuasion to emphasize its crucial distinction from the American jeremiad. In privileging motive over act, the scene of pure persuasion does not recall agents from the nation's past but demands that agents as well as their actions imitate inspiring motives. The second person does not commemorate the heroic deeds performed by characters from the nation's past. Instead, he calls individuals to aspire to actions indistinguishable from the motivational power of the orator's figures of will. In Emerson's remarkable turn, the Revolutionary Fathers, instead of remaining ideals to be imitated, became effects of the self-reliant man's inspiring words, embodiments of the motivating power of his speech. As a result of the claims implicit in Emerson's rhetoric, the people were able to internalize within the sovereign will not only the idealized Revolutionary Fathers but also the biblical figures who in the form of the American jeremiad provided the Fathers with their Divine Rights. Which is to say that in Emerson's rhetoric even God's words become indistinguishable from the sovereign will of the nation's second person.

This same absorptive power – the presumption of the sovereign will seemingly to claim every preexisting cultural authority as an effect of its power – introduces another dimension in the relationship between sovereign will and action. For although, as we stated, the sovereign will separated any particular action from the infinite capability of the sovereign will, that same sovereign will could claim any action as an effect of its motivating power. In this context, heroic deeds need not be conceived as motives that became actions (which would threaten the superiority of motive in relation to deed) but could be conceived as actions that were indistinguishable from the motivating power to act. Orators secured this equivalence by converting certain actions in the world into tropes of pure persuasion. So whenever an individual "acted out" the inspiring power of the orator's motives, he became a figure of will indistinguishable from the inner life of the self-reliant man and earned, as was the case with Ahab, the right to speak as the national second person he, in his personal life, had already become. He could motivate others, in short, because he had already equated their inner motivation with his public action.

Such national second persons as Ahab were the subject not only of legends that assimilated the excesses of the orator's rhetoric into human shape but also of tall tales that, like de Tocqueville's "humorous" observations, de-created these legendary figures by exposing their apparently heroic deeds as mere "stretchers." Here the distinction needs to be made between demystifying a rhetorical position and telling a tall tale. For the latter – telling a tall tale – displaces the need to do the former. Instead of wishing to acknowledge the rhetorical status of a tall tale, the teller never wants to get outside its format. For if he did, he would not have the pleasure of "taking in" a third person. This third person, in his turn, does not recognize what it is that has taken him in, but simply experiences the pleasure of "taking in" another third person with another tall tale. The legend and the tall tale, then, establish what we might (in our memory of the national second person) call a "second first" and a "second third" person who never become skeptical or even self-conscious about the rhetoric of pure persuasion, but who wish instead to claim their second person privileges and remain in the position of persons addressed by the nation's second person.

But if narrativity functions as a motive to remain within the form of address of the nation's second person, reading narratives became an occasion to locate the power of this will to address. Reading, in other words, offered an occasion to turn what is read – that is, words as motive forces – into what does the reading. Or, what is the same thing, reading became a means of internalizing and so, following the logic we found at work in the doctrine of self-reliance, making sovereign, what we have called the nation's second person.

The interrelationship between Americans engaged in the activities of listening, speaking, arguing, and reading – activities valued most, on at least one cultural level, when most indicative of a certain independence of mind – and what we have called the sovereign will of mind, releases an alarming recognition. When accompanying the "democratic" operations acclaimed as proof of the power of individual Americans to make up their own minds, the sovereign will turned these operations into expressions of a national compulsion. When turned toward the national scene on which compulsion could do its work, individual Americans did not make up their own minds but witnessed the scene on which their minds were made up for them as an "experience" of each American's self-reliance.

Perhaps this recognition will have its greatest value if we imagine it stated by the F. O. Matthiessen who led us to it: not the one who used Emerson's doctrine of self-reliance to form the consensus he called the *American Renaissance,* but the one whose dissenting political opinions were silenced by *Art and Expression in the Age of Emerson and Whitman.* Because we began to hear this Matthiessen who was not persuaded by the scene of cultural persuasion in his reading of the quarterdeck scene of *Moby-Dick,* perhaps we can use this scene as an oppositional one. And because the narrative of *Moby-Dick* offers an occasion for Matthiessen to signal opinions in conflict, we should expand the context of this oppositional scene by differentiating Melville's narrative vision from *Art and Expression in the Age of Emerson and Whitman.*

At around the time of the composition of *Moby-Dick,* Melville imagined a reading experience utterly at odds with what we have described as the internalization of the sovereign will.[21] Moreover, he discovered what he called the "will of the people" by reading not Emerson or Thoreau but a figure Matthiessen included as another (subsidiary) voice in the American Renaissance. Reading Hawthorne's *Mosses from an Old Manse,* a work attentive enough to the value of different opinions to provoke in the reader a series of conflicting attitudes, Melville conceived a review in which he *staged* the release of conflicting reactions. Recorded over a two-day period by a Virginian vacationing in Vermont, the review dramatizes a protocol the reverse of what we have called a scene of public persuasion. Instead of finding *his* mind already made up in the figure of Hawthorne's tales, this southerner vacationing in the heart of the abolitionist Northeast discovers a whole range of conflicting reactions to these tales: with each reaction possessed of sufficient self-consciousness to organize itself into an articulate opinion and each opinion accompanied by a second thought – the shocking recognition of the limits of that single opinion. In an intricate series of moves, Melville reads neither as an individual nor quite as a general will but as the conflicting opinions within a reading public – not a ready-made consensus but a consensus in the process of formulation, or what Melville calls a "plurality of men of genius" released in reading Hawthorne's twice-told tales.

In other words, Melville, at the time of his composition of *Moby-Dick,* imagined the release of the reading public from the sovereign will of the national second person. Moreover, he released that public by giving multiple voices, each with the possibility of "parity," to the conflicts silenced by that sovereign will. We got some indication of the dimensions of those conflicts when we analyzed what resulted when the rhetorical figure of Ahab was used to voice opposed political views. But as Alan Heimert in the past and Michael Paul Rogin in the present have pointed out, the other two principles in *Moby-Dick* – the figures of Ishmael and the Leviathan – were also deployed, in all their rich biblical allusiveness, to voice contrary political positions on the issues of abolitionism, secession, and manifest destiny in the form of the American jeremiad.[22]

In our previous discussion we suggested that the loss by these rhetorical figures of the power to contain conflict in the jeremiad form resulted in the public's need to actualize this conflict in the Civil War. In *Moby-Dick,* Melville, instead of actualizing this conflict, turns the rhetorical figures of Ahab, Ishmael, and the Leviathan, the orators used to contain it, into actual characters. Then in a massive alienation effect that estranges the second-person powers presuming to make up the public's mind for it, he lets them act out their felt alienation from the power legitimately to secure consent. Moreover, because Ahab and Ishmael share, as it were, the privileges of the second person, Melville revokes those privileges by exposing the compulsion at work in their rhetoric.

If we can imagine, in the broad context of a scene of cultural persuasion, the political conjuncture elemented by the different issues of slavery, succession, and expansionism, then if we imagine the three Ahabs, three Ishmaels, and three Leviathans used to word these issues into jeremiads, we can see how conflicted had become the space that was used to achieve consensus. If such cultural forms as the jeremiad, pure persuasion, the legend, and the tall tale had been used to "work through" the conflicts in the general will, Melville, in characterizing the contradictory relations among these forms, released the conflicts at work in the general will.

The "great tradition" of American literature founded by the *American*

Renaissance silenced these contradictory relations by converting all of them into the opposition between Ishmael's freedom and Ahab's totalitarian will. And this contradiction resolves the felt force of the contradiction by converting it into an "ideal conflict," a (Cold) War whose appropriate outcome has already been determined. In his analysis of the quarterdeck scene, however, Matthiessen displays a contradictory relation, a contradictory attitude unresolvable by the ideal opposition between Ahab and Ishmael. In his analysis, Matthiessen identifies Ahab as both totalitarian will and the freedom a self-reliant man must use to oppose it. Put another way, through the figure of Ahab, Matthiessen reads the feared compulsion at work in what he formerly regarded as the sovereign freedom of the self-reliant man.

He reads the compulsion, but, as we'll recall, he reads it in terms of Shakespeare's blank verse. And whereas Melville represented Ahab's use of Shakespearean language as a sign of his power over the crew, Matthiessen treats this language as a sign of Shakespeare's power over Melville. By reading Ahab's silencing of Starbuck's dissent as disclosure of the power Shakespeare wielded over Melville's prose, Matthiessen of course acknowledges the political power of Shakespeare's language. (Shakespeare, in the politics of canon formation, had, after all, functioned as Matthiessen's means of securing English Renaissance validity for American Renaissance figures.) But he displaces the context for the display of this power, moving it from the relation between Ahab and the crew to the relation between Melville and Shakespeare. And in doing so, Matthiessen simultaneously praises (through his mastery of Shakespeare's language) the Ahab he condemns (as the proponent of a totalitarian will). More specifically, Matthiessen in his one-dimensional reading of Ahab's totalitarian will, also reenacts Starbuck's scenario. For Ahab performs for Matthiessen the same function he performs for Starbuck: In embodying compulsion as his inner life alone, he releases Matthiessen from the need to find compulsion at work in the doctrine of self-reliance, the Emersonian will to virtue informing the body of his work.

We might say that the contradictory attitudes released by Matthiessen's reading disclose his doubts about, rather than the effectiveness of, both scenes of cultural persuasion. Earlier we suggested that the scene of cultural persuasion exists to displace political dissent experienced in the public sphere onto another scene, where the contradiction disappears into the ground terms, or where the principles sanctioning the right to dissent replace the specific terms of dissent. In Matthiessen's reading, the political contradictions existing at the time Melville wrote (between democratic ideals and the principle of self-reliance) turn into the opposition (between the totalitarian will and individual freedom) sanctioned by the Civil War. But Matthiessen's discovery of the agency of individual freedom (Emerson's "will to virtue") within Ahab's totalitarian will indicates only the failure of the scene of persuasion to resolve the contradiction.

The contradictions released by Matthiessen's reading, however, do not simply point up his conflicting responses to the character of Ahab. Because these contradictions appear at the point at which Matthiessen fails to remain persuaded in the scene (*American Renaissance*) he used to appropriate nineteenth-century America, these same contradictions opened up a cultural space, answerable neither to the scenes of persuasion operative in Melville's nor Matthiessen's (nor, by extension, our own) time. Since these contradictions are released within the character of Ahab's totalitarian will and are concerned by extension with his canonical opposition to Ishmael's "freedom," perhaps we should conclude with a consideration of that relation.

Let us begin with an observation missing from Matthiessen's concentration on Ahab's totalitarian will. Ahab's very power to silence dissent also causes him to reexperience his sense of loss. Unlike the spokesmen for the American jeremiad, Ahab cannot depend on Divine Writ to sanction his words. Consequently, a dual recognition accompanies his every act of persuasion: the terrible doubt that it may be without foundation, and the "experience" of his separation from another. Both recognitions remind him of the loss of his leg. And it is Ahab's need to justify this sense of loss – to make it his, rather than God's or Fate's – that leads him to turn his will, which in each act of persuasion repeats that separation of his body from his leg, into the ground for his existence.

Indeed, all of Ahab's actions – his dependence on omens, black magic, thaumaturgy – work as regressions to a more fundamental power of the human will. They constitute his efforts to provide a basis *in* the human will for a rhetoric that has lost all other sanction. Ahab, in short, attempts to turn the coercion at work in his rhetoric into Fate, a principle of order in a universe without it. But since this will is grounded in the sense of loss, it is fated to perfect that loss in an act of total destruction.

That final cataclysmic image of total destruction motivated Matthiessen and forty years of Cold War critics to turn to Ishmael, who in surviving *must,* the logic would have it, have survived as the principle of America's freedom who hands over to us our surviving heritage. When juxtaposed to Ahab, Ishmael is said to recover freedom in the midst of fixation; a sense of the present in a world in which Ahab's revenge makes the future indistinguishable from the past; and the free play of indeterminate possibility in a world forced to reflect Ahab's fixed meanings.

Given this juxtaposition, we should take the occasion to notice that if Ahab was a figure who ambivalently recalled the scene of persuasion in the American jeremiad, Ishmael recalls nothing if not the pure persuasion at work in Emerson's rhetoric. As does Emerson, Ishmael uncouples the actions that occur from the motives giving rise to them, thereby turning virtually all events in the narrative into an opportunity to display the powers of eloquence capable of taking possession of them. Indeed, nothing and no one resist Ishmael's power to convert the world that he sees into the forms of rhetoric that he wants. The question remains, however, whether Ishmael, in his need to convert all the facts in his world and all the events in his life into a persuasive power capable of recoining them as the money of his mind, is possessed of a will any less totalizing than Ahab's. Is a will capable of moving from one intellectual model to another–to seize each, to invest each with the subjunctive power of his personality, then, in a display of restlessness no eloquence can arrest, to turn away from each model as if it existed only for this ever-unsatisfied movement of attention–is such a will any less totalitarian, however indeterminate its local exertions, than a will to convert all the world into a single struggle?

Because, in a certain sense, Ishmael puts his will to work by converting Ahab's terrifying legend into cadences familiar from the tall tales, we might take this occasion to differentiate Ishmael's tall tale from those we have analyzed earlier in the chapter. In telling his tale, the Ishmael who was taken in by Ahab's rhetoric does not, as was the case with other narrators of the tall tales, use the tale to work through the excesses in Ahab's rhetoric. Instead, the extraordinary nature of Ahab's words and deeds legitimizes elements of Ishmael's narrative that might otherwise seem inflationary. As the figure whose excesses in word and deed cause him literally to be read out of Ishmael's narrative, Ahab turns into the figure who enables the reader to rule out the charge of excess in Ishmael's rhetoric. Ishmael occupies three different spaces in his narrative. As the victim of Ahab's narrative, he exists as a third person. As the narrator of his own tale, as a first person. And as the subject of such urgent addresses as "Call Me Ishmael," a second person. But because, as a first-person narrator, he turns Ahab into the figure who has victimized Ishmael, Ishmael does not have to be perceived as taking anyone else in. Ishmael turns Ahab into both the *definitive third-person* victim and the perfect *first-person* victimizer. In perfecting both roles, Ahab becomes Ishmael's means of exempting his narrative in advance of the charge of trying to victimize anyone. Moreover, because, in Ishmael's case, first-person narratives always turn into pretexts for second-person sermons, Ahab, the locus for all false rhetoric, also becomes Ishmael's means of redeeming *his second person* by exempting it in advance from all charges of mystification.

As Ishmael's means of purifying his individual acts of persuasion of any actantial component, Ahab, in his conflation of victim and agent, motive and deed, also turns out to be the second-person *power:* the figure of will who performs actions absolutely indistinguishable from the motive powers (released by an orator's address) within Ishmael's rhetorical exercise. In Ishmael's rhetoric, each individual act of perception turns into the occasion for an exercise of persuasive power. Through Ahab's death, Ishmael of course exempts these occasions from any charge of coercion (which has been perfected by Ahab).

The sensed loss of Ahab, however, results in another, less desirable state of affairs. Through Ahab, Ishmael experiences the one figure in his narrative capable of realizing inspired words in matching deeds.[23] Buried within Ishmael's display of remarkable oratorical power is his reiterated demand that the world be indistinguishable from the will of his words: Buried within Ishmael's narrative is the one figure capable of making these words consequential. In reaction to the fate befalling Ahab, the man who would make deed as consequential as his words demanded, Ishmael retreats into endless local performances of rhetorical exercises, with each performance invested with the desperate complaint that the world will be consequential enough. Each of these performances – these momentary indulgences in a sense of power superior to the given structures of the world – becomes Ishmael's means for the reappearance of the force if not the person of Ahab.

In speaking with the force of Ahab's demand for a world indistinguishable from human will but *free of* the consequences of that will, Ishmael can discover pleasure not quite in another world but in a *prior world,* in which the endless proliferation of possible deeds displaces the need for any definitive action. The pleasure in this *prior* world results from the economization of ends over means, and the capacity to experience this economy as pleasure (rather than frustration) also derives from Ahab. The fate befalling Ahab's decisive conversion of word into deed determines Ishmael's need for a realm in which the indeterminate play of endless possible reactions overdetermines his *in*decision.

We can begin to understand all of this better when we turn to the crucial distinctions that critics during the Cold War drew between Ishmael and Ahab. In their view, Ishmael, in his rhetoric, frees us from Ahab's fixation by returning all things to their status as pure possibilities. What we now must add is that Ishmael has also invested all the rest of the world of fact with possibility, then invests possibility with the voice of conviction. And when all the world turns out to be invested with the indeterminate interplay of possibility, it does not seem free but replicates what Ishmael called the hypos and what we call boredom (the need for intense action without any action to perform) that motivated the Ishmael who felt the "drizzly November in his soul" to feel attracted to Ahab in the first place. This interpolation of an excess of indeterminacy between motive and act displaces Ahab's fixation but in doing so causes Ishmael to develop a need for Ahab. In short, Ishmael's form of freedom does not oppose Ahab but compels him to need Ahab – not only as the purification of his style, but as the cure for a boredom verging on despair. Only in Ahab's final act can the Ishmael who has in his rhetoric converted the external world into an exact replica of the restless displacements of endlessly mobile energies of attention that we formerly identified with the sovereign will, find a means to give all these energies a final, fatal discharge. Ahab's fatal, decisive deed permits Ishmael to feel the excessive force of *Ahab's decision over*determine his exercises in indecision. Put more simply, Ahab's compulsion to decide *compels* Ishmael *not* to decide.

At this point, however, Ishmael cannot be said to oppose Ahab as freedom would totalitarianism. But the form of his narrative does anticipate the totalizing logic we saw at work in the Cold War scenario. For in identifying all coercion as the work of Ahab's totalitarian will, and not his own boredom, Ishmael is free to multiply his scenes of persuasion with the knowledge that all of them will be free in advance of the charge of coercion. Because in Ishmael's rendition it is Ahab alone who controls us against our will, we are "free" to read Ishmael's own obsessive multiplication of occasions to compel our attention as the work of Ahab.

Thus *Moby-Dick* does not limit its exposure to that of the scene of cultural persuasion in its own time. Ever since Matthiessen's reading of it as the sign of the power of the freedom of figures in the American Renaissance to oppose totalitarianism, *Moby-Dick* has been a Cold War text, one that secures in Ishmael's survival a sign of the free world's triumph over a totalitarian power. But Melville, in the organization of the narrative relation as a self-conflicted will, instead of letting Ishmael remain in opposition to Ahab, reveals the way in which Ishmael's obsession depends on Ahab's compulsion. Nor does he alienate opposition by positioning all opinions within the conflict between Ishmael and Ahab. Instead he "works through" the vicious circulation informing the conflicted will at work in Ishmael and Ahab. If the Cold War consensus would turn *Moby-Dick* into a figure through which it could read the free world's survival in the future struggle with totalitarianism, Melville, as it were, speaks back through the same figure, asking us if we can survive the free world that Ishmael has handed down to us.

Notes

1 Herman Melville, *Moby-Dick,* ed. Harrison Hayford and Hershel Parker (New York: Norton, 1967), p. 144. Subsequent references are to this edition.
2 See "Hawthorne and His Mosses," in *The Literary World,* August 17 and 20, 1850.
3 In its capacity to bring about consensus, through the intersection of a variety of different lines of intellectual, emotional, and psychological force, this Cold War logic may recall what Gramsci called hegemony. But what differentiates it is the Cold War drama's ability to empty out any thematic value. So that the Cold War releases what we might call the *force* of persuasion, a force that, like prejudice, works best by economizing on the work of choosing. When within the Cold War arena, we feel "chosen" as a result of the choices we (do not need to) make.
4 The progress followed here is interesting: The Cold War appears first as a mode of structuring an otherwise chaotic world, but the *neutral* binary opposition informing the structure becomes charged, and the victory of one side in relation to the other promises itself as the outcome–but the outcome *within* the opposition.
    What we call deconstruction finds acceptance consequent to the prior reduction of the world into this super-opposition. But the inverting, displacing operations of deconstruction do not dislodge this structure so much as they rationalize it. In acting out the logic of this opposition as if it were a revolutionary activity, deconstruction only maintains its cultural power.
5 See, for example, the review "Cause for a Writ de Lunatico," *The Southern Quarterly Review* 5 (January 1852), 262; or William Harrison Ainsworth, "Maniacal Style and Furibund Story," *New Monthly Magazine* (July 1853), 307–8.
6 I realize that Matthiessen was not writing during the time of the Cold War, but I wish to argue that his American Renaissance helped to create the postwar consensus on American literature as Cold War texts.
7 F. O. Matthiessen, *American Renaissance: Art and Expression in the Age of Emerson and Whitman* (New York: Oxford University Press, 1941), p. 656.
8 See, for example, Irving Howe, "The Sentimental Fellow Travelling of F. O. Matthiessen," *Partisan Review* 15 (1948): 1125–29.
9 See Sacvan Bercovitch, *The American Jeremiad* (Madison: University of Wisconsin Press, 1978).
10 Theodore Parker, *A Sermon on the Mexican War: Preached . . . June 25th, 1848* (Boston, 1848), p. 1.
11 Here we begin to acknowledge the "absolute" power of the paradigm: Having already made *all* the decisions, it enables the individual to conceive the state of being deprived of choice as the freedom from the need to choose.
12 For a compilation of the other jeremiads authorized by the Ahab figure, see

Alan Heimert, "*Moby-Dick* and American Political Symbolism," *American Quarterly* 15 (Winter 1963): 498–534. Heimert compiles this information with a remarkable sense of the interrelationship, but he does not, I think, have much sensitivity to the explosive power of the material he compiles.

13 The use of the "dramatic stage" as a context in which to discuss social and cultural issues presupposes the relation between social life and *theatrical distraction,* a relationship that may in itself serve certain political interests. We begin to sense the power of this context when we notice how an individual who feels alienated from himself when in society can, through *the* dramatic metaphor, reexperience alienation from self as the discovery of an opportunity to perform a variety of roles. The metaphor, however, cannot address the dramatic actor's distress over the number of roles inviting performance.

14 See Matthiessen, *American Renaissance,* p. 426.

15 Ibid., p. 430.

16 Ibid., p. 307. Although this appears in Matthiessen's discussion of Hawthorne, I would argue that Melville and Hawthorne serve as locations for Matthiessen's dissent from the "vital doctrines" of Emerson and Whitman.

17 See *Selections from Ralph Waldo Emerson,* ed. Stephen Whicher (Boston: Houghton Mifflin, 1960), p. 146.

18 Garfield's account is cited in Ralph Leslie Rusk's *The Life of Ralph Waldo Emerson* (New York: Scribner, 1949), p. 385. Conway's can be be found in *Remembrances of Emerson* (New York: Cooke, 1903) and John Jay Chapman's in "Emerson," in *The Shock of Recognition,* ed. Edmund Wilson (New York: Doubleday, 1943), p. 615.

19 *Walden and Other Writings of Henry David Thoreau,* ed. B. Atkinson (New York: Random House, 1937), pp. 357, 380, 386.

20 Matthiessen, *American Renaissance,* p. 20.

21 Of course, Emerson also permits a series of conflicting voices to speak in his essays, but in effectively depriving them of a context in which the voice can appear as anything other than a conflict *in* voice, he effectively converts these modulations in voice back into the motive powers of pure persuasion.

22 See Heimert, "*Moby-Dick* and American Political Symbolism," and Michael Paul Rogin in *Subversive Genealogy: The Politics and Art of Herman Melville* (New York: Knopf, 1983). Rogin needs to generate a Freudo-Marxist context in which to snare Melville, but this context reveals more of Rogin's nostalgia for the reappearance of that context (in something other than his father's political period) than it reveals about either the politics or the art of Melville.

23 Ishmael makes clear the connection when he evokes Ahab as his ideal addressee: "Oh, Ahab! What shall be grand in thee, it must needs be plucked at from the skies, and dived for in the deep, and featured in the unbodied air."

18

Afterword

SACVAN BERCOVITCH

The essays in this book explore the implications in literature and culture of what has been termed "the American ideology." The term itself may be somewhat misleading. It suggests something almost allegorical – some abstract corporate monolith – whereas, of course, the ideology in question reflects a particular set of interests and assumptions, the power structures and conceptual forms of modern middle-class society in the United States, as these evolved through three centuries of contradictions and discontinuities. So considered, "America" is not an overarching synthesis, *e pluribus unum,* but a rhetorical battleground, a symbol that has been made to stand for alternative and sometimes mutually antagonistic outlooks. The essays in this book interpret the conflicts in various ways, they posit various definitions of ideology, and they draw upon a variety of literary and paraliterary approaches. What links them is a common set of problems – literary offspring of the thorny and divisive issues that have attended the study of ideology in our time. The effect is that of a dialogue in the making, and I have organized this Afterword accordingly. In what follows I proceed not in the topical sequence of the table of contents, but in terms of what I take to be the central concerns of the dialogue implicit among the authors in this volume. Specifically, I refer to their concern with the way myths give shape to history and history generates the production of myths; with the constricting and enabling effects in literature of social values; with the relation between art and politics, symbols and ideas, culture and society; with the radical implications of our classic texts, and the cultural limitations inherent in any mode of scholarship, including ideological analysis.[1]

As Myra Jehlen's Introduction makes clear, these concerns have a direct bearing on recent developments in literary studies. They have a special claim on American literature, I think, because that literature, from its origins, is so often obsessed with the idea of America, and because that idea, as it was made the exclusive property of the United States, is so transparently ideological. What could be a clearer demonstration of ideas in the service of power than the system of beliefs that the early colonists imposed on the so-called New World? What clearer demonstration of the shaping power of ideology than the procession of declarations through which the republic was consecrated as New Israel, Nature's Nation in the Land of Futurity? "America" is a laboratory for examining the shifting connections between politics (in the broadest sense) and cultural expression. This is nowhere more evident than in the mid-nineteenth century, when the process of consecration was reaching its apotheosis; when, accordingly, the conflicts inherent in the symbol of America became most pronounced; and when, under pressure of vast economic change and impending civil war, the culture found expression, in all its contradictions and all its power of compelling allegiance, in a self-consciously *American* literary renaissance. Broadly speaking, the consensus that emerged during this period is what we have come to recognize as the American ideology. And the conditions for exploring the connections it involves, between literature, politics, and culture, were never more auspicious than they are now, when that ideological consensus seems to be breaking down, or at any rate seeking to reconstitute itself under the pressure once again of historical change and economic and social transformation.

Gerald Graff suggests something of the impact of the old consensus on American literary criticism. His main focus is contemporary: the "increasingly deceptive Left–Right antithesis" spawned by academic consumerism, which he relates persuasively to our "shopping mall society." But he shows, too, that this "culture-industry" has a long ideological foreground – antedating the American literary renaissance, and beginning, appropriately, in the ideological origins of the American Revolution.[2] The colonial power structure, we know, included Whigs and Tories alike. Although they fought a war over the question of independence, both sides shared the libertarian values of what was to become middle-class American society. And they framed the question of independence accordingly. The option presented to the colonists was not one of oppositional or alternative forms of social organization (as it was, say, in revolutionary France and Latin America), but of variant forms of the same dominant culture: Should our allegiance be imperial or national? Anglo-American or (in the "true Anglo-American spirit") self-determined? This was the ideological context of the debate in the early republic about "the mission of American literature." In this context, subsequent generations of critics continued the debate as Brahmin Conservatives or Young Americans, as genteel "reactionaries" or "reform-minded Realists." No doubt there were genuine polarities here, political and intellectual as well as aesthetic, but they were polarities within the same ideological spectrum, the East Egg and West Egg of American literary discourse – antagonisms designed as it were by cultural reflex to direct all forms of conflict toward the needs of the same open-market society.

To varying degrees, this strategy of fusion through fragmentation informs the entire course of American literary criticism. It may be seen as a central reason (in addition to those Graff mentions) for "the defeat of literary leftism in the thirties," perhaps the most creative decade of European literary leftism. In any case, the impress of that strategy is apparent upon most of the twentieth-century landmarks on his "ideological map": the Anglophobia of Van Wyck Brooks and the Anglophilia of the southern New Critics (who justified their conservatism as the tradition of Jefferson); the united front of right-wing humanists and left-wing Culture Critics against the betrayal of the American dream; Vernon Parrington's manichean vision of the Puritan–Republican struggle for America; and most recently the similarities in argumentation among our leading "synoptic" critics, whose arguments, Graff observes, build from different perspectives toward a celebration and/or elegy over a few interrelated ideals (Adamic innocence, agrarian harmony, personal freedom, the unbounded frontiers of thought and language), each of these rooted in the rhetoric of American identity.

It is *against* this background that the essays of this volume redefine our mid-nineteenth-century literary classics. The historians from George Bancroft to Daniel Boorstin who described the United States as a country without an ideology were speaking for a system of values so deeply ingrained they could assume it was simply common sense. The cultural commentators from Oliver Wendell Holmes to Louis Hartz who saw nothing in America but an expanding middle class were speaking for a way of life so completely internalized that its members could define America, tautologically, by excluding from it all Americans who were not middle class. The scholars who for two centuries have debated the nature of America's uniqueness have been arguing from within a certain long-nourished, richly endowed dominant culture, one that made the ritual terms of its ascendance – individualism, progress, and the American Way – appear no less self-evident, no less true to sacred and natural law, than the once eternal truths of hierarchy, providence, and the Catholic Church. The authors in this volume represent an ideological self-awareness that may reshape our views not only of our literary tradition but, in time, of our culture at large.

Perhaps the most dramatic testimony in this respect comes from Henry Nash Smith. When he wrote *Virgin Land,* Smith tells us, he failed to consider certain "tragic dimensions of the Westward Movement" because they were cloaked in ideas so familiar as to be "almost inaccessible to critical examination." His reconsideration is valuable not only as a critique of the single most influential book in American Studies but, more largely, as a commentary on the effects of ideology in both history and historiography. For, of course, the same ideas ("civilization," "free land," "frontier individualism") that obscured his view of the past also served in the past to rationalize the worst aspects of the westward movement: to mask oppression, facilitate greed, legitimize racism and violence. Smith's essay is eloquent and exemplary in its recognition of the ideological dimensions of scholarship.

Above all it is exemplary for what we might call the pejorative or adversary use of ideological analysis. No doubt this is inherent in the approach itself, encoded in its very terms as we've inherited these from Marxism and the social sciences. According to this tradition (which Jehlen outlines in the Introduction), ideology is necessarily suspect because it is intrinsically limiting, and analysis seeks to expose those limits through a process of unmasking, "inter-rupting," demystifying. In this case the process deserves special emphasis for the contrast it suggests between myth criticism and ideological analysis. Like ideology, myth is inherently suspect, and for much the same reasons: It is (among other things) a vehicle of culturally prescribed directives for thought and behavior. Literary critics, however, have tended to avoid the parallel by enforcing a sort of exegetical imperative of inversion. Because ideology pretends to truth, the task of analysis is to uncover, rationally, the sinister effects of its fictions. Because myths are fictions, the task is to display, empathetically, their "deeper truths" – the abiding values embedded in simple plots, the range and richness of formulaic metaphors. This double standard reflects the familiar Kantian distinction between the aesthetic and the cognitive faculties. To criticize a myth is to "appreciate" it from within, to explicate it "intrinsically," in its own "organic" terms. To criticize a piece of ideology is to see through it, to expose its historical functions, necessarily from an extrinsic, and usually from a hostile, perspective.

Hence the corrective import of "ideology" in Smith's essay. *Virgin Land* is a major work of literary and cultural history that is nonetheless freighted with the biases of myth criticism. The problem is not that Smith separated "historical consequences" from "imaginative and emotional realities," as some social historians have charged. It's that the separation involved a set of assumptions that obscured the function of the ideas in the myths he examined. *That* separation signals more than a scholar's self-imposed limits. It is an image of ideology in process – a mirror reflection of the way culture works, by imaginative and emotional appeal, to mask the effects of the ideas it promulgates, the unexamined (because internalized) values and beliefs that sustain the social order. Smith's essay offers a way of undoing those effects, an approach to the image–idea of "virgin land" that illuminates its historical consequences both in the nineteenth-century garden-deserts of the West and in our twentieth-century consumer-groves of academia. What he suggests, in sum, is a method by which the literary scholar can distance himself from cultural preconceptions, so as to make the study of myth a mode of cognitive criticism.

So considered, the essay records a significant shift in American studies. Smith outlines its new directions in his survey of recent scholarship; Richard Slotkin sets out its theoretical premises. His approach is integrative (as distinct from eclectic), and notable for its discriminating use of social science. On one hand, he incorporates Northrop Frye's mythography while insisting on its grounding in history. On the other hand, he rejects quantitative scientism while adopting a "skeptical-scientific" view that recognizes the fictionality of its own metaphoric structures. The result is a relativistic, dynamic mode of analysis, whose categories reflect the complex processes they describe. As Slotkin unfolds their meanings, myth, history, and ideology continually interact and redefine each other: myth as historical narrative with ideological import; ideology as a reaction against the historical constraints of myth; myth as a source of resistance to ideology; myth and ideology as the bases of social consensus *and* as the vehicles of contradictions that give rise to new forms of expression.

In all this, to recall, Slotkin's stance is pejorative, even adversary. His method is "diagnostic"; his main example, the "ordered lunacy" of cowboy-and-Indian games; his intention, to provide a defense against the "culture's battery of interpretive weapons." It may be well to remark, therefore, that his approach does not necessarily imply a hostility to ideology in general, not even the American ideology. I suggested earlier that the pejorative bias inheres in the method – it begins in the positivism of Destutt de Tracy and continues in the scientific-progressivist faith that links Marx and the French *idéologues* – but none of the essays in this volume, including those that might be termed Marxist, falls simply into this category. The point of departure, it is true, is often, as in Smith's case, a sense of cultural restriction (rather than, say, some "strangely neglected aspect of the text") and in that sense the examples offered of the American ideology might be said to be significant for what they exclude: the rhetoric of civil rights, for example, or the ideals of conservationism, or the appeal to liberty and equality, or for that matter the creative energies (social, economic, and imaginative) unleashed by the culture. One benefit of Slotkin's essay is that it clearly shows that this sort of exclusion is a choice of focus rather than a narrowness of perspective inherent in the view itself. Indeed, the very breadth and flexibility of Slotkin's analysis *invite* different perspectives. Ideology, he emphasizes, enacts the purposes of "societies in their totality"; and it does so not just by distortion and deceit, but by exposé, irony, and "cultural resistance." In short, ideology (by any definition) is not a system of ideas in the service of evil. It is a system of ideas wedded, for good and evil, to a certain social order. Ideology involves the networks of meaning through which a society, any society, elicits or enforces allegiance; and accordingly, ideological analysis can lead to a variety of views, including a positive and even partisan stance toward ideology. Two compelling examples, because they combine the adversarial and the partisan extremes, are the essays by Houston Baker and Jane Tompkins.

Their adversarial stance is certainly the more prominent. Black Studies and Women's Studies have contributed in many ways to American literary scholarship: by recovering unduly neglected authors and texts, by challenging unduly pervasive habits of mind, by opening new perspectives on the literary process itself. But the most important contribution has been ideological. I don't think we will ever again be able to feel so pure about our acts of canonization, or so innocently to claim that our models of literary development embody the American Spirit. This fortunate fall into history is the *donné* of Tompkin's essay and of Baker's. The intention, in each case, is not simply to add another "American classic" to the reading list; it is to bring the term "classic," and indeed the term "American," down from the realm of universals and back into history. Ideology thrives on the metamorphosis of type into archetype: a particular kind of man into mankind; a particular race or class into a moral abstraction; a particular set of values into a metaphysics of the Good. Ideological analysis tends in precisely the opposite direction. It seeks to de-sacrilize the archetypes by examining them as cultural artifacts, in terms of their specific forms and functions. This is not at all to deny their power as "universals." On the contrary, it is to affirm that power in all its manifold capacities, including its capacity to conceal, exclude, and repress.

Baker and Tompkins describe the process of exclusion and repression in detail. But they also describe (each from a very different angle) the positive and enabling aspects of ideology. Indeed, for Tompkins these are virtually identical with a feminist perspective. Her recovery of *Uncle Tom's Cabin* celebrates the "system of beliefs that undergirds . . . sentimental fiction," the great "storehouse of assumptions" about religion, politics, the family, and national mission that together "constitute the novel's ideological framework." No doubt she is aware that that ideology, like any other ideology, lent itself to many kinds of abuse. But because she sees it intrinsically, as a source of personal and social revitalization, she can understand its aesthetic complexity and appreciate the factors that made it work, the needs and aspirations it expressed. Thus she can show how the novel's most traditional components are also its most disruptive – how its agrarian, family-centered, Protestant values made *Uncle Tom's Cabin* (and by extension, the neglected literary genre it represents) a radical critique not only of slavery but of America's dominant "patriarchal" free enterprise culture.

It is a provocative instance of what I referred to earlier as the discrepant value-systems inherent in the symbol of America. Tompkins treats a moment of cultural transition, and the argument she makes about ideologies in conflict reaches beyond Stowe's work to the genre of sentimental fiction at large and beyond that to the cultural factors connecting high and popular fiction in mid-nineteenth-century America. By implication, Tompkins invites comparisons between *Uncle Tom's Cabin* and other major writings of the time – between, that is, once popular but now neglected works of art and once neglected but now established classics, like *Walden* and *Moby-Dick* – which have similarly been said to invoke precapitalist visions of "cooperation and harmony," and to direct these against the dominant forms of patriarchy and free enterprise. I would add, further, that any such comparisons between (say) Stowe and Thoreau are likely to yield evidence of ideological continuity as well as conflict; that the cultural factors linking "popular" and "elite" writing reveal continuities as well as disjunctions between agrarian and industrial America. As Tompkins explains it, Stowe's critique brings together a variety of contradictory currents of the age. *Uncle Tom's Cabin* is a visionary synthesis of the embattled parties of memory and hope; an integrated work of art whose "message" is economically nostalgic, culturally populist, and theologically progressivist – though remarkable, in its progressivism, for its heterodox idea of the future: a matriarchy under the lordship of Christ, a "radical transformation" of middle-class institutions that somehow "represents the interests of middle-class women." Altogether, it comes to seem (under Tompkins's analysis) a kaleidoscope of political and social change in mid-nineteenth-century America. But it is worth stressing that change itself also attests to the persistence of basic social and cultural patterns. These patterns take many forms in the novel; perhaps the most convenient example – the most striking emblem of the *reciprocities* Stowe implies between continuity and change – is the two kinds of utopia she offers in the novel as the sole redemptive alternatives, this side of heaven, to the lowly life in Uncle Tom's cabin: the outmoded Quaker community that shelters George Harris on his way to freedom, and the free-enterprise republic that he projects at the end of the novel, in fulfillment of his (and Stowe's) dream.

But the major effect of Tompkins's essay is to show the repressive force of the dominant culture. In this respect her essay may be seen to contrast with Houston Baker's. Both of the slave narratives that Baker examines attest, as it were inadvertently, to the *liberating* force of free enterprise ideology. The narratives themselves, that is, demonstrate the profound appeal of middle-class American culture during its decisive period of development, from 1789, the year of the Constitution and Vassa's *Life,* through 1845, when Frederic Douglass presented his classic *Narrative* to a nation moving inexorably toward its industrial–commercial Armageddon. Baker himself does not set out to vindicate that development, of course. On the contrary, he shows how Vassa and Douglass turned the metaphor of commercial deportation against itself by invoking Christian myth to justify their flight. And as Baker himself elucidates the metaphor, "archaeologically," it serves to invert the standard tropes for Americanization – one thinks here of Hawthorne's striking image of the *Mayflower,* delivering first the Pilgrims and then a cargo of slaves to the New World – and Baker supports this far-reaching inversion of canonical tradition with a wide variety of materials (folk songs, graphics, log cabins) and through various perspectives, from semiotics to economics.

It is a tribute to the integrity of Baker's method that, nonetheless, the affirmative qualities of free enterprise ideology emerge from the texts themselves as he analyzes them. If, as he shows, Vassa and Douglass were on some level manipulating the rhetoric they inherited, using the commercial argument to assert their right to "self-possession," surely, too, on some other level they were being manipulated in turn by the rhetoric, and energized by it. For as Baker also shows, both men believed deeply enough in what they said to define freedom itself in the same terms: to make those commercial catchwords – self-possesion, contract society, upward mobility, free trade, open opportunity – the key to their most private aspirations and most urgent social visions. Vassa meant his *Life* to demonstrate the benefits of a "superior" white society; and to the extent that Douglass did not, it was to rebuke that society for not being true to its own "sacred principles." For both men, as Baker portrays them, the free enterprise system represents political order, not *a* society, but Society – subject to human failings in practice, but in theory *the* form of social organization, reasonable, moral, and (through Scripture) divinely sanctioned. And seen in this light, the two autobiographies take on an almost ritual aspect. Alongside their radical implications – within the framework of defiance and dissent – they read like cultural morality plays; or, considered together, like an ideological *Pilgrim's Progress:* the sacred–secular journey of Self-Made Man from the economics of slavery toward the Armageddon of the Yankee bourgeoisie.

The effect is ironic for many reasons, including those for which Douglass's *Narrative,* like Stowe's novel, has until recently been denied serious literary study. Ideologically, the irony is all the richer in that it involves the traditional separation I alluded to, earlier in the After-word, of high art from popular culture. In American Studies this tradition has expressed itself through an almost dogmatic application of the distinction I made earlier between intrinsic and extrinsic criticism. Our classic writers are honored as keepers of the American myth; all other writers (especially the popular ones) are unmasked as representatives, on different levels, of the American ideology. When Robert Rantoul invokes the tenets of laissez-faire to attack social abuses, we point out that he is divided in his ideological loyalties. When John O'Sullivan advances the principles of minimal government and manifest destiny, we accuse him of using ideology to veil oppression. When Emerson and Thoreau advance those tenets, attack those abuses, and express that ambivalence, we say they're transcending, prophesying, and creating ambiguities.

I am not forgetting the vast differences between these men in mind and imagination; nor do I mean in any way to deny the important differences in their relation to the American ideology. My point is to call into question the well-worn dichotomy between art and society. In some sense, certainly, a work of art transcends; it may be said to be trans-historical, or trans-cultural, or even trans-canonical. But it can no more transcend ideology than an artist's mind can transcend psychology; and I would suggest that the writers who transform political into universal norms may be no less implicated than the others in the dominant culture, and in the long run perhaps more useful in perpetuating it. This is not at all to denigrate their achievement. Nor is it to deny that these writers may have used "America," imaginatively, to expose the contradictions inherent in the symbol, and so effectually to turn the cultural symbology (as several essays in this volume contend) against the dominant culture. Nor, finally, is it to forget the special capacities of language in some sense to break free of social restrictions, and through its own dynamics to undermine the power structures it seems to reflect. On the contrary, I would suggest that ideological analysis can help us see more clearly, and to define more precisely, what we have perceived as being extraordinary, irreducible, and uncontained about our classic texts. Obviously, any defense of literature (as art) that requires a pejorative view of popular culture (as ideology) is itself ideological, part of a strategy designed to reinforce the separation of "spheres of influence": culture from Culture, politics from art, public from private. Like other apologias for literature as handmaid to theology or servant to the state, this one is neither divine nor natural, but historical. And here as elsewhere, the more distance we get from inherited assumptions, the more fully we will be able to understand the functions of literary texts in their own time and in ours.

I have in mind a cultural dialectic, mediating between the pejorative and partisan uses of ideological analysis, attuned to the power of language no less than the language of power, sensitive to the appeal of ideology while insisting on the cognitive dimensions of art. That seems to me both subject and import of Alan Trachtenberg's essay on *Democratic Vistas*. He shows how the idea of America, which blurred Whitman's view of the country – which disabled Whitman from examining "the political terrain in terms themselves political or ideological" – also provided him with a profoundly radical vision of "culture in its political essence." It was a vision built on the interchangeable meanings of the words "America," "democracy," and "culture," and it expressed itself through an ideological "programme" that invested all three words with a transformative political power, creating in them the "ground for a historically new relation of culture to its society." This "politics of culture," Trachtenberg points out, became a major legacy to American Studies. His own analysis develops its implications into an interdisciplinary approach. Trachtenberg brings together the methods of social and humanistic studies, extrinsic and intrinsic criticism, in a challenging exploration of "culture as process," where "culture" serves both cognitively, "as a principle of historical explanation," and politically, "as an image of integration and interrelatedness." In fact, his essay offers an ideological programme of its own: one that makes literary analysis integral to the study of culture, and the problem of "our usable past" a problematic of political action.

For Trachtenberg, that problematic carries with it what he sees as the fundamentally radical impulse of Whitman's concept of culture. Thus he joins the debate implicit in many of these essays about the politics of our classic writings. The debate itself is central to this volume. It indicates not only the diversity of views, but the distinctive revisionary character of the venture as a whole. It returns us to the question I began with, concerning the multivalence of the symbol of America, and the comprehensiveness of "*the* American ideology." And it reminds us that the established views of our literary tradition, here often under attack, themselves began in a political reassessment of our classic writers. The reassessment was often couched in New Critical terms, to be sure, or at any rate in terms of intrinsic literary merit. But there were unmistakable cultural and social implications. The canon that substituted *Song of Myself* for *The Song of Hiawatha* (and *Democratic Vistas* for *The Bigelow Papers*) also sanctified Whitman as outsider and nonconformist. The literary establishment that raised *Moby-Dick* from cetology catalogues (as James Kavanagh points out) to sudden epic prominence proceeded to acclaim Melville for his No-in-thunder to the powers of the earth. Directly and indirectly, revaluation tended to valorize the subversive: duplicity in Hawthorne, protest in Thoreau, marginality in Poe, antinomianism in Emerson. All this, be it noted, in the name of a *national* tradition, an American literature newly recovered for its quintessential "Americanness."

The debate I just referred to may be said to center on the paradox of an antagonistic literature that is somehow also culturally representative. That did not really trouble an earlier generation of critics, because they tended to separate the America of the spirit, represented by our classic writers, from the realities of American life, represented by ideologues and their victims. By and large, the essays in this volume take it as a major challenge to connect these two forms of representation. The America they speak of lies neither in the "open air" of some quasi-Platonic Frontier Republic (or quasi-Christian New World Democracy), nor in a linguistic maze of self-reflexive symbology, nor in the mythic realm of biblical, moral, and psychological antinomies (Old Serpent and New Adam, Innocence and Experience, Eros and Thanatos). Rather, to repeat, it is a burgeoning political–economic–ideational system, neither monolithic in its culture nor teleological in its social development, conflicted in many ways, discontinuous in others, but expanding with remarkable energy and conviction toward what seemed to its adherents, much of the time, the fulfillment of a promise, and to our classic writers, at least some of the time, the desecration of an ideal. Essentially, this is the basis for the wide-ranging claims made in the section on "perspectives." The continuities and changes traced there constitute a new framework for examining our tradition of literary dissent and its problematic relation to "America." They also suggest new ways of examining that tradition in terms of the problematic relation of American intellectuals – writers, critics, academics, and others – to the culture that sustains them and that they have served to sustain (sometimes in spite of themselves).

For Leo Marx, the key to that doubly problematic relation lies in the persistence of American pastoralism. From its beginnings, he observes, the New World pastoral was at once a literary mode and an effort to shape a certain way of life; and accordingly his analysis focuses simultaneously on form and content. Considered both as a system of belief and as a literary genre, pastoralism, Marx writes, sought to make adventure a function of the "recovery of the natural," and material abundance subordinate to the quest for the good society. This vision our classic writers inherited, transmuted into the language of Romanticism, and bequeathed to the culture at large. Marx describes it as an ideology of the "ambiguous middle state," a mode of moral and social criticism opposed both to the fantasies of primitivism and to the imperatives of material progress, especially in their later technocratic forms. The ideal it advanced – a participatory democracy based on the primacy of organic self-realization – repudiated the faith in progress per se even while it welcomed the opportunities for economic, political, and scientific improvement. For although our classic writers drew upon "residual or past-oriented elements of culture," they did so, Marx points out, "not to renounce the amenities of modern life" but to enhance the modern through the recovery of a simpler, more natural way of life.

Hence the peculiar Americanness of their radical thought: It was the product of a precapitalist world view adapted to and then shaped by the conditions of the New World. And hence the peculiar role of our classic writers in the history of American radicalism: It was they, most conspicuously, who sustained the pastoral vision through the country's industrial transformation. In Europe at this time pastoralism was largely absorbed into the dominant culture – merged with a series of false rhetorical oppositions (country–city, nature–technology) that served to mystify industrial growth as the progress of mankind. Marx recognizes that it served that purpose in the United States as well; but he argues that here as nowhere else, or differently from anywhere else, the pastoral also assumed a contrary, subversive function. And he notes that in the past half century, especially after the failure of the Old Left, it has offered an increasingly plausible basis for social action: "an alternative way" conceived in opposition to the faith in bigness, organization, and growth that vitiated the spread of socialism in other "advanced" countries. Theoretically, Marx replaces the tautologies of "American exceptionalism" with a richly comparatist concept of difference. In practical terms, his discussion of literary dissent makes textual

S. Bercovitch

interpretation a form of political analysis, and literary-political analysis, so conceived, a form of moral commitment.

For Marx, the context of dissent is an adversary, nonprogressive residual culture. For Carolyn Porter it is the dominant culture itself. In what is probably the most lucid account we have of reification in nineteenth-century America, she describes our literary tradition as an increasingly effective struggle within and against the world created by industrial capitalism, a world of alienated objects – natural, human, mechanical – governed by what was made to seem the logic of impersonal and immutable law. Her approach is dialectical, developmental. Out of their very involvement in the culture, she argues, our writers forged a critical method that gradually expanded from an exposé of social contradictions to a wholly new mode of perception and action. The argument is illuminating in many ways. For my present purpose, I want to extrapolate three of these that I find to be characteristic of the critical tendencies of the volume in general. First, Porter makes explicit what many of the other authors here suggest, that our classic texts are "social to the core." They record an insistent engagement with society, rather than a recurrent flight from it. This view draws on earlier scholarship (including that of critics represented here, like Leo Marx); but the revision it implies in our concept of background, context, and influence – presented as this revision is throughout the volume from various angles and with new force and sophistication – takes on an importance that can hardly be overestimated. It relocates the American Renaissance firmly where it belongs, at the center of the antebellum movement toward industrialization, incorporation, and civil war.

Second, Porter draws out a theory of representation inherent in this shift of perspective. She sees literary texts in dynamic relation to the culture – neither as mirrors of their times nor as lamps of the creative imagination, but as works of *ideological* mimesis, produced by "participant-observers" who are implicated in the world they interpret, and yet capable, precisely by recognizing their complicity, of understanding, resisting, and in some cases "overcoming alienation."

Finally, Porter's essay highlights two main approaches to literary radicalism. One is essentially visionary, the new way of "seeing and being" that she infers from Faulkner's major novels. The other is essentially diagnostic – criticism that lays bare the root contradictions of the culture. Porter's prime example here is Emerson's *Nature;* Robert Byer offers another instance in Poe's "Man of the Crowd." Indeed, his essay is something of a diagnostic tour de force, a "close reading" that opens into an anatomy of urban alienation. Byer's use of stylistic techniques – his decoding (via Benjamin and Baudelaire) of Poe's decoding of the "mysteries of the city" – recalls Jehlen's comments in the Introduction about the contributions of literary theory to the study of ideology. But his essay also suggests that the advantages might be reciprocal. I refer in particular to his insistent historicism. Byer's analysis of the story's ambiguities leads outward, away from the self-enclosed symbolic harmonies of the New Criticism – and from the endless because self-generating verbal indeterminacies of the *new* New Criticism – to the conditions of Jacksonian life: the psychopathology of crowds, the "mechanization of daily routine," the doubleness of community and privacy, the symbiosis of criminal and conformist. In effect, Byer uses recent literary techniques to historicize Poe, or more accurately to rehistoricize him as a central figure of the period – central for his art, for the "depth of [his] engagement with his culture," and in both these respects for his radical exposé of "modernity and its ideology."

Poe takes his place here with Emerson, as Byer remarks. Except, of course, that Emerson the prophet is inseparable from the social critic: The Transcendental dream of regeneration – of individuals reintegrated with nature and society, and thereby empowered with the confidence to make their own world – is fundamental to Emerson's legacy of protest. I called this the visionary emphasis in Porter's critique because, by implication at least, it argues for the radical function of utopian thought. The argument is implicit as well in several other essays in this volume and may be briefly stated. All utopian visions – pastoral, matriarchal, millennial, whatever – express powerful feelings of social discontent; many are adopted by repressed or ascendant groups to challenge the status quo; and although some of them are thus incorporated into the ideology of a new social order, nonetheless, *as* utopian visions, even these remain a potential source of social unrest, a standing invitation to resistance and revolt. Every ideology, that is, breeds its own opposition, every culture its own counterculture. The same ideals that at one point nourish the system may later become the basis of a new revolutionary consensus, one that invokes those ideals on behalf of an entirely different way of life.

This perspective is common to several authors in this volume, and it leads them at times to invest the text with an almost noumenal quality, a sort of visionary knowledge associated with truths that (independent of authorial activity) provide a vital access to reality. In some respects, their view may be compared to that of traditional humanism – literature as a criticism of life. But there is a crucial difference. For, say, Philip Sidney and Matthew Arnold, the ideals embodied in literature convey the abiding norms of morality and the spirit, by which life invariably falls short. For the authors in this volume, those ideals, considered as a criticism of life, serve to engage us in the dynamics of history. In its negative or pejorative form, ideological analysis begins on the other side of humanist absolutes, in a recognition of the material processes that the *rhetoric* of morality and the spirit seeks to conceal or disguise. In its positive or empathic form, ideological analysis locates in those absolutes a utopian criticism of the status quo, a vision of human possibilities that provides the ground for reconstituting the moral and material norms of society—or else, as Michael Gilmore argues in his essay on Thoreau, for undertaking a personal, exemplary revolt against society for having betrayed its own founding principles.

Gilmore's essay is a cultural guide to American utopianism from Monticello to Walden Pond. He locates the origins of Thoreau's dissent—the principles behind his July Fourth secession from the Union—in the tradition of civic humanism, and specifically in the conflict between that tradition and the Jacksonian marketplace. Gilmore reads *Walden,* that is, as an ironic enactment of a growing cultural schizophrenia. For, as he notes, civic humanism was a cornerstone of American nationhood. The vision it embodied of agrarian harmony had provided an impetus to revolution, a rhetoric of social cohesion, and a rationale for the political structures of the young republic. As the economy expanded, those structures shifted, and the rhetoric shifted accordingly, to accommodate the new commercial interests. But the continuities were too strong, too basic, for the old ideals to be discarded. They were the ideals of national independence, after all, the self-evident truths of liberal democracy. So the rhetoric of civic humanism persisted, haunting the antebellum marketplace with memories of unkept promises. And thus divested of its social *function,* that rhetoric appealed now with the greater purity, as the vehicle of disinterested universal truth. In sum, the civic tradition that had helped establish the nation became, in the utopian form of memory and promise, a fundamental challenge to the established order. And in *Walden* the challenge found its classic literary expression. Both as an ideological critique and prophetic summons, Thoreau's work turns the ideals of the American Way—independence, liberty, enterprise, opportunity, individualism, expansion, "America" itself—against the United States.

We might see in this, with Trachtenberg, the basis for an emergent socialism; or with Porter, the beginning of a radically new way of seeing and being; or with Leo Marx, the rhetoric of a genuinely "alternative way" to both European socialism and American capitalism. But the ironies Gilmore traces—which in fact lie at the very heart of *Walden*—require us to consider a different prospect as well. I refer in particular to what he calls "Thoreau's complicity in the ideological

universe he abhorred" (as in *Walden*'s myth of self-reliance, or its transformation of politics into "a series of withdrawals from history"). I
refer also to the possibility that these strategies of accommodation contributed to the success of *Walden,* not only in the marketplace, but as a
sacred text of American dissent. Most largely, I refer to the historical
fact to which both these ironies point, that characteristically, as a matter
of course, the dominant culture adopts utopia for its own purposes. It
does not simply endorse the trans-historical ideals of harmony and
regeneration; it absorbs and redefines these in ways that support the
social system. It molds the "archetypes" of organic community to fit its
distinctive system of values. It re-creates the Eden of the "racial unconscious" in its own image. It ritualizes the egalitarian energies of the
liminal process in such a way as to control discontent and harness
anarchy itself to the social enterprise.

So molded, ritualized, and controlled, utopianism has served often
enough to diffuse or deflect dissent, or actually to transmute it into a
vehicle of socialization. Indeed, it is not too much to see this as ideology's chief weapon. Ideology represses alternative or oppositional
forms when these arise. But it seeks first of all to preempt them, and it
does so most effectively by *drawing out* protest, *encouraging* the contrast
between utopia and the status quo. The method is as old as ideology
itself. Any form of protest, utopian or other, threatens society most
fundamentally when it calls into question the claims of that society to
represent things as they ought to be (by divine right, natural law, the
dictates of Scripture, the Forms of reason). Fundamental protest, that
is, involves a historicist, relativistic perspective on the claims of ideology. And the immemorial response of ideology, what we might call its
instinctive defense, has been to redefine protest in terms of the system,
as a complaint about shortcomings from the ideal. Thus the very act of
identifying malfunction becomes an appeal for cohesion. To that end,
ideology seeks to focus attention on the distance between vision and
fact, or between theory and practice. To denounce Christian immoral-
ity through the precepts of Christ is to define morality itself as Christian; just as the contrast between Christianity and the various forms of
"paganism" excludes the very possibility of non-Christian (let alone
anti-Christian) ideals. To define injustice through particular violations
of free enterprise (or its constituent elements, such as social mobility,
open opportunity, and self-fulfillment) is to consecrate free enterprise as
the just society.

Hence the enormous conservative, restraining power in the alliance
between utopia and ideology. It allows the dominant culture not
merely to enforce rules of conduct, but to circumscribe the bounds of

perception, thought, and desire. And if that culture dominates not by coercion but by consent – if its rituals are not traditional but newly formed, *and "new" as well by cultural fiat* (new rituals of a self-proclaimed New People in a New World); if the population, moreover, is broadly heterogeneous (and again, *heterogeneous as well by cultural fiat,* the self-proclaimed Heir of the Ages); if its power, therefore, depends on myths and values to which all levels of society subscribe, *especially the excluded and repressed* (because to subscribe thus is the promised way to acceptance and power); and if, finally, it is a culture founded on the principles of contract, voluntarism, and self-interest – a culture whose primary unit is the self, and whose primary rites, accordingly, encourage the *implicitly radical, potentially subversive* doctrine of individualism (with its insidious claims for freedom, equality, and multiple interpretation) – if the culture, that is, combines the conditions of modernization in the United States with the principles of liberal democracy, then the need to preclude alternatives a priori assumes special urgency. We might say that the American ideology was made to fill that need. It undertakes above all, as a condition of its nurture and design, to turn what might be conflict between secular goals (personal and social) and moral or spiritual ideals into a mode of symbolic reconciliation. And according to several authors in this volume, it has accomplished this most effectively through its rhetoric of dissent.

This view is expressed most broadly in Myra Jehlen's essay on the "New World epic." In contrast to Gilmore and Porter, she sees our classic texts as examples par excellence of a triumphant middle-class hegemony. Their message, she writes, is that basic change is impossible, except as apocalypse; their symbolic and narrative strategies, far from subverting the status quo, attest to the capacities of the dominant culture "to co-opt oppositional and alternative forms," to the point of making alternatives virtually unthinkable. Jehlen does not at all minimize their protest. Her point is not that they have no quarrrel with America, but that they seem to have nothing *but* that to quarrel about. Having adopted their culture's *controlling* metaphor – "America" as synonym for human possibility – and having made this the ground of radical dissent, they effectually redefine radicalism as an affirmation of cultural values. For the metaphor, thus universalized, does not transcend ideology. It portrays the American ideology, as all ideology yearns to be portrayed, in the transcendent colors of utopia. Thus Stowe (it might be argued) portrays George Harris's free enterprise errand into the Liberian wilderness; thus Emerson and Thoreau (in their optative moods) sketch out the "nation of individuals" to come; and thus Whitman (in one view of *Democratic Vistas*) identifies the American future as utopia, and utopia, therefore, as the essence and telos of the American Way.

According to Jehlen, the same method applies, *mutatis mutandis,* to the novels of Hawthorne and Melville. Our classic novelists perceived evil in many forms, and they had a remarkable gift for seeing through those forms to metaphysical issues; but their insight was attended by an equally remarkable blindness to social limits. What they could not see all too often was that the issues themselves were culturally determined; that the universals they invoked might obscure or disguise the evils they attacked; that the United States was neither utopia at best nor dystopia at worst, neither "the world's fairest hope," as Melville put it, nor "man's foulest crime," but a certain political system; that *in principle* no less than in practice the American Way was neither inevitable nor providential nor "simply natural" but one of many possible forms of society.

Jehlen develops her argument into a general reappraisal of our "romance tradition" in the novel. Her essay is nicely complemented in this respect by Jonathan Arac's study of the A-politics of *The Scarlet Letter.* Arac's essay is the obverse of Byers's, as Jehlen's is of Porter's. For him the text embodies (rather than decodes) a process of mystification, so that he is less concerned, explicitly, with social than with rhetorical structures. His explication leads out from the problem of meaning into an anatomy of liberal co-optation. *Interpretation as co-optation:* From this vantage point, Arac relates *The Scarlet Letter* to the major issues of its time and to cultural patterns that reach back to the country's founding texts (the Declaration of Independence, the Federalist Papers, and the Constitution) and forward from Hawthorne to Hartman and Hirsch. In all cases, he finds essentially the same logic of "(in)action." To interpret is to perceive ambiguity; ambiguity requires us to acknowledge multiplicity; and that acknowledgment can be turned to positive ends, rescued (so to speak) from its own counsel of despair, only by the affirmation of some benevolent overarching design. As in Adam Smith's theory of free enterprise (or the doctrines of states' rights and balance of power), the ruling assumption is the tendency of competing interpretations to flow "naturally," of their own accord, into some "larger," "truer" interpretation. In this larger view, process *is* progress, and progress, a continual harmony-in-diversity, diversity-in-harmony – a benevolent, expanding process in which conflict is obviated (as in Poe's *Eureka*) by the alternation of the one into the many and the many into the one.

It amounts to a hermeneutics of laissez-faire, as Arac points out, and it carries with it a pointedly circumscribed set of moral–economic–aesthetic imperatives: "*Issues* have no part in the discourse of established parties"; what really counts is character; what really works is compromise; the only reliable viewpoint is one that recognizes the dangers inherent in self-assertion; the only proper interchange of ideas is one that prevents the sort of divisiveness that leads to radical social change. These are the imperatives, of course, behind the entire process of Americanization, from the doctrine of individualism to the corporate concept of "continuing revolution." Arac applies this to Hester Prynne's conversion, at the end of *The Scarlet Letter,* from rebel outcast to agent of socialization. We might apply it, in different ways, to other voices of protest in our classic texts: those of reformers, like Hawthorne's Holgrave, who interpret change as continuity; or of dissidents, like *Walden's* Thoreau, who interpret nature as free enterprise spiritualized; or of prophets, like Whitman's Walt, who interpret *themselves* as pluralism incarnate (and pluralism in turn as an image of the American self); or of rebel-isolatoes, like Poe's Pym, through whom perversity is interpreted as an inalienable personal right; or of blasphemers, like Ahab, who interpret *away* social protest as metaphysical outrage; or of daemonic originals, like Emerson's Native Genius, who interpret America simultaneously as progress, the soul, the farthest point in the development of the Anglo-Saxon race, and the triumph of democratic liberalism. This sort of radical stance, according to Arac, Jehlen, and others in this volume, is indeed "representative," *American:* It is the aesthetic flowering of an ideology adopted from the start precisely for its capacity to transmute radicalism of all forms, from religious protest to revolutionary war, into forms of cultural consensus.

Let me emphasize again that this view is disputed elsewhere in this volume, directly as well as indirectly. My point is not to offer still another ready and easy road to reconciliation, but on the contrary to call attention to the dispute and its implications – among these, the variety of views to which ideological analysis lends itself.[3] It may be that in this respect the authors here are closer than they acknowledge to the tenets of liberalism and the pressures of the academic shopping mall. Nonetheless, their concern with ideology makes a difference. In Porter's terms, the indeterminacy of the critic–appreciator is replaced by the relativism of the observer–participant. Interpretation remains as before an invitation to difference, but the terms of difference shift, from process to dialectics, and hence from a self-enclosed circle of multiple perspectives to an open-ended engagement between history, the reader, and the text.

This sense of engagement seems to me the common ground between what are otherwise four rather disparate views of Melville. The essays in this section effectually set out the parameters of diversity in ideological analysis. They may be read, for example, as an application to a particular writer of the various issues raised in this volume. Thus James Kavanagh argues that the art of "Benito Cereno" lies in its adversary ideological analysis of the distortions of discourse; Paul Royster explains *Moby-Dick* as the aesthetic triumph of the language of the dominant culture (and thereby enhances its affinities to epics of other cultures); Emory Elliott discusses *Pierre* as a sweeping critique of the American ideology, from its utopian fantasies of domesticity to its alienating "mysteries of the city"; and Donald Pease examines aspects of Melville's criticism through "scenes of cultural persuasion" that demonstrate the interaction of culture and society, aesthetic and political concerns. Or again, the four essays might be read as examples of the diverse influences on the study of ideology as Jehlen outlines these in her Introduction: Marxist and neo-Marxist approaches (Kavanagh); social and symbolic anthropology (Royster); deconstruction, semiotics, and reader-response theory (Pease); cultural and intellectual history (Elliott).

All this diversity and more. But these essays also insist on the evasions implicit in the recourse to multiple perspective per se. As Royster points out, Pip's famous commentary on the meaning of the doubloon ("I look, you look, he looks; we look, ye look, they look") proposes a theory of interpretive democracy that masks a hierarchy leading *down* to Pip, by fixed steps, from captain to officers to crew. Ideological analysis, that is, reminds us that multiplicity is not necessarily opposite to hegemony; the two may simply be different sides of the same coin. This should perhaps go without saying in a discussion of American culture, because the very rhetoric of union is grounded in appeals to diversity, separateness, and tolerance. But here as elsewhere, the obvious is a function of the assumed – the unexamined foundations of thought and expression that these essays set out to explore, and, in doing so, set themselves apart from other recent ventures in revision. I refer now not to literary theory but to what might be considered its counterpart in cultural studies, the trend toward pluralism. Or, more accurately, toward the new pluralism, for the trend itself is part of a long-established cycle in American scholarship of pluralism and consensus. It was once said, in reaction against those who sought to define America "intellectually," that America was really the product of process; the intellectuals had the American idea, and "the people" had "the American experience." Now it is said, in reaction against those who speak of an American literature or a national culture, that this country is sheer heterogeneity. The ruling elite has an American ideology; the people have their own patchwork-quilt (rather than melting-pot) American multifariousness: "America" is – many forms of ethnicity, many patterns of thought, many ways of life, many cultures, many American literatures.

It is a particular strength of the essays in this volume that they make use of the best insights of this new pluralism without succumbing to the ideological trap it signals. The insights are those that challenge the dominance of cultural norms: as in Pease's concept of persuasion, Kavanagh's use of oppositional contexts, Elliott's and Royster's analysis of popular "sentimental" literature in *Pierre,* and the suspicion with which all of them treat the terms "canon" and "classic." The trap lies in the way that the challenge itself may become the means for avoiding the issue of dominance. Every ideology construes its own form of this trap. The American form, I have suggested, is to turn potential conflict into a debate about fusion or fragmentation – in effect, to turn what might have been a confrontation of alternatives into an alternation of opposites. This does not necessarily apply to any specific study in pluralism. What I have in mind is the enterprise in its theoretical fullness, the prospect of a diversity of scholars, of every race and creed, all bent on capturing the heterogeneity of America, like that motley *Pequod*'s crew bent on the ubiquitous white whale; or more accurately, like so many Ishmaels explaining the pursuit as though Ahab were largely irrelevant, the representative of a tiny elite, the voice merely of an articulate few, or (as Pip has it) just one of many points of view.

This aspect of the new pluralism is part of the background I mentioned earlier, *against* which the essays in this volume define themselves. Together they demonstrate that to recognize the limitations of ideology is to open up interpretation; whereas, conversely, to deny those limitations is to subject interpretation to ideology. The option is not multiplicity or consensus. It is whether to make use of the categories of culture or to be used by them. I do not claim that the essays here altogether avoid the peculiar cultural traps embedded in the quest for "America," in either its multiple or its unitary guises. Indeed, I am aware that what at the start of this Afterword I called a dialogue in the making has itself the makings, *in potentia,* of still another example of the special genius of the rhetoric of American consensus, which is to co-opt the energies of radicalism: to absorb the very terms of opposition into the promise of the New, that long-nurtured vision of Futurity that carries us forever back, through a procession of sacred landmarks – the Gettysburg Address, "The American Scholar," the Declaration of Independence, the legendary *Mayflower* Compact, the imagined Discovery of America – to the ideological premises of modern democratic liberalism. I am aware, too, that some of the central concerns of the dialogue, as I outlined these at the start, may be even more problematic than their treatments in this volume suggest. I think, for instance, of the problem in locating our radical tradition in a literature obsessed with an *American* dream; or of the problem in locating that dream, considered as our *radical* tradition, in the realm of literature; or again, of the problem in locating a radical discourse about American culture in what is after all a rather *traditional* exchange among professional *literary* critics.

I mention these problems partly to highlight what I consider to be limitations of this volume, partly to suggest that those limitations may have a distinctive value of their own in setting directions for the study of American literature and culture. Ideological analysis does not promise to lead us out of the wilderness of ideology into a Canaan of unmediated truth. Quite the opposite, it reminds us that that promise is itself a function of ideology (variously mediated by religion, science, and art), and so enables us to see the ways of the wilderness more clearly. These essays are no less important for the questions they raise than for the answers they provide. Basically, indeed, all these authors share a *resistance* to solutions, a skepticism that begins in their suspicion of the formulaic, the "natural," and the "already-said." They tend to see in totalizing answers, as in self-evident truths, the traces of ideological snares or blunders. That almost programmatic suspiciousness is the negative side of ideological analysis. The other, complementary side lies in the freshness of perspective that the resistance provokes – the richness of the problems at issue, the methodological and practical challenges involved in these inquiries. I would like to think (in spite of the reservations I just voiced) that among these is the challenge of alternative *historical* possibilities, including alternative ways of intellectual, moral, and political commitment. To some extent at least, that hope, too, is implicit in the essays in this volume, and in the common venture they represent.

Notes

1 The dialogue extends far beyond the contributors to this particular volume. It applies to the entire range of American literature and it includes scholars outside the field who use American materials – among others, John Diggins (Intellectual History) on Thoreau; David Noble (American Studies) on nineteenth-century American literature; Michael Rogin (Political Science) on Melville; Edward Said (Comparative Literature) on American literary radicalism; and Warren Susman (Cultural History) on modern American literature. It also includes what might be termed right-wing and polemically "conservative" scholars – Kenneth Lynn and Peter Shaw, for example – although it should be stated openly that for the most part the

dialogue I refer to falls within the left-wing of the political spectrum, and that that bias is reflected in this volume. Even so, and even when the focus is narrowed (as it is here) specifically to the area of mid-nineteenth-century American literary scholarship, the interest in ideological analysis has made for a large, diverse, and growing corpus of criticism. This includes established scholars as well as some of the most interesting and productive younger scholars and critics: for example, Joyce Adler, Peter Antelyes, Nina Baym, Mitchell Breitweiser, Gillian Brown, John Cawelti, Bell Chevigny, Eric Cheyfitz, Michael Denning, Ann Douglas, Paul Ericson, Jay Fliegelman, Bruce Franklin, Sam Girgus, Irving Howe, Amy Kaplan, Carolyn Karcher, Anne Kibbey, Annette Kolodny, Michael Kramer, Mark Krupnik, Amy Lang, Frank Lentricchia, Kathryne Lindberg, Christopher Looby, Stephen Mailloux, Wendy Martin, John Peacock, John Carlos Rowe, Mark Seltzer, Doris Summer, Eric Sundquist, Brook Thomas, Cecilia Tichi, Priscilla Wald, James Wallace, Donald Weber, R. A. Yoder, and Larzer Ziff. I should perhaps stress the qualification–*for example*–that precedes this long list of names. The length is not a sign of inclusiveness. It is meant simply to suggest the richness (in quality and quantity) of the work currently under way in ideology and mid-nineteenth-century American literature. My apologies to those critics and scholars whom I have inadvertently omitted. And my thanks to those among the critics just cited who have read the Afterword and made useful suggestions.

Let me add, in this connection, that the contributors to this volume were selected not only for the excellence of their work but for the variety of their perspectives. I would like to thank them all for helpful comments, pro and con, on this Afterword. I would also like to make public an apology to several of them. Because this Afterword is designed as a discussion of the issues involved in ideological criticism, I have not attempted to evaluate the essays on their own merits; rather I have used them to exemplify the sorts of concerns that all the contributors share. In doing so I hope I have not misrepresented any of them. But I did find it expedient to skew the representation to my special purposes–sometimes dwelling on the implicit at the expense of the explicit (as in my treatments of the essays by Houston Baker and Gerald Graff); sometimes slighting individual statements by focusing on a group of essays (as in the case of those in the Melville section). My thanks to the contributors for generously agreeing to indulge me in this matter.

2   The historical studies of the ideology of the Revolution mark an important development in our understanding not only of that period but of the colonial background to nationhood and the country's subsequent growth through the Civil War. Although this historical scholarship differs in many ways from the sort of ideological analysis found in this volume, students interested in the ideological context (and substance) of American literature will find illuminating and provocative the works in this field by such historians as Bernard Bailyn, Lance Banning, Richard Buel, Pauline Maier,

Mary Beth Norton, Caroline Robbins, and Gordon Wood. On the subject of colonial ideology, students should consult (for example) the work of Joyce Appleby, Robert Brown, Nancy Cott, Jack P. Greene, Robert A. Gross, James Henretta, Rhys Isaac, and J. R. Pole. Historians who have examined ideology in the Jacksonian and antebellum periods include (among others) Rowland Berthoff, David Brion Davis, George M. Frederickson, John Higham, Robert Kelley, Gary Nash, David Noble, Dorothy Ross, Carroll Smith-Rosenberg, and Rush Welter. The ideology of "civic humanism" is most fully discussed by J. G. A. Pocock. Representative Marxist perspectives will be found in the work of Eric Foner, Eugene Genovese, Jesse Lemisch, Stoughton Lind, Edward Pessen, and Alfred F. Young.

3 Many of these differing views of ideology are suggested in the footnotes to these essays, in Jehlen's Introduction, and in our Selected Bibliography. It may be well to emphasize, however, that these citations have been kept to a minimum. A full list would include the work of anthropologists like Marshall Sahlins and historians like E. P. Thompson; it would range from proponents of cultural relativism like Wilhelm Dilthey, Emile Durkheim, Talcott Parsons, and Max Weber to various forms of Marxism (or neo-Marxism) represented by, say, Etienne Balibar, Lucien Goldmann, Jürgen Habermas, and Herbert Marcuse; it would note the influence of Jean-Paul Sartre (in the area of literary theory as well as philosophy); it would recognize the work of earlier Marxist literary critics, like Christopher Caldwell, Ralph Fox, Granville Hicks, and Arnold Kettle; it would recognize, too, the astute critique of ideological analysis by Michel Foucault; and for present purposes, it would draw special attention to the affinities of ideological criticism in diverse areas of literary theory – for example, in the work of Roland Barthes (semiotics), Mikhail Bakhtin (Russian formalism), Wolfgang Iser and Hans Robert Jauss (reader response), and Jacques Derrida and Paul de Man (deconstruction). Furthermore, any adequate discussion of differing views of ideology would call attention to what might be called bibliographical moot points in the field: which of Marx's works most fully or fruitfully represents his views of ideology; the controversies over and within the Frankfurt School (and the debates about its legacy, as in the studies of David Held, Martin Jay, and Raymond Geuss); the contributions of political figures, like Leon Trotsky; the problem of Lukács's changing perspectives; and so on. Students would do well in this respect to consult various conference proceedings, such as that of the University of Essex, July 1976, published in Francis Parker, ed., *Literature, Society, and the Sociology of Literature* (Colchester: University of Essex, 1977), and such journals as *Ideology and Consciousness* and *New Left Review,* as well as special journal-issues that involve questions on ideology: for example, the essays from *Working Papers in Cultural Studies* issued from the Centre for Contemporary Cultural Studies at the University of Birmingham as *On Ideology* (London: Hutchinson, 1978), the essays from *Critical Inquiry* in *Canons,* ed.

Robert von Hallberg (Chicago: University of Chicago Press, 1983), and the essays from *Signs* in *Feminist Theory: A Critique of Ideology,* ed. Nannerl O. Keohane, Michelle Z. Rosaldo, and Barbara C. Gelpi (Chicago: University of Chicago Press, 1982). Students should also consult the valuable bibliographic guides (as well as pertinent substantive discussions) in various recent studies: for example, by Catherine Belsey, *Critical Practice* (London: Methuen, 1980); Tony Bennett, *Formalism and Marxism* (London: Methuen, 1979); John Fekete, *The Critical Twilight: Explorations in the Ideology of Anglo-American Literary Theory from Eliot to McLuhan* (Boston: Routledge & Kegan Paul, 1977); and Susan Rubin Suleiman, *Authoritarian Fictions: The Ideological Novel as a Literary Genre* (New York: Columbia University Press, 1983). These are basically studies in literature. Different sorts of bibliographical maps are provided, for example, in the philosophical studies by James R. Flynn, *Humanism and Ideology: An Aristotelian View* (Boston: Routledge & Kegan Paul, 1973) and Alan Ryan, *The Philosophy of the Social Sciences* (New York: Macmillan, 1970); in the political studies by Nigel Harris, *Beliefs in Society: The Problem of Ideology* (London: Watts, 1968), and Donald G. Macrae, *Ideology and Society: Papers in Sociology and Politics* (London: Heinemann, 1961); in the critiques of Marxism by Alvin W. Gouldner, *The Dialectic of Ideology and Technology: The Origins, Grammar and Future of Ideology* (New York: Seabury, 1976), Lewis S. Feuer, *Ideology and the Ideologists* (New York: Harper & Row, 1975), Louis J. Halle, *The Ideological Imagination* (London: Chatto & Windus, 1972), Franz Jakubowski, *Ideology and Superstructure in Historical Materialism* (1936), trans. Anne Booth (London: Allison & Busby, 1978), and John P. Plamenatz, *Ideology* (New York: Macmillan, 1970); and in studies in semantics, law, political philosophy, and political psychology by Patrick Corbett, *Ideologies* (New York: Harcourt Brace Jovanovich, 1965), Paul Hirst, *On Law and Ideology* (New York: Macmillan, 1979), A. C. McIntyre, *Secularism and Moral Change: The Riddell Memorial Lectures* (New York: Oxford University Press, 1967), and Arne Naess, *Democracy, Ideology, and Objectivity: Studies in the Semantics and Cognitive Analysis of Ideological Controversy* (Oslo: University Press, 1956).

Selected Bibliography

This is a minimal list of readings for students who would like to explore further the background and implications of the arguments and themes developed in this volume. They should also consult, of course, the notes to the essays, including those to the Introduction and the Afterword.

A. INTRODUCTORY OVERVIEWS

Norman Birnbaum, "The Sociological Study of Ideology (1940–60): A Trend Report and Bibliography," *Current Sociology* 9 (1960): 91–172.

Ben Halperin, " 'Myth' and 'Ideology' in Modern Usage," *History and Theory* 1 (1961): 129–49.

Jorge Larrain, *The Concept of Ideology* (Athens: University of Georgia Press, 1979).

George Lichtheim, "The Concept of Ideology," in *The Concept of Ideology and Other Essays* (New York: Random House, 1963), pp. 3–46.

J. S. Roucek, "A History of the Concept of Ideology," *Journal of the History of Ideas* 5 (1944): 482–98.

Edward Shils, "Ideology," *International Encyclopedia of the Social Sciences* (New York: Macmillan, 1968), 7: 66–75.

B. GENERAL COLLECTIONS

David E. Apter, ed., *Ideology and Discontent* (New York: Free Press, 1964).

Jonathan Arac, ed., *Engagements: Post-Modernism, Marxism, Politics* (Binghamton: State University of New York, 1983), vols. 11 and 12 of *Boundary 2*.

Robin Blackburn, ed., *Ideology in Social Science* (New York: Fontana Collins, 1972).

Ernst Bloch et al., *Aesthetics and Politics* (London: NLB, 1977).

James M. Heath, ed., *Literature and Ideology,* (Lewisburg, Pa.: Bucknell University Press, 1982), vol. 27 of *Bucknell Review*.

Herbert G. Reid, ed., *Up the Mainstream: A Critique of Ideology in American Politics and Everyday Life* (New York: McKay, 1974).

C. SPECIALIZED STUDIES

Louis Althusser, "Ideology and Ideological State Apparatuses," in *Lenin and Philosophy and Other Essays,* tr. Ben Brewster (New York: Monthly Review Press, 1971), pp. 123–73.

Describes the function of ideology as organizing the reproduction of the conditions of production, and ideology itself as the medium in which the material world realizes itself, thereby implying an analogous material role for literature.

Daniel Bell, *The End of Ideology: On the Exhaustion of Political Ideas in the Fifties* (New York: Free Press, 1960; rev. ed. New York: Collier, 1961).

A widely debated study that finds ideological terms reductively programmatic and narrowly political, and in both respects unsuited for an understanding of America's pluralistic culture.

Walter Benjamin, *Illuminations,* tr. Harry Zohn (New York: Harcourt Brace Jovanovich, 1968).

Includes "The Work of Art in the Age of Mechanical Reproduction," perhaps Benjamin's most cited essay, as well as germinal studies of Kafka, Baudelaire, and Proust. Benjamin links the Modernist concern with the power of language to the search for principles of cultural order and integration.

John Berger, *Ways of Seeing* (New York: Viking, 1972).

Clear, sophisticated, and wide-ranging discussion (admirably free of jargon) of the way ideology shapes how we see, by an art historian who has been influential among literary critics. (Co-authors: Sven Blomberg, Chris Fox, Michael Dibb, and Richard Hollis.)

Kenneth Burke, *Attitudes Towards History* (New York: New Republic, 1937).

Implicit ideological criticism of a variety of American texts, informed by a keen sense of the social situation in which art arises and functions, and concerned throughout with the way literature works to organize community around accepted values and perceptions. These concerns are far more broadly developed in Burke's *The Philosophy of Aesthetic Form: Studies in Symbolic Action* (Baton Rouge: Louisiana State University Press, 1941).

Terry Eagleton, *Criticism and Ideology: A Study in Marxist Literary Theory* (New York: Schocken, 1978).

A Marxist approach, incorporating semiology and deconstruction, and proposing a critical method that mediates between a materialist account of "literary modes of production" and an examination of authorial subjectivity.

Clifford Geertz, "Ideology as a Cultural System," in *The Interpretation of Cultures: Selected Essays* (New York: Basic, 1973), pp. 193–223.

Anthropological method widely adapted by literary critics, which seeks to combine the methods of social science with those of symbolic and linguistic analysis. Essentially, it renders ideology as itself a text to be analyzed in terms of complex structures of meaning.

Antonio Gramsci, *Selections from the Prison Notebooks,* tr. Quentin Hoare and Geoffrey N. Smith (New York: International Publishers, 1972).

Seldom concerned directly with aesthetics, but the view of hegemony it advances has been widely influential in the study of the way culture embodies ideology and participates in its development.

Max Horkheimer and Theodor W. Adorno, *Dialectic of Enlightenment,* tr. John Cumming (New York: Herder, 1972).

Examines the contradictory capacity of the Enlightenment concept of thought to permit an unprecedented freedom but also to rationalize its destruction. Written during the growth of German Fascism, the book illustrates (in a relatively accessible style) the passionate engagement of the "Frankfurt School" with issues of politics, art, and society.

Fredric Jameson, *The Political Unconscious: Narrative as a Socially Symbolic Act* (Ithaca, N.Y.: Cornell University Press, 1981).

Imports the psychological concept of the unconscious in order to suggest the pervasive workings of ideology as it generates and encodes the language of literature; Jameson's Marxist analysis of trans-historical reading posits an ongoing "narrative" that is at once the story and the reality of history.

Georg Lukács, *The Theory of the Novel: A Historico-Philosophical Essay on the Forms of Great Epic Literature,* tr. Anna Bostock (Cambridge, Mass.: MIT Press, 1971).

Written when, according to some, Lukács was more Hegelian than Marxist, this book sets out his criticism of bourgeois culture as profoundly distorted by alienation, so that even its art is incapable of the integration and wholeness of earlier traditions. It thus places the novel in the context of Western history, and suggests how literary study can reveal the forms of social reality.

Pierre Macherey, *A Theory of Literary Production,* tr. Geoffrey Wall (Boston: Routledge & Kegan Paul, 1978).

Structuralist interpretation of Marx, which focuses on the literary product as a material entity rather than the subjective "creation" of its author.

Karl Mannheim, *Ideology and Utopia: An Introduction to the Sociology of Knowledge,* tr. Louis Wirth and Edward Shils (New York: Harcourt Brace, 1936).

Contrasts "ideology" and "utopia" as terms that respectively rationalize an established social order and project its alternative. So understood, all knowledge may be said to arise in ideology, because the intellectual processes by which we order our world also offer a language in which we imagine it otherwise.

Raymond Williams, *Marxism and Literature* (New York: Oxford University Press, 1977).

A wide-ranging and authoritative study of ideology, both in its own complex meanings and in relation to theories of culture, literature, and language.

Index

Aaron, Daniel, 101
Adams, Henry 99, 104, 145, 189, 197, 199, 200, 206–10, 214, 215, 248
Adorno, Theodor, 7, 8, 188
Althusser, Louis, 8, 146
Anderson, John, 26
Anderson, Quentin, 128
Arac, Jonathan, 243n6, 435–6
Arendt, Hannah, 17n18
Arnold, Matthew, 172–5, 177–80, 183, 184, 185, 250, 431
Arvin, Newton, 203
Auden, Wystan Hugh, 300

Babbitt, Irving, 100
Baker, Houston, 423–6, 440n1
Balzac, Honoré de, 137, 138, 139, 188
Bancroft, George, 24, 420
Barque, George, 197
Barthes, Roland, 33n8, 80, 84, 335n8
Baudelaire, Charles, 221, 226, 229, 240, 430
Beecher, Catherine, 285, 286, 287
Bell, Daniel, 13, 14
Bellow, Saul, 54
Benjamin, Walter, 7, 8, 17n17, 221, 226, 228, 229, 231, 243n12, 247–8, 262, 430
Bercovitch, Sacvan, 23, 109, 177, 183, 257, 282, 349n2, 393, 394, 398, 399, 407
Berger, John, 196
Berkhofer, Robert Frederick, 34n20, 35n30
Bernstein, Bernard, 32n2
Berthoff, Warner, 108
Beyle, Marie-Henri, see Stendhal
Billington, Ray Allen, 34n24
Blackmur, Richard Palmer, 101
Blassingame, John, 153
Bohr, Niels, 197, 216n15
Boone, Daniel, 34n20

Boorstin, Daniel, 32n2, 420
Bourne, Randolph, 99
Brackenridge, Hugh Henry, 338
Bradford, William, 148
Brecht, Bertolt, 7, 8, 17n17
Brooks, Cleanth, 104, 149
Brooks, Van Wyck, 1, 2, 15, 99, 106, 185, 186, 420
Brown, Charles Brockden, 338
Brumm, Ursula, 28, 34n27
Buffalo Bill, 25, 26
Bunyan, John, 329
Burke, Kenneth, 67n3, 185, 398
Burnett, Frances Hodgson, 268
Byer, Robert, 430, 431
Byron, George Gordon, Lord, 342, 367

Calhoun, John, 396
Cather, Willa, 107
Cawelti, John, 4, 29, 35n33
Chapman, John Jay, 403, 406
Charters, Samuel, 153
Charvat, William, 15n1, 96, 98, 108
Chase, Richard, 16n6, 106, 107, 125, 133, 268
Chaucer, Geoffrey, 129
Childs, David Lee, 396
Chomsky, Noam, 390
Chopin, Frédéric François, 267
Clemens, Samuel Langhorne, see Twain, Mark
Cody, William Frederick, see Buffalo Bill
Coleridge, Samuel Taylor, 106, 250, 300
Conway, Moncure, 404, 406
Cooper, James Fenimore, 54, 72, 107, 108, 125, 129, 137, 141, 335n6
Cowley, Malcolm, 2, 99–101
Crews, Frederick, 249
Crockett, David, 150
Curie, Eve, 207

447